SCOOT

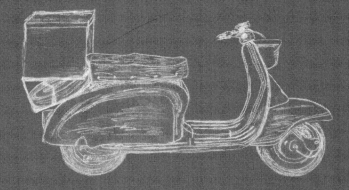

AURELEO ROSANO

© 2016, 2017, 2020 Aureleo Rosano. All Rights Reserved.
Available for purchase on lulu.com

ABOUT THE WRITING OF THE SCOOTER STORY

In the Spring of 2015, Ryan Smith, President of 3-FORM LIGHT ART, visited my wife Angela Rose and me at our studios in the desert boondocks northwest of Tucson, Arizona. Ryan was on the Southwest leg of his Ignite/Create Van Tour of the USA and interviewed and talked with me about Creativity. During that interview (http://illuminate.3-form.com/ignitecreate-interview-aureleo-rosano-artist/), filmed and edited by photographer Dominic Arizona Bonuccelli, we briefly talked of my scooter trip across the USA fifty years before. After that interview as we enjoyed a little Italian food, both Ryan and Dominic mentioned that the scooter trip seemed genuinely interesting and further, that I should write about it. To me, it was just one of the 'things' I had done in my life ... but I wrote two brief chapters in the week following the interview. To gauge response, I published the two chapters on Facebook and they were well-received. So I began a third chapter ... that's how we got here.

Looking back, this is what I wrote in February of 2016:

It was a bit more than a year ago that I began to put onto paper the experience of this scooter trip across a major part of the USA. Why do it? Not sure. Certainly people have crossed the US using zanier methods and in braver or more demanding circumstances. After posting two or three brief chapters on Facebook, and finding favorable response, I decided a few people might enjoy the story and more important, a few might, in fact, be encouraged to try something, anything, to bring excitement to their lives or to the lives of others. Perhaps writing it was for my children, now adults, to read and learn some of what helped form their unorthodox father.

My hope is that a decent balance was reached between being accurate and providing too many details. Consequently, many small incidents, a number of lesser side trips, and quite a few conversations were omitted. The zig-zag route across the country was accurate, though there were some road changes during the more-than-half-century between the riding and the writing.

The story has been written in a conversational manner, as if you the reader, and I, the storyteller, were sitting in a living room, having a drink or two, and telling tales. Understand that I can be a bit of a grammar stormtrooper and a spelling screwball, but enjoy equally, the breaking of grammatical rules, sometimes scattering punctuation here and there as I go along. Also enjoy creating new words occasionally.

The story of my journey is not brief, it just is.
Enjoy.

—AURELEO ROSANO 2/29/16

SCOOT
ACROSS THE USA

DEDICATION

To those persons willing
to try an unbeaten path ...

To the misfits of our world,
the creative, the innovative,
the adventurous.

Feeling so fortunate to have people
close to me who are included in this group:
my wife Angela Rose,
my four children:
Teresa, Dante, Marco, + Tony Rosano,
and two newer friends:
Dominic Arizona Bonuccelli + Christopher Stamos.

PART ONE
TUCSON TO DENVER

Trying to recall events, circumstances, and impressions from 55 years before is a challenge.

In 1960 I drove an Italian motor scooter from Tucson (near the border of Mexico) in Southern Arizona on a zig-zag path across the USA to Boston, Massachusetts on the East Coast. The maps say it can be done in approximately 2,500 road miles (4,000 km). I missed that mark by 4,000 or 5,000 miles (8,000 km).

My intent is to tell the tale as truthfully as I can from memory. There was no diary or log, no camera for recording images, and no financial or mileage journal kept. So ... that puts the two of us – you, the reader, and me, the storyteller, in a position where we must rely on my memory. And that's risky. And that's my disclaimer.

And that's the forward to this tale.

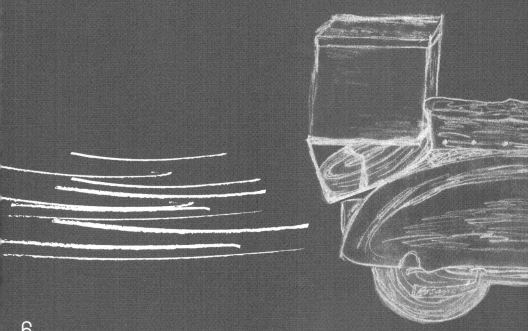

CHAPTER 1

SCOOT ACROSS THE USA

SETTING THE STAGE

April 1960: Twenty years old and seeking adventure. I had abandoned New England four months earlier, taken a flight to Southern Arizona based on the deliberate decision to allow the flip of a coin to tell me where to land. All of that is a separate story which I will relate soon… in the next paragraph actually. Suffice it to say, it's April in Tucson. The winter residents, usually called "snowbirds", have returned to their more northern homes, my job as a waiter at a resort hotel is ending for the season, my younger sister Phyllis will be married at the end of June back east in Connecticut, and I'm expected to be part of the wedding party. How did I get to Tucson, Arizona? Raised in Connecticut, floundering around in various colleges, having some monumental encounters with and becoming intimate friends with both Jim Beam and Jack Daniels, I looked out the window of my crummy little apartment in Boston. The semester at Boston University was just beginning and I was supposed to register, but everything outside was gray, nasty, and cold. There was snow, spattered with slush, and a layer of exhaust soot and city dirt lightly blanketed everything. I was sober, and hugely irritated to have to go outside at all. Instead of going to register for any classes, I grumbled my way to a nearby bookstore where I grabbed a map of the United States and paid the pretty young woman at the cash register. Since no one else was in line, I unfolded the map, tore off the upper half (the northern part of the map) and gave it to the cashier. I remember saying "Sell this to somebody else. I don't want to look at it." With the southern half, I returned to my room, and looked at cities in the South … Miami, New Orleans, Houston, San Antonio,

7

Albuquerque, Tucson, and San Diego. The last two seemed to pull at me. Carefully considering all the positives and negatives that the two towns offered, I flipped a coin and Tucson came up heads. Within an hour, I had packed my things, paid the little bit of rent due on my hovel, got into my car and started down the road to Connecticut, stopped at the airport north of Hartford, and bought a ticket for the next day's flight. I asked my friend to drive me to the airport for the early morning flight. "Where're you going?" Answer: "Tucson, Arizona." A few more questions and answers and then "When are you coming back?" Answer: "I'm not. I may not stay there, but I'm not coming back." In Tucson, in January, I had purchased an almost new 1959 Lambretta 125 motor scooter. It seemed to be a very reliable, well-crafted, and efficient machine ... reasonably quiet and rather comfortable. Italian made, the Lambretta is very similar to the better-known Vespa ("wasp" in Italian, probably for it buzzing sound or perhaps because it can dart in and out of traffic). Top speed about 42 miles per hour (67 kmh) with the windshield and probably a bit faster without. So now I've told you a little about the man and a little about the machine and now for the madness of my plan to cross this big nation, the USA. Any decent plan considers quite a number of factors. My plan did not and was largely based on three considerations: (1) generally aim the Lambretta (now named 'Tony') north and eastward; (2) try to arrive a day or two prior to June 29th in Connecticut (the date of my sister's wedding); and (3) invite at least one new thing or adventure each day while experiencing this exotic thing called 'America.' While I was 'going back to New England' as I had vowed not to do, I knew it was for a very brief period and not a valid vow breaker. Jack Kerouac was a French-Canadian American 'Beat Generation' author. His book 'On the Road' (a great read, written on a 120-ft roll with no paragraphs, but with a driven energy) had caused me to think about crossing the US two years before. Here was the chance to do it, to try something different. I'm sure some people have walked and bicycled and maybe even roller skated across the country, so to scooter across was not hugely brave ... just a bit unusual, and except for (1) and (2) above, the plan was to go with no plan. Just go. Just Go!

CHAPTER 2

PREPARATIONS + DEPARTURE

So ... the decision was made to use the 1959 Lambretta to cross the USA from Tucson, AZ to Boston, MA, a map distance of 2500 miles. Of course, preparations are necessary. One doesn't just start out willy-nilly on such a jaunt, but I wanted to stay as close to willy-nilly as possible. Preparations were few and quickly accomplished.

A two-compartment metal box was a found treasure – about a 16in height, 18in width, and 14in depth and it was bolted behind the passenger seat. The smaller compartment (which was sealed separately) would contain a metal quart container of gasoline along with oil and measuring cup. The Lambretta used a two-cycle engine requiring a 4 to 5% addition of motor oil mixed with the gasoline. Later, I understand the ratio changed to 2%, but 4% was the minimum used on this little excursion. The quart container served as my mixing chamber and also as the 'reserve' reserve tank, since the scooter had a built-in reserve of a pint or so of fuel. The larger compartment of the metal box held a small nylon mountaineer's tent (supposedly waterproof), a few tools, a diminutive 2-cup coffee pot and coffee (great word ... 'diminutive'). A waterproof bag holding all my clothing was tied to the passenger seat. One critical item was water. Now accustomed to the incredibly dry Arizona Sonoran desert air, I knew the enjoyment of this gorgeous place depended on having enough water to drink. One of the side effects of water shortage in Arizona is death, which I hoped to avoid on this trip. A water bag would do nicely. Most people today have no idea what a water bag is or was. Essentially it's a tightly woven canvas bag with a capped filling and drinking spout. When the bag is first filled, the canvas bag will leak water fairly quickly. As the canvas fibers swell after a few hours, the weave becomes so tight that only tiny amounts of water wick to the outside surface of the bag. As that small amount of water evaporates, (remember "latent heat" from your high school physics?) the remaining water is cooled and becomes refreshing for drinking. The one-gallon water bag was tied to the front of the scooter both for easy access and for evaporative cooling by the wind. The trick is never to allow the bag to dry completely. Empty it for fresh water, but refill it promptly. The idea of all this was that I wanted to 'camp out' most nights and only take a motel room once a week to do laundry, rest from the road, do scooter maintenance, etc.

People often speak of the basic necessities as being food, clothing, and shelter. While that might have been a complete list for our cave-dwelling ancestors, the list had to be expanded for a scooter trip across the USA (technically a more advanced activity than an average day of cave-dwelling). To carry food would be a constant nuisance except for a bag of nuts and some dried fruits. Water, of course, but what about those other basic and critical biological necessities? ... chocolate and coffee. Chocolate would have to be purchased on the way because of the melting problem. Coffee requirements could be handled by the small brewing pot in which two cups of water could be campfire boiled and ground coffee directly added to make some nice strong, black coffee ... no strainer, no filter, no cream, no sugar (just my opinion, but all those trimmings are strictly for wimps). Sometimes that's called 'cowboy coffee.' Whatever the name, it's good stuff. Two good cups of coffee in the morning and two or three along the way at a café or diner, as much to take a break and talk with people as to just buy another caffeine fix. It was easy to meet people over a cup of coffee in 1960 and it still is today.

Food. The thought was to purchase all required food along the way, always keeping the small lightweight bag of nuts and dried fruit (constantly consumed and refilled) for reserve purposes or just for treats now and then. Bread (usually Italian or French), cheese, occasionally a little meat from a delicatessen (never pre-packaged), various fruits, olives, and veggies. Usually at three or four in the afternoon, I'd start looking for a deli with either a Greek, Italian or Jewish name (if it was Moshe's Market or Dante's Deli, I would stop). That just shows my food prejudices. And yeah, yeah, yeah. I know now and knew then, it was terrible white bread which I was eating on a daily basis and that I should have selected a nice, dense loaf of 38-grain bread with alfalfa sprouts, chia seeds, ground watermelon rinds, and all the other silly stuff. However, my bread had to taste like bread. It had to feed my soul first, then my stomach, the soul being far more important.

Scooter maintenance. That's one subject I can really 'get into' some other day, primarily because I knew so little about this machine. My ignorance was almost limitless, knowing the principles of internal combustion engines (4-stroke and 2-stroke) and knowing also how to make a fair number of repairs on the big fire-breathing monsters of Detroit. This Lambretta, however, was like a gasoline powered sewing machine to me and seemed marvelous that it functioned at all. In the less than three months in my possession, the scooter had taught me how to change and repair its tires, how to keep filters clean (air and fuel), how to clean its spark plug and perhaps one or two additional tidbits. Beyond that ... zero. But ... in the sparkling and magic days of youth, there was no fear of jumping enthusiastically into something about which nothing was known.

Earlier, I referred to Kerouac's Beat Generation novel 'On The Road' which fostered a sense of adventure without care... that free spirit sort of feeling. I greatly admired that and 'Beat' poets, writers, and artists. One thing, however, was disturbing. To me, there seemed to be a sense amongst the beatniks, and later, the hippies, that 'freeloading is OK.' That part of the Beat Generation separated me from fully accepting them and probably the reverse as well. Too ingrained with the work ethic, I worked my butt off at any job with the immediate goal of wanting my boss, whoever it might be, to openly weep whenever I said "I'll be leaving this job. I'm giving you two weeks' notice."

So, money had been saved from my waiter's job and leaving some amount in the bank, I put $400.00 in my pockets. 1960 dollars were worth about 8 times our 2015 dollars. Doing the math gives today's equivalent of $3200 US. To me, the supply of money was in third place after water and fuel. It was time to leave and I started out, took Oracle Road north out of Tucson and I was, in fact, on the road, three magic words – on the road. In movies, poetry, in music, often in the minds of Americans at that time, there was a meaning, a yearning, and a certain satisfaction which accompanied that phrase 'on the road'.

CHAPTER 3

THAT FIRST DAY

April in the Sonoran Desert (where Tucson is located) is a wondrous place and time of year. I've always felt tourists left too early in the season, but of course, spring season is welcomed and beautiful almost everywhere. Leaving Tucson, my first mini goal was Denver, Colorado for several reasons: (1) that would take me out of the southern deserts where it was growing warmer and I would be exposed to every weather as it occurred; (2) I had never seen the higher mountains of the Rocky Mountain Chain, 9,200 feet (2,800 meters) being the elevation max near Tucson; and (3) looking at that southern portion of the map I had purchased in Boston, it seemed there were so many interesting places en route. I pointed the Lambretta north on Oracle Road and was soon out of town and heading up Route 77 towards Catalina, AZ and Oracle Junction at a blistering pace with wind tearing at my hair.

Well, that's really not quite accurate. The pace was 43mph on flat road and less on any incline longer than a tennis court and that bit about the hair was simply a lie ... my hair was rather short, a helmet covered nearly all of it, and the wind was more akin to a moderately stiff breeze because of the windshield.

The first hours were a time of learning and adjustment. Get a feel for this thing. Watch the fuel gauge. Listen more carefully to engine sounds. In some ways 43mph in town was quite different from the same speed out on the highway. While more speed seemed a better idea initially, I reminded myself there was no rush at all. The idea was to enjoy every bit of the trip as much as possible and there was no schedule and 43 was, in fact, swift enough to miss quite a number of things anyway. I knew to move to the right when traffic was behind me, sometimes pulling off the road entirely to allow vehicles to pass on uphill portions of a narrow road, and learned to prepare myself when large rigs shot past me, first their air pressure pushing me aside (and almost off the road in some cases) and then, as they passed, pulling me into their draft. At times, more than a little freaky (double trailer rigs encountered later were the worst).

Within an hour of our (Tony Lambretta's and mine) exit from Tucson, we were passing the road intersection called Oracle Junction, where supposedly, a big mafia-controlled gambling setup operated at the inn and restaurant. If we took the northward leg (Rt. 79) toward the prison town of Florence, we would pass the spot where Tom Mix, a famous movie cowboy died in a car crash after visiting with the Pima County Sheriff. We instead continued on Rt. 77 turning slightly eastward toward Oracle and San Manuel, a town built by the copper mining industry there. This enormous and relatively lush high desert was a visual treat for any eye. Seeing the remarkable differences in vegetation while traveling just a few highway miles can be a surprise to a visitor, but occurs often as one travels in the deserts of the Southwest. Well-known and sometimes troubled Biosphere II is along this stretch of road today, but didn't exist in 1960. What did exist, however, was the incredibly large smokestack of the San Manuel copper smelter operation, about 20ft (6m) in diameter and more than 500feet (150m) in height. The constant cloud of gases drifting across the sky was mesmerizing if one could just look at it and not experience the sulfurous fumes poisoning the entire valley. Time for a swig of water and a smoke. At the time, I smoked Parliaments or other brands – about six a day. So I smoked and so did the copper smelter. Tony Lambretta and I put the enormous smokestack behind us and headed north.

Now it is time to talk of the name Tony Lambretta. Certainly there are real people who are named Tony Lambretta, but MY Tony Lambretta was complete fiction. Blame it all on my deceased mother because, indeed, it was all her fault. An explanation seems due about now, to explain that. My mother was a typical, small, strong, loving mother with a quick temper (augmented at times with a wooden spoon) and a certain way of driving me completely crazy. Of Italian Roman Catholic origin, she was a perfect example of a good Jewish mother. (Reading hint: "How To Be a Jewish Mother", by Dan Greenburg, first published in 1964 – a genuine hoot of a book). One talent of hers was certainly unmatched by anyone in the 1900's (try looking for this in The Guinness Book of Records) and far surpassed even the most notorious of Jewish mothers in the 'worrying' category. My mom knew how to worry, worry about anything at all. She could worry about too much snow in New York, or not enough snow in Vermont. When we had a string of warm sunny days in New England, she would worry about farmers not getting enough rain. On one occasion, as I crammed some blue jeans into a bag for a spelunking trip to Virginia and West Virginia, she said she should iron the jeans first. Explaining they would be worn as I crawled through underground caves lined with bat guano, I said ironing really wasn't necessary. Mom said "But I would worry." Probably looking at my puzzled stance, she said "Your friends might think I don't take good care of my family, and that would worry me the whole time you're gone." So … you can imagine how she'd be if she knew I was heading toward my old home from distant Arizona on a putt-putt two-wheeled scooter. So … I created a story (this is sometimes called telling a big lie) in which a friend "named Lambretta, Tony Lambretta" and I, would be touring our country and would arrive home in time for my younger sister Phyllis's wedding (and in the meantime, my mother could worry about wedding things, and not about me). Given that Lambretta is a well-known Italian name, a first name of Gunter, Lars, or Wamsley wouldn't fit so well, so Tony it was. Throughout my journey I mailed postcards at 8 or 10 day intervals saying things like "Tony and I will be heading to Amarillo, Texas for the next leg of this trip. I'll send you guys a card from there." Those were the blessed days of no cell phones or other electronic leashes. No need to explain your phone had accidentally been turned off for a month.

Traveling north from the smokestack of San Manuel, AZ on Rt. 77, one starts to pass a few small settlements and a few mining towns and perhaps hundreds of failed mining efforts, abandoned mine shafts, or exploratory tunnels. About a year after this trip I hesitantly explored three or four different sites. Although having more underground experience than the average person might, there was an overwhelming feeling that spelunking or cave-crawling was much safer than old mineshaft exploration. Nature, that powerful architect, creates holes here and there on our planet which are relatively safe compared to manmade earth holes which are excavated in places unintended by the earth's forces. Nature doesn't like man's intrusions and will eventually win these little conflicts. Anyway, this was hot, dry, copper mining country with mining towns scattered along the way on my left. One settlement was named Christmas, a small mining settlement with few people, but a functioning post office where people could bring their thousands of Christmas cards to be processed with the Christmas, AZ postmark. Another town, named Snowflake, further north in Arizona and which remains viable today, used to do the same sort of thing, but now, Christmas, Arizona is vacant. Within an hour I was scootering almost parallel to a section of the Gila River, which had a moderate flow of water, always a refreshing sight here in the desert. The landscape became more severely mountainous. The scooter needed its lower gears to carry its burden up steeper grades and finally to a slope of downhill terrain where the Lambretta could use neutral and then coast for several miles, ending at a highway junction, taking me into the town of Globe, Arizona. Coasting downhill was a huge relief, both for the scooter's engine and for my nerves. My blood pressure was probably moving in parallel to the scooter RPM's.

Too steep a down grade could be treacherous, however, as I would discover soon enough. But here I was in Globe, a thriving little town and after the three previous hours, I needed a rest and a restroom. If I knew how to write the sound of a big sigh of relief, it would appear here.

CHAPTER 4

THE FIRST STOP AND A WILD AFTERNOON

Globe, Arizona High Noon (as they say in the Westerns) and it was time to consider what had already happened. A few more than 100 miles had been covered in a bit less than 4 hours, including a break in a town called Winkleman. Therefore my effective rate of travel had been 25 mph which could carry me across the country in 100 hours if I were a machine needing no sleep, no maintenance and with no thoughts of experiencing the journey.

The first thing to be done was to refuel... first the machine, then the person. Pulled into a gas station, emptied the one-quart container (into which enough 2-cycle oil for a tankful had already been mixed) into the gas tank and asked the attendant, an older guy, to "fill 'er up please." As I was paying the small amount of money, the old man asked "You from around here?" I said "Tucson." "Heading home are you?" Answer: "No, heading to Boston." After quite a pause, he said, "Never heard of any town named Boston in Arizona." I answered "Neither have I. Boston, Massachusetts." A longer pause and then, "On THAT?" I nodded yes. He then walked all around the scooter and asked, "Got a minute?" "Sure I do." "Let's go in the office." "OK." He sat down. From the way he walked, I guessed his feet were hurting badly. As he sat down, gesturing to a wooden chair for me, he said, "You know, lots of guys working in mines around here live in Tucson and most of them drive pickup trucks. They come in here all the time. I'll bet that if you offered someone a few dollars, they'd take you and that contraption of yours back to Tucson." I said something appreciating his concern, but explained that wasn't part of the plan. Another pause and then he laughed gently and said something I heard again and again all across the nation, with little variation. "I always wanted to do something crazy like that ... but I got married instead." With him shaking his head, still laughing, and me, hungry and badly in need of coffee, we waved adios and I putt-putted into town and its sister town Miami, AZ is search of a café or food store or better than that, both. Found a café and while drinking a cup of coffee and having another smoke, looked out the window at my scooter, with its metal box up high on the back end, and my sleeping bag on top of that. Only then did I realize this rig presented an image which seemed very peculiar to most people here in the US. That seemed no problem at all to me.

Note to readers: That paragraph above is quite accurate ... except I've deleted some cursing and rough language. Swearing and cussing are fine with me, and can be really colorful at times, but be notified that any conversation recalled in future chapters will probably be sanitized. Not always, but much of the time.

One problem I knew I had ... was the scooter's throttle – a swiveling spring-loaded affair built into the handlebar grip. For a few hours, it had been tolerable, but the spring was too strong for long hours of driving, my hand already feeling some strain. After a sandwich and coffee at the café, there was a stop at a grocer for a few food items, then a stop at what used to be called a 'Five and Dime' (five and ten cent store) where I purchased some strong rubber bands. My final stop was a small park-like spot near the National Guard Armory, where I rigged rubbers bands on the throttle grip to relieve most of the strain and rested on the patch of cool Bermuda grass for almost an hour.

Time to return to highway travel. In the approximately three months I had lived in Arizona, I had never been north of Globe. The last ten miles leading into Globe-Miami was routed through the Tonto National Forest and soon after heading north out of those twin towns, I found myself back in Tonto, which means 'wild', or 'crazy' in Spanish. The more southern Chiricahua (pronounced cheer-eh-KAH-wah) Apaches called their northern relatives in this area 'foolish' and the Navajo (NA-va-hoe) picked up the Spanish word and the area was named. This Tonto had nothing to do with the Lone Ranger's faithful Indian companion, Tonto. That character was actually played by a Canadian Mohawk named Jay Silverheels.

Jay Silverheels was a smart, well-spoken, and highly regarded actor. I remember seeing him on The Jack Parr Show in a now famous interview where it was mentioned that he was married to an Italian woman. Host Jack Parr asked how a North American Indian came to be married to an Italian girl. Silverheels answers, "As an Indian, I'd been looking all my life for a way to get even with Columbus."

Traveling northward and slightly eastward out of Globe, still on Rte. 77, I was enjoying the desert's spring wildflowers which can put on a remarkable show, dependent on the rainfall of the previous months. The flowers had been lining my route the entire distance from Tucson. Not a dazzling show at this time, but showy enough. The land was sloping upward slightly. Less than an hour had passed and perhaps 20 miles, when highway signs began to warn that brakes should be tested and a steep downgrade was ahead. The frequency of warnings increased. A few more miles and a modest sign announced The Salt River Canyon. So … big deal, thought I. Never having heard of The Salt River Canyon, I thought, "OK. No big deal. Let's have a look!" There were several more brake advisory signs, one telling truckers to stop their rigs for a thorough inspection of brakes and tires. Two more miles and the land leveled briefly and then sloped downward ever so gently and then a little steeper and then … "Holy Shit!" Sorry, but there are no other words to describe my reaction. This indeed was a canyon, a very big canyon, and to someone from New England it was simply staggering. It was, in fact, a very big deal and at first glance, a daunting, unanticipated surprise. Pulling over, I stopped to catch the enormity of it all and my breath as well, and brace my thinking into something resembling reasonable. This was a first for me.

Having lived in Arizona for three and one-half months, I had taken this Lambretta up and down the Mount Lemmon highway to an elevation of 9,000+ feet (2,800 meters) and we (the scooter had not yet been given the Tony name) both behaved prudently and well. I had previously driven the Mount Lemmon road in a car, and while a bit unnerving at times, all went well. So that was a plus. But this Salt River Canyon stunned me into silence (which is some respectable stunning). Never had seen anything quite so steep, except for the skyscrapers of New York City. The fact that I had never heard of this canyon (Our Grand Canyon far outshines it in every way) only pointed to my profound ignorance of this place we call 'Out West'. Evidently, from the highway signs, the greatest fear was overheating a vehicle's brakes resulting in a runaway situation which could possibly be halted by a highway device I had also never heard of … a runaway ramp, an upward sloping ramp of earth carved into the side of a downward sloping road. It's designed to stop any vehicle which has overheated its brakes, making them useless. My thought was "Well, you wanted adventure. Here's one right before your eyes. C'mon Tony, it's showbiz! Let's do it! Let's give 'er hell."

And we gave her hell … but very slow hell, and rather cautious hell at that. In second gear much of the time, and even then, the rpms increased uncomfortably. We were able to pass the few runaway ramps available and the scooter brakes were used sparsely. Of course, with the slow descent into the canyon, there was ample time to catch the scenery. There were a few viewing cutouts where people could rest, run through some camera film to take bad photos of Aunt Beatrice in the polka-dot dress she had worn in all the photos of the past three weeks. The views along the length of the canyon and across to the opposite side were splendid and varied. And this was early afternoon. They'd be more so as the sun lowered its place in our enormous western sky and shadows became more dramatic. Turning this way and that, curving to the right and then left, and now, down at the road's lowest point, a two-lane bridge crossed to the other side of the Salt River. The river's flow was moderate, I guessed, from markings along the bank. In later years, I would see this same Salt River, positively roaring through the Metropolitan Phoenix valley (a hundred miles west of this canyon), taking out or threatening the bridges. This day it was tame. A few feet beyond the bridge lay a restaurant/café/tourist stop which had a large parking area. That's where we would pause, stretch and shake off the stress of the descent, have something to drink, and just watch people for a short time.

Aside from my own immediate needs, I was determined to buy as little as possible the entire trip, for three reasons: (1) Limited space available in or on this rig, (2) additional weight was detrimental to scooter performance, and (3) I was a tightwad and wanted to use my available money conservatively or waste it in an entertaining manner. So I didn't buy anything in the gift shop/tourist snare at the bottom of the canyon, but had looked at photography on the hundreds of postcards available ... some remarkable photos and no Photoshop in those times.

To leave the parking area and head north again, the upward slope to climb out of the canyon looked steeper than the downhill run. Staying in low gear and increasing rpms considerably, we began the climb for just a few yards as rpms diminished swiftly and we almost stalled. Turn around now and go back to the parking lot to start again. The next attempt was to run alongside the scooter, operating the throttle until I could run no faster and hop on. And it was done with speed, grace, agility, and style. The resulting slowdown was much slower paced than my first attempt but results after a two minute struggle were the same. It seemed the scooter named Tony could not haul us out of the canyon. Now turn the whole rig around again and return to the parking area. Time to think. It would be simplest to beg a lift from one of the many pickup truck drivers. If I could get Tony to give me just a few more rpms, I believed we could make it. How to do that? So again, at as high a speed as I could get and only be marginally unsafe, we shot out of the parking area and headed south, banging back across the bridge and up the way we had come and traveled uphill as far as possible. Now do a 180 degree turn and head downhill once more, bang northward across that bridge again at the highest speed and highest rpms possible, jam into the lowest gear, and with the engine racing faster than I had ever asked of it, we made it, all the way, to the top of the canyon road, in first gear. A slow painful ascent for us, but nevertheless, an adventure of sorts.

CHAPTER 5

ON TO SHOW LOW

And so it was a long slow climb out of Salt River Canyon. A long slow-paced journey allows generous time for thoughts of any description to ricochet here and there inside one's head. While gorgeous scenery is genuinely appreciated, it has never held my attention for long periods of time and thoughts turn to the geological or weather phenomena that created that scenery. While the canyon views were captivating to my eye, my mind was elsewhere, first being occupied with the wildflowers proliferating along our roadways, most densely growing next to the pavement where they received more than their fair share of any rain runoff. Then, thinking back a few minutes to wildflowers pictured on postcards back in the gift shop, I was certain those displays shown on the cards did not occur every year. So … if I were a photographer, and if the wildflower season was exceptional, and if I knew of a suitable area of densely packed blossoms, and if I could call in sick at my day job without getting fired, I'd take photos of that flower grouping from a hundred different angles, and with as much variance in sunlight as possible. I'd stay with those flowers for at least a full day (from sunrise to sunset) and take a twelve-foot ladder with me to get photos from yet more angles. Assuming some of these photos would be exceptional, I'd try to sell them to every possible outlet for years, maybe decades to come. Postcard photos are usually taken at peak photogenic moments during a location's life cycle. Imagine you are a photographer in Seattle. On the rare sunny day in Seattle, you would be out snapping so many photos your snapper would wear out. Of course, these are the photos appearing on postcards. Very rarely does one see, on a postcard, an image of dirty slush-spattered snow along roadways lit by grey drizzle. In Portland, Oregon and probably in Seattle, photographers must stumble over each other taking shots of buildings and places no one sees except three times a year when the sun makes an appearance. I imagined the photographers shooshing each other out of the way, shouting "Get out of the way! I don't need another picture of your camera! Hurry up, before the sun disappears! Nobody with a camera was around when I was pouring a pan of hot water on my car door, frozen shut by an ice storm. The camera people waited until the gleam of sunshine lit the artistically ice-covered twig. Despite the visual appeal of the compact cloud of water vapor emanating from my defrosting pan, it was the twig that became the post card.

Next, my thoughts turned to the employees selling those postcards and working in all the businesses at the bottom of the canyon I was leaving behind. Did they live there? Did they drive up and down that canyon road every day? Then ... what about the people who built the road? Amazing planning and engineering. Think of people going ahead of the construction crews, marking the way where no road existed. Every phase of building this road was a minor human miracle. There are things equal to this or bigger in scale than this everywhere in this country we call the USA. Actually, all over this world of ours. Humans can be complete jackasses and fools, but we can also be magnificent thinking creatures.

In the previous two paragraphs, you have seen results of excessive idle time for meditation. There would be many hours of thinking time ahead.

Salt River Canyon road, (which was my old Rte. 77, which had merged with State route 60 back there in Globe), diminished its steepness as it neared the top of the canyon, and one by one, I was able to use higher gears and travel as close to a normal pace as was possible. The road down into the canyon and up out was in the Fort Apache Indian Reservation, though I noticed little difference except for highway signage announcing this. What was noticeable was a distinct change in vegetation as the land slowly climbed higher, with tall evergreens and aspens becoming the prominent trees. There was more shade on the roadway and the coolth was welcome (my Microsoft program says coolth is not a word by underlining with a squiggly red line, but I like the word, and it is real, and everyone understands it, and Microsoft just has to 'get with it'). From the canyon top northward to the next town, Show Low, was about 40 miles (65km), a leisurely drive of an hour or so in a car and in decent weather.

The weather was perfect and Tony and I did that leg in three hours instead of just one, pulling off the road a short distance, leaning Tony against one of the Ponderosa pines, smelling the forest, taking a leak in the woods (pees on earth), having a smoke, having a snack, some water, and generally just cooling it. A beautiful day to be enjoyed with no urgency at all. It was always a relief to remove safety helmet, sunglasses, and sometimes my sports coat. The white helmet was comfortable and no problem except that it existed, was not collapsible, and probably subject to theft since I had no way to lock it up. Each state had its own laws regarding helmets. Arizona might have a different law from Utah. Both states could differ from Colorado or New Mexico, and I did not want the hassle of getting a traffic ticket or penalty. More importantly, not wearing a helmet seemed too risky, having seen a cyclist accident occur a month or two before. Even a slow speed crash can do immense damage to a person's head. For this trip, I had never considered not wearing one. Sunglasses were of immense importance. Wearing goggles was anathema, too tight and uncomfortable, triggering an intense headache in less than an hour each time I tried. Wraparound sunglasses, of moderately light shading, loose enough to allow some air circulation and able to close to a relatively flat configuration when not in use, these were the considerations for eye protection. I had discovered a sport jacket, medium gray, with two pockets on each side, all four pockets having flaps. A good, light-colored shirt (from my waiter's garb), darker gray pants, and dark gray roughout boots. That was my daily appearance, the more formal shirt and jacket certainly set me aside from most travelers on the road that summer.

Returning to the highway after break, hardly two miles had been traveled, when a motorcyclist on a Harley Davidson blasted past me. All higher powered two-wheelers got a small wave from me either as they approached from the opposite direction or as they flew past at twice my speed. This guy returned the wave and disappeared over the next little hill. Then, there he was, with his bike parked, waving his arms slowly as I putt-putted toward him. The situation was disconcerting, me being rather vulnerable, and not having the capacity to escape at any speed faster than the average wheelchair. He had not seen me taking a break and so I pretended that it was a welcome opportunity to stop and have a smoke, though I had just finished one.

Offering this guy a smoke, I greeted him, with "Hey man, you want a smoke, 'cause I need a break. That canyon just about killed me?" As he accepted and tore the filter off the end, I said, "Hey, my name's Rosano, you?" As we lit up, he said "Duffy. The name is Duffy, and man, I just had to see your rig up close and ask what in hell you were doing." He looked at my setup while I admired the huge Harley. We talked for a few minutes, usual stuff about what a nutty thing I was doing. He asked, "Rosano, you Italian?" I nodded yes. He said "Great artists the Italians, terrific food, and a bunch of criminals." He had just given me the major impressions of Italian-Americans prevalent in the minds of many non-Italian-Americans at that time. "Mafia?" he asked. I said, "Never heard of them." Then he said more quietly, "You connected?" After I considered this question for a moment, with what I thought was just the right amount of pause, I said. "Not directly." Then I said, "Duffy? That Irish?" he said, "Yeah, kind of." I said, "Irish ... terrible cooks, but great writers, poets, and singers." Then, he changed to a more relaxed posture, and asked "Where you headed now?" "Only up to Show Low. I've had enough for today." He said, "Hey, maybe I'll see you there. Thanks for the smoke." Duffy looked to be 30 or 35 years old, with a bit of a Hell's Angels' look, except he was skinny with no beer belly. He easily climbed onto his machine, hit the start button, waved and was back to his road. I did the same, but had to kickstart my little machine and was back on my road, a much slower road than Duffy's.

So, thinking of Duffy, I had, for a short time, felt threatened. Almost 21 years old and I was strong, and could be, when the occasion demanded it, tough, nasty, and belligerent. I knew well, however, that my circumstances made me easy pickin's ... to what I could only guess. Robbery? A beating? Who could know? This Italian 'thing' including the Mafia part ... how could it best serve me? What if Duffy had harbored bad thoughts? Was my answer "Not directly" a veiled threat toward him to counteract the possible danger I felt? I'd have to think about that ... what might I do, if anything, to neutralize a potentially menacing situation? The scooter couldn't outrun anything. I would be unable to lock myself inside for protection, as one might do with a car (convertibles excepted) and I carried no weapons other that a modestly-sized utilitarian pocket knife.

Note: Honestly, I never learned how a religious group such as the Utilitarians got so involved in design of small pocket knives ... probably for the income generated. There was a rumor that the Utilitarians had some dispute in their ranks. The rebel group supposedly separated and independently began working on other things ... among them cement products, eventually becoming what today is known as the Concretationists. That's what I heard years ago, but am unable to confirm any of the details.

As I approached Show Low, I knew it was time to end installment 5 of a possible book I might be writing more than 50 years later.

CHAPTER 6

FIRST NIGHT OUT

So this was Show Low, a small town, a popular summer recreation and resort area, but also an agricultural and logging center. Pine trees were everywhere, big pines and little ones. I had traveled about 100 miles from Globe. Not yet six o'clock and about two hours of daylight remained. Highway signs said we were in the Apache Sitgreaves National Forest, just north of the Fort Apache Reservation. First thing to do, always, was to refuel man and machine. Second thing, cruise around town to get a feel for the place. Since this would be my first night of camping, my intent was to scout out a good spot, near water if possible, for pitching my little tent and sleeping. Having heard of nearby places called Lakeside and Pinetop, my ignorance of this area seemed vast.

Of course, everyone asks how this place called Show Low got its name. It resulted from a card game involving two neighbors. When? I can't find that (probably the 1880's). But these two guys, Corydon E. Cooley and Marion Clark had been neighbors for a short time and both agreed the area was getting too crowded and one of them had to move. The issue would be settled with cards. A game, called Seven-Up, where the lowest card wins, was popular then. The game ended when Clark said to Cooley as he dealt the last hand, "If you can show low, you win." Cooley turned up the deuce of clubs and won. He named the town 'Show Low' to commemorate that card game. The main street in Show Low is called 'Deuce of Clubs.' That's the story we all learn.

Show Low was a town of 35,000 in 1960, having a good little business area along the Deuce of Clubs. After getting fuel into the scooter, I stopped at a hardware store for a few nuts and bolts and asked the middle-aged man where would be a good spot to camp alone, not with a bunch of people around. He suggested I take the road south to that Lakeside and Pinetop area, along the Show Low Creek. He said there'd be a thousand places to camp not far from the road, where I could drive the scooter and no one would know I was there. And I did exactly that. But first, some coffee and some food at a café would be good. I could buy a few groceries in the morning.

While having another coffee and sandwich and then looking for a campsite, thoughts went back a few centuries to that morning, actually only twelve hours and two hundred miles ago. A quick visual inventory scrolled through my mind: two or three different types of desert, three or four mining communities, two rivers, an impressive canyon, two Indian reservations, two or three different kinds of woodlands, a jillion wildflowers and I was exhausted. While I had considered myself about an 85 on the 0-100 toughness scale, I knew I had overdone it this day. Tonight would be a time for rest, tomorrow's travel would be half or less of today's. The hardware guy was right. It was no trouble finding a suitable place to camp, almost level ground, under a few small trees, firewood and water available within arm's reach.

For shelter, from rain, insects and serpents, (which seem to like cuddling up to sleeping humans), I had purchased a "mountaineer's" tent, made of water repellent nylon (very thin and very strong) with a rubberized nylon floor which did not leak, an adjustable screened opening for ventilation as needed. Two collapsible lightweight curved metal supports formed arches at the two ends, essentially causing the tent to become 40 inches in height (1 meter), the same in width, and 80 inches in length (2 meters). While this could be a self-supporting structure, it was not heavy enough, at two and one-fourth pounds (1 kilo) to stand through anything more than a strong breeze. To offset that feature, there were six or eight grommeted tabs on the exterior where ropes could be tied to help keep everything upright. I had purchased this tent and tested it while in Tucson, actually covering the inside floor with an inch of water to see if any leaked out. None did. A strange looking affair, it seemed acceptable, and when stored in its nylon sack was remarkably compact, a most attractive feature for the trip. Less than five minutes was required for pitching and perhaps twice that for teardown and good storage, rolling the fabric tightly.

The tent was unfurled and set between two small pines in a stand of young trees. The Lambretta, Tony, was leaned up against one of the pines and tied to it with one of the half dozen short lengths of small nylon rope included in my tool kit. The kickstand was useless in soft earth and also on sun-softened pavement. Using a large stick (my organic, gluten-free shovel), small trenches were scratched in the loose earth to guide water around the tent in case of rain. A small circle of stones on cleared ground would support the coffee pot in the morning and a supply of small twigs and small branches was gathered and positioned for easy ignition in the morning, enough firewood to boil the two or three cups of water vital for bringing me to reasonably intelligent consciousness in the morning. Crawling on all fours through the entrance, I pushed the sleeping bag ahead of me. Unzipped it. And then ....

It was morning. My guess was 10 or 11 hours had passed. There was some light filtering through the tent fabric. That and bladder pressure probably pushed me awake. First, look outside the tent flap to see if any critters awaited my arrival. Then pee on a tree. Then it was time for coffee. Light the prearranged fire. The pot held almost two and one-half cups. Two cups of water from the water bag went into the pot, three scoops of fine ground coffee followed. Then onto the fire. Wash hands and face and brush teeth. With the higher elevation, (Show Low was at 7,400 ft.), the water boiled more quickly, but was not quite as hot. In a few minutes, I had two cups of delicious coffee (with a little texture because of grounds). I didn't like to wait for coffee to "settle." No need to get dressed because I had never undressed the previous night.

Not before, but after coffee, it was a time to plan this day which was already surrounding me. There was more of Show Low to see, I was camping in either Pinetop or Lakeside (not sure which or if there was any distinction). Arizona real estate had begun to interest me ... though not yet legally able to sign a contract, it would be less than two months before I could. Thought I might be on the road again at noon, and, let me see, it is now ... oh, I forgot, I have no watch. It was purposely left back in Tucson to avoid having a timepiece (other than the sun) to alter my thinking or cause me to change my activities in any way on the way. The next spot to land would be ... yes, the Petrified Forest, a little less than 100 miles north and east. That could be cool. Before that, I wanted to wash and change clothing. There was water available a few steps away, I had soap and a washcloth and the water would be shocking and I might die of thermal deprivation, but not until later in the morning, at least until the air warmed up a few degrees. So, explore the local scene first, return to camp, wash, and then head out.

Sounds like a plan, except... did I want to pack up everything, then unpack to wash, then repack or ... should I leave and hope everything would be there on my return. How could an unlocked tent, sleeping bag, etc. be made more secure when the owner (me) is elsewhere and not in sight? Taking the last sip of now-cold coffee, I dipped the coffee pot into the creek, swirled the water around and threw the grounds onto the pine needles covering the soft earth and wrote a short note on one of the 4 x 6 inch filing cards out of the small pack I carried. The note was rolled up loosely and tied to one of the drawstring cords used to close the tent entrance.

The note went like this:

> Hey Big Lovie—
> Hang loose for a few minutes
> Be back real quick
> Getting ammo
> Joey

So that was my security. We traveled slowly on the main road south of Show Low looking at Pinetop and Lakeside, both areas being thickly wooded, with wood cabins dotted here and there. Tried this side road for a mile and that side road for two miles and everything looked beautiful and after an hour or so, rather boring. It was a bit of a fad at the time, for people from hot desert areas of Tucson and Phoenix to buy "summer cabins" in these pine-forested White Mountains of Arizona and prices for plots of land and house lots were increasing strongly. Turning north again, I returned to Show Low, to a café for pancakes, another cup or two of coffee, conversation with the waitress, and use of the restroom. Then, it was back to the hardware store. One item needed was a small, strong garden trowel for digging … the small pit for my campfire, trenches around the tent, and a deeper hole to be used as a latrine. Said hello to the same guy as yesterday, couldn't find a suitable trowel , but thanked him again for his recommendation for camping, said it was perfect, and said "See you later" knowing that I probably wouldn't. The road heading north out of town would soon be seeing us. Show Low seemed a friendly little town … but it was time to go.

Time to go back to the little temporary camp spot and time to see if my stuff was still there. It was indeed, and undisturbed. Now was the time for terror … time to get clean using unheated creek water, soap, a washcloth, and a small towel. My whole body was covered by a warm, perfectly comfortable layer of road dust, dried perspiration, and body dirt. And it was all to be removed along with the clothing that helped hold it all together. That just does not make sense. I was about to risk arrest by some local authorities for stripping naked and rubbing my body with water straight from the artic. It would be quick, but thorough and painful. First, the preparations … fresh underwear and socks unpacked and laid out, and of course, the tools of torture (washcloth, etc.). Then the tent was tied between two pines to form a sort of privacy barrier, which was useless since there was no 'my side' or 'inside' or 'your side' or 'outside'. The privacy barrier was strictly for explanation purposes if local law enforcement happened by, with me saying in an imaginary conversation, "You see, sir (always use the sir or ma'am word), I tried to stay covered and washed and got dressed as quickly as possible." Time to do the deed. Slowly strip down to my underwear, place the clothing to be worn in exactly the right place, etc. Knowing that the anticipation was always worse than the doing, I stepped to the edge of the creek and furiously began sloshing and soaping and washing and groping and scrubbing and rubbing and let's get the hell out of this water, kick the polar bears out of the way, and dry off. And it needs telling, it was, in fact, even worse than anticipated. The body was clean and fitted with fresh underwear, the spirit was only slightly damaged, and the frostbite would heal. The rest was easy. Everything was OK.

So my little camp had been untouched during my absence. Did my note to Big Louie have any effect? If it did, I would never know. If it didn't work, it would be all too noticeable. As the sleeping bag was rolled up, and the tent was compressed to near original size, my thoughts turned to Duffy from yesterday's meeting, and then to this morning's purposely misleading note to "Big Louie" signed by "Joey." Without thinking about it, I was using "this Italian thing" to my advantage, this partially unknown, somewhat unpredictable, slightly threatening quality that many people attributed to Italian-Americans. I would think about that, as again, my faithful steed Tony Lambretta would be pointed north toward The Petrified Forest.

CHAPTER 7

PETRIFIED

Leaving the campsite in as close to original condition as possible, we, Tony Lambretta and I, scootered north again to Show Low to buy food at a grocer's for the next day or two or three. My diet would change dramatically on this trip, being accustomed to a large variety of excellent food while working as a waiter in a high-dollar hotel. Now it would be back to basics, very basic basics. The next town was Snowflake, Arizona, 20 or 25 miles away, then Holbrook, another 25 or 30 miles, and then, yet another dozen miles or so to the Petrified Forest for a camping spot ... rather lean pickings when fine dining is considered. Good food would be needed to stay healthy, sufficient calories, too. To some very small degree, this was a survival trek. There was a moderately-sized food store on Deuce of Clubs Avenue and I stopped. Into my basket went a small bag of almonds, a box of prunes, a small box of raisins, two cans of string beans, a loaf of French bread, and a few pieces of fresh fruit. While not a vegetarian, my normal meat intake was hardly ever more than six or eight ounces (200 grams) per week, and perhaps the same for cheese. There was no accounting for ice cream since it would be consumed at almost every opportunity. Big surprise – this store had a real meat counter with a guy who appeared to be a butcher, with a name tag which said Achilles. A Greek, for sure. Looking at me from inside the meat case was four small sausage-looking things that looked at least semi-dried, with no label or price. Me: "Excuse me. Mister Achilles, what kind of meat are those little ones in the corner?" Him: "Achilles is my given name, not my family name, but that's OK." Me: "OK, SIR Achilles." Him: "That's better!" and we both laughed. "Anyway, those are cacciatore salami, imported from Italy." Me: "Never heard of that, chicken cacciatore from the hunter ... yes, but this ... no." So he described them as very dry, slightly sweet, and very spicy. Sounded perfect. We chatted for a few minutes, about the store, the scooter trip, the town, and how I knew cacciatore (cah cha TOR eh) meant hunter in Italian. And then asking if he had a hard dried cheese that would keep without refrigeration for a few days, I waved at the packaged meats and cheeses, over there against the wall, making a negative face. He said "Myzithra." (pronounced mee-Zee-thra). I shook my head as he held up about a half-pound chunk. "Myzithra, it's a hard Greek cheese, similar to the hard Italian Pecorino and this piece would cost $2.00 and I'll donate the cacciatore." Together they were a great bargain. I asked why and he said. "Look, I'll never sell these sophisticated foods to these people around here. They're not ready for it. If it doesn't come from a cow they're not interested unless it's bacon. So my mistake is your gain. Enjoy. And enjoy your trip. And say hello to New York!" I paid for my all the food at the front of the store, walked back again to the meat counter, and I shook his hand, said again "Sir Achilles." He looked over the top of his glasses and I said, "Ciao, my friend." I felt kindred to this man. Seemed like a good guy.

Note to readers: As I write these paragraphs, you should be advised of at least three inaccuracies (there are certainly more than that): (1) mileages quoted are close estimates, (2) dollar amounts are wild estimates, and (3) except for me, Duffy, the scooter named Tony Lambretta, and a few others, all personal names have been changed.

Back on Show Low's Deuce of Clubs then a turn north onto my familiar Route 77 heading to Snowflake. After 3 or 4 miles, vegetation became thinner and more "scrubby" with pinòn, juniper, cedar, and maybe pin oak. Within ten miles, we were driving through some semi-desolate areas. What would account for that? Elevation was nearly the same, with precipitation and temperatures probably pretty close to Show Low's numbers. Maybe it was a different type of soil. Though being semi-knowledgeable in gardening stuff, I was puzzled. There were a few cattle grazing here and there and (heel of hand bumping against my forehead) that was probably it. Grazing. The land was being constantly stripped. So while distant views from the scooter to the horizons were picturesque, close-up views were depressing and neither was postcard material – not total devastation, but not so pretty either. There were some green areas where Show Low creek and the highway were close to each other and where people were doing some commercial planting, probably animal fodder.

An hour after leaving Show Low, I was rolling into the vibrant metropolis of Snowflake, Arizona, except there wasn't much 'into' about it. A farming and cattle community, it had a population just over 1000. Taking a left into town, I putt-putted here and there just looking at this community. That took almost 5 minutes. From a short distance away the LDS (Mormon) Temple looked better than anything else in town, and that same sort of thing occurs all over the world. Back to the main route for a break, off my bottom, to stretch my legs, have a smoke, and some water, and with the intention to pee somewhere up the road where people weren't. Lighting up a cigarette immediately identifies a person as an outsider in a Mormon community. Of course, the strangeness of my scooter had already done that to anyone who might be interested. A few vehicles passed by on the highway, most ignoring me completely, others slowing down with drivers or passengers squinting out the window in my direction. The beautiful name of the town of Snowflake, Arizona, very well-known in The Worldwide Interesting Name Society (WINS) would most likely have been named from some beautiful incident or poetic quote. No such luck. Erastus Snow and William Flake, two pioneers in 1878, settled the area and gave it the name. Not a very exciting story. Not when compared to the origins of Buttfrozen, Alaska.

Smoked as much of the cigarette as I wanted, extinguished and field-stripped it, and was ready to start Tony again, when what should appear, but a tiny ... First, let me tell those of you who have never smoked and have never been in the military, what field stripping is. It's a way to make a cigarette butt disappear and not litter the landscape. When you're done smoking, step on the end to extinguish the glowing portion of tobacco. Next, you split the paper or flick it a few times to spill and disperse the shreds of tobacco onto the grass or the ground where they are absorbed in some manner by nature. The paper and filter go into your pocket for later disposal at a waste basket or trash can. So what did appear? A shiny triangle in the roadside dirt. Nudging it with my boot, no movement. Pushed some dirt away, then more. Now digging with the toe of my boot, I got it to move much more and then out of the ground ... an aluminum scoop like those used in bulk food departments. About five inches wide, eight inches long and quite strong, but the handle had been broken off at its narrowest point, leaving about an inch still attached to the scooping part. This strong lightweight scoop, not the trowel I had sought to buy, would be my camping shovel. A treasure! How could I ever repay this debt to Snowflake? It would be rather simply taken care of by not charging the town for trash removal. We'd call it even.

Time to hit the highway for an hour or so to Holbrook, AZ on famous Route 66. Holbrook, at 3,300 people, was about three times the size of Snowflake and if it had three times the 'action', it would still have no action at all, but maybe there was a cafe. On the one-hour drive to Holbrook, my thoughts turned to the many subjects I knew so little about. These crops I was seeing along the way ... couldn't name them or recognize them. Cattle, of course, I did recognize but actual knowledge was sparse. Mormons ... I knew almost nothing about that group. New England didn't cover much about them in school or anywhere else. My impression was they were a strange bunch of people out in Utah. The fact that my boss, manager of the resort back in Tucson was a Mormon, did little to educate me and here

I was 'in Mormon country' as ignorant as ever, bringing me to good place for a rant...

... about growing up in the educational system in Connecticut. My complaint concerns the study of History, specifically American history. There was so much history that had occurred in western regions of the US, Canada, and in Mexico, not ever mentioned. It was as if everything west of Pennsylvania was just miles and miles of sand where nothing ever happened ... no Conquistadores, no Padres Kino and Serra, no Apaches or Navajo, no Lewis and Clark, and on and on ... but of course we made up for it by covering the pilgrims every year, year after year. Got sent to the principal's office the first day of school, tenth or eleventh grade, for loudly complaining in class "Oh no. Not those goddamn pilgrims AGAIN." Comments and suggestions of this sort were not welcomed in those days. Perhaps it was my delivery rather than the content of my message. The phrase did catch on for a short time at school with a few braver souls occasionally saying "Oh no! Those goddamn pilgrims again." In all those years, we used one or two class sessions on our Civil War and there was only a briefest mention of World War I. WW II, ending just a decade previously, didn't exist as far as our school system was concerned. And here I was 'Out West', filled with impressions of the place, impressions that were, most likely, badly distorted if not completely wrong. That's my rant. Overall, in public school from kindergarten through high school, I received an otherwise excellent education by US standards, with a splendid background in sciences and math. Later in life, I would try catching up on my history, starting with WWII

The road from Snowflake to Holbrook was smooth, straight, and boring, to me at least. This was desert, but a higher and often cold desert very different from the Sonora Desert where Tucson, much of Southern Arizona, and parts of Mexico enjoyed warmth and sunshine most of the year. This more northern desert was a scrubby tree and sparse grass terrain. Any dramatic landscapes seemed at quite a distance. Tony Lambretta purred steadily and contentedly as we moved northward. This was a leisurely day, badly needed after a long, exciting, and jam-packed yesterday. A day to just take it easy.

Traveling the few miles toward Holbrook was uneventful, with little traffic. On the south edge of town ran the Little Colorado River, sometimes powerful, sometimes dry, but a small to moderate flow as we crossed the bridge into town. The Little Colorado eventually adds its contribution to its larger brother, the Colorado River, creator and sculptor of our Grand Canyon.

The road eastward from Holbrook, on Route 66 and Interstate 40, looked a little on the lean side as far as creature comfort and conveniences were concerned. It would be best to stay as full as possible for the Lambretta and perhaps myself. I looked for a café for a sandwich. Food purchased back in Show Low from Sir Achilles would be consumed in the Petrified Forest and beyond.

A large sign on a small building said "EAT DRINK" ... straight-forward advertising catering to my exact wishes, for the moment at least. Evidently, late morning was not a busy time at EAT DRINK. A slightly plump, pleasant-faced young woman was using tape to attach an announcement for the day's "special" to the napkin holders. It was a steak sandwich, fried potatoes, and a pickle, very reasonably priced. The woman smiled as she approached, said "Hello, what can I get you for lunch?" I said the special sounded good and asked if it had onions. No, onions would be extra. "OK then, a steak sandwich, plain, and a cup of black coffee, please." Then her smile vanished and a blank look covered her face in less than a second and words sounded "We don't have coffee." The words were in the same voice, but her lips didn't seem to move. Hmmm. Not being known for my sensitivity, but open to suggestion, I asked, "What do you normally serve?" The answer was milk. "Great! A steak sandwich and a glass of chocolate milk." The look remained. And I swear, words appeared in the air above her head, saying "We don't have chocolate." About to ask what kind of place would ever be without chocolate, it finally penetrated thick fog in my head ... Oh, this woman was one of an exotic tribe of people called Mormons. Oh brother, oh sister, talk about dense, I won the prize that day. Recovering, and saying, "Water will be fine," and truly not intending to say it, I added, "Holy water." Both of us were surprised. She almost smiled.

After that sandwich, that very good sandwich, it would be a natural action for me to have a cup of coffee and a smoke, but having enough flexibility can be helpful. My goal was to get to the Petrified Forest, about 25 miles (40km) east of Holbrook, which was an hour's drive. Before that, I thought I'd noodle around Holbrook for a bit, since I might never return. The now very famous Route 66 went straight through Holbrook. It was called America's Highway and went 2,500 miles (4,000 km) from Chicago to Los Angeles and across the entire width of northern Arizona. The song Route 66 was known, but not an enormous hit in 1960. Holbrook was one of the places along the way which was not mentioned in the song. The TV series, with two guys blasting around in a Corvette convertible, would begin after my trip was done. Route 66 was a real mixture of scenic road and shabby places catering to tourists and travelers of every description. Holbrook was not a pretty place, just average. There was a motel called the Wigwam motel, with perhaps eight or ten cone-shaped structures, plastered or finished with stucco. Teepee Motel seemed a more accurate name, but differentiation between wigwam, teepee, and wikiup structures was unknown to me. If The Wigwam Motel was the biggest hit in town, it was time to leave and head eastward to the Petrified Forest to look at rocks and do some reading. Top off the fuel tank and go, but not before the gas station guy said, "Damn. All the way to Boston? Shoulda done something big and stupid like that, but I got married." An hour later, after two or three quick stops to gather a small bundle of firewood, we were taking a right hand turn, going southward into the Petrified Forest.

CHAPTER 8

BADLANDS

At the intersection of Route 66 and Petrified Forest Road, sat a yellow pickup truck, a shade rigged up on one side, some signs announcing availability of Indian jewelry, blankets, fry bread and petrified rocks. There were two Indians attending this portable store (we did not yet call them Native Americans). Though I didn't ask, my first question was "which tribe?" They ranged from A to Z, literally. This huge Painted Desert land, which included the Petrified Forest, had at least four major tribes on its bordering lands – Apache, Hopi, Navajo, and Zuni. On the road from Holbrook to this highway junction, there were a dozen or more shops selling everything imaginable to the tourist trade. The huge expanse of Painted Desert was visually stunning and geologically fascinating. While having done rock-hounding and spelunking in the eastern US, the Southwest seemed almost unbelievable in its variety of minerals and formations as well as its easy accessibility for any rock hound or mineral collector. In Massachusetts, easiest pickin's for rock hounds were highway cuts. The Massachusetts turnpike was a great place to chip away at rock faces, but if we stopped for too long a time, a State Police vehicle would almost certainly pull up behind us. The officer would explain that despite being off the roadway, we were not allowed to stop except at rest stops, etc. Most of those guys were good about it. A few were jackasses, and spouted and fumed, but we never got a ticket or a written warning. Of course, there had been some deception involved at times. We carried four one-quart soda bottles full of water in the trunk of the car. When we stopped at a highway cut, we'd lift the car's hood part way, pour about half a bottle of water on the radiator cap to cool it, then do our rock sampling. When a patrol car approached one of us would climb down the rock face, feel the car's radiator, and holler at the other one, "OK, it's cool enough! Let's get going." None of that ruse was necessary out here in the west.

Within two or three miles south of the intersection with Route 66, a small sign pointed to Newspaper Rock, down a small road to the right.   Just a few hundred feet by scooter and a few steps on foot and I was looking at petroglyphs crafted by some artist or reporter or advertising executive from a distant past. So many designs and pictures all pecked into moderately dark stone, exposing lighter stone material underneath. Here's a spiral, here's a sunburst sort of thing. Here's a guy with a large penis, here's another without, here a sunrise or sunset, here a lizard type animal. This engraving in stone was not an easy or casual thing to accomplish ... not just a magic marker or spray paint type of quick graffiti. Someone had to have been patient and determined to record a message in stone. Or ... perhaps it was just art, abstract or realistic. And the person pecking on this stone was just feeling an urge to create, thinking "Some goats would look good right here." There were a few designs in stone in the Tortolita Mountains near Tucson, just a mile or two from my home, but 400 miles to the south of where Newspaper Rock sat. Not having seen any petroglyphs done by Indians in the more Eastern states, these, in front of me, were fascinating and, at the same time, puzzling to me. Since we have found no Rosetta Stone keyed to petroglyphs, they're sure to be a mystery to almost everybody. My guess is that today's archeologist or scholar might write thousands of pages about these drawings in stone (until the grant money runs out), without ever actually knowing their meaning or purpose.

 Wanting to see more, I got back on the scooter, kickstarted it, and returned to the road leading south. Books tell me this entire area was part of an earth formation we call Chinle (about 200 million years of history, give or take 50 million years). Scattered everywhere were variously sized, from modest to enormous, horizontally-striped cones, where layers of earth of different colors (mostly reds and grays) had been eroded by wind and water. Some of these had been seen from the highway on the drive from Holbrook. Slowly scootering past these cones, some of which were called "The Teepees," gave a slowly changing landscape and a constantly evolving perspective of their shapes and sizes. This land was eroded into uncountable natural sculptures, each unique, each with its own ancient designer. Being an artist involved in mosaics, but not yet 'into' sculpture (that would begin a few years later), these nature-made artworks were simply mesmerizing. Timeless.

 Prior to entering Petrified Forest, my impression was there was no vegetation in that forbidding place, none at all. Of course, my impression was wrong, but not by much. There were small bushes and there was some grass. Friendly campsites with water were not to be had. This was tough country for plants, for beasts, and for mankind. This was called 'badlands' with good reason. As is common in the desert, along the now dry rivers or dry washes were probably the best places to stay for a few hours ... along, not in. A chance rainstorm, even miles away, can wipe you out in seconds as the so-called wall of water decides to pass through your campsite in the bottom of the wash, where, of course, you might have chosen to camp to lessen the effects of an annoying wind. Tony Lambretta and I noodled along, taking a short sidepath for a few hundred feet this way and another sidepath going that way, while surrounding geology became more and more overwhelming and I still hadn't seen the Petrified Forest. On one of the side journeys toward a dry wash, there was a former campsite off the road about 100 feet, marked by a small piece of yellow cloth. Someone had marked this site with that small ribbon of cloth purposely tied to one of the slender branches. Taking the scooter along an already existing footpath, I found three clumps of scrub brush growing together, one of them almost four feet tall. That could provide a bit of shade for the remainder of the afternoon. Needing a break, I'd make some coffee (unavailable at EAT DRINK, remember?), have a snack, make a camp for the night, and do a little reading. Petrified wood could be seen in the morning. There was no urgency, since getting on the road early in the morning when you're traveling eastward means you'll be staring directly into bright sunshine. So mid-morning is a better time to start, and a day ends more gently with sun and wind at your back. Setting up camp so my small tent would be shaded as much as possible took only a few minutes. A few minutes more and a small fire was burning for coffee. Started on a snack, including some of that cacciatore salami, washed it down with some coffee, and settled down to read one of two pocket edition paperbacks that had been packed for this trip. Hoping my books appreciated use of precious cargo room on their behalf, I started on Steinbeck.

Since childhood, reading was my friend, my major source of entertainment, and my major source of education. Reading anything at all was heaven to me ... labels on food packages, the Book of Knowledge encyclopedia, newspapers, Reader's Digest fillers (those little stories or jokes at the end of an article) ... almost anything. To this day, in my seventy-five years, I have tried to read at least one book a week. That's three or four thousand books or more. In my normal life, there were usually five or six books in progress and I would switch from one to another and read until I dropped, always resisting and resenting the need to sleep. The only two books which began this trip with me were Steinbeck's "Of Mice and Men" and Michener's "Tales of the South Pacific." When one was finished, it would be time to stop at a used book store and find a replacement. Michener's work was pulling me in, by his style of writing, but more compelling, by the extensive research I knew had gone into his book before words were put on paper. "Of Mice and Men" by John Steinbeck kept me occupied for perhaps two hours, taking me three-fourths of the way through this Steinbeck novel. Our sun was dropping to the west, and soon my reading would stop, having no battery-powered light with sufficient power for reading for any length of time.

The day had been perfect ... almost no wind, temperature (low 70's my guess, 22deg C) and now the rapid cooling of the dry desert would begin (probably into the mid 30's, 2 deg C). Now would begin a strong, silent, powerful light show of the setting sun on these wildly carved earth parts. Now, very quiet. Thought I heard some bird sounds but was unsure. Heard a distant howl, immediately thinking coyote, but not quite the same as I heard in Tucson. Maybe coyotes in different locations had different accents or dialects. The light became more red, livening the already reddish stripes of the cones, and making the grey stripes a murky pink. The howl sounded again, a bit louder and closer. Two minutes later, I saw him, her, whichever – a very large coyote? A German Shepard? No, it couldn't be a wolf, could it? There! Down in the creek bed, visible, but fading as daylight continued to diminish. Decided to light a few more small pieces of firewood. Was this my protection? Don't know. Decided the second cup of coffee needed reheating ... that was why I rekindled the fire, oh sure. Tried to protect my eyes from firelight, and strained to see into that creek bed, but the image had vanished.

Had that been a stray shepherd dog from some nearby settlement? Seemed too big for a coyote. Had some government agency relocated wolves to this part of the desert? My thinking went in several directions. Despite knowing my almost total vulnerability, I felt only mildly threatened and merely hoped that this "wolf" didn't like Italian food, meaning me. Then, imagining wolf couples who might have been transplanted into this barren landscape, their reactions might have gone like this: "Oh man, what a bummer. See this place? Nothingsville! A million acres of kitty litter! Damn, we were doing pretty good back at the compound ... and now this? And that wolf couple who were already here ... have you heard their accents? Wonder where the hell they're from."

Thoughts turned back to the Mormon café, but of course, without coffee it couldn't really be called a café. A diner, then, a diner named EAT DRINK. A diner serving highway trade, but with no coffee for salesmen driving to the next appointment or for the tourist needing to wake up from the hypnotizing effects of road travel. To me, the Mormon stimulant thing seemed simply absurd. Absurd, that is, until I considered some of the Jewish food laws also serving as health measures, or the insanity of the Roman Catholic teaching "no meat on Friday." All these religious inconsistencies, ridiculous. The use of wine was one that I thought was more than funny. To drink wine was forbidden until you were an 'adult' and maybe forbidden forever, dependent on which group of crazies had their hooks into you. Celebrate the New Testament miracle of turning water into wine (which reportedly was done by a guy named Jesus), but if the Gallo brothers or Carlo Rossi did the same thing in California, it became subject to holy censure. Being skeptical, it all smacked of sleazy manipulation to me. But then, wasn't that the purpose of religion? Manipulation and control and getting you to tithe.

While setting up this night's little camp area, I had found two flat stones of decent size and placed them under the "feet" of Tony Lambretta's kickstand. Since there was nothing of any height to which the scooter could be tied, I could only hope there would be no strong wind to knock it over. This machine had performed well these past two days and we both seemed content, for the moment at least. This Lambretta, and the Vespa as well, were marvels of practical mechanical engineering. My rough estimate was that we were traveling about 80 miles (125km) on one US gallon of fuel. Hats Off! to those people responsible, those mechanical engineers in Milan, Italy.

Too dark to read, it was a time to look at the sky and uncountable stars poking little holes in the darkness. That lasted until night cooled to a point where it would be more comfortable inside the little tent, whose tie-string opening was aimed to the east, just as the ancients might have done with their little rubberized nylon tents.

CHAPTER 9

TO GALLUP

Morning of the third day and it was chilly and it was dawn. The coffeepot had managed to crawl onto my tiny campfire, while I walked some meters away and used that precious scoop to dig a 12-inch deep latrine spot. Very easy digging and even easier covering the hole after the paperwork was complete. As the night's warmth left my clothing and sleeping bag, water in the pot could be heard close to boiling point. Now, as the sun rose in the east, that most sacred of all mankind's rituals, performed slowly and deliberately, came to its conclusion with me holding that morning's first cup of coffee. Thank the Gods (in this case named Chock Full o' Nuts) for this vital sustenance. The last ounce or two of that first cup of coffee was savored while mentally planning the day. Since traveling would be south along Petrified Forest Road, I could start early and not stare into the sun and soon I would indeed see The Petrified Forest. Wasting no time, the camp was packed up and now it was time for that lesser, but still necessary, ritual, performed with enthusiasm – that second cup of coffee. Next …fire out and cool. No trash left behind. An apple core, one string bean which looked discolored, a tiny bit of sausage skin, and a few raisins accidentally dropped onto the sandy ground … these I did not consider trash and placed them at the base of a bush. It would be food for some critter. A new and falsely prompted civilization would probably not spring forth from the bounty of one apple core. The can from the string beans was flattened and stashed for disposal at the next fuel stop.

On the forest road and traveling slowly, enjoying the rising sun on my left, scooter quietly purring, we bypassed Agate Bridge and Jasper Forest, instead heading directly to Crystal Forest, to me, a quietly astounding collection of fossilized tree sections, colorful and gleaming in the light of this early day. Having an interest in geology for five or six years, I had read of the formation of this petrified wood. I was neither a paleontologist nor a 'fossilographer' or 'fossilologist' (my own words with Microsoft's squiggly and persistent red line underneath). Briefly, here's how it happened. These rather large trees grew in a low-lying area, some falling over onto the ground (by wind? by volcanic eruption?). Flooding then occurred, covering these fallen trees with one or more layers of silt before animals, insects, or microbes could cause decomposition. After that, mineral-bearing water moved through the silt, and slowly replaced the wood with those minerals, creating a stone or mineral fossil mimicking the original wood. Later, the land rose in elevation and became eroded by wind and water. The fossils were harder than the surrounding soils and were left on top of the surface where we find them today. That's as brief as I can make it. Bear in mind, this whole process didn't occur on a weekend, but rather over many, many thousands of years. This Crystal Forest was magic. It was as if an enormous and ancient being had scattered contents of its costume jewelry box across the landscape. Here now was a collection of ancient baubles and unstrung beads, each having its own beauty — a variety of colors, some pale, some intense. Sections of mineralized tree trunks scattered, some seeming to have their own source of light. Walking to this grouping or that, wondering at events which had initiated this rock forest, imagining histories these rocks had seen, I felt mildly possessed by a distant past which would never be truly known.

The morning sun's warmth and dryness in my throat pulled me back into this world, toward the water bag. Certainly this had been one adventure for me for today, and this day was still young. Perhaps two hours had passed looking at, touching, and empathizing with this bunch of rocks. A person has to be a bit loony for that sort of thing, right? Well yes, but so be it. A few miles further south along this Petrified Forest road would take me to Agate house, a structure made entirely of petrified wood chucks used as bricks. There would also be an area of fossilized tree trunks of longer length. My curiosity had been satisfied, however. Leaving Agate House and the Long Woods for others to see, heading back at a slow pace, enjoying the surroundings in a much different light from the previous afternoon, we made our way out of the park. The magic of the place had been wrapped up and put into my sack of experiences.

At the junction of Route 66, there were two or three people setting up the same yellow pickup truck and canopy as yesterday. Waving a good morning greeting as we passed, I headed east on 66. Then came the realization that these were the only people I had seen since entering the Petrified Forest ... inside the park not a soul, nor even the sound of a vehicle. There were other petrified wood deposits elsewhere in the world, even perhaps in the US, but certainly this was the most popular, the best known in the world, yet it seemed I was alone today. Maybe a troop of 400 cub scouts entered just after my exit. Maybe I had timed it perfectly.

There was more scenic Painted Desert terrain as we headed eastward, but again the harshness of this high desert was apparent with sparse vegetation, intense sunlight, and sun-bleached rocks and soil. It really was magnificent stuff, this painted and sculpted desert land. With 7,500 square miles of area (20,000 sq. km), it seemed endless and timeless. Of course, every so often, there would be a tourist shop, selling anything a tourist might purchase. And that was OK as far as I was concerned, except for the petrified wood ... incredible amounts for sale, each piece with its price. Where had all this come from? Certainly some had come from the National Park that I had just left. If allowed, stupid people would cart off all the petrified wood and the National Park would cease to exist. Hopefully, protection would become more effective. While the Lambretta purred along this relatively barren ground, imaginary conversation between two tourists played in my head, with Abel saying, "Hey, look Honey, here's some of that petrified wood that looks like it has a heart shape on it." Mabel then says, "Hmmm." Abel says "Maybe we should buy it to remind us of this trip." Mabel: "What would you do with it once it was at the house, 'cause I don't want anything I have to dust every week." Abel: "Hey, we could put it right near the front door next to the seashells from California. That way, people would know where we've been." Mable says, "Since we've been to Mount Rushmore, maybe we should go back and get a chunk of stone out of Washington's nose." Abel: "Oh, Mable, don't be ridiculous, I just think this is unusual." Mabel says, "Oh, alright Abel, maybe you should go ahead and buy your precious wood before there isn't any left out there."

We had traveled perhaps thirty miles since leaving the Petrified Forest. There was some highway construction where Route 66 was being transformed into Interstate 40. This was part of the Interstate Highway program ramrodded into being in the Eisenhower presidency, in 1956, four years previously. It would, in later years, become an enormous system costing billions of dollars, allowing much easier travel across the US. It would also create a number of ghost towns or ghost communities as it bypassed them. Two places which, as far as I was concerned, were very nearly ghost towns already were Sanders and Chambers, both of which were just intersections with Route 191, one leg of which went north from Chambers off to some unseen destination, the other leg, 5 miles further east, pointed south from Sanders, where I saw a small cloud of dust a very short distance off 66.

Time to take a break. Have a smoke. South of 66, less than a mile, was the source of the dust ... a small collection of corrals and people doing calf roping. This rodeo skill involves dexterity with a rope, a well-trained horse, and a good deal of courage beside. A calf is released from a chute and runs like hell, a split second later, rider and horse begin the chase, rider with rope in hand trying to lasso the calf around the neck. If successful, the rider dismounts and tries to tie three legs of the calf together, temporarily disabling the unsuspecting victim. All this is timed, usually taking 7 or 8 seconds if it's a good run (the world record being 6 seconds). Watching for a while, it was apparent this was not a competition, rather just a "practice" I was witness to. On one release, the calf, instead of running directly out of the chute, took a sharp turn to the right and ran alongside the corral fence. The lasso seemed to circle the neck OK, but rider and calf crashed into the fence with an impact I felt would surely kill both beast and man. Finally, the calf was tied and while the time probably was not a good one, all participants survived amidst the dust cloud raised. While I watched at a little distance, two pickup trucks pulling horse trailers passed by and pulled in amongst the rodeo group. None of the people I saw looked like Indians ... they all looked like cowboys ... some blonde, some darker skinned, a real mix, but they all looked like western cowboys to me, the displaced waiter. No war bonnets or feathers that I could see.

We were in Navajo lands, with the Zuni Tribe not far away. Evidently there were disputes between the two tribes which I had little knowledge of, the tribes or the disputes. Later in life I would work with a few Apaches, a few Pima and Papagos, and several from the Navajo nation at Fort Defiance and Window Rock, both communities being north of Sanders. Eastward from Sanders, another 15 or 20 miles would take me to the Arizona border with New Mexico. Two-and-a-half days of travel and I was still in Arizona. Man, these western states were huge. On an auto trip in New England, one could travel through three or four states in one day without trying.

After a snack of cacciatore salami, myzithra cheese, water, and a smoke, it would be twenty miles to the border and another twenty to Gallup, NM, where there would be a stop for fuel, and water. Only a cup or a little more water remained in the bag and I didn't want the water bag to dry out if it could be avoided. So I would wait to reach Gallup before drinking much more. Back onto Route 66, and heading east, actually northeast, for the border. On my right, from the highway, railroad tracks, which paralleled the road, were almost always in view. Not far beyond the tracks, serpentining across the high desert, was a dry river bed. Trains traveling this stretch seemed to have no less than 50 cars (sometimes twice that number) trailing behind the engines with a caboose announcing the end of the train. It became a game to count to cars as they passed in either direction. Always, I'd give a wave to the engineer upfront with the engines and to the brakeman or 'cabooseman' (my word) and sometimes the greeting would be returned and not often, but occasionally, a tiny touch of that huge train horn would sound. Counting railroad cars of a moving train while you yourself are moving can be a bit of a challenge since so many cars looked identical. Difficult to keep your place when you have to look at the road you're driving on occasionally.

As the border came into view, Arizona signs said "Hope You Enjoyed Your Visit" and "Come Back Soon to The Grand Canyon State." The signs for New Mexico welcomed me to the "Land of Enchantment." On the westbound side was an Inspection and Weighing Station for all vehicles entering Arizona. At the time, agricultural inspection was trying to prevent the entrance of any citrus product into Arizona for fear of contaminating our citrus crops with a blight or some insect invasion. If you had any citrus in your vehicle, you'd be given the choice to abandon it at the inspection point or pull your vehicle to the side and begin to consume your cargo. Of course, as soon as you finished eating your crateful of grapefruit, you could enter Arizona tanked up with Vitamin C, with blessings from the inspectors, and maybe a little applause as well.

The highway in New Mexico was long and straight for miles. At one point, one could see the downhill slope of the highway (this part was being called I-40) for perhaps five or six miles, maybe more, and beyond that see an equal amount of the upward slope of the same highway as it climbed the other side of an immense valley. Looking to that far end, my guess was that we could be there in an hour and would make an imaginary appointment with that spot in the road. At the beginning of the downward slope, three double-trailer rigs, one close behind the next and then the next, came roaring past me at what seemed like the speed of sound, nearing pushing me off the road with the pressure of the wind they created and then sucking the scooter and me into their backdraft, the windshield probably acting as an effective sail of sorts. While trying to maintain my position on the pavement, the miles per hour on the speedometer and the rpm's had never been higher and I snapped the scooter out of gear to ride it out. Pretty dangerous situation for the unprepared. My thoughts had been elsewhere and the rigs approaching from the rear had been a complete surprise. It wasn't long before suburbs of Gallup, NM were in view, the suburbs being some tourist shops, a café, a gas station or two, the usual unpretty signs of the Route 66 civilization. Unpretty unless you had need for fuel, water, or coffee, the three travel essentials.

Pulling into a gas station, the scooter and I were not heavy enough to activate the alarm cable strung across the driveway. Because no attendant appeared, I walked to the 'office', walked in, and called out "hello! hello?" From the rear door, a call said, "Just a minute, be right there!" A middle-aged guy came through the door and said, "Hi, Sorry, Out back working on my car. Didn't hear the bell." Pointing to the scooter out front, he said.

"Oh, I see why, Need some gas?" I said, "Yeah, hate to bother you, but all I need is a gallon or so. That, and a bathroom, too." As we walked toward the scooter parked at the pump, he said, "No problem at all, no problem at all. What kind of scooter is that? Doesn't look like a Cushman." "No, a Lambretta, like a Vespa, Italian made." He laughed and said, "but you're supposed to have four people and a picnic basket on there and you're all by yourself." I said, "You've been to Italy?" "Nope, but my son spent a little time there with the Navy. He told me about these scooters. How far do you go on a gallon?" I told him my guess ... somewhere between 70 and 90 miles, I had never kept a record. He said, "Here's the key to the bathroom, over there on the left. Before you leave would you be willing to help me for a minute or two with my car?" I said "If I can, sure." I started the scooter and drove away from the gas pump to the rear of the building, used the bathroom, splashed some very cold water on my face, went outside, got the water bag and filled it to the brim, put it back on the scooter and then walked over to his car, a beautiful 1948 Ford coupe, black and shiny. He said, "I'd just like you to try the starter when I say so, just bump it." I climbed behind the wheel of this perfectly clean auto. Clutch in, neutral. Brake applied. As he leaned into the engine compartment …"OK, now. Ok, again. Perfect. Thanks." I said, "Is that it? I need to pay you for the gas." "The hell with it, my friend, thanks for your help." I complimented him on his car and we talked for 15 or 20 minutes in the office about hot rods, and scooters and his son. I asked about a good café and maybe a motel. He recommended a café, but no motel. When I asked about Gallup, he paused for a bit, and said, "It's garbage. Except for the Library. Could be a decent town, but it isn't and probably never will be. So much crime and it's constant and never slows down. Makes me sad. I'm married to a Zuni woman, nice woman, smart, but she won't leave her family, so here we sit. Hope my son never comes back here for more than a weekend." On that sad note, we said our goodbyes. He headed back to his car, I to the scooter, a wave and then off to the café, to have a meal, and after, explore Gallup, my imagery of the town (which I had never seen before) placed in doubt.

    A little café with six or seven booths, a small counter with a few nice stools. Warm and pleasant, with a nice perfume of food. As I took one of the stools at the counter, I asked the waitress what she recommended for this traveler. Without hesitating she said, "A minute-steak sandwich and a bowl of vegetable soup. As she placed silverware in front of me, she asked "Do you know what minute-steak is?" I nodded yes, and as I switched the spoon and fork into their more correct positions ... "thinly sliced beef, about half-fried and half-poached. On whole wheat toast, if you could." "Certainly, young man", she smiled and curtsied just a bit and chuckled and said "shall we start with soup?" "Please," said I, and we continued this overly courteous vignette until it was time for coffee and a smoke and for me to pay the bill. She joined me with coffee, and we talked a bit about me being a waiter, and her excellent vegetable soup, and the beautiful aroma of the whole café. In quiet confidence, she revealed ... "That's because I never use onions, or even allow them in the café. Ever." Almost choking, I told her we were kindred spirits and how strongly I felt about onions. A good laugh together. Then I asked about Gallup, telling her what I had imagined it might be, never having seen it. She merely said, "It isn't like that at all. It's much rougher." So here I was, on the edge of Gallup, having already met two friendly people and neither had said anything good about the place. Fueled and fed, Tony Lambretta and I would travel into Gallup.

CHAPTER 10

GALLUP AND BEYOND

What was my image of Gallup, New Mexico? With that name Gallup, which I thought was quirky, it had to have some character at least in its beginnings. I knew population was about 14,000 and guessed that it was a tightly knit community, and also had given it an artsy attitude, probably transferring some of Scottsdale's old town charm or Santa Fe's art reputation to Gallup. All of this imagining had little or no factual basis. The weather was perfect. The stomach was full, as was Tony Lambretta's gas tank. We purred along 66 and arbitrarily took a right, and we were in town. A left turn put us on Coal Avenue, which seemed to be the main business street – a typical town's business area. Just noodling (my word for poking here and there), I tried this street and then that street, a few modest housing areas, some well kept, some quite neglected. The county courthouse was old and beautiful in its simple architectural style. Two things seemed disturbing to me: one was the feeling I got that this was not a friendly place. Why did I feel that? Was it the way people looked at me or avoided looking at me? Just a bone marrow feeling, which I try to ignore, but almost never do. Had my waitress and gas station guy influenced my thinking? Something else ... the litter. It was unending ... a little pile of trash here, a little more over there. Pieces of broken glass were everywhere. Scraps of discarded papers and wrappers always in your path. My conclusion – this was a sad community. It was ill. Perhaps I wasn't being fair, forming this opinion while having been in town less than an hour. Not a "feel good" situation. That bone marrow talking again – I just didn't belong here. Already it was time to leave, and so little had been seen, but maybe, too much had been seen. Pulling over near the Catholic church, I dragged the half-map out of my jacket pocket, looked at Gallup, traced route 66 all the way to Albuquerque, about 140 miles to the east. Damn. Too far. Thought about taking a motel room for the night, which would be pretty cold since we were at a higher elevation. A closer look now. About 50 miles to the east (on the way to Albuquerque) was a place called Bluewater Lake State Park. Now, that sounded so refreshing after witnessing the dinginess and debris of Gallup. Later I learned that the name Gallup had no really entertaining story attached to it. More like Snowflake's story with one guy named Snow and another named Flake. Gallup was merely the last name of the paymaster for the railroad way back in the 1800's. Oh well. A fertile imagination can, at times, lead to disappointment.

Back to 66 and time to head for Bluewater Lake. My guess was that it would take less than two hours to reach the lake if all went well. The scooter named Tony had so far been completely reliable and from time to time I would quietly thank those engineers in Milan, Italy. Our elevation was now about 7,500 ft. (2,285 meters), 5,000 ft. higher than where we started back in Tucson, AZ and there seemed no profound difference in the scooter's performance. A good machine, though not really designed for the American highway. Now, that splendid '48 Ford could move along the US highway system with ease and grace. That car was relatively simple to operate, maintain, and repair. Quite powerful with its small V8 engine and a sought-after model for the hot rodders and car customizers. I had been a member, and then president of a hot rod club in Connecticut during my teen years, and was keenly interested in building a street machine of moderate design. That goal had never been achieved, and probably would never be. Some club members, me included, had been active in drag racing in Agawam, Massachusetts at an old airport up there. The days of the 'shade-tree' or 'backyard' mechanic's involvement in drag racing were numbered as people with big money invaded the sport. The so-called little guy would no longer be able to compete. Reaching the goal of building my own street hot rod would never happen. My major problem was having too many goals. The realization just beginning to take shape was that I could not do everything I dreamed or thought of doing. Some ideas just had to be put aside, at least temporarily, though reluctantly.

The countryside between Gallup and Bluewater Lake was scattered with pinon and juniper, both trees being rather short, perhaps due to the harshness of this desert. Cold and dry in the winter with little if any snow blanket. Hot and a little more moist in the summer.   Those delicious pine nuts (pinons) are harvested from trees like these. All pine trees produce edible nuts, but only a few varieties have big enough seeds to be worth the effort of harvest. All US pine nuts are harvested by American Indians, some sort of agreement allowing that. I've been told it's the Hopi Indians who do the gathering in this area. Ahead, as we traveled east from Gallup, some darker colored mountains could be seen to the southeast. This was the Zuni Forest, on the Zuni Reservation I assumed. Bluewater Lake was at the foot of these mountains, but still ahead of us about 30 miles. Evidently there are logging operations in the Zuni Forest, so the trees must be sized accordingly. Quite beautiful to see these mountains against that huge western sky, but that was also the case with any outcropping of Painted Desert rock ... magnificent and constantly changing. It would be a tough job being a landscape photographer out here, the toughest part being to know where to start and when to stop ... too many great choices. The parade of names of rock formations never ceases for very long ... Pyramid Rock, Church Rock, Red Rock, Fire Rock, etc.

Before reaching my turnoff to Bluewater Lake, there was a widening in the road, with a few small buildings and a trading post, probably filled with piles of touristy things – tchotchkes (New York Yiddish inspired slang for knick-knacks). I wanted to thoroughly see one (but only one) of these so-called 'trading posts.' However, today was not the day. This place was called Continental Divide (an official name for this spot?), but it was, in fact, on the line which is called The Continental Divide. What is that? Actually, it's someone's pretty cool idea. It's a line on a map, from way up north in Alaska to the tip of South America, through all of North, Central, and South America. A continuous squiggly line that divides the western hemisphere, essentially into two major water drainage zones. On the east side of this line, all water from rainfall, springs, glaciers, etc. will somehow make its way to the Atlantic Ocean, including the Gulf of Mexico and the Caribbean. So theoretically, I could pee east of this line and some of it would end up in Miami Beach. That's cool. From the west side of this line (sometimes called the Great Divide), all waters drain into the Pacific Ocean. Quite a concept, but I know of no practical use. Knowing of this line since I was a kid, I was finally at that very line where it crossed Route 66. Not that I expected a parade, but it was a rather dull spot for such elevated status. And since living in the dryness of Southern Arizona, I wondered at the definition since water flowing through Tucson probably never makes the entire trip to the Pacific. Rivers in Arizona grow smaller, not larger as they travel across our desert.

A few miles east of the Continental Divide, putt-putting through the settlement of Thoreau was the signal to start looking for signs to Bluewater Lake and they soon appeared. Turning off 66 and taking the road south, I'd have to travel six or seven miles to eventually get to the lake. Up and down various hills on this road through the lower forest, I saw no other vehicles. Was I going to repeat the isolation experienced at Petrified Forest? Coasting downhill toward the lake, the vegetation thinned out and Bluewater Lake was there facing me and asking me, "What are you going to do now, Rosano?" Answering, I held the water bag up, turned off the scooter, broke out the pack of smokes, and stretched. It was time for a break from the driving. The air was cool, but not cold ... yet. That would come soon enough this evening. There was little or no breeze, at the moment anyway. Most of the day the wind had been somewhat stronger than gentle and it was a relief to experience the near calm.

Quietly smoking, I noted the dam (which had formed this lake years ago) was to my left, most of the lake seemed to be to my right. There were a few campsites with small stone fireplaces, and the water really did look blue. Bluer than expected. Almost gem quality. And I still hadn't seen or heard any humans since leaving Route 66. Then, through the trees, on my left I saw the shine of a camper or camp trailer. So I was not really alone, and that made me decide to turn to the right. The scooter was started and we cruised slowly to the right. A small road guided us around one section of the lake and there were a few more fireplaces marking informal campsites. The least noticeable fireplace and the one most distant from the water's edge had some trash around it. Yuk! Got closer and noticed the trash was a bag of charcoal briquettes, about half full, its label faded and scruffy, and this was inside a sad-looking and dented aluminum pan about 8 inches (20 cm) deep and much wider than usual, maybe 20 or 22 inches (50 to 55 cm) in diameter. The pile of trash was not trash at all. It was a pile of firewood not so neatly piled but a small treasure for the evening. That was going to be my camping place and there would be a real fire that evening, not just a coffeepot fire. Just to stay in practice, however, I started a quick little coffeepot fire in the little stone fireplace and brewed two cups of that precious fluid. The scooter was tied to one of the trees. After coffee, I set up the tent as usual, but tied a few of the tabs to some of the slender pines. As the sky was beginning to darken, I added a few pieces of wood to the small fire to encourage a bigger heat source. Looking at the pan, wondering what it might be used for, I held it up against the sky and then toward the firelight and it looked OK. Walking to the edge of the lake, I noticed how clean the water looked, maybe not suitable for drinking, but clear, not at all murky. Lightly scrubbing the pan with sand from the lake's edge, I rinsed it and filled it with lake water, walked to the fireplace and began to heat the water and added more firewood, thinking, in my high school physics logic, that water holds a bunch of BTUs and makes a pretty good heat storage medium. Water in the lake was nearly the temperature of ice, but water in my new-found pan was getting warm rather quickly. And there was the added feature of a steady rhythm, a steady 'pfff, pfff, pfff', as drops of water passed through a tiny hole in the bottom of the pan and into the fire below. And that's why the pan had been left behind by someone. And to hell with heat storage and high school physics ... I would wash myself with real hot water next to a good-sized fire. Talk about luxury! Grabbed my washcloth and soap. A few more minutes and the water was hot enough to start and so the stripping started and I didn't pretend to shield myself from any newcomers who might happen by, just stood near the fire and started washing at an almost leisurely pace, enjoying the complete exterior cleansing immensely. Nothing quite like being freshly clean, with clean clothing to climb into. Similar to a hermit crab getting a brand new shell. If you want to conquer the world, change your underwear first. How's that for a quotable: "To Conquer the World, First Change Your Underwear."

Time for a fancy dinner. Remove the label and open the can of string beans and put it on the fire. Steamed string beans will be the appetizer. Slice up half the remaining cacciatore salami, cut and break up some pieces of myzithra cheese, put those items on a clean flat rock, and then what. Throw away bath water (no baby to save at the moment), rinse pan in the lake, turn pan upside down and place slices of spicy meat on its flat bottom. String beans in the can are just beginning to make bubbling noises, throw the meat slices on the up-turned bottom of the pan, they start sizzling almost immediately, so toss on the small cheese chucks, they melt a little reluctantly, but fine. Using my spork, I scraped the fried mixture back onto that clean rock, sat down on a wide piece of firewood and started eating supper not far from the fire. Note: The reader should understand the idea of a spork. It is a utensil for eating ... a combination of spoon and fork, which really means it's a spoon with three or four tines. This very clever device is one of the more stupid inventions and I had one. It is neither an effective spoon nor is it a decent fork. Add a sharpened edge to one side of the spoon for cutting food, and it can become a treacherous weapon as well. Imagine a combination funnel, hammer, and spatula ... so versatile it becomes useless ... has many functions and can't perform any of them well. Finished eating the meat and cheese and scaled the flat rock out into the lake, trying to get seven or eight skips on the water's surface, but as soon as the rock left the light of my fire, it disappeared. Using two small sticks as tongs, I fished the can of string beans off the fire and again using my spork, I managed to spear one bean at a time. So my appetizer was out of sequence. A large white-faced dog ran left-to-right across my field of vision near the edge of the lake. Taken completely by surprise, my thoughts were: What the hell, oh, a dog, big, white head, what a strange shape, no, it's carrying something, something white. And it disappeared into the darkness with almost no sound. Quick and confusing. What the hell was it and what the hell was being carried? A big food wrapper? A piece of cloth? Not being certain of what I had seen, I tried to replay it visually in my mind, but still could not extract a clear picture. And so, it would remain a mystery. Finishing my lightly boiled string beans, I was ready to end the day. The can was flattened and stashed. I took the big pan about 100 feet away, along the water's edge in the direction the dog and white thing had disappeared, intending to return it to the fireplace when I left, sometime in the morning. Walking in the woods or in the desert in the dark always felt creepy. Even then, and to this day, a half-century later, I avoid it whenever possible. Insects? Rattlesnakes? Who knows? The odor of meat and cheese might attract an unwanted visitor and at least that attraction would not be at the front door of my tiny tent. Returning to camp, sitting again on the wide piece of firewood, I smoked and listened to the quiet of a very gentle breeze. Cigarette done now. I'll field strip it in the morning. And a small light appeared across the lake. That must be the camper I thought I saw when I arrived a few hours ago. Then … a human voice? Again. Unintelligible, but sounding like a woman's voice. Then quiet. Now two lights. Moving? Now two voices, the second lower than the first. Probably woman and man. A minute or two passes. The same voices again. The lights across this section of the lake moved to my left, along the opposite shore. A short time later I could discern the two voices were calling out Ya Ya! Here Ya Ya … again and again. And I was already putting the puzzle pieces together. Ya Ya was getting an all-expenses-paid tour of the lake and the woods by a large coyote or small wolf, if there were wolves in the area. Ya Ya, I suspect, was going to be the guest of honor at a coyote luncheon, which might already be in progress. Only a matter of minutes later, two lights were approaching my campsite, a woman's voice asking "We saw your campfire. Can we approach?" Oh Geez, Louise! This was going to be a bad scene. "Of course." I stood up. Then closer, "Thank you." Then in my firelight, a young couple approached, he said "Hi" and she said, "Hello, sorry to bother you, but …" Now, what does Rosano do with this? Guessing they're about to say we're looking for Ya Ya, our pet something or other. Have you seen him/her/it? Do I just avoid the question and say no, haven't seen anything unusual. That would keep them searching. Maybe all night, with identical or worse results in the morning. Or do I let them in on the truth? And if the truth … how does one present that, knowing people can be as emotional about their pets as they are about people in their lives. I don't agree with it, don't share it, but I do understand it. Uh oh, here it comes. "Hello, sorry to bother you, but we're looking for our toy poodle. His name is Partner and he's all white." So … the name was Partner, not Ya Ya. And now, I had to tell them about Partner's demise. An approach both simple and straight forward seemed best. "Look people, your dog is almost certainly dead. A large coyote ran just in front of my campsite about a half hour ago, carrying something white and about this big (using my hands to size and shape some air). So sorry, I thought it might be a rabbit, but there are no white rabbits around here."

The two of them looked stunned and both semi-collapsed on the ground in front of my campfire. They cried and whimpered and I just watched for two or three minutes until a suitable pause occurred. And I asked "Where are you guys from?" She sniffled, "Philadelphia." Telling them of my recent relocation from the East Coast, I said "No city dog, especially a small dog, can survive out here for very long. Your dog died very quickly."

After a time they both composed themselves and each other. Red-faced, red-eyed and still sniffling, the young woman said, "We can't even have a funeral." I just nodded in agreement. Though they had received no physical injury, they started limping back to their campsite, flashlights still waving back and forth, but more slowly now. She turned around and said, half calling out, "Thank you, thank you for being honest." Answering loudly, I said, "Take care," and returned to my fire.

It was getting cold, but there was no intention to keep a fire through the night. My coffeepot fire would be critical for morning and so it was prepared with small wood, tufts of grass, reverence and care. Crawling into the tent with sleeping bag ready and waiting, my thoughts turned to the couple now grieving their dog, Partner. What a memory from your camping trip to take back to your Philadelphia home! Of course, local animals would know the territory and its opportunities and would probably check this and other campgrounds on a regular basis. And Partner probably ran right up to that coyote wagging its tail. That's what dogs do and chomp is what coyotes do. Anything which appeared to be a possible lunch would be snapped up in an instant. It's not an easy life in the high desert. Not for the wild ones and not for invading pets either. What could have been worse than hearing their dog had been taken? Worse would be if they hadn't heard that, had searched all night, and at some time be forced to 'abandon' their lost pet ... a psychological journey of some length and depth.

Removing only my jacket before crawling into the sleeping bag, I stayed warm. Again, I wanted to read, but didn't have a good light source. Did I really want the hassle of flashlight and batteries and for what period of time would I read each evening? An hour? Half of that? Maybe two minutes before I fell asleep with the flashlight on, and with batteries dying by the minute as I snoozed. And snoozing was the very next thing on the agenda.

Sometime during the night, noises brought me out of a sound sleep. Listening and doing nothing with as much intensity as possible, I finally heard the voices of cattle ... two or three. Looking at the tent flap, I thought I saw light, but wasn't sure, and resumed sleeping. Sometime later, a vehicle's sound, quite clear, and I peeked outside. It was first light and a vehicle pulling a small camp trailer was moving toward the access road. It was certainly the couple with the sad dog story leaving, probably thinking this place was too emotionally draining to stay. More sleep. Then, a bunch of sounds. There were horses nearby. Poked my head through the tent flap into the cold air. Eight or nine horses were at the water's edge directly between the tent and the lake. A few drinking from the lake, one or two pacing around, heads bobbing, a few neighs and some snorts, lots of condensation in the air, slowly drifting upward from the group. Quite a scene. Beautiful. A busy morning here at Bluewater. Time to get up. No rush. Do the sacred blessing of the coffee ceremony. Pack up camp. Make a tentative plan and move on.

CHAPTER 11

ALBUQUERQUE

Earlier than usual and cold, above freezing, but cold. Bright and sunny, but cold. Wondered if the Lambretta would start. Bam! First halfhearted kick and it started, giving off some blue smoke, but running well and warming up. Time to head to The Big City. When Tony Lambretta and I left Tucson a few days ago, that town had a population of approximately 100,000, which was somebody's guess and a number which people would discuss because it was growing so fast. No one could really agree on what constituted Tucson. Did that include Pima County ... but 100,000 would do as a nice comparison to Albuquerque, NM which was boasting about twice that. An acceptable number with no argument from me. Albuquerque was 100 miles east of Bluewater Lake. Slowly, we worked our way back along the access road; the sun climbed a bit higher in the sky, and was shining directly in my eyes as we joined Route 66 again. Stop, put the sunglasses on, button up the jacket a little tighter and drive a little slower to lose less of my body heat and absorb more sunlight. This was one of those situations where the windshield was advantageous and appreciated as it took the brunt of the breeze as we putted along. Still, I froze my butt, and my fingers and nose weren't doing so well either. After an hour of beautiful scenery which I appreciated not at all, we cruised through the village of Milan and into the settlement of Grants, where a small diner and a large cup of coffee loomed large in my thoughts. It was late April outside, but January in my bones as I ordered a large, black coffee and an order of dollar-sized pancakes. These were pancakes two or three inches in diameter vaguely reminiscent of a US silver dollar in size. Fewer and fewer diners or restaurants were offering them. With a very small amount of butter and just a little maple syrup, well-cooked dollarsized were a simple treat for me. That isn't a typo ... one could still say, "an order of dollarsize, please" and a breakfast place would know. And these folks in Grants knew and their pancakes were wonderful. As was a second cup of coffee. The restroom and the third coffee, too, with a smoke. No rush to get out in that cold again. Resolved never to start early on a chilly morning ever again. Ever. Ever. For the rest of my life. And I was only 20.

From the window of the diner, a gas station could be seen and that was my next stop. While not critical at the moment, the gas tank should never be allowed to go empty for at least two reasons: one being the effort and embarrassment of having to transport that which should be transporting me, and two, if there were debris at the bottom of the tank, it would be best to avoid pulling it into the fuel filter. While exact capacity of the fuel tank was not known, my guess was about one and three-fourths of a gallon, including the reserve. Construction of the reserve was also a mystery to me, not knowing if fuel sat idly there forever or was constantly refreshed with each fuel addition. It was my practice to use a few miles worth of reserve gasoline at least once per day to 'freshen' the reserve tank. Did that make sense? Don't know, even to this day, but that's what was done. The reserve tank could be brought into play with a simple twist handle on a little three-way valve. Leaving a pretty good tip for the waitress, then climbing onto the scooter, I started it and in less than a minute was at the pump ready to buy some gasoline. Seeing the attendant walking over, I said my usual, "Sorry to bother you, but I need just a bit of gasoline, and as I poured my premixed quart into the tank, "Can you fill the tank, and this can, too, but not quite full. I need some room for oil." He was a middle-aged guy. He said, "Is that one of those Vespas? Looks like one, but not quite." "No, it's a Lambretta, pretty close to the same thing. Actually a competitor to the Vespa." Nodding, he said, "those two-stroke engines can be a pain in the ass at times, and usually it's the spark plug." "That's right, but I haven't had any problem so far." The tank was full, he took the quart can from my hand, set it on the ground, poked a funnel into the opening, filled it perfectly and said, "That ought to do it." Then he saw the Arizona license plate, and asked "How far you going?" The usual answer "Boston." He just nodded. I said, "kind of dumb, no?" He answered "Yep, kinda dumb, but not as dumb as what I tried." "Oh? What was that?" Since we were standing in the sunshine absorbing some heat, I was willing to continue listening and he seemed willing to talk. And his short story went like this: "Fourteen years ago, 1946, right after we got back from the war in the Pacific, my two buddies and I were having a few beers in Champaign-Urbana. Know where that is?" Not waiting for an answer, he said, "Illinois. We were young and strong as hell and a little drunk and a little crazy and we decided to go to California, mind you, – on our bicycles – and we, just like that, started out. No preparations of any kind. From the bar, the three of us, we just started peddling to California. We probably took three hours to go fifteen miles and got thirsty as hell and one of my buddies had a friend who lived on a farm not far from where we were. This friend was really in the moonshine business, not the farming business. We started sampling three different batches of moonshine liquor and tried to compare their finer qualities. After some time, we found ourselves in Monticello, a small town not far down the road from the farm, and the cops were keeping us company. No, that's not right, they were just keeping us, period. We weren't in jail, we were just sitting on a bench in a room somewhere. Seems that the three of us were trying to do fancy bicycle tricks in one of Monticello's public parks and attracted a little crowd. After some time, and after sobering up some, one of my buddies negotiated with the police, saying that if they arrested us and put us in jail and made us pay fines, and all of that formal stuff ... then, we'd have no more money and would have to stay in Monticello forever and ever, but ... IF they would allow us to donate our bicycles to some kids who really needed them, and IF they would agree to put us on a bus back to Champaign-Urbana, we would promise never to bother them again. They took the deal. And that was that. So ... we headed to California and didn't even make it as far as Decatur, 50 miles away. So what you're doing makes perfect sense to me, but I'm probably not the one to judge." He started laughing and I did too. Crazy. He made a most peculiar noise on the inbreath and that made me laugh. So he laughed more and sounded again on the intake. Cracked me up. We laughed and snorted like two baboons and laughed some more, he with tears running down his cheeks. Like two school kids, we were still at it when a station wagon pulled up on the other side of the pump. I paid and he said, "Good Luck, Buddy, and watch out for those cops in Monticello. They drive a hard bargain." And we both started laughing again.

Damn, that was a blast, and warmed me up, too, and I was on my way to Albuquerque, about 65 miles and less than three hours away. Probably get there at noon. Leaving Grants, on my right, to the south, were more of those mountains that cradled Bluewater Lake. Just a bit further east was El Malpais (The Badlands) and the Acoma Pueblo Indian Tribal area (not sure if it was called a reservation). On my left, to the north, were a higher bunch of mountains, which included the famous Mount Taylor (which I had never heard of before) and the Laguna Pueblo Indian Tribe and the settlement of Laguna was straight ahead. Acoma Pueblo and Laguna Pueblo were new names to me. Both seemed to be distinct from the Navaho Tribe. How many tribes did the US actually have in its borders ... 500, 1,000? It was somewhat overwhelming. After an hour and a half, I took a break at a road junction with something called Indian Service Road which went off to the horizon and an unknown place. Time to take a leak, drink some water, have a smoke and stretch and stretch some more. A few miles before Albuquerque, there would be the opportunity to experience Petroglyph

National Monument, which was a chain of rock drawings by Spanish explorers as well as native Indians. There were supposed to be about 15 miles of trails for tourists and hikers to follow leading to thousands of drawings. Having seen petroglyphs at Petrified Forest not so many hours before, my preference was for something more modern … maybe art galleries in Albuquerque and Santa Fe. Later I would learn more of the various cultures that were here in the West before Spaniards and horses arrived. So … I opted out of the Petroglyphs and can't tell you much about the National Monument that contains and protects them. Maybe another nut case on a scooter can do that for you someday.

Approaching Albuquerque from the west, one crosses the famous Rio Grande, the same river that people down there in El Paso, Texas (275 miles or 440 km south) sing about all the time. Driving into a real city lifted my spirits a bit. While nature's displays are gorgeous and variable and unending and cause poets and painters to swoon by the thousands, it is the city, with its bookstores, art galleries, hardware stores and record shops which is more suited to my tastes. Route 66 went right through Albuquerque, close to the Old Town center, then past the University and then farther east. Old Town would be my first stop. There was a tentative list in my head of things that needed doing, before seeking out any rowdiness or mischief making. There was dire need for another cup of coffee and immediate food to go with it. There was also the need for some food to carry on the scooter (I had consumed everything), so it was time to keep a deli in mind while exploring this good-looking town. Since carrying the helmet everywhere was a genuine nuisance, a locking system for it and the scooter itself was needed. A reading light, if suitable, could be a small, but much appreciated luxury … thinking it would be more likely found in a bookstore than a hardware store. And … it was time to do domestic chores, in this case, the laundry.

First, something to eat. Found a small café on one of the little streets which advertised "Breakfast All Day" which was, at the moment, exactly aimed at me. Stopped for coffee and a big breakfast. Having passed at least one art gallery, I retraced my path, stopped and, carrying my helmet, entered. Everything in the place was Cowboys, Indians, Horses, or Roadrunners. Everything. Some of the work was excellent, capturing the spirit of the subject (except for the roadrunners which were all junk in my opinion) and it beat the hell out of petroglyphs. The woman tending the gallery immediately recognized that I was not a buyer, but she had a nice and cordial manner and invited me to please take my time. Left the gallery to drive a few miles toward the University, to find a bookstore and perhaps find a hardware store.

Found a bookstore, and began looking for reading lights and lamps, while ignoring all the books. A bookstore is death to my wallet, me being addicted without doubt, and there's only one cure. Found a small display of three or four different lights, all of which were 110 volt and none battery-powered. Putting on my blinders to avoid printed distractions and focusing intensely on the escape hatch, I left the bookstore behind and decided to do some noodling, while hoping to chance on either a hardware store or a delicatessen for a food stash. Circled around the University Area, saw some fine-looking young women. Since this was not a fishing expedition, at least at the moment, I continued driving and worked my way back and forth for almost an hour as I generally moved north. Albuquerque was one of those towns I had considered before flipping a coin between Tucson and San Diego. Now, almost a half year later, my feeling was this town might have been a good choice. There were a few areas that were slummy, but overall, my impression was favorable. Most likely it was the more northern location that had dissuaded me.

A hardware store window said "Great Value" and it was time to find a suitable locking system. Having already decided on a small but sturdy padlock, along with a cable having a loop at each end, it was just a matter of selection. The loop had to be small enough to pass through one of the vent slots in the helmet. If anyone wanted to steal the helmet, they'd be forced to ruin it first. Nothing would positively prevent true thievery, and someone had said to me "A lock helps an honest man stay that way, and makes a thief look for an easier target." There seemed to be some truth there. In the store, there was a young guy who asked if he could help me. When I explained what I was up to, he said they had just what was needed. I followed him down the aisle to spools of wires, chains, ropes, and handed me the end of some cable, which looked very thin, a bit more than 1/8 inch (.33cm) diameter very flexible cable. Skepticism probably covered my face, and he said, "This stuff is some type of aircraft cable and it was an order mistake, but it's almost impossible to cut. We use an abrasive wheel to cut it, because it ruins our nippers and wire cutters and bolt cutters, too." Mentioning the needed loops, he looked around the store and said, "No one else here right now, I'll crimp some sleeves on the ends for you. How long a cable do you want?" About six feet, I thought. I could wind any excess around the pole or around part of the scooter. In less than five minutes, he had my cable ready while I chose a padlock. Paying for my things, I shook his hand, thanking him and pointing to the sign, and saying it was a great value just like the sign says. Nice guy.

After tucking the cable and lock away, I took three or four good swallows from the water bag to wash down two aspirins. A headache, not severe, but annoying. It was middle afternoon or beyond and it was necessary to get some food and find a camp space somewhere. Started the Lambretta and again it was on the first try. Kept a hawkeye out for a food store. Found a Mexican market with most of the signs in Spanish, a fair amount of which I understood, but that's not what I wanted right now. Five or six minutes later, a deli advertising 'the world's best pastrami sandwich' appeared and I was immediately hooked and a certain victim. My heart was in the west, but my stomach was still East Coast. Mexican food was tasty, but at times, I could taste or feel the lard, and I really disliked that mucho mucho. One Mexican lady I knew would make tortillas with sunflower oil instead of lard, and that was much preferred. A Mexicano would say, "But … that's not Mexican" and I'd have to agree, but I would silently think "but it will be someday, because this lard thing won't go on forever, it's so bad for you."

But man, oh man, that deli smelled good. My food shopping would be done here. Got a hand basket, and in a few minutes, got a half-dozen bread rolls, a can of asparagus spears, a jar of black olives and a jar of green olives, again some prunes, almonds, dried fruit, and two or three pieces of fresh fruit. Next … to get some cold cuts and cheese I went to the meat counter. The young guy behind the counter says, "what can I do you for?" Hadn't heard that expression for a while. I said, "I'd like to get some hard, dry sausage or salami and some hard dry cheese, about a half pound each." He said, "We have some really good Polish kielbasa. Want to try some?" Sure, I'd try. With a knife, he cut a slice so thin it was transparent. I recognized that as a skilled move and ate that slice and while not a huge fan of kielbasa, it did have an OK taste. Then he said, "This morning I got some hard Genoa salami in, but haven't had a minute to try it." "Let's try it," I said, "but if you're not ready, that's OK." "One minute, be right back" and he disappeared toward the back at the same time a good looking woman appeared behind the counter and she said "Ciao! Is Morris helping you?" Just joking I said "Buon Pomeriggio (Good Afternoon). Si!" She laughed and said "I knew it, you're Italian, right? Nodding yes, I said "East Coast, just like you guys." She laughed again, then Morris appeared again, but she asked, "Our accents, right?" Again, yes. She asked, "You speak Italian?" "Only a little" was my standard answer for that question even though the true answer was "Almost zero." She leaned down and said, "Vien 'aca," using the Italian and picking up a very cute little girl, three or four years old. Then she said, "At first, you looked Mexican, but I knew different. The beard and mustache make you look Mexican." I said, "Yeah, today I saw myself in a mirror and didn't recognize me. But what about you guys? You're both from New York, but he's a Morris and says 'what can I do you for' and the first word you say is 'Ciao' and there's a good story here, that's for sure. Morris laughed and handed me a slice of salami. And the woman laughed such a good friendly laugh and said, "Boy! You had us pegged in a minute. Morris is a Jew and I'm a Dago and we fell in love. Both our families went completely cuckoo and stayed that way for too long. So, one night, we just packed our things, headed to a place we knew nothing about and where nobody knew us. We drove all night, and here we are! Yeah, and here we are … our own family and happy as clams. And we're raising our kids to be … something called Good People and that's it … no particular religion." Morris then piped in and said, "And she was pregnant. We had a few dollars saved. And the rest is history." Me: "That's cool. I was secretly in love with a Jewish girl for a while. We got along so well. Even asked her out, but she'd have none of it." So then I started with "The Genoa is excellent, big congratulations to both of you, what a gorgeous child, and you guys are OK and what have I missed? Morris laughed and said, "You have to order something or we'll all starve." So I asked for a half pound of the Genoa, not sliced, and what do you have for a hard cheese. He said, "I have some great Romano, very strong tasting, and some Myzithra, somewhat milder." I interrupted and said, "Greek. The Myzithra salesman must really be pushing hard." Morris said, "Nobody knows about this cheese. And yet you know. How does that happen?" I said, "I learned from Sir Achilles down in Show Low, Arizona. That's what I've been eating for about three days. He has a place something like this one." This time, I'll get the Romano, about a half pound piece, please." He wrapped that up and asked, "Anything else?" That should do it I thought, and was about to say so, when I thought about what brought me to this place. "Yeah, you bet. If that Pastrami is as good as you say it is, I'd like a big pastrami sandwich. I'll sit at one of those little tables. Is that OK with you guys?" Morris said, "Sure it is, you want something to drink?" Me: "If you have any coffee, I'd love a cup of black coffee." He said, "It's coffee time, anyway. Liana, honey, could you make a small pot of coffee for us while I make this man a sandwich?" Then, holding up one hand wide, "Five minutes." So I wandered the store for another minute, used the restroom when I spied it, and sat down at the tiny table, as Morris, bringing a plate and Liana, with a small tray and coffee makings and the child dragging along approached and he said, "Mind if we join you?" I said, "Onorato, I'm honored." After a truly beautiful half-hour or more, I paid for my food and said my goodbyes to these fine courageous people and the gorgeous child named Angelina.

Outside the deli, with headache still bothering me, the decision was made: to hell with nature's beauty and the exquisite simplicity of camping, a motel would have to be a lowly regarded substitute. Forget the reading light search, also. Find a motel. That became the immediate goal, and toward the northwest part of Albuquerque on the main route out of town, there was just that which I sought – an older, clean-looking motel and it was very cheap. Very plain. Very welcome.

Got all my clothes, my two little books, and my food into the motel room. Went back out and used my lock and cable for the first time. Back inside, the big hand was on the ten and the little hand was almost at the five and checkout time was noon the next day, which meant I could wash my clothes and they would easily dry by morning. Got into the shower still in my underwear and started washing everything in sight and some things that were out of sight. Reached outside the shower, got the rest of my laundry and dragged it into the shower and worked on it. Maybe I wasn't wealthy, but dammit, I was clean, and after a little while, clean and wrinkly. Rolled a set of underwear and a pair of socks in a towel and got as much water out as possible and then got dressed in the damp clothes. I would become their personal drier. Strongly ringing out the rest of the laundry, I went outside and draped them over the wooden rail of the little porch-like landing which was attached to each of the rooms. Dragged a wooden rocking chair out of the room and put it on the porch, got a glass of water and another aspirin, sat down and lit up a smoke.

The guy next door came out onto his little porch carrying a chair and a six-pack of beer, Mexican beer, Pacifico. And I thought that's classy, that's good beer. He looked at my laundry draped all over the rail and grinned and said, "Hey Bud, want a beer?" I said, "Hey Man, thanks, but I've got a goddamn headache and a brew isn't gonna help it." "Well, if you do, holler, cause I'm gonna drink three of these babies and the rest are yours. Just say so." "That's a generous offer, but I'll pass for now. Hey my name is Rosano." I offered my hand and he reached across the wood rail that separated our two porches. "Barney", he said, "just call me Barney." We talked for a fifteen or twenty minutes before he opened the second beer. He asked what I thought of Albuquerque. I mentioned the nice guy in the hardware store and the cool couple in the deli and said that overall, I was very favorable toward Albuquerque, but was disappointed that I totally crapped out and didn't get a chance to hang around the University yet, but saw a bunch of nice looking coeds there, earlier in the day." "Isn't that the truth," he said. "Drives you bonkers. I go there one semester and then work a semester, then classes for a semester and so forth. Civil Engineering. I know a bunch of young crazy beauties there, and they're a blast and a half. "That's exactly what I'm looking for!" said I, "but I just couldn't handle it tonight ... but I'm game for tomorrow, anytime, just tell me when." Barney said "Oh Man, we gotta leave early in the morning for a job up near Las Vegas. My two buddies will get me early tomorrow morning and we'll drive to the job. We're doing carpentry work up there, some housing. Pays pretty good." Me: "Las Vegas, haven't been there yet, but that is a long way from here..." Barney said, "No, Las Vegas, New Mexico, not Nevada. Not too far from here, but far enough where we don't want to drive every day. My buddy moved a house trailer up near there yesterday." He had finished his third beer, held the now 3-pack toward me and asked "You sure?" "Positive, thanks again, any other time, I'd say yes." Barney said, "no problem. They're coming to get me at four-thirty AM, so I'm gonna hit the sack. You staying in town?" I answered, "Maybe. I'll decide in the morning because no big decisions should ever be made while wearing wet underwear. Good meeting you. Take care." He casually saluted, took his chair inside and was gone. Gathering my laundry and taking it inside, I distributed it here and there, wherever I could, went back outside, grabbed the chair and likewise, was gone from that porch scene.

So it had been a day of no real adventure, but really a good day because of good people I had met ... the guy in the gas station, the young guy in the hardware store, that great couple in the deli, just now this Barney had seemed to be good guy, serious in a way, and a little on the crazy side, but that was a definite plus.

Still early, I read some of Michener's "South Pacific" while enjoying the quiet hum of the highway, the luxuries of a good bedside lamp, and a real bed with no lumps.

CHAPTER 12

SANTA FE, THEN A GREAT DISASTER

Awake, middle of the night. Insomnia? Not this time. Just a full bladder. Not yet dawn. Glass of water. Laundry all over the room and it's all dry. Good, gather it and fold it. Open the motel room door. Cool outside, nice. Back inside. Put your pants on. Grab a smoke and light up and go back outside to sit on the rail. Make sure the Lambretta is still there. It is. Quiet night. Occasional car out on the highway. Halfway through my smoke and a car, no, a truck, leaves the highway slowly and drives straight at me and then turns. Pickup truck, '51 or '52 Ford, can't tell which, still blinded by the headlights. Must be Barney's construction buddies, must be around 4:30 AM. One guy gets out of the truck and raps on Barney's door. And raps again. The door opens and Barney says, "Damn it, I slept through the alarm. Give me three minutes." Then the guy turns towards me and says "You going to work early, too?" Me: "No, just couldn't sleep. Hey, what kind of camshaft are you running in that truck? Sounds a little wild." A little laugh and he says "You know about camshafts? That's good." Me: "I know only a little and have helped build up two or three flatheads, but wouldn't trust myself alone." He says, "It's an Iskenderian, a moderate one, but that's a running machine. Looks like hell because of the paint, but not much can touch us on the street." I ask, "How much weight do you carry in the back?" He says, "Two hundred" as Barney comes out the door carrying his stuff. He heads to the truck, throws everything in back, looks at me and says, "Rosano, hey, sorry if we woke you up? Gotta go. Have a good crazy trip and if you ever can find me, I'll be holding those three beers for you. Adios, man." They pile into the truck and are gone. Time for me to catch more snooze. Do not want to start this day this early.

Three hours later, I leave the motel to seek out that dispenser of hot black holy water. No cowboy coffee this morning, thank you, I'll be drinking 'civilized coffee.' Too early for breakfast, just get the coffee and rejoin the human race. Two full cups and back to the motel room. Gather my things, pack them onto the Lambretta. Seems OK, but leave it locked. Back into the room, use the bathroom, rest on the bed for ten more minutes, then leave a tip for the maid. Decided Albuquerque was a good place and might return one day ... but not today. Today was for Santa Fe, the famous Santa Fe. Should be there around noon.

Back on the road heading north with the Rio Grande on my left. The valley is very green in strong contrast to the deserts hills just beyond. There are a number of agricultural rectangles in various stages of green dress, then a small town, Bernalillo, really a suburb of Albuquerque I suppose. A sign tells me the road underneath me is called the Pan American Highway, though I'm not sure what that means. It's supposed to be a highway system from somewhere in Canada to the tip of Argentina. It goes north to Denver, where my idea is to then head eastward across the prairie to the East Coast. My impression is that no one seems too serious about the Pan Am Highway. More farmland and the day is mostly sunny, cool and breezy. Ten miles past Bernalillo and it seems we are getting more distant from the Rio Grande as it continues northward to its source in the mountains of Colorado and we head in a more northeast direction, past the Mormon Battalion marker, to the artsy town of Santa Fe. From a magazine article I knew the Mormon Battalion was part of the US Army at one time. A determined bunch, they had marched all over the west and were important in the history of the west. I'd have to look that up at the library, if I stopped at one. Now the countryside is drier, though still having its own beauty. This is a demanding landscape, the word often used is ... unforgiving. The breeze is a little stronger and I have to lean to starboard to offset its pressure on me and the machine. That's really no problem unless the breeze suddenly diminishes or stops. Then ... you'd better correct your posture very quickly or you'll wreck. A stop now for a roadside breakfast (food from yesterday's deli stop) included a small chuck of Genoa, an equal size of Pecorino, a small handful of almonds, pieces of dried fruit and a fresh pear. This was lunch, not breakfast. Breakfast will have to wait until sometime after lunch. Time for a smoke, too. Lit up and watched the sparse traffic until break time was over. Less than an hour to go for Santa Fe. And while the landscape was tough-looking, it was greener and somewhat softer than the Painted Desert back in Arizona. Back on the road, partly cloudy, warmer, wind has lessened and Tony Lambretta and I are on our way into Santa Fe. First things first, however, time to gas up and wash up and get my bearings. Got to the pump, filled up, and refilled my one-quart spare. No reaction at all from the attendant. None. Almost zero acknowledgement that I was even there. I asked about a small map of Santa Fe, he points to the office and says "Tourist stuff in there." So I went 'in there' and found a tourist brochure with a simplified map. While 'in there' I ask if I could use the restroom. He hands me a key tied to a board big enough for a game of checkers, points to a white-painted door and says "In there." So I go 'in there' (a different 'in there' than before). Leaving 'in there,' I give him the board with the key (is it a keyboard?) say my thanks and see ya sort of thing. He moved his head at a 45deg angle somewhere between yes and no and hello and goodbye. Maybe he was having a bad day. On the other hand, maybe this was a good day for him. Either way, I silently dubbed him "Mr. Personality." And soon enough I was in town.

    Not much time is needed to figure out that almost every building in town was pueblo adobe (or stylized adobe) or Spanish-influenced frontier style. The next thing that struck me was the number of art galleries. They were everywhere it seemed. Knowing that the town had an artsy reputation, it was still surprising to see so many. What a great place! I found a spot to park the scooter and lock it and the helmet to a metal street sign. Now I could walk into a gallery without carrying my helmet ... a decided improvement. And there were three or four different galleries in a very small distance. Art Galleries rank high on my list of good places, up there with book stores and record shops, but not quite up to the level of Italian bakeries. Slowly toured and thoroughly enjoyed two galleries. There were a number of good quality pieces showing strong talent ... drawings, paintings and sculptures ... most being in a Western theme. That was what sold, evidently. Window shopped two more galleries which also had Cowboys and Indians and Horses as their predominant themes. So, to see something different, I would look for a modern or contemporary gallery since I can get overloaded with Western stuff, especially road runners. Walked around a bit more, returned to the scooter, then putt-putted around town for ten or twenty minutes. There's a good feel to Santa Fe, at least to me there is. Here I was, just beginning to get serious about mosaic work and all these talented artists are already showing in fine galleries. Feeling a little jealous, my thoughts were, yeah, fine portraits in charcoal, excellent cowboys on horses painted on canvas, and well-crafted Indians in bronze sculpture, but nobody was doing fine work with mosaics. That secret would be well kept by me. Found a modern/contemporary gallery. Went in. Quite an experience. Some pieces appealed to me and there would be some sense of identity or understanding. Other pieces were so "far out" as to provoke puzzlement or even a dislike. A few caused me to feel that the artist, in cahoots with the gallery director, was just trying to scam the public.

    Having eaten lunch in the morning, it was time for breakfast, and with a bit of scooter-poking here and there, found a small restaurant near the highway. Being hungry, but not ravenous, the order was a 'short stack' of pancakes well done (they didn't do dollarsize), a side order of spinach (if they would, please, gotta have some veggies) and a cup of black coffee. Meanwhile, I thought back to the modern/contemporary art I had viewed. Whatever my feeling was about the works, there were only two or three out of the fifty or sixty that didn't get some reaction from me. And, to me that's what it was all about ... a reaction from the viewer. And as I thought these profound things, my well-cooked short stack appeared and no longer did it seem a bit pricey. Each of the three pancakes was the size of a serving platter. This would be a pancake gluttonfest. In situations like this, a person mustn't be hasty, but rather be patient and persistent, and dedicated wouldn't hurt either. As the waitress passed my booth, I asked how much bigger than the short stack was the 'standard' order. She said, "Twice as big, hon." Impressive. As I slowly ate and drank coffee, my favorable view of Santa Fe made me vow to return some day. Should I see more galleries? It was early afternoon. I'd like to hang out in a town for two or three days, maybe meet a young woman, maybe an older one and have some fun. For now at least, I didn't feel that type of good vibration in this place, some day perhaps. So I would move on after having a delightful few hours here and start making my way to Denver, 400 miles east and north by road.

Started my faithful scooter and rode out of town. Santa Fe, a magnificent place! My plan was to cruise along Rt. 84 eastward until it was time to make a camp for the night. Damn, should have taken the time to find a decent reading light. Beautiful afternoon, a steady breeze at my back, a few wild-looking clouds in the sky, mountains on my left, smaller ones on my right. Within an hour I saw signs to Pecos, a small settlement that had some ruins nearby. Pecos is a famous name, made famous by stories of Pecos Bill. He was a super-cowboy of sorts. As a kid, stories of Pecos Bill would put me into a near trance. In these tall tales, he could do almost anything and do it well. There was a Pecos River which, in its own squiggly fashion paralleled the road I was traveling. So many well-known names in this part of New Mexico. Now the wind died down and a few more clouds were looking down at me. Felt one or two drops of rain. No big deal. After another half-hour the wind became a headwind, and I had to drop the Lambretta into a lower gear and the pace slowed, I passed over the bridge where the Pecos River turned south and went on its squiggly way. Now the headwind had increased and Tony Lambretta was struggling. This windshield was shelter for me but certainly added to wind resistance. Now in second gear, top speed of 20 and it was time to pull over, rest, and see if this wind would drop down a few notches.

Just a few feet off the highway, there was a grouping of scrubby pines twice my height or a bit more and they offered fair shelter from this persistent wind. Tied the scooter to one tree, leaned against another and smoked a Parliament. Wind was the same, maybe a little stronger. Scooter almost toppled. Another tie from the scooter to another little tree. A very irritable, gritty, wind-blown half-hour later, my patience was just about gone. Screw it. Set up camp and get inside the tent and try to take a little snooze. This will be my camp spot tonight. Hell, with the wind, there's nothing else to do, even if there is plenty of daytime remaining. After the tent was set up, ditches dug around it, and securely tied in about six places (not so easy to do in this mild tornado). I took the waterproof sleeping bag bag and the clothing bag into the tent to use as pillows. Took my jacket off and stuffed it into the clothing bag. Settled down and actually slept ... for perhaps a whole minute. The first raindrop hit the tent with a 'fwap'... silence, then another. Fortunately, this was a mountaineer's tent, waterproof floor and all that. It would be OK this first time in the rain. A few more 'fwaps', more than a few after that. Within two minutes, I was sitting in this little tent, on top of the genuinely waterproof clothing bag and the truly waterproof sleeping bag bag, and I was surrounded by what closely resembled a mini-moat. And my water resistant mountaineer tent had three inches of water inside. I'm sure none of that water leaked out because I had tested the floor of the tent back in Tucson. The mist created by water drops hitting the tent fabric was probably an ideal moisturizing skin treatment and I'd consider going for a patent someday, but right now I was a desert rat in serious jeopardy of drowning in my own nifty little shelter. Open the flap which matters not a whit. Crawl outside into the driving rain (can't get any wetter), reach in and extract my two authentically waterproof bags, prop them upside down to prevent any rain from entering the openings. The scooter has not fallen over, but has not stood upright either, and lists at a 45 degree angle, straining on the two cords and with its wheels half-buried in mud. So now what? What's the best move? Stay where I am and ride it out? And for how long? The trees now offer almost no protection and I am soaking wet and slowly slipping and oozing into the mud along with Tony the Lambretta. The decision is made: get back onto firm pavement. After that is accomplished, I could make some other sort of decision. Easier stated than accomplished. Still raining but much less fiercely. Get the scooter vertical once again. Now pull it out of the mud, one wheel at a time. Wind has quit for the most part, so I can move the scooter to the paved highway shoulder. Dragging it through the mud (too slippery to drive) just about killed me. Back to the trees to empty the tent, which still held a respectable pool of water and which had already proved its worth as a rain strainer, should one ever need such a thing. Untie, empty, and then collapse the squishy tent and grab the two impermeable bags containing the only dryness for miles around. Now on the highway shoulder trying to roll up and tie up the soaked and muddy tent. Then tie all this back onto Tony as the rain lessens and finally stops. So I'm soaked, semi-exhausted, cold, and confronted by the big question. What now? Go into the clothing bag, paw around in the jacket, find your pack of Parliaments. Take one out. Light up. Relax. List your options. Choose one. A black car passes by, and then a powder blue Chevy. Can't hitchhike. Probably have to set up camp somewhere else. Pickup truck coming and slows down and slows some more and pulls alongside me. The voice of the driver says, "Want one of those beers now?" It's Barney from the motel. Unbelievable! The truck pulled up in front of me. Barney got out saying, "Well, I'll be damned, 'tis Rosano, the Happy Wanderer, how the hell are you, man?" He looked at me and said, "I just wanted to congratulate you. Rosano, you look like shit, man." His buddy got out of the passenger door and Barney introduced us. This was Vincent. Not Vinny, Vincent. Shaking his hand, "We met this morning at the motel," I said. The three of us chatted for less than a minute before Barney said "Man, what a goddamn mess. What happened?" After hearing about the brief, but wild storm and my story of the last hour and a half, and that I was thinking of setting up camp again, he was snorting and laughing. "You ought to go on stage with that story ... that moat business ... with no sharks or no alligators ... really funny as hell." Walking around the scooter, he asked, "How much does all this weigh?" I answered "About three hundred pounds." Barney said "Want to stay in a dry place tonight?" "Sounds like heaven right now" I said. Vincent said, "Let's throw your trash collection into the back of the truck and we'll get going." Three of us did it easily and I climbed up and tied the scooter here and there. Barney said, "Watch out for all that booze up there." And I noticed half-a-dozen carefully cushioned one-gallon bottles with labels I recognized from Mexican liquor stores across the border (300 miles to the south) ... rum, tequila, maybe some vodka. In no time at all I was seated between the two as we headed northeast, me with a Pacifico beer in my hand, but I wasn't complaining about the cold. I had been rescued. Physically and spiritually saved by carpenters. Hmmm. Lordy Lordy.

After thanks to the two and telling them they had really saved my butt, I asked where we were going. Back to Las Vegas, not that Las Vegas, this Las Vegas. They had a small mobile home there, the three of them. Dan had towed the forty-foot trailer and placed it two days before. He was at the construction jobsite waiting for two truckloads of lumber from Montana to be delivered. Without lumber, there was no work, which is why these two, Barney and Vincent were out on the highway when they stumbled across me. I said I hadn't met Dan yet. Vincent said, "Yeah, he was driving this morning when we saw you at the motel. He's a good guy ... not crazy like you, Lone Ranger." And the two of them spent the next ten or fifteen minutes laughing and dreaming up what they thought were appropriate names for me, names like the Scoot Stalker, Wetter Wonder, Splash, Monsoon Man, etc. And actually, it WAS pretty funny.

We pulled off the highway onto a gravel road and then into an area where there were a dozen camp trailers and mobile homes scattered about, each next to a paved slab. As we passed a small trailer we could see its awning had been torn away and most of it was gone. Another small camp trailer was on its side. We stopped. Barney jumped out, ran to it and shouted, "OK in there? Anyone in there? Helloooo." From a parked car, a voice said, "Hey! Yeah, we're OK. When the wind started howling, we, my wife and I got in the car." The older man got out of the car and said, "I've got some help coming shortly. So, we'll be fine. But thanks for checkin' on us." So it had been quite a storm. And I wasn't the only displaced person.

Back in the truck, Barney drove another 20 or 30 yards, made a partial left turn, slowed to a crawl and said, "Oh shit, will you look at that!" The pickup was pointed straight toward the white mobile home which had suffered some wind damage ... specifically that the front door opening had only half its frame and the forward six or eight feet of the front wall, including the door, had been peeled from the main structure and was laying twisted in the mud four or five paces away, the whole disaster seemed decorated by the drinking glasses, dishes, cups and saucers that had been in a cupboard which no longer existed. This part had been the living room/dining area just a day before. The roof was still there but sagging considerably at the corner. We got out of the truck, walked to the shiny blue front steps still in place, climbed the three brightly painted blue steps and walked through the half doorway, and looked inside. Barney walked through a narrow hallway into the back rooms and after a minute or so returned to the open area. Vincent had in the meantime walked over to the kitchen sink, tried the water, and the overhead light. Both seemed OK. I was looking at the area where the wall had separated and told Vincent that there were two 3-wire electrical cables that had been badly damaged and could possibly set the whole mess on fire. We should cut them and tape the wires ... now. Vincent asked if I knew how to do that and I nodded yes. All I needed was some decent tape since I had a knife and cutting pliers in the scooter. He went to the pickup, came back and handed me tape, wire nippers, and a razor knife. I found the electrical hookup, killed the power, made the temporary repairs, restored the power, and we were back in business so to speak. Even the refrigerator was still functioning.

Barney said, "It's getting dark and I have to go get Dan. Let's get that scooter down off the truck, the three of us. I'll be back in about half an hour."

Vincent and I cleaned up the broken glass and the debris in the living room area. Aside from the wall being gone, things didn't look too bad at all. There was little or no wind now and the trailer was really quite clean, that included a small bathroom with a smaller shower stall, the hot water still available. Turned on a few lights. Took off my boots and took out my smokes, offered one to Vincent. Accepted. We sat down to smoke at the dinette set.

Vincent said, "I only smoke two or three a day, and usually I bum them." I said, "Four, five, or six a day for me." He asked me about this scooter trip and said Barney had talked about my insane little journey that morning. "We wondered how you were doing," he said, "I guess we found out, eh? Think you can find a place to sleep here tonight?" I said, "This is like the Taj Mahal, except with a covered patio." I pointed at the sagging ceiling. A little joke there, but then I said, "Hey, we ought to find a pole or something to prop that corner up or it'll bend more of the roof." He jumped up, put the cigarette out and went outside. Banging the boots together got rid of most of the mud and I was putting the boots on when Vincent hollered into the trailer, "Help me with this thing." I went down the blue steps and Vincent had a large square clothesline assembly with a pair of socks still hanging onto one of the wires. From outside, we stuck the pole under the corner of the roof. On an agreed signal, we'd both lift like hell and try to move the roof upward to its original position and damned if we didn't do just that with the base of the clothesline pole sitting on the trailer's frame, with half the assembly inside the trailer (the part with the socks) and the other half exposed to the stars. Vincent said, "Good Idea, buddy." I said, "Nice hunting, for being in the dark. Who's missing their socks?" He held his index finger to his lips in a shushing gesture and we laughed.

"Now, tell me about this scooter of yours." He got all the information that was available in my mind. He listened very carefully, asked a few technical questions, some of which I actually had answers for, others I had to say I didn't know. He asked what seemed the best thing about it. My answer was, "So far ... reliability. This machine never fails to start and the engine always sounds smooth-running, even under a strain." The next question: What's the biggest problem? My answer: "Lack of power. I could use twice as much horsepower, but if I were in a hurry, I wouldn't have chosen a scooter in the first place." I made my crack about not being able to outrun the average wheelchair. He got a good laugh out of that. Next, I mentioned that on the uphill, I had to pull to the right to allow pedestrians to pass. He almost choked on that. Vince then said, "You praise the reliability, and complain about lack of horsepower. They go with each other. It won't always be so, but for now, I suspect it's what the Italians thought might be the best compromise." That's when the truck got back and I met Dan. He looked at all the damage, shook our clothesline a bit, and sat without saying a word. He seemed to be the leader of the trio, though I wasn't sure. I wanted to check the scooter and went outside, moved it against a small, but sturdy telephone pole and tied it. In just a few minutes, back at the dinette set, Dan finally stirred and said "I have a suggestion and really don't want a bunch of discussion unless you guys see something really wrong with it. Barney here has a God-given talent to create a party and he has a ton of female connections. I just stocked up on food and the fridge is OK. We already have the booze, gallons of it. All we need is some glasses and some girls. What say you?" It was heartily and unanimously approved. Dan handed the truck keys to Barney and said, "Do your job, and do it well. The rest of us should clean up and get some food ready. Rosano the Road Renegade, you want in the shower first?" Me: "I'm the dirtiest, so I'll go last. And I'll take my clothes into the shower with me, and lucky for me, we have a brand new clothesline in the living room. And in the meantime, I'll start on food prep. Whatever you have, I can make a good meal of it." While Dan and Vincent got cleaned up, I started arranging supper. He had bought two pounds of ground round steak, I found a dozen eggs and added four of them to the beef, so the main part of the meal was three large beef patties and one smaller one, that being mine. I had gone out to the scooter, gotten the salami and grated some and mixed it in the ground beef and then returned it to the scooter. Found some fennel seed, a little old and put a generous amount of that in there too. From down the hall, one of them hollered, "Hey Storm King, the shower is yours." I hollered back, "As soon as I'm clean, I'll cook."

Into the shower, surprise ... plenty of hot water, wash all the mud off my clothes, then washed me, put on all dry clothes except for the wet pants, brush teeth, do everything necessary and return to the kitchen. Barney is back with good news. Four beauties will be here in two hours with all the trimmings for a grand party. I say, "Four beauties, eh?" Vince pipes up and says, "You think he's kidding? In two hours you'll see." Me: "That's perfect. You guys want supper? Set the table." After a little pause, Barney says "With what? No dishes left." I said, "Get the silverware and something to drink and maybe some napkins so we don't have use our shirt sleeves, and I'll get the dishes." In less than ten minutes, I had broiled the meat on a cookie sheet, fried a big pile of thinly sliced potatoes, had a big bunch of cut up veggies in a fry pan (in place of a serving platter) and made up another cookie sheet full of garlic bread to be toasted as soon as the meat was done. On the table, were four bottles of beer and napkins and silverware. I went to each place at this small table and put down a 12 inch square of aluminum foil and said, "Be careful with your knives, the dishes are so delicate." Then I served supper and we had an excellent meal almost under the night sky. Dan said, "Damn, you damn sure know how to cook, my friend. Where'd you learn that?" I said, "If you grow up with Italians, you KNOW how to cook, even if you never LEARNED how to cook. Capisci?" Barney says, "Time for me to get clean, that way I don't have to do the dishes." Vincent said, "Around here, we don't do the dishes, we can afford to just throw them away." Then he rumpled one of the aluminum foils and tossed in into the sink, and said "I'll do the dishes."

So we're going to have a party. So the whole tent disaster turned out great. So the question then becomes: Is a disaster which turns out great … a great disaster? Dan said, "Hey Rainmaker, why don't you just rest for a few minutes. You have to save your strength for our parties. You just can't do it justice if you're not well-rested." I said, "Can't wait, but it would be better if I had some dry pants, at least to start with. Nobody should start a serious party with wet pants. Anybody have some pants I can wear?"

CHAPTER 13

BARNEY DOES QUITE WELL

The mobile home (in my mind they were still called 'trailers') had two bedrooms, the furthest aft was fair-sized with two full-sized mattresses on the floor and a walking 'path' at the foot end of both mattresses. It was wall-to-wall mattresses. There was a large pile of pillows and blankets and quilts against the far wall. The smaller bedroom was considerably smaller and had a bunk bed arrangement with one twin-size mattress above the other. Vince had said there was an extra pair of jeans on the lower bunk. I changed into them. They were about a football field too long but they were dry. Since I had been warned to rest up, I flopped onto the lower bunk and sailed off to La La Land in an estimated three or four seconds.

What brought me back to consciousness was the smell of coffee. Upright and zombielike, with outstretched arms I staggered to the kitchen. Dan was pouring cups of coffee. I said, "Where did you get the cups?" He said, "Out in the mud, found three unbroken and washed them, want one?" Me: "Much obliged. Oh, man, coffee, that's perfect." He added, "You'll probably need it." As I savored dark, strong coffee, I asked, "So tell me about these women. What should I know?" Dan laughed, "Usually in their twenties, usually from wealthy families, always well-built and Miss America material-gorgeous, and almost always smart as hell. You know, Barney is one smart cookie. He hides it some." I said, "That's the impression I got last night after we talked for only a short time on the porch at the motel." Dan said, "One of these days he'll be a fine engineer, but what I was talking about is that Barney simply cannot stand stupid people, least of all his own family. Even gorgeous stupid people. In a way, it's a personality defect, and yet … " He trailed off and then said, "Hey, Rain Dancer, don't worry, you must be OK or he would never have stopped for you on the highway this afternoon. Anyway, Barney is like a magnet for beauty. Vincent and I are accustomed to it by now. You can bet they'll be knockouts."

Indeed they were. I had just finished brushing my teeth for the eleventh time when they arrived in a white Lincoln convertible, with the top down, though it was chilly that evening. And that's when all the greetings and hugs and introductions and more hugs and kisses and yet more hugs got started as everyone made their way into our 'open air living room' with built-in clothesline assembly. Everyone was talking at once.

Note to reader: I've never been very good at recalling names, and the names of these girls floated into one ear, disappeared, and never reached that memory morsel in my brain, all the power of which had been sidetracked by the exquisite picture of these four truly stunning young women. So ... to help you keep your characters straight and help you follow the action, I'll arbitrarily assign four easily remembered names. The names will be: Christie, Cristy, Kristey, and Kristi, in no particular order.

Dan had set up and was half tending bar, now that Christy had brought some glasses. And some liquor had begun to trickle into the group. The girls had brought and set out some munchies. Kristee said the four of them had planned the party games on the way from Santa Fe and would start "when the time was right." Dan asked how they could plan a party with the wind howling around their ears as they drove. She said, "You know how important appearances are. Well, we put the top down about two minutes before we got here." We laughed and agreed, for appearance's sake, it damn sure was a grand entrance. She said not to worry; they had indeed planned a good, fun party.

There were many and varied jokes about the remodel job on the front of the trailer and the laundry lines and the pair of socks still hanging there. There were so many questions about the Tucson to Boston scooter thing that I couldn't answer fast enough. Everyone seemed to be having an energetically enjoyable time. Barney could be heard laughing while describing me having just emerged from the mud, saying go ahead, ask him about the moat. In my own head, I thought I would really take it easy on the booze and try not to get very drunk. Just maintain a tiny buzz. At the time I really enjoyed drinking whiskey, but tonight, that rum from Mexico was the closest drink to whiskey. Making very weak drinks for myself, mild rum and cokes, I maintained a good balance. Christie called for attention and said hey everybody sit down. There were four dinette chairs and someone, probably Dan, had provided four good stout wooden milk cartons with thick towels on top which made effective stools, one of which beaconed me to sit down next to Cristi. Christie asked if everyone had a place to sit. Yes we did. She said we're going to play a party game. Vincent says what game. She says I don't know yet ... the special guest from Arizona, our Downpour Dude, will pick the game. Taken by surprise, I ask what did she have in mind and the answer was ... anything that everyone can do to make a fool of themselves in front of everybody else. After a minute or so I said, OK, each person has to sing a song, any kind of song imaginable – for not less than one full minute nor more than three minutes. Someone has to be the timer and someone has to start. Kristy says she'll be the timer and I, the Arizona Waterboy would have to go first. Everybody laughs at that little twist. So I do a phony Satchmo arrangement of 'The Begat' from the Broadway show, 'Finian's Rainbow' and there was some applause and Barney said, "Get it? Get it? ... Rainbow ... Rain ... soaked ...?" Cristey was next and did a very sultry version of 'Itsy Bitsy Spider' and earned rousing applause. Dan tried 'Rudolf the Red Nosed Reindeer' and screwed up the lyrics and started making them up until the one-minute mark was reached, but he suspected it was closer to two full minutes. One after the other everyone gave it their best shot. This was a competitive bunch of people and spontaneous and resourceful at the same time. Kristy did a credible version of 'Hail, Hail, The Gang's All Here.' And so it went as we sang and laughed and did some more booze. Cristy said, "It's cold out here in your open air living room. Let's go in the back, but everyone has to take their shoes off. Leave your shoes in the kitchen, but bring your drinks."

Eight people in stocking feet sitting on two sheet-covered mattresses makes for an interesting mix. Kristy said each one of us should tell a little story. Dan said he would start and he did, saying he was a little sad to see the mobile home damaged, but it could be fixed. He said it was a special trailer because more than a year ago, he had ripped out all the propane gas pipes for the wall heaters, the stove and oven, and the hot water heater. He had replaced it all with very heavy duty, very safe electrical service. The hot water heater was 50 or 60 gallon fast recovery. He asked why did I do that? Because when the three of us, Barney, Vincent, and I, are on a jobsite and get to this trailer after work, we can take showers, one after the other after the other, without waiting for a puny little heater to catch up. Barney laughed and said I think you're drunk. Dan said no, well maybe a little, but he had brought up the hot water heater because if anyone here wanted to take a shower anytime, there would be plenty of hot water and he would be glad to shower with them to make sure nothing went haywire. Barney laughed again and said I still think you're drunk, but the thought was good. And he said Rosano is next, the Rain Ranger, who will tell us about the magic tent and the moat, right? Since something approaching a comedy routine had already been concocted in my mind, I agreed and the tale began. Most likely it was the liquor, but people started laughing, especially when I described the deadly serpents lurking in the moat and that even after escaping uninjured, it was necessary to reach back into the tent, across and very near to the danger zone to retrieve my sleeping bag bag and clothing bag, demonstrating that even an average man can show great courage when a situation calls for it. Barney was laughing so loud that everyone was laughing at him and not necessarily at the story. Kristee began a tale of knitting a lightweight sweater for her dachshund. There were groans all around. She continued. The sweater was black and white and when it was fitted onto the dog, it caused the mutt to look very much like a skunk. Of course she enjoyed reactions of people when taking the pooch out for a walk, as they either avoided her or just fled leaving all social graces behind. Other dogs being walked had little or no reactions other than their usual stuff. The best response came when she walked into the veterinarian's waiting room for pooch's appointment. The place emptied out as three or four people dragged their pets outside, allowing Kristee and her skunk to see the vet immediately. Now that was very crafty and she got a bunch of Attaboys from us. A few more stories and a few more drinks and most of us were at least mildly sloshed. Looking around at this remarkable female quartet, and being a bit oiled up from a few mild drinks, it would be easy to slip and fall into love with any of the four, at least for this one evening.

That's when Cristi said it was time for The Second of Three Games. This is a contest to see which of us four girls will win Miss Congeniality. Everyone ready? Of course everyone was ready! OK, here's how we play. The guys stand up and we blindfold them. And she had a paper sack in her hand and gave out strips of dark cloth and each of us was blindfolded by one of the girls. Now she explained that as soon as we started there was to be absolutely no talking. It was Vincent who started to say something and she said Shut UP. Then she said again – no talking. You guys have to remember us in order, from A to D. First, A will approach you. Then B, and C, and so on. One minute per turn. So you, Vincent, on the end, you will have to wait for three minutes before A approaches you. When all four of us have finished with all four of you guys, then you get to vote, but no talking. At all. Not even after the voting. Tonight you guys will be using the Braille method, that is, touching. You use your hands to find your personal favorite Miss Congeniality. Everyone understand? Without waiting for a response she said Good. Shhhh! And the room went nearly silent. Trying to remember being third in line, or maybe ... oh, who gives a damn, this is so incredibly cool. Now, understand, to be blindfolded and to stand on a slightly springy mattress is difficult, but with a drink or two or three, for a whole minute or two, it gets a little dicey. So I waited and maintained my balance. Hearing or sensing some movement to my right, I turned my head slightly in that direction just as a pair of cool, gentle hands got hold of my face ...

Note to reader: This impromptu, yet planned party was one of the best in which I've ever taken part. We were eight young healthy people. A considerable amount of booze was involved and more than a considerable amount of love-making occurred. So ... if you don't want the virtuousness of your reading glasses to be compromised, you should stop reading at this point, just for a moment, in order to skip past the remainder of this chapter and go directly to the fourteenth installment/chapter of this story and for those who prefer to maintain their purity and avoid reading about this little get-together, know that you'll be missing one excellent party. The impure among you should continue reading normally.

... got hold of my face, turned it forward again and contestant A kissed my lips two or three times softly as I put my hands on her waist and oh, what a beautiful waist! It stopped my breathing. What a gorgeous sensation! Miss Congeniality Contestant A placed her hands over mine, pushed them downward until both hands were squarely on her bottom. For just a moment. Her right hand moved my left hand upward along her ribcage, under her blouse and pressed that most fortunate of all left hands against her naked breast and caused me a full coronary stop and then she was gone. Coherent thoughts – none. Trying to force my mind to process anything at all was interrupted as Contestant B put her hands on my shoulder and pulled me to her, kissed my neck, rubbed herself upward against my whole body length while her hands pressed against my back. Indescribable. I was stunned. Though it had been less than two weeks, it seemed so long ago that I had touched a woman. But right now this had stopped my heart, and it was time to die because heaven had already been reached. And poof, Congeniality B was no longer there. I wanted to reach for her. Several very empty seconds flew past and Contestant C put her hand on the top of my head and gently backed herself into me so that we were, in fact, spooning while standing, with her arms holding mine firmly around her torso as she moved to the left a bit and to the right a bit, again to the left and once more to the right. All was well with the world. Too soon, she parted my arms and left me. I was just catching on to this most sensuous of games when Miss Congeniality D put her hands behind my neck, drew me to her and she kissed my blindfold and her breath moved against my face, her breath so warm and soft. When a little kiss touched my cheekbone, I felt the gentle and steady pressure of her hand against my genitals and slowly now, she kissed the other cheekbone and she also had gone away. I had always felt some personal identification with the Rock of Gibraltar, but now, in the span of four minutes, I had become a Block of Jell-O. This was impossible. What a ride! Two or three silent minutes later. A female voice said softly: Now everybody listen. Don't talk. You can vote for your favorite in a little while. First, we're going to remove your blindfolds, and everybody will go into the kitchen for another round of refreshments and everyone can talk about anything except the games. Half hour break. After that we will play the Third Game. Gentle hands untied my blindfold. One of those hands took my hand and guided me to the kitchen.

    The thinking part of my brain had ceased functioning, probably starved for blood since the aroused parts of my body took all that was available. Finally, a few social graces started filtering into my head and I said to Kristee, "Can I fix you a drink?" She asked what I was drinking. "Normally I drink whiskey and water, good US or Canadian whiskey, but now I'm drinking rum and Coca Cola, same as in the song." She said, "Is it strong?" Thinking, 'What a gorgeous creature.' I said, "Doesn't have to be, want to try a mild one?" She nodded yes. As I mixed, she kept one arm lightly around my waist. I was so hard, but didn't try to hide it, figuring that's what this is all about, anyway. Finally got the drink assembled, took a taste, offered it to her. "Here, try this one." As she carefully tasted, I could not take my gaze from her face. She looked surprised, saying, "Oooh, that's good." Me: "Yeah, a little on the sweet side and a little bit weak, just like me. Look, usually it's stronger than that, but there is no way that I'm getting drunk tonight. This is worth being sober for." Laughing she said, "This is just fine. Do you want to mix another or can we just share? And ….Is there really a song called 'Rum and Coke'?" I said, "It's actually called 'Rum and Coca Cola'. It's a calypso from … I forget where in the Caribbean." Kristee said, "Sing it." Christi, who had joined us said she knew at least part of the song and started to sing it. Pleasant voice. These two beautiful women are for real and so poised. And, of course, I was a complete shambles. And I had to take a leak so badly. And that's what I said. "Excuse me ladies, but I just have to pee," and I headed for the hallway. Christi said "Me too!" and Kristee said "Me too! The two trailed behind me, but one got in front and into the bathroom first. Before the door was shut, the one behind me pushed me right into the bathroom and closed the door with the three of us inside. Christi first sat on the pot and peed, then tended to her tush with paper and the second sat right down and did the same. When she stood up, she said "Now it's your turn." And they both laughed. "Go ahead, go ahead." So I sat down and peed too. One of them said, "Hey! No Fair! We thought you'd put the seat up and pee standing up!" I said, "In my condition, there's no telling where the stream would go. That's why I sat." Now I stood up and the other said "Well, isn't that so nice." I tucked myself back in as best I could and thought maybe I am just a wee bit drunk after all. Back to the kitchen, where there were more conversations … me complimenting Barney on his choices and getting a thumbs up in return. We finished our shared drink just as Kristy was saying, "OK people, OK people," as she rapped on the side of a glass. "Ready for Game Three?" There were no objections. She said same rules: "Finish your drinks and leave the glasses here. Guys, you get back in line." That took a minute or two, but now I was last in line. Vincent was having trouble standing still and was rocking back and forth. I was guessing Vincent was quite drunk by now. Barney was quietly murmuring "alright, alright, alright," until Kristy told him to be quiet. She said, "Ladies, put the blindfolds back on these guys." And from behind the blindfold was tied around my head. "Now Ladies, tie their hands. So you guys have to cross your hands together behind your back. Vincent, in back not in front." I felt a ribbon or strap tied around my wrists, but not very tightly. Kristy was saying, "Here's the deal. Same progression as before, one minute per move, A through D. You get to vote later. Now you have to select your favorite Miss Congeniality without using your hands. When you feel her touch your nose, start to find out all you can for that one minute, but … the only thing you get to use this time … is your nose. Rosano, you're last so you get to wait three minutes." For a quiet party, this was the wildest. Your nose. My nose. Good thing I have a big Roman one. Oh man, this is something else, this is stratospheric! To my right, I hear a few soft grunts and groans, a couple of big thuds (probably Vincent falling down). I'm thinking Fantastic Delicious Craziness when I feel the first touch on my nose. Oh this is so delectable. And I nuzzled Contestant A on both sides of her face, and rubbed noses, and worked my way downward across her neck to one armpit, I now realized she was naked, oh sweetness of heaven, I nuzzled across one naked breast and the other, downward to one side of her navel, across the navel now the far side of the navel and finally downward into the fur line for just a second or two before the minute was over. After a few seconds and still leaning down, I felt the touch of Miss Congeniality B lift my head and then lightly tapped my nose. A perfect, simple invitation and I accepted, repeating the course I had followed with A, but just a bit more quickly to allow a few extra time for finishing touches. I felt B catch her breath, push against my nose for the briefest moment and then she also disappeared. Contestant C elevated my head and put her finger on my nose. What exquisite torture this was! As I walked that trail for the third time, embracing as much as possible, C kept rubbing my head so tenderly. Was I keeping a mental record for voting purposes? Hell, no. They were all so completely and superbly naked that … Oh, it was Congeniality D who now touched my nose, and guided my head to where she wanted it to be and that completed the final minute. This was such an irrational fantasy it would have to continue just to keep the universe in alignment and prevent galaxies from exploding. That beautiful female voice said it was time to untie the hands, but leave the blindfolds and that was done. Now it said to give each of the men a quilt to hold. That was done and I so loved the touch of those gentle hands giving me the quilt. And now the instructions said voting would happen later ... and that we were to remember the four contestants as best we could. In the meantime we could return to the kitchen for another round of drinks, or use the bathroom, or just recline on the mattress where we were and take a little rest. And that would be my choice if there were a female with me. The voice said to remove the blindfold. I thought I would see four naked young women and I was wrong. Each was wearing a long nightshirt, like a muu-muu. No one moved for a second or two. Lowering myself to the mattress, I sat quietly as a few of the eight started back into the hallway.

Such an unusual gathering ... good looking people, good conversation, fantastic sexy games, lots of drinking and yet, there was no loud or belligerent behavior ... just tipsy, peaceful, open friendliness. Such a good thing. Kristee sat beside me and asked if I wanted to make another drink to share. I said no. I'd like to just rest for a bit, and that I felt a little cold. She reached back and dragged a couple of pillows toward us, covered our legs with the quilt and then began to unbutton my shirt and helped me take it off and the tee shirt was next, and the trousers and the underwear and socks and of course I cooperated and tried to be as helpful as possible and tugged at her nightshirt. Now we were naked under the quilt with her head half supported by my chest. Two people were standing and talking near us, but that mattered not at all. Soon we were kissing lightly, touching and exploring. Touching and exploring everything. Gentle and beautiful. In time I pulled her on top of me, whispering she could have more control that way, that I didn't want to hurt her, and asked shouldn't we use some protection. She said not to worry, everyone was on the pill. And carefully and slowly, she melted on top of me. Beautiful things happened and everything was splendid, everything was perfect.

Warm and comfortable under the oversized quilt, Kristee slowly returned to my side, settled into the crook of my right arm and we slept. Felt movement on my left side. Christi had pulled a pillow over, gotten under our quilt, snuggled against my other side and we all stayed warm and slept again. Some time had passed when I became aware that Christi was manipulating the situation for her own purposes. Since I've always admired initiative, there was certainly no protest from me. She asked if she got a turn? About to respond, I stopped when I heard when Kristee said, Go ahead, honey, he's so considerate. So Christi and I made love and lingered and deeply enjoyed while Kristee dozed, occasionally petted and dozed again. Eventually, the three of us slept contentedly. The Goddess of Love,

Aphrodite herself, might have become jealous of us and asked her god friend Hypnos to force sleep upon us.

My foot was shaking, no, someone was shaking my foot. It was Dan saying "Time to wake up and the coffee's ready in two minutes." It was as if I had been in a distant land in a different century, disoriented, disconnected and completely out of focus. Finally, I was able to zero in a bit more on the present world and looked for my two beautiful partners. Not there. Walked to the bathroom and peed and woke up some more. Back to the bedroom, put on pants and a shirt and socks since it was so chilly and walked into the kitchen, expecting to see a bunch of people and there was Dan alone with a coffee pot and a cup and a question on his face. I nodded yes, and said thanks. He said everyone has left for the day. I felt genuinely sad, since I so wanted to be with those two women again. After most of that first cup of coffee, Dan asked "Are you leaving today?" I asked "Are the girls coming back?" He shook his head no. "They're back in Santa Fe and maybe even Albuquerque by now." So I said softly, "That was so incredibly fine, almost unbelievable. Thanks to you guys, absolutely, thanks a million. Yeah, I'll leave today as soon as I dry out that tent." Dan nodded and poured more coffee and said "It's almost 10 o'clock, while you're packing up, could you do me a favor?" "Of course," I said, "anything, that's the least I could do for you people." Dan explained that an insurance agent was supposed to come by to look at the damage, but wouldn't look at it unless someone was here. Could I possibly wait for him, but no later than 1:00 PM. He said if he wasn't here by that time, it meant he wasn't coming today. I said, "Be glad to do that. Can't lock a place that's missing a wall, anyway, so I'll leave at one." Dan said, "Thanks, I should really be at work right now, so I'm leaving. Rain Man, those two girls are in love with you. Nice going. Anyway, a real pleasure to know you. Bon voyage." He offered his hand and I shook it and said "Tell the two girls I fell in love with both of them. Say Good-bye to all the others, and take care and thanks again." Dan left.

My pants had dried from yesterday's rain. I finished dressing, went outside into bright sunshine. How painful reality can be. Untied the tent, rolled it out on the concrete slab and returned to the back bedroom, folded the quilt, just the tiniest scent of three people loving and resting. Put the quilt against the wall. To the kitchen for more coffee, which I drank as I washed the few dishes remaining. Went back outside, checked the scooter over. Tires a little muddy, but other than that, everything seemed OK. I'd get gas first chance. Shook some of the mud off the tent. Even that wasn't bad and the tent was drying quickly, the dry air doing its thing. The insurance guy arrived at 11:00 and asked for Dan. I explained, he looked around for a minute or two, asked me to sign a paper saying he had been there, put a copy on the kitchen counter and was gone. The whole deal took less than five minutes. My thought was 'Gee, tough job.' I decided on one more shower with hot water before getting back to my journey. And that's what happened.

CHAPTER 14

NORTHWARD AGAIN

Showered and clean, waterbag freshened, the tent dried and repacked, I put on my very wrinkled permaprest jacket (at least I had kept it dry during the tent fiasco). Las Vegas, New Mexico, not Las Vegas, Nevada, was just a few miles north. I would stop for gas, a pack of smokes, maybe a snack. Smoke one now? Yeah, hadn't had one since the one with Vincent. Lighting up, I walked around a bit and thought of writing a note of thanks, but no, that just didn't fit. This was just one of those terrific times and now it's done. Put out the smoke and got onto the scooter, started it up first try. Remarkable little machine. Leaving the wounded, but blessed mobile home behind, it seemed that an entire decade had passed while I was there, but it had been less than 24 hours.

In less than a half-hour, I was refueling the scooter. Bought a pack of Marlboro's since they seem to fit the landscape better (who says advertising doesn't work) and two Snickers bars (did the Marlboro man eat Snickers bars?). Cruised through town and was back on Route 87, no, I thought it was 85, heading north. When did that happen? Talk about being distracted. Hardly saw the town at all, being so mentally derailed by the party of the night before. Raton, NM was my target for today, about 100 miles north, unless a mental second wind struck me. In that case, Trinidad, Colorado, twenty miles north of Raton, would be it. The towns, roads, the train tracks, all seemed to follow this course northward along the base of the Rocky Mountain chain. Foothills, forested hills and distant mountains to the west, plains on my right to the east. All of it quite scenic, but not sufficient to pull my attention away from my own thoughts. After the glorious night just experienced, the winding down was just that, a big letdown. My mood had to change. How would that happen? Have to think about something funny and far-removed. Later, when camp was made for the night, there would be reading, a couple of aspirin, and hopefully, a good snooze. So it was time to remember and think about something funny. So I thought about something which happened in church when I was a kid.

So here goes: Raised in an Italian Roman Catholic household. My mother was a devout Catholic and my father thought the entire church thing (didn't matter which religion) was a big farce and that any "man of the cloth" was at the least, a scam artist, and probably worse than that. But still, I was a holy kid for a few years. This had to have happened when I was nine years old, in fourth grade of elementary school, not Catholic school, public school. At the time (late 1940's) kids in Connecticut public schools had one hour of "religious instruction" per week. They would leave the school one hour early, travel to the church of their respective religion and get their holy time in. The Catholic church was a two-minute walk from our school. One sunny Wednesday afternoon, after a good snowfall, Ray Arronnell and I started our walk to the church. I gathered up a handful of snow, quickly formed a snowball and hit him squarely in the back of the head, some of the snow dropping down into his collar. The snow was perfect, absolutely perfect for snowball fabrication. And oh, the two of us did fabricate and the snowball war was on. Great time, but it had to end and we knew we'd be a half-hour late to our Religious Education session at the church, where the nun, the evil, foul-tempered dragon, awaited us. At the door of the church, before we went in, we agreed that we'd have to dream up some excuse, an individual excuse, for being late. Kids who were raised as Catholics in those times will understand the terror that we faced. The nuns were more to be feared than the police or the school Principal. These nuns were the new-age inquisitors. Ray and I took a minute or two, prepared our ridiculous stories, went into the church, used the holy water to bless ourselves, and while I never thought Ray was exceptionally bright, he neatly outmaneuvered me as we walked down the aisle, putting me up to bat first. Understand that the nun was totally pissed off at me from weeks before because I hadn't studied my Catechism. So she breathed some fire toward me, and said very slowly, and very dis-tinct-ly, "Master Ro-sa-no (that's the title they used, Master), explain why you are late arriving at God's House!" And thoughts are traveling through my head like rockets on the 4th of July ... oh god what a stupid story oh man she'll never believe me oh shit I'm going to hell for sure, etc. But I had to plow onward. Pushing my knee against the side of the pew to stop the tremors, I spoke. "I'm so sorry, Sister Catherine, I thought there was enough time to run home and let our cat, Mittens, out of our house. But when I tried to grab her, she thought I was playing and ran under the bed and it took so long to catch her, and that's why I'm so late." Whew! The story was out, and we both knew I was telling a big lie right here in front of Jesus, right here in God's House. She looked at me silently for a very painful five seconds, each of which felt like a decade. Then the black-robed executioner vowed "I will deal with you later." Then she hissed, "Ssssit down!" At least this time, I was eager to comply. "Master Arronnell, What is your story?" Ray, of course, had let me take the nun's first flames, and the steam jets, and the death ray vision, as he hid behind me. Now it was his turn. Safely seated, I was anxious to hear his story. Let's see if he could beat my 'cat under the bed' story. Ray cleared his throat and said, "Same thing for me, sister, only it was my dog."

Having relived this story a few hundred times over the years, I still laugh every time. Then a question arises, given that the big sin had already been committed, the big sin of being late to God's House (because that sneaky god had tested us with perfect snow). The question arises what could I have done? I could have told the truth, but of course, that would have put Ray at the mercy of this terrifying black lagoon creature, in effect 'ratting him out.' There was some code of honor amongst us big church liars, so that really wasn't an option. I could have said, "No excuse, Sister," and taken the punishment that was certain. But no, you've read my tale. In retrospect, of course, I made a poor choice, but remembering it always elevates my spirits. While I have honestly tried to remember any punishment that might have been earned, I cannot. And to be honest, I don't think the monster, known as Sister Catherine ever did actually 'deal with me later.' There is something special about being raised Catholic. Good or Bad, not my call, but different for sure. There must be two or three million funny stories. I've been involved in only three or four. Now you've heard one of them. Soon I'll tell you about the Catechism thing. Not a funny story ... just a story about a kid growing up.

Tony the Lambretta had done its job without a pause and we had passed some mountains called Turkey Mountains and a few miles later a sign pointed to The Wagon Mound, a small forested bump on the earth which reminded early white guys of a Conestoga wagon. We traveled past a settlement called Wagon Mound and then past a small salt lake, grey in color. We were in Kiowa Grassland Territory. Probably cattle ranching was the major economic activity. Traveling through these little towns, sometimes so remote, always prompted me to wonder what the kids did as they grew up. The library had to be pretty limited if they actually had one. Did these kids ever go to concerts? I grew up in a small city, but near to New York and Boston. There were so many things so easily available ... theatres, concerts, major league baseball parks, museums, jazz clubs, Broadway, and more. This terrain was so huge, this grassland. It meant these people just had to travel much farther to experience some of the cultural things, and so would most likely see fewer.

Just south of Springer, a town of seven or eight hundred, I thought I'd take a break. Still had most of the food purchased in Albuquerque and hadn't eaten very much since Santa Fe. A Snickers bar would hold me until campfire time. This grassland extended for miles and miles. Was this the same thing as the prairie? Suspected they were similar if not actually the same thing. I'd have to look that up. Either way, this was Marlboro Country, and I lit one up. Might have hummed the theme song, but couldn't remember it. The afternoon was huge, with an enormous sky, white clouds like abstract paintings all over it, lit up by a bright sun, with a very light breeze. Very different than my Southern Arizona desert, though both were equally staggering in scope. The clouds continually morphed into different shapes, playing their own games, having a good time.

Thinking ahead a few miles, there would be a small town called Maxwell, then my target town of Raton where I would camp. The plan was to find a camping spot just before Raton. Make some coffee, have some of that deli food, read and then sleep. I'd try to finish Steinbeck's "Of Mice and Men". Field stripped the Marlboro 'cause break was over.

Tony and I headed north once more. Easy traveling for about an hour and we were near Raton. Found some scrubby trees, enough for a little protection from the wind, should it increase. Caution was the key word traveling off road, for at least two reasons. One was the rattlesnake threat, to which I had become very attentive since moving to Tucson. The second was scooter tires. While excellent and comfortable on paved roads (though I drove at a slower rate when the pavement was wet), they really were not designed for traversing the raw desert or prairie. Perhaps there were available some heavy duty tires. Should I look for tires in Denver if there was a scooter place? If there was, should I have the scooter thoroughly serviced? Second thoughts about both were: The tires looked nearly new with very few miles having been traveled. Despite all the adventure, it had been only a thousand miles since I'd left Tucson. Though not far from the highway, I was hidden from it, but at the same time could watch vehicles traveling along its length into and out of Raton. The tent was set up, and a camp firepit was dug. Camp was made, there was enough small wood around for a coffeepot fire. I'd make coffee now. Damn, I make good coffee, always have.

There was remaining in the day at least an hour of daylight suitable for reading. I'll finish "Of Mice and Men". And I did. Steinbeck told the tale in such a way as to hold my attention all the way through. Part of that was the number of different themes and streams of thought running through the story, a heartbreaker of a story. A fine contribution to our world, John Steinbeck. Bravo. When I get to Denver, maybe I'll replace it with another one of your books. Anticipating a stay of a few days in Denver, I couldn't really give a reason for doing so, except that it was a big Western city and it would be sure to have good things ... libraries, bookstores, etc.

Drank only one cup of coffee. The second cup would be reheated in the morning before I went into Raton for a decent breakfast and fuel for Tony. Supper was food from those good people in the deli in Albuquerque. My second Snickers bar would be dessert. This quiet night would be my last night in New Mexico for quite a while. It had been an eventful few days and my good fortune to have met such a string of likeable people. And, of course, there would always be the memory of last night and two especially beautiful people. But never would I try contacting any of those that I felt so attracted to, having learned in my teens to never attempt to relive special moments or times. People and settings and feelings all change ... better a good memory than a sad disappointment. So I was leaving The Land of Enchantment and, with the exception of Gallup, it had indeed been that for me. As enchanting as New Mexico had been, its cooler climate would prevent me from ever living there. In a few short months back in Tucson, desert rat hood had become my way of life, thoroughly enjoying the intense heat. Despite the anticipation of traveling to and being in Denver for a few days, I would never live there because of cold weather, though I suspected it might be a great "summer" city for me.

So far on this little cross-country jaunt, the nights had been rather cold, above freezing temperature but not much above. Typically in the dry desert, there was considerable warming during the day, 35 degrees Fahrenheit (22 C) difference being common. The large sleeping bag did excellent service, by keeping me quite warm, to the point where it would not have to be zipped up all the way and left partially open. Though I featured myself as being an avid camper, later in life I would avoid it whenever possible, genuinely resenting waking in the morning until sunshine started doing its job. A tent site was always chosen that would have sunshine as soon as the sun decided to do its daily duty. A little sunshine on the tent fabric warmed the inside very quickly. With enough stored body heat in my clothing, I had survived each morning long enough to brew that life-giving coffee. There are creatures among us who seem to not need coffee to begin functioning in the morning. These, of course, are not really people, and are, in fact, the beings from outer space that we're constantly seeking. And they're right in front of us.

The goal for tomorrow was modest. Get to Pueblo, Colorado, unless something more interesting turned up. Pueblo was about 110 miles north, four to six leisurely hours of scootering along the base of the gorgeous Rocky Mountain Chain. First, there would be the town of Ratòn, NM, 4,000 or 5,000 people. Twenty-five miles north of that – the town of Trinidad, Colorado, about the same population. The population size could be of importance as an indication of what services might be available. For example, later in my trip, in a small village, the gas station was open Monday, Wednesday, and Friday mornings from 9:00 AM 'till Noon. And it was Tuesday, and Tony had a nearly empty gas tank. Might tell you about that later, but what was in my mind was two immediate items: One, buy another pair of pants, so I could wash the ones I'd been wearing for a week, and Two, find a lightweight, but well-constructed waterproof cover for the tent for protection from the rain. Maybe one of the two towns had these, and maybe not. Certainly, Denver did. So, it wasn't urgent, at least until it rained again.

Tomorrow morning, then, Raton, NM would be a place for breakfast, enabling me to say for the rest of my life that I had had breakfast in Rat, New Mexico. The question arises: Why would anyone name their town 'Rat' or if the Spanish translation was 'mouse', why would anyone name their town Mouse, New Mexico. I had heard of Boca Raton, Florida translated as 'Rat's Mouth' and I suppose that's not as bad as something like Manure, Minnesota or Snotty Waddy, Washington, but not much better either.

Imagine now, a meeting of a town's founding members, the most prominent amongst them saying, "Now fellas, you have to admit that if we call our town Turd Pile, Texas, there likely will never be another town by that name ... and no one will ever forget the name of our town." There would be a brief discussion as to whether it should be one word or two. They would agree two words was probably better, and given that the liquor jug was being passed around and given that almost everyone owed at least some money to Mr. Prominent Citizen, it would be adopted (by unanimous vote, no less). Later, when Turd Pile did not grow and prosper, a salesman would say to one of the founders, "... but no one wants to live in a place called Turd Pile. Why did you guys give it that name anyway?" The response would have to be "well, we thought it was a good idea at the time."

A few days later, I learned that Raton, NM referred to the many chipmunks, not rats or mice, which inhabited the area. In that case, use of the English word Chipmunk, NM might be an improvement.

With the sky darkening and the air cooling, it was time for day windering downering. Had a last Marlboro, brushed my teeth with two or three swigs of water from the waterbag, peed, washed down two aspirins, and crawled into my nest for the night.

CHAPTER 15

BANANA BELT

Morning arrived earlier than usual that day or maybe it was just my imagination. Crawled out of the tent, did a few necessary things in the half light of dawn. Then started the little fire for the coffee, the leftover cup from last night. It had not suffered during the night and was well received by everyone attending the presentation. The air was cool, but certainly not as cold as I had already witnessed. Since it was just a few miles into Raton, aka Chipmunk, NM, I thought I'd pack up and get on to a café to have a decent breakfast with hot coffee. There was a moderate breeze from the south, not quite warm, but comfortable. It didn't take long to pack up and lash everything to the Lambretta. Slowly and carefully, I retraced my steps of the evening before to regain the highway. Within twenty minutes, I was pulling up in front of a diner. The usual ... a short stack and black coffee. An unremarkable place, except the pancakes were perfectly done and the coffee was almost as good as mine. Used the restroom, and dallied over the second cup of coffee with a Marlboro. It was too early for stores to be opened and the older woman waiting the tables didn't have much to say even after staring out the window at the scooter for a minute or two. So there would be no conversation. Left a tip and paid the bill. I'd drive right through this town, which seemed a pleasant enough place.

In a very few miles I'd be saying goodbye to New Mexico, and heading to Trinidad, Colorado. The road was more hilly and more forested as we made our way northward through a mountain pass. The wind almost directly at my back made traveling easier.

This area Raton to Trinidad had much history attached to it. It was the highest elevation (7,800 feet, 2,377 meters) of the famous Atchison, Topeka, and Santa Fe Railroad with a railroad tunnel which eventually became an historical landmark. Pioneer cowboy Kit Carson most likely traveled this route a number of times. Gamblers of the Old West probably traveled this route occasionally as they moved from Tombstone and Tucson in Southern Arizona Territory, to other gambling centers like Denver or Leadville, in the Colorado Rockies. Still seeing interesting rock formations, with greener forest and lush springtime vegetation in the background, occasional patches of grassland and more forests and hills. A genuine mixture of everything. This area I suppose would be considered foothills of the Rockies, the east face of the Rocky Mountains. This was a fine morning I was experiencing. The scooter maintained a pretty good rate and seemed to be resting at the same time ... a fine morning with warmth in the air, the tailwind gently pushing, and after a while, a long scenic descent into the Town of Trinidad, an Old West town, the first Colorado town I'd ever visited.

No need for gasoline or coffee, so that meant it was "noodling" time. Trinidad was a town of 7,000 people (my guess) and semi-famous for a couple of things, the most prominent being the fact that Bat Masterson was the town Marshall for a time in the late 1800's. Nice-looking town, well-kept, rather quiet, built up on both sides of the Purgatoire River, not a huge river, but it did have water, something many Arizona rivers didn't have, much of the time being dry riverbeds instead of rivers. Driving through a few randomly selected side streets, my feelings didn't change. If I saw a military surplus store or men's clothing store open, I'd stop to try buying another pair of pants, but no such luck. Putted northward through town, and the urge to use this beautiful day for scenic views and traveling took over. Stop on the northern outskirts of Trinidad to take a leak and have a Marlboro, just like a man of the West should. And I did. And headed north again toward Pueblo. The day was warm, that beautiful wind was at my back and I thought 'Life is pretty peachy.'

Speaking of 'peachy' ... As I purchased food on this trip, I always tried to buy a few pieces of fresh fruit, not too many, because they'd spoil very easily. Almost always, I would have with me some dried fruit and nuts, usually almonds, either raw or toasted. From childhood, almonds were a favorite, to the point where I did some research on this nut when I was eleven or twelve years old. Well, you can't do much reading about almonds without reading about peaches, plums, and apricots, because they're all from the same genus, Prunus (cherries are closely related also). So I learned that the flesh of the almond fruit is not so good to eat because of cyanide concentration. The same is true of the pits of peaches and apricots. So that means that the peach (with good flesh and bad pits) is the 'opposite' of the almond (with bad flesh and good pits). Not many fruits have an opposite, for example, what is the opposite of a banana? This is the sort of thinking that would rattle around inside my head while traveling long miles, whether with Lambretta or, in later years, Alitalia. In this case maybe it was the vibration which triggered this sort of thinking.

There once lived a great man, a self-taught horticulturist named Luther Burbank. He cross-pollinated and hybridized so many different plants, including peaches and plums, 'inventing' the nectarine. Fascinating life Luther Burbank. Ever heard of Burbank, California? Well, it is not named in his honor, it was named after a different Burbank, a dentist, I believe.

Pueblo was about 80 miles north from Trinidad. About halfway was the small town of Walsenburg. Maybe 1,500 population, towns of this size puzzled me. For a time this was the home of Bob Ford, the guy who nailed Jesse James. But a town cannot live on that alone. I would guess the economic base would be agriculture, but I didn't see much farmland or animal facilities. Maybe the town existed solely because it is an intersection of four or five roads. This was grassland. Without the splendid views way off in the distance, this would have been a rather boring place. Today, however, the distant scenery was splendid and I was still enjoying the ease with which Tony Lambretta and I passed the miles. The tail wind persisted and I would not easily interrupt such smoothness. North of Walsenburg was grassland almost all the way to Colorado City and then to Pueblo. This was part of the Western edge of the Great Prairie.

Thinking about and laughing once more at the 'Cat Under the Bed' story (in the last chapter, 14), I remembered that Sister Catherine, the awful black-robed creature, had already been very angry with me, and it was all about Catechism. For those who do not know the word catechism, it can be defined simply as an elementary book of the principles of the church, in question and answer form (in this case, the church being the Roman Catholic church). As part of our "religious education" in public elementary school, we traveled to our respective churches for this instruction. Sister Catherine presided over this class of 30 or 40 kids. Part of our assignment (as good Catholic kids) was to memorize the Catechism, word for word, question by question, answer by answer, and chapter by chapter. Before going any farther, let me mention that by age nine, I was a pretty good reader, and would read anything and lots of it. Able to read the Reader's Digest, which I often did, the New York Times occasionally, the encyclopedia constantly and anything that happened into my vision ... the jacket of a long-play record or bag-changing instructions for the vacuum cleaner. Now, here comes The Catechism which, of course, God wants us to know backward and forward, and if we don't ... uh oh. God wanting us to know this would be incentive enough, but Sister Catherine, the Holy Witch, was enforcing God's wishes. We were all given a new copy of the First Volume and told to 'know by heart' and 'know with your heart' the first twenty questions (almost two full lessons) before next week's religious education class. OK, not so bad, we had to memorize various things in 'regular' school ... the state capitals, the multiplication tables, Pledge of Allegiance, etc. In church we memorized the Our Father, of course, and other prayers.

In addition, as an altar boy, I had memorized all the Latin necessary to serve Mass. We could repeat all the sounds without really a thought as to their meanings, but no big deal. Now, here was The Catechism, which I took home with the intention to study diligently. After supper, I began to read this new book. Read the first twenty questions and answers and began to … began to what? This seemed a little bit dumb to me. Two things bothered me: One, if it's in the book why memorize it … this is not just a short prayer, it's a whole book. Two, the questions and answers really made little sense, so that logic wouldn't help you remember anything. OK, look ahead, at more advanced questions and answers. Question: Does God see us? Answer: God sees us and watches over us with loving care. At age nine, I was familiar with enough of WWII to know that God totally missed watching over about 9 or 10 million people in Europe alone. Question: What do we mean by the Blessed Trinity? Answer: This answer and subsequent answers were convoluted doozies, I decided, and made no sense whatsoever … The Father, The Son, and The Holy Ghost were all separate and all equal and yet they were all the same person (later in my youth I referred to them as Daddy-O, JC, & The Spook). Here is what happened: After long deliberation (at least for a nine year old), I decided I would not spend my effort memorizing this nonsense. Instead I would try to just fake it, slide by, and hope the whole catastrophe would pass over my head and leave me untouched. So I was a reasonably happy kid until the following Wednesday afternoon when the formidable Sister Catherine uncovered my plot on one of the first and easiest questions, at which I had not even bothered to look. Tried to fake some answer, obviously not even close to what was wanted. Sister Catherine said she knew I hadn't studied and that the following week I was to know the lessons or something terrible beyond my imagination would occur. That was Week One. Week Two was a week of misery for me. Studying this was not going to happen, that I knew, and something terrible beyond my imagination would happen, that I also knew. So Wednesday of Week Two, the Steaming Sister Catherine latched onto this skinny, pathetic, little Italian kid, like a spider with a fly, with instructions to start reciting all the questions and answers of the Catechism lessons. Of course, I couldn't even begin and just stood there, mute. She asked four or five questions of me and I stood mute. The kids in the class were silent and scared and so was I. Finally, she asked loudly, "Right now, in front of Jesus On The Cross, will you promise to study for next week?" I shook my head and finally said, "No, Sister." Silence. She reached into some hidden compartment of her black habit (that's what nuns used to wear) and, as a magician might, produced a pad and pencil and energetically wrote something. Handing it to me, she said (for all the class to hear, of course) "This is a note to your mother. She needs to answer this note and you WILL return with her answer next week. For now, you can stand in shame, over there." This could have been a bad move by the good Sister ... I knew a dozen ways to completely distract a classroom of kids by just standing still. She lucked out (God must have been watching over her with loving care) because I was genuinely frightened of her, and would not do any of my little, devious, clown things. The following Saturday (note that I waited a few days), I gave the written note to my mother. Naturally, my mother blew her cork and went on and on, as only she could, almost ending with "How embarrassing!" and actually ending with "Now just sit down now and study this!" And I said "No, it's ridiculous. I won't study it." So this was a big crisis for me, and it really tested my mother for a day or two, but I would not even pretend to study. Not often as a kid, but occasionally, I would get unmovingly stubborn about something, and 'all the King's horses and all the King's men' could not get me to budge from my position. This was one of those times. My mother tried eleven different ways to get me to change my mind and I would not. Finally, she spoke to my father, maybe on the Monday or Tuesday night before her answer was due. I was in an adjacent room, but heard them talking, half in English and half in Italian. Pretending to be engrossed in something else, I seemingly paid no attention to them at all. My father evidently asked to see this catechism because my mother handed it to him. Understand that my father had only one year of school, first grade, in Italy, had taught himself to read in Italian and English, though quite slowly, and semi-aloud and with that Italian accent he never lost despite his many years in America. He could, however, read and understand a real estate contract, for example, or read and understand a complex political article in the newspaper. So it took some time for him to sample these catechism teachings. After a long, long time, he called out, "Annie." (I won't try to type out this whole conversation in an Italian accent, so readers will have to do their best to 'hear' this as it was spoken. Well, I'll help a little.) My mother came in from the kitchen and said "What do you think?" My father said, "That kid is right. It's too stupid to waste the time." My mother asked, "Well, what am I going to say to the nun?" My father laughed and said, "you say you husband trewa damn ting away and I pay for ita, but no wanna nudder one-a." Wednesday morning, before I went to school, my mother gave me a sealed envelope to be delivered to Sister Catherine that afternoon. She made me promise not to open it. And it was delivered unopened to the Wicked Witch of the West, who opened and read the note silently in front of the class. She told me softly to sit down and I never heard another word about catechism directed to me. Ever. Not a fun-filled story, actually a very big stress for me, a normally happy kid.

So Tony Lambretta and I are 'flying' today, up and down gentle rolling terrain, straight across the flatter land. We pass through Colorado City, which seems a little greener than the lands surrounding it. In less than an hour, we'll hit the southern portions of Pueblo. So far, despite the repetition of the grassland images, this State of Colorado was genuinely beautiful. If it had been only grassland or prairie, it would be the sort of thing that encouraged madness. Just as the views of the Painted Desert landscape continually changed, these mountains to the west presented an ever-changing image, each area having its own visual drama. The things of civilization increased substantially as we approached Pueblo and gradually we, my faithful putt-putt and I, were in a city. Almost without a break, we had already traveled a bit more than 100 miles today and it seemed like half that distance. Now it was time for a meal, a lunch or supper, not a breakfast. Early afternoon, lunch was just over for most people. Locking the helmet to the scooter, roughing up my hair which could get matted under the helmet's weight, and removing my sunglasses, I walked into a diner named Enrico's.

A middle-aged guy behind the counter said, "Good afternoon, take any seat you like." I said, "Thanks, you mind if I use a booth instead of a stool?" He replied, "You are my guest, your choice." Sitting down, and without looking at the menu, I said I'd like some sort of light meal, with greens if available, and some bread perhaps. He said, "I can give you today's Lunch Special which was chicken and red peppers, and I could add some Swiss chard on the side with a couple of slices of French bread. How's that sound?" I said, "You must be reading my mind. That sounds perfect. That and a cup of black coffee, please. Let me go wash my hands." Used the restroom, and my meal was being served as I took my seat again. I looked at the food for maybe a moment too long and he asked, "Is anything wrong?" I said "No, not at all. Here I am, in a strange place and the food looks and smells so familiar. You must be Enrico, and are you Italian ... because nobody else ever serves Swiss chard, not even the Swiss!" He laughed out loud. "Only half Italian, my father was Cuban and Portuguese, but I learned food from my mother. And you, when I said Swiss chard, you didn't bat an eye. I cook that for my family and a few friends. Nobody else around here knows what to do with it. So you must be at least part Italian." I said, "Sicilian, the worst kind or the best kind of Italian, depending on your point of view, I suppose." He laughed again, saying "… and here you come on that Vespa, from how far?" I answered, "Tucson, Arizona, about 800 miles from here. That's a competitor of the Vespa, a Lambretta." He said "Eight hundred miles, Madon! Go ahead, you eat in peace and later we can talk. I gotta clean up some stuff first." After twenty minutes and an excellent lunch, Enrico approached with the coffee pot, and an extra cup, refilled my cup and sat down opposite me asking "Is this OK?" I responded, "You are my guest." Then we introduced ourselves, shaking hands as if we were long lost friends. Smiling he asked, "The food. OK?" I said, "Superb. Can I buy you a cup of coffee?" He filled his own cup. We started talking and that lasted about a half-hour until two couples came into the diner. He greeted them, served coffee to all four, and returned to my booth, saying, "They come in here often and just drink coffee, so it's OK." We resumed our talking and I mentioned that this morning the warm wind was a nice change. He mentioned that we were in the 'banana belt' of the Rockies, that it always seemed to be a friendlier climate than the surrounding areas. That 'banana belt' business was a new one for me. Asked if he was spoofing me. No, it's for real. I asked him about a hardware store and also a good place to camp tonight and got advice on both. He offered to let me stay at his house, but he lived 20 miles or so in the wrong direction. I paid my bill, probably underpriced. Shaking hands warmly, we said our goodbyes, me in English, him saying, "Ciao, amico mio."

And I headed into Pueblo, following his suggested route. Very shortly later, I was at a hardware store asking about plastic sheeting or a small waterproof tarpaulin. There was a plastic tarp with grommeted holes which would do OK for me, except it seemed a bit heavy and also a little pricey, both of which I mentioned. The guy looked straight into my eyes and said, "Are you asking me for a twenty percent discount?" Surprised, I finally said, "Yes, I am." He said "Why on earth should I give you such a discount?" Playing along, I said, "Because I'm good-looking and might become a regular customer." He said, "OK, you talked me into it. You're quite a talker, young man." And the deal was made. And the tarp folded and stashed in my clothing bag, which was getting bigger. What a nice little scenario! Able to find something very close to what was sought, and at decent price. He sold an article and made some profit. And ... both parties played a little word game and could smile. Too bad that more of life isn't as simple, as give and take, and profitable and pleasant.

Enrico had suggested that I head north on the main drag through town, cross the Arkansas River, which he said could be pretty nice, but that Fountain Creek, which the highway followed was even nicer and had a million places for camping out. At the same time wanting a rest, I wanted to see more of Pueblo, having already crossed the Arkansas, and still pointed north, was now in constant view of Fountain Creek (which could easily qualify as a full-fledged river in Southern Arizona). Spotted a number of pretty good camping spots with the usual pines. Arbitrarily picked a place, drove carefully off the road and parked under the pines. Nice peaceful day, perfect temperature, maybe time for a snooze. Dragged out my new possession, the grey-green tarp, unfolded it and spread it out. It was a little larger than I wanted, but seemed like a good cover for the tent. Folded it in half, sat on it, used the clothing bag as a pillow, got my copy of South Pacific, opened it and immediately fell asleep. For about an hour, hour and a half. Woke up with a start. What the hell? Oh! Two red tail hawks, maybe 20 feet away on the bleached limb of a dead tree. Beautiful birds, but they really needed some remedial voice training. The screeching, scraping, screaming sounds seem impossible coming from such sleek creatures. No shortage of volume either. There was no hint as to whether they were glad to see each other or mad at one another, but there was quite a long conversation and I had never been so close for so long a time. They quieted after a while. I continued to watch. Finally, one left on wide wings, then the other followed. I'll see Pueblo tomorrow. Now ... I'll make camp, do some reading, have some food later, and just enjoy the evening. Fountain Creek was less than 100 feet away. Light up a Marlboro and enjoy the West. I saw briefly at the hardware store a Denver newspaper predicted no rain for the area, so I decided not to cover my little non-water-resistant tent this evening. Before setting up the tent, I tried to guess where the morning sun would hit the rear of the tent, since the opening facing Fountain Creek looked to the west. No morning sun in my big picture window tomorrow. While I hadn't planned any food shopping in Pueblo, I would finish most of the food which I carried. So, I'll try to find a decent deli in this place which seemed to be a good-hearted working man's town. Towns have distinct personalities, sometimes more than one.

Walked over to the river's edge with washcloth and soap. Ai-yai-yai, the water was more than refreshing, but I did the best possible to get all my vital parts clean – a rather shocking process, but not so serious as to cause frostbite. Back to the tent, set up tomorrow's coffeepot fire. Settle in, read more of Michener, listen to some owls as the sky turns dark. Sleep.

CHAPTER 16

COOKIES PAVE THE WAY

Early mornings on this trip were proving to be the most leisurely part of the day ... the opposite of most people's work schedules. There was no enthusiasm to ride in the coldest part of the day and heading east, the sun directly into my eyes was unsafe and, at the very least, annoying and tiring. Driving north or south was easier. This morning I woke slowly, got my little coffeepot fire going, peed on a nearby tree (mark my territory – trying to keep all those other scooterists from crowding my space, donchaknow), returned to the sacred pot and poured a cup, sat down and just inhaled coffee fumes for a few moments, which reminded me I'd better buy a pound of coffee. Where the two red-tailed hawks had had their little meeting the evening before, there were now three bald eagles, silent, and now a fourth joined them (maybe they were trying to get a game of poker going or more likely, just thinking about lunch). The collective noun for a group of eagles is a 'convocation.' Does a gathering of four eagles qualify as a convocation? Do four cows constitute a herd? Probably not. So this was just a bunch. My hunch ... a lunch bunch.

As I packed up camp, I emptied each bag, and repacked, removing misplaced items or putting little trash items aside for disposal. Only one set of clean underwear remaining. Time to do laundry today or tomorrow. This had been a nice camping spot, but now, I'd go back south two or three miles to noodle around Pueblo. Back across Fountain Creek, and now heading south and now back across the Arkansas River. My reaction was similar to many people who spend time in the dry southwest deserts ... we were just not accustomed to crossing rivers with water in them. They were mesmerizing ... almost as much fun as the window in a front load washing machine (you can tell laundry is on my mind right now).

It was time to refuel the scooter, check tire pressures, get rid of the little bit of trash, refill the water bag, etc. Pulled off the highway into a gas station. The guy walked out of his little house and came over to me with a great big, "Good Morning!" I greeted him and went into my usual song and dance about not wanting to bother him for such a small amount of gas.

"Hell, doesn't matter to me, I'd fill a thimble if you asked." He saw the Arizona license plate on the Lambretta and, of course, that started the conversation I would have many times across the country, with him saying "I wish I could have done that, but I got married." Except he said, "I wish I could do something like that only ..." and he interrupted himself to ask, "How old are you?" I answered, "Twenty-one next month." Pausing, he said, "Hell, I'm only twenty-eight. My girlfriend wants to get married now." I splayed out both my hands in an 'I don't know' gesture. He looked so sincere and said, "What do you think?" I said, "I don't like to answer a question with another question, but here's a question I've been thinking about, because I have a girlfriend back in Tucson with the same thoughts as yours. The question is: 'Why is it so easy to get married and so difficult to get unmarried?' We were done fueling. Another customer pulled in. He said, "You stay right there. We gotta talk."   I said, "Let me use the restroom. I'll pull over at the office." Reaching in his pocket, he gave me a key. Did the restroom thing. Got rid of my trash. Then found the faucet on the outside of the little building, tasted the water from the bag, emptied it and refilled the water bag from the faucet. Using the air hose, I checked the tire pressures. Went into the office and lit up a Marlboro, started looking at tourist brochures, got Pueblo, Colorado Springs, and another for Denver, found a map of the Western United States, and the attendant walked into the office. I handed him the key, said thanks, and introduced myself, and offered him a smoke. Taking it and lighting up, he said his name was Zipper, and then had a million questions. A good twenty minutes of conversation later, he said, "You're like today's second sunrise." I'd never heard that expression before. Nice. Mentioning that I had seen a small sign for Gagliano's Deli on Elm Street, I asked where Elm Street was. He said, "Gag-lee-ah-nos? Gag's? You're almost there," and gave me directions. He said they have the best food there, not cheap, but really good tasting food and they've been there forever. I said, "Gag's? Oh jeez, you guys can really murder a name! It's better if you pronounce it like this: Gahl-YAHN-nose." I got up to go and said, "How much do I owe you? I'd like to take this map, too." "Man, are you kidding? I owe you bigtime. Don't worry about the gas and here"... he pulled a pack a Marlboros from the rack and handed it to me ..."I might see you on the road somewhere. Maybe we can have another smoke break together soon!" Wow!

   Wow, did I start something in his life? Less than ten minutes and I had found my way to Gagliano's Deli ... Gag's. They had just about everything a person could want in a deli. Beautiful smell to the place, spent a little bit of money and treated myself to two dozen Italian cookies ... soul food, a dozen in each bag. At the cash register, I paid my bill, grabbed a handful of napkins, took my loot outside and except for the cookies and the napkins, which I stashed in my jacket pockets for quick reference, I packed everything neatly in place.

Pockets bulging a bit, it was time for noodling. This was a very old neighborhood I was in. I putted here and there. Using the Pueblo brochure as a guide, I headed east on Northern Avenue then north on the business route. While the whole place had a good feel to it, nothing seemed to entice me, at the moment, to stay and spend some time. But one day I would hope to return. Very much though, I did want to see the Garden of the Gods up north about 50 miles in Colorado Springs. Back across the Arkansas River heading north. The business route out of Pueblo joined the main highway north. That's what was followed. Soon enough, within five or six miles, I was back on the edge of the prairie – this time on both sides of me. Immediately to the east ran Fountain Creek, beyond that – prairie, miles and miles of grassland. Directly to the west was a bit more grassland, then more distant but not too far away, the Rockies. The tailwind from yesterday did not reappear. Still, progress was smooth and steady on this gorgeous morning. A little more than an hour later, I was driving into the southernmost 'suburbs.' Time for a little break. A cookie break. After that, there would be a coffee break, since I wouldn't take my own cookies into a food establishment. Three cookies is what I chose, three different kinds of Italian cookies. Excellent, all three just plain excellent. Now find a café for some coffee. Driving into Colorado Springs was a neat experience – some big, wide streets, occasional rock formations, always the view of Pike's Peak, famous at 14,000+ ft. (4300 meters), but not the tallest in the US. Lots of military activities here, including the Air Force Academy, which graduated its first class a year or two before I putted through town. Many people don't know that The US Air Force is relatively young, as it grew out of the US Army in the late 1940's and early 1950's, at some time in that transition being known as the US Army Air Force. Stopped for coffee and a refill. Had a smoke. Then, generally noodled my way north and west until signs for Garden of the Gods appeared and followed them into West Colorado Springs.

A remarkable place visually and spiritually. I knew something of the geology and marveled at that. The balanced rocks, red rock formations, and sandstone spires could easily be interpreted into spiritual beings. At least a half-dozen Indian tribes considered this area sacred. Whether they fought over the area or agreed to truces, I'm not sure, probably both at one time or another. I scootered here and there in a rather large area getting different viewpoints as I did. There were hiking trails and small groups of people on the tops of one or two rock formations. Visually, a magnificent experience. Geologically, it was stunning. While I felt no spiritual stirrings, it was easily understood how the captivating aura of the place could give birth to any number of beneficent gods. A magnificent area and it was good to have used the effort to see it. For being so smart, I rewarded myself with three more cookies. Already half of one dozen gone. Italian cookies are certainly vulnerable to predators.

An impressive town, Colorado Springs, with an impressive number of creeks having a dozen different names. Wondered if they had extensive springtime flooding. Elevation was more than 6,000 feet, so that was fairly high ground, most likely with good runoff, though I didn't know. Aside from the few words necessary to buy coffee, I exchanged no conversation with anyone in town, but everyone seemed to have a little smile and that's OK. Having a beard in the 1960's was off-putting, I knew, to many people. The few times I caught my image in a mirror, I thought I did, in fact, appear to be at least unpredictable and maybe a little dangerous. As part of my job as a waiter, I was always clean-shaven. As a scooterman, having the beard helped protect facial skin from the constant wind. The odd appearance of the scooter had attracted some brave souls into conversation occasionally. So, much of my time was spent alone and that's never been a big problem for me. On this trip, 90% of my conversations had been with people dispensing fuel or food.

Noodled around Colorado Springs for a while, knowing that tomorrow I'd be in Denver, barring any huge happenings. Maybe I should get right on Denver's doorstep, about 40 miles north. My very tentative plan was to spend two or three days there. Was there a reason? Not really, just that it was a large western city. Rural was nice, but so was city. Enjoy the afternoon up in Castle Rock, just a stone's throw from Denver. Ok, let's do it! Heading north again toward Denver. The land becomes more hilly, more piney, and less flat grassland, and still with red rocks and grey ones, and open spaces ... a real mixture again and always entertainment for the eyes. Clouds were active and I felt a few droplets of rain, but looking around, saw nothing at all threatening. Buzzed on through the village of Larkspur. Castle Rock was next and was the name given to a rock formation, a butte, and later to the little town nearby, with a population of 1,000 or a bit more.

Just as I was entering the little town, it began to drizzle, and then a light rain started and I pulled the scooter into a small gas station with a large canopy overhang. Pulled up near the office, not the pump. A middle aged guy came out of the little glassed-in office and said, "Welcome, How're you doing?" I answered, "Thanks for asking. I'd sure like to use your roof for a while if you don't mind." He said, "Help yourself. Hey, where did you get the Lambretta?" I said, "Oh, you know the Lambretta? Everyone thinks it's a Vespa. How do you know Lambretta? Smiling he said, "... with the Navy and we were in an Italian port for the last two months of my enlistment … Naples … Napoli. That was 1957. What a great place Italy is! And I saw at least one million of these Lambrettas and Vespas. Damn, you have Arizona plates on that thing. Which part of Arizona?" I answered "Tucson." He said, "Damn, that's almost Mexico." I nodded yes. We introduced ourselves and shook hands. He said, "Rosano, I'm about to make coffee, care to join me?" Nodding, "That sounds great." He asked, "Should I make two cups or four, because I always drink two myself." I held up four fingers. "Sugar? I don't have any cream." "Black," I answered, "black is perfect, and Ron, I'll tell you I knew this would happen and I knew you'd invite me for coffee, so I brought the pastry." Reaching into my jacket pocket, I took out the six remaining cookies of the first dozen from Gagliano's in Pueblo. Eyes wide open, he said again, "Damn, those things are habit-forming. I've been all over this world and I really like pastries, and nobody even gets close to the Italians for desserts, no one, not even close." I was nodding in agreement as he poured coffee and he said, "Crazy people, but they do try to enjoy life. Even their arguments are fun." I laughed and said, "Yeah, I know." He looked at me and said "You're Mexican, right?" Shaking my head no, I said, "Sicilian." He laughed out loud, "I shoulda known, and you with light eyes." We drank two cups of coffee and talked for a little over an hour. The rain had stopped. Finally, I said, "I have to find a place to pitch my little tent tonight, what can you suggest around here?" A customer pulled in at the pump. He said, "I'll be right back." Five minutes later, he said, "I got just the place for you." Guiding me outside, he said, "You see that car there?" and he pointed to a Nash or Hudson sedan delivery, similar to a station wagon, parked near the side of the building. I said, "Yeah, but …" Interrupting he said, "It's my nephew's car and as clean as a whistle, cleaner than a whistle for sure. I worry that it's here and told him to park it at the house, but no… Look, can you stay in there? I'll give you the key to the bathroom … no shower, just a toilet and a sink with hot and cold water. Listen, I'd invite you to the house, but my wife would get totally squirrelly. You'd be doing me a favor. Someone's going to steal that thing, so I'm going to move it tomorrow. But for tonight … at least I wouldn't worry, and you'd be out of the rain. Damn, I'll even bring you breakfast in bed." Funny, and I laughed. "OK, it's a deal." He laughed and said, "I was just kidding about the breakfast." "Yeah, I knew you'd weasel out of that one," I said. "C'mon," he said waving his hand, "let's finish our coffee." So we went inside. He fiddled with some keys for a minute or two, then gave me a key ring with two keys on it. "This is for the bathroom. This one's for the car door. Let's run a drop light into the back so you can see." We did that. Then he said, "I have to stay open another hour. More coffee?" I held up one finger. "Perfect, and I'll join you and you can tell me more about your trip." As I mentioned this part of the trip or that part, he would say, "Damn, Good for You." But I kept asking him questions, too. As he answered questions, he seemed to be a thoughtful person, always considering the view of people in the various areas of the world he had visited. The hour absolutely flew.

So I was set for this evening. With a reading light, and hot water! Luxury unlimited. And I had spent a major part of three hours, and three cups of coffee, talking with a stranger about so many different things. He was a good guy and was now a friend instead of a stranger. He had been round the globe two or three times. When I mentioned that the Lambretta was originally purchased in Guam at a Base Exchange and then flown to Tucson's Davis-Montham Air Force Base on a US Bomber, he said he'd probably bought a few things at the same Exchange. Small world. I purchased it from a pilot who had ridden it about 600 miles and it was a screaming bargain. After he closed up his office and locked the pumps, he said, "Sleep well. What time do you get up in the morning?" Answering, "It doesn't matter at all. I'll be here whatever time you get here in the morning. And Ron, if you don't want a hobo hanging around in the morning, kick my ass out of here. Take care and thanks." I waved. Used my lock and cable to secure Tony to a concrete post next to the building. Got out some food, the Michener book, clothing bag, sleeping bag, and the water bag and stashed all of it into the vehicle. Got my washcloth and soap, unlocked the bathroom, a small room, but recently painted and spotlessly clean (Navy training sticks to a man). The smell of the paint reminded me of that old phrase (but relatively new to me at the time) from the Navy ... 'If you can't move it, paint it.' Washed myself as thoroughly as possible using that miraculous life-sustaining hot water. Great invention.

As the reddish glow of sunset lost its light and the sky darkened, I ate a small meal from my food stash, with my feet hanging out the back end of the delivery wagon. No dessert (had already eaten nine cookies which was probably enough), but had a piece of fresh fruit and would have the other in the morning. There were some owls nearby, practicing their hooting. Had semi-identified with owls, since childhood. I couldn't see where they might be, nor could I guess at the number. Throughout the day, since seeing the eagles, there was a constant mini-search in my head for collective nouns, and I did remember that a gathering of owls was called a parliament of owls, but still wondered at who assigned these words to groups of animals ... a school of fish, etc. The most appropriate group name remembered was ... a congress of baboons. So, the day had begun with eagles and ended with owls.

CHAPTER 17

THERE WAS THIS GIRL

Last night, on top of the sleeping bag, rolled-out on the floor of the delivery wagon, I read Michener's "Tales of the South Pacific" using the drop light. A minor contest occurred to see which happened first, my eyes closing shut in sleep or finishing the book. My memory included turning out the light, but not necessarily any of the last page or two.

Not quite sunrise and I'm up taking a leak, but still want to sleep some more despite having had seven or eight hours. This scooter driving was probably more tiring than I wanted to admit. Returned to at least a half-snoozing state.

Until Ron rapped on the side panel. "Morning," I said. Through the driver's side window he motioned as if drinking from a cup, "Coffee?" I said, "I was wondering when our waiter would show up. Coffee would be great." So I climbed out of the rear door of the vehicle, stretched, and stumbled into the office where the smell of coffee illuminated the world. He poured me a cup and said, "It's pretty busy in the morning here, people making their way into the big city. Let me check out the bathroom. Sleep OK?" I said, "Ron, I wiped the bathroom down so that it's just as clean as when I entered it, mirror and all. It's OK. And yeah, I slept like a stone. Here's your keys." Two cars pulled in at the same time at the pumps. "They'll keep me hoppin' for an hour or two, so no time to talk." "Well," I said, "I'll pack up and be going and thanks so much. That saved me a bunch of hassle. A pleasure knowing you. So long." As we shook hands once more, he said, "You did me the favor, friend. Arrivederci." I finished my coffee, took about 15 minutes to pack, then used the bathroom one last time. Got on the scooter named Tony Lambretta and putted over to the pumps where Ron was pumping fuel. "Don't forget, the car and the bathroom are still unlocked. Ciao, Ron." He gave a thumbs up as I turned to the road.

Two or three miles north of Castle Rock, I took Route 85 slightly to the west, but from this point all roads headed to Denver and its satellites towns. 85 was called Canam Highway, and Santa Fe Drive too. No shortage of names for this road. Fair amount of traffic and this was what I could usually avoid by starting later in the morning, but at the same time, I hadn't wanted to overstay my welcome back at Ron's station. Earlier in the trip, Englewood, Colorado, just south of Denver itself, seemed to call me and I hadn't the foggiest reason as to why. Vaguely I remembered that my family knew a family from Englewood, so big deal. But Englewood it was, about 30 miles north, about an hour's travel. It was fairly chilly, but tolerable this morning. Upon reaching Englewood, I'd gas up again, stop for more coffee, and figure out why I wanted to go to Denver so badly. How's that for advanced planning which continually incorporated a good measure of willy-nilly. On my left, to the west, was Plum Creek. But I thought East Plum Creek was to the West. It seemed to be everywhere at once. Perhaps all those cookies were affecting me.

Cruising through Littleton and then stopping for gas, I asked the attendant which might be the best approach to Englewood and Denver. He asked if I was in a hurry, then laughed as he pointed at the scooter. Turn here, go east to South Broadway, turn left to head north. That would take me to both places. Wasn't sure if he was making a fun of me or not. For sure, though, was the fact that I was in a large city and no longer out on the plains. There were all sorts of city things around – minimarkets, a pawnshop, a bakery, one or two liquor stores, a repair garage, a car sales lot, etc. Hadn't seen much of this stuff since Albuquerque. This area (was I in Littleton or Englewood?) was a little on the rough side, but OK. Cruised north, slowly, looking here and there, and Hey!

Thank the gods! They knew I would arrive sometime … there, on the corner … a coin-op, a coin-operated laundry! And here I am with no more clean underwear. And God must have thought, "As soon as I'm done with this little bunch of universes over here, that kid will need some attention. Among other things, that kid will need some clean underwear, so he needs a laundry. So there. Poof! There's your laundry, and You're Welcome." Now I'd spend some time getting cleaner and reading the brochures I'd picked up. Pulled in on the side street side of the building, put the scooter up on its kickstand. Noticed a young woman across the street walking with a purse and one cloth bag over her shoulder and another bag, which seemed heavy, she held just an inch or two up off the sidewalk. She stopped for maybe a full minute (and I watched without staring or being intrusive I hoped) and then she started toward me, crossing the side street diagonally and limping more than a little. I stopped what I was doing and half-trotted toward her and asked, "Can I help you?" Red-faced and nodding yes, she said, "Oh thank you, yes, yes." "To the laundry?" She nodded yes. "C'mon, I'll help you. Let me have that. And take my arm." And we went into the coin-op where she practically fell into one of the chairs fastened to the floor. "Can I get you some water?" She nodded yes. Looking around, there was a restroom but no drinking fountain, and no cups. I said, "One minute, OK?" Again, she just nodded. Out to the scooter, got my coffee cup, washed it and filled it with water from the rest room sink, brought it to her and sat beside her and stayed quiet. Got her a second helping of water after a few minutes. As five more minutes passed, her color returned to something more normal. She had caught her breath and brushed the hair away from her face. This was a beautiful woman now, not frowny and sweaty and blotchy. Very dark hair and very light skin. Remarkably pretty, a cross between Queen Nefertiti and Audrey Hepburn. I said, "I'll be right back." Out to the scooter, got my clothing bag, and went back inside. Sat next to her again and asked "If you're OK, how OK are you – fifty percent? seventy-five …?"

She smiled. That was good. And told me the story briefly: She was living at her cousin's house, had started a large load of laundry, the washing machine started smoking like hell, so she shut it off. But the laundry was soaking wet and the machine wouldn't drain and that's the large load in the heavy bag and she thought she could easily walk the six blocks to the coin-op to finish the laundry, but her leg gave out (an injury from ice skating about a year before). Things went from bad to worse in a hurry and that's the mess I found her in across the street.

"Well," I said, "you look a hundred percent better now. Are you alright taking aspirin?" She nodded yes. Reached into my jacket and took a very small bottle out and gave her two and got more water for her. "That'll help with your leg. Now, my name is Rosano, and your name is …" "Stella Beauchamp … Stella," she said. "A heavenly name," said I. (that was a little word-play there, and I don't know if she 'got' it). What's the plan now?" She just shrugged, her chin wrinkled a bit, and she shuddered lightly. I said, "Is there anyone I can call to help you?" She shook her head no. After another few seconds I asked, "Do you want me to help make a plan?" Again, she nodded. "My next question is 'Can you walk a little bit?' or does it hurt too much."? She stood up and walked carefully. I said, "OK Stella, let's do this. Let's get the laundry done, washed and dried – yours and mine, while we rest your leg and give the aspirin a chance to do some good. After that, we'll make a further plan. How's that?" She said, "OK, I really don't want to let those clothes get ruined." Holding up my laundry bag, I said, "I want to wash everything I own right now, including this jacket. We've got plenty of washing machines and plenty of driers and I have far too much change in my pocket. So now, you lead the way and start giving me orders and we'll get it all started. Then we can rest while the machines do the work." She stood then, and I grabbed the heavy bag and we walked over to the machines and started loading, she having two loads and me with just one. Three machines. After my clothes were in, I walked to the restroom and came back out with my underwear and socks and added them to the load and then emptied all the treasures from my jacket, filled up one of the chairs with them, and tossed the jacket into the machine, and next was my normal shirt, leaving me with boots (no socks), pants (no undies) and a tee shirt. She coin-fed all three machines, started them cranking, and sat down. I said, "Across the street is a little corner market. They must have coffee. Would you like some?" "That sounds terrific," she said. "How do you like it," I asked. She said, "Just black." I'm sure I smiled and said something like "You just stole my heart with that black coffee. That means we don't need a chemistry set. I'll get it now." First however, I walked over to an elderly woman seated at the other end of the row of chairs and said, "Hi, excuse me, but I'm going across the street for coffee, would you like me to get a cup for you … my treat." The old lady seem dazed, then recovering, she said, "Oh my, what a nice offer, but my drier is almost done, and I'll be going, but thank you, thank you so much."

So … in a few minutes, I was back with two black coffees and sat down next to Stella and the old lady was waving goodbye and threw a big smile and a little kiss our way. Stella smiled, looking at the jacket debris on the chair, said, "That's quite a bit for one jacket, some Marlboros, an aspirin bottle, napkins, even a toothbrush. Would you happen to have an ironing board there somewhere?" I said I'd look and reached over, picked up the bag of cookies and a few napkins, opened the bag and offered it to her. She looked inside, then reached inside, took out one of the cookies lightly wrapped in thin paper, tasted it, and said "Holy Cow!" I took one and bit it and said, "Holy Cow is right." We drank coffee and each of us finished our cookie and I offered another to her and she accepted saying "These are so-o-o good." I nodded yes, and said "The best."

Stella ate three cookies in all, which now seemed to be a normal serving. She refused a fourth and asked, "Who are you, I mean beside being the knight on a white horse, no, on a white motorcycle?" I filled her in, told her something about me, of what I had done in the past week. Two of the washing machines stopped, the ones with the small loads, and we got up and moved the clothes to driers. The third was a large load and would take a few minutes longer and we sat once more. I had pretty much finished my little tale, leaving out most of the party stuff in New Mexico. She asked how long I'd be in Denver and what would I do after that. Explaining that I didn't know, but two, three, or four days seemed reasonable … there was no rush. And I wanted to see the Gulf of Mexico, travel along the

Mississippi River at least to where the Ohio River joins it, maybe see one of the Great Lakes, and the South, I wanted to see some of the southern states. Same old thing, I needed to get to Connecticut by the end of June for my little sister Phyllis's wedding. Third machine was done with its washing. Transfer the clothes to a drier and start it going.

So, Stella, tell me about you. C'mon, we'll be here at least another half hour. And she did. She was a practical nurse and good at taking care of old people. She was gentle and they liked her. Raised in Louisiana, in the swamp land, part of the time, and still had a bunch of family there. But an aunt, a librarian lived in Missouri and took her for the summers when she was a kid, and then full time when she turned eleven. Her aunt's husband was an engineer, some sort of agricultural engineer, and a really good guy who always pushed her into educational things and would support her through school if she wanted. She would revisit her Louisiana family from time to time, but when she turned nineteen, she left them permanently, later joined her cousin Broderick up in Denver, well Englewood, about two-and-a-half years ago. She had worked two jobs, one fulltime for a healthcare agency and a fair amount of private part-time work. Had taken an indefinite leave of absence from her full-time job and there were four more days remaining for her remaining part-time job taking care of the Fergusons. The old man was ninety-two or three and the wife was in her middle 80's. They were sweet people and the new helper couldn't start until that time. She had to take care of some family business down in Louisiana in a month or so and after that … who knows. And it was cousin Broderick's washing machine which had smoked up the house that morning. In the meantime, two driers had stopped, one of them mine.

Took the clothes out, folded most of my stuff and returned it to the bag. Took some underwear and socks into the restroom and got dressed 'properly.' Put my jacket back on, sorted out all the valuables that still sat on the chair, threw away little bits of trash, reloaded the jacket, and was ready for the next stage of whatever it was we were doing. Stella did the same with her smaller load of laundry and we sat down for the third drier. I asked, "Do you date much? Do you have a boyfriend?" She said she had gotten rid of her boyfriend six months ago and there was nobody since then. I said he must have been a stupid bastard to allow that to happen. She said, stupid no, but bastard yes – he had a mean streak that she couldn't tolerate. I told her to never put up with any of that, never, because it never gets better, only worse. She just nodded. We talked more and laughed a little. The third drier was winding down. I helped her get all the clothes onto the folding table and repacked into the laundry bag, now much, much lighter.

"OK Stella, want to hear the next stage of a possible plan." This time she laughed, and said "Go ahead, White Knight, go ahead." I said, "Here's the proposed plan. I take you and your laundry back to your house, wherever that is. You call the Fergusons and tell them you can't work today. Then I take you out to a lunch of Italian food." Without waiting for an answer, I asked if she had ever ridden on a scooter. No. Had she ever ridden on a bicycle? Of course. I said, almost the same, but instead of handlebars, you have to hold onto me and … She interrupted me saying, "If you could get me back to the house with my laundry, I would be most grateful, and we can argue about the rest of your proposed plan there." I said "Fair enough. Let's go outside." I grabbed all three laundry bags. She held onto her purse, rather tightly I thought. "Now here's the procedure. I take your laundry bags and tie them to the top of the box carrier, which I am now calling the 'trunk.' Then I tie my laundry to the front of the box so you can use it as a back cushion. Then you get onto the seat and skootch to the rear part of the seat, but easy, so we don't tip over. Then I'll get on and start this thing up. When we get going, it's sometimes difficult for me to hear, so you have to lean forward and give me hand signals for directions. You OK with that?" She nodded. I demonstrated a few basic hand signals. "By the way, the scooter's name is Tony, Tony Lambretta." I put my helmet on and we started, and without so much as a tiny wobble. The light pressure of her hands on my ribcage felt so good. We made it to her house, no Broderick's house, without incident. No problem at all. She pointed into the driveway and I followed her directions. Just as I had taught her, she gave me a clenched fist signal, meaning 'hold it right there.' And I shut Tony Lambretta down. "That was a blast. Now that was fun," she said. "Let me help you with this stuff," I said, and she limped and I walked to the front door with the laundry. She unlocked the door, and tossed the two laundry bags inside, one at a time. Leaving the door half open, she said, "Look, I will go to work today. They are old people and are so frail, and they need me for these next few days. When no one shows up, they suffer. Boy, I don't ever want to get old. Anyway, the work is easy, so my leg will be fine." I said, "OK, I understand that. I personally have almost never missed work. If you think your leg will hold up, just take care of it so that it will indeed hold up. Now, how are you getting to work and how far is it?" She said, "It's a little less than three miles and I usually walk. Sometimes, I borrow the neighbor's bicycle, but today I'll have to call a cab." "No cab," I said, "let's get some lunch. You can rest your leg some more, and I'll take you to your job. Sometime, though, you have to show me two places, if they exist around here." She said, "Two places? Which are …" I filled in … a book store and an army-navy store or men's clothing store. Need to buy another pair of pants so these can get washed. They're kinda grubby." She said, "Get your things from the scooter, and lock it, and then come inside," pushing the door open "and I'll make us a little sandwich."

As I got my stuff and locked the scooter and helmet to a metal fence post, my thoughts were something like this: Rosano, only in town for three hours and already you're inside a beautiful lady's cousin's house. How many people can say that? So I brought my things into the front little hallway and left them on the floor there and closed the door. The house was not large, but was neat as a pin. It had the smell of an electrical fire or burning rubber. Stella was in the kitchen, had already arranged two small plates, each with a small ham and cheese sandwich. There was mustard, mayo, and ketchup on the table and she asked what I might want to drink. Water would be good. And so we sat.

"This is a nice little house," I said, "so well kept. Your cousin ... what does he do for a living." She said he was a designer and I asked ... aircraft? buildings? toasters? She said windows, display windows. I'm thinking ... bulletin boards, meat counters, glass and frames, etc. and she says Fashion Display Windows like in department stores. Oh, that's neat stuff. That can be interesting. I've noticed those displays. She said quietly "And he's gay." I must have looked blank, probably because my mind was blank. "Gay?" Hmmm. "What's that?" She said, "You really don't know, do you? Gay means he's a homosexual, a queer." She paused for a response, I suppose. I just shrugged to indicate 'So, who cares?' Finally, I said, "OK. I never heard that word that way before. Is that a new use or am I just ignorant?" She laughed gently and said "Probably neither." We finished our sandwiches and she said she wanted to rest her leg a little more. I suggested she take another aspirin now that she had food in her tummy and yet another just before going to work. Walking into the living room, she stopped and picked up the phone book, opened the yellow pages and sat in a stuffed chair. I pushed the matching foot rest toward her. She lifted her leg onto it. I took a seat on the couch. In the yellow pages, she scanned saying "Books, books," pause, "books." She had a pad and pencil and wrote briefly. Then, "clothing, clothing men's, clothing men's" and she wrote a few more things. She said, "That's what I need, a good book." I walked into the hallway and reached into the sleeping bag bag, pulled out the two books I had finished in the last few days and handed both to her. "Both are excellent, but for different reasons. You might like Steinbeck better than Michener, but you should know at least a little of both if you don't already." She gave me the page from her notebook. Here are four addresses, two book stores ... one new and one used, and two clothing stores ... one has military surplus, one is moderate men's clothing. I'll show you all four when you take me to work this afternoon. Where do you plan to camp out tonight?" Of course, those were welcome words to hear … that meant we weren't going to say goodbyes just yet. Oh man, this was one gorgeous girl. I answered that I didn't know yet, but last night I slept in a station wagon and most nights I slept in a campground of one sort or another, with an occasional motel room thrown in. She started to speak, then paused, and then said, if I liked, I could sleep on the couch instead of in a campground. Of course, my spirits soared past the lower heavens at least. That meant I'd pick her up from work, too. I said, "if it's OK with Broderick, it's super for me." She said, "Broderick will be OK with it." I said she ought to rest for an hour and then get ready for work and I would take her and pick her up. Did she need to eat anything before work? No, she usually had a little snack while the Fergusons ate supper. I asked if I could use the bathroom, she said go ahead and that she wanted to shower before work. I said good, but be careful for that leg. I half-snoozed sitting upright on the couch as she got ready for her four-hour shift. I cleaned up what little mess we had made in the kitchen and washed the two dishes, two glasses, and a couple of utensils. She was ready. I said "If you're OK, let's go."

Back outside, walked past the carefully tended, almost manicured garden and got to the scooter. I said, "You don't have a backrest and that box is hard as hell, so lean slightly forward." She got on, backed onto the passenger part of the seat. I got on, started the scooter on the first try, pushed forward to get off the kickstand and we putted out onto the little side street, she giving hand signals that I had taught her. We turned North on Broadway towards Denver. She gave me the 'slow down' sign and then pointed to a clothing store, and almost next door, the used book store. She gave me the 'increase speed' sign. After three or four minutes, she gave the slow down sign again, then pointed to a military surplus store. Around the corner and down the street a bit, there was a bookstore saying 'no trade-ins' in the window. She indicated that place and gave it a "thumbs up." We took a left on South Logan and went a few blocks and then the clenched fist stop signal. This was the Ferguson house. She had started to lift her leg over the seat and I stopped her, shaking my finger in a no-no way, then I got off and still holding the scooter waved her forward so she could dismount easily. I said take it easy and that I would be back a little before the 7:00 PM end of her shift. She kissed her index finger and pressed it onto my nose and walked into the house. Stunning, and more beautiful by the minute. An absolute doll.

Turning around, I memorized the street and house number. Retracing my steps, I was slowly and carefully observant so as not to forget where I should return. I tried the 'thumbs up' bookstore. Bookstores are a delight and a pain. Of course, I want to read everything and want to do it now. I spotted about four dozen books I should have, but instead settled on looking at a battery reading light – florescent (supposed to save on battery life). I clicked it on … nothing. Very light weight probably because there was no battery. And there were no other battery-driven lights on display. Next stop the military surplus store. Often, these places were not really involved in military surplus and were normal retail outlets. This store was about half and half and that's fair game. Found some good sturdy canvas pants in dark grey which fit my waist, but were a little baggy in style and a little long in the leg and that was perfect for the camp scene. Yea! Go now to the used book store a few miles away. Since I wore no watch, I kept an eye on everybody else's timepieces. It was close to 6:00 PM and there were two books in my hands … "Twelve Angry Men", by Reginald Rose, about whom I knew nothing other than this authorship, and "Fahrenheit 451", by Ray Bradbury. Paid for the books, went outside and stashed them in the trunk. Had to remember to refrigerate food I had purchased the morning before.

    Tony the scooter had behaved almost as well with two passengers as it had with only one person on board. On the flat, it was nearly the same, except for braking distance, which increased substantially. Acceleration was considerably slower, and now I would joke that I had to pull to the right to allow the snails to pass. I would add a bit more air to the rear tire to compensate for the added weight of Stella. Tomorrow, not now. Now I would have a smoke, which I hadn't had since morning. Lit up a Marlboro and visions of a big cattle drive danced in my head. I'd buy some chewing gum at the corner market. I walked back into the book store, there was a young woman and a younger looking guy behind the counter. I asked if they could recommend a decent Italian restaurant somewhere nearby. Looking at each other, they asked each other, "Gemelli's?" She said, pretty good food, very modest prices, nice atmosphere if you like subdued lighting. Sounds perfect. Where is it? Got directions and said my thanks. So … it would be Gemelli's.

    Putted down to a mini-market, bought some minty gum. Followed the book store directions to Gemelli's, which was only a mile or so off the route to the Ferguson place. The aromas of an Italian kitchen were in the air as I drove past, then turned around and headed off to get the injured lady, Stella. Parked in front of the house for five minutes or so before she appeared, purse on her shoulder and a big smile on her face. I was standing by the scooter and saying only "Good evening, Madam," I swept my arm low to invite her to the scooter. Saying only "Thank you," she stepped onto the scooter platform and slid back gracefully to the passenger seat. On the driver's seat, started up (again, on the first try) and began driving. She gave no signals until I headed to Gemelli's instead of taking the route home. When she did signal, I gave her the finger wagging no-no signal in return and we putted our way to Gemelli's where I pulled into a parking place in front. Dismounting, I held the imaginary door open for her, she paused, then slid forward and stepped down. She said, "You don't have to do this." I said, "You have been kidnapped and I'll hold you for ransom. Don't do anything foolish and no one will get hurt." She laughed as I looped my cable thru the helmet, around the scooter and around the 2-HR parking sign. "Shall we? I, for one, am hungry."

Gemelli's was a relaxed place with quiet, solid feel to it. We ordered food and I suggested she have some wine, saying "A little wine can do a lot of good, a lot of wine can't do any good." When I didn't order wine, she noticed and asked. I said when I was driving I never touched alcohol. We talked about many things that first hour. I mentioned she had a very mild southern drawl, then asked about what event would take her back to Louisiana.

She said it was a big family reunion every year on Memorial Day. I said something like "Well, that should be fun." Her face darkened some and she said, "I really hate the whole bunch of them. They are stingy and mean and treacherous people." I said, "Wow, you don't have to tell me about it." She said, off the subject, "What do you think of gay people?" Boy, that was a switch! This was confusing. "Oh, there's that word again ... gay. This time I understand. I'll do my best. What do I think of gay people? I really don't know very much. Not really close friends with any that I know of. One thing I do know is that life can be tough for anybody, and the queer people have another layer of tough to have to deal with. It must be a very difficult life. Everyone's against them ... their schools, their churches, their families, everyone. The few queer people, gay people, that I know, all seem to be pretty nice people, maybe overly gentle, but certainly not harmful. But Stella, I'm talking about something I know almost nothing about. In high school, I was friendly to everyone, and never played the popularity game. So I was kind of a magnet for the school's oddballs, the misfits. But I always said 'Hello, how're doing?' and I'd shake hands. I knew some of them were queer, and I knew other people were watching and disapproved, but I just didn't give a hoot. Since I was really good at math and science I'd help them with that during study periods, and that was frowned upon, but I never have given one good goddamn what people thought of that. Anyway, how did we get on this subject?" She just sat back and looked at me. Finally, she said, "When we get to the house I want to tell you a story. And after that, I may want your ideas and maybe your advice. Is that OK with you?" Then I looked at her and said, "An exquisitely beautiful woman wants to talk to me. How could I ever refuse this?" As we finished our meal, I asked "Dessert?" She said "If you think it will be good, sure." The waiter was walking past and I stopped him. "Do you have Tortoni?" He said, "Ma, certo." "Due, per favore, anche il conto," I said. So two tortoni arrived. When she tasted, her eyes lit up. "Oh my god! This is unbelievable. And this is ... tortoni?" "Yeah, I named my scooter after it." She didn't get my little lame joke.

We left Gemelli's, got onto Tony Lambretta's back, and started off for Broderick's house, cousin Broderick, the 'gay' guy. Noticed that the Lambretta's headlight was not really very effective. I almost never drove it at night and if I did, there always seemed to be street lights where I traveled. Soon, however, we were back on the main drag where street lights grew and thrived and everything was OK. As we pulled into the driveway, she signaled 'straight ahead' and I guided the scooter right up to the garage door, before shutting down. We got off the scooter and she used her key to unlock the garage, I jumped forward to open the door and the garage was empty. She said we could lock it in here tonight. So I walked the scooter into the garage as she turned on the light. I asked if Broderick had a car. She answered that he did, but it was at the airport for a week while he was traveling. So I wouldn't see Broderick which was why the house was dark when we arrived. She started to close the garage door and I finished doing it and threw the latch as she opened a door into the house. I said there was some food in my trunk that I would like to refrigerate if possible. That was OK. And it was done. The rest of my stuff was still in the hallway.

First thing she said was "What does ma-chair-toe mean? I laughed and said "Tonight, you heard me use just about every Italian word I know, but when the waiter said, 'Ma, certo,' that was not one word, but two words ... ma meaning 'but' and certo meaning 'certain'. I asked if he had tortoni, he responded 'But, of course.' She said, "Sounds a lot better in Italian." I said, "Most things do."

She asked if I wanted a beer. I asked if we could split one. Sure. She then asked if I was as kind a person as I appeared to be. My reply was truthful, I'm very kind until someone screws with me and then I can get pretty nasty, but what's important was that the little things pass over my head with hardly a thought. For example, I don't care if someone cuts me off in traffic. Not worth getting aggravated over small stupid things like that. Now Stella, tell me the story you mentioned at dinner.

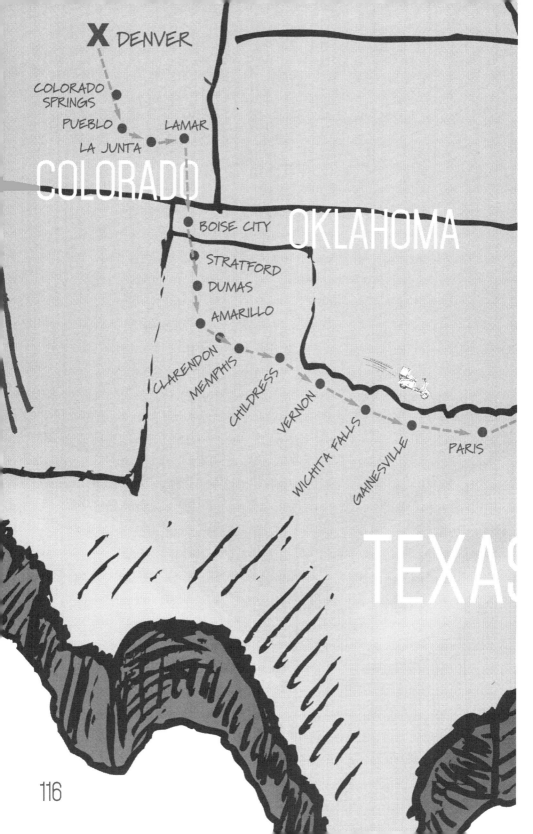

PART TWO
DENVER TO NEW ORLEANS

CHAPTER 18

MA, CERTO

So Stella told me her story. And it went like this: She grew up in Bayou Country in southern Louisiana, some distance from the town of Houma. Her family was poor but not destitute. They earned money doing various things. Real rednecks who hated everyone who wasn't like them. They belonged to some wild offshoot of a hate-peddling fundamentalist church which she thought was normal until she was about age eight. Then, an aunt, the librarian from Missouri, visited the family during one of these Memorial Day reunions. The aunt didn't seem to fit in with her family at all, but Stella liked her anyway. The aunt asked her mother if Stella could drive back to Missouri with her and her husband. Her mother said, "shit yeah!", but she had to be back in school in September. The aunt had purchased a brand new little suitcase and helped Stella pack her clothes and they were on the road to Kansas City, Missouri. All that summer, the aunt gently encouraged Stella toward reading and traveling to museums, art galleries, or the zoo and then writing about those experiences, sometimes just a small paragraph, sometimes more. She learned to always wash and comb or brush her hair, had clean clothes and learned to wash them herself, with the washing machine and also by hand. The aunt took her to a number of different churches where people didn't scream and holler and faint and fall down during services, but instead talked and sang. The aunt and her husband never got drunk, never had a fist fight, never raised their voices to each other and were always kind, loving and respectful toward Stella. And to top it all, she had her own private bedroom which no one would enter without knocking first. The first week of September they drove her back to the bayou in time for school's starting. And the aunt cried. There were two more years of this summertime trade-off. The aunt had given Stella a small, but thick notebook with many thin pages. On one of the middle pages, she wrote the address and phone numbers in Kansas City. She also wrote instructions for calling her 'collect' to Kansas City, to both the house and library where she worked. All of this information was also written on a separate piece of paper which Stella should hide in case someone made off with her notebook. She was not to mention any of this to anyone. It would be a secret they could always share. Each summer spent in Missouri pulled her farther away from her swamp family's values or lack of such. At age eleven, a week before the Memorial Day Family Reunion, Stella, who was just leaving childhood and entering womanhood, was asleep when she felt movement near her knees. Waking, but not moving, she saw her father's face and her Uncle Billie's face looking at her where they had lifted the nightgown up to her waist. The two of them were staring at her. Uncle Billie said "Yep she's just about ready." Her father said "Couple more weeks." Stella saw them and heard them clearly, slept no more that night, and in the morning told her mother all about it. Her mother said, "Shit, they didn't mean nothin' by that, honey." Later that morning is when she called collect to Kansas City. Her aunt listened to her carefully and said, "Listen precious, get a few of your favorite things together, but don't let it look like you're packing. We'll pay a surprise visit to the family tomorrow sometime, probably late in the afternoon, and we'll work things out from there. Be safe, please be alert, and we'll be there tomorrow. You'll be coming home with us, but not a word to anyone, not even your closest friend". Stella didn't sleep at all that night, just waited for dawn, then for noon. True to her words, in the middle of the afternoon the aunt and her husband showed up, greeted the family for a few minutes, very matter-of-factly with the aunt saying "Stella, I found the prettiest little dress for you in town, let's go get it before someone else buys it." Quietly, and aside, the aunt told her to put her special things into this bag (giving her a cloth bag), leave the suitcase behind, and get into the car. In two minutes, they were on their way back to Kansas City, which, in time, became her home town. As far as Stella knew, her Louisiana family never asked about her.

    Stella lived in Kansas City with her new family through her teen years, doing well in high school and taking some practical nursing courses. She began working and saving some money. She felt somehow obligated to attend the family reunion each year and she would return to the Louisiana swamp for a day. Her Missouri family would drive down and back each year until Stella was sixteen. After that, it would be by Greyhound Bus, alone. That first year, at age sixteen, she met her cousin Broderick. They were the same age, got along well, and to some extent were separate from the rest of the family. Broderick read books, more than she did. He was thoughtful and polite, unlike most of the teenagers she knew. Hanging around together for a day or two was a pleasure for both. The following year, the next reunion they did pretty much the same, but there were a few comments by other family members, comments that seemed out of place to Stella. "Well, maybe there is hope for him." "She's pretty enough to cure him, if anybody can." Actually Broderick was the only bright spot of that entire family and had become the only reason Stella would even bother to take the long bus ride down to Louisiana and back. The summer they turned nineteen, Stella, taking a nap inside the little house, could hear Uncle Billie, Broderick's father and a third man (she couldn't tell who the third one was) talking on the other side of the thin wall. They were sitting on a side porch. She could not hear everything, but caught much of what was said … phrases like "that goddamn faggot – pure embarrassment," "beat the living shit – Broderick queer piece of garbage," "if he gets killed, it don't matter – cover it somehow," "- better off without that homo." Stella was super awake now. Waiting for two or three minutes, she quietly left the house, found Broderick at a shabby picnic table reading. She sat next to him and said. "How's the book?" He began to respond and she said, "Broderick, please listen to me, but don't react to anything I'm going to say, and please believe what I'm going to say. OK?" He nodded yes. "Broderick, your father and Uncle Billie, and someone else, I don't know who, are planning to beat the shit out of you and maybe even kill you and I'm so very serious and so scared. Will you do something for me?" Again, he slowly nodded yes. She said, "I want the two of us to go to town, right now. Do you have your wallet with you?" A yes nod. "Good. Just take your book, I'll get my purse. We'll go to town together. If anyone asks and they probably won't, we're checking on my bus ticket. Just be casual and I'll get us a ride." That is what actually happened. One of the women gave them a ride into town. After the cheery thank you and a wave, they walked into the bus station and got tickets for a bus leaving in twenty minutes. She was holding her breath the entire time. Broderick just sat quietly. Afraid to talk openly, she waited till they were seated on the bus, away from the other passengers, and finally asked "Why would your father want to beat the shit out of you?" Broderick said "Because I'm gay, a homo, a faggot." That was the first time Stella had heard the word 'gay' used that way. She just said, "Yeah, I thought so. I never wanted to pry." Broderick said, "He detests me and has said, so many times, that everyone, including me, would be better off if I were dead. So you see, I believed you when you said they were planning to kill me. Stella, you have probably saved my life and I'll always owe that to you. Thank you, thank you so much. You're so strong and I've always admired you for that. I can never, ever, go back to that place now, and to those people, my own family, who can't hide their disgust every time I appear." He stopped for composure, Stella sat quietly, then Broderick continued, "Their minds are poisoned with deadly things called ignorance and hate and half of it comes from that sleazy criminal son-of-a-bitch they call a preacher." So Stella had rescued her cousin in a manner similar to the way she herself had been rescued.

They made it back to Kansas City. Broderick stayed with them for only a week or so and then announced that he had gotten a job in Denver working for a department store chain. He borrowed a little bit of money from Stella, got a bus to Denver, and was gone, leaving only an address and phone number which no one else was ever supposed to see. Every month or two, Broderick would write a letter (with never a return address) to Stella, updating her on his doings. Three years later, he mailed a newspaper to her with a photo and brief article about one of the award-winning show windows he had designed. She thought that was really nice, but what really got her attention was an ad seeking practical medical assistants and advertising wages considerably above what she was making. She followed up and within a month was packing a few things to take to Denver with her. She would sorely miss her aunt and her husband. Meanwhile Broderick wrote that he had just bought a used car and a little house near Denver.

That's the story Stella told me, as best I can remember, and that had happened two or three years before she and I had dinner at Gemelli's. Doing the math, I figured Stella was twenty-four or twenty-five years old. I would never ask.

She asked if I wanted another beer or did I want to split another one. Split another one would be better but I would like to ask a favor first. Could I possibly take a shower instead of just a washcloth cleaning? "Ma, certo," she said laughing. "Rosano, I will never, until I hit the grave, forget those two words. Ma, certo! Let me get a towel for you." I grabbed my clothing bag and my sleeping bag and took them into the small bathroom. She handed me a large towel, a washcloth and a bar of soap.

Out of the bathroom now, clean and refreshed, dressed in my new pants, and a tee shirt. I asked if she might like my new trousers with or without the price tag and laundry instructions. She thought without might be better, but thought they were a rather big for me. I said these were for camping and would be better for that purpose than pants that were well-tailored. Also, could I wash my other pants in the bathtub? OK, she said, and got up, and gave me some liquid laundry soap. It took me five minutes to run some hot water into the tub, wash and ring out the pants, and hang them over the shower curtain rod to dry. Then we sat down in the kitchen with a few potato chips and another beer to split.

Stella said thanks for Gemelli's tonight and she had really enjoyed the scooter rides so far and asked if I had ever spilled. I said yes, twice. Both times at near zero miles per hour. First time occurred when I was surrounded by one of Tucson's notorious 'dust devils', which are like mini-tornados. There was so much dust, grit and crap in the air that I was blinded and tried to pull over to the curb, but not being able to see it, I hit it a little too hard, and slowly spilled over with the scooter almost on top of me. Very dirty and dusty, but neither of us (the human or the machine) suffered much damage. The second time happened in very slippery clay mud, with very similar results. When conditions are not good ... wet pavement, or sand on the road, I go as slowly as any respectable old lady school teacher might, and it is a 'thing' with me to never be in a hurry on the scooter.

We talked of many different things for the next few hours, until we both began to yawn. She told me to think about the story she had related and she would ask me about it in the morning. Would I be OK sleeping on the couch? That would be fine I said and I do appreciate not having to find a campground. I reminded her to take another aspirin or two before she went to bed, she would sleep better and it would help that leg business. She asked again if the couch would be OK. Before I could respond, she asked if a real bed might be better. When I said that'd be great, she took my hand, and wordlessly took me into her small bedroom and said we should get ready for bed and she started to undress, then turned, pulled at my tee shirt just a little, then turned back and continued to undress, saying she wanted to shower first. Oh, gods in the heavens, she had to be one of the world's most beautiful creatures ever. Despite being in a state of mild shock, I asked if I could join her in the shower. "Ma, certo." she said softly. We helped each other bathe, slowly and carefully.

Morning arrived as expected. She was in the crook of my left arm, awake. My arm, however, was completely asleep. She said, "Compatible, Rosano, no doubt, we are compatible. Last night was a beautiful thing." I said, "Ma, certo," and she laughed so sweetly and asked "Coffee?" "Please and thank you." But at the moment, I would have stayed until my arm fell off.

In not too many minutes, there was the smell of coffee in the air. Half dressed, I made my way to the bathroom and from there to the little kitchen table. She poured two cups and we sat silently and drank. Finally awake, I asked, "Are you OK?" She said "Very OK, thank you, and you?" "Me? A very happy camper, thank you." Stella asked "What should we have for breakfast?" I stood up, found my jacket in the living room, found the small paper sack in the jacket pocket, and returned to the table. "Cookies, we should have cookies for breakfast, before they go bad." She laughed aloud, saying "Some 'White Knight' you are. You'll kill me with cookies before you're done." Then, pouring second cups for both, she quietly said, "Thank you so much for all of yesterday. You really were the White Knight." I said, "Yeah, and you really were the Beautiful Princess." She asked "What are your plans today." And I asked, "Would you like me to make a proposed plan?" She chuckled and nodded a yes. "OK, here's my proposal. I drive and you navigate using the hand signals. This morning you can guide me on a tour of Denver, which I haven't seen yet. We should see at least one art museum or gallery, maybe a zoo or botanical garden, and anything else that you find attractive, like another coin-operated laundry. Then I take you back here to rest and get ready for work. While you're at work, I want to visit a tire shop and do one or two little chores. That is, if you allow me to stay another night here. How's that for a tentative plan?"

The silence was paralyzing. At last she smiled and said "That sounds like a good time. I say yes, except … now seriously listen to me. No bullshit, Rosano, here's the deal: I know you don't have a lot of money and Gemelli's last night was perfect, but extravagant, and I did need that so badly, but I want to tell you that I have a big bunch of money, not just a little, a lot. Broderick has a good-paying job and he will not accept any rent money from me, or money for food or utilities. I've worked two jobs, have no car, and saved practically everything for more than two years. So again, here's the deal: You pay for all scooter expenses, and I pay for everything else … everything, got it? Don't even try to pay for anything other than the scooter. Everything … or there's no deal at all. If you can accept this, we can have a great time for the next few days."

Since there were so many issues involved here, with unseen ramifications and unknown consequences, it was almost two seconds before I said "How could I possibly refuse?" But, in turn, I had a requirement … the first thing we would do when we went out later this morning, would be to find a suitable helmet for her to wear. She paused. I said, "I just want to keep you well." She nodded yes. Sealed with a kiss, a little one. "Then let's get dressed and go out for a while."

As I opened the garage door, she pointed with her toe to an unusually-shaped black rock in a bunch of other rocks near the corner of the building. "Under that rock is a key to the house if you need one, and here's one to carry with you," she said while handing me a key on a little silver ring. Out on the driveway, I closed the garage door and she locked it with her key.

Pointing to the front door and then back to the garage door, she said quietly, "Same key." Thumbs up from me.

We headed to Denver, but had driven only a few minutes, when the slow down signal was given, then a left turn signal and we were in a small strip mall. She indicated a place to park. A flower shop? A pet shop? No, it was a sports shop she wanted. She said, "Would you mind staying here while I try to find a suitable helmet?" Of course I wouldn't and I'd have a smoke while she did that. "OK, good, I won't be long." Ten minutes later she emerged from the store with a protective helmet that matched the scooter paint job and said, pointing her index finger to the sky, "Onward, White Knight." Off we went, into the heart of Denver, unstoppable, blazing past a lawn mower here, a stopped city bus there, a kiddy's trike and a few gray-haired pedestrians. We turned this way and that, and eventually she gave the direction signal to a parking space and the clenched fist stop signal. What a team! And I was just melting and swimming in a sea of good vibrations. To think, that if I didn't screw things up, this stunning beauty would be all mine for two or three more days! Incomprehensibly good fortune was mine! This was the lottery paying off!

We were in an arts district with two or three galleries in immediate view. Shutting the scooter down, dismounting and putting it up on the stand, I said, "Nice hat, Miss." She saw me stringing the cable through my helmet and handed me hers and with a little bit of pushing was able to include hers in the confusing collection of locked items which also included the parking meter. She asked what kind of art I liked best. The answer was several kinds but I tended more to what I would call 'classical modern stuff', and some of the wilder, less conventional art. She said she didn't know much about art terminology and my response was I didn't either, and felt at least half of the 'artspeak' we might encounter was absolute bullshit anyway. "Let's try two or three galleries," I said, "anything more gets to be overkill." And we started. One gallery so-so and the next one with a number of excellent pieces, modern in style and well-crafted. A pleasure to view. Time for coffee? It's always time for coffee. The day was gorgeous, the girl was more than gorgeous, and I was drunk on her beauty. As we sat, Stella asked what I had thought of her story of the night before. I had a few thoughts and would like to sit with her and tell her my feelings. But first, I wanted to ask a few questions of her, not many, but this afternoon or this evening when we were alone with no distractions. She just squeezed my hand for a moment. As we finished our coffee, she asked, "What's next?" I suggested one more gallery and then we have some lunch. The next art gallery was small but had superb paintings and several sculptures, and every piece in the gallery had some innovative twist to it. Excellent.

For lunch? I said, in the fridge back at the house, we had some salami and cheese from yesterday that I had stashed, and if we picked up some bread, added a few cut up veggies, we could have a nice lunch there. Or we could use that stuff for late night snacking and stop somewhere for a bowl of soup. She said, "Soup."

Hand signals got us to a Chinese place. Stella told me to hold it right there. Went in and two minutes later came out with a quart Mason canning jar of soup. I took the soup as she got repositioned on the passenger seat, then handed her the jar and she said "Take us home, White Knight."

And so we had Wonton soup with half-stale bread broken up into it, a good little lunch. As we finished she asked "Next?" "Well, we have some time, so I thought we could quickly shower, then explore this compatibility thing, and then talk about your story."

Within a minute, the shower water was running as we peeled down to skin, washed energetically, dried haphazardly and joined together in a semi-raucous fun-filled romp. Two anxious energies, colliding and fusing to reach some critical combination – a goal attained and savored. Then, after a time, after settling down, another gentle washing and drying. For sure, compatible we were indeed.

Half sitting up in bed with a single sheet over our lower halves, I started. "Your story, sounds like a bad movie in a way, but I have a few questions and then a few thoughts. First question: Does anyone ever call the law on some of that stuff?" Stella said, "No. Uncle Billie is the law in that area." Oh wow, I hadn't planned on that one. "OK, second question: When you were a little kid … four, five six years old … did anyone in your family help you with reading, or music, or making things, or collecting something, or any hobby?" She answered, "No, they would help the boys with a few things, but the girls … no, nothing, nothing at all." "Then it was your Missouri aunt who first showed you some decent attention and taught you to take care of yourself and all that?" She said, "That's true. That's true." I felt so badly for that little girl I never knew, but I asked, "Last question. Do you still talk to your aunt or write to her?" And that's when her eyes got watery and she said, "About four months ago, I took the bus to Kansas City to see her, but she didn't recognize me, she thought I came to use the library, and then told me she had sold the library. Something has happened in her brain, a stroke or something else quite serious. Now her husband cares for her. He has helpers, similar to what I'm doing for the Fergusons. It's so sad."

I wanted to think a little more about her upbringing and told her so and suggested we take a ten minute snooze and then she'd have to get ready for work. We could talk some this evening. "Good idea," she said and snuggled up and snooze we did.

On the way to the Ferguson's house, she gave me a little extra squeeze and of course, as any young child might be, I was thrilled. Leaving her off at work, I headed to Denver's Main Library, a fairly new and large building. Beautiful place, quiet at this time of day. I decided to read some newspaper articles, since being separated from radio, television and newspaper for more than a week. Before leaving Tucson for this trip, I had just started becoming something of a news junkie. That would have to wait a few months. After reading a few international and national news items, local newspapers caught my eye. Flipped through the Denver Post and then a smaller newspaper, an independent, I guessed. Overall, there was the impression that Denver was a thriving and changing and modernizing community. There was a good feel to it. Someone had left a book on the edge of the newspaper rack, a small book about the prairie. Spent about a half-hour reading and skipping pages and reading more. Interesting place this prairie. But that's enough for now. On returning to the parked scooter, the Civic Center seemed receptive to people in the late afternoon light. Enjoyed a quiet smoke just watching people walk here and there.

Having passed a tire store on the way here, I thought I'd return to it and ask about heavy duty tires for this scooter. Found the place and walked in. Nice looking woman behind the counter asked if she could help me. I told her what I was driving and asked if there were any heavy duty tires made in that size for highway travel and was surprised that she knew quite a lot about the scooter and its friendly competitor, the Vespa. She said she had just exactly what I was looking for, but that I wouldn't like it at all. How's that for a sales pitch? They had a set of tires which had already been rejected by two different scooter owners. Of course, my question: Why? She explained the tires were far too noisy, the whining sound on pavement was unacceptable to scooter owners, who preferred quieter operation. The crazies, the off-road people would tolerate anything that might give them better performance, but scooter people were a different breed. Not only that, but Americans were always trying to do something with a machine beyond its capacity. Did I live in the Denver area? No, Arizona. You didn't drive here on that, did you? Yes I did. That's what I mean ... beyond the capacity. These scooters were made for Italian cities, not American highways and she laughed. Where are you headed. Boston. Oh good lord. Anyway, original tires were my best bet. So that was that. I would stick with originals.

Not quite, but almost time to get Stella. Did a few minutes of noodling, trying this street and that, and then made my way over to the Ferguson house. By my count, Stella had two more shifts. Certainly it would be sad to leave her, but so immensely fine to have been with her. Hearing the door to the house open, I turned to see that beautiful face, and it was smiling. Oops, I pointed to my head, tapping it three or four times. She stopped, turned around, went back into the house and then emerged with her helmet in one hand and her purse in the other. Again, I held the imaginary door wide open, and she moved onto the seat. As she got the helmet on, she said "I'm Navigator, you are Pilot, and you follow my directions. Mr. Ferguson said that's the way it is when you're near the target." He must have been on aircraft in the military. She gave directions, eventually pointed to a pizza place, and gave a clenched fist signal.

We sat at a booth in this East Coast semi-traditional looking restaurant, maybe a little noisy, but comfortable and great-smelling. A waitress came to the booth with two glasses of water, said hello, asked if we wanted to start with a drink. Stella said no, we would order first, and then figure out what we wanted to drink. Without looking at a menu she ordered an extra-large pizza with olives, basil, green peppers, and spinach. And asked me, "Is that OK?" I nodded a hearty yes. Then she said, "He would like a black coffee and I would like red wine." When the waitress asked what type, Stella looked a little puzzled. So I jumped in and asked, "Do you have a good house wine or table wine?" The answer was yes. Then I said "Why don't we try a glass of that." Stella smiled and as the waitress left, she asked "Is this place OK?" Again, I nodded yes. "Would you like anything else on your pizza?" I laughed and said "Oh no, it'll be perfect … as long as there's no onions … there probably isn't any room on it anyway. And now we don't have to order salad." Laughing again and shaking her head she asked, "You don't like onions?" I shook my head, and said I really, really don't like them. To me the smell is just penetrating, dreadful, and sour, and all sorts of bad things. And I know that is strange for an Italian, and I try to hide it sometimes, but deep down I really hated onions. She snorted and laughed "I know what you mean. You never eat them, do you?" I said, "That's right." She went on "I knew it, I knew it, because you always smell so good. Even when you say you're dirty or sweaty, and that's why you still smell good. I can't stand onions myself." And I replied, "Stella, we are, in fact, most compatible. Listen, our waitress said pizza would take twenty-five minutes. OK if I tell you my thoughts on your story of growing up? Or would you rather wait?" "Now is good," she said.

Was it OK if I just talked, and got my thoughts out? After that, we could discuss. I said there were five or six items to consider. One: You have to understand that I was about the least qualified person in the nation to comment on psychological things. Two: Cousin Broderick feels he can never really repay you for saving his life. And it's quite likely you did. He loves providing a clean, safe place for you now. Don't ever deny him that.

Never insist on helping with rent. Just thank him and give him a hug from time to time. I don't know him, but from the few things you've mentioned, he's really a good guy. Just accept that with no conditions. Three: While I'm sorry about your aunt, recognize that she has done a lot of good in this world, by your rescue, sure, but also with her job. She probably was able to nudge hundreds of kids in a better direction during her career. And now her time has passed and it's OK. That's the fate of all of us. Four: Your family in Louisiana is not your family in any good sense. You don't owe them a damn thing. They, in fact, deprived you of so much as a kid, so much that your aunt tried to make up for in her limited time with you, and so much that you'll have to get on your own. Whether they did it out of ignorance, meanness, selfishness or plain laziness is not important. What is important is number Five: That you put all that stupidity and ignorance behind you, leave it in the swamp, and begin to blossom, yourself, without that anchor holding you down. That's it, that's my collection of thoughts. Now, you think about what I've said, and we can talk about a few details later. And later, I have one big question for you. She had sat quietly and listened intently, occasionally taking a small sip of her wine. She remained silent for a minute or two and finally said, "Wow, you did a lot of thinking, didn't you?" I nodded yes.

She said, "Our pizza will be here in a minute, so let's eat, but first, tell me what you know about this house wine. It's delicious. How did you know?" My answer was: Back in Tucson, as a waiter, I was just beginning to learn a fair amount about wines. I was learning from the Bar Manager of the hotel where I worked. More important than that, we were in an Italian restaurant which really had an 'old world' feel to it, which probably meant the owners were old timers or children of old timers. Traditionally, Italian restaurants always have a good tasting table wine, it is their 'calling card' and might not be expensive wine, but always good tasting. A bad-tasting table wine would be unforgivable, shameful, and word would get around immediately. So, unless you're very knowledgeable about wine and want something specific, it's always best to get the house table wine ... and a sip of yours, if I might? A fine taste.

The pizza arrived, excellent, and we ate slowly. Stella asked, "Why the big smile, Rosano?" "Look," I said, "I'm sitting across the table from an exquisitely beautiful woman, in front of me is pizza which is nature's perfect food, and I'm remembering pizza back in Connecticut where we used to grow them when I was a kid. We couldn't grow them this big, not even close. Since the growing season is so short, we could only grow the small size, sometimes we could actually get medium sized pizzas from the trees, that is, if the weather was good. Late in the season, when it came near time to harvest, people would get a little anxious and keep an eye on the sky in case of rain. And if it started raining we'd all have to run like hell outside and harvest as many pizzas as we could. Sometimes it got a little wild, but it was worth doing. As I continued, she started to laugh and laughed more, tried to quiet down, then tried to say something, then totally cracked up while I was sitting like a dunce saying, "What ... what?"

CHAPTER 19

MY INVITATION

So this beautiful lady was laughing like hell, with me playing dumb, not too daunting a task under most conditions. While she seemed so mild-mannered, compassionate, and sociable, there was a small element of darkness also. The darkness seemed to disappear completely as she laughed at my little jokes. Catching her breath, she said, "Oh God, I haven't laughed like that for a long, long time, maybe forever. You actually had me believing that nonsense for a short while. You are a genuine nutcase, and I feel so lucky." "Stella, tonight we are both lucky. We still have half a pizza and I'm full. Could we have pizza for breakfast instead of cookies?" She thought she could arrange that. I asked if she would mind if I had a smoke here, before we started home. No, she would join me if I didn't mind. We smoked and chatted and finished our drinks as the waitress packed up the extra pizza. Stella asked for the bill and I didn't make a stab for it, so everything was fine. We had agreed.

In the cool of evening we made our way back to Broderick's place, into the garage, and into the house itself. She put the pizza into the fridge. I said thanks for a wonderful supper, that she was an excellent cook, and leftovers always seemed to taste better the following day. She asked what I might like to do in the morning. I said, first thing to be done was to either drain the washing machine or call a repairman. I was afraid water remaining in the machine would get pretty nasty if it stayed too long. I knew enough to be able to drain the thing. She said OK, if I could. After that, I'd like to go down to the Civic Center just to look around. (I hadn't told her that I had already spent some time there). She said that sounds good. Then I asked if we could sit down and split a beer if there were any left. She said there was at least a six pack left, but she didn't know if she should have any more alcohol - that I might try to take advantage of her. I agreed the possibility was there, but certainly it would be worth the risk. Let's sit down.

After a few sips of our mini-beers, I said there were actually two major questions, not just one. First question ... what was her reaction to what I had said regarding her upbringing? She started with Broderick, and said she hadn't thought that providing this house was his way of trying to repay her. Now she felt my suggestion would be best ... to accept something good without questioning or examining. She said she felt I was right about the aunt she owed so much to, that the aunt's time had indeed passed, but she wanted to see her one last time, just for quietly saying goodbye in person. That seemed important. About not owing the family anything ... I was probably mostly right about that, too. Not so much that they denied, but they never offered anything to their kids and made them feel guilty about needing simple school supplies, or got mad when kids got sick because "doctors cost money, too." But they always had enough money for beer, and liquor and tobacco. And lastly, you are right on the money ... I think about those people far too much and have to get them out of my head and that's what I have trouble doing and it drives me crazy. You know something, White Knight, the only time I don't think about them is when you're talking with me and making me laugh. And that is such a good feeling.

We each took final sips from our glasses. I said that's enough psychological stuff for tonight. But first, how was the leg doing? Much better, she said, much quieter. I said to keep taking some aspirin from time to time. Let's get showered and then just hang around and read for a while. Are you game for that? She agreed. We washed each other in a warm shower and climbed into bed with books and extra pillows. She began "Of Mice and Men" and I started "Fahrenheit 451" by Bradbury. A half-hour of reading, some gentle contact, and then sleep.

One of the world's best ways to wake up in the morning is to have aromas of coffee stir your being into wakefulness. And that's what happened. After a quick bathroom visit and some personal maintenance, I zombied into the kitchen where the Beautiful Princess was pouring coffee for me. Softly, a touch on my face, a good morning, then sitting opposite me, a smile. What could be better than that? Two cups of coffee and a piece of pizza from last night put me into focus. I asked if Cousin Broderick had some tools since I had only a few on the scooter. Stella took me into the laundry area and opened a small drawer and said this was it. Not very many, but maybe enough basic tools to drain the washer. Fifteen minutes later, the washer was drained and the floor was mildly flooded, but for only a short time, as I mopped up the mess with an old towel and wrung it out in a small sink a dozen times. Wrote a note to the future repairman alerting to the disconnected drain hose leading to the pump. And that either pump or solenoid was probably bad.

Stella asked, "More coffee?" Sounded good. "Sure, got time for my last question?" She got coffee for the two of us and sat down. Then I started with "You don't have to answer if you prefer not to, but here's my last question in several parts: One ...Why are you planning to return to your swamp family in a month? Two ... What do you plan to do there? Three ... Do you plan to separate yourself from that place, and if so, how? Again, you don't have to give me an answer. You can tell me to mind my own goddamn business and I will, but you will have to eventually answer these questions for yourself." It was obvious that she was upset with my questions and I quickly asked "Want to talk later?" She gave me the 'yes' nod and I said, "Let's get ready and go downtown, OK?"

Again, in the driveway, Tony Lambretta started on the first kick (very seldom was more than one kick necessary). It was a glorious morning as we made our way northward from Englewood into Denver, just a few miles away. This time she held onto me tightly. We were down into the area of the Civic Center. We found a parking place easily and tied up Tony and the helmets. Let's just take a little walk, an easy walk for a few minutes, and then we can go into the library for a few minutes. Is that OK? Oh sure she said. And we did.

As we headed into the library, I asked if her aunt took her to the library in Kansas City often. She said not really, because there were so many books at home. I told her I wanted to research something for a few minutes. Would she help me? Thumbs up. I told her that libraries could be the most important buildings in her life. That libraries were one of the paths to freedom. Had she been here before? No, not really. I said this building is full of treasures and I was going to show her just a few. So first, I dragged her over to the newspaper area, a reading area. Look, they have newspapers from major cities in the US, and from some foreign countries. Here's Paris, Munich, Rome, Mexico City. You might want to know more about these places someday. Here's some business newspapers from London and New York. OK, look here, Yellow Pages from large US and Canadian cities. That could be very handy some time. Over here, here is a huge collection of information about American companies. This set of books is called the Thomas' Register and this is where I could use a little help. I want to make a list of Lambretta scooter dealers in this part of the country, in case I have a major breakdown. So I start looking it up, and pretty soon, we're onto correct pages. I had a few sheets of typewriter paper and a pen and pencil. I told her which states I wanted to do and if there were no Lambretta entries, we make a note of it and then check Vespa entries. In a half hour or so, we had a pretty good list. I want to show you a genuine treasure, walking her over to the music recordings. One day, not now, but sometime, you might find so much enjoyment here. Some of the best music in the world is right here in Denver, right here in this room. I just want you to know that it is here, waiting for anyone including you.

OK, that's enough, what do you want to do next? She mentioned the Botanic Gardens, not too far from here. Let's do it. And we did.

On arrival there, she explained the place was relatively new and lots of construction work was happening, but there were wonderful flowers already planted and blooming and she was beginning to get really interested in garden plants. It was good to see her eyes light up with enthusiasm for this place. We wandered alongside the plantings and sat on a bench for a long time. I started to make the motion of getting up and she said "Please stay. This place is so peaceful and I want to talk with you here. Is that OK?" "Absolutely, I answered." She said, "Let's have a smoke first. Look in that portable attic that you wear and find your Marlboros." I did, and we lit up and smoked almost without speaking until I crushed my cigarette and then took hers and did the same, field-stripped them both, and put the filters in my pocket. She then said she wanted to answer my questions from this morning, if she could. It was almost exactly a month from now that she would be at the family reunion in Louisiana on Memorial Day. She wanted it to be the last reunion she would ever attend and wanted to sever her ties to the whole family as a group and she wanted them to know why. And she wanted it to be dramatic and final. She was trying to work out details, but felt determined and nothing on this earth was going to stop her from doing it. Then … "Well, White Knight, what do you think?" She was going to do it, for sure. So first I said, "Sounds like you should do something like that if it can truly end the whole connection, with no loose ends." She said, "You really think so, don't you? You're not just saying that just because … " I shook my head, "No, you really should do something with some fireworks, so you can finally say "to hell with you, the total bunch of you no-good bastards." Stella, from what you have told me … the only two members of the group who are decent and kind people are your aunt, who is ill now, and your cousin Broderick. So really, Broderick is your new family and you and he are fortunate to have each other. So now you have a basic plan and that's good. But why are you leaving so early?" Her response surprised me, but she knew her own makeup better than anyone did. She said, "I don't want to be here when Broderick returns from his trip. He'll try to stop me, to convince me not to do it, but I really must. Also, he'll be upset beyond belief if he knows where I'll be going and I don't want to make him worry. And he really would. He would make himself ill. He has already separated himself completely from that clan, but I haven't been able to yet. They're still in the back of my mind constantly and I really want to be able to say 'piss on the whole lot of you' and then be gone from that scene forever. And something beats on my head and demands that I do it in person and in a big way."

Standing, I leaned toward her, took her face in my hands and kissed her on the forehead, and I said, "Exactly ... you need to do that and be done with it. I'm really happy for you and I'm glad you're going to do this forceful split with them. They are poisonous and you'll be simply marvelous without them. You'll be as beautiful inside your soul as all these flowers are, all around us. How can I help you?" Stella said "Just be with me and talk with me. Let's talk some more at lunch while we have a sandwich." She stood and gave me a big smooch and said, "Let's saddle up, Oh White Knight." Putting on helmets and getting onto the back of our steed, I felt like a million dollars, no, two million. She navigated and I drove and we ended up at some sandwich shop where she said the sandwiches were great and the patio was too. Correct on both.

We talked more. I mentioned that at least one thought occurred to me as she was talking back there at the Botanical Garden ... that she should not go the reunion alone, but should have one or two other people with her, for safety's sake. She had already considered this and had contacted two of the teachers in her school, from more than a decade ago, who remembered her very well and had genuinely liked her. These two men, she knew, disliked her family intensely, and had argued with them several times in the years before she left for Kansas City. One of them was now Principal of the school. The other was now teaching at a small college nearby. They had been buddies for years and both remembered her accurately and had recognized her as being different from the rest of her family. Both were willing to accompany her on her Memorial Day mission. It wouldn't take very long, anyway. In fact, they had discussed it with each other and were actually looking forward to a little confrontation with that group, if it were necessary. Man, that was impressive. And I told her just that. She had had foresight to arrange this. Brava! Excellent! I told her, despite not knowing many details, I felt she was going to be just fine. She was smarter than the whole friggin' pile of them put together. Good for you, Stella.

"What would you like to do now," I asked. She laughed a little, "Last night, in the middle of the night, I believe you took advantage of me. I'm not sure that's fair." My reply was "You were warned of the risk involved. Besides, I was a bit sleepy and could swear that I had help, though I'm not certain." "Well," she said, "Now I think we should go back to the house, so I can get even." Vengeance can be so sweet.(Revenge is not always a dish best served cold)

So we putt-putted to the house, showered, and enjoyed each other's energies, eventually deciding to rest. She needed to work her next-to-last shift with the Fergusons. We were showering once more and preparing to travel to their house. She asked what I would be doing during the four hour shift. "Part of the time, I'd be 'noodling' and the rest of the time, who knows?" "What exactly is noodling," she asked. Well, it used to mean "doing an aimless or silly thing, but I believe it's more than that now. I described trying to push a noodle across your plate. Sometimes it goes where you aim it and sometimes it chooses its own direction. It was similar with the scooter and was a way to see quite a lot of a town or city without actually making a plan ... not a tourist thing so much as an explorer thing. It's what I wanted to do this evening, but a little farther north and west. And ... while you're having a little snack with the old folks, I'll see if I can find an ice cream shop. I'll give myself a treat for being such a nice guy. "So," I said, "I'll come get you after work this evening, and maybe I'll be full of ice cream and maybe not."

    A little later, we made our way to the Ferguson house and as she dismounted from the scooter, gave me a hug, and said, "Good noodling, see you later." So off into Denver I went, first stop a pharmacy to buy some postcards. Bought a pack of five scenic cards and some three-cent stamps. Also bought an emergency Snicker's Bar. Never can tell when you really need one. Wandered north and then west going through commercial areas, two or three residential neighborhoods, past some public buildings and eventually ended up next to the South Platte River. Denver was a genuine mix of modern, some not so modern, and even a fair amount of Victorian styling. That surprised me. Just didn't expect to see Victorian out here in the wild and wooly west. Shows my ignorance. South Platte River, flowing thru Denver was impressive. But wasn't this a river that flooded like crazy from time to time? I wasn't sure, but thought I had read about that. Being a desert rat, I had to remind myself that this river actually got bigger as it went along picking up tributaries and itself being a tributary to an even larger river system. Actually did spot an ice cream place, stopped and had a small Sundae. Good and refreshing, but not noteworthy. Thought I take Stella out for ice cream tomorrow. While at the ice cream shop, I wrote a brief message on four postcards. Got stamps onto them, ready for mailing. Soon it would be time to gather Beautiful Princess. Half-noodled my way back toward that side of town. Actually, I had seen enough of Denver. Much greener than I expected. A good feel to the place despite some air pollution, but they would work on that. Denver seemed vibrant and gave me a good feeling generally. Time to get Stella.

    After saying hello, she put the helmet on while getting onto the scooter. Then she said, "Where to?" I thought for a moment and asked, "Are there any veggies at the house?" She nodded and said "Enough for plenty of nibbles." I asked, "How about we just go home and eat whatever we have there?" That was a yes. And we did. I had begun cutting and slicing when the phone rang. Stella answered it, had a five minute conversation, none of which I heard. After disconnecting she came into the kitchen and also began slicing, first some cheese, then some of my Genoa, while I continued with veggies. Soon we had quite a platter full. "If we can add a few crackers and something to drink, we'll have a complete meal." Stella had some wheat crackers and asked if I wanted beer. I opted for water, just some cold water. We sat, clinked our glasses, and hadn't quite started to eat when she said that was a call from Broderick. I asked if he was OK. Yes. And when is he coming home? In three days. And ...? She said, "I told him I might be gone by then. He knows I want to take a month or two off from work. He thinks it's a vacation. I suppose it is, really." We took pieces of this and that and slowly munched our way through part of the food. I mentioned she had one more day with the Fergusons. What was she going to do after that? There would be a month before the reunion? She shrugged an 'I don't know' kind of shrug and said, "Totally unplanned, blank. I don't know what to do, or where to go." We were both silent for minute or so. I said I knew exactly how she should spend at least some of the next two days. Want to hear my proposed plan? "Sure," she said, "go ahead."

The plan started like this: "That time should be used to prepare for a minimum 5-week vacation, six would be better. You should pack one soft bag, not a suitcase, a bag light enough to carry over one shoulder without straining either your shoulder or your back. Any more than that and the purse you normally carry makes you too dependent and too vulnerable. Make certain you have all the contact numbers you need ... Broderick's, your aunt's, your Doctor's, your bank's number, your lawyer if you have one, your work number. Put one copy in your bag and one on your person and possibly one in your purse. Make sure you have enough money to carry you through and some extra for emergency stuff. Split your traveling money into several different places. If someone steals your bag, you still have some money. The same with the purse. Also, always have some coins for the phone since sometimes, you need a coin just to get to an operator. Write a note to Broderick, tell him not to worry, tell him about the washing machine or anything else that's different since he's been gone. Toss out all of the old food. Are you ready for the rest of the plan?" A big smile and a nod yes.

Continuing, I said "The following morning you should get on the back of my scooter and let me take you to New Orleans, which is close to where you're going. That's the plan."

She was stunned and sat perfectly still. Then tears formed in her eyes. Finally she asked so softly, "You would actually do that?" I nodded yes and said "It would be my honor and my pleasure." She said "Tell me more." I said I would, but first we should finish our supper, and have desert. She smiled a little and asked "Did you find some more cookies?" We had nearly finished the food. Then I served slices of the Snickers Bar. She asked if I wanted more coffee. I asked if there was any tea in the house, and if so, that would be a refreshing change. She said Broderick drinks tea fairly often. She'd find some and we could have tea for two. While you do that, I would straighten up the kitchen and wash dishes. After a few minutes, the kitchen was clean, tea was made and on a little tray which Stella brought into the living room. We sat on the couch with tea in front of us.

After a few sips, I said, "You haven't rejected my idea yet, you haven't accepted either. What are your thoughts?" She answered that she really wasn't thinking too deeply, but she knew we should not say goodbye this soon and my idea had taken her completely by surprise.

"Look Stella," I started, "I'm going to tell you more, just as you asked. As part of my trip, I wanted to see Denver and that's done. Also want to see the Mississippi River, or at least a good part of it. Whether I start at the northern part and work my way south or vice versa, New Orleans will see me one way or the other at some time. Why not begin there, at the outlet into the Gulf of Mexico? From Denver to New Orleans is about 1400 miles. If you and I are on the scooter and do only ninety or one hundred miles per day, that would get us into New Orleans in just over two weeks. That's the logistics. If, at any time, you wanted out of that trip, I would leave you in any town which has a Greyhound Bus Station. We could say our goodbyes and from there you could grab a bus to anywhere and we'd each be on our separate path. We're going to do that anyway. So now, without getting sloppy about it, I want to tell you that I don't know if we are 'in love' or not. It seems to be so. But for sure, I so deeply enjoy being with you and I don't want to say goodbye, either. The time for goodbyes will come too soon as it is. It doesn't need to be rushed. So, that's one kind of love, isn't it? Besides that, I have purely selfish reasons."

Almost smiling, but not quite, she looked at me, saying, "Which are … ?" Holding one finger up, I said "Our conversations are good-hearted, honest, and interesting," and holding up the second finger, I said "and I completely enjoy taking advantage of that gorgeous body of yours and testing our 'compatibility' to its limits." She looked at me, squinted a bit, and asked, "Can I think about all this for a while?" What was I going to say … I said, "Ma, certo." She left the room. I sat back and closed my eyes and thought if this is tough for me, imagine how tough it is for her. On the other hand, she has strength, she's smart, and determined. She will be OK either way.

After a time, she sat beside me. She said, "Listen Rosano, I have a lot of questions, but just details. So I'm telling you this: Same Deal or No Deal." It took a few seconds to figure out what she was referring to, but I was able to say "You mean about money?" She said, "Yep, you got it … Same Deal or No Deal." I said two or three weeks will be a big drain on your wallet, especially if we're going to be traveling in the very 'high style' to which I have become accustomed. Stella said, "Rosano, cut the bullshit. Same Deal or No Deal. Which is it?" I asked if there was any "in between." She said again, "Same Deal or No Deal." I said, "OK, same deal. So you think you're such a tough cookie, eh?" She laughed and said "When I have to be. Now I want to tell you something. I told you I have saved a bunch of money, right? Can you guess how much I have saved in over two years?" I might have been able to do some rough estimate, but I just shook my head instead. "I'm going to tell you because I don't want you to have to think about money or about saving money. Ready?" I nodded yes. "A little over nineteen thousand dollars." (Note for readers: approximate equivalent in 2015 dollars is $150,000) For a young woman who had inherited nothing, and earned every penny, this was truly impressive. I said, "Wow! My congratulations! That's just staggering. That spells freedom for you. Now … when you get your mind cleared of this other garbage, your soul can soar with the eagles. You are going to be a great lady one day and that's exciting. And never let anyone hold you back! You'll be a grand lady, I'm certain." She practically mauled me and said "Let's get clean and do some more compatibility testing. I'm so, so, so happy we'll be together, My Dear White Knight, my dear friend."

CHAPTER 20

GOODBYE, DENVER

The decision had been made. She would ride with me 1,300 miles (2,100km) or more as we made our way to New Orleans. We were both elated as we showered and started to play under the stream of water. I mentioned that if we spent too much time in the water we'd start looking wrinkled like pale prunes. She said she liked the fact that I was always pushing to be clean, but if we ended up looking like anemic prunes, she would blame me. The two of us, I feel, were a little delirious with not having to separate. My guess was that despite our knowing each other for just a few days, the upcoming farewell had been weighing on the two of us. So this was a happy, playful, quietly joyful evening. Too excited to read, we talked of so many different things, got up again, drank more tea, returned to the bed, played, and eventually slept.

Morning was almost wordless until we were sitting with coffee. Then she said she had a million questions, having never gone camping before. This trip, I explained, involved bare bones camping with very few extras, no cooking, and while I had a fair amount of experience with camping, I was, by no means, an 'expert,' whatever that might be. The sleeping bag will hold two people if they're friendly. The ground may be lumpy at times. By the time we get to New Orleans, we'll know what we're doing, but this morning we needed to do a few chores that involved her. This afternoon, while she did her last shift at the Ferguson house, I could do the few things which needed attention from me. She asked about her things to do. My suggestion was: Let's make a written list. We did and it wasn't very long, but included the pharmacy for medicines she might need to take with her, the bank for the enormous pile of money we might need, and she should prepare in advance for having money wired to her in case it might be necessary, and we should go to the military surplus store for a waterproof travel bag. She should put her address list on her prep list even though we don't need to buy anything for that (and don't forget addresses and phone numbers of the two teachers, your guardians, in Louisiana).

OK, what food is left in the fridge? Not much, not enough for a meal. So ... you do the navigating and I'll do the driving and let's go down the list after we clean up and sometime this morning we'll go out for a little breakfast. So we showered once more, dressed, spent two minutes to straighten kitchen stuff. Soon after that, we were opening the garage door for our preparation run.

The bank was just opening as we parked. She said this might take a little bit of time. I said I'd have a smoke. A young bank clerk held the door open for her. It was less than ten minutes. Field-stripping the Marlboro, I waited just another minute when she appeared, smiling, climbed onto the scooter and whispered "They helped me make up four little packets." I asked, "Four?" She said, "One for my body, one for my bag, one for my purse, and one for the nag." "The nag?" She said, "You know ... the nag ... the horse ... the scooter. Besides, it rhymed with 'bag'." "O-o-oh. I just didn't catch that, probably need more coffee." Pointing, she gave the go signal and two minutes later, we were in front of the drug store. "Need anything?" she asked. "Yes, I need some more aspirin, not necessarily today, though." She said, "That's what I came here for ... be right back." Next was the Army-Navy surplus store. I said, "They had some waterproof equipment bags and also some nice-looking canvas bags that I'm sure are not military surplus. But let's look. Also, don't forget you have to pack a towel and a washcloth." They actually had two types of canvas bags, one quite heavy-duty, one of lighter canvas, both pretty good looking. She asked which would be better. Indicating the lighter one, I explained there were two reasons: One: the shoulder strap on the heavy-duty one was narrower and would tend to cut into her shoulder more and it was fastened on the ends of the bag, which meant the bag would tend to bow down in the middle. Two: The lighter duty bag weighed a little less, and had a strap twice as wide as the other and fastened one-fourth of the distance from each end, but more important, it was softer and would make a better pillow for sleeping. She said that made sense but it wasn't water-proof. I told her to check the zipper and the snaps to find the best of the four bags available. Next we went to another display table. I explained we wanted a large enough waterproof bag to put inside the canvas bag. If there was a downpour, only the canvas would get wet, and she would have dry clothes to change into. This arrangement also allowed her to put her dirty laundry outside the waterproof bag, but inside the canvas bag, separating the soiled from the clean clothing. Found one and tried it inside the canvas bag. Seemed to work pretty well. Let's get two of these. There was one more thing, we needed two forks and two spoons, stainless steel and lightweight. They might have them here. Looking around here and there, found some kitchen stuff and then found a half dozen mini mess kits, military style, except for kids. They were lightweight stainless steel and had no sharp edges. I didn't know such a thing existed. Very inexpensive. Let's get two of these. We were done with chores for a while. "Let's have a little breakfast. What would you like, Princess, cookies or ice cream?" "He's trying to kill me with cookies again," she said. "No, I'm just trying to take advantage of you again." We gathered up our selections, she paid the bill, stuffed everything inside the canvas bag, and we walked out to the scooter.

She gave directions to a little café. Pancakes and coffee for me. She had a more balanced breakfast. We lingered over coffee, me enjoying the splendid sight of this fine woman. She started to talk, stopped, and then started again. "You have been a very good thing for me, Rosano. The closest thing to an adventure I've had, in my whole life, was coming to Denver to join Broderick. I've worked so hard these past few years, not so much to get a pile of money, but because I was afraid to try anything else except work. And here you come along, like gangbusters, and open a whole new world of thinking and action to me, right from the start, in that laundry. I thought you were putting on some sort of act, but when you offered to buy coffee for that older lady, that really was you, wasn't it?" I said, "But it really was an act, I was using you to try to make her jealous because I wanted to take advantage of her. But she was too smart." Stella began to laugh, and could not stop long enough to sip some coffee. She had to put the cup down two or three times. Of course, I was thrilled to be able to cause that kind of laughter, but I deadpanned it for a while, which, of course, make her laugh all the more. Finally, as we finished breakfast and coffee, our waitress came over with the tab, and I was already saying … "and if you're not willing to pay for breakfast, I'll end up washing dishes here in the café and that's not fair." The waitress gave us the strangest look and Stella cracked up yet again. As we left, I suggested we go back to the house and prepare a little further for our trip. Stella said, "I'm the navigator, you do as I say when we get near the target, remember?" So we got onto the scooter. She directed us down this street and across to another, and down a third street and finally pointed and gave the clenched fist. It was a Greek/Italian deli. "Food for the first leg of our journey," she said. "C'mon, I might need some advice." I said, "I doubt that."

She selected all the right things for snacking, that needed no cooking, that were good tasting and healthy, and she had gotten, in addition, a dozen Italian cookies. We were going to be fine. She said, "Now, take us home, O White Knight." I said, "Ma, certo."

As we approached the house, she asked, "What next?" My answer was, "We get as ready as we can for tomorrow's mid-morning departure. For me, that means a trip to the laundry, since we don't have a washing machine. We should probably do that now and ... maybe someone really beautiful might show up." She said, "I had forgotten about doing laundry already. So let's do that, take your book and read, and I'll get my addresses and phone numbers listed and write a note to Broderick while the dryer does its work." No new people at the laundry. She said, "This is where you did the White Knight act." I said, "Yes, I've fooled everyone. Tomorrow at noon, they're having a parade in my honor, but we're going to miss it ... we'll be on the road." It was rather nice to use those words again ... on the road. She wrote and I read while the dryer gently toasted and tossed our combined laundry. Now it was time to rest before her final shift.

Took a bit of snooze and when Stella started getting ready for work, I went into the garage and took everything out of the scooter's trunk. Sorted out everything, refolded the tent, discarded a few items, including the spork. Wiped everything clean. Went to the kitchen and washed the two little mess kits and packed them. Stella was ready to head to work. Might she have a little gift for the Fergusons? Oops, she had meant to, but forgot in all the excitement. I suggested she give them half the cookies, wrapped up, if she could. Yes she'd do that, surprised that I'd be willing to give up cookies to strangers. Told her I tried to be generous, but wasn't crazy, that there were Italian cookies one day's travel away, and if we didn't run out of gas, we wouldn't run out of cookies. She got a little gift package ready and into her purse. She asked what we should do for supper ... how about some pasta? Told her I liked her thinking. Eased the scooter out of the garage and we were off for her last shift. After delivering her and getting a big smooch for doing so, I putt-putted over to a filling station for fuel.

Here's the attendant, scratching his head, saying "If that isn't the craziest looking contraption I ever did see ... how many miles a gallon do you get ... and goddam, you ain't really from Arizona, are you ... and are you going to or coming from ... this thing's from where ... Italy? ... I always wanted to do something like that except ... " the usual. Eventually, the scooter was refueled. I'd been checking the rear tire visually for the past few days with the second passenger aboard. For highway, the tire pressure would be increased slightly and 2 psi was added. That should be good. The highways were not yet as hot as they would be later in the summer. That could be a problem with two people. Back at Broderick's, there was time to maintenance check everything I could for the scooter and repack the trunk as far as possible. The rest would have to wait for the morning. One daily chore I had been doing was to empty and refresh the water bag and that was done again. Each time it was emptied, I'd taste the water. If it ever tasted peculiar, I might add a drop of chlorine bleach, but hadn't needed to do that so far. Never let the water bag go stale, for it will never taste the same, no matter what you might try to renew it.

Soon I was on my way to gather Stella from her work site a few minutes early, and Stella was coming down the walk with tears in her eyes. She gave me a little hug and said "I'm going to miss them. They are sweet, but they are declining almost daily." I said, "You know, you were a bright spot in their days, and that's all you could possibly do for them. Be happy that you made them happy. They probably really loved you. Who wouldn't?" She gave me the signal to go and navigated us to a small restaurant, which said 'A Touch of Sicily' in neon in a small front window. She said "We can get some pasta here, I bet." As we were seated she said, "My cousin and I come here once in a while. He says this place is 'unpretentious' and has just ordinary good-natured food. We try to do something together once a week or so. I'm his only family and now with my aunt losing her mind, he is my only family, or will be very shortly." We ordered two different salads, two different veggies, and two different pasta dishes and then shared everything. As we ate, I said "Broderick is going to miss you. Whether you know it or not, you are his 'anchor,' you are his starting point. It's none of my business, but I'd like to suggest something … while we're traveling, try to drop him a letter or post card every few days. That way he'll still feel connected to someone … not adrift. And don't forget, to Broderick, you are the source of his life … without you and your quick thinking way back then …" Stella said softly, "I know you're right. I'll always connect to him." We ate the good-natured food and it was just right. Stella said, "You eat Italian food most of the time, don't you?" I said, "Only when I can get it. When I can't get it, I have to make due with second-rate substitutes." She laughed, "But you can always get it, right?" Shaking my head, "Not always, and I suspect when we cross the prairie, I'll have withdrawal symptoms. I've known a few families from Iowa and Nebraska and Montana, and I swear, they do not know how to cook. Everything is meat and potatoes smothered in that crude, awful, brown gravy, or sloshing around in a pool of melted butter, rather boring food actually, but it keeps them alive and it keeps them fat." Stella said to tell her about the prairie.

You want to know what little I know of the prairie. OK, but tomorrow we'll see the Western edge of it because it starts at the base of the Rocky Mountains here in the US and in Canada, and maybe some in Mexico, too. It's called the prairie, the plains, or the grasslands. Those words are interchangeable, I believe, but not certain of that. Essentially it's land covered by grass with very few trees. Maybe a third of the US land is prairie. It's enormous. Huge. In some ways it is fascinating, but most people don't really want to learn different types of grassland, the variations, and how it came to be. They want scenery, something for the camera, an interesting view and that's where the great grassland comes up short, especially compared to the Rockies or Southwest Deserts or the coastlines, lakes, forests, etc. Translate that to say 'it's boring.' So tomorrow, instead of going directly from Denver eastward across the prairie, we should go south along the base of the Rockies until we hit Pueblo, then head east along the Arkansas River for 100 or 150 miles. That river cuts through the prairie which we will see plenty of before we see Louisiana. And we'll be going slow enough to have a leisurely look, believe me. Tonight, we'll look at a map.

We had eaten little more than half our meal. The waitress brought some containers, and we put tomorrow's breakfast in them. Saddled up and headed to the house.

There was more preparation, but not much, tossed out the little bit of food we wouldn't be using, and packed, as far as possible, our clothing bags. "Clothing bag' was not quite accurate, because it held everything else in addition ... toiletries, books, etc. She asked if there would be time in the morning to check over our packing. I said we're never in a rush, anytime, on this whole trip. This little journey is for fun. We'll have a good time, a slow time, but good for our inner spirits. I explained the day was divided into four basic parts: 'mid-morning', 'noon or thereabouts', 'mid-afternoon', and 'evening'. Everything else, like 'early morning' or 'midnight' almost didn't exist. Anyway, tomorrow 'mid morning' would be good. Not cold, not a lot of traffic, etc. Let's take a look at the map. And we did and she saw, as I pointed, Colorado Springs, and south of that, the town of Pueblo, and then the Arkansas River. Retracing the last 100 plus miles I had traveled getting to Denver, but this would all be new to Stella.

Well, my Beautiful Princess, this is my last night in Denver, and I'd like to sleep through at least part of it. How shall we start? She suggested a mutual shower for starters. Damn that girl is a good thinker. We played a bit in the warm water and washed each other, slowly and purposely, and for a moment, just a moment, she was a famous painting, or perhaps an ancient sculpture ... real, but somewhere other than here. Closing my eyes, I shook my head, and forced my mind back into the present reality, a place where I was hungry to continue my journey and hungry for this woman with her beautiful softness and she was hungry to begin a new adventure and hungry for me. All of this crashed and smashed us together in a feast of pleasure.

Again, a quick shower, and again in bed with tea to drink, and books to read if we wanted. Too keyed up to read so let's talk a little. Ok. Stella, how much traveling have you done? Outside of trips between Kansas City and Louisiana, almost none. There was the bus trip from Kansas City to Denver, but most of that was in nighttime, and she saw very little beside a few Greyhound stations. Have you ever been to Colorado Springs? No, she hadn't. You're a little afraid of traveling, aren't you? She nodded yes. Well, don't worry about it. It's natural to feel that. Traveling takes you out of your comfortable little nest. You'll see, pretty soon you'll enjoy the adventure and challenge of it all. Right now, you're still trying to protect yourself from something threatening, but you'll be past that soon … whenever you rid yourself of that family and memories of them. You'll be great. Gonna have the world on a plate. Startin' here. Startin' now … and I continued with lyrics to Everything's Coming Up Roses, in a decent, but soft lower tenor voice. A song from Gypsy, which I had seen on Broadway about a year earlier. We were both surprised at that. She gave me a light round of applause and said "You're a little crazy and I love it!" I said it must be the tea. She got up, turned off the light, left a hallway light on at my request so I wouldn't smash into something in the middle of the night and then snuggled back into bed.

No matter how comfortable we might be, and with no regard for the good vibrations being shared, morning began to intrude. Fully awake now, it was time to do a few last-minute things and start the new adventure. Start for her, restart for me. We finished last night's supper with coffee and smiles and more coffee and more smiles. I returned keys she had given me. Let's get everything packed, don't forget washcloth and towel, carry your toothbrush where you can get at it easily. A little more coffee. She was just prancing around with anticipation. I'll start fastening everything to the scooter. She'd do a final kitchen thing. First, pack our food into the trunk, except the cookies (they go in my jacket pocket, in case we need an emergency cookie). Last thing into the trunk is the digging scoop. The two clothing bags are tied to the sides of the trunk with the sleeping bag bag tied to the front of it, providing a cushioned backrest for the passenger. Stella would carry her purse on her lap with the strap going over her shoulder and across her back. The leather purse seemed a little boxy and rigid, but it was OK. She also had a lightweight jacket, with only two pockets, not a portable, wearable storeroom such as mine. Well, it's 8:20 AM, almost mid-morning, shall we go? Got your helmet and sunglasses, right? She checked the doors to the house, we went into the garage, opened its door and I pushed Tony Lambretta out onto the driveway and into the daylight. Have we forgotten anything? I wish us a good journey. Let's saddle up, Princess. Again on the first kick, the scooter started with a tiny bit of blue smoke. As we started down the street I was thinking, "Goodbye, Denver, you're a great place and you've been so good to me. Someday I'll be back for another visit."

CHAPTER 21

A TINY TENT FOR TWO

On the road again, out of Denver, south along Route 85 or is it 87, but this time with a pretty passenger. Heading to Colorado Springs, the Lambretta behaving well as always. We would be encountering some hills, but what was lost on the uphill, could, as least partially be regained on downward slopes and our rate of travel would allow for enjoyment. An added bonus this morning was the closeness of Stella and the partial protection from cool breezes her presence offered. That and the welcome touch of one hand, then the other, and sometimes both hands on my rib cage or back. Oh Lordy, this was one sweet morning. One new hand signal we agreed to was a scissoring motion of the index and middle fingers to indicate that a break was needed. We could use voice communication, but it was a bit of a strain and really not a conversational thing.

We were traveling along that in-between area, between the Rockies on our right and grasslands on our left. It was mixed terrain, and various bumps on the earth's surface had names like Rattlesnake Mountain, Bald Mountain, True Mountain, each with its own little bit of history. There were scattered patches of evergreen forest, probably juniper and pinòn, and some agricultural fields. We had gorgeous sunshine and a hint of warmth coming into the air. I signaled a break with the scissors imitation and pulled into a café parking lot on the northern outskirts of Colorado Springs. We had driven almost two hours and covered 50 miles. Removing my helmet and glasses I told Stella, we would almost never travel that long without a break. Was she OK so far? She leaned into my face and said "Delighted, perfectly content." Reaching into my jacket, "Cookie?" So we ate a few cookies each while we talked. I mentioned that when we hit a café, we should always use the restroom, sometimes twice ... maybe once before we sit down and order, and always just before we leave. Would she like to have a small meal or just coffee or ... "just some coffee, sir." In that case, I won't lock the helmets to the scooter and all that. We'll just carry them. Went in and sat at the counter and she said "Just two black coffees, please." And as we sipped coffee, I explained that Colorado Springs was an upscale town

... there were many high salary people living there. I wanted her to see the Garden of the Gods, which I had seen on the way up to Denver. On the west edge of town. We could spend as much time as she liked noodling around there, after we finished our coffee and used the restroom. We are never in a hurry, I emphasized. At the scooter, we saddled up, she gave me a big hug and said loudly 'Onward to the Garden of the Gods, O White Knight.' And we started on our way. But damn, those hugs felt so fine. So very fine.

Continuing south, not long afterward, we were in the northern parts of Colorado Springs. Turning right, we headed west until the red rock formations became prominent, which meant we were in the Garden of the Gods. I had explained that this was not just a little compact park. It was a sprawling area, with vehicle roads, paved footpaths, dirt footpaths, and lots of red sandstone formations. Whenever a stop was called for, Stella should signal me. We stopped three or four times to look at particular formations. A moderate number of people were doing the same ... some looked dressed for long hikes, others in everyday clothing. I pointed out Pikes Peak and she asked how far away, it seemed so close. Ten or twelve miles. Her favorites were the formations called Cathedral Spires and the Three Graces. My suggestion was that we keep the scooter in sight but that we walk around a little more, since one's legs are nearly immobile while riding a scooter. Gentle exercise would be good for her leg which she still favored a bit from time to time. We talked of the spirituality of this area. It reminded me a bit of Sedona back in Arizona – also a spiritual center of some significance. She asked if I felt anything religious here in the Garden. My answer was a waffle ... no, not religious like the western man's churches, but I could see how various Indian tribes which encountered this area would feel attached to this and genuinely feel a spiritual attachment. Me, I just appreciate the incredible geology and I guess that, in a way, is more like the Indians' regard for this place than the white man's. These rocks are 200 or 300 million years old. Imagine. In comparison, our religions are nothing but freckles on a flea's ass. She got a blast out of that remark. Oh, what a beautiful sight when she laughed. That's what I call sight-seeing at its best.

Hey Beautiful Princess, are you hungry? It's approximately lunchtime. She asked if we had any cookies left? Ma, certo! Now, I've got you hooked on cookies. Now I can do whatever I want with you. Let's have a few cookies and we'll head down to Pueblo, about two hours from here. I know a place where the food is wholesome, tasty, and just unbeatable. If Enrico is there, we'll have the best meal attainable in all of Colorado. Got the water bag from the scooter, the cookies were in my jacket, all we needed was a friendly rock to sit on. As we nibbled cookies and took sips of water, she asked why I wasn't fat since I liked cookies so much. I explained that good Italian cookies did not add to the weight of a person, that they fed the soul and everyone knows the soul doesn't have any weight. Any lesser cookie, of course, is fattening. She thought that was a perfect explanation and chuckling, just shook her head while I was saying "What? What?" How I loved making this girl smile.

Now making our way out of Colorado Springs and southward, retracing the trip back to Pueblo. Fountain Creek was on our left and the Rocky Mountains were on our right and all was well with the world. The scenery seemed particularly splendid this fine day. On some upgrades, I had to drop to a lower gear for a distance, but I thought we'd pretty much done the steep grade stuff. After about an hour of buzzing along, I gave the scissors signal, indicating a break, and finding a likely place near some greenery, pulled off the road.

"We should have stopped for coffee before we left Colorado Springs. Time to wee-wee now." She said, "Good idea." "Urgent?" I asked. She said no. So I walked into the brush and took a leak. On returning, she asked the procedure. I took out a small handful of café paper napkins. "First, find a loose stone of decent size. You can use it for leaning on without putting your hand in the dirt. Then, after you pee, tend to your tush with these and then put the used ones under that stone. They'll decompose very quickly. Pooping is more involved. I'll explain that later. Right now, I'd like to have a smoke." She said, "I'll join you." As we talked and smoked, I asked her how she liked the day so far. She said "Absolutely magical. It seems I've seen more today than in the rest of my life." I explained, on the other side of the road was Fountain Creek which empties into the Arkansas River at Pueblo. We'll camp alongside this creek tonight, if that's OK with you. She said I was the trail boss.

Back to our roadway and a few hugs from behind me. Then a bit of a shoulder rub. Then a little tug on each earlobe. Time seemed to fly as we drove across the bridge spanning the Arkansas, she for the first time, me for about the fourth time. Pointing down river, I said, "Tomorrow, we'll begin to follow it ... for a day or two." Now, down through Pueblo, past the hardware store where I had bought the tarp. Soon we pulled into Enrico's.

Removing helmets, stretching, shaking our hair out, locking helmets to the scooter, we made our way into that extraordinary, ordinary-looking café. Mid-afternoon, a few customers there and we took a booth. Enrico himself soon appeared from the kitchen, paused for a moment, and almost shouted, "Unbelievable! Unbelievable! I have thought about you five hundred times since you left. Enrico seemed to be dancing. Who's this?" Leaning toward Stella, he said, "I'm Enrico." She said, "My name is Stella." She extended her hand and he took hers, gave it a little kiss and said, "What a perfect name for such a beautiful young woman! Oh, you two are a picture!" So I pipe in and say, "Let me introduce you"... and they both laugh. Enrico said, "I thought I'd never see you again. What are you doing back here?" I explained that Stella needed a ride to New Orleans and I couldn't refuse such good-looking girl, could I? He said, "New Orleans! New Orleans? You're some wonderful kind of crazy. I thought you'd be in Chicago by now." I said, "How could I go to Chicago without having some more of your food. Do you remember what you fed me?" He said, "But of course ..." Stella said quietly, "Ma, certo." Enrico looked at Stella, "You speak Italian? I wish I could." And he went on without pause ... "Yes, yes, you had chicken and red peppers, Swiss chard on the side and some bread and coffee." I looked at Stella, "Sound OK to you?" She smiled and nodded yes. Enrico had this sad look on his face. "Oh, what a shame," he said, "I don't have chicken and red peppers" and then immediately, a big smile, "I have chicken with asparagus and roasted green peppers instead of red ... and ... I have Swiss chard, too. Is that OK?" "Enrico, that's sounds perfect, will you join us for lunch or supper, whichever it is?" He said, "How about I join you for coffee like the last time?" I said, "It would be my honor."

Enrico served our meal and we slowly enjoyed every bit of it. He finally came over with coffee and an extra cup for himself. He cleared a few dishes, and Stella got up and helped him. Then he came over with the coffee pot and an extra cup and sat down with us. "The food was OK?" he asked. "Enrico, it was delightful and it was needed. I'm happy I was able to get back here." He asked, "You're really headed to New Orleans?" I nodded yes and said we planned to reach it in two or three weeks and just enjoy the whole experience. We talked for an hour or more. He had so many questions and finally he said, "I'm going to imagine you two every day for the next two weeks. A little piece of my soul will be with you the entire trip. Listen, I haven't known you a long time, but I love you both." I said I knew exactly what he meant. I asked for the tab, he waved me away, and I said that wasn't fair. Let me use the restroom and then we could argue. First, I went out and got the water bag, took it to the sink and filled it. On my way back to the table, Stella met me half way and said so quietly, "He won't bill us. How much should I leave?" "Ten, I whispered." When I got back to the table, I told him we'd be camping out tonight in the same area that he recommended a week ago and thanked him so much. As we got ready to leave, he gave Stella a big hug. Then he gave me an emotional hug and while I was shaking his hand, I felt he was crying inside when he said "Good Luck to the two of you. You are such magnificent people!"

Stella and I headed to the scooter, and she said, "Let's hurry before he finds the money I left." And we made good our escape from that beautiful place and headed to that other beautiful place along Fountain Creek to make our camp for the night. I would get fuel for Tony the Lambretta in the morning. All this was breaking rules normally followed. Usually, the scooter fuel was first consideration, but this afternoon was special.

Back across the Arkansas River heading northward now, take a right, and eventually get back to the place where I had camped a week before. Could not believe only a week had passed. This had to be a time warp. The past week seemed half a lifetime.

Now it was time to set up camp amongst the small trees and shrubs near Fountain Creek. First thing, stabilize footing for the scooter and tie it off to two small trees. Of course, Stella wanted to help with everything. I suggested it would be better to let me go through my routine unassisted, which would require about fifteen minutes, and she could watch and next time, help with it. That was fine with her, but she really was a bit anxious to jump into this camping. I mentioned again that this was not 'normal' camping, but rather primitive with very few luxuries involved. She could, in a few minutes, help me with the new tarpaulin. Set up the tent very quickly and just as quickly had shallow trenches dug around it. Having told her of my fiasco of the New Mexico rainstorm experience, she understood the tarp business immediately. Finally, I retrieved the tarp from the trunk of the scooter, opened the package and Stella helped me spread it out and we draped it over the tent. There was a generous amount of overhang. OK, let's try to find six rocks about this big and I shaped the air into a football sized chunk. If they're a little more oblong, that's even better. That took about five minutes. Not a tough job, here near the river bed. Tied the four corners of the tarp to stones, then a center one on each side, always trying to keep as low a profile as possible. I knew what the force of wind could do, having studied and worked a few math problems which involved low pressures over large surface areas in high school physics. So that did it. We had a camp with a tent. And only a very slight breeze. Now get the sleeping bag bag, and the clothing bags and arrange the inside. The dull color grayish green of the tarp blended well with the surroundings and so far, I was satisfied with it. Ok, next step is to gather two small piles of wood for coffeepot fires, one for this evening, one for the morning. That done, it was time to sit down and rest or talk or read. I pointed out the dead tree where the hawks and eagles had been. We still had an hour or more of daylight. I mentioned we had a river to get bathing water from, but were limited to a gallon for drinking, coffee-making and tooth-brushing. Resting and talking we could do with the reduced light of evening, but reading would have to be done now. She said she would prefer to do a little writing in her notebook. Good, I'd like to read. Haven't done much this week.

Thought I'd read Bradbury's 'Fahrenheit 451,' which I had just begun two or three years before and had been interrupted, and had never gone back. But I was always trying to read a half dozen books at a time, anyway. We began and spent a half-hour in near silence at the entrance 'doormat' of the little tent, in reality just a thin fabric flap. She closed her notebook and I noticed it was small and thick. Was that the same notebook her aunt had given her when she was a little girl. She nodded yes and said she would never leave it behind.

While we have some daylight, let's walk near the Creek. Beautiful place, despite being not too far from the highway and railroad tracks on the other side of the creek and close to a residential area on this side. I explained how I washed using a washcloth and a bar of soap the week before and very nearly froze my ass off. She laughed and said, "Tonight then, we go to bed dirty, if you don't mind too much." I said it wasn't normally my style, but neither was frostbite. As we walked back to the tent, I grabbed the water bag from the scooter and asked if she wanted more coffee. She said no, let's do coffee in the morning and just brush our teeth and wash our faces tonight. I asked if she thought she might want a midnight snack, if so, better get it now while we can still see. And better to pee now, too. We took care of that business, then sat and talked on the doormat for a while as the air cooled, daylight diminished, and starlight gained the night sky. Then it was time to crawl inside the tent for the evening. This was a new experience for me, two people in this little tent. We managed to get comfortable, half sitting up with the sleeping bag rolled out under us, using the clothing bags as cushions, and opening the little vents for breathing air.

With my arm half way around her, I asked, "So, Princess, how was your day?" She started with, "This has been the best day of my life. The scooter riding is just the right pace. I see so much as we go past. I cannot tell you how good this has been ... the cookies, towns, mountains, clouds, and the restaurant ... such simple, splendid food. And you know what, Rosano? That man, Enrico, you have given him a new look at life. He'll start some adventure in his life, and soon. You did that for me, too. And what about you ... how was your day?" "Stella, it was a memorable, beautiful day for me. The journey northward, I shared with you, but in reverse, as we moved southward. On the scooter was one of the ten most beautiful women in the world touching me almost all day. And this beautiful woman laughed at most of my ridiculous jokes. Nobody on earth can top that." "Oh yes," she said, "I can top that if you don't object to getting in bed with some dirty little woman from out of town." I said, "Sometimes, we just have to be tolerant and accepting."

"Princess, I got something bothering me. Just listen. On my way up to Colorado, I realized that I was really vulnerable and almost without any defense if I needed it. Now, with you, I feel doubly exposed. Tomorrow, I want to return to the hardware store and buy a machete. I saw some there. I can't carry a firearm, because each state has its own laws, maybe each county or township, so that's a sure way to get in trouble over nothing. But having a machete goes with camping and the tent and all that. So that's what I'll do. I just don't want you to get too concerned about all this." She answered, "Tomorrow, when we have more light, I will show you something. And tomorrow, let's get a better flashlight, too."

We talked for a while, touching on many subjects, this trip included. Tomorrow we would start across prairie land, though for a day or two we would never be far from the Arkansas River. She asked where the river went eventually. The source, was some springs, about 150 miles west of us, up into the Rockies we had just driven past. It finally emptied its water into the Mississippi River. It total length was about 1500 miles as it meandered this way and that way across four or five states. Now you know as much as I do. The Arkansas is absolutely loaded with history, maybe one day I'll look it up. Starting tomorrow, everything we encounter is new to both of us, that is, until we reach Louisiana, where you know much more than I do. She said no, she really didn't know much at all, since as kids, all they did was hang around and try to avoid the adults, because they seemed to think kids were just so much trash. My childhood wasn't terrible compared to some kids, but it was scary and dull at the same time. Actually, my whole life has been pretty dull. And Rosano, you've already changed that, in just a week.

My response was something like this: "Look, I'll take a tiny bit of credit for that, but give yourself far more credit, because you are ready for big changes in your life. Listen, you took leave of absence from your fulltime job, you've quit your part time job, all in preparation to go to that family reunion just so you can sever your family ties for once and for all. So you see, you've decided, no one else did, it was you, and you're all set. You don't know what you want to do with your life, but that's no problem at all. That will eventually resolve itself. More important is that you know what you don't want, what you won't do. So I come along and completely luck out by finding you in a coin-op laundry and we become lovers and at least halfway fall in love in a matter of days and it has been a glorious time. So we'll be going in different directions soon and you'll start recreating yourself and I'm going to suggest one thing which could be very helpful in your mind. You should change your name. Stella Beauchamp. Stella, meaning star, is a splendid name, so you must keep that. Beauchamp, which means beautiful meadow, is also a fine name, so you should keep that, too. What you should change, I believe, is the pronunciation of Beauchamp. You pronounce it 'beachim' to rhyme with 'reach him.' The Brits do crazy crap like that. Sometimes they purposely obscure the language, I swear. Try 'bow Shom' with a little push on the second syllable. That does two things: one, it just sounds far more elegant and matches your elegant appearance, and two, it separates you from all that childhood family garbage, it splits you apart from the people, the 'beachims' you dislike so intensely. If you have a different name, the split becomes more valid in your own mind, and your own heart, and that's where it counts the most."

She sat quietly. Then, a question, "What does Champs-Élysées mean?" Oh wow, I didn't expect that. I said, "Sounds gorgeous, right?" She said yes. I said it refers to a Greek paradise, the Elysian Fields or Meadows, a place for heroes who have gone to heaven, but I have no idea how to say it in Greek. I'm really weak on Greek history and mythology. For a while though, I was pretty strong on Metaxa and Ouzo. Anyway, say it ... "bow Shom." And she did, and even though I couldn't see her in the darkness, I know she smiled ... and quietly said it again, "bow Shom." "There you go, Miss Beauchamp, the old spelling but a new name. And you don't have to change any paperwork."

After more talk, she asked for the water bag, took a sip of water, and said, "I think you should get naked." Hmmm ... I wonder what's on her mind, after all, she's already had a lot to deal with today. I asked if she would join me and she said, "When the time is right." This was the first night with two people in this tiny tent. And it was a doozie with a capital 'dooz.'

CHAPTER 22

SERIOUS PRAIRIE START

Body heat in the small confines of the mountaineer tent kept us comfortable during the chilly night. Only partially covered by the sleeping bag, we slept reasonably well. Half draped over each other, waking was a long, rather enjoyable, process. Eventually, she said quietly, "I have to pee." I said, "How romantic, I do, too. I'll go first and drive the bears and the lions away so you'll be safe." She said, "That's what White Knights are for." Dressing in a tee shirt, pants, and boots, I opened the tent flap to find the morning just beginning to get serious. Took a leak, returned, handed Stella a few café napkins and said to just get a rock from one corner of the tent and proceed normally, that nobody seemed to be near us. She, dressed in only a shirt, went and returned, and we sat for a minute or two. "I'll make the coffee." Crawled out and lit the fire prepared last night and hurried back to the tent and began pulling my clothes outside and dressing as quickly as I could. Brisk and crispy fresh air in the morning is really dreadful no matter what the woodspeople say. Into the scooter trunk, get the ground coffee, wait for the boiling sound, measure the right amount into the pot and create a personal miracle called that 'first cup of coffee.' Just about to pour the first cup when 'she' emerged from the tent fully clothed. Filling the first cup woke me to the fact there was no 'her' cup. I asked if she had packed one, she shook her head 'no'. Taking a sip, I remarked on how unfortunate that was, now that she could have no coffee until I was finished. Then, trying to avoid any serious injury, I handed her the cup and we traded sips. She was captivating in early morning light, as we both huddled over one cup of coffee. Two minutes later, cup nearly empty, it was refilled and we resumed sipping and looking at one another, smiling sometimes, faces nearly touching. So good, so good.

Another pot? No, that's enough for now. What's next, Captain? Let's do a little maintenance. We need to shake out the sleeping bag each morning, if possible, to air it out and insure that no critters might have gotten in. Critters? Well, insects actually. I think we would have noticed a blue jay, squirrel, or raccoon. Out of the tent comes the sleeping bag, we unzip it completely and each of us takes a side and we flap it up and down and then drape it over the tent. Now, personal maintenance. First brush teeth with water from the water bag. Next, coffeepot, soap, washcloth and towel, down to the edge of Fountain Creek, which is gurgling merrily. Coffeepot first, wash with sand or dirt and water to get rid of the carbon from the fire. The inside is done less vigorously. Now fill the coffeepot and set it aside. That water will be used to extinguish the fire, if it's still alive. Now dip the washcloth in the clear running water, rub the soap on it, and then scrub whichever part of you can stand the coldness. After you've washed, it's time to rinse with unsoapy water from the creek, then the towel. Now back to the scooter and tent. From the trunk, I take out the aluminum scoop and explain the process for a poop. If we make camp early enough, I can fashion a substitute toilet seat if there is wood available and a machete to use as a tool, but the process remains pretty much the same. Let's take our clothing bags out of the tent and repack them if necessary and tie them up for the day with the most needed items, like the mini mess kits, packed last. Washcloths I tie to the scooter separately so they'll dry out. Next, let's roll up the sleeping bag and put it in the sleeping bag bag. Next, we tightly fold and roll the tarp and make it as compact as possible. Now we pack the tent. Finally, we tie everything to the scooter in a secure manner that allows Stella to lean back against the trunk and still be comfortable. Seems like a lot to do, but really only ten or fifteen minutes, big if, if you've had at least one cup of coffee. Final thing is to check the campfire to make certain it's out.

Before we resume our journey, we have four stops: a café, Gagliano's deli, hardware store, and then fuel for the scooter. Start the Lambretta, pull out of our camping area, get back onto the main road going south across the Arkansas River again, stop at a café, I'd like to have a few pancakes, coffee, and a smoke. Stella orders a bigger breakfast and coffee. Sounds weird, but we should try to use the restroom as much as possible. We have our breakfast and talk. Well, Beautiful Princess, how do you like 'camping out?' "First time, fun, different. We really live in luxury and never appreciate it, especially the hot water for cleaning ourselves." I agreed and said that after two or three days in campgrounds, a hot shower seemed to be the ultimate luxury, but, I thought perhaps it was an 'American' thing. Other cultures just don't seem to demand the same easy access to hot water and soap. Breakfast is done, use the restroom again, pay the bill, get back onto the scooter and drive less than a half mile to the hardware store. I said this will only be a minute, walked in, picked up one of those surplus machetes with a canvas scabbard, paid the guy at the register, and was back at the scooter. Took the time to carefully tie the machete scabbard to the scooter's trunk. Now off to Gagliano's, which I said was a secret magic kingdom where cookies are located. She chuckled and said, how many dozen, Captain. I suggested two dozen would last us three days, then we go on famine rations. By the third day, they get pretty hard, but still taste splendid. After that, they begin to decline and should not be taken. Also we should get a hefty supply of dried figs, dried peaches or apricots, maybe a few other things, anything that she might find. Into Gagliano's, she told me later, she felt she was entering another world or at least another country. Everything was a little strange, everything smelled so good, she chose the cookies, nuts, bags of figs and apricots, and after wandering around decided we were OK, let's check out. One minute, and I almost doubled the amount of the dried fruit, and added two cans of Kadota figs and two cans of canned peaches and we went to the register. She paid the bill as agreed. Back to the scooter we packed everything as best we could, she asking about the canned figs and peaches, which are heavy. I said that's our next snack. We need these things to keep our intestines doing their job and moving along. Very uncomfortable to be constipated and then riding any distance at all. OK, let's get some fuel for Tony and we'll head out across the prairie. Drove to the same station where I had refueled the week before. A guy came out of the little building and I knew it wasn't my twenty-minute friend Zipper. I did my normal 'sorry to bother you thing' and had already poured my reserve mixture into the tank. As he fueled the scooter tank and took the smaller can to fill, he said, "Arizona. Where in Arizona?" Told him Tucson. "Then you must be the guy Zipper was talking about just before he quit." I acted surprised and thought it was a little surprising, but not shocking. "Did he quit? "Hell yes, he quit. Couldn't wait to 'get on the road.' and try to catch up with that crazy, little sonuvabitch, that's what he called you." I asked, "Did it put you in a bind?" "Hell no, it turned my part time job into a fulltime job." Well, OK then. I paid the man, we got onto the scooter and putt-putted over to the little building, refreshed our water bag, then headed out of the station. All those chores took a bit of time, but now it was time to restart our journey.

Today we would travel eastward through Pueblo, Colorado for about fifteen miles. Agricultural rectangles were everywhere. Of course, this would have been prairie years before. The question arises: Would the prairie still exist in 2060, a century from now. How much of it will be 'domesticated' and when? As we leave Pueblo behind, we begin to cross a part of this Great American Grassland, The Prairie, The Plains. The Arkansas River, running with cold fresh waters from springs and snow runoff from the Rockies would be just north of us, sometimes just a few feet, sometimes a mile as it took a wandering path across the land. With these agricultural fields each dipping its straw into this river, I wonder how it can possibly have any water to empty into the Mississippi.

Stella was leaning on me a little and occasionally giving a gentle squeeze as we headed eastward on a very straight road alongside a very curvy river. Not too many miles after leaving Pueblo, between two small towns, Boone, and Fowler and looking south, we had a taste of what people call 'endless' prairie, where a telegraph pole became the most significant visual point. It was here that contrast between the intense green of trees along the river and the dry sandy blonde color of dried prairie grass was most defined. This lack of trees out in the grasslands was intriguing. After driving for a little more than an hour, I scissored my fingers and pulled over near a small area of brush. Time to pee, for both of us. Want a little fruit break? Stella said that would be good. Figs? Great. OK, let's get the mess kits. Let's just use the forks and eat from the container. She was OK with that. Oh, wow, she had never had that kind of fig ... Kadota. Quite sweet, delicious. We talked a short time and I asked if she preferred camping or a motel tonight. The choice was camping. In that case, we could probably stay at a place called the John Martin Reservoir, after we passed through the towns of La Junta and Las Animas. Stella asked what kind of town La Junta would be. I said, probably a farming community, I thought population was about a thousand people, but didn't know where I had gotten that impression. Probably would have a few stores ... a pharmacy, maybe a hardware store, a café, maybe a grocer or a general store ... just a guess. She said, if they have a hardware store or general store, she wanted to buy something. In a short time, we were there. La Junta was larger than I imagined. We parked in front of a mercantile store. She asked what's a mercantile. I told her it was a cross between a general store, a hardware store, a clothing store or almost any kind of store imaginable. Depends on the ideas of the owner. First, I have to empty all our trash into the barrel outside the store. Now let's go in and see if they have this mystery item. We walked around a bit and she found the pots and pans department and selected a large aluminum saucepan. I asked her, "For heating water?" She grinned and said, "How did you know?" I said it seems we had the same idea. I picked up a few pots, pushed a few aside, and picked out an aluminum roasting pan with a lid. This is better, I said. With a lid, the water heats faster, using less fuel and the oval shape lets us pack it onto the scooter more efficiently. The sauce pan has a wooden handle, not so great for putting on a wood fire. She agreed. Up to the front of the store, I reached for my money and she stopped my hand. I said I would be using this pan for the entire trip even after New Orleans, so please. She relaxed and said OK. Out to the scooter, untied a few things, repacked and she said, "Oops, ... forgot" and trotted back into the store. Came out with a bigger flashlight and a pack of batteries. We were ready to roll again. About an hour to go before we get to the reservoir, want coffee break now or …? Let's find a tree for shade and have a few cookies. Oh boy, that'll stop me, every time.

While munching on cookies, she said, "Tell me why water boils faster if there's a lid on the pan. I know it's about evaporation, but what do you know about it?" So I start: "You're on the right path. Did you ever hear the phrase 'A watched pot never boils?' We take it to mean that …anything we impatiently wait for, seems to take forever, right? OK, but if you think of it actually involving a real pot or kettle of water, it does take much longer if you watch the water, because you take the lid off to see. Wild, eh? So you know about molecules and how they vibrate and bang around faster if heat is added and the temperature is raised. Well, the hottest or the most active molecules of water escape into the atmosphere first and we call that … steam … so if the hottest molecules are allowed to break free, they are carrying the most heat away from the body or pan of water while you're trying to get to a boiling point. So boiling and evaporation are approximately the same thing. What we call evaporation is just slower because it happens at a lower temperature. If the lid is kept on the pot, far fewer molecules can escape and so the water gets hotter faster. Does that make sense to you?"

She nodded yes and said now she could picture it happening. Told her 'A watched pot never boils' is an old expression. But now we have some glass pot lids, so it just makes my story a little tougher to sell. "Yes," she said, "but your explanations are really clear and make sense, easy to understand."

Let's get going. Now, this part of the journey was new to the two of us. So here's the map, and every navigator is in charge of maps. So she began to navigate, pointing eastward out of La Junta and a short time later through the smaller town called Las Animas, Spanish for 'the spirits' or 'the souls.' Twenty minutes after Las Animas, she signaled right onto a small paved road, numbered #24, where there was a micro town called Hasty. A few little buildings, including a very small post office building. Stella finally directed us to a point where we could see the reservoir and said it was up to me to find a camp spot. Looking around, I saw what I thought would be the best opportunities for a campsite reasonably near the water. We had run out of pavement and our campsite would be off road. Took about twenty minutes to look and decide. It would be off road and hidden from it. We would be OK, but I wouldn't risk the tires, especially with extra weight of a second passenger, so I'm going to half walk and half drive the scooter about 100 feet and you, Beautiful Princess, are going to have to walk. We don't want to lame the horse.

A low place between two rises sloping downward to the reservoir was chosen. There was a group of small shrubby trees and we weren't far from the water's edge. We hadn't seen or heard another person and the immediate area showed no evidence of recent use. Good. Secure the scooter to a short, but stout tree. Early afternoon and the sun is warm. Before we get started, let's eat some of those canned peaches. We sat quietly, trading the peaches back and forth, enjoying the almost total quiet of the reservoir.

Time to set up camp. First remove my jacket, then start untying everything from the scooter. Next, changed into my camping pants. Gave the tent and the scoop to Stella and told her to go ahead and set it up and dig some trenches around it, while I get some firewood. But first, and most important ... we both must move slowly and stay super alert to any rattlesnakes which very well might be about. Do nothing quickly, and don't put any part of you where you cannot see ... don't reach behind anything or under anything ... don't take a step without seeing where your foot will be landing, etc. Up into that group of trees, finding enough firewood was no problem. Probably no one had been in this spot for years. Actually found two pieces, each a little more than two inches in diameter ... too valuable for firewood, they could be used to fashion a reasonable toilet seat. Talk about luxury of the highest order. Using that wood and some large rocks, a latrine with a seat resulted. I cleared two or three feet around the pit just so we could see more easily. Then gathering a big armful of firewood, I returned to see the tent upright, with trenches surrounding it, and the tarp already draped over it and anchored by sizable rocks. Stella was beaming, "How did I do?" I looked things over and said "Very good, Princess. Need to do two more things. One is to tie these tent tabs to the trees to help keep this thing upright in the wind. Second, is to make sure the trenches can drain downhill, so you have to dig a little more to guide any water down the hill. You tie the tent and I'll finish digging. That'll make things as good as we can expect. Go ahead, do whatever else you think might need doing, maybe even prepare a lunch for us, using our mess kits. I'll make up a fire pit and we can brew some coffee, too. Back to the latrine and dug a good sized hole and piled the dirt alongside. Back to the fire. Gathering a good selection of five or six stones, I made a star-shaped resting place for the new pan we had purchased and the coffeepot to be heated at the same time. Also got three or four good sized flat rocks to make reasonable seating. Got the new machete and started chopping firewood into manageable pieces. Got a fire started while Stella prepared the coffeepot with waterbag water and filled the roasting pan full of lake water. I stayed with gathering firewood as she prepared two mess kits with sliced salami, little chunks of cheese, the other can of figs, some nuts. There was a respectable pile of wood by the time she announced "Lunch is served." It was so good to share this activity with this very fine woman. Hoped she was as pleased as I was. We ate slowly, enjoying the food, the sun, and the peacefulness. Coffee pot sounded almost ready, and soon enough, we had my world-famous cowboy coffee available. Gave it a few minutes to settle, and we shared the first cup, between bites of food. The remaining coffee was all mine. Finishing the food remaining in the mess kits, she said, "What's next?" I said, "I'll do the dishes, while you use the latrine. When you're done with your paperwork at the latrine, just kick some of the dirt over the paper. Be alert. No daydreaming. After that, we'll wash using that pan of hot water. OK with you?" She said, "Good plan." Now with the mess kits and coffee pot, down to the water's edge, wash the mess kits, though not much washing needed, wash the coffee pot inside and refill it to the brim. Back to the fire, add some wood, coffeepot back on the fire. Emerging from the thicket of trees, Stella was smiling and congratulated me. "Very clever toilet seat, maestro. More comfortable than I imagined. Now, how do we wash?" Glad she asked.

So here's what we do. Since it's a warm day, there's no need to really rush. As far as I know there's nobody else around, but if you prefer, we can put up the tarp for privacy. OK, no tarp, so let's get ready. First get the clothes you're going to wear after your bath and stack them on this rock. Then get your washcloth, your towel and the bar of soap and bring them here, near the fire. OK. Now, wash your face and your neck by dipping about a third of the washcloth into the hot water. Be careful, it's pretty hot right now. OK, let it cool a little, rub some soap on the cloth and start cleaning your face and neck. You may want to do that two or three times. How's the water, hot, but not too hot, good. Now the fun starts, because now you should get naked and I'm going to help you wash and rinse and dry. You do the front side using the washcloth and I do the back side using my hands. Your legs and feet, we do last. Touching the water, I found it a bit too hot for my hands, so I added a little water from the coffee pot to tone it down. Then dipping my hands into the water, I took the bar of soap, rubbed in on my hands and then started to wash her shoulders and her back, then her bottom, then her butt crack and she groaned lightly. My hands are back in the water, rinsing themselves, then cupping water onto her shoulders, I hand-squeegee the little bit of soap off and rub her with the clean water. Meanwhile she has finished soaping and scrubbing the front side and says quietly, "Rinse me, and then you can dry me." Oh my, this must be one of those foreign movies I'm in. I cradle the roasting pan in one arm, and gently splash water onto her chest and rinse my way down, gently tending to every bit of this small, statuesque body, and she's making delicious little sounds. The coffee pot water is warm and I pour some of this over her shoulders for a final little rinse, then kneel to do her legs, first the soaping and then rinsing and we are both in some magic kingdom where it's OK to be clean and naked in the sun. Take her towel and begin to pat her dry. Take the washcloth, rinse it well, then fold it in half, place it onto one of the flat rocks and guide her to sit on it, while I wash her feet and rinse. "Rosano, you're deadly," she said so quietly. I put some more wood on the fire. Got the roasting pan and walked to the lake's edge, refilled it, walked back and put it on the fire and said, "When the water is warm enough ... I'm next." Dug my clean clothes out of the clothing bag and laid them out on one of the rocks.

"The water is perfect," she said. Stripping, I said that after I did my face and neck, she could do both front and backsides of me while I just watched to see if she did acceptable work, just supervise if that was OK. She said, "Better start washing your face then."

This reservoir, this man-made lake had been formed years before by damming or diverting water from the Arkansas River. At this point the river itself had a long way to flow to reach the Mississippi. Over 1,000 miles from where we were standing and everyone along the way dipping into it. Sometime I'd have to learn more about this river and this whole entity we call the prairie, which this river flows through. Stella and I were going through a small part of it and already it seemed a little menacing, well maybe that's too strong a word.

How did I get side-tracked like that? I was washing my face and neck and then this beautiful little goddess assumed the remainder of the task. Of course, I was fully capable of washing myself and usually preferred that arrangement. Tried not to be too rigid in this kind of situation, but just couldn't help it given the circumstances. Certainly though, this was all good clean fun ... a detailed and complete exterior cleaning. After I regained consciousness and recovered to some extent, I took her hand and led the way to the tent which had the sleeping bag already rolled out (how convenient). A sense of 'Compatibility' was in the air. We reclined, touching each other, each of us scented with the tiniest hint of that perfume called eau du café. How we both loved the taste of coffee that afternoon.

Loving, then snoozing, then awakening, and it was still afternoon with an hour or two of daylight available. Let's make coffee and have cookies and then do some reading. Later, we can talk and eat. Agreed. Half dressed, I poured two cups of water from the water bag into the coffee pot, got a small fire going, dug the book out of the clothing bag and sat on one of the flat rocks near the coffee pot. She joined me as the coffeepot was sounding its 'ready' sound. Put the scoops of coffee into the water, pull the pot back most of the way from the fire and just wait while the magic happens. Stella had brought her book, her towel, and a half-dozen cookies. We shared coffee, ate cookies, and read our books for an hour or so. Time to stretch, move around, refilled the pan and the coffeepot from the lake and put them both on the fire, added some wood. She asked what I was planning. Really nothing, but it couldn't hurt to have a little extra water already boiled. After it boiled I would let it cool down and not try to maintain the fire.

"Rosano, I have a question for you." I said, "Me first, last night you were going to show me something when there was enough light. Now's the time. Do you have to get undressed to show me?" She really laughed, then walked over to the tent, brought her purse back with her, and handed it to me. "Do you like this pocketbook?" It was leather, with decorative details everywhere, about a foot long and a little boxy with a strong leather strap, also intricately tooled. I looked it over and said, "Whoever did this leatherwork was a fine craftsman. That's excellent work. Can I peek inside?" I did, briefly, and handed it back. It felt slightly on the heavy side, but I attributed that to the thick leather. She said, "Now, watch me." She put the strap over her shoulder, held the pocket book lightly under her left arm and against her waist in a casual manner, and with a quick movement of her right arm was suddenly holding a nine-inch dagger in her right hand. Then passed it to me, handle first. It was razor sharp on both edges and the point was almost a needle. "Impressive," I said, "concealed so well." She said, "Last night, when you said you felt doubly vulnerable now that I was with you, I knew better. We were not totally defenseless. The machete is a good thing to have, too, and I see how you tie it to the scooter so you can have instant access. I love that you want to protect me. You don't know how important that is to me." I said, "Where and how did you get this?"

She told me another growing up story, this one brief and involved a negro girl, who is now a friend with whom she exchanges letters once or twice a year. While in high school, each day after school, she would have to wait for a bus to take her home. At the same time, the colored girl (that's another word used then) would wait at the same stop, but for a different bus. Each couldn't help noticing the other and after a few days they began talking ... eventually about so many things ... sometimes for just a minute, sometimes for as much as fifteen minutes. In time, Stella talked of why she had left Louisiana and of those men (she didn't say who they were, just 'relatives') looking under her nightshirt. The dark-skinned girl, said, "Honey, they were getting ready to rape you, but you know that already." Stella asked, "That ever happen to you?" Her friend said, "NO, no, no. My Mom and Dad were very, very protective of us kids. They made sure we knew what was going on around us. And not to let anyone touch us in a bad way. My Dad made one of these for each of his daughters, for me and my two sisters. And he and my mom gave us lessons on what to say and do. She held up her pocketbook. Stella must have looked puzzled. Then, looking around to make sure no other people were around, in an eye blink, she held a big dagger in her hand, so that Stella could see. One of their buses was approaching the stop. The dagger was returned into its place quickly. "See you tomorrow." "Yeah, OK." On the way home, Stella thought about the pocketbook dagger and wanted to take a closer look and would ask her tomorrow. She could hardly wait to see her friend the following day. That's when the pocketbook was examined closely and when Stella asked if the girl's father could make one for her and to please tell her the price. Within two weeks Stella was the owner of the pocketbook which I had just held. The two girls became friends through high school and were friends still. After this approaching Memorial Day reunion down in Louisiana, Stella wanted to more or less say Goodbye to her failing aunt and Hello again to her dark-skinned friend.

OK Stella, now you had a question. Stella smiled and said, "You are a cookie-nut, and I can understand why. These cookies are out of this world. So I have a question or two. Are there any 'American' cookies you like and think are good? And, why doesn't every nationality just copy the Italians when it comes to cookies? Can't wait to hear your answers, I really can't." So I tried to answer: "Last question first: Why doesn't everyone imitate … ? Haven't thought about that much. Part of it must be strictly cultural. For example, have you ever heard of anyone's mouth watering at the thought of going to a Norwegian delicatessen? No. It's just not their 'thing.' Delicatessens are for Greeks, Italians, and Jews. They know what to do and how to do it. Ever see any big sign advertising a Lithuanian bakery? No. Again, it isn't their 'thing'. Here in the US, there are so many different openings for food of any kind to take hold … Cuban, Mexican, German, East Indian, Chinese. Ever, ever, hear of an English restaurant? Of course not. And you never will. For all their really impressive stores of knowledge, and believe me, they have accomplished enormously great things, the Brits never learned to cook. So … Italians are totally involved in desserts of many kinds and no one can match them. Beautiful-looking and super-tasting cookies is part of that tradition. So it's really a cultural thing. Second major reason: The Italians use the best ingredients available and that becomes rather expensive and not many people here want to pay for expensive little cookies, especially if they have to fill a teenager's stomach. Now the first question: Any 'American' cookies … the best one I can think of right now is

Fig Newtons. Nothing to get excited about, but they are reasonably good tasting and probably good for you, too. Oreos is certainly not one. Very popular, OK tasting, but really disgusting on closer look ... two heavily sugared and starched pastry slabs with a layer of sugar and lard in between. Yucky. And not good for you, either."

Daylight was ending. Better if we use the latrine in the daylight if possible. More coffee? No? Ok, I'll get the coffeepot fire ready for brewing tomorrow's transfusion. It was so convenient that the two of us liked our coffee black. Thank God, it meant we could brew and pour, and use one cup, with no need to mess with the extra paraphernalia of cream and sugar, and spoons, and getting the right balance. The Lord works in mysterious ways! Oh yes! And religion fails us in so many other ways! Oh no! Having attended a number of different churches, quite a few different denominations, I had found not one, not a single one, which sought to convert people to black coffee consumption in place of the altered stuff. They were really missing the boat. They hardly ever consult me which, of course, is where they all go wrong.

As daylight was failing, a small boat moved down the length of the lake, eastward toward the dam and civilization which we had completely avoided. The multiple V-shaped wake organized the sunlight's reflection into a geometric image. Stella asked why we couldn't hear the boat. My guess was that it had a battery-powered electric trolling motor. They were almost silent, not very powerful, but very quiet. I remember some gasoline-fueled boat motors on the Connecticut shore, powerful and loud. Had never gotten involved with boating to any appreciable degree. Did a little sailing, but that's a whole 'nother deal. Viewing the lake's water, we are transported from the prairieness of our location in Southeastern Colorado. Tomorrow would be different. No lake, no river, and after we head south out of the town of Lamar, not much but grass ... for a hundred miles and then ... a hundred more. Right now was a time for a little food, a bunch of talking, some loving, and perhaps some sleeping.

CHAPTER 23

OKLAHOMA

The sun was up and starting its working day. Cool outside, but not quite a cool as previous days. Perfectly comfortable inside the tent with the body heat of two people. Looking through barely open eyes at my companion of a week, my half-awake brain was again seeing strong resemblance to the famous bust of Queen Nefertiti. As good an image to wake to as could be hoped. Strong urge to hold and protect her. Gathered her into my arms and saved her from the world ... while I snoozed a bit more.

This was going to be one gorgeous morning. Peeking through the screen of the tent entrance, there were only a few dinosaurs and dragons out there ... nothing that I couldn't easily manage while I peed and started the coffee fire. It was the diamondbacks and now, possibly, the prairie rattlesnake which I tried always to be alert to, though in fact, I hadn't seen one. Not seeing them can be a rather creepy condition, too. Does it mean they're not nearby or does it mean we're not being sufficiently observant? Reaching into the tent, I pulled enough clothing out to get myself dressed. In time, I was measuring the ground coffee into the boiling water. Allow 90 seconds for the brew to 'age' a bit, and then pour, inhale, sip, and know that survival is likely, for a short time at least. Drank about half that first cup and went to see my friend in the cocoon. "Hey, Princess, breakfast in bed!" She was already awake, but not yet dressed ... a genuine delight to gaze upon. Smiling, she reached for the cup and quietly took a few sips. Then a few more and handed the cup back and said, "I'll be out in a minute or two." And she was and joined me at the fire for more coffee. We traded the cup back and forth without talking. The reservoir lake had not a ripple on its surface. A peaceful time.

"Are we in any hurry?" Answering, I said, "Never." "Where are you taking us today?" "To a strange place ... to the real prairie. More coffee?" "That would be great." "Good. I'll brew another pot. Let's just air out the sleeping bag while we're waiting." Got the sleeping bag out, fluffed up and draped over the tent, poured the dregs of the old pot out and added water from the water bag into the coffeepot, added wood to the fire, and sat on one of the stones. She sat next to me and gave me a hug, then a little face nuzzle. As the water heated, I said we ought to have a few cookies and call that breakfast. Then, if we were late enough getting to the next town, named Lamar, we could try to have a good lunch with as many veggies as possible before we go on the highway. So there was no rush. Second pot ready. Add the coffee. This time allow two full minutes for aging the brew. Then pour and take with cookies, two or three different flavors ... to help get a balanced diet. Again we traded the coffee cup to and fro and told her I liked sipping from the same cup because with that arrangement I could see her up close, always a fine image ... and there were fewer dishes to wash.

Tonight, I'd like to stay at a motel. Could use the hot water to wash my hair and beard. OK with you? We could ask about one at the restaurant this morning or just take our chances. Either way, I don't think there's a river or lake where we're headed or even a campground. She said a motel would be good. That cleanliness is next to godliness, and that I could certainly use a bigger helping of godliness. Funny, funny.

We began packing up at a leisurely pace. I showed her how to do the tent. We always tied the entrance netting, whether we were inside or outside the tent. That way, nothing would decide to make it a home. Most concerned with the rattlesnakes. So the procedure for packing up the tent was this: First: Roll the rocks off the tarp. Then, making sure you're clear behind you, grab the tarp by the top center and pull it off the tent a pretty good distance. Visually check that nothing is crawling around, and carefully fold the tarp. Next: Untie the straps from the tent to the trees. Then, again making sure the area to your rear is clear, grab the tent by the top front tab and drag it a good distance away from where it sat. That's the most likely time to see a snake ... nesting under a corner of the tent. But you are safely away. Each time I pack the tent, just before folding it, I poke my head inside and look for any holes which might have appeared. So far ... none. So we're safe. Packing up really doesn't take much time. But we check the area we've used for two things, any of our stuff which may have gotten misplaced ... and any trash we must gather and take with us. She asked me about the latrine. I explained that as we leave this site, we kick the remaining dirt back into the hole and we leave the wood as is, so future archeologists can have a job someday imagining an entire civilization from two pieces of wood and a bit of poop. She paused, then laughed, saying, "You're not faking it, Rosano, you really are crazy. The things you think about!" Me: "What. What!"

So we were packed. I handed the helmets to Stella, and told her that because she called me crazy, she could damn well walk to the next town.

Got on the scooter, started it, then very carefully maneuvered it back to the little road, with her giggling and snorting a bit as she followed behind me. So enjoyable to see this beautiful woman laugh. Getting our helmets on and getting onto the scooter, we prepared to launch into a new adventure. Moved back to route 50, which eventually ended near the eastern coast of the US. But we would take it only a dozen miles into Lamar, Colorado, where we would pick up route 287 heading south. But first, find a restaurant which serves lunch early. Lamar was a good-sized town of 7000 people, most of them probably involved in agriculture. Driving to town we crossed the Arkansas River, as we headed south. The river paid no attention to us and continued its eastward course. Not much available for restaurants … pizza place not yet open, hamburger joint which didn't look or smell very good. A small breakfast shop seemed like our best bet. It looks like breakfast time again, surprise, surprise. And so it was, and it was pretty good for breakfast, which they served until 1:00PM, but they didn't serve lunch. So it was pancakes and coffee for me again, plus a large orange juice. Stella always had a bigger breakfast than I would. We had a good supply of dried fruit and nuts with us. While I wanted some veggies this morning, we could do without until later. As breakfast was being served, Stella asked what more did I know of this prairie we were about to 'really get into.'

What more did I know. Well, a few days before, I read some info at the Denver Library … not many details, but I had learned the grasslands were divided generally into three divisions … long grass, short grass, and something in the middle (couldn't remember the term used). Because fires on the prairie were frequent, there were few trees that survived. I was sidetracked into reading about prairie fires.

As a kid in Connecticut, I'd see people occasionally burning dried grass and leaves on their lawn or vacant lots or small fields. People said it would improve the soil. So when I first read about a prairie fire, I thought 'no big deal' because you could just hop over the fire line or run through it to the part already burnt or just walk away from it when it started by accident or was started purposely. Later, when I was a little older, I realized the prairie grasses were not like the stuff I was accustomed to in New England. They were grassier, if that's a word, thicker and still I thought, if a prairie fire started, people facing such a thing could just walk away from it. Didn't give it much thought until this trip. Then, in the Denver library I read that a prairie fire, if driven by the wind, could spread as fast as a horse could run, that sometimes the grasses were five or six feet tall or more. That information made me change my ideas completely and I understood the devastation that a prairie fire could and did cause to settlers' buildings, the houses, barns, stables, wagons, haystacks and stacked firewood. The fire would burn until it rained, or it ran out of fuel, or reached a barrier such as a river. The only defense for a farmer was to keep a 50 to 100 foot strip of land around his farm free of grass. That was done mostly by preburning, in a sense, fighting fire with fire. But sometimes it was these preventative fires which escaped and burned the prairie. That was in earlier years. Now, with so much of the prairie being farmed and controlled, prairie fires were much reduced and would probably not ever occur in future years. Anyway this thing called The Prairie covered about a third of the US. Huge. We'll get a good taste soon after breakfast, I suspect.

A leisurely breakfast, with good coffee, and a clean restroom, was always a big plus while traveling. Left the breakfast shop and drove a short distance to a gas station. Did my 'sorry to bother you' bit. The guy said 'no bother.' I asked about having any 2-cycle oil and yes, he did. One quart would do. I packed the oil while Stella refreshed the water bag.

Lamar would be the last Colorado town of any size that we would see. We were leaving the Arkansas River and its green influence on the scenery. Driving southward just a few miles put us out on the highway surrounded by prairie, where, at times, one could almost forget the color green existed. Travelers in autos would be moving at 60 or 70 miles per hour, we were averaging about 30 mph. This was a land of big dimensions with an almost limitless, almost uninterrupted, flat horizon. When traveling across these expanses, one cannot help but think of the pioneers, the hopeful adventurers, who covered terrain like this at just a few miles per day, no faster than oxen could walk. Amazing to me that more of these early ones didn't go completely berserk. Perhaps they did and we just didn't get that sort of information. In less than an hour, the vastness of the prairie was becoming apparent. We were constantly seeing man's mark on the land, however, the highway itself being the most apparent. There were distant agricultural things, too, windmills, power poles, etc. Still, the wide, almost unchanging scene made its impression. It was a horizontal world. After some miles, a sign appeared saying, 'The Knolls – 6 miles.'

In ten minutes we approached 'The Knolls' with a rest area for viewing. A knoll is a mound, usually of earth, rising from a relatively flat terrain. In almost any other landscape, these would not have been announced. Unimpressive. A bit more interesting were some rock structures which seemed to be poking their noses above the surface of the earth. However, after seeing the Painted Desert and the Rocky mountains in the past two weeks, these were also a yawn. We paused for a glance and were back on the road. How jaded we can become in such a short time. After another half hour, the navigator gave the scissors signal which meant break time. I gave a thumbs up signal and spotted some greenery a mile or two in front of us and pulled off the highway as we approached a small gully with a bridge taking the highway across. Later, I learned this was part of Springfield, Colorado. We were really just interested in peeing. This was not a great place for taking a break. A low bridge, a few scrubs of little consequence, no shade. "Hey Princess, should we have something to eat?" Shaking her head no, "Just a drink of water. You were right, if nothing else, this prairie is big."

Back onto Tony Lambretta, faithful scooter, and southward again. For another half hour and then into the small town called Springfield. This seemed like such a refreshing place. They actually had some trees and a park and a library. Neat little town, probably farming and ranching, and a wonderful place for a break ... the city park. Follow the sign to the park, one block away from the main route through town. Bring the scooter to a rest under some trees.

"Hey Princess, I reserved a table for the afternoon. And the entertainment committee put up a couple of swings for us." She stretched, taking off the helmet, and said, "Wow, that was something." I told her we had traveled a little less than 60 miles this morning, just a tiny fragment of the grasslands. This afternoon we had about 50 miles to go ... 30 of it in Colorado and 20 miles in Oklahoma, about 2 hours total. So ... let's have a nice break, drink some cool water from the fountain over there. I'm going to check out that little building for restrooms. She started digging out some snacks, got the cup. Yes, two restrooms, his and hers, his was clean, I assumed hers would be also. The stretching and walking around in the shade were a welcome change from this morning's travel. We nibbled at some fruit, had a few nuts, and drank some water. And walked around again. Let's try the swings. They were strong and could carry adults easily. So we went back and forth for a while and talked, with me asking how she was enjoying this camping adventure. She said "Everything is so amazing to me. You seem to just enjoy it, and take it in stride, while I'm really overwhelmed by it all." I said, "Before you get too excited, this afternoon we'll be going through some very unchanging grassland. Two hours of sameness. We need a break halfway, so I propose we do that on the state line separating Colorado and Oklahoma. Can we call it a plan?" She nodded, "A plan it is." Back to the picnic table for a few more snacks and more water. It would be good to have a cup of coffee, but not critical ... yet. Let's go sit against that tree and I'll put my arms around you and we can semi-snooze for a few minutes. And we did that and I enjoyed holding her.

When semi-snooze was over, we exchanged a few light-weight smooches and began to repack. We'll use the restrooms and be on our way. Back to the main road through town and Hey! A diner! Let's get a cup of coffee! Thumbs up from the navigator. We stop. Carry our helmets inside, sit at a vacant booth. Nice-looking woman comes over with two glasses of water. Stella says "Just two coffees, please, black." There's that vacant look again, I saw it in Arizona. Nice-looking woman's brain has gone into neutral and her mouth is saying "We don't serve coffee here." And I get up and say to the waitress, "Of course, I'm over-reacting ... but that should be illegal. Thank you, anyway." And Stella is grinning. And I'm a little irritated that these Mormons, with their jackass idea of no coffee, are allowed to advertise the word 'Diner' without saying on the same sign, 'no coffee served here because Jesus wouldn't like it.' And I say exactly that to the navigator and she completely loses it, laughing long and loudly, saying, "That's a pretty big sign. And funny, too." Back onto the scooter and we're both laughing as we put our helmets on and I say "Mormons are good people ... but only sometimes."

So off we go and in no time at all, we're surrounded by the prairie. A half-hour later, it seems as if we haven't traveled at all because there has been almost no change in the scenery, despite the fact that the scenery is moving past. In a way, it's a little creepy, as if the plainness of the plains is purposely trying to hypnotize you, to engulf, swallow and eventually digest you. Fortunately, the scooter has no such thoughts and continues on the very straight road with no deviation from a straight line directly south for fifteen miles, then a tiny bend to the east. As a habit, I continually check our rearview mirror and if a vehicle approaches from the rear, I move to the right before it passes. As if sensing the mesmerizing effect, Stella continually pets and massages and lightly pinches me here and there. And we are approaching the state line, decelerate and stop halfway across. It is break time. Time again for both of us to stretch, have a smoke, and look around at almost unbelievable continuity. Stella said that back at the café, I was a riot ... it was a perfect display of reasonable unreasonableness and she had a few questions to ask me later on in the day. I told her it was time to say goodbye to Colorado, then kissed my fingers and waved them to the north and called, "Goodbye, my friend Colorado, you gave me a Princess. My Deepest Thanks." Perhaps overly dramatic, but genuine sentiment nonetheless. Princess was crying just a little and trying to smile as I gave her a hug and we returned to our journey southward. Reached back and caught her right hand and put it around my waist and then the left hand came around without my guidance.

Now we were in Oklahoma and nothing else had changed. The prairie prevailed. This was Oklahoma's panhandle, and we were heading to Boise City, a town of 4000, almost exactly in the center of nowhere. And we had to pass a lot of grass to get there. An hour's worth of grass. It is not surprising to me that so many of the ancients thought the earth to be flat, especially looking at this terrain. But eventually we were seeing human activities called agriculture and buildings and we were entering the town and I felt a sigh of relief escape me before it could be checked. To me, and much against my will and reason, the enormity of the grassland was a weight on my shoulders.

Taking a right onto Route 385 would take me into the center of Boise City. In a minute, we were in town. Well, look at me, folks. I got us across the prairie (this teensy part of it anyway) with no problem. Let's have a cup of coffee, a smoke, ask about a motel, or whatever you want to do. She gave me a big hug. She said we need some coffee. Now there's a girl who trying to take advantage of me. So coffee it was at a 'real' café, not one of those imposter cafes the Mormons use as a lure. We sat down at a little table. When the waitress arrived, Stella said "Two coffees, please, black ... and do you have any pies with fruit?" Yes, indeed, they had peach pie and blueberry pie. Stella ordered one of each. I said, "Two pieces, eh?" She said, "We're all out of cookies, you know." I said, "Yeah, I know, and I won't see them again until I hit Chicago." Stella asked "Chicago? Have you ever been there?" I shook my head no. "And you're going there?" I nodded my head yes. "And you're not afraid?" Again, no. After a pause, she said she needed to talk with me more. Gave her the thumbs up as our order arrived. Before the waitress could leave, Stella asked which motel in town might be our best bet. And which restaurant might serve the best vegetables. That could be good information she was gathering. We drank coffee and ate about half the pie, then switched plates, drank more coffee and finished the pie. And decided that was a good system we had just invented. No real discussion, just coffee and pie, and let's get a room.

One more thing first. Need to gas up Tony. This Lambretta has been the most reliable small engine I've ever been involved with for any length of time. Long, uninterrupted miles with two people aboard and didn't miss a beat. It deserves a medal. For now, however, I'll just feed it normally. She started hand signals pointing this way. As we moved along, I pointed to a gas station, stopped, and did the refueling thing and she began with signals again. A few minutes later, we pulled up to a motel office. Stella took a good look at the license plate and then went into the office. I waited outside and lit a Marlboro. Several minutes later, from the office, she walked toward the rooms with the clerk leading the way. Extinguished the smoke and field-stripped it. Less than a minute later, she returned to the office, and came out to the scooter and said, "Follow me, White Knight." And I said, "Ma certo, Principessa." And I did. And parked at the front of the room which door she had opened. She invited me in, and I graciously accepted and walked inside. She grabbed my two ears, gave me a smooch and said that we should get all our stuff off the scooter, lock it to the lamppost and come inside for showers and recreation. For sure, I was OK with that idea. Went outside, got everything untied, got our stuff inside, locked up the Lambretta, and flopped into the chair by the window.

This was no time to relax evidently, as she began pulling at my boots, saying "Time to get clean … then, we can relax." Right. I finished taking my boots off and started dropping clothing on the way to the shower, where there were strange things from another world … multiple washcloths, towels, paper-wrapped bars of soap, even little bottles of shampoo and a stream of beautifully warm water. Together and individually we washed hair, scrubbed backs and bottoms, and feet. Time to dry off, brush teeth, and get into the bed, lightly holding one another and instantly nodding off in sleep.

Awakening only to find my wrists pinned to the bed by an overwhelming force, and a voice saying to do exactly as I was told. Protesting, I would fight every step of the way. After some indeterminate time, Stella said, "Not much of a fight, Rosano." "Well, you've weakened me, with that sleeping potion disguised as fruit aroma, rendered me limp and feeble. Alas." She laughed and said, "Such baloney … the aroma is the citrus in the soap, and limp is hardly the appropriate word right now." Meekly, I said, "Anyway, you smell delicious." And then, surprising her, I grabbed her and did fight valiantly and there was a raucous battle, in the middle of the afternoon. Shameful.

After a time, we talked quietly of many things: vegetables, rattlesnakes, lovemaking, camping, religion, music. She laughed again at my reaction to the café without coffee. I explained they did use the word diner instead of 'café.' But if they weren't in business there, someone else most likely would be … someone who had no dumb-ass idea about coffee. So Stella laughed again and asked "You don't have much regard for religion, do you?" "Before I answer, how do you feel about it?" She paused and said, "To me, it's two different things. Religion down in the swamp was frightening. There was so much hating and hell and fire and I thought those people really were evil, but I was always afraid to say anything at all. During services, I just stood there like a jerk and watched and a few people criticized me for that, but I was a girl and nobody really gave a damn one way or another about a girl child. Then later, my aunt took me to various churches in Kansas City, but they all seemed like social gatherings. At least they were peaceful and people were considerate. But I have felt no connection to God in either place. Just nothing. And you're the first person I've ever said that to."

"Thanks for that honor and I'm sincere about that. And … and congratulations and I'm sincere about that, too." She looked puzzled.

Continuing, I said, "Some people spend their entire lifespan trying to shake loose of that churchy brain clutter, and you've already achieved that. Think about you, and your attitude toward other people. You have no inclination to want to harm anybody or anything. Look at your attitude toward your cousin, or toward the Fergusons, and probably anyone else you have had dealings with. You carry no malice in your heart. Now think about this question: What if everyone, everyone in the world, had that same spirit? No malice. The world, of course, wouldn't be perfect, but it would certainly improve immensely. So, you have no need for some artificial Big Guy in the Sky. Spiritually, you're in the top 1 percent. You are at the top."

Stella looked at me directly and said, "Wow, you really believe that, don't you?" I said, "Absolutely. To me, morality has nothing to do with churches, or god, or religions. Have you ever heard of a church or one of these religious leaders saying 'Hey, you're a good person, you don't need to come here every week and put money in the basket. You might stop in once or twice a year for a get-together and maybe a little spiritual checkup. That's all you need.' No, you'll never hear that. Look, I feel lucky. Raised as a Roman Catholic, mother very devout, but my father thought the church was just a big scam. So I saw two sides of the issue from the beginning. So I was a 'holy' kid, altar boy and all that. Holy, until I began applying logic and asking questions, and at some point, maybe twelve years old, I refused to 'just have faith' in what was told to me. The church was always pushing this God thing. That's what they do. God the all-powerful, God the all-knowing, God the all-merciful, etc. But this God demanded that we love him, and love him unconditionally, and if we didn't love him well enough, this all-merciful God would really kick our asses and we could end up in an eternal barbeque pit called Hell. How's that for mercy? Well, if that isn't just the biggest load of heavenly horseshit. Man-made heavenly horseshit for the sole purpose of keeping everybody in line. So one of these days, I'll tell you how I divorced myself from the church circus. So, you're right, I have little regard for religions. I say that, but still like to go to High Mass occasionally, to enjoy all the candles, and the sometimes excellent music, all the pomp and ceremony, the great vestments, and all that murmuring and singing in Latin, as long as I don't have to hear their half-assed message in English. It's like a good magic show once or twice a year. The rest of the time would be just a colossal waste of time."

Stella said, "All of this ... it's amazing to me, it's all new to me. You're younger than I am, but you've been dealing with these things and thinking about them for a long time. And I haven't thought about much at all and I'm puzzled and thrilled at the same time. You just don't know what you've done to the inside of my head." My response was "You're right, I don't know, but I can guess. You remember a few days ago, I said that you were short-changed in your childhood, that your aunt took you away from that cruddy bunch down in the swamp. Over the few years she had with you, I suspect she was just trying to nurture you and give you the tools to start sorting out your mind and your thinking. She led you to books, where you can now explore everything. You're excellent with basic mathematics. So, while you were in Louisiana, you were not exposed to many good things which you should have been, and you probably saw a lot of not-so-good things. My guess is that you were in a cautious, defensive frame of mind, for most of that eleven years before the move to your aunt's house. And you did survive, but that's all. You really began your growing in Kansas City, but were still cautious and defensive. So now, Miss Beauchamp ... so now, it's time for you to blossom, to fill your mind, but first ... we have to fill our stomachs. What shall we do for supper?"

CHAPTER 24

BOISE BOISE

"The desk clerk said there was a good restaurant just down the street ... they always had three different vegetables for the evening meal. And we can walk." Stella was taking charge and that was good for both of us. I asked if we should get dressed or stay naked. She said we might get farther if we were dressed. So she's just starting to make jokes. Little ones, not wildly hilarious like mine (which I enjoy so much) but jokes nonetheless.

As we walked the less than half mile to the restaurant, I put my hand lightly around her waist. She told me that she liked me to touch her, that she felt strength and energy going into her as that happened. My idea was that the strength and energy were already hers and that I was just the trigger from time to time. When I said that, she looked at me and before she could say anything, I said it was good to see her growing so strongly each day, and I was glad to be a small part of it.

We sat at a small booth and looked at the menu. Tonight's special was a cube steak, potatoes, and two vegetables. What veggies were available? String beans, lima beans, corn and squash. Oh man, the jackpot! Stella thought that would be good for her. And for me as well I said.

Stella said that I had really surprised her with that top 1 percent spiritual rating. I said I had meant it. Then she asked what percent I was. I said if she got a grade of 99, an A+, then I was perhaps an 80, maybe a little higher, a B. She said that was a surprise to her also. Did I have some sort of spiritual problem? Yes, I thought so. Question on her face. Did she remember me saying I let all the little crap fly over my head, like being cut off in traffic, etc. She remembered very well. My question continued, do you also remember when I said I could get nasty sometimes? She said yes, she remembered, but didn't believe me. I said, believe me. If I feel someone has personally and deliberately done me wrong, it does not pass. I do seek revenge. Again and again until that person is defeated, not just defeated, but demolished. So that they'll never think of doing anything like that again, not to me, not to anybody. And (here's the worst part) I enjoy that revenge and yet, believe it to be a fault. So if that opportunity presents itself in my life again, I'll have to work it out. And that's my big bad confession.

We finished our meal, took a pass on desert, and headed back to our room as the sky grew dark with nightfall. We had decided to do the three R's, reading, relaxation, and recreation. I asked what might we do for recreation. Her answer: Did you forget to tie the croquet set onto the scooter? Another joke ... I hoped.

She asked what the difference was between the diamondback rattlesnake and the prairie rattlesnake. It seemed to me they were about the same in behavior, neither being super aggressive, but capable of doing a lot of damage with a strike. I explained they really didn't want to waste their venom on a human. A human was just too big to make a decent meal, so they would try to avoid getting into a fight with us. Of course, if they felt threatened ... As far as I knew they were pretty close to being the same creature and I wouldn't be surprised if they interbred where their territories overlapped. Didn't know if that would be possible, however. Way, way back, even before the cave man stage, we were, I felt, programmed by nature to avoid serpents. And of course, the snake or serpent is used by the Bible people to introduce a 'bad' thing in the Garden of Eden. Our fear of serpents came long before the snake in the Garden of Eden because our fear is ancient and that story was concocted just a few thousand years ago ... and it's just a story.

Back at our room, I asked if I should get any food out of our scooter trunk for a midnight snack. Sure, just some fruit and nuts. The salami and cheese would be better outside in the cool of nighttime. Mentioned that I should gather some firewood for the morning coffeepot. She said we had survived the prairie and now we could go for a 'continental breakfast' at 6:00 AM, where they have coffee, really Rosano, they'll have coffee. Let's have a smoke outside before we go into the room for the night. We watched our little clouds drift upward. I pointed to the North Star, saying it was hardly noticeable, especially with the light around us. Did she know how to find it? Not really, but something in the Big Dipper pointed to the Little Dipper, she thought. That's right, one of these camping nights, if the sky is clear enough, I'll show you. OK?

It had been a long day. We sat quietly on the edge of the bed. Who wants to use the bathroom first? It doesn't matter. OK, you go first. And she did. And, in time, I did also. On emerging, I found her naked and reading 'Of Mice and Men'. A beautiful sight ... the physical with an intellectual flair. Got my book and joined her. No words exchanged for quite a while. She asked "George really likes Lenny, doesn't he?" I said "Yeah, I think he more than likes him. George is not really educated, but he is Lenny's protection from society, where Lenny really can't function normally. At the same time, though, George gets pretty pissed off at Lenny. I found it helpful to read this book twice. First time, really quickly, get a feel for the whole tale, because I recognized early that each character seemed fairly complex. Then I went back to the beginning and started to examine each character more closely. Anyway, an excellent book." She said "That's for sure. What about your book?" "Oh," I said, "This is a wild one, sci-fi. About a society in the not too distant future where books are banned, and the job of firemen is not to put fires out, but to start fires and burn books. The title is the temperature at which paper is supposed to burst into flame … 'Fahrenheit 451'. Exciting story." "So," she asked, "burning the books prevents people from learning about all sorts of things." "Exactly, it helps prevent people from thinking about all sorts of things and thinking people are trouble-makers. They disrupt everybody's comfort level. Remember when we were in the library in Denver and I said something like 'This place is your freedom?' Well, I meant it. You'll find out for yourself. Now, I want you to think about something that can make life better for you, for anyone. These paperback books are so cheap and so lightweight that you should always have one with you. The train is delayed, so you can read. The car breaks down, so you can read. The doctor is running late with too many patients, so you can read. Really worth doing to have one always available." That's when she surprised me a bit. She said her aunt had stressed reading also, but had given her some rather boring 'classics' to read and they were OK but not very inviting. Would I give her a list of ten or twelve books she might enjoy and were worth reading. What a great request! Atta girl, you bet I would.

Taking the book from her hands, I told her that reading was one of humankind's finest activities, but that too much reading was probably not good for one's eyes and the only thing that can offset some of the damage is a bottom rub, so would she please roll over and that could be attended to more easily. She complied, but questioned the validity of that statement. My suggestion was that she not worry about such things and there would be a more detailed explanation soon. Bottom rubbing and reading are similar in that both can easily lead to other activities.

Early, too early in the morning, still dark, we are both suddenly wide awake. What has happened? A sound? Why do I ask "Are you OK?" She says, "Yes, are you?" Then I ask, "Did something just happen?' She say she didn't know. Strange. Get up to pee. Then just walk into the shower and half wash and half rinse and half wake up for real this time. She follows and gets into the shower with me. We trade washing backs. Dry off and flop down in bed. Rest and snuggle some. Fully awake. She asks, besides coffee, what is a Continental breakfast? I tell her depends on the place offering it. Always a hot drink like coffee and tea. Sometimes, a cold drink like milk or juice. Usually some sort of bread thing, with butter and jam available, sometimes a pastry, sometimes cereal. Why the name Continental Breakfast? Have no clue. Just meaningless marketing, I suspect. Maybe the opposite of 'Big American Breakfast.' She said let's go check it out. I said, you're hungry, you have the look of a predator on the prowl.

As we made our way the short distance to the lobby, I glanced at her several times and was stunned anew by this woman's beauty. She seemed to radiate some newfound confidence. In the room off the lobby was the Continental breakfast. Black coffee and plain toast for me. Stella had coffee, a small box of cereal, with milk. We looked at each other across the little table. I said, we have separate cups this morning, we don't have to share. She mentioned that it seemed strange and we form habits quickly. Then she said she was surprised that I didn't just grab three or four sweet rolls instead of plain toast. Yeah, but they look like they're made of butter, and when people use that much butter, it's an indication they don't know how to cook anything at all. Just my opinion. I think the Italian cookies have ruined me for any of the normal stuff. She got up and got one of the sweet rolls on a little plate. Cutting it with the edge of her fork, she took a bite and chewed and said "Yes, very heavy. How did you know?" I said they just looked as if any touch of finesse or elegance was left out of the mixture. And I couldn't explain. We talked a little of the prairie and her reaction and this town and other towns like it. Then she said, "Rosano, you said you were in no hurry to get to the East Coast, right?" I nod yes and she continued, "I want to do something different today." I give her one of those immigrant gestures that says 'Go ahead, tell me.' She said, "I want to stay right here for the day and read and talk with you. How does that sound?" I'm nodding in agreement when she adds "... and screw your brains out." And she looked at my little surprised look with a smirk and a "Well?" I said, "Ma certo! How could I refuse? Will I need anything stronger than coffee?" Without a word, she got up, walked over to me and gave me a big enthusiastic smooch and three or four other motel guests in the breakfast room applauded. This girl was really something! As we finished our Continental breakfast and took our dishes up, I reached into the breakfast bar and took four little juice cans out of the basket and stuffed them in my jacket pockets. Stella walked up to the desk and made arrangements for another day ... and no maid service, please.

Back in our room, I said, "You understand there is nothing to do in this town. Nothing. So we are our own source of entertainment." She understood. There must be 10 or 20 thousand towns like this in the US.

Each one tries to claim something unique to stand out from the rest. And advertise on the road coming into town. 'Home of the world's largest collection of Bolivian whale oil lanterns', or 'Birthplace of Olivia Bluelace, 1st runner-up Miss Pumpkin USA 1954." On the prairie, these are the towns where the highway overpass or the grain elevator becomes the most important landmark. Personally, I can't imagine living in a place like this. And yet, so many people live and prosper there. This town is not near any other city of significant size. Denver and Albuquerque are both 300 miles away, Oklahoma City is a little more than that, and Dallas, Texas, a big roaring town is 500 miles away ... a long, hard day's driving. Amarillo, TX is the nearest big deal (at 120 miles) and it's no big deal.

That's when she asked where we were headed tomorrow. I said I thought we should head toward Amarillo and stop just short of it and camp out on the prairie or close to it so that each of us could say we did that, you know, put it on our life's resume, so to speak. She said "Let's do it. But today, there are other things to do. First thing, I want to have a little more snoozing and nap with you and just hold you for a while." And we slept for another hour or more.

On wakening she said, "Today, I wanted to keep you here strictly for selfish reasons. There are a thousand questions in my mind. Ready?" Not ready, need to pee and need to brush my teeth. Then I'll be ready. OK, now. She said, "What made you decide to take this little scooter across the country?" "Well, a few different reasons, and I've asked myself that question many times: One, I was working as a waiter, doing reasonably well, but the tourist season was over and Tucson gets pretty damn quiet in the summer, so essentially my job was ending for the summer, though I was asked to stay on, it would be a lean time. Two, I was not going back to school for the foreseeable future ... just could not discipline myself to sit down and study when so much life was going on around me. I was going to Mexico, only 60 miles south, quite often, I was looking at real estate, interested deeply in the desert plants. No time for school. Three, I have the draft hanging over my head. This country has an enormous war machine. Does anyone think they're not going to use it? They have to use it, if for nothing else, to practice war, and raise their own ranks and salaries while weapon sellers rip off the taxpayer. So, with this draft, I have no idea where I'm headed. Four, I've read so much about various areas of this country, but seeing, smelling, and experiencing has to be immensely better. Five, I bought this great little scooter and have taken it to Mexico two or three times. And ... since I have to be in Connecticut at the end of June ... I thought ... why the hell not? So with almost no planning, I got on the scooter, met a beautiful creature at a laundry in Denver and fell under her spell and here we are, you and I. Not simple, not complicated either. I want to experience things before going into the service and thought I'd better do it now."

"Oh my, what if they draft you while you're in the middle of this trip?" I said, "No one can reach me while I'm traveling because no one knows where I'm going to be and that includes me, at least until the end of June. Now ... turnabout is fair play. Tell me what caused you to take this part of the journey with me?"

She paused and said nothing for perhaps two minutes, which seemed like an hour, and we remained silent. She cleared her throat and said very quietly, "Several things: One, I told you before I didn't want Broderick to know what I was up to, with my job leave of absence. He was sure to know something was up. So I wanted to be gone when he came back from his trip. Two, I didn't know what to do in the month, the interim, before the reunion. I was determined and still am determined to sever myself from those people. Honestly, I think they would be murderers by now. And I'm going to do it and I'm still working on that. And you, Rosano, you're right, you can tell it has been on my mind. Three, from the first moment you and I met, and in the few days we were together, you were always so kind, and so protective of me ... more than anybody in my entire life ... ever, ever. Always so gentle. And, Oh God help me, I just didn't want to lose you so quickly. It was tearing my heart out, Rosano, and then, then out of the blue, you said so magically and confidently, 'Come with me ... we'll be OK.' You didn't know it then, but you rescued me from a nothingness, and I love you so deeply for that. In these days together, I have always felt safe and secure with you, and in your quiet way, and with your lovely craziness, you have given me a new look at the world, and really, a new life. Did you know that? You do that to people, not just me."

And I said quietly, "Wow, I did all that? And I wasn't really working at it." Stella was crying and then crying some more and then laughing a little and her nose was running and I suppose I felt weepy because I'm a sucker for that sort of thing, except my nose, as big as it was, was OK. I went to my jacket draped over a chair, reached in a pocket, pulled out a few napkins and one of the little juice cans, opened it and offered it to her. She looked at me and at it and laughed and shook her head, and I said "What are friends for? What are jackets for?"

Do we still have time to hit the Continental Breakfast room? She said we had a half hour left. I said I could use another dose of medicinal coffee. Let's do it. Walked into the breakfast room and she said she'd bring the coffee over and she did ... only one cup. Probably had a question on my face because she said "We can share. The coffee tastes better when we share." "Princess, everything tastes better when we share. When I started this trip, I could not have imagined the good fortune of meeting and then sharing with someone like you. We have become part of one another for a reason, it seems, but we'll never know what that reason is. We are in some kind of love and that makes everything so splendid. So, I thank you." Stella leaned a little closer and said "Rosano, we are compatible." We traded sips and started another half cup as they started to close the breakfast room.

So we were having a love affair which could be described as 'torrid' by some writers. We were both aware this was an unusual love affair, felt so strongly by both, yet knowing it was temporary, with different directions and different lives to pursue. And we had agreed in advance, neither would pursue the other after we said goodbye down in Louisiana not too many days in the future. Enjoyment of each other seemed complete and unbounded and together we relished that precious time.

On the way back to the room, I visited Tony Lambretta. Unlocked and loosened the cable a bit and kickstarted the engine, again on the first try, ran it for a minute and then shut it down. Opened the trunk, took some food out, then secured the whole thing again. She asked if starting the scooter everyday was helpful. Of course it was helpful, this way the scooter doesn't feel neglected and it knows that I'm not ignoring it. They can get touchy if they feel slighted. In return, I can get a daily dose of blue exhaust smoke, which in large quantities is poisonous, but I felt if we didn't get a bit of poison each day, we would not be in tune with our environment. Laughing and shaking her head, she opened the door to our room and asked "Care to explore some compatibility?" I reminded her that she had mentioned 'turning my mind about' or something like that and I wanted more details. "No, no, no, she said, "It was 'screwing your brains out'," "Oh … my mistake." And then things got very exciting.

After a time she was whispering in my ear. "Hey, White Knight, you OK?" Quietly I said, "With those new meds and all the help from the ambulance guys, I should be better soon." Again she was quietly laughing, something so enjoyable for me. She nuzzled for another few minutes and said she wanted to read more of her book, then reminded me that I was supposed to give her a list of books. Oh, I would, I definitely would. And I asked her to remember that I urged her always to carry one with her. She nodded yes and I said there were a few others things I suggest … one was to give the book away so that someone else can use it. When you're done and you feel you are not going to reread any part of it, leave the book wherever you are … the dentist's waiting room, on the bus, at the laundry … someone will get it and maybe read it and in that way, you've improved their life. Maybe it's the janitor, maybe the bus driver, maybe a tired businessman in an airport ... it doesn't matter. Right now you're reading "Of Mice and Men." Imagine just finding it on the city bus or the subway. Wouldn't you be curious? Wouldn't just the title get your interest and then you'd see the author's name and hey, you've heard that name. Now ... if there were a note inside saying 'great book, read it, and pass it on." Well, you see what I mean.

After reading quietly for more than an hour, I got up, took a mess kit out of our stuff, washed and prepared a variety of snacks. Weather was warming up, and evening temperatures were no longer close to freezing. I thought I'd have to change my portable meat selection from salami to jerky. And that wasn't as optional as it appeared. There was little likelihood I could find a decent hard salami or good hard cheese in all of western Oklahoma or east Texas. It just wasn't in the everyday experience of the prairie dwellers. In addition, jerky needed no refrigeration at all. My meat consumption was small, but I felt the calories and proteins were beneficial and it would require a wagonload of veggies to equal a small chunk of meat. A year or two before I had read a novel entitled 'Pemmican' by an author named Fisher (whose name seemed perfectly inappropriate for the title of the book. Pemmican was dried meat prepared by various Indian tribes). Each time I thought about jerky, I would think of this book and also think of the Mexican dish 'carne seca', another semi-dried meat preparation. Certainly, many calories were also available in the almonds, pecans, and pistachio nuts, all of which I carried continuously. The nuts and the meats were all high-energy, lightweight foods perfect for a scooter journey.

We munched on food snacks and talked of various things as we sat in bed. I asked if she remembered hearing or knowing anything about WWII, since I remembered quite a few isolated pieces of information, that war having ended when I turned 5 years of age. She recalled almost nothing except a few men showed up in uniform in her area and they were there because some war ended, and that was all. With Stella being about 4 years older than I, that would put her at nine or ten years old when WWII ended, meaning she had been totally oblivious to that enormous international conflict. Later she learned who the Nazis were and where the war in the Pacific was and eventually learned of Japanese surrender after the A-Bomb. She knew a few things about President Truman, but had learned them from her Kansas City aunt who was proud that Truman also came from Missouri ... Independence, Missouri. So Stella had had a rather empty childhood. For me, who had been exposed to so much as a kid, it was difficult to imagine a vacant upbringing. But now, this beautiful and kind woman was just beginning to get involved with the world. A pleasure to witness her joy of discovery and be a small part in it!

Mid-afternoon and I need either a cup of coffee or some snooze time. Let's do a little snoozing, Princess. OK? Without saying a word, she snuggled alongside. There is something intrinsically marvelous about two naked people sleeping and holding each other ... a feeling of contentment and oneness. Stella seemed always to press lightly against me and gently pull my arms around her even while deeply asleep. My guess was she still sought protection of a kind. I just enjoyed holding and touching a beautiful naked woman, and a huge bonus was enjoying her companionship and the sharing of everything on our journey toward New Orleans. This beautiful love affair would end there and she would be missed so intensely. Tomorrow we would be back on the prairie heading toward Amarillo, Texas. For now at least, there was nothing better than holding my friend as we slept.

We began stirring and noticed the light around the curtains lessening. As the day moved toward evening, we showered once more in preparation for another visit to the restaurant. On the way, I said to the scooter, "I know you feel neglected, but tomorrow you'll be busy again, and did you notice what I've got with me. Isn't she something? And tomorrow you'll get to feel her butt on your back again. Promisso!" Stella was pretending outrage and then she laughed and said, "pro-ME-so?" "That means 'I promise'." She chuckled and said, "Let me get this straight. You promised your buddy here, that he could feel my butt tomorrow and you didn't ask my permission? Is that right?" I said that was true, and it sounded pretty bad, but I was still working on my social skills. Give a guy a break!

Outside the restaurant, a newspaper rack showed headlines saying Tornados: Eastern OK, Arkansas, Red River. Whoa! I fed the coin slot, but the rack wouldn't unlatch, so no newspaper. We'll ask the waitress. And we did. She said it was that time of year again and those damn tornados were unpredictable. Just keep an eye on the sky and if you see one drive sideways to its path if you could, that is, if you could tell which way the damn thing was traveling. If you thought you couldn't avoid it, the best thing was to find a depression in the earth's surface, like a drainage ditch or a real low spot and lie down and protect your face and head and hope for the best. Wow. I'd never been in one. The closest I had ever been was 100 miles away when they had a big one in Worcester, Mass if you can believe that. The sky looked very peculiar in Connecticut that afternoon, but we had no idea a tornado was raging a hundred miles north of us in Massachusetts. Tornados? They were 'out west somewhere. Of course, that's New England thinking, but here we actually were "out west somewhere.' And there were tornados about. I asked the waitress if she had ever been in one. She said hurricanes, yes, but tornados, no. But they're the same thing, except one is wetter. She was from South Carolina and had been here in Oklahoma only a year. We ordered our meals and talked about what we might do. My thought was to continue as we had been doing, keep our eyes open and if we did get trapped in the open by one of these tornados, we would quickly search out a low place, lay the scooter down on its side, keep our helmets on and stick our heads in the area between the front wheel and the engine and hopefully gain some protection that way, and wait for it to pass over. These things were so incredibly fierce and so completely destructive to any human activity. Maybe you could get your family into an underground shelter, but your livestock, your crops, buildings, etc. could all be devastated in a minute or two. Frightening, and yet, here we go, traveling through one or another of the tornado alleys during 'the season' with a minimum of thought and no protection at all. Tomorrow we would be on the road crossing some monotonous terrain, and would have plenty of opportunity to keep an eye on the sky.

    We were working our way through a decent meal, pretty ordinary food, but nutritious would be my guess. Almost finished, I asked Stella if she wanted any dessert. No, not tonight. How was your meal, Princess? She said it was OK, not exciting, but OK. I said, "exactly." You see why I always try to eat Italian? How did this meal compare to what we ate at Gemelli's? Or Enrico's? She said, "No comparison, none at all. Why is that?" I said, "It's the difference between a domestic chore and an art form. We just ate a domestic chore because we needed it. This is decent food that will keep us in reasonable shape, but there is no spark, no pizzazz, or originality. There was little or no art in the food we just finished." Stella then said, "That I understand and agree with, but why just the Italians?" My reply went something like this: "But it's not just the Italians, there are others. The Greeks have some splendid dishes. Some of the Mexican foods and Cuban dishes are truly splendid, the cooks from India have great foods with excellent spices, the Chinese have some excellent dishes. Maybe your question is really this question: 'Why haven't others copied, stolen, or borrowed those good food ideas?' And that's my question, too. It just baffles me. I cannot understand why this restaurant and thousands of others put out millions of so-so, boring meals every day. I know people running these places and working in these places have been exposed to food with personality. An Italian will fry an egg and it will be a tiny masterpiece, maybe with a few basil flakes or rosemary, a touch of salt and pepper. A Midwesterner will fry an egg and think he's done a great flavoring job if he uses bacon grease instead of lard to fry it. The Brits, who have put enormous efforts into exploring all the world's lands and cultures, and who are so admirable in so many ways, are just dreadful with food.

How could they not borrow more ideas from their colonies in Asia, Africa, the Caribbean? Except maybe, just maybe, ... tradition ... the sort of thinking that says 'my mother made especially awful porridge and so will I.' It baffles me." We finished our ordinary, ho-hum meal and walked back toward our room. As we passed by, I patted the Lambretta on the seat, and said "See you in the morning, my friend."

Back in the room, we relaxed, did some reading and finished our books almost simultaneously. Stella had some questions about 'Of Mice and Men', questions about my book, "Fahrenheit 451", and another question about Italian food. I said that was enough questioning for the moment, that it was time for dessert. She asked what did I bring for dessert? I answered, "You, I brought you. You are dessert."

CHAPTER 25

TEXAS PANHANDLE

We enjoyed dessert, then washed, and slept. A peaceful night. Touching and resting. Waking as the sun rose, I say "Good morning, Princess. Shall I start the coffeepot fire?" She said sleepily, "Go ahead, and I'll just call the fire department now." We got out of bed, got dressed, and made our way down to the Continental Breakfast area for that first cup of coffee, always welcome. As we drank, she said she liked my coffee better. So did I, but this was certainly more convenient. With our second rounds of coffee, we ate a few little goodies. Relaxed, had a smoke, talked very little. With hardly a word, we walked back to the room. A beautiful morning was in bloom. She asked, "Back to the prairie?" I nodded yes, "... but we should stop at a grocer's first. Pick up a few items. We'll stop just north of Amarillo and there's not much going on between here and there. We'll camp on the prairie somewhere, so we have to be sure of food, fuel, and water. Fuel is OK, let's refresh our water again this morning, and as we pack, we take a mental inventory of our food. When we take a motel room, we get out of the habit of checking everything. So, let's be thorough in our packing, and we'll hit the breakfast room again on our way out. Then the grocer, then the prairie. OK with you, Princess?" She smiled. There's that eye-opening smile. She said, "Don't forget your lance and your sword, Oh White Knight!" As we packed, I scrutinized our food supplies, to ensure against any spoilage being consumed. Tossed away a few small amounts. The nuts and dried fruits were always OK. We'd get a few canned veggies, some jerky, a three or four ounce piece of cheese, maybe some bread, maybe some Fig Newtons. Weather was warming and it was best to be more cautious. Carefully we got everything packed and ready to tie to the scooter. We'd leave everything in the room, visit the breakfast room again, drink some more coffee, then return here for last bathroom break, tooth brushing, etc. and then back on the road. Get back into the swing of things. Again, we shared a cup of coffee, again I took a couple of juices. Stella talked to the desk guy before we returned to the room. A half-hour later, everything was tied in place on the scooter, we vacated the room, and we were headed east to pick up route 287 southeast to Texas. Two days in Boise City had been good for the two of us. Now we'd check a grocer first. Small market, but they did have some smoked jerky, probably not the best thing for us, but probably peppery and tasty. Got two cans of veggies and a can of black olives. They had Fig Newtons, but stale and rather hard. Instead, we bought some crackers and a small jar of plum jam, though I preferred not buying anything in glass jars, just too fragile. So it had to been packed safely. We were set. It required almost three minutes to reach 'out of town' which meant we were back on the prairie heading southeast and would leave Oklahoma and enter Texas in an hour or a little more.

Absolutely beautiful morning, not hot yet. My passenger playing little games on my back. Occasionally she would reach up and hold my earlobe, or gently pull on my beard, always slowly though, so as not to startle me. The scene was almost a continuous picture. We were in a grassland that had a name though there was no difference between the nameless area and the area which had a name. A light breeze was moving the grass and provided some visual action. An occasional vehicle would pass or approach us, sometimes throwing up a pebble. I had instructed Stella to duck behind me whenever a vehicle was encountered. The windshield protected me to a great extent, and I guessed she might be more vulnerable to debris thrown up by vehicles. To our right, just west of us, was a railroad track as little as fifty feet away, but most of the time farther than that. Occasionally, a small dirt track would lead off the road to some unknown spot, probably a water catchment or loading facility for cattle. Close to an hour of traveling and my passenger had her arms lightly around my chest, then slowly rubbing my tummy and then upward and gently she pinched my nipples and I had to laugh from the helplessness of my position. I just gave her a finger-wagging no-no signal, and she stopped and resumed more benign activity. But it was quietly zany, surprising, and to me, genuinely funny. Not long after that we crossed from Oklahoma into Texas with only a highway sign telling us of the occasion. Another sign announced that we were 14 miles from Stratford, Texas. I didn't recall ever having heard of it, but it seemed a good place to take a little break, especially if they had a real live tree. Maybe that's the thing most troubling about the prairie ... the lack of trees. What's worse is the lack of trees in some of the small towns of the prairie. People settled there, maybe even fought and died for that land, but to not plant trees seemed backward to me. That situation is not the usual. Most of the little towns have at least a small park, perhaps with a baseball diamond and a grove or two of trees. When a town has none of these, I judge it to be a depressed place and am really not interested in seeing the town nor meeting any of the inhabitants. That's being close-minded for sure, but I'm allowed my prejudices. Trees seem as precious on the prairie as they do in my desert. Perhaps I'm missing something or don't understand something important. We putt-putted into Stratford, Texas. Stella gave hand signals which sent us eastward for a short distance. She had spotted the tree tops of a small park where we would take a break.

Stretching and groaning a bit, we removed our helmets ... always a relief. We had a sip or two of water. Four or five juice containers in my jacket were starting to weigh on me. We each drank one. I told Stella I really appreciated her keeping the monotony of the scenery at bay with her petting and rubbing. I thought we might try letting her drive the next leg of the journey so that I might have a chance to seek out her pinchable parts. She just chuckled quietly and said there might be a chance later. Neither of us wanted a meal just then. We just needed a little rest, maybe a small snack. Let's get horizontal on the picnic table benches for a few minutes. Maybe this town has a café where we can have a coffee and use the restroom ... that is, if the Mormons haven't taken control of the place. Stella laughed and said, "You're never going to forgive them, are you?" I said "Hell, no. They'll have to meet their maker someday and explain why they're so stupid about coffee. And I'd like to see them point to their bible and read God's words and passages about coffee, or even decaf, those jerks." Stella became totally unglued with laughing. Finally, she said, "Rosano, you are so reasonably unreasonable and I know I've said that before, but that's one reason why I love being with you so much, so very much." "Hey Princess, you have filled my heart with good things, and it feels absolutely perfect to be with you, but most of all, I enjoy the way you laugh at my jokes. Almost no one else does." We rested ten or fifteen minutes and had the last two Marlboros.

Back onto Tony Lambretta's back. Within five minutes, we had a diner and a convenience market in sight. Let's do the convenience market first. Into the market, we bought a pack of Viceroys and a quart of orange juice. Carefully packed the juice into the trunk, stashed the smokes in my jacket and headed to the café just a stone's toss away. And, surprise! ... there was coffee ... imagine! We ordered coffees and two pieces of pie. Took turns in the restroom. Sat down and began our snack. As was the habit we had developed, each ate half of the pie serving and then switched plates. Before we started, I urged her to really pay attention to the pie, all aspects of it. As we ate pie, she asked me what I thought about during a long, relatively boring stretch of road. It varies ... sometimes about the book I'm reading, sometimes about places already visited, lately I've thought of you and your life and how vastly different from mine, sometimes I just do little math problems in my head, and sometimes I play word games, which is what I want you to try this afternoon after we finish here. Let me explain: I want you to think about 'collective nouns'. Do you know what they are? She hesitated and I said "a word for a group of animals like a 'herd' of cattle or" … She interrupted me saying "… or a school of fish or a pride of lions? You want me to think about those?" I answered, "In a way, yes, but not exactly. When we're purring across prairie, we need to be more creative than that. So, here's what I'm going to be doing: This question popped into my head: 'What if we named groups of people, not based on their hair color … like blondes or brunettes, or their heights …like six-footers and shorties, but based on their occupations or activities?' Here's a few I thought of this morning: A buzz of scooterists (which started this minor insanity), a beaker of chemists, a spark of welders. Got the idea?" Stella said "Yes, I do. What a great idea! No wonder I think you're crazy. But I'll work on this project this afternoon, as long as I can keep twiddling you this afternoon as we drive."

We finished our pie and coffee, revisited the restroom, paid our bill and were back on Route 287 heading southeast toward Amarillo. The plan was to stop short of Amarillo, camp the night on the prairie, and then go into town. That meant about 75 miles of prairie this afternoon. Amarillo was the biggest town in the Texas Panhandle at over 100,000 people. We would take a break about halfway there, maybe in Dumas, Texas. Stella continued her 'twiddlings' as she called them, rubbing on my back, or my neck, while I drove and enjoyed the little attentions.

In a matter of minutes, most of the agricultural marks on the terrain were behind us. This was prairie again, again with few trees, most of them planted by human hand I suspect. We had a light breeze crossing our path, but more behind than toward us so it was a slight assist. A strong breeze is OK when steady, but if too changeable, it first becomes a nuisance and then a danger. But we were just fine in sunshine and the breeze. Landmarks were man-made … a windmill, a water tank, sometimes a fence or little road going off somewhere. Something triggered the word 'pampas' in my mind. I knew of Pampas Grass, a feathery grass landscaping accent, used in Tucson and Phoenix and elsewhere I'm sure. Was 'pampas' the word for the plains in Paraguay or Argentina? And was that the same as the 'steppes' in Russia and Asia or the 'savannah' in Africa? Did the Australians have a word for it? The word 'outback' wasn't quite the same, or was it? Have to research that. I say that to myself, knowing I'll research a tenth of what I intend. My impression was that they all shared this wide, extended, enormity of grass, into which one could disappear leaving no trace whatsoever. This was 'Twilight Zone' stuff. Pulling my thinking back into normalcy, was a little hug from my pretty passenger and a sign which said 'Dumas 5 miles.'

Route 287 was the main street through this nice little town, population about 12,000. The town was neat and seemed more prosperous than many of these places. It was 50 miles north of Amarillo, so maybe some money spilled over. In recesses of my mind, words scrolled through saying Dumas, Dumas, how do I know Dumas? Was there a movie star with that name? A major league ballplayer? Then came the clarification. A popular song when I was a kid was "I'm A Ding Dong Daddy from Dumas (and You Ought to See Me Do My Stuff)." Fairly catchy rhythm and tune. So this is what triggered it? Just as I was recalling this, a signal came from the caboose saying turn left. And we did. And there was a little park with trees. Break time.

Again, off with the helmets, and stretch our bodies, drink some water. I ask Stella if she still wants to camp on the prairie or get closer to Amarillo and find a formal campground or at least a small pond or lake, or a decent sized tree. She said to follow our plan and do the prairie thing at least once. That's OK with me ... but I am going to refuel the scooter before it's actually needed and I'm not sure why. Do we want to eat anything now? No, the pie at the last place filled us and we're OK. Let's just rest. We do a little walking since we spend so much time sitting on the scooter. I ask if she has worked on the collective nouns. As a matter of fact she has. Do I want to hear some? No, save them for tonight in the tent. As we walk around the little park, the breeze continues its steady push. The sun is warm. The shade of the trees is welcome. I do a few deep knee bends and just stretch and try to regain flexibility. There's no rush, so let's have a smoke. OK. Lighting up, we talk of various things, and she asks what is the bravest thing I've ever done. Was it this trip? No, not even close. I'll tell you tonight. Put the smokes out then tossed the butts into the trash. Trash cans in parks always seem to be painted green. Did some national committee agree on that color?

Back on the scooter, into a gas station, refuel the scooter and refill the water bag. We'll drive southeast for about forty miles and look for a camping spot on the prairie. Leaving Dumas and going south puts one on the plainest plains imaginable. Flat or very gently rolling terrain, an almost flat constant color of tan. The highway itself is a visual relief. This land is so hugely far-flung that the enormous openness seems paradoxically confining ... as if to say there's no running away because there's nothing to run to. Stella continued her little touches and pettings, all of which were appreciated. If I wanted to be honest, I would have opted to forgo the camping on the prairie thing and driven into Amarillo to a campground or lake or reservoir. But we're going to endure, no we would enjoy, this prairie thing tonight. The highway crossed a riverbed and the sign announced

'Canadian River'. This was the kind of river I was now accustomed to seeing in Southern Arizona ... it didn't have any water flowing, although there was some greenery associated with the edges of the riverbed. I would normally choose a spot like that for camping but felt, at least for tonight, that to do so would be cheating a little. Another ten miles would put us about ten miles north of Amarillo. Reducing our speed a bit, the hunt was on for a suitable earth depression in which to camp. In twenty or thirty minutes, I pulled off the highway onto a small dirt road and followed it for about a mile. There was a lot of land and no problem finding a flat spot for the tent. My guess was that we could not be seen from the highway due to the slight rolling nature of the terrain. Of course, this was not 'untouched' prairie, if for no other evidence, the dirt road itself spoke to that.

Stopped the scooter and before we dismounted, I warned Stella to look where she was going to walk, always. If you want to look at the sky, first stop, then look. We then dismounted from Tony Lambretta, that faithful, untiring servant. There were a dozen or more iron stakes in a row almost six feet in height and twelve feet apart. Might that have been a fence years ago, but why so tall? Asked Stella to hang on and balance the scooter while I cleared the grass from around one pole. Using the machete, I trimmed the grass closely, while not hitting the earth with the machete, to the point where I could see the ground easily. Then moved the scooter to the cleared area and tied it upright to the pole. Changed into my camping pants and then, in ten minutes, I cropped a generous area of grass to the same shortness for our tent location between two of the rusted iron poles. Tied the tent tabs to help the tent stay upright in the strong breeze. No tarp tonight, very little chance of rain. There was no wood to be had for a coffeepot fire. The grass trimmings had all been saved, most likely sufficient to keep a fire going long enough for two cups of water. It was the wind which prevented starting of a fire, which could get away from us in an instant. So ... no coffee this afternoon. We'd have some juice or water. No wood or rocks for a makeshift toilet seat either. I'd just scoop out a hole in the dirt and it was squat time. The latrine area also had to be cleared enough to see any critters. Here we were, with perhaps two or more hours of daylight left. The tent opening had been aimed to the east, putting the wind at our backs if we sat on the front flap. Stella had put our things in the tent. The flashlight could be important if we needed to do toilet stuff during the night. This was the prairie. I wondered how much of it remained as prairie and not yet been converted to farmland.

When the latrine was dug, it was obvious that there was much organic material, rootlets and such, as part of the soil. Maybe being too careful, I thought if we actually got a little fire going in a shallow pit, it might be very difficult to insure the fire was extinguished once we were done. I have seen fire travel underground and emerge elsewhere. Just not worth the risk. So ... no coffee in the morning either. This was quickly turning into a treacherous survival situation ... no coffee. Decided to experiment with coffee ... cold coffee ... making it cold and drinking it cold. Got the coffeepot, put in two cups of water from the water bag, then added a normal amount of ground coffee and then 10% more to compensate for lack of temperature. After a good stirring it would be left overnight and we would try drinking it in the morning. Was I so desperate? Absolutely, the genetic mutants among us ... those who do not use coffee ... do not understand that the same substance which makes us smarter and more alert than average people, does have a drawback ... and in medical and technical literature is called 'caffeine withdrawal headache of monstrous proportions.' So, yes, I would try to drink cold coffee in the morning.

    Stella said it was time for a bite to eat. Something in the line of veggies, or ... how about the can of asparagus. That we did and added a little stick of jerky to our menu. Survival food, but reasonably healthy and somewhat tasty. We talked about the pie we had eaten earlier. I asked her opinion. She felt they were OK, but just OK, and too heavy on the sugar or syrup or whatever they used. The main taste was sweetness, not necessarily the fruit. What did she think of the bread part ... the crust. Very heavy on the butter or lard, almost waterproof. Then I pointed out the main difference between those pies and cookies we had enjoyed for those days. Remember the Italian cookies in the laundromat? She smiled and said what a surprise they were ... lightly delightful. So I asked if she remembered my rant about people not even having the sense to imitate good cooking and differences between cooking as a domestic chore and cooking as an art form. Yes, she remembered it very well, and while she had to laugh a bit at my ranting, I, in fact, seemed to make sense. Did she remember asking why Italian cooking was so popular? I thought about that during part of our drive down here. Why so popular? First and most important, even the simplest of their dishes are delicious, there is enjoyment in the eating, in the chewing and tasting, not just something to keep you going. Second ... Almost always, there's a certain spontaneity in the creation of a meal. Leftovers are turned into an exploration experience. Italians use a wide variety of ingredients and all are of excellent quality and that variety makes for good health. Third ... All those things combined with the willingness to break all the rules at the drop of a hat, make the cook a creator, not just a preparer or processing agent, but an innovator. Do you remember what we had to eat in Pueblo at Enrico's place? Sure, you remember, and you will for a long time. How long will it be before you forget last night's meal? Almost immediately. And there is the difference, you see? Now, instead of those wonderful cookies, all we have for desert is crackers and what looks like it might be pretty good plum jam. Pretty basic, but we're into a survival camping mode, right? Shall we try some?

We ate crackers with plum jam applied in small amounts and enjoyed this very basic snack with sips of water. I had poured a cup of water and rested it on the tent flap between us and the surface of the water soon had a light coating of dust and a few plant parts. It was the steady wind which carried this almost microscopic debris into our cup and everywhere else, too. This breeze had continued all day. Not gusty, but steady, and now becoming a little annoying. Stella asked why I had chosen that jam instead of another. My answer was that the amount of fruit was higher than in the other brands available. That is, if the label was accurate and sometimes I questioned that. She then said my comparison between Enrico's food a few days ago and last night's meal was true, but she had a question ... how did all this get started?

Good question! There was a theory I had read a few years back. Written by a Spanish, Swedish, or Swiss historian ... can't remember ... it seemed to explain the popularity of Italian cooking. Just a theory and it went something like this: Around 750 BC, small groups of Latins, were living on hilltops where Rome is now located. Hilltops offered some protection from attackers. The groups banded together to farm the Tiber River valley where soil was richer and cooperated in some manner of mutual defense. As any community gained in wealth, such as having a surplus of food, or large herds of animals, it became a more attractive target for marauders. For this community to grow itself, for protection reasons, it started taking in more stray travelers ... stranded seamen, refugees from Greek city-states, outcasts of various sorts from various places ... taking them in, rather than chasing them away. Looking at a map of the Mediterranean, one sees that the Italian peninsula (along with the island of Sicily), sticks out into the middle and would be accessible, either by plan or accident, to any group at sea. As Rome grew and conquered its neighbors, the Romans made a habit of taking the talented persons from the conquered groups or tribes and sending them back to Rome, whether they were craftsmen, poets, scribes, engineers, accountants, etc., accomplishing several goals simultaneously ... depriving the conquered group of potential leadership, augmenting talent available in Rome itself, and bringing into the Roman experience, new ideas, new arts, different methods for doing the community's work, new genes, and all those, in turn, fostered innovation and all that goes with it. Over the centuries, through triumph and defeat, that willingness to absorb foreign influence and try an untried path, became part of the genetic fabric of what is now Italy.

You can see it in everyday life. Where there are two clearly defined lines of auto traffic laid out on an Italian street, the Italians will make five lanes of traffic out of it. And if the sidewalk isn't too crowded they'll drive on it, too. That creativity and sense of individualistic style make them almost ungovernable. And it shows up in everything, but especially in their cooking. There are, in the Italian cooking repertoire, many traditional foods, which Italians regard only as suggestions, not rules. That imagination, that creativity, combined with an enormous variety of available ingredients, helped make Italian food one of the world's favored cuisines. How accurate is that theory? Who can really be the judge of that? I'll tell you who ... the world is the judge of that.

You know what? This wind is irritating. I'm going to pee, brush my teeth, wash my face because it feels so dusty and get inside that tent. I know it's not quite dark yet, but the wind just tires me out. She said she'd do the same, and in the same order. And that's what happened. We got ourselves situated inside the tent, on top of the sleeping bag. Did some hugging and rubbing. Noise of the wind against the sides of the tent, while not very loud, would prevent us from hearing anything outside the tent. Didn't care for that situation, but there was little to be done about that problem. Imagine hearing wind non-stop for days and days. On the prairie, especially up in more northern states, the wind would continue for weeks, an enormous stress on everyone. I heard that in September, the US Air Force adds extra psychologists to their staff at Ellsworth Air Force Base in South Dakota to help counteract effects of the cold prairie wind for all the winter months. They are there to tend to the mental health of personnel stationed there. Here, the mild wind had done its thing, and in only a dozen hours, had already aggravated me. Geez, what a wimp!

Hey, Princess! I've got a great idea! With the two of us in the tent, it stays pretty warm, so ... I think we should get naked and then you can tell me the results of our word game. It's just much easier to hear if our clothing isn't absorbing the sound of our voices. Right? What? What?

Stella said, "At first, of course, I thought you were truly coo-coo. Then, as we buzzed along, ideas started forming, and then after a while, I couldn't stop. Ready for my contributions?" "Ready? You bet. I'll file them away in a back closets of my brain and someday, I might even put them in a book." She started. "OK ... a brief of lawyers, a sweep of janitors," ... and pausing for effect between each new revelation, she continued, "... a field of farmers, a crock of cooks, a ream of writers, a cracking of chiropractors, a prod of proctologists, a leap of gymnasts, a swarm of beekeepers, a palette of painters. So ... that's ten and I'm working on more. How's that for starters?" "Actually, I'm pleasantly surprised. You have some good ones ...

I particularly like the 'sweep of janitors', 'field of farmers', a 'ream of writers,' and 'leap of gymnasts', where they seem so natural. You see, now you might actually be creating little parts of our language."

We talked of this and that as darkness completed its takeover of the sky. This day had tired me more than normally. Unceasing wind probably made a huge difference though I would hesitate to admit such. I told my dear friend to hand me the flashlight, that I wanted to go outside to pee and asked if she'd like to join me. She laughed, saying, "Are you asking me out tonight?" Answering, I said "Yes, but don't dress up, it's rather informal." She returned the banter saying, "Well, that sounds good, I won't have to wash my hair." "No," I said, "not if you're careful when you pee." We were both giggling as I crawled out of the little tent into the darkness. Leading with the flashlight gave me a view of a medium-sized snake eight or ten feet from the tent. Big sigh of relief. Not a rattler. Standing up then, I told Stella there was a snake, but non-poisonous so don't be frightened and it was OK to come outside. The snake stayed where it was and seemed not to be disturbed at our movements or the flashlight. Anyway, it was probably a healthy reminder to stay alert. We took turns holding the flashlight and emptying our bladders before crawling back into our tent. Stella had tied the netting closed and had to untie it to return inside and I complimented her on that precaution. The inconsiderate wind never paused long enough for us to pee peacefully. Back inside our protective shell, and ready for a little snooze, we undressed and lay down, me with my arms around her. "Well, how was your day?" I asked. She said today was really different than any other, that any day with me was different than any other and that today was the first time she had ever peed with two sets of eyes watching. I told her there might have been more than two sets, but mine weren't part of the crowd because I wasn't watching … I was only listening. That earned a little chuckle. I thought it warranted more than that, but comedy is a tough game.

CHAPTER 26

AMARILLO

There were three or four hours of sleep, disturbed by wind sweeping across the tent fabric. Had to go through the pee routine again, first putting shoes on to walk outside naked into the cool breeze. The snake wasn't attending the event this time and we returned to our shelter for more rest, both of us more fatigued than expected from the previous day. First, another small juice container to share, and then back to embracing and half-sleep until first light, that initial lighting in the sky before dawn. We were semi-awake, but it was just too damn early to get up. We continued snuggling and quiet resting until full daylight was available. We had camped out one night in the middle of the prairie, in a manner of speaking, and had survived. In comparison to the covered wagon travelers, we were indeed wimps. Neither of us had rested well, but we were OK. My teeth needed brushing badly and taking a leak was taking precedence over any other thoughts. And of course, there was the experimental cold coffee waiting for us. So, we'll start the day. A bit groggily, and we agreed that for the two of us, there was a feeling of being lightly coated with fine grit and dust.

Going outside after being inside the tent for several hours was a little like being born again, not in the religious sense, but in the physical. Even the tent opening had its resemblances. Now standing in the cool morning breeze seemed a refreshing change to a small degree. The breeze was much gentler, a great improvement. 'Don't piss into the wind' the saying goes, and I didn't. Taking sips from our water bag, I brushed my teeth, twice. Stella was doing the same sort of morning maintenance with me waiting for the appropriate moment, I asked "Coffee, miss?" She almost winced, but managed a smile and a gracious nod. I poured, and offered her the cup. Gently she pushed it back with "After you, kind sir." I bowed slightly and then sipped the experimental non-fired coffee, which had had more than twelve hours to 'settle.' It wasn't very good, but neither was it very bad. Except for the expected temperature, it actually was a tolerable cup of coffee. I deemed the experiment a success, if not a roaring success, at least a strong positive and certainly not a failure. In an emergency, and adding yet another ten percent ground coffee, I would certainly repeat the process, and expressed my opinion. Stella, gathering her courage, also drank from the cup, paused, and agreed with my opinion. Some of us are born leaders.

Giving Stella a big dusty hug, and looking over her shoulder, I noticed the image of the scooter looked peculiar. A step or two closer and I could clearly see a large snake, with a color matching the landscape, and this one was indeed a rattler coiled under the scooter near the kickstand. Holding Stella firmly, I described the situation. I told her to carefully move toward the tent, reach inside, retrieve the machete, and give it to me, while I kept my eye on the snake. Having dealt with rattlers in Tucson, there was no big fear, but certainly a healthy respect. My intent was to just drive this creature away, but there were no qualms about killing it, if it headed in what I thought was the wrong direction, that is, toward the tent. I told Stella to stay behind me, but slightly off to one side, so she could be aware of what was happening. I approached the snake, stomping the ground as I got nearer. There was its rattling warning, rather loud, and a movement of its coiled position. I stomped a few more times. Slowly it began to uncoil and move away from me. I watched for perhaps two minutes as it continued in what it felt might be safer direction. The stomping probably warned the serpent 'too big to eat, best move away'. And so the two humans would pack up camp and give up claim to that patch of ground. Drank more of the cold coffee, then poured the little remaining out onto the ground. Needless to say, we went about our business very cautiously. Double checked the scooter before I started tying anything to it. After a while, we were 'good to go' and with a kick and a little puff of blue smoke, we were on our way ... very slowly along the dirt road, then back onto highway 287. We were within ten miles of Amarillo. In a short time, the prairie was receding as we cruised into town.

Princess and I had agreed that the first thing we would do would be to have some breakfast with a bathtub full of hot coffee. She gave me a hand signal directing us to a restaurant which had a sign out front announcing "open for breakfast" with a neatly trimmed green hedge lining the path to the front door. I locked up Tony and the helmets (that could be the name of a singing group – Tony and the Helmets). We dusted ourselves off as best we could and allowed the green hedge to guide us to the entrance. We were seated at a corner table with comfortable, upholstered chairs. Luxury unlimited. When the waitress returned with menus, Stella asked if we could just have two black coffees for starters and we would order in a few minutes if that was OK. The waitress looked at us and said "Absolutely no problem." I'll bring your coffee now."

We sipped coffee for a minute or two before I exchanged our cups and said coffee always tasted better when it had a tiny touch of Stella with it. A few more sips and she asked "Well, that was the prairie. So, what do you think?" I said, "About what I expected, and to tell the truth, I've enjoyed as much of this prairie as I can stand." It's not so bad if there's a tree or river or something other than just grass. That 'amber waves of grain' thing is much overrated. She laughed and said, "You're tired and I am, too. We'll have breakfast and see what that does for us. Not much sleep with all that wind." We drank coffee, used the restroom, ordered breakfasts, ate slowly, used the restrooms again, and had more coffee along with a welcome Viceroy. Stella took care of the bill and as we left the restaurant asked "OK White Knight, what next." I didn't want to try to do anything enlightening or entertaining at the moment. "How about if we go back up the street to the coin-op laundry we just passed and get our clothes clean?" That would take an hour or more and in the meantime we could decide what to do this morning. That sounded reasonable and clean clothes sounded inviting.

North about a half mile and we were in front of a do-it-yourself coin-operated laundry. We had met in a similar place and I felt surely it was on our minds as we began to go through clothing. I leaned over and gave her a little kiss and she returned it and raised the stakes a notch. Same procedure as a week or so before, went into the restroom, removed my underwear and socks, and tossed them into the machine. Then I started to empty the jacket and went through that exercise once again, filling one of the plastic seated chairs. Got everything into the machine, she put the detergent in and fed some coins into the slot and started the washer. We sat down. Stella looked at my pile of stuff on the chair, chuckled, and said, "This is where you take out the little sack of drugged cookies, right?" Snapped my fingers, "Damn, I forgot about that. How about if I just kiss your butt ten or twelve times?" She yelped, choked a bit, and whirled around to see if anyone else was near. I said, "Careful, careful, you can hurt your neck doing that." She laughed more and more as I said "What, what?" After a decent time interval, she said, "Always a little surprise with Rosano." Another little interval and she said "And besides, you owe me a story."

What story? She said she had asked me the bravest thing I had ever done. Having thought about that since she had asked a day or two ago, my answer went something like this. I didn't know the bravest thing I had ever done, but I knew when I had been the most scared. It had to do with the Catholic Church and all that God and Jesus stuff, all of which I fervently believed for a time as a child, but which I began to question starting at age 7 approximately. That's when I starting seeing inconsistencies in the teachings. The doubts were not reduced by a priest saying "One must believe, one must have faith." Trouble began to accelerate a bit as the nuns, those frightening black-clad creatures tried to hammer God and Jesus into our heads. At age 10 or 11, with serious doubts stewing in my head, I asked what I thought was a reasonable question. The nun in front of our religious education class (probably Sister Catherine) stated that what she had just read (and I've forgotten the specifics) was "The Word of God!" Now, you have to understand that at this point, I did really believe in this God, strongly. So, in sincerity, I asked if God had said that in English. The nun looked at me and snarled "Of course not, English had not been invented yet." She seemed instantly and greatly irritated with me. So I asked, or rather said, if English wasn't used at that time, what she read was really a translation of something by a human person and not actually "The Word of God Himself." This was a technical point, but valid, I thought. The nun, this servant of God told me to sit down and keep my mouth shut. There's nothing quite as frightening as a pissed-off nun to a skinny little Italian kid in the middle of an almost totally Irish church.

There were more incidents after that, but ... all that's just background for the actual story, and here's the story: That church had five masses every Sunday at 7, 8, 9, 10, and 11:00 AM with the last one always being a 'high mass.' The normal routine for our family was that my father would drive us to church for the 9 or 10:00 o'clock mass. A few weeks before my thirteenth birthday, on a Sunday morning, my mother said we'd be going to the 10:00 AM mass. I said I would go to the 9:00 AM and would walk, it was a beautiful day and a fifteen minute walk, etc. That was not unusual and there was no notice taken. However, instead of going to St. Francis of Assisi Church, I walked to the drug store and bought a New York Times and then walked to Stanley Quarter Park where I sat on a bench in the open sunshine so that God could have a clear view and a clear shot. And I had this one-way conversation. "Look God, if you're really there ... I'm going to miss mass this morning intentionally, on purpose, with no excuses, and I know it's supposed to be a big sin, a 'mortal' sin. So God, if you exist and if you're not too big a shot, too big a cannon, to mess around with us little shots, us bee-bees, then I expect you to strike me dead or least give me a serious sign that you're pissed off about this. So ... I'm going to miss mass and read this newspaper. And if I don't get a sign from you in the next hour before your church bells announce the end of mass, you can just forget about me. I've been an altar boy for seven or eight years and at one time, believed all the stuff your priests and your nuns told me and now I believe it's all man-made bullshit. So make your move anytime. When the bells ring, I'm going home. And I'll never believe any of that garbage again. OK God. That's all I have to say. So do your stuff."

Stella had listened patiently and said she could appreciate, to some extent, what I had faced, but since she herself had never been deeply involved in the church, maybe some of what I did was lost on her. While her family insisted boys go to church services, they really didn't care if girl children did or didn't attend.

Listen, Princess. My little speech to God seems melodramatic and childlike. The truth is I was deeply and genuinely frightened. I had worked on that little speech and practiced and of course, if God knew everything he was supposed to know, he'd not be surprised. What if this God guy decided to fry me on the spot? ... a real possibility in my mind at the time. How would that affect my family? What a sad ending that would be. Still, I was unwilling to continue this 'not knowing' state of religion with all the hocus-pocus and I felt priests and nuns had their own doubts. As a Roman Catholic, we had church doctrine drilled into us, and we were not much exposed to Biblical training. When I finally had some long discussions with Bible thumpers, they seemed yet more deceptive and even more convoluted in their reasoning than the crazy-assed nuns if that were possible. So was I brave? Courageous? Or just selfish and lazy in not wanting to deal with religious nonsense the rest of my life? Maybe we'll know someday and maybe we won't. I'm almost 21 now and I made my bet eight years ago and I'll stick with it. (Reader's note: Now it is more than 60 years later and I have indeed stuck with it.)

The washer was done after a half hour and we transferred our clothing to the dryer. It would be about 45 minutes. Stella asked how I was doing. I answered by tilting my hand back and forth in a so-so or così-così fashion. She said, now that our clothes were clean, we should get our bodies clean. Oh man, that's sounds so good. She said we should get a room and wash up and get some decent sleep. She got a thumbs up from me. We waited patiently for the dryer. I took her hands in mine and gave each a little kiss and said thanks to each hand for tending to me for all those miles. The dryer decided it had witnessed enough of this schmaltz and sounded its buzzer bringing an end to the dreamy stuff. Removed the warm clothing, and while Stella folded it into proper piles, I reloaded my jacket/attic with all our little goodies. Discarded the debris, repacked the clothing into our bags, secured everything to the scooter and we were ready. Just knowing we would be clean soon lifted my spirits as we headed south into Amarillo. We were going to intersect again with famous Route 66, with parts of it now called Interstate 40. Before actually reaching 66, Stella gave the slowdown signal for a turn, and pointed to a motel. And there we stopped.

Not a particularly unusual place in concept. Old-fashioned, with individual cabins, each having its own covered carport for parking. What was unusual was the open space between cabins, fifty or sixty feet, meaning that the length of the line of nine or ten cabins, arranged in a gentle arc, was equal to two football fields, the 'office' cabin being centermost. Stella walked in the front door and within two minutes came back out and said for us to check cabin #3. We drove to it, she walked in, then out in a minute, gave a thumbs up and told me to go to the office. I waited there while she walked half a football length back to the office. She walked over to me and said softly, "First we get clean, then we get dirty." Quite a talker that girl. And a planner. Had me convinced before I really knew what was happening. Into the office, she made a deal with the old man, came out, hopped onto Tony Lambretta, saying, "Yessir, Number 3, please." Number 3 it was. I told Stella to go ahead, use the bathroom while I unpacked, locked up Tony and the Helmets. It wasn't long before we two refugees from the prairie got into the shower. Hair first, then the two of us scrubbing each other's backs and soaping and rinsing and just enjoying the occasion. Finally, toweling dry, then brushing teeth, and reclining on the bed. Next was some welcome, non-dusty groping and wrestling, and soon, with my arms around this beauty, we were sleeping soundly.

What was it that was so tiring about our little run through prairieland? Was it the relentless wind we had experienced? Granted we were not accustomed to the wind noises at night and so had had little actual sleep. The level of fatigue seemed far greater than was justified. And how incredibly bad was the dust bowl of the 1930's? Insanity must have been an enormous factor to counteract. Now, however, we rested well.

After a time, I was waking because my friend, the Princess, was gently pulling on my ear. And again, this time the other ear. Finally awake, but with eyes closed, I said, "Hello-o-o, Who i-i-is it?" She said, "Rosano, you have been drugged and rendered helpless. You are now under my control. Do not resist. There can only be harm in trying. And you will not speak." And my thoughts were ... 'Again? This happens to me far too often ... an exquisitely beautiful woman incapacitates me and uses me for her purposes with no regard for my modesty or sensitivity. Life can be brutal.' But of course, talking was forbidden. Whatever happened in the next half-hour, or more, was to be endured without complaint. What a trooper I could be under duress!

The deed done, and after decent interval, she kissed me on the lips several times and asked "Is this how mouth-to-mouth rescue is done?" I answered it wasn't done exactly that way, but it was a good start and offered thanks for her saving me from that Wicked Woman who had been here earlier and where was she now? Stella said she had chased her off, but one could never tell ... she might return.

Stretching and groaning, I said there was no reason for me to be so tired. Stella, "Oh yes, Rosano, there is a good reason ... you slept almost not at all last night. You kept your arms around me all night long. When I tried to change positions, you wouldn't let me. Why not?" I just shrugged and she continued "You know why? ... because you tried to protect me all night long, that's why. I got some sleep, but you didn't. And that's why you're a bit of a wreck today." "Just wanted to make sure you were OK", I said, "that's all." She said, "Exactly! And you don't know how much that does for me. You can't imagine how much I love you for that. But that's why you're so tired."

Listen, Princess. It's still early. Let's go do something in town, something relaxing. I've heard Amarillo is a pretty good town. How about a movie and a little meal or vice versa? To tell the truth, after that prairie, I need a culture injection. That grassland affected me much more than I guessed." Stella said she had noticed a little newspaper in the motel office. Maybe it had movie listings. She'd run down there and get it while I took another quick shower. When she returned, I was already drying off. She showered while I read the little weekly. Found at least one decent offering ... 'On The Beach' ... an Aussie/Brit film. I had read the book, by Nevil Shute. A quietly staggering story taking place after a world-wide nuclear fiasco sometime in the not too distant future. Reading the book was an experience as I followed the relentless progress of the tragedy. Hoped the movie did it justice. Stella appeared, naked save for a towel around her head (that Nefertiti look again), and that just stopped my heart for half-a-dozen beats. An amazing sight. A stunning beauty. After I got my heart restarted (it was similar to the scooter, requiring only one kick), I described the movie, which might really be worth seeing. This one had been around for three or four months and reviews were very favorable. She said whatever I chose would be fine with her. And what kind of food would we find. My guess was that Italian food was a no-no. There was probably Chinese food available, Mexican or Tex-Mex, and most prevalent might be barbequed beef of some variety or another. Well OK, let's give it a go. We got ourselves dressed, straightened the room a bit, and prepared to take Tony to town. As we left, Stella couldn't get the cabin door locked. She looked a little exasperated, handed me the key and asked me to try and I was equally unsuccessful. Just close the door and we'll go to the office and find out what to do. We scootered toward the office and the old man was sitting in a rocking chair on the front porch of his 'office' cabin. I explained the problem was that we wanted to go into town for a movie and a meal, but our door wouldn't lock and I didn't want to lose any of our stuff. The old man said, "Durn, my man was supposed to fix that." He paused, then said "Son, look that way toward your cabin and beyond to the next two, and now look the other way at the other cabins. What do you see?" What did I see? Hmmm. "I see a row of cabins, arranged in an arc, with lots of space between them and each one turned a little more than the one before it." "Well," he said, "that's better than what most folks might see. What you might have seen, but didn't mention is ... that from this here veranda, I can see each of the front doors." I nodded OK. "And that means I can hit any of those front doors with this" and he reached to his left and grabbed a rifle which had been leaning against the wall. Now, son, you take that pretty little woman and go see your picture show and have a peaceable meal, 'cause ain't nobody gonna touch your stuff. I guarantee that. And I'll get that lock repaired first thing in the morning." If that wasn't pure Texas!

Stella had been standing alongside me and asked the old man, "Are there any Italian restaurants in town?" He squinted just a little as he looked back and forth between the two of us. "Eye-talian? You Eye-talian?" Stella said no, but he is, tilting her head toward me. He said, "Oh my, my. I hear there're two different ones and neither is very good, so I couldn't say to try one or t'other." Stella said, "What about Chinese?" He said, "There're also two of them and people say they're pretty good. Ask the movie house people about that. They'll know." Stella asked for directions and we climbed onto the Lambretta, waved, and putted off with Stella navigating.

We found the movie theatre, were about forty-five minutes early and they were just opening for the afternoon and evening. Looking up the street and down, I spotted a drug store. Hey Princess, I want to get a few postcards and stamps, let's go get a cup of coffee and have a smoke. Most pharmacies had a little lunch counter and this was no exception. Stella ordered coffee for two while I took a minute and bought four postcards and stamps. I spent a few minutes, wrote a few words and pasted a stamp on each. We sipped coffee, lit up two Viceroys and just smiled back and forth. I gave her a preview of the movie, along with my summary of the Cold War positions of the US and the Soviet Union and explained the MAD (mutual assured destruction) concept. All that is the setting for this movie called 'On the Beach'. As we finished our coffee and paid the counterwoman, Stella asked about the Chinese Restaurants. Postcards were dropped into a box on the counter designated as 'Outgoing Mail.' Finally, back up the street to where the scooter and the helmets were locked to a parking sign, to the box office for tickets and into the theatre for the film.

Stella had her hand under or on my arm from the movie's opening frames. Not fiddling, nor moving much at all, but touching and holding steadily. While there are famous actors in the film, the star of the film is the story itself. Guessing that having read the book, I might be searching for differences between the book's rendition and the film, but that was not the case for me. The story is overwhelmingly relentless and holds one's attention to the very end, where everyone is swallowing suicide pills and saying goodbye and the audience realizes there is no hope at all for mankind's survival. After the film's ending, the crowd leaving the theatre that afternoon was silent, stunned. Stella's grip on my arm was uninterrupted until we got to the scooter. Finally, she asked, "Supper?" I nodded yes. "Chinese?" Again, yes. By drawing a U in the air, she signaled to go in the opposite direction from where we headed. The slow down signal came two blocks later, then the clenched fist and she pointed to The Lotus Garden. I secured the scooter and headgear to a wrought iron fence and we entered.

Mid-afternoon was quiet in the restaurant and the only other people seated were Asians, probably the family or staff, probably descendants of railroad workers from China, a century ago. Sure enough, one rose and came to greet us, ushered us to a table, gave us menus, and said "one moment, please," with no trace of accent and left us. Returning two minutes later, she poured a small cup of tea for each of us. We ordered and ate quietly, the somberness of the movie still affecting us.

Stella asked, "Do you think that could ever happen?" Slowly, I nodded yes. "What do you think are the chances?" With a shrug, I said. "Fifty-fifty ... just because I wouldn't know which other number combination to use. Both sides have to love their children and their grandchildren more than they hate 'the enemy'. So that's one requirement. Another big one is that no one in power becomes deranged enough to start that sort of thing. A third requirement is that there be no 'accidents'. There is supposed to be safeguards against this sort of thing, but who really knows how effective." Stella quietly said "How sad. So very sad." I nodded yes. As we continued eating quietly, Stella said, "That story ... the author of the book created something really shocking." I said, "Unfortunately, he has taken an existing situation and extended it to one of its possible conclusions. There might have been a dozen different endings, each as valid as the next. He chose one and did a superb job in following it through and holding everyone's attention while he did it. Just very effective story-telling and writing. There were a few differences between the book and the movie, but hardly worth discussing."

Stella asked, "Are we back on the prairie tomorrow?" I said, "I don't know, do you want to be?" She said, "I figured out we have plenty of days left to get to New Orleans. Would you stay another day here in Amarillo, if I asked you?" I replied, "Ma certo, Principessa. Actually, a waitress I worked with in Tucson, said if I ever got near Amarillo, not to miss Palo Duro

Canyon. Even though, 'palo duro' means 'hard stick', she said they called it 'Little Grand Canyon' and there was some excellent sightseeing to be had. It's about a half hour south of town. So we can pack a picnic lunch and take a little trip. Are you game for that?" Stella said "certo, certo."

The Chinese food was probably perfect for us that afternoon. As we finished, she asked, "Dessert?" I said, "Let's get some dessert somewhere else. Chinese are excellent with many foods, but, aside from their fortune cookies, dessert is just not their thing. Now, if they learned to stuff fortune cookies with something tasty, instead of those little notes, they'd have something. But, believe it or not, they never have asked me for advice. How about a little ice cream on the way home?" Good.

The Lambretta was patiently waiting for us. After unlocking, we climbed on and with the navigator signaling, we headed to the motel. At a stop sign, she asked, "Ice cream later?" Thumbs up from me. At the next stop, I asked "How about just a Snicker's bar? She gave a thumbs up and in a moment we were in front of a convenience market. Stella hopped off and disappeared inside, returned with a smiling face, and said, "Hey Tony, Hey Rosano, I've got something for each of you. Let's go." We made our way back to the motel and parked and locked up the Lambretta, except for the trunk. Found the cottage locked. We looked around at the office and the old man waved. Stella had the key, opened up, returned the wave. While there was a bit of evening light available, I took some of our food stash out of the trunk and closed it. Make sure the water bag is inside and can't forget to refresh it. Easy to forget when we're in a civilized situation.

Hey Princess, let's have a smoke out here on our front porch. We lit up two Viceroys and enjoyed the peace and warmth of early evening. I said if it were darker, I'd show her how to find the North Star. Next time we're camping we could probably do that. As we sat and relaxed her hand was on my back, then on the back of my neck, then behind my ear and I loved it. Told her that all that touching felt so good when we were driving and I hoped she never tired of it. She said, "Rosano, you don't understand. Let me explain something to you. Being with you has made a huge difference in my life … made me a much stronger person than I was when we met. How long ago was that … only ten days? When you and I are talking about anything, my thinking comes alive and starts moving in different directions. When I'm touching you, I gain strength from you. When you wrap me up in your arms, my spirit grows, and when we make love, I gain your energy and you never seem to run out. That's why I'm always touching you if you're near, like now or when we're driving or at the movies. It's so strange … you're like a battery charger that never diminishes, even when you're sleeping." So I touch you and pet you for selfish reasons, not because of any silly love stuff." She leaned over, gave me a big smooch on the side of my face and said "Let's go inside, White Knight."

We were in for the evening. It had been a day different from others. A quiet day, somewhat closer to other peoples' 'normal.'

CHAPTER 27

LITTLE GRAND CANYON

The tranquil day and peaceful evening in Amarillo was time beautifully spent. We talked and touched and laughed and loved and snacked and slept. After I prompted her to talk of her work, she hesitated initially. A few more gentle questions and she began to warm up to the subject, expressing her feelings toward the job, toward her patients, toward the system. With only an occasional question from me, she spoke for nearly an hour, almost as if I weren't there listening. What I saw as she talked was an excellent balance between 'heart' things and 'head' things. As unknowledgeable as I was about the medical field, I could see she had an organized and probably accurate view of care for terminally ill. Remarkable, I thought, for a woman in her mid-twenties, as she spoke of one phase of her work and then another.

We talked more about the movie 'On the Beach' which we had seen only hours before. She saw a great deal of sadness as part of her work with mortally ill patients and would most likely feel the emotions of the movie characters, perhaps more intensely than most people. That, of course, is not easily measured. Stella said that she wouldn't know how to handle the situation presented in the film. My thought was that radiation poisoning, and dealing with the sickness that accompanies it, would lead one to take the pill with all-encompassing sadness, there being few alternatives. It would be little comfort to know that all love, with few exceptions, ends in one form of sadness or another. Stella asked if I really meant that. Princess, let's think about it. Love between grandparent and grandchild must end in some manner of sadness. The same with parent and child ... hopefully with a normal death of the older person, but possibly with neglect or worse, bitterness. Siblings who love each other may drift apart, or die, and sadness remains with the one who survives. Lovers will part with venom or with great tenderness as time changes them and circumstances surrounding them. And ... you and I will part and that will be sad, and at the same time, I'll be happy for having affected you and for having known you and having spent some splendid time with you. But it's still holds, love almost always ends in some sadness. For us, now is not a time for sadness. Now is a time for us just to celebrate us. Look how lucky we are. We're on a journey we'll both remember forever. Tomorrow, we take a little side trip and there's time for more side trips. I told you before we started that we'd be OK and we will be. But now, it is time to hold each other and sleep.

In Texas, as in most other places, morning is relentless. In Texas, as in other places, coffee is a vital requirement. Miss Beauchamp, did you happen to notice the nearest source of the sacred substance? She had, in fact. We could walk there in less than ten minutes. Miss Beauchamp, you know ten minutes is my absolute limit. Aren't we cutting it a bit close? She put her arms around me, moved her face closer to mine so lovingly and said "Don't be such a wimp, and don't worry. I'll lead the way." As we left the little cottage I remarked that I hoped Mormons hadn't bought the place during the night. That drew a smile and a small laugh and she asked if I would ever forgive them for not having coffee in their diner. Of course I could forgive them, as soon as they changed their ways. We had a beautiful breakfast with dollar size pancakes and coffee. Finished breakfast with a smoke and a few more swallows of coffee. She said tell me about Hard Stick Canyon. I didn't know much except that it was recommended to me and was called "Little Grand Canyon" and since I had not yet seen the big brother, this would probably be good. Oh, and this one, the Palo Duro Canyon was about 100 miles long. We'll just see a few good parts, have a little picnic, and noodle around. I didn't want to spend too much time riding because I thought the day after might be a long one. So, if you're OK with it, let's eat lunch from our stash and replenish our supplies on the way back and get ready for tomorrow's run across mixed prairie and somewhat greener rolling hill country. She gave me thumbs up. We drank more coffee, settled the bill, and as we walked back, we stopped at the motel office and paid for today's stay and said "no maid service, thank you." The old man wasn't in the office yet.

At the cottage, we prepared for the morning's outing ... straightened bed linens, and organized the room. Stella arranged for our picnic lunch while I refreshed the water bag and checked the scooter. We were getting a little earlier start than usual. The morning was still cool, though we might hit 80 degrees later today. We would head south on Route 87 and follow signs to Route 217 to the Palo Duro Canyon State Park. There was some traffic, Amarillo being a town of 100,000 or more, but we made our way with little delay. We actually crossed the upper part of the canyon before we reached 217. Then traveled 8 or 10 miles eastward through farmland and prairie to the entrance of the park. A Ranger or a tour guide waved us through without stopping us and we were on state park roads and soon descending gradually toward the floor of the canyon. We slowly traveled the road looking at distinctly colored layers of rock two or three hundred million years old, now exposed by the Red River cutting through the land. This western geology seemed so stunning in appearance in comparison to that of New England, which now, in my memory, seemed perpetually gray and rather dull. This was truly vibrant in the mid-morning light. We putt-putted along the park road, occasionally passing a few campsites, a smattering of them occupied. There were few people here this day. Rock formations reminded me of the Painted Desert from a few weeks ago and was also reminiscent of the Garden of the Gods, just a few days ago. Truly magnificent and magical, and surprisingly little known, being greatly overshadowed by Arizona's Grand Canyon. Of course, I intended to see that one day, perhaps in the autumn of this year. We had driven about five miles into the canyon. At that point, on our left, or east of us, was a Formation called Fortress Cliff and on our right to the west was a beautiful formation called Lighthouse Rock, a multi-layered vertical, squared off spire. Was this a rock form called a hoodoo? We continued for another mile or two. Miss Beauchamp, let's go back a mile or so and find a good picnic spot away from other people, if we can. That way we could continue viewing both the Lighthouse and the Fortress during our snack. She was an observant navigator and noticed so many things which I missed.

Within a few minutes, she gave a slow-down, then a stop signal. She dismounted, walked onto a footpath, disappeared into some rocks and small trees, then returned in a minute and said to follow her. I did. What a fine selection! Here was a small clearing, from which we could see all around and yet remain almost unseen. Then let's have a picnic with a view of the Fortress and the Lighthouse. Opened the Lambretta's 'trunk' to remove the food, got the tarp and opened it halfway, placed it on the ground, taking advantage of some shade provided by the short trees. Soon there were seven or eight food items arranged like a smorgasbord on our tarp. That, with a water bag, was a minor feast. We sat quietly and grazed on our bounty and looked around us. This was big, an expansive and varied canyon. Stella said Fortress Cliff was so impressive it was frightening in a way. Try imagining what it is like from above, from the flat prairie, it would have to be a heart-stopping dropoff. This had turned out to be a perfect day for a picnic. Not too hot, some haze in the sky tempering the sun, and now, a cardinal watching us. Just hanging around, occasionally making a sharp quick chirp, a hard single note. Appearing not exactly like cardinals in Tucson, but close enough. I tossed half an almond off to one side, not directly at the bird. We watched, continued to talk softly for five minutes or so, and that bright splash of color hopped onto the ground, two or three more hops and it was at the almond half, scrutinizing and smelling I guessed, and then a peck. The almond piece broke into several pieces. One piece was selected and carried off. While we watched, two more feathered spirits watched us ... some species of oriel in the lower branches of the trees and up high, near the top of one tree, a small hawk or kestrel. Not being a birder, I might identify species with a picture in front of me, but there'd be little chance without such an aid. We wondered if the cardinal would return for additional almond fragments.

That brings a question to mind. Why do people enjoy feeding wild animals, like that cardinal or a squirrel in a city park, or ducks on a lake or fish in pond? Are we wired to do that or is it just to pleasure ourselves. Stella thought we fed them to see them up close, for our own curiosity and pleasure. My feeling was that there was something in our brain which caused humans to 'care' for animals, despite the fact that we hunted animals or raised them for food. Why did we want to give a peanut to a squirrel (or an almond to a cardinal)? Were we trying to give nature a little boost, a helping hand? Would we want to do that if we ourselves were genuinely hungry? Would I eat the peanut instead and then try to catch and eat the squirrel, too? Stella thought not, saying I was too much of a 'soft touch'. My response was that a hamburger, or roast chicken, or salami, or beef jerky was part of my diet. She felt that was something different. If we think about this long enough, it becomes a very complex issue, but only if the thinker is not terribly hungry. She asked if my thinking leaned toward taking 'care' of small creatures. Had to say yes, but how much of it was some sort of instinct or was it a cultural or learned influence. My mother always remarked at how I tried to 'rescue' every injured animal when I was a kid. Or feed every stray. Stella laughed so gently and kindly and said, "Don't you see? That's what you did with me." That statement came with a minor mauling and a major smooch.

We had finished a good share of the food. Reclined for short time and actually napped for a ten or fifteen minutes. Life seemed idyllic and it was. We agreed that it was time to do a little noodling with the scooter on our way out of the canyon. Then, a time for scooter fuel, get some groceries, and head back to the cottage for a little compatibility testing. We were repacking the Lambretta when our red cardinal returned, hopped around a bit, and made off with another almond fragment.

On the way out, there wasn't much noodling room. We would either be on the park road or off into ground that I preferred to avoid for the sake of our tires. Prickly pear needles could work their way into tires causing slow, almost unnoticeable leaks. Staying in the lowest gear, we climbed gradually out of Palo Duro Canyon and returned to grassland level.

Heading west toward the small town of Canyon, we then turned northward instead, back to Amarillo, to do our chores.

We agreed that we'd continue our grazing of our present stash of food this evening. This afternoon we'd buy snack foods for two days travel, which would take us to Wichita Falls, Texas. Did we need more skin lotion? There was more humidity, but scooter traveling was very drying to facial skin, even with my beard, which, of course, Stella lacked. Flashlight batteries? We were OK for now. Finding a good deli seemed a lost cause ... we settled for an ordinary supermarket. With a selection of a fresh fruit, dried fruit, a few canned goods, crackers, and beef jerky, we were able to gather enough for two days, the fresh fruit to be consumed that night and the following morning. We were getting efficient with our shopping. Back onto to Tony Lambretta, the faithful scooter. Let's get fuel for Tony, check tires, clean the windshield. The scooter was getting a bit dirty and dusty and needed a washing, but not this evening. Stella gave a slowdown signal and pointed to a gas station. And in we went. The old man tending the pumps said 'ain't no trouble" when I did my 'sorry to bother you routine.' I assumed it would be a nuisance to pump so little gas, but that was offset somewhat by curiosity when the scooter pulled in. We did the fueling and the old man asked where we were heading. I said New Orleans. He asked if I thought we could make it riding 'that there grasscutter.' Told him we were gonna give it a try. Checked the tires, the windshield, the engine. Everything looked OK. Now heading back to the motel and Stella gives a slowdown sign and points to a little ice cream shop. Good thinking. We stop. Ice cream is always an attractive thing, a demanding thing, and needs attention from time to time ... a small strawberry sundae for her and a hot fudge sundae with coffee ice cream for me. And in addition, I would have a cup of hot coffee. Hit the spot. A treat. Since we're leaving Amarillo in the morning, we'll do a little scooter noodling before we return to the cottage. Zig-zagged our way back. Felt mildly, favorably impressed by Amarillo, despite its depressed areas. While weather had been so perfect for us, I knew this could be an annoyingly windy place. Also, too damn cold a winter for me, for sure.

Back at our little cottage, new food purchases went into the scooter's trunk for tomorrow's eastward jaunt, as we took most of what was left of the old food and brought it into the room. Brushed teeth, kicked off shoes and socks. I told her since we were going across more prairie tomorrow and would not be sure of decent washing facilities where we camped, we should take three or four showers before we got on the road. She said she knew I liked to be clean, but that number of showers seemed excessive. Well, that might be true, but there was some enjoyment to be had in washing her and getting washed. She laughed, gave me a little hug, said I was a screwball and a dangerous one at that. Well... Well what? How about getting clean? Without saying anything, she walked to the shower and started the water. Taking showers and getting clean had become a major activity and a preliminary proceeding for us, with the main event happening not long after. But first, so carefully, I washed her ears, and behind her ears, and her neck, working my way downhill, careful not to miss anything, until with one knee on the shower floor I washed her legs down to her toes, each toe receiving individual attention. A job well done. Then it was my turn to be washed ... an uplifting and outstanding experience.

The main event was a fierce frolic ... a wild, no-holds-barred bout. Serious competitors cooperating. Nearing exhaustion, we began laughing at ourselves and each other. After calming down a bit, we just held each other gently for some time, enjoying our own insulated place of refuge in the Panhandle of Texas. We were deeply compatible, for sure. Tomorrow morning we would rejoin the world to travel eastward, but the remainder of the afternoon, and all the hours 'till morning would be ours to enjoy.

In time, Stella said, "I would like to start reading the book you just finished. Is that OK?" That would be fine with me because as you start "Fahrenheit 451", I'd get into "Twelve Angry Men", the jury-room drama. And so we leaned on each and read our books for perhaps an hour. She said, as she put her book aside, "Rosano, did you ever put a list of books together for me?" I said "I've got a list going. Still working on it, but maybe I ought to give you what I have, in case I die during one of our compatibility testing sessions." That cracked her up. "Die? Die? Do you think I'm trying to kill you?" I said if I died, it probably couldn't be called murder, but accidental homicide might be an accurate description. Get a decent sheet of paper and a pencil and we'll get started. I got up, rummaged through all my jacket stuff and came up with a rumpled scrap of paper and a little stub of a pencil. She had her notebook and a mechanical pencil ready. I told her these were in no particular order and I might add more titles as they came to mind. The list:

1. EXODUS, by Leon Uris, about the founding of Israel
2. ANIMAL FARM, by George Orwell,
    a satire, social and economic
3. Any book by Alexander King, a writer/
    story-teller, seen on the Jack Paar Show
4. THE CATCHER IN THE RYE, by J.D. Salinger,
    a troubled kid and his thoughts
5. MAIN STREET, by Sinclair Lewis,
    a satire of small-town American life

6. 1984 by George Orwell, a scary scenario
     of a future "perfect" society
7. MOBY DICK, by Herman Melville, a captain's
     self-destructive pursuit of a whale
8. LIFE WITH FIORELLO, by Cuneo; Fiorello Laguardia,
     NYC mayor, a unique character,
9. A TREE GROWS IN BROOKLYN, by Betty Smith,
     a poor Irish-American girl matures

"OK Princess, Here's a list of nine and I'll probably add a few more, and now you've already read 'Of Mice and Men' and you have Michener's 'Tales of the South Pacific' and you'll have started 'Fahrenheit 451'. If you finish my list, you will forever be ... a reader. Congratulations in advance!"

"Miss Beauchamp, do you realize that tomorrow, if and when we reach the town of Childress, Texas, we will have covered exactly half the distance from Denver to New Orleans in eight days. What do you think about that?" Stella looked at me, saying "To me, there are at least three remarkable things about this whole trip ... first, in my wildest dreams, before we met just two weeks ago, I could not have imagined such an adventure ... second, it sounds crazy, but you, Rosano, you really could, and actually did dream up such a trip, without hesitation or fear, and ... third, I never could have imagined trusting anyone so completely and loving anyone so intensely and that's all for now or I'll end up crying." So I said, "OK, different subject." She said, "OK, go ahead."

"First, I'll say you do not have to answer any of my questions or tell me anything. At any time you can tell me to mind my own business. That's fair game with me. So ... Miss Beauchamp, easy question first ... how do you like your new name?" Big smile from the lady and "I've said it to myself a thousand times in the last week and I'm getting accustomed to the sound of it ... Bow-shom'... and now that is my new me." That was good. Essential, in fact. "So Miss Beauchamp, whenever anyone needs to write your name, you'll have to spell it. So start doing that automatically. OK next question, you said you were working on some plan for a final severance from your former family, the swamp family. Do you want to tell me about it?" She said, "I haven't finished my thinking and honestly, I haven't thought much about it the last few days, which has been a relief, but maybe, in a day or two, we'll talk and I'll get your ideas, too. OK?" That was OK.

We spent the rest of the evening snacking, scratching or stroking each other's this or that, reading, conversing and eventually folding into each other and sleeping in preparation for the following day.

CHAPTER 28

HALFWAY TO NEW ORLEANS

The Texans think they're so damn special, and maybe rightly so, but they couldn't prevent morning from arriving. And so the two happy vagabonds stirred, did the routine stuff and one walked and the other staggered to the little restaurant we had visited yesterday. The restaurant did have dollar-sized pancakes and coffee which meant that I could have dollar-sized pancakes and coffee. How beautiful. Miss Beauchamp had a larger, more balanced meal. We had plenty of time before beginning the day's run, especially because we were heading almost directly eastward. The sun would look straight into our eyes until 8:30 or 9:00 AM. Time for an extra ration of coffee and a smoke. A tranquil time for us. On the walk back to the cottage, I suggested that since I had little idea of what we might encounter for tonight's camping spot, we should shower before leaving this morning. She just laughed and squeezed my arm and said, "Incorrigible."

On return to the cottage, we brushed teeth, played a bit, showered, and packed up. Here was a TV in the room that neither of us had looked at for a moment. TV just seemed to completely nonfit our mood and our methods. TV just seemed like so much garbage, an intrusion into real life. "You have our map, Princess? You know where we're going?" She gave me two thumbs up. We had everything ready for securing to the scooter. Everything was packed, we locked the room, climbed onto the scooter, and putt-putted to the office. She dismounted, returned the key, said adios, and we were back to our journey. "Onward, White Knight!" came the cry from the rear seating section of the Lambretta.

There was some traffic, but in not too many minutes, we were on Route 66, now being converted into US 40 in many places. We would travel on good old 66 for a few miles until we intersected with our Route 287, which, instead of heading directly east, took us southeast toward Louisiana. It required about eight miles to transition from city to suburbs to an ever-changing mixture of prairie and agriculture and rolling hill terrain. Everything seemed somewhat greener than we had experienced north of Amarillo. Weather was warmer, humidity higher and there were a few more trees (probably people-planted). Without doubt, the landscape was more interesting visually. In addition, the light breeze was almost directly from the rear, meaning that Tony Lambretta just didn't have to work quite so hard. Princess was singing something, which I couldn't identify, and was keeping time on my back. All three of us seemed rather happy and content. In less than an hour, we were going into a small town named Claude, Texas. I gave my passenger a signal combination by drawing an imaginary question mark in the air, followed by our scissors sign ... the pair of signs asking 'Do you want a break?' She waved her no-no sign back, so there was no stopping, just a slowing down as we passed through the farming town with some grain elevators and about a thousand people, my guess. Definite prairie surroundings, but seemed not as depressing as a few days ago. Just my impression and feeling. Perhaps it was the beat of a music tempo on my back from the woman sitting behind me. All seemed right with the world that morning. The scooter performed its task admirably, taking the few gentle hills in stride, never needing to use a lower gear. Just buzzed along, seeing more prairie, then some cultivated acreage, then prairie again. My thought was these farmers or ranchers had to travel many miles to tend to their acres, or livestock or whatever it was they were raising. Also, I guessed school kids had to spend hours and hours on busses. Depressing. We were approaching a town named Clarendon, twice the size of Claude, so that meant the two towns 35 miles apart had a total of 3000 people. Being a city boy, it made me wonder what life would be in these towns. As we drove into Clarendon and slowed down, I signaled a break. We had traveled about 65 miles in just a few minutes less than two hours. Overdue for a stretch and a snack. Putt-putt-putting into town, Stella directed us to take a left and pointed to a good-sized bunch of trees. We pulled up under some trees. Dismounting, I asked how she liked our longish run this morning. She said it was absolutely delightful and gave me a big hug. A little too soon to gas up, but the next town was Hedley, about two hundred population and I had no idea if there was a service station or not. Let's look at the map. Beyond Hedley was Memphis, Texas which I had never heard of, but the population was just over three thousand. It would take about an hour to reach there. And there would be gas there. So, we'll stretch, get some coffee and pie, if they have it, and write off the Hedley village as a supply source for anything.

What song was she singing for the last fifty miles? She said she didn't know the name of it. Sing a little of it now that we're not on the scooter. She did. There must have been a strange look on my face because she asked if I knew it. Shook my head no. She laughed a little and said I didn't think she sang very well, did I? I said, one day, she would have a great career in nursing. We stretched out, walked around a bit, had a smoke, and walked around more. How about some coffee and pie? Or would you rather snack on our food. Coffee and pie sounded good. OK, hop on. Down the street we went to a small restaurant. Tied up the helmets and the scooter. Ordered pie and coffee for two, then used the restroom. At the table, we did our usual thing with pies by each eating half the serving and then trading plates. We talked of various things ... camping, music, high school, etc. I interrupted the conversation by asking if she remembered we were supposed to keep an eye on the sky for possible storms and a possible tornado. She said she had remembered and was alert from the time we left the motel this morning. I said not to forget to look behind us also. We finished out little treat, the pie was better than most, the coffee excellent. Restrooms again and then back to Tony Lambretta. Got ready to roll, one kick, a little puff of bluish smoke with its unique 2-stroke perfume and we were on our way to Memphis ... Memphis, Texas, that is.

We had traveled for about 20 miles through alternating landscapes of prairie and farmland, when Stella tapped on my left shoulder to get my attention and pointed to the northeast. At first not seeing anything unusual, I stared and finally saw small column of dust quite distant. I nodded yes and pointed to my eyes and then toward the column. Ten minutes later, it appeared considerably closer. Rather large in scale, and carrying some debris. It was what I would call a 'dust devil' similar to what I had experienced in Tucson, Arizona. There seemed to be no supporting cloud structure above or near it. Certainly proved that my passenger was awake and vigilant. Two or three minutes later, it started giving up its debris and dissipated before we got close enough to feel its effects. Not much to worry about. I gave Stella a 'thumbs up' signal. She tickled both my ears. Putted through Hedley without seeing one person. There were a few trees scattered in lower areas of the passing scenery. I wasn't sure if this was called Texas 'hill country' or was it still 'prairie' we were traveling through. We had a continuing light breeze behind us, the day was warm, and we were in fine spirits. There were no other signs of dust devils or tornados. Stella continued to sing her song and beat a rhythm on my back. Fortunately, I was unable to hear her song, but thought it a very good sign that she was singing. We would stop in Memphis for gas and food.

As we neared small towns like Memphis, the first visible manmade objects were usually structures such as grain elevators and water towers. Before we did anything, I wanted to refuel the scooter, just one more thing not to think about. As we entered the town, something seemed different, in a comfortable way. There were some vacant buildings, but that was occurring in all rural areas of the country, maybe in much of the world, as more people migrated to cities, and fewer people were needed on farms. Before going in too far, I pulled into a gas station. Old guy comes out of the little building. I do my apology routine for not needing much gas, pour my oil and gas combo into the tank, and asked him to fill it. Measured some oil into my reserve can and asked him to fill it also. Did he have any two-cycle oil? Indeed he did. While Stella was refreshing the water bag, he got the quart of oil. Done with the refueling, I paid for the gas and oil. Then the old man said, "C'mon to the office. Can I buy you a coke?" I said that would be good. Then the old man started asking questions about the scooter, how it behaved, what kind of gas mileage it got, how fast could it go, was the balancing difficult, etc. He said (and I won't try to imitate his Southern/Texan accent) "I knew those eye-talians made a bunch of high performance race cars, but never knew about the scooters." Stella was listening as the old man fed a few coins into the Coke machine and handed a coke to her and one to me. I said, "Don't get a third one, you take this one we'll split this other one." He said OK and asked about five or six more questions about the scooter and traveling and yes, he noticed the Arizona license plate. One question I couldn't answer was 'How many horsepower.' The cubic centimeters I knew. How it translated into horsepower, I didn't know.

Then I said that we had seen a number of small towns on our journey, and Memphis seemed nice. What was it? The old man said the town used to be over 4000 people and had lost about a fourth of that, so now it was about 3000. He said what seemed good about the town was that people took care of things, didn't leave trash around, that sort of thing. He said to go a little further into town and take a little spin around the courthouse and we would see what he meant. People have some pride here, he continued. Some years back, for instance, the train people didn't want to stop here in Memphis, so the townspeople greased the rails so the train had no traction and couldn't go forward and couldn't leave town. Eventually the town got the railroad to agree to stop in Memphis. We finished our coke, Stella and I taking alternate sips. Shook hands with the old man and said my thanks. As we got back onto the scooter, I asked if we were going to snack from our food stash or hit a café. It was still early afternoon. She opted for café. We headed further into town and spotted what we guessed was the courthouse. And the pavement was red brick. Wow. Very unusual in the US to have such an extensive area of brickwork. I wondered what had prompted this. There had to be an interesting story here. I'd have to look it up. We noodled around, following some of the bricked streets. Stella spotted a small restaurant as we neared the courthouse again. We stopped, tied up the helmets and the scooter and went inside.

Comfortable, medium sized place, looked clean. Waitress came over to us and seated us, poured ice water into our glasses, gave us menus and said she'd be back in a minute. She was back in two, asked if we wanted something to drink beside water. I ordered black coffee. Waitress said the lunch special was a cup of vegetable soup, a very lean 6 ounce hamburger, with green beans and French fries. Stella needed a minute and I should go ahead. The special sounded great, cooked medium, hold the onion, and could the cook please sprinkle it pretty heavy with oregano. The waitress winced a bit, and said the hamburger was rather tough, so I should be forewarned. That was good with me and I didn't care how tough. Stella ordered meat loaf.

Before the meal came, she asked about the dust column we had seen earlier. I said that was a dust devil or at least that's what they were called in Southern Arizona. They had other names in other places. Similar to a tornado, but much, much smaller, not nearly as powerful and hardly ever lasted more than five or ten minutes and usually shorter than that. Remember when I said I had fallen off the scooter because of a dust devil. Well, the one we saw today was a pretty good sized one, and fairly long-lasting, but we watched as it just collapsed and then all its dirt and debris fell from the sky. She had heard the name, but had never seen one before nor had she ever seen a real tornado either. I mentioned that a friend in Arizona, who did a lot of flying said the dust devils could be rather dangerous to small aircraft up high (2 or 3 thousand feet) where swirling air columns were invisible, because dirt or the pieces of paper, grass, and leaves often didn't get up that high.

We started with soup and that was a nice change for us. When our food arrived, we began, and Stella paused, tasted her meat loaf and made a little face. A problem? She said it had lots of onions in it. Without saying a word, and using my spoon, I pushed the offending food onto my coffee cup saucer, and moved it to the far side of the table. I cut my hamburger in half and put half on her plate. She didn't protest. After taking a small bite of my food, she smiled and said, "Much, much better." I said yes, especially for later on, that I didn't like love-making with a clothespin on my nose. That cracked her up. She was laughing and saying, "What a crazy image. That's wild. That could be a comedy bit for a TV show." We finished our meal slowly, passed on any dessert, drank more coffee and had another smoke. I asked the waitress about camping near Childress, the next town. She said she knew there were two or three different commercial parks on the east side of that town ... RV parks or campgrounds. She wasn't sure of any details. That was OK, we'd give it a try. Stella took care of the bill.

Back on our faithful Lambretta, we had about an hour to go and that would be enough traveling for the day. One kick, a little puff of blue exhaust and we were starting on the last leg. It had been an easy day so far. As we left the good little town of Memphis, we had about fifteen miles to go before we crossed the Red River or specifically the Prairie Dog Fork of the Red River. No that's not quite it ... actually, the Prairie Dog Town Fork of the Red River. I suspect that name was used to help keep the sign painters employed. Nonetheless we would be crossing it before we reached Childress, Texas. My passenger was leaning lightly against my back, probably sneaking little mini-naps. The terrain was flat and the sky was clear, and sure enough, within the half-hour we were driving on the bridge spanning the river bed, less than half of which had water flowing. I wondered for how many more years. The farming and ranching industries were insatiable for water. I knew from Southern Arizona that one acre of cotton used as much water as 20,000 or 50,000 people (whatever the number, it was a staggering amount). Still it was indeed a refreshing sight to see water flowing (Arizona does that to a person). Stella was awake and giving little hugs, probably trying to insure that I was awake. No problem there. As soon as I felt the smallest bit of drowsiness, I would stop, take a break, walk around, do some deep knee bends, etc. That also worked very well with the philosophy that, while scootering, to never ever be in a hurry. Crossing the bridge from north to south puts one into the village of Estilline, but it hardly deserved the word village. 'Ragtag collection' would be more in keeping. Just a pile of junk and was happy to get through it in such a short time. As we putted our way toward Childress, my thinking turned to the mountains of the southern Arizona desert and what a focal point they always provided as one's eye swept the landscape. Not quite as majestic as Colorado Rockies, Arizona's Rockies were nonetheless stunning and ever-changing in the intense sunlight. This part of Texas, without such a visual resting place, seemed always to urge one's eyes to go beyond the horizon, to seek something else, something more.

We were entering the outskirts of Childress, a neatly kept town of 5,000 or 6,000 people. We stopped at a small market, bought a pack of Winstons and some orange juice. We had more than enough food to carry us into the following day and beyond, if necessary. Childress, the midpoint of our trek between Denver and New Orleans was a typical agricultural town, not really remarkable. It seemed to mark our exit from the Texas panhandle. So it was time to look for a camping spot. First, we spied a little diner with a large coffee cup painted on a sign (bless their hearts, truly. They might be dreadful scoundrels, but that was permissible if they had coffee) and I blessed them with the sign of the cross just the way the priests would. Stella laughed loud enough for me to hear. A mile further and a small sign on the north side of the highway said "Camping – Very Clean Restrooms – Very Clean Showers – Fireplaces." Stella spotted the sign and the two 'Verys' sold me. We stopped in, the fee was fifty cents for a tent site with no electricity. A small concrete block building contained restrooms and showers. The showers were coin-operated and charcoal and wood were available cheaply. The small area was well-planted with trees. We entered and putted over to our assigned spot. Just a few other campers around. Within twenty minutes, we had camp set up, I had a coffee pot fire built but not lit. Got our helmets and the scooter secured and then suggested we use the restrooms and right after, take showers. Stella thought that was a plan worth following. And we did just that. And the restrooms were honestly very clean and the showers, too. And again, we washed each other slowly and carefully and occasionally fed another coin into the timer. A warm, pleasant middle afternoon in the middle of May in the middle of our trip to New Orleans. And we were clean and fed. We sat on some wooden lawn furniture arranged in a conversational semi-circle.

Hey Princess, what did you think of today's run? She said it was a splendid day, a relaxing day, except for that last little place right after the bridge. She said there was something almost evil about it. You felt it too, I said. Something is wrong there, but I don't care to find out specifics. What is it about certain places that give off so-called 'bad vibes' which are like a bad odor that you can't quite identify, but you know something stinks? All very unscientific and viewed by me with deep skepticism, but something was felt by the two of us simultaneously. Something ungood.

We've got good daylight remaining. Read for a while? That sounds fine. We got our books from the tent and read for about 45 minutes, but dozing off was a better description than reading for the last 15 minutes. Time to get inside the tent and take a short, but a real snooze. Stella said I was just full of good ideas and joined me. Zonked out, with most of my mind in some other galaxy. Remarkable though, that a tiny portion of that mind stays behind, in reserve, and says or senses that 'things are OK and you're holding and guarding and protecting your friend. Rest and be peaceful.'

CHAPTER 29

DROP INTO WICHITA FALLS

We passed late afternoon and evening in Childress, Texas, quietly and uneventfully. Stella and I talked of camping and traveling. She assumed that I really enjoyed camping in order to be closer to nature. I had, in fact, camped out in quite a few places in New England, and down the eastern seaboard. Camped two or three times in Mexico. Did I do it to be closer to nature? I wasn't convinced of that. Perhaps the challenge of not being 'contained' in some manmade structure or building was that which attracted me. Not sure. Truthfully, I always slept better in a motel, but few 'campers' ever admit to that. For me, two major drawbacks to this 'camping out' activity were (1) personal cleanliness (one day without a good cleaning was tolerable, two days was borderline, the third day was madness) and (2) mosquitos ... I just hated the little bastards, and they just loved me. If ever I ventured outside for more than ten seconds, they passed the word "Hey, he's outside!" and for miles around they began their individual migrations toward me, bypassing most other people, trying to get a sample, and leaving a big welt behind. The most effective repellant I found was dish detergent. It also seemed to relieve the irritation of the little pricks on my hide (some word play there, if you hadn't noticed). On this trip, the tent was equipped with mosquito netting on the entry and the air vents. And I'd visually inspect these nettings each time I set up camp. Thus far, on this cross country jaunt, I had not yet encountered a mosquito. That's one splendid aspect of the dry air in the west. Now heading into eastern Texas, we were experiencing wetter and warmer air, and soon would leave mosquito-free zones behind.

Stella asked what the plans were for tomorrow. I said I'd like to make it to Wichita Falls, about 110 miles, and visit a bookstore and do one or two cultural things if possible ... because I was having culture withdrawal symptoms. Stella suggested that since Wichita Falls was pretty fair sized at 100,000 people, it might be a good place to spend two days if I didn't object and if we liked it. Ma Certo, Principessa, d'accordo. "OK Rosano, that's a new word. Explain." So I explained, "it means we're in accord ... we agree or maybe it means I agree, but I'm not sure which." For the evening meal, we snacked on our collection of foods ... jerky, dried fruits, nuts, one can of peaches, and orange juice and water. The coffee was out there, ready to be made, but we elected to wait 'till morning. Let's get the flashlight and walk over to the restrooms. We'll refresh the water bag also. Back inside our little secure cocoon, inside the sleeping bag, we talked more, embraced, petted, played and finally slept.

During the night ... Boom, then another ... Boom. Thunder. Then, the patter of rain. With the tarp having been secured well, I felt we'd be fine in a rainstorm. Hugging a little closer, we slept for another hour or two, waking at first light, before sunrise. We were warm and dry, but wide awake, probably having slept for a full eight or nine hours. I asked her to take a peek out the tent flap to see if I had to slay any monsters on the way to the restroom building. Untying the flap, she looked out and said it was still pretty dark and probably wouldn't be able to see the monsters if they were out there. I had turned the flashlight on. She reached for it and I wouldn't let her have it. She said, "What's going on?" I said I didn't know but the view of her bottom was just magnificent. It's good to start a day wrestling and laughing. Full bladders soon brought that to a tranquil end and we got dressed for the day, made our way to the restrooms and returned. I was about to start the coffee fire, when I realized we had no dry fuel with which to cook coffee. My mistake. There was enough woodsman lore in my brain so that I knew how to get a fire going, even starting with a pile of wet wood. But survivability in these circumstances was greatly enhanced by the presence of a café just up the road. How about we just pack up everything and drive back to that blessed diner and we'll get rolling early and see what happens? She said "D'accordo. Certo." Less than a half-hour later, we started the scooter and rode back to the café for a beautiful breakfast as a subdued sunrise was softly lighting up the sky. An overcast day and there were a few small stormy-looking clouds scattered here and there. After tanking up on coffee, we left the café, and walked into a cool morning.

We got aboard Tony the Lambretta and started eastward out of town on semi-dry pavement. A very light breeze was at our back, the sunrise was a bright glow in the east, softened by cloudiness and not at all piercing. Ten miles north of us, to our left, was the Red River, forming the state boundary between Texas and Oklahoma. Land we were passing through was much the same as yesterday's, but seemed a bit greener and, of course, was wetter due to the rain. Did our scooter run a bit quieter in humid air? I wasn't sure. Perhaps a tiny bit. The best scenery was in the sky this morning, great cloudscapes everywhere. We buzzed along for nearly an hour with little or no change. There was a row of clouds directly in front of us. We were making excellent progress and the road became wetter as we gained on that small cloud bank. I began to feel droplets on my face and now there were no more dry spots on the pavement. And now, more droplets as we got closer. I lessened the pace, and these actions began retreating. Three or four minutes later, I increased the pace again, and again the pavement became wetter as droplets began. We repeated this cycle three or four more times. In fact, we were heading almost exactly in the same direction as the cloud bank and were 'playing tag' with it. A quietly exciting and fun experience. We were approaching Vernon, TX and would need fuel. Evidently that friendly group of clouds had a bigger fuel tank than ours and continued its eastward journey as Stella waved goodbye. We had covered 60 miles in 90 minutes of very easy traveling.

Route 287 crossed the Pease River just west of Vernon. As we crossed the bridge, the river was running a respectable flow, probably helped by this morning's rain. It emptied into the Red River eight or ten miles north of town. Vernon itself was a rather quiet agricultural town of 10,000 or 12,000 people. I suggested, as we were fueling the scooter, trying a little coffee at a local non-Mormon café, if Stella was game for that. She smiled, grabbed me by the ears, said "You are the most wonderfully stubborn nutcase I have ever known", and gave me a big smooch on the nose. The young guy at the gas pump looked a little embarrassed, but stayed at his task, grinning widely. When he saw the Arizona plate, he asked if we had driven all that way from Arizona. To simplify things, I just said "That's right." He said "Well I'll be damned if you ain't the luckiest. All that way with this gorgeous young lady, who obviously likes you a whole lot. Mister, you have already made it to heaven. My hat's off to you for sure." He took his cap off and held it over his heart and stood at attention. And all three of us were laughing. A good guy and a good feeling. As I was paying him, I asked about the café right next door. He said he didn't know about their food, but their coffee was great. I thanked him, shook his hand, and said "A pleasure meeting you." He returned with "Likewise, I'm sure. Have a good trip."

At the café, we ordered two coffees, Stella asked if I would split a piece of pie, and I said "Certo." Use the restrooms, then the pie and coffee, then some more coffee and a smoke, and I said, without thinking about it, "Damn, I miss those cookies." She asked if we might find them in Wichita Falls and my answer was 'not likely'. And maybe not so good if we did. I wouldn't conduct any search for them. We wouldn't even find the Falls of Wichita Falls. She thought surely we could manage that. And I said maybe not, one never knows. We had about fifty miles to go to reach that town. Let's say two hours, being generous. We got such an early start this morning, we'll reach our goal before noon, most likely. Stella paid for our coffee and we remounted our faithful steed, the Lambretta. And we were off again on Route 287, continuing the transition from prairie to 'Hill Country' or 'Piney Woods Country' on this easiest of traveling days. Within an hour or so, we had passed through much agricultural land, crossed a few creeks, slowed down through a few settlements and found ourselves in the town or suburb of Iowa Park, ten miles from Wichita Falls. Landscapes had gotten greener. There was more road traffic. In a few minutes we were about to enter town when Stella gave signals to pull over and stop, the clenched fist signal. She hopped off, saying, "Take a break. Have a smoke … be right back." She walked back two or three doors to a real estate office. I lit up a Winston and wondered what she was cooking up. After finishing my smoke and field-stripping the remnant, I waited patiently. She reappeared, shaking her head, saying "You knew, you knew all along there was no waterfall in Wichita Falls. And I was going to prove you wrong. How did you know?" Laughing, I told her about a friend in Tucson who had grown up in Beaumont, Texas. He had mentioned once or twice there were no falls in Wichita Falls. That's a tough one to forget. No falls in Wichita Falls doesn't mean no one falls in Wichita Falls, etc. She said she had found a nice place for us to stay. OK, Princess, time to navigate. She directed us just a short distance to a large U-shaped complex of cabins with a restaurant in the opening of the U, and gardens, a playground, a swimming pool, and a service building in the center of the U. We stopped at the office, she went in and five minutes later emerged with keys in her hand and said "Four." I putted down to Number Four and shut the scooter down. It was a few minutes before noon.

Into a large room, with table and two chairs, two upholstered chairs, a king-size bed, TV, telephone, reading lamps, an alarm clock, and other goodies. Plus some tourist brochures. Rather plush after a mountaineer tent. A bit of a culture shock, but manageable. I said, "You're right, it's a very nice place. Two days?" She nodded yes and said, "If we want. C'mon, before we unpack, let's just walk around the grounds for a few minutes … we've been sitting in one place or the other all morning." And so we did. A service building had a good looking laundry room for the guests. Garden sections were loaded with a variety of flowers with blossoms everywhere. Wooden outdoor furniture was arranged in a few groups. A very pleasant, very civilized place. We walked around and stretched, checked out the restaurant menu. It would be reasonably good, my guess.

We headed back to Number Four, untied our things from the scooter, and brought them into the room. Time to relax for a bit. Want to shower? That would be good start for an afternoon. The shower was not so much sensual as it was maintenance and cleaning. After drying ourselves and tooth brushing, we pulled back the bed sheets and just rested for a while, gently holding each other, awake, with no conversation. Two people comfortable with each other.

After some fine time together, Stella quietly asked what we might do this afternoon. I said I'd like to spend an hour or possibly two in a book store, preferably a used book store. What would you like? She said she'd like to go out in the evening, for a change, and have a drink in a place with a live band. I said that sounds great, but no alcohol for me if I was driving, but that was OK with me ... I did that fairly often in Tucson. So ... first, we'll get dressed and go to the office and ask about a book store and possibly find out what's at local nightclubs. Then we'll hit a bookstore and decide what's next. Sound like a plan, a partial plan at least? Stella said she loved the way I made these plans ... so definite and so open at the same time. Let's get started and remember, you are the navigator. First, she says, we check the Yellow Pages, then the office. Agreed. Got directions for two bookstores, got onto the scooter and she directed us to one of them in ten minutes. Wichita Falls seemed like a pretty good town, similar in size to my town of Tucson, each also having an Air Force base on the edges of town. A pleasant afternoon with flowers blooming everywhere. The street layout was a bit of an uncomfortable puzzle for me. I liked the grid system typical of so many cities in the west, but this town had grid systems at 45 degree angles to each other, making for too many intersections where half-right or 45 degree turns or 135 degree turns were required. Wonder who dreamed up that one.

Entering a bookstore gave me the same thrill as stepping into a magnificent concert hall. There is a thing so special, the look and smell and taste of the place. Have always enjoyed the mild induced trance of being surrounded by books. Stella asked where we should start. I said I was going to wander around, but she might start by reading jackets of books in what I would call 'modern classics' section. Ask people behind the counter, they just love getting asked about books. Tell them books you have just read. They'll get the idea. Moving through the aisles slowly, my mind was trying to absorb everything. How I treasure bookstores and hardware stores and record shops! A shelf labeled 'PLAYS' caught my attention. Finally, it was 'A Streetcar Named Desire' by Tennessee Williams which was saying 'me, me, choose me' with the most force. It won, and would leave with me. Walked around a bit more and found my beauty sitting on a little stool with half a dozen paperbacks in front of her. She looked up at me, smiled gently and said "Isn't this just a wonderful place!" I said "Holier than any church." She nodded yes slowly. "Hey Princess, have you chosen anything?" She said "I think so ... two books, but I'd like you to see." She showed me 'Auntie Mame' by Patrick Dennis, and 'Lord Of The Flies' by William Golding. "Wow! It would be hard to choose two books more different from each other than these two. 'Mame' is a hoot and 'Flies' is a real heavy. Excellent! You'll enjoy both. Good choices. Now, want to keep looking?" She said no, this was just perfect and we walked over to the register. I picked up a Dallas newspaper and reached into my pocket for ... and she stopped me with her hand and a frown and said "These are mine, all of them." "OK." What I thought was a half-hour had been nearly one-and-a-half. Exiting the bookstore, I asked what was next. She said she was Navigator and I would just have to follow her signals. She was able to get her two books into her purse and I stashed my pocket edition in my jacket and wedged the newspaper between the seat and the body of the scooter. We got on Tony Lambretta, 'OneKick Tony' I had started to call it, and with the little familiar puff of two-stroke smoke, we were on our way with our Navigator calling the shots. Two minutes later, she signaled for a stop and pointed to ... an ice cream shop. This woman was not only beautiful, she was smart as hell, alert to basic needs of humanity, ice cream being prominent on the list.

We stopped and I said, "How did you know?" She said, "Rosano, you're suffering from cookie withdrawal and it shows. Ice cream is a pretty good habit maintenance measure – like a painkiller substitute." We ordered sundaes and sat down. She asked, "How on earth did you know the two books I had chosen?" I said I had read them both ... and not only that but had seen the movie "Auntie Mame." Big fun book and movie. "Lord Of The Flies" was a dark study into human nature. No movie of that one, not yet. Both would provide a number of topics to think about. She said, "No, not those two books, all the books, how do you do it?" My answer: "I'm not a fast reader, but I read all the time, anything and everything. If I don't have a beautiful Princess to sleep with, I'll read until I absolutely drop ... and try to read at least one book a week, often there will be two books and I've been doing that since little kidhood. I got that from my little runt of an uneducated Italian mother, but that's another story I'll tell you sometime later." She said "I have a long way to go." I said, "There is no end to that reading road, it is just a good path to be on, a good path to be following. You've just started in the last two weeks and I think you're already hooked. You had a respectable collection in front of you back at the bookstore. You'll begin to choose favorite authors from that list we're preparing. Nothing is going to stop you. You'll see." We ate ice cream, enjoyed it, and as we were finishing she asked what we should do next. "Want to hear a plan?" She said "Sure." My suggestion was that we return to that nice room she had secured, then try some sweet and strong and sweaty lovemaking, then shower once again and make further plans at that time. She stood up from the table, came around to where she could whisper in my ear and said softly "D'accordo, agreed."

And that's what happened in exactly that sequence and it was a glorious event. The word was … Compatible. That we were, indeed.

The phone chimed once and again. Stella reached over, picked up, and said "Hello … Calypso … one minute … Rosano, do you like Calypso music … Yes, that would be great … and … Thank you so much." Then she said "Want to know what's happening? The desk clerk called around and found out where there might be live music tonight. There's a Calypso band playing at a lounge not too far from here. They start at eight o'clock. Want to try it?" Sure I would.

Rosano, what book did you get? I told her "A Streetcar Named Desire" which was a Tennessee Williams play from ten or twelve years ago. Seven or eight years ago, a pretty good movie was made of it, more than pretty good. I had seen the movie, but never read the play. Takes place in New Orleans. Of course, I'll be leaving the book with you and you'll be reading it soon enough.

Rosano, I want your opinion on something, no, your advice. Ready? I nodded yes. She said she was still planning to say something and do something dramatic in her "Farewell to the NoGoods, and she might or might not tell me about it. "Listen, Rosano, what should I do AFTER I make my grand gesture." I know I should leave immediately, but what do you think I should do … and how should I do it?"

Here's how I started. "First things first. You bought a book today called 'Auntie Mame' and you should start to read it now. Mame is a special woman, zany, but with an element of style, grace, and fearlessness about her that would be unmatched except by a very few. Read the book, enjoy Mame, and some of her will rub off on you. Second, I assume you've taken plenty of money with you. Third, whatever you have in mind is probably going to piss off some people, so you're correct … you should do your thing and get the hell out … confidently, but without delay and with finality. OK, this is what I suggest. It's going to sound radical, but this will forever be a big bright spot in your life and might change your life immensely. Ready? … and she had her little book and a pencil poised. When you leave that gathering, you should have a ride to the airport in New Orleans already lined up. You should also have an airline ticket to New York City already reserved and paid for. When we get to New Orleans, we'll talk to a travel agent, get your airline ticket and a hotel room near Little Italy. So you should fly to New York City, check into your hotel, then … ask the concierge or the bell captain to arrange to get a seat for the Broadway musicals 'Fiorello' and

'Gypsy'. "Fiorello" is an excellent show about a great character (remember that he's on the reading list). 'Gypsy' with Ethel Merman is the greatest show I've ever seen or heard of and will be remembered as one of the best Broadway musicals ever. That bell captain can also arrange for you to take a guided bus tour of the city to get an overall feel for the place. See a couple of other things, but don't try to do the whole city, just get a taste of it and eat some great Italian food in Little Italy. If you just use the few Italian words you know, they'll treat you like royalty. And buy a few cookies in one of their bakeries and look back in time for a moment at the two of us and our journey. Next, get on an airplane and fly to Chicago, spend one whole day at the Museum of Science and Industry. You'll get an education there. Amazing place. Then see a one or two other big attractions, maybe the art museum, maybe something else. While you're in Chicago, ask about three or four things to do in San Francisco, a great town which I haven't been to yet, but I know they have wonderful Italian food there and a million art galleries. From Chicago, you can fly to Kansas City to say your goodbyes to your aunt and then, that same day fly to San Francisco. From there, you can fly back to Denver or do another city, I would suggest Los Angeles or Las Vegas or both. This is about a two week circuit I've outlined. By the time you drag yourself back to Denver, you will have become a 'Worldly Woman.' And you can decide how your life might go from there. And, more important, you will have had one heluva time. What a blast!"

Stella was shocked and she was silent. After a very long minute, I broke the silence by asking? "Any questions?" She blinked and slowly nodded her head 'yes.' "What makes you able to imagine such an adventure? That's one question. The second is ... Do you think I could actually do it?"

"The first question I'll try to answer some other time. So ... second question first. You and I have been acquaintances, friends and lovers for two weeks ... more than a week of that on the road, with about another week to go. You have changed so much in such a short amount of time. Believe it or not, you have an adventurous seed in your spirit. You've just held your spirit in reserve, close to yourself, afraid for it to show. Princess, you're like a flower bud, ready to bloom and you will, for sure. There's no stopping now. So don't be afraid of it. Let it all happen. If you could tolerate all the new stuff you've been exposed to in the last two weeks, you're doing better than most people could dream of doing. You can handle yourself anywhere I'm sure... just need some practice without me in your way. Remember when I sang that song for you ... 'Everything's Coming Up Roses', well that's what's happening to you and I'm delighted to be witness to it. And ... You're going to hear that song on the New York stage and you'll never, ever, forget it."

The two of us simmered down and began reading ... she started 'Auntie Mame' and I was finishing with 'Twelve Angry Men'. After a time, she asked me if I would do her a favor tomorrow morning. "Ma, certo!" She said she would like to make a few phone calls tomorrow and preferred I not hear them. Two of the calls would be to her two 'protectors' down in Louisiana. I said "The school teachers?" She nodded yes. "Good, is two hours enough time?" Again she nodded. "Princess, here's a plan ... we go to breakfast and return here. I get the laundry and walk over there and read the newspaper we bought. A day or two old doesn't matter since I'm at least a month behind anyway." She gave me a hug and said "You're a Prince." And, of course I said, "No, I'm the White Knight ... Let me introduce myself."

Later, we walked the mile and a half to the saloon, let's call it a nightclub. Four musicians did some beautiful work up there on a very small stage. Calypso had been so popular just a few years before, but was being overwhelmed by rock and roll just as Jazz had been all but smothered also. We had two drinks each over a two hour period. Just two people enjoying a relaxed atmosphere of Caribbean rhythms. Stella must have tipped the waitress and band very well because each of them gave her a hug and all but threw flowers at us as we left and returned to our room, with echoes of 'Day-O' and 'Brown Skin Girl' still in our heads.

CHAPTER 30

MORE FALLS

Our second morning in Wichita Falls was loosely scheduled, quite a change from the usual non-scheduled format. We would catch breakfast at the restaurant in the front of the motel, then return to the room, where I'd get the laundry, take it over to the service building, while Stella spent an hour or more with the telephone. At breakfast, Stella mentioned the four new drinks she had shared with me, each of us drinking half of each drink, similar to the pie routine we had developed. Before we ordered from the cocktail waitress, I had told her that I preferred slightly sweet drinks, usually with a good US or Canadian Whiskey or US Bourbon. She thought she'd like to try whatever I was having, since she had no idea what drink she would order, very seldom drinking anything at all. So, over the almost three hours, we had been served and shared, a Whiskey Sour, a Manhattan, an Old-Fashioned, and a Bourbon and Ginger. I explained also that these were not the drinks of the "sophisticated" folks, who drank scotch, vodka, and gin. Scotch was OK, but vodka and gin were for people who had run out of antifreeze and couldn't find any after-shave lotion to tide themselves over… just my opinion, of course. She got a good laugh out of that, saying "Rosano, 'subtle' is not your strong suit." A fun breakfast, then back to the room, use the bathroom, grab the laundry (do I have everything of yours? Yes, you do) and the newspaper, and go to the central area, get the washing machine to begin its assigned task, find a chair in the garden, open the day-old newspaper and see how the world had misbehaved as we crossed the US prairie.

While I listened for the machine going through its paces, there seemed to be more positive news than negative. How refreshing! For one, Nashville, Tennessee was desegregating its lunch counters. Raised in New England, then moving to Arizona, I wasn't much aware of legal segregation. Of course, I knew of de facto segregation or separation. It would take a quite a while, but that segregation insanity would end. So that was good. Second, President Eisenhower took full responsibility for the U-2 spy-plane flights over Soviet territory. Ike said it was justified because everyone knew what a bunch of sneaky bastards the Russians were and everyone knew they were the bad guys and we were the good guys, and if Ike said that, it was probably right. (Washing machine is done, take the clothes out, detwist some of them and toss them into the dryer. I'd try thirty minutes at the lowest heat, feed a few coins into the machine and return to the newspaper). Third, Enovid, or 'The Pill' was finally being approved for contraception, instead of just for menstrual pain or female cycle 'regulation'. This was the source of huge controversy with the makers of the pill never saying the word contraception and the religious Neanderthals screaming, as they are so capable of doing, that God wouldn't want us to do any of that shit. Months earlier, in the few discussions in which I had been involved, the lively talk would fizzle whenever I asked how many 'unwanted children' the would-be deniers had adopted or would adopt and provide care and nourishment for. All depends on whose ox is being gored with the self-righteous soul-saver set. But the dryer needed another 10 minutes, probably because intake air was pretty humid, not like the desert southwest, where a dryer was hardly ever needed.

In that paper there was an article about weather in that part of Texas. It sounded pretty rough in some ways. Today was great, warm, a bit humid, but I had become a lizard in the Tucson dry. However, I read that Wichita Falls could become almost as hot as our southwest desert and be humid at the same time. That's not good. In addition, the winters could get below zero, and that's terrible. Add to that nonsense the big tornado factor, and I would just call it a nice place to visit … it seemed OK … today, but my bet was that it could wear pretty thin pretty quickly. The laundry was finished except for folding, so I took my own sweet time, did a credible job of folding my clothes and hers and returned to our room. Knocked and entered and asked "Coast clear?" She was writing in her little book, nodded yes, smiled widely, and said "C'mon, Let's go for more coffee." Setting the laundry on one of the chairs, I breathed deeply and said "A woman's work is never done." She laughed lightly. For me, there are few rewards greater that causing a beautiful woman to smile … to cause a beautiful woman to laugh, even softly, was one of those.

As we walked to the restaurant, she asked what I'd like to do in the afternoon. I mentioned that the little walk of last night felt good, maybe we could take a stroll alongside that Wichita River. That would be a little change. Also, I felt there was damn little else for tourists in this town, unless we wanted to visit one of the nearby lakes, but a river in the middle of a city seemed intriguing. Growing up in the eastern US, I never paid much attention to rivers, except of course, when they flooded. Now, having adopted the desert southwest as home, I became keenly aware of rivers, and which way they flowed or didn't flow. Anyway, an afternoon walk sounded good. We'd take the Lambretta, noodle around town a bit, find a good place to stroll, and just leisure a while. Hey, how about a picnic? Isn't that what we've been doing? True, but we've called it 'camping' or 'snacking.' Today, we'll call it a picnic, just for variety's sake. As we drank our coffee, she finally asked "Are you going to ask me about my phone calls this morning?" I said yes I'll ask right now. "Did your calls go OK for you this morning?" She answered, "Yes, quite well." I said "Good for you. Now, are you going to ask me how the laundry went?" She laughed loudly and snorted just a little coffee through her nose into the napkin. As she was recovering, I continued, "You know, getting laundry done can be quite a procedure and there are always costs which we do not anticipate ... for example, most washing machines require water, soap, electric power (in this case, enabled by coin insert), and one sock. The machines almost always require one sock, and they will take that sock if the opportunity arises. But ... I was alert to this sort of thing, and diligently retrieved all the clothing, including all the socks. The trick, of course, is to accurately count the socks before they are introduced into the washing cycle, count them again as they enter the drying phase, rounding up any strays, and then take a final roll call as they are withdrawn from the dryer, ready for foot patrol. This morning, I'm pleased to report, the process went perfectly." The Princess smiled, saying "Rosano, you sweet young man, we can get help for you."

And so we went noodling, with her giving directions this way and that, just experiencing some of Wichita Falls, Texas. Such a splendid time, the scooter behaving perfectly, and this lovely person holding me lightly, twiddling my ears or neck or beard now and then. Part of the time, we were alongside the river. She gave me a signal to stop at a mini-market. Came out with two cold cans, which I assumed were beers. She signaled and two or three minutes later, we were parking the scooter near the river. "Picnic Time," she said and displayed the two cans of cold Club Soda. Perfect. We had a cup for sharing, and some jerky, and dried fruit, some pistachios, and a box of whole wheat crackers. What more could a person ask? I locked the helmets to the scooter and secured everything to a sign post. Sitting on a low concrete wall, we watched the river flowing steadily to the north and east where it eventually emptied into the Red River. We had our food between us and traded cold sips of soda as we ate slowly and talked. It didn't require too many minutes for two or three ducks to begin their investigation to find how much of a sucker one of us might be for their maak-maak-maaking. Stella caved in, broke two or three crackers into pieces and tossed them on the ground, from which they disappeared faster than the telling. These were some veteran beggars. We finished our little picnic under the watchful eyes of the beggar birds, and returned the remaining food to the scooter. "Princess, let's take a little stroll. I enjoyed last night's walk to the pub. I'd like to do a little more." We strolled downriver and hardly spoke, just enjoyed being alive and being friends on a day perfectly tailored for a gentle walk. A young couple, maybe middle 30's walked toward us with three or four kids speaking rapidly in Spanish, and I nodded and said "Buenas Tardes." The couple smiled and returned the greeting and one of the boys asked "Sei Zorro de las peliculas?" Surprised, I said, "Mi.? Zorro? No, no, pero, somos amigos." The couple laughed as we passed and the kids hollered "Patos!" and started chasing the ducks. Stella then asked me, "That kid, he asked if you were Zorro from what?" I said "Zorro from the movies, I think. So I said, 'no, but we are friends.'" She said "How much Spanish do you know?" My answer was very little, but I was just beginning to understand and it seemed so difficult because they speak so rapidly. By the time I figure out one thing. They've said seven more.

We walked at a leisurely pace for perhaps a half-mile without talking, but always touching. Turning about to retrace our steps, she asked what I had read in the newspaper that morning. To make it brief, the U-2 incident has the US and the Soviets trying to bring the end of our world soon, but a lot of people were going to miss seeing it because The Pill was being approved as a legal birth control method. She said that was good because almost everyone who was using it was telling a lie to their doctor and the doctors knew it and lied right back. I recognized it as a big charade because of the crazy 'churchies' of various descriptions and persuasions with misguided 'Jesus Christ' ideas, and sleazy legislators each having a different price at which he would sell his soul.

Back to that reliable little machine, Tony Lambretta, and Stella asked, "What's next, White Knight?" I answered, "Fuel for Tony, and food for our run tomorrow." She said "Lead the charge!" And it happened. As we gassed up and shopped at a market for food items, I felt people looking at us for a bit longer or perhaps slightly more intensely than at any previous time on this entire trip. Unless very obvious, that sort of thing is elusive and little attention was paid ... just a mental note. We returned to our luxury room at the motel, stashed the food, refreshed the water bag, and grabbed our books, lay down and promptly snoozed with arms and legs draped here and there, neither of us, it seemed, wanting to detach from the other. Time passed.

On wakening, we discovered it was still afternoon. Stella sat up, said "Me, first." and disappeared into the bathroom. Nudging me awake again, she said "You, next." Got up and eventually got the shower going and said "Me, wash" and she jumped up with "Me, too." We bathed and became so hungry for each other. We had to be the best thing happening that day in all of Wichita Falls, maybe in the whole state of Texas. A monumental merger. After a time, she asked if I wanted to shower again. I said no. I preferred to wear her scent a while longer. We rested.

After a decent interval, she asked, "Rosano, what do you think you might do in your life ... or with your life ... however you want to say it ... and you don't have to answer if you don't want to. But I'd like to hear your thinking." Oh my. So I began and it was no big deal for me. It was, however, the most enormous deal for my parents, who never got used to having a son, their only son, who was such a screwup and wouldn't conform to any of their or anybody else's expectations. Having tried their idea of a good 'path for a good life' for far too long, I no longer would. Presently, I was trying to come up with a way to let them down gently if that were possible. The upcoming wedding would be a joyous occasion for my gorgeous younger sister, Phyllis, and the entire family. But when the bride and groom left, I would remain behind with my parents who would eagerly seek some encouraging signs from me. That wasn't going to happen. But enough of that stuff. What were my intentions? Simple, I would just try a number of things and not be in a rush to latch onto anything too firmly, unless of course, it really grabbed me. The possibility of a military draft hung over me, but there were a few positives going for me ... I knew I was a bit more creative than many people, and thoroughly enjoyed mathematics and the sciences, and, most important, I wasn't afraid of failing ... and genuinely enjoyed doing things that I wasn't trained for. Crazy, no? So my plan, already in progress, was to try a wide variety of things and make more plans afterward, which seemed to be my plan for everything ... plan to try different things and make more plans at a later time. If it required five years or ten years, then that would have to be. Stella nodded in acknowledgement. Of course, I didn't mention that a parallel intention, with that 'different things' approach was my determination to be with as many different women as possible before 'settling down' and I had yet to tell my 'girlfriend' back in Tucson, to 'fageddabowditdaholting' (East coast dialect : 'forget about it, the whole thing.) Somehow a postcard from Wichita Falls seemed an inappropriate way to end an affair. Time to write a letter, I suppose. I'd do it tomorrow ... maybe.

Now I had a question, nothing too deep. Did she remember our collective nouns and the question 'What if we named groups of people based on their occupations or activities?' Had she thought of any others? She grinned and said "Rosano, as we buzz down the highway and my hands stay busy pulling your ears or scratching your back, do you think my mind is idle?" Shocked, I said, "Ma, non certo!" Laughing, she said, "Hey, I understood that! And yes, I have a few more. Ready?" I nodded yes. "OK, how about ... a piping of plumbers, or a net of fishermen, a slice of surgeons, or a carpet of weavers, a stitch of tailors, a surge of electricians, or a cut of butchers." That was some good word playing. I'd have to give her a good grade on her report card.

"Ready for some supper?" I nodded yes, got up, and quickly rinsed in the shower. She was there to towel me down. This lovely lady was going to take me out for our evening meal. What more could a traveling stranger ask? We walked over to the restaurant, waited several minutes to be seated despite the fact that half the tables were vacant. As we sat down, a middle-aged couple stood up two tables away and left in a hurried manner and stared pointedly at me as they did. I looked at Stella, probably with a question on my face. Quietly she said, "It's probably your beard which has them annoyed and probably a little scared, too." After appraising that for a moment, my hunch tells me she's right, but there's one more factor, unspoken ... they probably think I'm Mexican. Just my guess. I really do look Mexican and we're in Texas, after all (remember the Alamo and all that), and not in Southern Arizona where it's OK to be Mexican. In Tucson, a most prestigious social club was part of the scene at the hotel where I worked and it had a Mexican-American as President. This was 1960 and the beatniks were fading and the hippies were just starting and bearded people were becoming prominent on the scene, more often than not, seen in a strongly negative manner. Having a beard or mustache just pissed off some of the folks who should know better. Stella and I ordered our food. At my suggestion, one of us ordered Texas Bar-B-Q and we split it. Tasty stuff and I liked the intensity of the spicing, but thought the whole thing was far too sweet and sticky. Stella asked if I knew about Cajun food or Creole cooking. Yeah, but just a little. I knew a little because at the hotel in Tucson, they were having a Fat Tuesday (Marti Gras) banquet and I would be working it as a waiter. I had heard of both Cajun and Creole cooking, but didn't know the differences between them. The hotel brought in a "special guest chef for the event" and she took over the kitchen for about two days. I stayed as close to the kitchen as possible those two days and really tried to learn a few things, even hanging around during my 'off' hours. At the end of the two days, I still didn't know any major differences between the two. I thought both were too heavy on the onions, but maybe that's my weirdness coming through. The food seemed tasty enough, but not 'knock your socks off' tasty. Stella asked if I thought Cajun or Creole would ever 'catch on' as a major food style. My opinion was that it didn't have a prayer. One or two dishes might get popular, but I felt there was more 'sweet talk' than substance, more mystique than meat. It was good, but not great. So here I've formed an opinion based on the food from only a single chef, who was not in her home territory, and that's not quite fair. On the other hand ... she was 'the authority' and highly paid at that. If I had paid her fee, I would have felt cheated.

What did Stella remember of food preparation down in the south of Louisiana, home to both Creole and Cajun and something called Louisiana Cuisine. She hesitated, thought about how to respond, and quietly said, "There was never quite enough. The grownups talked about the Jambalaya or Gumbo and how it had to be the best ever, but the only way the kids could fill their stomachs was with corn bread. We didn't starve, but we were never satisfied either. And we didn't really taste our food, we ate very quickly, almost like animals. My Kansas City aunt taught me proper table manners and how to be 'civilized' at mealtime ... and always made sure there was enough food, in plain sight, for second helpings."

We ate slowly and talked on various topics. Stella said she might want to take some courses at the University in Denver when she returned there ... if she decided to stay. Who knows ... after she saw a bit of New York City and some of Chicago and San Francisco. Interrupting her, I said, "So, you've decided to try that little circuit. Good for you! Man, that's exciting just to think about it. You are going to have the time of your life! Congratulations to you, Miss Stella Beauchamp, within a month you will have become ... a 'Woman of the world'!" She grinned and bowed slightly as if to acknowledge the applause. "Rosano, I want to ask you about College courses." I said "Soon. Later, I'll have to think about that. Right now let's just celebrate a little."

Finishing our meal, we passed on dessert having had enough of the sweetness with the Bar-B-Q. As we left she said, "Tomorrow we're back to the highway. Where to?" I explained, "We had essentially two choices. We could stay on old familiar Route 287, continue southeast and get into the Dallas area, or start on 287 and switch to Route 82, and head more directly east to Gainesville. The second choice was the more northern route, probably a bit cooler, certainly more rural. With either choice, we'd have to be aware this was tornado country, the North Central Plains, at the tornado time of year. What's your pleasure, Principessa?" She said, "Cooler sounds better right now."

We began to 'settle in' for the evening. I had just a few pages to finish "Twelve Angry Men" before starting "Streetcar named Desire." Stella was just opening "Auntie Mame" and seemed anxious to get into that audacious character. I thought we might have more relaxed reading if our clothes weren't restricting us. With a big smile, she started unbuttoning my shirt and continued in this helpful and rather sultry manner until I was naked.

With a bigger smile, she asked "Better?" I nodded a big yes. She said softly, "Good." And lay down, fully clothed, and began to read. Very funny. I could feel her laughing silently. After some time, I rolled over, put my arm around this lovely lady, saying "Pay attention to Mame. She was based on a real person. As a book character she is so many desirable things ... zany, glamorous and sophisticated, and if you take your clothes off, I'll tell you more about Mame." Miss Beauchamp got out of bed, stood beside it, and said "You just think I'm 'easy pickin's', right? Well, mister, I can drive a hard bargain when necessary. So ... you're going to have to tell me two more things before I show you my good luck charms." Responding, I said slowly, "...and Mame was irreverent, that's one, and good-hearted just like me, and that's two. And I know you have 'charms' so now it's time to keep your part of the bargain."

CHAPTER 31

THE REST OF TEXAS

Luxurious sleeping. That's what the ordinary motel offers to anyone who is camping and sleeping on the ground. And we had had two rewarding nights of it. Looking at my deeply sleeping companion in my own half sleep, the resemblance to "Anya" or Princess Ann, played by Audrey Hepburn is so strong, I become disoriented for a moment or two and pictured her on the motor scooter in the movie 'Roman Holiday.' The little grey gears in my brain begin to mesh properly and normal function makes a muddled return, but not immediately. Coffee would certainly aid in this process. Without the coffee, Geez Louise, confusion. Finally, I bushwhacked my way through the groggy, put my arm around my friend. Taking my arm, she pulled it a little tighter around her and we lightly snoozed on.

Rising a bit later, and with almost no talking, we prepared ourselves for the world in general, but in particular, for the restaurant and its coffee. We were able to walk the thirty or forty yards entirely without incident. The First Cup Holy Sacrament was in progress when the Princess leaned over, planted a little smooch and said "Good Morning, White Knight!" Leaning toward her, and as tenderly as possible, I said, "Shhhh." We drank coffee with her in full grin mode. Food arrived and my pancakes were excellent. Her breakfast, suitable in size for the average lumberjack, was handled easily. "Thanks for last night." I raised my eyebrows, "Oh?" She said "It was lovely." Looking at her I asked, "Where was I?" She started to giggle, and stated "I wasn't exactly sure where you were." And she was laughing lightly. When I asked "Did WE have YOURself a good time?" That got to her for sure and she was laughing loudly and trying to muffle it with her napkin, and snorted a bit of coffee through her nose, just for effect, I suppose. The couple seated at the next table began to laugh at her laughing. A family of four on the other side of us joined in, and the waitress did too. I tried to be deadpan but had to laugh, too. A loud bunch of people we were. Other people at more distant tables looked at us and had to smile. If we knew what we were laughing at, we might have told them. Everything simmered down in time. One of those silly and splendid moments amongst strangers.

We were finishing breakfast, having a smoke, and drinking final cups of coffee, when Stella asked "Which route are we taking this morning?" Essentially, we had two choices, go southeast through Bowie, the Dallas-Fort Worth area, southward to Houston, then east along the gulf coast toward Louisiana. Second major option, more northerly, was to head directly east, staying just south of the Red River and the Texas-Oklahoma border, making our way to the corner of Arkansas and then south to Shreveport, Louisiana. Second choice was probably a few degrees cooler. We had already talked about this the day before, and Stella said cooler sounded better. Answering, I said "Northern choice wins. We'll head to Gainesville, a little less than 100 miles from here. Probably get there early, so we can go to the Zoo, spend a little time in the library, and catch a concert, and end up watching boat races on the river." She started laughing again, and shaking her head, saying "In where? In Gainesville? Quite an agenda, Rosano. Good luck to us."

Back to our room. Let's shower, because we may not get a chance tonight when we camp out. We washed, dried and dressed. In one way, it seemed a year had passed since we were on the highway. What the brain does to time and vice versa, I suppose, is unexplainable. Seems to be truth in the expression 'Time flies when you're having fun.' We did our little packing, with food and clean clothing, a refreshed water bag, and a sense of adventure. We were on the scooter and soon back onto our old friend, Route 287, but not for long. We would travel for about 20 miles into Henrietta, Texas, a town of 2000, and take our new path, Route 82, through a half-dozen additional towns before reaching Gainesville, TX, our stopping point for the day. Neither of us was anxious to travel many miles per day, but rather there was a certain contentment just to view and enjoy our surroundings as we passed by at a leisurely pace. Leaving Wichita Falls, there seemed to me to be a decided change, feeling strongly that we had left the 'American West' behind and were now in transition to the 'Southland' or 'Dixie' or whatever name is used. This, despite having three days and three hundred miles of Texas still ahead of us. Texas is a big state, especially for a person with a New England mindset. The distance in Texas we intended to travel in the next three days would take us from New York City, through three or four states, to Portland, Maine if we were on the East coast. Texas seems especially expansive when traveling on a scooter with that top speed of 43 miles per hour. Always best to keep in mind that the traveling part was, in fact, the destination. The final landing place is not our destination. Our journey is itself the destination.

We had reached Henrietta, Texas where our old friend Route 287 and Route 82 parted ways, with 82 taking a more easterly direction. That would be our route. My passenger, who had been doing her always welcome twiddling, paused, and gave signals taking us through the center of town. As we putt-putted our way, I signaled with a question mark in the air and the scissor imitation with my fingers – 'do you want a break?' She returned with the finger-wagging 'no-no' signal and there was no pause as we were leaving Henrietta behind and aiming our road rocket to something far more mysterious and exotic ... Belcherville, Texas. Traveling eastward from Henrietta, the countryside became slightly more hilly and greener. I didn't remember many oil rigs back in the Oklahoma Panhandle. In the Texas Panhandle near Amarillo there had been scatterings of these tireless beasts dipping into the earth. Now they appeared more often, with service roads leading to them. This terrain no longer seemed part of the legendary American West. We were definitely in the south, at least in my mind. Having seen Belcherville on a map, and never having heard of it before, I was mildly intrigued only by the name and wondered if the people claimed they were from Bel-Chur-ville (as in stomach upset) or Bel-Ker-ville (as in stomach not upset). We continued along Route 82 with my passenger doing her twiddlings and the two of us enjoying a fine and peaceful morning, with a lightly overcast sky, and the Lambretta behaving perfectly. Traveling through Ringgold, a small community with a handful of people and five miles later, there it was ... or wasn't ... Belcherville. We paused, without shutting the scooter down. There were a few abandoned buildings and no sign of people inhabiting this tiny town. If it was, in fact, a town, it would be a ghost town, or close to it. Neither of us saw any people ... rather a strange feeling. Stella leaned forward to say quietly, "Let's get out of here ... now, please." And we did. My thought was, the difference between Bel-CHUR-ville and Bel-KER-ville made no difference at all since there were no people. Another ten minutes and we were in Nocona, Texas, where I signaled for a coffee break (scissors signal plus a tipped cup signal). The ever-alert Princess navigated us to a café. We had already traveled half the intended distance for the day.

After restrooms, we got seated, ordered black coffee, pie too? Sure, why not. "You didn't care for that abandoned village, did you?" She answered "I felt threatened there, didn't you feel it?" I said it had a sadness more than a threatening feel, but if either of us feels something not good, we'll get the hell out. In part, that's what 'compatibility' is all about. She gave my arm a little squeeze. As was our habit, we traded our half-eaten pie pieces and continued. The coffee tasted great. "Well, Miss Beauchamp, you with the sharp eyes, what did you notice back there in Henrietta? Did anything strike you?" She thought for a short time and said, "Nothing really outstanding about that town. Lots of churches, though." "That's it", I said,

"That and the fact that there were no bookstores evident. Not a one. Says something about the place, doesn't it? There might be a library, but I didn't see one, nor a sign pointing to one. A dozen or more churches is a bit much for fewer than 3000 people. This must be the Western edge of what they call the 'Bible Belt, but I'm not sure."

We finished our break with another round of coffee and a smoke and as always, a second visit to the restroom. Outside, we walked around a bit, stretched. She looked at my face, as if there were something to scrutinize, then grabbed my ears and gave me a big smooch and a smile to go with it. We were soon back on the highway. A perfect day climate-wise, sky without any threatening clouds, just a slight haze. We were less than two hours from Gainesville. Hilly, wooded terrain with a mixture of tree types, picturesque. These wooded hills gave way to more level grazing land, pastures, and a string of small communities or towns, interesting to see, and prompting the same question which I had while traveling the prairie ... how limited were the educational resources for the young people living here ... much dependent on the quality and enthusiasm of their teachers, I would guess.

As we approached Gainesville, there were a dozen signs for various campgrounds and I suspect on the other side of town there were a dozen more. I pulled over near the intersection of Route 82 and north-south Route 77 for a fuel stop. The station attendant was a young guy. Talked with him briefly while I did my oil and gas mixture routine. He remarked on the Arizona license plate and said he was thinking of applying to the U of A in Tucson. Right now he was finishing a few classes at a local Junior College. I asked if he had ever been to Tucson. No, not yet. Go there and look around, I think you'll love it, but for sure, get out of this area, this is dead-ends-ville. He nodded his head. We talked a few more minutes ... about going to New Orleans and other things. He asked if I had read 'On The Road' by Jack Kerouac. I said yes, for sure. Had he read 'Dharma Bums' or 'Subterraneans' by Kerouac? No, too busy with school. Yeah, I understand. He then asked about the scooter. He knew the Lambretta and the Vespa were about the same, not exactly, but close enough. How was it on the highway? Perfect, I said, if you have no schedule. Quite slow, but excellent for around town in a mild climate. Stella asked him about the zoo, the library, and campgrounds and restaurants. Yes, she had noticed the zoo. That girl could gather more useful information in the shortest time ... and remember it all.

Fueling complete, I paid the man, shook his hand, said "Thanks, Best of Luck to you." Stella asked, "What's the plan, Oh White Knight?" I said I wasn't hungry yet, could always use a cup of coffee, though. How about coffee and then an hour or two in the local library? After that we could have a meal and decide what to do. A plan? She said, "A plan." First kick on the scooter got it going and we drove less than a mile to a café, sat at the counter had coffee and a smoke.

Then she navigated us south about a mile to the Cooke County Library where we parked, tied up our helmets and locked up the scooter. Nice-looking 2-story brick building. Up a dozen stairs and through the entrance. Let's just wander a while. Entering the library gave a shocking change of scene ... no highway, no scooter buzz, no grassland, no wind. Books and a nice lady in charge of them who says "Hello," and asks "Can I help you find something?" Me: "Good Afternoon, thank you, but I just want to try osmosis for a few minutes." That nice lady smiles and says "I understand. Please, go right ahead." and I begin to wander, and see and smell and experience. Stella starts to ask a question which I don't hear. Not looking for a particular title or subject, I finally pull a book from a display table ... about the Bayou and the American alligator and American crocodile and other critters. Sitting in a lounge chair, I read small parts of three or four books. What a wondrous thing a book can be. Those little squiggles of ink can make you laugh or cry or be frightened or be informed. It's an amazing thing humans have developed. How I really treasured libraries ... what they contained and what they represented. Climbing out of that comfortable chair, I began to wander again. The librarian asked if I had enough of the osmosis treatment. Before I could answer, Stella's voice said "There you are." I said "Hello Princess, do you want to stay longer or are you ready to go?" She said "I'm hungry. Let's go for food." I turned to the librarian, saying "Thanks so much. You and other librarians do such important work." Then Stella said to her "Thanks for your help. That was exactly what I needed" and gave the woman a little hug. Our librarian said "Bon Voyage ... to both of you!"

Out of the library and back into the world. Onto our faithful Tony Lambretta, again started on the first kick. Navigated to a restaurant for a midafternoon meal. Removing and locking up the helmets and scooter as Stella asks "What's that song you're singing under your breath?" "Oh, that's a good little song by Jimmy Durante. Ever heard of him?" She nodded yes, "He's the one with the big nose, right?" I said "Hey, be careful, be careful." She laughed, tweaked my nose, and said, "That's the first place one of my little kisses landed on you, remember?" I said, "Yes, but that was just the easiest thing to reach." Stella (damn, she was beautiful) said, "The song, Rosano, the song, tell me." I said, "Let's go inside and order and by then, I might remember more of it." So into the diner we went, took a booth, and sat down. Stella was hungry, but I wanted very little to eat. We ordered coffee and food and I said the song is called 'The Day I Read a Book.' I started to sing it softly ...

I'll never forget the day I read a book.
It was contagious, seventy pages.
There were pictures here and there,
Ya da da da da dah,
The day I read a book.
It's a shame I don't recall the name of the book.
It wasn't a history, Ya da da da da da dah,
It wasn't a mystery, Ya da da da da da dah,
The day I read a book? I can't remember when,
But one of these days, I'm gonna do it again.

Well that's the best I can do. Not too strong on lyrics, but I especially like the way he rhymed 'pages' with 'contagious.' The Library triggered all this business. Man, how I love libraries. They are sacred spots on this earth. And what about you, Princess, find anything interesting?" She said "You know well enough I did, with the Librarian's help. I read about New York City and Chicago and San Francisco, because that's where I'm going ... exactly as you suggested." Oh man, I was so tickled and super pleased, saying "Good for you! Good for you! Congratulations, so good for you!" And she was crying again, but happy crying ... I think. Never really sure about these things.

As we ate, we talked quietly of various things with Stella finally asking, "Where to next?" I asked about a campground suggested by the gas station guy. Did it have a shower, etc? She said it sounded quite clean, secure, and a good place to stay. In that case, I said we should forget about the Zoo, and the Concert, and the Boat Races along the river and just make camp, make certain we had enough coins, make our coffee fire ready, make ourselves clean and then play, and then sleep. And ... that's what occupied two travelers until early the following morning. That's when we would begin to see the rest of Texas.

CHAPTER 32

PARIS AND SEGREGATION

Waking up in Gainesville, TX, in the middle of May is not so bad, I thought. With a little effort, and a little time, there would be life-saving coffee available. My companion was still sleeping. With a full bladder, however, choices are limited. Get up and slowly get dressed, enough at least, to get to the bathhouse restrooms without getting arrested. Lit the coffeepot fire, half watched and half dozed while it prepared itself. Ah, it sounds done. Count to 100 to give it time to age, then pour. Small blessings are so important, even if self-generated. And, as delightful as my companion could be, I would drink this first cup quietly, without sharing. I mean, love is one thing, but coffee …

Setting the coffee pot to the edge of the fire where it could still gain a bit of heat, I went back to the little tent, crawled in and took my beautiful friend into my arms and held her quietly until she stirred. When finally she sat up, I gave her a little smooch and asked "Coffee?" She smiled, eyes closed, and nodded "yes". Then coffee was served by a charming Italian waiter who greeted the Princess softly with "Buon Giorno, Principessa."

There were times when we could talk energetically for long periods of time about so many different subjects. Other times, hardly a word was exchanged. Those times seemed to coincide, fortunately. This was one of the quiet times as Stella finished her coffee, rose, dressed, used the restroom at the bathhouse and returned. In the meantime, I had started a second pot of coffee, because my coffee was so damn good, good for your body, and good for your soul. Stella came over to the fire, where I sat on one of the sawn tree trunk sections that served as chairs, and put her arms over my shoulders and just held me from behind for a few minutes without speaking. The coffeepot broke the spell as it said 'almost ready' with its gurgling sound. How much better could life get? The sound stopped when the pot was moved off the fire and the count to 100 began. Stella asked "Aging process?" I said," Yes, it has to 'breathe' for a moment or two." I poured, she sat beside me and we shared and everything was hunky dory. She asked "Are we going to see Paris, Texas today?" I said if there were no major glitches, we would. It was about 100 miles from where we were ... about three hours of scooter time. In that 100 miles, we would drop 150 feet in elevation or 18 inches per mile. That's a gradual slope.

Early mornings on the road, if you're driving to the east, can be tough because of the sun looking directly at you. So we packed up camp at a careful and leisurely pace (which always included freshening the water bag), got onto Tony Lambretta's back, gave it one kickstart, which was returned, in friendly fashion, by the usual puff of bluish smoke and we were off to a local breakfast shop. After breakfast, a stop at a corner market, which was trying to become a supermarket. Bought some fresh fruit, some snack items, canned peaches, canned figs, and a small bottle of dish detergent for mosquito wars. In front of the market, after we packed our food, got our sunglasses and helmets on, Stella semi-mauled me with a good natured smooch, saying, "Rosano, I really love being with you. So now, White Knight, I would like to go to Paris." A minute later we were back onto our Route 82. This was the Piney Woods area of Texas, quite green, the morning was mild, humid, almost no wind. Weather had been very favorable during most of trip from Denver. We were traveling in so-called 'Tornado Alley' which was an area of Kansas, Oklahoma, and Texas where tornados happened most frequently. For sure, people in other states felt they had equal claim to Tornado Alley status, especially given the wild unpredictability of these devastating storms. We had been spared any dangerous weather in our journey so far. We kept watch skyward to get as much advanced warning as possible, in case bad stuff was brewing. No radio or TV meant we were insulated from news of quick-moving events. We would never know about bridge collapses, train wrecks, floods, or tornados until we happened on them.

Arizona living, even for that short time, had made me a confirmed lizard. That dry air, with humidity levels usually in the teens, but often with a humidity reading in the single digits ... 5% not unusual, was in strong contrast to this stuff with 70 -80% which I was now breathing. The precious water bag was not producing the cool water I was accustomed to. It was elementary physics ... now there was a much slower rate of evaporation, resulting in warmer water. Even with a much-reduced cooling effect, the unbreakable water bag was still a convenient method of thirst quenching. It still needed to be refreshed on a daily basis.

After driving through four or five small towns in 60 miles, and nearly two hours later, it was time for a restroom and coffee break. What was this little burg called? Bonham, Texas. We ordered coffee and two different fruit pies, did our usual switching at the halfway point of the pie pieces, paid the bill, used the restrooms, and returned to the scooter. There were four people having their breakfast at a picnic table just a few feet from where the scooter was parked. I gave a cheery "Good Morning, folks. How's it going?" There was a decided hesitation, and the older man said "A Good Morning to you." We got our sunglasses and helmets back onto our heads, started Tony Lambretta, waved, and we were back on the highway and I'm thinking it was a perfect morning to have breakfast outside, but since Stella and I were exposed to so much weather each day, being inside was always a break from the feel of wind and the noise constantly generated as it swirled around us as we rode, even at our relatively slow highway speed. We would be in Paris in less than two hours, to gas up, seek out a camping area, get a bite to eat, perhaps do something in town. Library? Movie? Bookstore?

Much of the land we traveled through was farmland, pasture with animals grazing, there was also some cotton. Pima Long Staple Cotton was huge in Arizona, where it grew superbly, so these fields near Paris, Texas seemed familiar. I had no idea which variety was grown here. Pima cotton was valued because of the length of fiber, its strength and uniformity, but used enormous amounts of water during its growth. Here in Texas, with forty or fifty inches of rainfall per year, growing cotton made more sense, I thought. But I was unknowledgeable in so many subjects in so many ways.

An hour of putt-putting through farmland was cause for a break. I pulled over near the sign pointing to the right which said Petty, population 200. Time for a drink of water and a smoke. My guess was Petty was named after someone with that family name. Having to say you were from Petty, Texas would be a challenge. One could say instead 'I live north of Dallas'. Stella and I did our walking and stretching before getting onto the Lambretta again. Less than an hour later, we were entering Paris, Texas. Pulling into the first gas station, I stopped at the pump and waited for the attendant to finish serving a customer. When he came over to us, the first thing he said was "Arizona? Arizona? You didn't drive from there in that, did you? " "Sure did," I said. Then he did the 'I always wanted to do something like that, only I got married' routine. Then he said, "Oh, excuse my big mouth talking. Are you two married?" Silence, then Stella said "Soon, perhaps." That was a better response than "Mind your own business" or "I'd rather not say." We fueled the scooter, and Stella asked about a campground and places to eat. As we were putting on helmets and glasses, Stella asked if there was something specific to see in Paris. I replied there was nothing I knew to be really outstanding or in the 'do not miss' category. Was she ready for food or would she prefer to make camp? I could go either way. She was a little hungry so we headed to a small restaurant, which would have some decent food. We parked at the rounded corner since there were already two or three cars parked in front. As I was stringing the cable thru our helmets I noticed four people standing around the front end of their car parked at the side of the building. A neatly dressed middle-aged couple and a very well-dressed elderly couple. They were eating food from paper plates, which were resting on the fenders of the car. This illogical picture made me pause. How peculiar! Without realizing, I stopped what I was doing long enough for Stella to touch my arm and say "C'mon Rosano." I asked her quietly, "What are they doing?" She said softly, "They can't eat inside because they're Colored." That floored me. I was stunned. I finally said "but those two old people … they shouldn't have to stand up to eat." What sense did that make? Trying to understand, something in my head said 'segregation' and my mind refused to function and I was aware that it wasn't working well, wasn't processing. And that is truly frightening. So goddamned shameful. I didn't know how to handle this. With a noisy roar in my ears, I was unstringing the helmets from the cable, and remembered saying "I want to get out of here … now!" Stella said not a word, got onto the scooter quickly and we were back on Route 82. We drove eastward for almost an hour, Stella gently rubbing or hugging me the entire time. It was one of those 'forevers', but eventually the cloud of turmoil was leaving my head and I began to forcefeed logic into my thinking. It was a slow regain of consciousness and there was no memory of those miles except for the feel of the woman who held me. Eventually, seeing a group of trees at the roadside far ahead, I pulled over slowly and glided slowly to a stop. And dismounted, removed my helmet and glasses, and apologized. "I'm so sorry. I must have scared the hell out of you. That will not happen again." She just gave me a hug, reached upward with a kiss and said "Let's have a drink of water and a smoke and we can wind down, OK?" And we did so. Stella started talking first. "All those hours of us talking together and we never talked about segregation. I assumed you knew far more than I did, especially when you mentioned the newspaper headline that Nashville was desegregating its lunch counters." I said, "I've read about this, heard about it, but never in 'real life', just on paper, in newspapers or books. The word 'segregation' was just a political word to me, I guess. But this, this is 'real life' and this is so goddamn appalling. I just wasn't prepared for it, at all … so completely stupid of me and ignorant, too. Unbelievable." Walking around removed more of the tangled web of thoughts in my mind. We were near a place called Clarksville. "Sorry we missed Paris, but I'll take you to Clarksville instead. Let's get some coffee and food." The Princess said, "Let's sit down for a slow meal and we should talk about this, this one area where I might help you for a change." And thus we drove the few miles into Clarkesville and found a diner that was almost empty at that time of the early afternoon.

We sat at a booth which blocked our view of almost everything except each other. Our food was delivered, we began eating slowly, and Stella asked "Which of us is going to talk first, except I think I should." Had to smile at that one and I gave a manual 'go ahead' signal. "Rosano, you are at a big disadvantage right now in dealing with this. You are the kindest, fairest person I've ever known. But you are one 'soft touch', for being a rough and tough knight and all that. Your mind couldn't handle what you saw back there because it was so unfair and there was nothing you could do about it. One small reserve part of your brain said 'I can't fix this and I can't stand it either, so we must leave this place.' Is that accurate?" Yeah, that's right. She had the whole thing summed up perfectly. Smart cookie, this lady. I had to agree ... she was right on the money. She went on, "Earlier this morning we had coffee and pie in Bonham. Did you think those people were sitting outside at the picnic table by choice?" I nodded yes and said "It was a perfect morning for a little picnic and I thought they were clever to do that." She said "I wondered what you thought was going on there." I said, "You know I was raised in New England, in Connecticut. I went to school, ate lunch, played sports, and music, with a wide mixture of people including Colored, a few Orientals, some Puerto Ricans, Jamaicans, and yeah, we would hear adults make all kinds of racial comments, and for the most part, just laughed at them both – the comments and the older people, ignored them or just quietly chalked it up to old ideas. And some of the Mayflower bunch were snotty small-minded jackasses. And I heard my share of Italian slurs, too, and if I felt someone was being a bit too nasty, I would sometimes get in a fight about it. Then I moved to Arizona, where again, there was a mixture of people of all kinds, two kinds were completely new to me ... Mexicans and Mormons, and except for the Mormon coffee thing, there were no major problems. So this segregation thing occupied very little space in my thinking until today. This is the first time I witnessed how dreadful this was. You know what image is stuck in my mind? Do you know what I see? That old woman's nice blue and white dress and the thin frail legs below that. And one of her ankles was bandaged and her leg was shaking a little as she tried to take some of the weight off it, and she, so dignified, yet I imagine she really needed to sit down. Terrible! I guess we truly are in the south, a south I know very little about." Then it was time for a question for Stella. How did she handle this shit when she was growing up in Louisiana?

Stella said, "First, Rosano, I have to tell you ... all these hours on the scooter have been just wonderful for me, wonderful meaning full of wonder. So many new things, new ideas, and you ... you just dive into life, and you talk to strangers, and are so unafraid and I'm jealous of that and I want some of that for myself and you get that from a very rich childhood, rich in culture, rich in heroes, and experiences. So ... you can understand only partly, the emptiness of my upbringing. I'm not sure I understand it myself, but for my entire childhood, I felt like a foreigner. I didn't belong anywhere. I walked around, almost in a daze, in a sea of people, some of them Colored, some of them White and I was far removed from any of them. I had no feelings at all for anyone, until finally when my Kansas City aunt came down to Louisiana and a little later, when I began to know my cousin Broderick. So, Rosano, you ask how did I handle this segregation thing when I was growing up. The fact is that I didn't handle it at all, just went along with whatever was happening that day. And looked at everything as an outsider. Insulated from everything, I just wasn't involved. So we can talk more about me some other time. I want to talk 'at' you and not 'with' you for a few minutes. You OK with that?" I remember taking a big breath and saying "Ma, Certo,"... to let the Princess know I was back in possession of my mind.

So this woman started talking. "Rosano, you started this little journey for several reasons, and you offered to take me to New Orleans for several reasons also. One of your important purposes was to 'see this place called America.' Part of that was to see a good part of the Mississippi River. And you will. But ... here's a problem. For a variety of reasons, you just seem to enter the lives of people so easily, my life included. I saw it in Pueblo, where that guy named Zip, in the gas station, just quit his job, quit his job, mind you, to follow a dream you presented to him. Or Enrico, at the restaurant, who just loved you immediately and then loved us together. So, for two thousand miles, you have been an observer of the land and people, but you were also a participant. Now, you're entering the south, and I am telling you, as strongly as I can, to reduce your participation and increase your observation. I know you well enough now to say, from this point in your travels, and until you get north of Kentucky somewhere, you are a foreigner in your own country. Rosano, in your mind and in your heart, you are not a suitable person for the south. And you were right when you bought the machete, back in Pueblo ... on this scooter you are so vulnerable. So now, Rosano, you have to be still more protective of the two of us and when we say our goodbyes, more protective of yourself, alone". She paused and looking straight into my eyes she said, "I'm telling you this and I am begging you, Rosano." And her eyes were watery as she went silent and lowered her head into her hands and she was crying and not just a little. I got up from my seat and sat beside her and put my arm around her waist. Some minutes later she said softly, "I just don't want you to get hurt. I really am begging you." And tears continued down her face.

Dragging my place setting to my new place at the booth, I slowly sipped coffee. After a long while, I asked "Are you going to be OK?" Slowly, she nodded yes. "Are you up for camping tonight? Because I don't want to drive any further today." She said yes, she would prefer that there were no other people around. "Can you ask the waitress for info on campgrounds?" She said she would. We finished our food, used the restrooms, drank more coffee, had a smoke, paid the bill and exited. Stella directed us to a campground with running water, clean restrooms, but no showers because they were just being built. That's OK with me for tonight. Within an hour, our tent was set up, and we were "settled in." It had been a tough, emotional afternoon for both. Still midafternoon and I needed a little shutdown time. From my jacket pocket, I fished out the little aspirin bottle and took four in my hand, offered my hand to my dear friend. She took one and I took three, we retreated to our tiny tent world and lay down, holding each other gently, staying in touch.

It was the squawk of a large bird, maybe a hawk or an eagle, which caused us to wake perhaps an hour later. With a little kiss, I asked if she would like some coffee if I made a pot. She said not yet, later, and pulled my arms around her more snuggly. From her sounds, I knew she was sleeping again. I was wide awake and my thinking gears were churning as I replayed the scene that prompted all this turmoil. If I felt sorry for myself, I'd have to compare my situation with the circumstances of those people standing around the front end of their car. They didn't have to think, they had to endure. I felt embarrassed that I had allowed emotions to take control and cause me to frighten my dear companion. She had appraised the situation as it occurred. She knew what had happened in my mind before I did. She would talk to me or 'at' me again, and I would indeed listen. I had already decided.

Some time passed before Stella turned toward me saying it was OK to make coffee now. Gave her a smooch and got out of the tent and arranged a fire in the small brick fireplace and got the coffee started. It was late afternoon and it seemed even the sun was weary. Stella joined me at the fireplace. Soon we could pour a cup and share it back and forth. How I loved doing that! She then said, "I want to ask you a question ... How much do you know about Communist China?" After thinking for a few seconds, I had to admit I knew damn little. She said, "Rosano, you are in China now. You are in a place where you know very little, and understand even less. So from now on, I want you to be just a tourist, just an observer, just an onlooker. No active role for you now. These people can be so incredibly mean-spirited and they can and they will hurt you. You can do something unintentionally and piss off one these brainless nitwits. Rosano, for the next few weeks, you are an alien, an outsider. You have to pretend that you're in China, a land where you know nothing. Can you do that, please, can you do that"? I said, "First, I have a question for you … when we separate and take our own paths in New Orleans, are you going to go to New York and Chicago and the rest of it? For sure?" She looked at me and said "Absolutely, absolutely. I can't wait. I told both of my schoolteacher friends your plan and that you had pushed it strongly. Do you what they both said, separate from each other? They said 'Oh, your Italian friend must really love you. Of course you should go'. So that's what I will do, for sure." She looked at me and said again, "For sure". That's when I said, "Listen, Princess, I know you're right about this. So, if you're going to New York … then I'll be in 'China', starting tomorrow." She just grabbed me, saying, "Listen, White Knight, no crusades for a while. Promise?" I did promise.

We finished the coffee, washed the pot and reloaded it for the morning fire, which I also arranged. Refreshed the water bag. Got the oval pan full of water so we could wash hands and face, since there would be no shower. Asked Stella to get a few food items from our scooter stash, if we wanted snacks later. The sun was setting. Day was ending, and I had run out of steam.

She and I talked quietly for an hour or more, covering many topics … this segregation thing that still existed, the cold war with the Soviet Union, my draft status and other topics. I thanked her for that afternoon's help. She was right … I had sought adventure. However, the form it took today was completely unexpected and miserably handled. We agreed, for the remainder of our journey to New Orleans, I would drive, but she would guide us in all things social. Of course, after New Orleans, I would be on my own.

CHAPTER 33

LOUISIANA

Waking in the morning with my arms around the Princess had been pleasant these past two weeks. She continued sleeping while I sorted out events of the previous day. We had talked of so many things before sleep got us. Again I apologized for my reaction to my first real exposure to 'real-life' segregation. Stella thought that yesterday's moment of weakness was just that, 'a moment', and no more than that. Holding me tightly, she asked if I had any idea as to how much stronger she was, just for having been with me for these weeks. I told her she always had the strength, she just had to learn that she did. And maybe that's why 'fates' had thrown us together. You know, 'the fates,' those mysterious spirits which I don't subscribe to. Maybe those little rascals decided that we were part of each other for a reason. In any event, I had decided to follow her lead for this remaining time together, that I would be a bit more reserved and certainly more cautious around 'rednecks' and unwaveringly polite to every one of every color, to avoid inadvertently creating a 'situation.' This was 1960. President Truman had declared an ending of segregation in the US Armed Forces a dozen years before. These Southerners, Colored and White, had too many years of crap to go through still, and I didn't want to become part of what might become an enormous pile of crap.

She was waking now. Eyes open, she asks "Rosano, you OK now?" I nod yes, say "I'm OK. We'll be fine. I told you before we began this trip ... we'll be fine." Stella asks "Time to get up?" I said there wasn't much choice. I had to pee, and would light a coffee fire, too. Dressed, lit the prearranged fire, grabbed my toothbrush, soap and washcloth, walked across the campground to the restroom and then back. Coffee nearly done. My companion followed in my footsteps and arrived as I was finishing my count to 100 (coffee 'aging' time). With two hands at the back of my neck, she planted 6 or 8 or more little kisses on my face, saying "The world needs you for a while, so you must take care. Understand?" I nodded and said "Coffee?" as I poured our first cup. Our habit of sharing a cup of coffee, back and forth, alternating sips, seemed a quiet celebration of ourselves. So personal. So pleasurable.

Our plan for today? Well, we pack up camp, and if our navigator takes us to a source of coffee, we should take advantage of that. Then, on the road for two hours should take us to the Texas border with Arkansas, at the town of Texarkana. At that point, we can make more plans. I don't see any exciting side trips worth pursuing, but our navigator might. One can never tell. The navigator gave me a kiss on the neck and said she liked the way I smelled even when I hadn't showered. I told her she smelled wonderful and I knew why. "Rosano, are you going to tell me the onion thing?" And she was laughing at me, not with me, at me. I know because I wasn't laughing. I said, "That's only part of it, the other part is the bigger secret, the real secret ... sh-h-h ... quiet ... don't tell anybody ... it is ... Italian cookies! We ate enough of them so that we'll smell good for at least another month. And you'll be able to get more in Little Italy in New York and I'll get some in Chicago. We're set for smell for a while, at least." I changed out of my 'camping' pants. Soon we were nearly packed, last step was to tie our washcloths on so that the wind would dry them. It was requiring more time to dry them in this humidity. Stella asked if we were ready. OK Cisco, let's went! (reader's note: research Cisco Kid and Pancho).

Coffee and pancakes for me. Coffee and a big breakfast for the lady. Without a word or plan, we set our coffee cups down and exchanged them. Compatible, we were indeed. Restrooms visited, we were on the road, heading out of Clarkesville and east on Route 82, a moderate day, a bit heavy on the humidity, but nothing to generate complaints. In an hour's travel, we passed through six or eight settlements or towns, with signs pointing to that many more. Agricultural fields almost all the way. On the side of one large farm building were painted two words, one over the other, in white letters perhaps three feet tall ... DAMNATION ... and under that ... SALVATION. It was time for a smoke. I gave the scissors sign to the navigator, got a thumb up in response and we stopped for break with a good view of that message. Lighting up, the question confronted us in bold fashion ... 'What on earth would possess someone to produce this huge sign?' Had to laugh at my use of 'on earth'... life here on earth wasn't the subject here. The lettering was credibly done, not sloppy at all. I thought the words might have traded places, in keeping with currently accepted placing of heaven and hell, but I'm no expert on either Damnation or Salvation. Someone had measured and spent time, effort and dollars to place this message. Maybe he was trying to earn brownie points for his idea of heaven. Maybe his Jesus figure would say "Yeah, that's what I meant." I asked Princess, what do you think? She just shook her head slowly and said "That hell and heaven thing is lost on me. All the labor that went into that sign. What if he (I assume it was a 'he') had used that time and energy and earned a few dollars and used it to buy some shoes for some of the kids around here? Instead, he just screws up scenery with that ridiculous sign." Well, she summed it up rather well, I thought.

So Princess, unless we stop in Texarkana, Texas, we will cross the border into Arkansas and we'll be done with Texas. Your impressions? She looked thoughtful for a moment, and said, "Mixed. Some good, some not so good." I said "That's my feeling too, I was in West Texas and El Paso back in February and I liked it despite it being a little rough around the edges. I expected something similar on this trip, but El Paso is eight hundred miles from here and very different from here. Big state, Texas. I hear the best place is Austin. Lots of good things supposed to be happening in Austin. Would you like to go to Austin? It's only four or five hundred miles out of the way. Or do you think we should continue east, leave Texas, and head to Arkansas?" I field stripped our smokes as usual. We climbed aboard. She pointed eastward. She was the navigator and that's where we headed.

Just as I was about to kickstart the Lambretta, an armadillo began crossing the highway from right to left 40 or 50 feet in front of us. It was my first time seeing one of these creatures and not just a photo of one. It was three-fourths across when an approaching pickup truck swerved toward the animal, hitting it, the impact causing it to flip up into the air and into weeds on the far side of the road. While that was happening, another one started crossing at a farther distance from us. This one made it safely across. I wasn't at all familiar with these creatures and frankly, didn't care to be. While I might have enjoyed handling an eagle or an owl or frog or a fawn, for me the armadillo was something to be kept at a distance. There was no clue as to why I felt that way.

As we approached Texarkana, road traffic increased somewhat, but not enough to be troublesome. So here were two towns melded into one community. Nothing remarkable or special about that. There were two towns, both called Nogales, one in the US and one in Mexico, split down the middle by an international border, with Customs and Inspections and that whole disaster. There were a number of shared towns along the Mexican border. But imagine if there were a town in the state of, let's say, Virginia called Viva, right on the seacoast and another town on the coast of Spain or Portugal, across the ocean, also called Viva, and the two towns were active in each other's affairs, now that would indeed, be unusual. A few signs announced that we were no longer in Texas and had entered the state of Arkansas, nicknamed 'The Wonder State' until a few years before when it was officially changed to 'The Land of Opportunity.' We would continue on Route 82 for a short distance, looking for signs to connect us to Route 71, heading south. The navigator kept us on track through downtown traffic and before long, we had made our way to 71. I signaled with a scissors and tilted cup sign. It was break time.

Stella gave a gentle slow down sign. We passed two or three cafes and finally she selected one with her finger pointed and closed fist signals. Pulled into the parking area, locked up the helmets and scooter, went inside and settled down. Not being hungry, I said "Something small, go ahead and order for me, while I hit the restroom." When I returned to the table, there was coffee waiting to be sipped, then Stella joined me. "Well Princess, I'm not sure on what basis you selected this restaurant, but that's OK. Listen, you don't have to worry about me and this segregation thing. I'm on my scooter trip now and not on any crusade. These people have a very long battle ahead of them and I'm not an active part of it yet. I've accepted that, so truly, I'm OK and will tend only to my own business." Stella said "OK, I believe you, but I'll still keep an eye on you. So Rosano, different subject ... can you guess what I liked best about Texas?" Looking to the ceiling for an answer, I shrugged and said "No clue." She said, "I'll tell you ... it was you, you were the best thing in Texas. And ... there will be no more discussion about that now." Our food arrived, mine was an empty plate, her's was a burger the size of a Frisbee, with a five-gallon bucket of French fries. She said "We're in cattle country, you know." She offered half and I waved her off, and indicated a fourth. She served me that and a generous handful of fries. Oh, and part of a huge pickle, too. And we enjoyed this with coffee. Stella asked if there was anything I was anxious to see in Texarkana. I said I had looked through the tourist pamphlets when we entered the restaurant, and there was nothing, but the newspaper had a small headline saying there was a new cold cut slicer at one of the markets and people could get to see that ... and there was no admission charge. The Princess got a pretty good laugh from that remark (shhh, don't say anything, it wasn't original).

OK, what's the next stop? If we go back onto Route 71, we will cross from Arkansas into Louisiana in about an hour of driving. A second hour's worth of driving would take us to Shreveport, Louisiana. That's a big city and a port (sort of). Want to try for it? She said yes, sounds better than Texarkana. I said that many things sound better than Texarkana, either the Texas part or the Arkansas part. How about we have a bit more coffee, a smoke, and then we'll adios this place and get fuel for the scooter. She nodded yes. So we lit up, the waitress poured a little more coffee.

She, of course, was in first place as to what I liked in Texas and I told her so. While we had been through a quite a lot of unexciting landscape, having her as a traveling companion had made the whole Texas trip a true delight. In second place was the movie we had seen "On the Beach", third place was held by Palo Duro Canyon and there was no fourth place. While she and I were enjoying the adventure and each other, realistically, the last four hundred miles would have been rather boring. Texas was so big, a person couldn't really pass judgement based on the small part we had covered. There were so many small towns (typical of agricultural areas), most of which were unknown to me. Most of these towns would languish or diminish in the coming years. That process had already started. Some would become ghost towns. Fewer people and animals were needed for farm work. That was the major factor. It was happening all over the country, and not only this country, but in many parts of the world.

Finishing our coffee, Stella asked for the tab, settled it, and we left. She said her tummy was full. Oh my, I wonder why. Onto the back of Tony the Lambretta and with our customary small puff of two-stroke, we pulled out of the parking lot and onto the road for less than a mile to a fuel station. I mentioned that the scooter was slower after she ate that burger. After fueling, we returned to our new route southeastward toward Louisiana (pronounced Looz-zan'-uh, and not Loo-whee-zee-ann'-uh). After a dozen miles, the highway headed more directly southward. Another dozen miles would take us to the Louisiana border. Very green country. Little ponds, lakes, water-filled ditches, everywhere. Did each one have its resident alligator? Hadn't seen one of those yet. We had made a 90 degree turn to the south as we passed through Texarkana. The Red River had done approximately the same and was now heading south a few miles to our left, just where it had been for the past 400 miles, a little to our left. Something that amazed me was the apparent lack of changes in elevation. So gradual. I knew that rivers flowed downhill most of the time, so there had to be a slope to the land, but I certainly couldn't see any. A mile or two north of the Arkansas-Louisiana border, a small highway sign announced the West Fork Kelly Bayou which meant I just had to stop. This was my first 'genuine' bayou or at least my first swamp called a bayou. Not necessarily a momentous occasion, but I was curious. Was there an enormous prehistoric beast lurking in the swamp that thought a Lambretta looked delicious, especially with two humans as dressing? Uh-oh, imagination running a bit wild. Poisonous serpents without rattles were on my worry list. At least the diamondback might announce itself with a fairly loud buzz, but these others were worrisome … moccasins and cottonmouths with no warning signal, just a bad attitude. Today the bayou looked like a swamp and nothing more or less. A few small surface ripples were not large enough to indicate any creature capable of swallowing a rhino or hippo. And most likely, not a

Lambretta either. Today, at least, it looked peaceful and benign. There were two large birds poking around in a small treeless area a hundred feet away. Large white bodies, and dark heads. Were these some species of crane or stork? Insects were everywhere. During the past two or three days of travel, there had been a substantial increase of insects and consequently, the Lambretta's windshield needed more cleaning. Even at our relatively slow pace, there were insect marks and parts and bodies stuck to windshield. Without that interference, a good portion of these critters would have been stuck to me. That would genuinely qualify as yucky.

Hey Princess, campground or motel tonight? The answer: motel tonight, campground tomorrow, was that OK? Certo, Principessa. Back onto the scooter for a final run into Shreveport, Louisiana. Just as I was preparing to kickstart the scooter, two or three mosquitos landed on the backs of my hands. Very quickly shaking them off before they got a taste, and starting the scooter, my thoughts were one ... so lucky not to have to deal with them so far, and two ... it would be best to begin using the detergent as a repellent. Starting up and driving south for two minutes put us into the State of Louisiana, Stella's home state.

Continuing on Route 71 brought us into northern parts of Shreveport, Louisiana, an interesting town of 150,000 people. We had putted through eight or ten little towns and settlements, including one named Belcher and saw a sign pointing east which could have taken us to Plain Dealing, if we so wished. There had to be some history that went with the name Plain Dealing, but I wasn't going to research it. We decided to stay the course and enter Shreveport. I could catch glimpses of the Red River, a half mile to my left. I decided to visit the river again. "Hey Princess, remember the Red River in Palo Duro Canyon?" She said "Yes, I do. It was a little more Red back there. Here it's a little greener and grayer. And slower." I guessed it turned a muddy red color when there's enough rain runoff dumping reddish clay soil into the stream.

"Coffee?" I asked. "Yes, but no pie for me." "Well, I can understand that. Your burger was about the size of a yearling calf, but I could enjoy a piece of pie while you ask the staff for information about a motel and maybe a bookstore or library or whatever." Stella said, "Sounds like a plan." And so it was. First the coffee at a small diner, then a motel, immediately into the shower to shed two days' worth of grit and grime, then, a brief but sound snooze, a nap in earnest.

A gentle tug on my ear and a 'Hey Rosano' brought me into the present. "I like your bookstore idea, and we still have time." Oh boy, I've helped create a monster, a strange person called a 'reader' and they are nothing but trouble. A few small smooches later, I agreed to the bookstore. Go ahead, twist my arm. We dressed, left the motel room, piled onto Tony Lambretta, our faithful scooter, and headed into the city. Since Stella was navigator, I just behaved myself and followed her directions. Sometimes, it was comfortable just being a driver. Soon enough we were parked in front of a bookstore – new and used books. Wandering and absorbing atmosphere for a few minutes was first, before any serious browsing. Bookstores were sacred places for me. So much knowledge available for such small expense. I picked up a book 'Cities of the South' and sampled my way through it for a short time, and then browsed. After an hour, Stella had chosen one book … Agatha Christie's 'And Then There Were None' and I had selected two books … 'I Robot' by Isaac Asimov, and 'The Last Hurrah' by Edwin O'Conner. After paying, and on the scooter, this sweet woman navigated us directly to an ice cream shop, saying as we dismounted, "Maintenance dose for your cookie withdrawal." As we ate our ice cream sundaes, large size, we talked of the books we had just purchased. I told her 'Hurrah' was about big city politics and that she should read it also. Her choice by Agatha Christie, was superb. She asked, "You've read it?" I nodded yes. She smiled, "I should have guessed". I said I would have put it on the list, but had simply forgotten Christie, the biggest selling author of all, male or female. Anyway Princess, what's next? Stella said, "Finish your ice cream, dearie. You're going to need your strength for what's next."

CHAPTER 34

EVENING IN SHREVEPORT

When we returned to the motel, Stella suggested we take a few snacks from the scooter, in case we got hungry later. Once inside, we took turns using the bathroom, brushing teeth, combing hair, etc. Stella offers to trim my hair and my beard and do a quick manicure and I gladly accept. Done with that personal maintenance, she says, "OK Rosano, since we're in the squeaky clean habit, let's get back in the shower, wash the hair trimmings off, and we'll get squeaky clean again and see what happens." Not only was this woman stunningly beautiful, but in the blink of an eye, she talked me into going with her into the shower with no clothes on. Can you imagine! And just from that alone, one could see she was a convincing speaker. Over the past few weeks, she and I had enjoyed some memorable showers together and this was one of the better ones. Our sporting events soon followed.

We had rested, holding each other quietly, without talking for quite some time. "Rosano, we don't have much time left together." She gave a gentle squeeze. "Yeah, I was having the same thought. You know I've enjoyed being with you so much, and there will be a big vacant place inside me, but I won't dwell on it. We've had such a delicious time of it, with more to go, so I just want to enjoy us for now. You OK with that?" She nodded slowly, saying, "But you owe me at least one story, so you'd better sit up." And I did, and asked "For which story are you holding me hostage?" Laughing, she said "You mentioned you would tell me about your mom and your reading."

So I started and it went something like this: When my mother was a young girl in fourth or fifth grade, her mother, my Italian grandmother from the old country, took her out of school believing that girls needed to know only the most basic math and only enough reading for cookbooks perhaps and little else. In other words, to educate a female was a total waste of time and money. Girls should know household things ... cooking, sewing, cleaning, etc. However, sometime and somewhere, in that few years of elementary school, my mother learned to love reading and all that it offered.

Grandma wouldn't allow my mom to have any books in the house, except for a cookbook and a prayer book. So my mother hid a book in the basement, another out in the garage, another in a closet, wherever she thought she might be able to sneak and read something. And that's the way it was for those years until my mother married my father. Now, get this ... my father had had only one year of school in Italy, but he was smart as hell, did well financially here in the US, and strongly pushed education and the arts onto his kids and the other kids in the extended family. When my parents married, my mother suddenly had her own house. Since she was now in charge, it became a place where books were welcomed, treasured, celebrated, and always available in a wide variety, which included two different sets of encyclopedias. So we kids, my two sisters and I, grew up with books. My mother would read to us at least one hour a day and usually a good deal more than that. In addition, once a week, we'd get onto the bus, go downtown, and walk the few blocks to the library where books were kept by the thousands. There was never a time in my life when there wasn't reading. Consequently, I was a pretty good reader in my kindergarten year. The little fillers at the ends of Reader's Digest articles were my treasure. Read them by the thousands. Didn't always understand them, but I could read them. Our school system didn't begin to teach reading until the first grade. It began with Dick and Jane. Entirely underwhelming! And, Oh brother, lethally boring. And Rosano and Forced Boredom was not a good combination. Dick and Jane almost made me weep. Sally and Spot almost made me puke. A few times, I thought my first grade teacher was going to kill me. She should have put me in another place in the classroom when it was reading time. Or out in the hallway. Or somewhere. My memory of that grade is hazy, but I must have been a complete and perfect pain in the ass, and the teacher was too stupid to find a solution, but insisted I sit with the rest of the class. So we both suffered through Dick and Jane et al. Suffered mightily. In any event, I had become a reader in spite of school. Reading anything, it seemed I couldn't pass anything printed ... the vacuum cleaner instructions, the dictionary, the cereal box, anything. And I've always tried to read at least one book a week. Been doing that since early childhood. You might not think that's such a big deal, but it's a big deal.

"So Princess, what are your thoughts." Stella leaned toward me, planted a little kiss, and said "Thank You." Answering, I said, "True story. Left out some details, but that's very close to what happened." She said, "Yes. Thanks for the story, but more important, thanks for infecting me with the 'reading bug'. I think that's what my aunt, as a librarian, tried to accomplish with me. But maybe I was just waiting for a little Italian guy with cookies, who knows? That's one of the big changes in my life that you're responsible for. In other words, it's all your fault." Answering her I said it was nobody's fault, it was just one of those 'cookie for nookie' situations which arise occasionally. And she jumped on me, wrestling me this way and that, got me in a headlock, and started roughing me up a little, and we struggled and nearly laughed ourselves sick.

Time to settle down. We decided to read. Princess would finish reading "Auntie Mame" and start "Lord of the Flies" while I would start "Last Hurrah" after reading the final few pages of "Streetcar Named Desire." Stella would take all four pocket editions with her when we parted. We had read for almost an hour when Stella closed her book and said "What a character Mame is! What a wonderful character!" Princess was just aglow. "So," I said, "Have you finished?" She nodded an enthusiastic yes. Continuing, I said, "Now you've read one of the most important books of your life, I suspect. Quite a story. First, before we talk about that character called Mame, think what a great job the author did. What a fun time anyone would have reading this story, and yet, he addresses quite a few social issues without being preachy. So, hat's off to Dennis Patrick for sure. And his character Mame is magnificent. Remember when I suggested you leave these books at the dentist's office or on a train, or any random place?" She said "Yes, someone will really get a kick out of this one." I said, "No, this book should be an exception for you. You should keep a copy ... read it once a year. It's my opinion, but here's why I say that ... because you, Princess, you Miss Stella Beauchamp, have the makings and, I think, the moxie, to become an Auntie Mame yourself, perhaps not as extravagant or audacious, but an Auntie Mame nonetheless. Yeah, that's right. You have smarts, the sparkle, vitality, and strength, and now I'm seeing more of a delightful devil in you. All this combined with a beautiful heart. Unbeatable. So hang onto this little book and use it as your spiritual guide."

"And now, Princess, we are now in your home state. How does it feel to be in Louisiana?" A strange, maybe a perplexed look on her face, and she said. "That's a good question, except I never have thought about this as my home state. In my mind, my home state is Missouri, where my aunt is ... Kansas City, Missouri. You know, Rosano, I'm almost as new to this area as you are. Even though my so-called family is from this area, I always felt I was another species from a distant planet or something. Gave this a lot of thought as we have traveled these past weeks. My life has divided itself into four parts ... first part ... eleven years, was here, as the alien species, here in Louisiana, until my aunt pulled me out of this and more or less installed me in Kansas City. So that was the second part, much better than the first, but I was still 'floating' and rather detached from my surroundings. Oh, I functioned pretty well and 'got along' pretty well, but nothing seemed quite real and certainly nothing felt important. When my cousin Broderick called me to Denver, I went. Why? Because he was really the first person I had ever felt 'attached' to, the first person I felt truly emotional toward. So these past few years in Denver are part three. Rosano, you are Part Four. How do like that ... being Part Four? You pulled me out of that shell. You're the magician and you make my head spin. These last three weeks with you have been an eye-opening heaven and a whole new life for me." Her eyes were getting a little watery and I interrupted her saying, "Listen Princess, it's been great for me, too. We've shared a genuinely unique experience. We've traveled about 1200 miles together, with a few hundred miles left to go, through some of the most boring terrain available, and we've had an enlightening, laughing, and loving time of it. Such a good thing for both the Princess and the Knight. And we'll remember it, for sure, and forever. And we'll both be OK."

My few minutes of reading in the bookstore allowed me to learn a bit about this town of Shreveport. It was more than 300 miles from the Gulf Coast and its elevation was 144 feet above sea level. That boggled my mind. Elevations in New England were not huge, but certainly easily recognizable ... hills were hills and they still went up and down. Arizona had its flat areas, but there were always two or three mountain ranges in view, the tallest peak at 12000 feet, with some impressive elevation changes ... full-grown mountains and canyons and valleys, but this flat wet terrain was new to me and visibility was much reduced from the hundred mile views of Arizona's desert. At one time, this Red River was navigable, usually by steamboat and usually with agricultural cargo. This river, if stretched out in a straight line, would probably be 2 or 3 times longer than the distance actually accomplished. That probably didn't help the steamboat folks when it came time to compete with the railroad folks, who were winners in the cargo shipping competition. So the question was 'If there are no decent sized boats coming in and out of Shreveport, is it a port at all? I didn't know. And I'm sure other people have argued that same subject. This was a key town for the Confederacy during the Civil War, but I knew so little about that entire disaster. One interesting fact I had read was this: In Connecticut, there was no 'virgin forest' remaining after the Civil War. The entire forest of the state had been harvested for war efforts against the South. What a waste! Of course, all of war is an enormous waste. That's the purpose of war ... to lay waste the other guys stuff before you waste all of your own stuff.

"Hey, Rosano. What are you thinking about? You have that faraway look." Reeled my mind back to the two of us. "I was thinking back to the beginnings of this trip. Arizona, New Mexico, Colorado, Oklahoma, Texas, a bit of Arkansas, and now Louisiana. Of all the maybe several hundred towns and villages encountered, which ones would I consider calling home, that is, if I could stand cold weather. Tucson, of course, but it would be Albuquerque, Santa Fe, Pueblo, Colorado Springs, and Denver and that's all so far. The rest I wouldn't consider. Just taking a mental inventory. That's all.

Stella had started 'Lord of the Flies' and was getting sleepy. I had opened 'The Last Hurrah' and had not yet read a word. Our books and our eyelids were drooping. "Princess, let's rinse off in the shower. Then we'll sleep. Is that a plan?" A gentle smile, "D'accordo." And we did brush teeth, rinse off, all the maintenance stuff, and returned to bed. Quietly, I asked, "Princess, how are you feeling?" She said, "Good, Knight."

CHAPTER 35

ALEXANDRIA

The two happy wanderers were waking. It was a bit past first light ... too early to start our day. As I quietly held my friend, she said, "Do you know that all last night, in your sleep, you were still trying to protect me? You know, that makes me feel ... valued. Such a comfortable feeling. And now, I'm going to reward you in one of the ways you most enjoy ... I'll take you out for coffee." The Princess knew priorities. The motel had a small coffee room where the so-called Continental breakfast was served. There was coffee, the most vital component, also hot water and various teabags, as well as doughnuts. I hadn't had doughnuts for a long time and they tasted great. So lucky that doughnuts are so good for one's body and health.

Stella asked where we would be going this day. Alexandria, I thought, maybe 130 miles south of Shreveport. She asked if I wanted to see more of Shreveport. Yes, but nothing specific. I'd like to do a bit of noodling, just for the feeling of the place. I knew that a person couldn't walk more than ten feet without running into a big hunk of history. While I, personally, was not inspired to study that history, other people scrutinized every document, grocery list, and scrap of paper from two hundred years ago to the present. She asked why not the history of the South ... it had to be interesting. My response was that the history of the region was fascinating, but that I knew a little bit of Greek history, a little more of the Roman centuries, and now, I had turned to the Second World War since I knew relatives and friends who had been through it. The First World War (WWI) was an unknown chaotic confusion in my mind, but I was getting a good grasp of WWII. The only other history I might pursue to any extent would be our Revolutionary War. Since I was neither a genius nor a fast reader, I had to limit myself ... so my choice was that I would first become at least semi-knowledgeable of WW II. The War Between the States would have to wait ... but noodling around Shreveport for a half hour couldn't hurt, and besides, we probably needed to pick up some groceries, and before we did that, I thought we should check out the flashlight batteries, especially if we were going to camp tonight.

We sat and exchanged the coffee cup easily two dozen times. This little exchange ritual of the coffee, and sometimes the pie and coffee, seemed an innocent, but heartfelt intimacy, and the two of us had come to prefer this. "Rosano, have you had enough coffee?" Nodding yes, "For now, at least." Almost in a whisper she said, "It's still early, let's go back to our room for some close contact, some compatibility." Taken by surprise, but recovering handily, and not wanting the lady to think I was unworldly, I asked, "Excuse me miss, but are you one of those bad women I've been warned about?" She laughed loud enough to make all heads in that little breakfast room turn toward us, gawking, but not smiling, which made me start laughing. Then, she said very quietly "It's your job to find out just how bad." The two of us were laughing quietly now, but no one else was smiling that I could see. Here's a swarthy, tanned, bearded guy with a beautiful, very light-skinned woman, far more beautiful than any of them, and we were obviously up to 'no good.' And they all looked like good solid, rather plain, unsmiling church people (resembling a herd of turtles for a just a moment). What a drag! Maybe I was reading too much into the whole thing. We took final sips, left the breakfast room, returned to our own room for R & R.

Later, after playing, showering once again, and packing, we were ready to start noodling. I said I could use another quick round of coffee. That we did on our way out and shortly after that, we were 'noodling' ... driving somewhat randomly here and there, in a residential neighborhood which seemed middle class, in another at a lower economic level, in yet another which seemed 'high dollar' and all shared at least three things: one, they were all intensely green with vegetation, two, the terrain was flat everywhere, the smallest rise in the land (usually created by a house-builder or contractor) became prominent, and three, there were plenty of insects flying around constantly. No shortage for sure. Bug-eating birds probably had an easy life there. Stella was navigating and knew we were due for fuel and groceries. At a stop sign, I asked "Enough noodling?" She said yes. Good. Gas, groceries, and then we were on Route 1 heading south out of town. Route 1 roughly paralleled the Red River as we headed south and east along the level road with moderate traffic. The morning was warm and humid. Breeze generated by the scooter was welcome as we traveled through farmland with a dozen or more different crops growing at full tilt. Is growing season 'year round' here? Don't know, but with careful selection, it probably could be. Parts of The Confederate Army had been based in this area, and Union troops had been through once or twice. There were Historical sites everywhere ... plantations, military mustering areas, battlefields, etc. The South has a long and intense military tradition and history, and the military is more honored and cherished here than in northern states.

As we putt-putted our way southward, it seemed Stella was holding onto me a bit more firmly than usual. My imagination? In almost two hours without a break, we had traveled nearly 75 miles. We were approaching Natchitoches, a town of ten or twelve thousand people. I pulled over into a fuel station. Alexandria was about sixty miles distant ... too far without a fuel stop. On the other hand, I didn't like buying less than one gallon of gas, but it was necessary. The windshield was a bit of a mess with all the bug debris. In fact the entire front panel of the scooter looked similar to a rough carpet with insect cadavers hitching a ride. I've got to wash this thing soon, I thought, and often. Asked Princess if she wanted a meal or a snack. A meal, Rosano, we've only had doughnuts, remember? What about crawfish, I asked. Was there a place to get them around here? The gas guy laughed and said we could get crawdads just about anywhere. Stella asked which café or restaurant might be a good place. I noticed her voice took on a little more Southern tone as she talked. Cool lady. She was announcing 'Hey, we're not complete strangers here', with her manner of speech. Staying on Route 1 was taking us through town. I was driving quite slowly. A short time later, Stella pointed and then gave a clenched fist signal and we were in front of a small restaurant. Locking up scooter and helmets, I mentioned we got such an early start, we had plenty of time. Stella indicated we could have a leisurely lunch, since we had no deadline. Life can be pleasant with no deadlines to meet. Maybe not so 'productive,' but pleasant.

After we ordered, Princess asked what I thought of Louisiana so far. My major impressions were that it was flat, and there were many poor people, judging from so much of the housing I had seen. Oh, and there was no shortage of water. Of course, that was from an Arizona viewpoint. What were her impressions? About the same ... it was wet, there were indeed many poor people, and she felt no part of this whole scene and was looking at it much as any tourist might. When our food arrived, its aromas were rather nice. My dish had two styles of crawdads, one bunch was simply buttered, the other had some sort of Louisiana hot sauce, and both were quite tasty, very similar to a New England lobster. Stella had ordered a seafood platter. We were about 300 miles from the Gulf of Mexico, allowing seafood to be kept fresh quite easily. A beautiful, quiet lunch, we exchanged plates after a while. We talked about books she had or would have with her. I advised her not to buy more just yet, to travel as light as possible. Books can get heavy in a hurry.

"Rosano, do you know about something called an 'oxbow lake'?" As a matter of fact, I did. Did she want to know? Of course she did. So began a little explanation: First, a quick look at rivers. If the terrain has some steepness, a river will take a relatively straight course downhill, with as little diversion as possible. If land is very gradually sloped, such as what we've been driving on for four or five days, the speed of the moving water is quite slow, sometimes nearly stagnant, and a river meanders and winds around and makes great loops in its lazy path toward the sea. We've seen that on the map this past week. OK, now here's this sleepy river, making its way in no hurry, when, far upstream, there comes a torrential rainstorm dropping lots of water. That water has to do something, get absorbed by the land, or flood across it, and eventually it tries to join a river and return to the sea, with gravity pulling on it constantly. Now the flow rate is much faster with more force and it eats into the far bank of one of the loops and is able to take a 'short cut' across the land and pour back into the river somewhere downstream, leaving one or more loops behind. Those loops get cut off from the river by sediment and so a crescent-shaped lake is often formed. That's called an ox-bow lake, similar in shape to the metal pin of the yoke put on teams of oxen. Did she understand that?

"White Knight, that was a clear, simple explanation, and yes I understood. How did you know about that? Oh, never mind, I know ... books." We both laughed. I said, "Yep, books, but also experience, since oxbow lakes are a fairly common phenomenon and occur all over the world, in the deserts, in the artic, everywhere. There's actually one in this town, sort of. When the Red River changed course, maybe a hundred years ago, it left a thirty mile long segment behind. It's called Cane River or Cane Lake. I read about it back in the library, was it in Gainesville? We can see it when we leave, but I don't think it could be a real crescent shape ... not if it's that long. Anyway this town's elevation is 120 feet above sea level, but we're about 300 miles from the ocean, the gulf. Doing a little bit of basic math, that means the downward slope is less than 6 inches per mile and that's why the river moves slowly and that's why it wanders all over. This Red River has probably created two or three dozen 'oxbow' lakes along its length. Interesting, actually."

We finished that excellent meal, passing on dessert, but opting for more coffee. How about dessert in Alexandria? Good idea! As we left and were preparing to get back onto the scooter named Tony Lambretta, I said "Princess, thanks for a beautiful lunch. You're a great cook." I gave the scooter its required single kick and was rewarded with a perfumed puff of two-stroke blue smoke. We drove less than a mile and crossed a bridge spanning the Cane River Lake, the one we had discussed. As we slowly made our way along the business route, my impression was that this was a thriving town, and it had more history per square foot than one could study in a lifetime. Even the general store was nearly 100 years old. Continued on our route slowly southward and crossed another bridge over Cane Lake, and into a rural area as we headed toward Alexandria.

A few minutes later we were passing through a village?, town?, suburb?, called Natchez. Three or four hundred people, maybe. But three, possibly four churches. My first thought and what I wanted to say to the Natchezarians was "What a waste! Don't you people see you can't afford four churches. And don't you think your God gets a bit weary of two or three billion prayers a day, even if some of them are set to music? Next time, start a small library. Put a steeple on it if you have to, and it will do more good than all the churches in town. Use your brains, people!" Of course, that was me silently screaming. Driving at the slow pace of the Lambretta allows the mind to wander. Eventually I resigned myself to thinking that if this holy stuff provided comfort ... it might not be all bad, but that would have to be shown to me.

The Princess and I were both enjoying the leisurely pace of the day. We had about two hours of travel before reaching Alexandria. Looked like it might rain, but then we would just get wet, I suppose. There was probably very little shelter along the way. The scenery was pleasant, not staggering like Arizona's Painted Desert or Colorado's Rockies, but green and lush. The Red River was three or four miles to the east of us. My thinking was that it wouldn't take much for the river to flood many, many square miles of land, along with all the houses, barns, schools, etc., since floods are not very selective. Now, if a house were built on a four foot elevated site, it would most likely be safer than 90% of the buildings I was seeing. However, building an elevated acre of land would certainly not be cheap, but would it be worth the expense? Suddenly we were out of the farmland and into a wooded area. That yielded a much different sound. The scooter noise was louder as it echoed from the woods, but still pleasant. What a great machine this has been so far. The area we were traveling through was a Land Management Area or something akin to that. A half hour later we were back into farmland.

The passenger in the rear seating compartment was doing her little fiddlings, hugging more than usual, but sometimes softly beating a rhythm on my back as she sang, which again, fortunately, I couldn't hear clearly. The scooter and the Red River were converging as Alexandria drew closer. Road traffic increased as we neared the northern limits of the city. Farther into town, Stella gave me the 'reduce speed' signal and pointed to ... yippee ... an ice cream shop, or rather shoppe. It is certainly a good thing to have a navigator whose priorities are in order. We ordered our sundaes, mine being Butter Pecan. Something in the back of my mind said Southerners do great things with pecans ... didn't know what, but I followed my inclination and it was indeed, very tasty and refreshing.

Was she going to find us a place to camp? Yes, she said. I said, I'd like to refuel yet again, because tomorrow's run was too long for what I had in the tank and we also needed a quart of two-stroke oil. Stella had talked for a short time with the two middle-aged women tending the ice cream place and thought she had info on a good campground. Onto the scooter and only a mile south we spotted a gas station that advertised car washes and detailing, which meant they had a power washer. Stopping at the pump, I apologized for needing so little gas, but did they have two-stroke oil? Yes, they did. Did they have a power washer? Yes, they did. Was is a steam cleaner? Only if they turned the heater on … it didn't have to be steam. Could they do this scooter quickly without harming the windshield. Damn right, they could. OK, then let's do it. Within fifteen minutes we were fueled up and cleaned up. The scooter looked so new and shiny. A whole new look. Well, Princess, now that we have new transportation, should we go out on the town? She said, "White Knight, we will camp just south of town. What I would like to do, if it's OK with you, is to slowly noodle our way through town, reach our campsite and set up for the evening. We have everything we need … coffee and snacks, and I just want to spend time with you. Is that OK?" She seemed to be talking slowly, softly and sincerely. "How could I refuse a request from the Princess … of course it's OK, it's perfect." We got onto the scooter, got my fix of two-stroke smoke, and we headed out. Tony Lambretta seemed to sound a little differently and seemed to drive a little more smoothly since the washing. Or was that my imagination? Anyway, well worth doing. All that bug debris was nasty. With Stella navigating, we noodled this way and that, sometimes close to the Red River, sometimes not. Population was supposed to be 35 or 40 thousand, but it seemed considerably more than that. Nice-looking town. Eventually Stella directed us onto a small side road where pay campsites were available. She made her deal with a woman in a small cottage/office and left carrying a roll of toilet tissue in her hands. Oh well, that was different. People must have been stealing the rolls provided.

The campground area for RV's and trailers had small concrete slabs. The area for tents had elevated areas (by about 8 inches) for pitching a tent. Pretty good selection the Princess made. Each also had a small stone fireplace with a built-in iron grille. Stella walked around to other tent sites and returned with two partial bags of charcoal and a small bundle of wood. We were the only tenters that night. We set up fairly easily, finding enough stones at other tent sites to have a relatively secure install. Stella put a few snacks in the tent. A moderate breeze was moving through the campground, probably keeping the mosquito delegation subdued. Still, I was prepared to apply my dish detergent/repellent if necessary. Sitting on a nearby small wooden bench, we rested, knowing the three of us had done well and enjoyed this day. Couldn't exclude our faithful scooter now, could we? Stella said she had a few things she wanted to talk about. I said, certainly we could talk, but it was shower time while we had daylight.

After locking the helmets and scooter to a large tree near the tent, we took our toiletries, towels, and a handful of coins to the bathhouse, performed all the routine personal maintenance, and then enjoyed a leisurely and complete washing of each other, always a delight. Washing my hair and beard was always welcome ... more than two days under a helmet and a good washing was needed. We two drifters settled in for the late afternoon. Should I build a coffee fire? Her answer: In a little while. Now that we were clean, we could do some snoozing and she could absorb more energy from me while we rested since she hadn't soaked up quite enough today despite her strong efforts to do so. Thought I felt some of that effort and enjoyed it for sure.

Inside our mini-world, we 'settled in' and rested. In time, she asked "OK Rosano, are you ready for Question Number One?" I gave her our manual 'go ahead' sign. She started with "I want to ask you about school for me. I want to get into better areas of nursing. I know you wouldn't know specific courses, but I bet you know an approach I could take." So I started my answer by saying "You know you're asking the least qualified person in the nation for advice ... a complete washout in college, but you already know that. You asked me more than a week ago about school and I said I'd think about it and I have. I'll try not to be long-winded, so here are my thoughts. I'll number them. Ready, Princess?"

Continue working, either full time or part time, but don't hurt yourself. You are physically small, and nursing can be very demanding physically. So sure, you start school, study, straight A's and all that. Great, but all that is meaningless if you get hurt. You must always, always, always, protect you. That's first priority.

As far as taking courses and classes, you'll have to talk with some counselor. And listen to their plan, but be flexible. School shouldn't be just a series of chores to be done. The point I'm onto is this ... take necessary classes, yes, but also take a few classes that you just enjoy for enjoyment ... maybe photography or philosophy, it doesn't matter. None of it is wasted. If it takes five years to earn a degree ... fine. If it takes ten years, that's also fine. So, enjoy and take your time. Similar to this scooter trip, we've never been in a hurry. And it's been pretty good so far, right?

Whatever class, course, seminar, program or activity you are involved with ... get the certificate, get the graduation stamp, get the diploma, get that paper which says you completed it. Guard this pile of acknowledgements.

These are your credentials. They could be very important in reaching a goal you've set. People who are hiring or promoting other people like to see credentials to justify their choice, which you hope is ... you.

So that's your three-layer cake. Pretty basic stuff. This fourth part is the frosting. Consider combining your nursing with something else. Maybe business administration, maybe photography, statistics, art, languages, law, insurance. Having a major in nursing with a minor in something else... turns you into a unique commodity. With much higher potential earnings. Consider it.

Now let's say it takes a dozen or more years to finish and you're forty years old when you finish. That's not too late at all. It means you only have twenty-five good working years left. Doesn't that sound ridiculous ... only twenty-five years? Ok, that's it. Not too bad. I gave it some serious thought as we rode along. Whatever you do, you're going to be great!"

CHAPTER 36

EVENING IN ALEXANDRIA

That steady breeze we had experienced brought a few drops of rain with it. We had made camp well and would be OK for the evening I thought. That tarp had been a necessary equipment addition and would do its job. We talked more.

"Now" she said, "Ready for Question Number Two?" Me: "Not yet, because I have a question for you. Ready?" She nodded yes. "Two parts: Part A: Have you figured out what you'll be doing for your dramatic exit from your swamp family? Part B: Do you want me to help you think it through?" She looked at me, saying "I was thinking about that just this morning during our ride, so … Part A answer is … not exactly. The Part B answer is … no, I don't want you to think about it anymore. You have done a beautiful thing for me, by pushing me to fly to New York City and the rest. The important part is done. So put it out of your mind. Is that OK with you?" My response: "Absolutely, that's your show and you're in charge. Do whatever you feel is best for you. Do it and be done. Then … it's New York City!"

OK, you had a Second Question. She said, "It's not really a question as much as it is a 'situation' at my job. Let me explain … There is a woman there, almost one of my supervisors, but not really … she just has more seniority. She says she is half Apache and half Ute. That's not a problem, but … she mentions, at every conceivable opportunity, bad crap the white man did to Indians … the diseases, the starvation, the broken treaties, the murders, etc., almost as if I had done it personally. Frankly, I'd really like her to just choose some other subject, because I don't know how to respond without either getting into an argument or hurting her feelings. She's not a bad person at all. I've tried a 'Gee, I don't know approach', but she just says 'Well I'll tell you.' And then she goes directly into her story. I don't know how can I deal with this? Or if I should just stay quiet." In my mind, I'm thinking 'some people just communicate too damn much. And this woman is just repeating what she had been exposed to.' I said "Princess, we have a relatively long run tomorrow to get to Baton Rouge. Let me think about this as we drive". And rain was steady now, temperature dropping comfortably. Despite the early hour, I was a little sleepy. Oh, that's right, we hadn't made an afternoon pot of coffee, hence, this sleepy business. Now, we curled up and snoozed to a steady sound of raindrops.

In my dream, someone was explaining that it was rain that made everything around here so green. Of course, I knew that and didn't need explanation, but I needed to pee anyway, no matter how much it rained. Now I was waking and tried to make sense of my dream. And now it was real life, and I really did need to pee. The rain had stopped. Stella said, "Rosano, are you awake?" I said "Yes, barely." She said, "I have to pee, but I don't want to walk all the way to the bathhouse alone." I said "Neither do I. Hand me the flashlight, we'll go not too far from the tent. Get a couple napkins for yourself. We should slip our shoes on, though." We made our way to the outside. There was a bit a moonlight, but not much. It seemed so peculiar to be outside, in cool darkness, naked except for shoes. Just as we finished, there was a pretty good crashing in the underbrush about 10 yards behind the tent. Flashlight aimed in that direction, we saw some movement of shrubs and plants, there was more noise, but neither of us saw a beast or beasties that caused this minor commotion ... pig, alligator, panther, nutria, cow? I had no clue, but nonetheless, it did cause heartbeats to increase considerably. "Princess, throw the napkins in the fireplace, I'll take care of them in the morning. Let's go back to sleep." After some mild snuggling and huggling, we returned to snoozling. We stayed 'in touch' and life was good.

At some ungodly early hour, before first light (I know because I peeked), I was fully awake, having slept my quota and then some. Also, I had strong beginnings of a caffeine withdrawal headache. No matter the hour, it was time to make coffee, which meant, in turn, it was time to get dressed. And I did. In the dark. Finally got the flashlight and walked to the bathhouse toilets, returned to the tent, dragged the little bundle of wood and the charcoal from under the tarp (played it smart this time) and quickly had a fire going and the coffeepot resting above it, warming up. This morning, the coffee would be simply exquisite, having medicinal application as well as normal sacred overtones. The brisk little fire was welcome in the cool, damp morning. Coffee almost done. I could hear a mosquito now and then. Time for detergent. Placed a few small pieces of wet wood on the fire to create some smoke. Smeared some detergent into the palm of my left hand, added some water from the water bag and applied the thin mix to my exposed skin areas. Meanwhile the coffee finished its process. Smoke was slowly drifting around since there was no breeze, and probably helped keep mosquitoes at bay. Conditions then were nearly perfect for one of mankind's favorite pastimes ... coffee drinking.

Had nearly finished the first cup when Sleepyhead appeared, gave me a hug, wordlessly took the flashlight, and walked to the bathhouse. I waited for her return, before pouring the second cup, which I handed to her, saying she could drink it all while I made a second pot, which I had on the fire in just a minute or two. She gave me a little peck on the cheek, saying "Morning, Knight." Neat little two-word joke. It wasn't long before a second pot was ready. Just had to count to 100 for the aging of it. We shared that cup, using our back and forth routine which I had come to enjoy immensely, and shared a fourth cup as well. Headache gone. Now we could see the false dawn through the trees. So early, but we had slept more than enough. "Well Princess, there is far more to do in Baton Rouge than here in Alexandria. Shall we pack up our camp and get some breakfast and hit the road?" She said, "Sounds good, and besides, I'm hungry." We had become rather efficient at camp setup and teardown. In not-too-many minutes, we were packed up, coffee pot cleaned and all the rest. Even in this very damp air, Tony Lambretta started on the first kick and gave us our 'fix' of pale blue smoke and we were putt-putting out of there just as dawn began serious thinking about starting up a new day. We rode in the semi-darkness a short distance.

Into a café for yet more coffee, with pancakes for me (what a surprise) and a big multifaceted breakfast for the navigator. She had an appetite that would, given time, transform me into a dirigible. Between bites, she talked of how much she enjoyed sleeping with me, noting that we had only slept 'inside' the sleeping bag two or three times, but instead, had slept 'on' the sleeping bag most of the time. The same held true when we had taken a motel room, sleeping 'on top of' bedding rather than 'in' bed. Being 'protected' by my arms being around her had been so comforting to her especially during that first week of our trip. Our 'staying in touch' as we did, seemed therapeutic and beneficial. Sipping my fourth or fifth cup of coffee for the morning, I said that was true for me as well. Sleeping with her was just a splendid thing ... and since we were naked most of the time, whenever I was awake in the middle of the night, I had a great scenic view of things without having to open the tent flaps. She laughed gently saying, "There will never be another ..."

After leaving the café, the navigator directed us to Route 71 south and we were back on the road heading south and slightly east, with about 80 miles to go before we intersected with Route 190. The pavement was dark with wetness and just beginning to dry a bit. So I'd be even more cautious than usual. We had parted ways with the Red River, which headed off to the east without consulting us, taking Route 1 with it. We were traveling through developed agricultural land, with very little traffic. There were water-filled ditches, little brooks and ponds everywhere. As we passed, a variety of larger elegant birds were here and there, usually standing in water. Herons, egrets, cranes, I didn't know specifically. But beautiful, and elegant creatures for certain. This had to be the wettest state of the 48. No, maybe not, maybe Washington or Oregon took that prize. Florida maybe?

My beautiful friend was singing softly, keeping rhythm on my back, and occasionally pulling on my earlobes or reaching under my jacket for some gentle pinching. Thinking about her American Indian co-worker had my attention. How does one respond to the question of white man's treatment of the North American Indians, no matter the tribe? In the most simple of descriptions, the white man of Western Europe simply overwhelmed many other groups or civilizations it encountered. There were the American Indians, the East Indians, the Pacific Islanders, the Central and South Americans, many African and Middle Eastern societies. So, in a sense, the White Western European became the Roman of the modern era. That thought got me started on the Romans, specifically in their dealings with the Carthaginians, during and after the Punic wars. I'd condense and summarize for the Princess. Just wanted her to have a general picture.

We had gone through a small town called Bunkie, believe it or not, and had not gone too far beyond, when I signaled for a break and pulled off the roadway and parked near a grove of trees. It was time to pee in earnest. Couldn't hold all that coffee much longer. Ohmyohmy, bladder relief is one of life's little pleasures. Stella said "Me next", and hid herself from the roadway behind one of the trees. In a minute or so, I heard, "Rosano, Rosano, there aren't any rocks to put on top of the napkins." Loudly I said, "OH NO, don't tell me you didn't bring any rocks. You've put this whole trip in jeopardy!" She started laughing and said "You Crazy Ass!" Still laughing, she said, "Well, now you have to take care of the paperwork. That's a Knight's work." I said, "I'll take care of it, but it won't take all night." The two of us were enjoying this little bit of stupidness. Went behind the tree, pulled up a medium-sized clump of grass, pushed the paper into the hole and replaced the grass. I suspect, with all this wetness and the growth rate of vegetation everywhere, the ground would heal itself in three minutes, max. There did seem to be a scarcity of rocks, plenty of mud, but rocks, no. Anyway, a rewarding little pause.

Onto the roadway again, I would pick up the pace a little bit with the road being drier. Very little traffic, very straight road. There was occasional farm equipment on the highway. If it was moving slowly enough I would pass when safety allowed. If it was moving at 30 mph or more, I would stay a goodly distance behind for several reasons ... one: to let that driver know I was not interested in passing, two: to avoid the debris like hay, or leaves or dirt clods that often flew through the air behind one of these rigs, and three: I had vowed to myself that I would never 'push the situation'. That meant I would never make an extra effort to get through a traffic signal. It meant I would wait for a train to go past instead of risking a quick crossing. It meant I would always wait to pull out into traffic. Back in Arizona, when I was first driving this scooter, I had noticed that drivers in cars often treated bicycles, motorcycles, and scooters as if they didn't exist and would pull out in front with no warning whatsoever. Never knew if it was their eyes or their brains malfunctioning.

We were approaching the intersection with Route 190, which would take us eastward toward Baton Rouge. Onto 190, we drove three or four miles to Krotz Springs, a small settlement with café. It was time to stretch. And it was still early morning. It had been a pleasant run with my passenger hugging me the entire time, causing me to believe she was doing a bit of snoozing back there. Stella and I walked around, did a few deep knee bends, touched toes a few times and waved our arms about. Time to use a restroom and get another cup of coffee and maybe, just maybe some fruit pie? She gave a thumbs up. And that's what we did. She laughed again at the rock thing, saying it was so ridiculous that it had merit. We talked of various things and I mentioned when we reached Baton Rouge, I needed to go to a pharmacy for some sinus stuff, and also, our laundry needed washing. Stella started a conversation with our waitress, asked about motels in or near Baton Rouge. Again, I noticed her accent a bit more pronounced when talking with a local person. Besides our coffees, we had split a piece of raspberry pie. And had a smoke, too. A good stop.

Back onto the scooter, again a whiff of two-stroke perfume. This rather neat and tidy town was on the west bank of the Atchafalaya River (probably a name from a local Indian tribe). Despite being within 30 or 40 miles of the Mississippi, this Atchafalaya River made its own way into the Gulf of Mexico, and had its own delta. We were on the north end of a wildlife sanctuary as we crossed the bridge spanning the river. The river was about 1000 feet from bank to bank, at least it was that day, at flooding it had to be considerably wider with bridgework maybe twice that length or more. From a vantage point on the bridge, the sanctuary area appeared to extend southward forever. There was something primeval and wondrous about that view. The farther south we traveled in this place called Louisiana, the more interesting it became to me. In just a short time in Southern Arizona, I had become a confirmed desert rat, treasuring the hot dry land. Living in that furnace caused one to appreciate the value of water. A friend, ranching near Tucson, said it required about 60 acres of land for one cow and calf. The stuff I was driving through could probably support a cow and calf on a plot of land the size of a dinner napkin. This place was just packed with living things, most of which I couldn't see, but existed nonetheless. This could never be a place to live for me, although the warm dampness was not as hostile as the wretched cold dampness of New England. Louisiana seemed more interesting than Texas, but ... I was comparing to what I guessed was the worst part of Texas, geographically and culturally ... East Texas. Dallas-Fort Worth and San Antonio were unknown to me, and there were glowing reports about Austin, which I had not yet experienced. So my comparison was unfair. Ignorance often accompanies youth.

Off the east end of the bridge we're back on the normal roadway, very straight and slightly elevated from surrounding wetlands. We were aimed directly east. One-fourth of a mile south of us, a railroad track was running a parallel route, having crossed on its separate bridge. Stella gave a slow-down signal and pointed. On the banks of a rivulet, gully, brook, stream, whatever they called it, were alligators, the first I had ever seen in the wild. There was some curiosity on my part, but, on the other hand ... Back in my high school days, in our Biology classroom, there was a terrarium which housed a small, live alligator, perhaps 14 inches long. Part of my task as a biology assistant was to tend to this terrarium, which by the way, smelled rather strongly. As I would attempt cleanup, the little beastie would always try to defend its territory, I supposed, and try to bite my hand or wrist, which I protected with a heavy glove. Powerful little so-and-so, it could snap a normal #2 pencil in half in an instant. I never trusted that creature. And I wondered if the ones I was seeing ever came up onto the highway. That could be a real nuisance if they were aggressive or, for that matter, a nuisance if they got run over by traffic. There was a great deal that I didn't know about alligators. Five or six miles after crossing the Atchafalaya River, still on Route 190, we were back into farmland with well-ordered acreages for the various crops. In about an hour, we'd be entering Baton Rouge ('red stick' or 'red pole' in French), capital city of Louisiana. We putt-putted through three or four settlements or towns. About ten miles before reaching the capital, our old highway, Route 1, rejoined us after having gone off on an adventure of its own. Baton Rouge was on the east bank of the Mississippi, but we were putting along toward the west side of the river, which meant, we would cross a bridge spanning the Mississippi River, a semi-momentous occasion for me, never having seen this huge river system, third biggest on earth, after the Nile and the Amazon. Road traffic had increased considerably in the late morning and then, the bridge, surprising me with its narrow lanes and congestion ... not much wiggle room. Staying alert was critical ... if something went awry, it would cause a big mess in a big hurry. The river itself seemed a quarter-mile wide, but again, as with the Atchafalaya, the bridge system seemed two or three times that length. Frankly, I couldn't enjoy the view at midstream, being afraid to take my eyes from the traffic for more than a glance or two. Soon, however we were onto normal city streets. It seemed a rather busy place ... not at all a sleepy southern town. In the city, having a navigator was delightful. Trying to read a map while driving a scooter was a dangerous, if not impossible, game to play. The navigator gave a 'slow down' signal, then pointed at a drug store, followed by the closed hand signal. A breather. Heavy traffic, even of short duration, fatigues me quickly. Taking off helmets, Stella asked if she should choose some over-the counter sinus medicine of the non-drowsy variety for me. That would be fine, her choice was probably better than mine. She said, "I'll be a few minutes. Take five." Lit up and enjoyed a leisurely smoke. She emerged from the store carrying a larger bag than I expected, climbed onto the scooter and said "Onward, White Knight", and indicated the direction. Ten minutes later, we were driving into a motor hotel parking space near the lobby. Again, she hopped off and entered the lobby, seven or eight minutes and back onto the Lambretta, carrying a newspaper and keys, indicating we should go around back. It was a good room and near the laundry machines. It was noon and we had shelter 'til the morrow.

CHAPTER 37

BATON ROUGE

Got our clothing bags into our room and unpacked Lambretta's trunk, to inventory our food stash, and toss out anything questionable. We had very little food, so that part was easy. In the room, Stella asked "Rosano, do you have a plan?" Answering, "Not a plan exactly, more of a suggestion … I'd like to do laundry first, to get it out of my mind, and read a little while machines work on it. Then we could do something in town, if you like, something urban, since we've seen so much rural. I'd also like to see some big ships in this port since it can handle any craft that can get through the Panama Canal. Sound OK? "Wow", she said. "Sounds terrific. Are you hungry?" I said, "No, not at all." Stella said, "Then let's get laundry going and while you read, I'll grab a little snack and make two phone calls to my friends." That was the outlined plan we followed. She had gotten a newspaper and that's what I was reading as the washing machine and dryer were doing their work. Caught up on international news a bit. Then saw that 'The Mouse That Roared' with Peter Sellers was playing at a movie house. We could easily catch an afternoon show and get out in time to do a little sight-seeing. Princess joined me in the laundry room, but we still had about ten minutes to go for drying. I asked if she was up for a movie. Definitely. I handed her the movie listing and asked her to find out where this theatre was and I would join her in the room in a few minutes.

Gave her a big hug and asked about the movie timing. We had time, the movie house being about three miles away. Was she OK for hungry? She had a pretty good snack, but we had nothing remaining. Used a few minutes to fold the laundry, dividing it into his and hers, then washed my face, brushed teeth, etc. She said, "Without spoiling things, tell me about the movie." I said "Well, the reviews have been excellent and the film is a satire about the nuclear arms race of the super powers and a big spoof of US politics. A light-hearted story. Excellent actor Peter Sellers, a British comedian." She said, "Your mind goes in many directions. How do you keep things straight?" I said, "Yep, but far too many directions, and I don't keep things straight at all. That's one reason this trip is valuable to me, it's something I've decided to 'stick with', a thing I feel compelled to complete. It's important that I do that at least once in a while." She gave me a little smooch, and said "OK White Knight, I would like to be escorted to the Theatre, please."

Into a warm afternoon, we traveled busy streets toward the theatre with Stella giving signals. I noticed, while stopped at a traffic light, a sign reading 'Muffalettas' which tried to trigger a memory in my mind. But I could not 'make a connection' to a memory, if indeed there was one. Oh well, had to take care of driving through this traffic. Busy town, quite a change after nearly three weeks and a thousand miles of relatively tranquil traffic atmosphere. The theatre was air-conditioned and only half full. I said I'd like to sit where I could elevate my legs up on a seat in front of me. Stella chose our seats toward the back of the theatre and we settled in. 'Mouse That Roared' was a delight with Sellers taking three different roles. A good-hearted film and very funny in its poking at US political attitudes and actions. Sellers was quietly zany in all his roles. A fine actor, I thought. Stella thought the whole thing was a blast and said she would never have seen it on her own.

What's next, she asks. I asked if she had ever heard the word 'Muffaletta'? She said she had, and thought it was a sandwich. I had been trying to remember the word and half-way through the movie, I thought I remembered it as a bread. C'mon, let's find out which. She said "onward, Oh White Knight!" And we onwarded (that's not a typo). Retraced our path back to the store advertising 'muffalettas', which appeared to be a grocery/deli. It was almost an Italian market, not quite, but close enough ... after the cultural barrenness of Oklahoma, East Texas, and Arkansas, this store seemed like Rome itself. They had two or three small tables with chairs. First, let me find out what muffaletta is about. Behind a deli counter a middle aged woman was working. Got her attention, said good afternoon and then asked what a muffaletta was. She asked where I was from. I answered Arizona. She said a muffaletta was a flat 10-inch round equivalent to a submarine sandwich, except there was usually an olive salad as one of the ingredients. Oh. I told her I thought it was a type of bread. She answered yes, it also meant a loaf of bread which was used to make the sandwich. She held a 10 inch diameter loaf, not like a pizza, but about three inches thick. So Stella was right and so was I. How long does it take to make one and could we eat it there? It took about twenty minutes to make and heat up in the oven to 'perfection', which seemed desirable. Let's go for it. Did they have coffee? Absolutely, standard and espresso. Stella mentioned onions. The woman said, no onions. We would do our food shopping in the meantime. We could have coffee in a minute or two ... a fresh pot was close to finishing. Great. Stella had a shopping basket in hand and said she would start. I wandered over to the small bakery department. There was a good selection of breads, but not much in pastries (I was looking for cookies). Soon, we heard "Cof-fee-e-e. Nice and Hot!" Seated, we started sipping that beautiful fluid, so welcome this late afternoon. Stella and I talked quietly. She absolutely loved the movie, but she didn't want to see the ships this afternoon. She wanted to go back to our room and just be together. Would that be OK? I got out of my chair, moved closer to her, gave her a little smooch on the lips and said, "Ma Certo, Principessa." The muffaletta was enormous, cut into fourths, tasted, and found to be delicious. We would take half of it with us. "Good find, Rosano! That was wonderful food. I'd almost forgotten." I said, "Not me. The bland and tasteless prairie diet is strictly for ignorant people, I swear, so damn boring. Hey Princess, different subject: When we go back to the motel, let's ask if we can stay a couple of extra hours tomorrow morning. They're only half full, so it should be no problem. Tomorrow's run is relatively short so we shouldn't start early. We were up too early this morning." She said "D'Accordo."

We finished our meal, finished our shopping, took our faithful scooter back to the motel, stopped at the office, with Stella asking permission, then onto our room, Stella saying "We have 'till 2:30 PM. Now, Rosano, let's get in the shower and use some of that new shampoo I bought." I responded, "There you go, talking me into dangerous situations again."

Washing each other and using a good shampoo to wash head hair and beard was beyond description. Drying, brushing teeth, and finally reclining on clean sheets, a quiet entanglement of arms and legs and the two of us fell asleep in seconds. It had been a long day, a very fine day, and it was not yet sunset.

Some unknown amount of time later, there was pressure from some unknown person's nose being pushed into that hollow spot behind my ear. At some unknown distance there were words being spoken, difficult to discern, but sounding vaguely like "Hey Rosano, time to get up. Can't waste your whole life sleeping." These were followed by a few near-distance light smooches and several more nosey ear pokes, and believe it or not, I was awake, asking how long we had slept. Nearly an hour she guessed. I rolled over and gathered her into my arms and held her for a while.

Breaking the spell, she said, "Tomorrow we will reach New Orleans." I said I'd like to stop just short of that, at LaPlace or Metrairie. First, I wanted to see a bit more of Baton Rouge, then travel south, a little less than a hundred miles, get the scooter fueled, ourselves too, take a room, get clean, and then see what we want to do. Was she OK with that? She nodded yes and then asked what I knew about Dixieland music.

From a scholarly standpoint, I knew a few things, but more important, I had listened to a fair amount of Dixieland band music, some of it fairly obscure. Had also played a little while in high school. The popular stuff, like Dukes of Dixieland, was fine. That was a group that had been together for ten or twelve years and were putting out albums and probably making some substantial money. Al Hirt was a fine trumpeter, very well known, who could hold his own with any Dixie group. Pete Fountain, a splendid clarinetist, French Canadian I think, also widely known. The obscure stuff was probably one of the sources for the popularized music. 'Obscure' almost translates to 'colored' musicians, who were not given a fair shake in the whole scheme of things, and very often not even given credit for their original works. Anyway, it's all part of that unique and important contribution to civilization ... Jazz. Dixieland was one of the early forms of Jazz. And Jazz was one of two major American contributions to a better life for all the world. "So, Princess, when we get to listen to some Dixie, I'll explain a few basics. Is that OK?" She said, "Yes, that's great. What's the second?" "Second?" "Yeah, Rosano, the second contribution."

"Oh ... it's called 'plumbing.' The Romans knew how to handle water and made it easily available ... for rich people, at least, and also available at public fountains and public baths. But it was the Americans who took plumbing and made it available and popular for average people. It was Americans who started washing themselves often and demanding bathrooms in every hotel room. The Europeans were still in the dark ages, the French were still shitting on the staircase at Versailles Palace. Stella laughed and said "You're kidding, right?" Answering, I said I wasn't joking, we could probably look it up somewhere, but I didn't know if we would look under 'shit' or under 'staircase.' They both started with 's' and that was helpful. She started laughing, saying I was outrageous, that she had laughed more in the last three weeks ... etc. and that I deserved a treat. A good thought ... I almost always deserved a treat ... what did she have in mind? She got the bag from the morning's drugstore stop, reached in, and handed me a Snicker's Bar, a small one. She had bought a pack of mini-bars. Indeed a Princess.

We ate the candy as I walked around and stretched. She asked if I'd like another. Sure, I took the bag, opening it and took out a box of tampons. Oh, is it that time? She said it was tough to predict exactly ... close, in the next few days. I said I thought so, doing some rough math. Jokingly I said, don't worry, we can still be friends. She remained quiet.

She straightened out the room though it wasn't needed, fussed with the clothing bag, got a book out and didn't read it, and then took my hand, led me to the bed, pushed me down onto my stomach, and lay down half on top of me. She said quietly, "I want to absorb as much of your energy as I can, so just be still." Eventually, though, we moved this way and that, and things progressed to a gentle and loving conclusion.

Back in the shower, rinsing and playing a bit, she asked if I had thought about her Utache or Apachute friend. And the White Man versus the American Indian. Yes, I had. My thinking was much broader than she probably guessed, so she would have to be patient ... as soon as we got out of the shower. We dried off, brushed teeth yet again, and sat down.

First it helps to understand where we came from, we human beings. The church folks keep pushing the fairy tale that the big guy in the sky created us in his own image. That's just church-sponsored stupidity ... some illogical and ridiculous story for the gullible so they can be manipulated and talked into shoving money in the basket every week. From prehistoric man-like creatures, we descended not from the kindest, most gentle individuals, but from aggressive, belligerent, vicious ones. So, it was those individuals of early man who grabbed food from the others, who screwed anything they could, and who killed any other individual who got in their way, and who probably ate them, too. That's where present day mankind came from ... not from the genteel, the 'after you' type, but from the 'me first' sonsofbitches bunch. From the winners of the fights. From the survivors. Understand that mankind has been slaughtering its own members from the very beginnings. It's nothing new.

Now, fast forward an eon or two, to the hundred-year long (about 200 BC) struggle between two powerful societies, the Romans, so powerful on land, and the Carthaginians, the strongest naval power in the Mediterranean. It was inevitable that they clashed. That series of conflicts is called The Punic Wars ... the 'Hannibal crossing the Alps with the Elephants' wars that we all hear about. The Romans could really be a bunch of pricks (by today's standards) when they wanted to be. In terms of just plain viciousness, though, the Carthaginians took the cake and set new standards, sacrificing their own children to some mysterious gods. It was normal procedure for them to seize a foreign ship, immediately drown all the people aboard, and keep the ship and its cargo. That was routine. They came close to really tearing up Rome when they got into the Alps from Spain. But Rome was able to hang in there and became yet stronger over the years, until ... the Roman Senate (there's a relatively new idea ... having a senate and not just a supreme ruler... idea borrowed from the Greeks) decided that since Carthage (located near Tunis in today's Tunisia) was in a weakened state, it should be destroyed (after all, we've been screwing with those bastards for a century, I could almost hear them say). So the Roman Senate voted to fund an army, go to North Africa and eradicate Carthage, not just defeat them, rather cause them to cease to exist. The marching orders stated that no two stones shall remain together. It took a few years, but Rome actually did that, dismantled the entire city, and not only that, but also plowed salt into the soil, so that no crops would ever grow there and sold off all the inhabitants into slavery (many were allowed to live, not to be free, but to be alive and work). Carthage no longer existed. It was history, a history written by the winner, Rome. So the question arises ... who were "the Bad Guys" ... the Romans or the Carthaginians? This was just one of the thousands of examples of one society simply overwhelming another, pushing it out or wiping it out, and subduing it completely.

Fast forward again, this time two thousand years to the White Man vs. The American Indian. The Western European White Man, landing on the shores of this new place, saw opportunity. These Indians, that's what we'll call them, had none of the basic tools of western civilization ... no gunpowder, no rudimentary machines, no fences, they didn't even have the wheel. They had little or no written language, far too many spoken languages and they didn't get along with each other and spent a fair amount of time killing and eating each other. So ... the White Man was able to do whatever was necessary to get this annoying, but deadly bunch of natives out of the way. I mean who gives a damn about them? We are the important ones. But we'll let some of them still live in some place that we don't care about. That was the prevailing attitude and the White Man's actions followed that attitude.

Now you, Princess, are working with an American Indian woman who constantly refers to the White Man's transgressions. How do you handle it? I would say this ... don't apologize, but consider a different approach. Try not feel or think defensively. Feel and think matter-of-factly. Don't try to defend or explain the 'white man's actions. It's just something that happened. It is history. You could say, "Yeah, you're right ... the 'White guys really screwed over the Indian, killed a lot of them, stole the land, ignored treaties when convenient, forced them onto some wretched reservations. That's true, for sure. Now you could ask, how did these Apaches or Utes or Navaho get this land? From whom did they get it and how did they get it? They overwhelmed and either absorbed or eliminated another tribe or group, that's how. Hadn't the Comanche overrun, kill, and then enslaved entire villages of Mexicans?

But all of that is just information for you. It doesn't help with your half-Apache, half-Ute friend. After you consider everything I have just very roughly summarized, you might say to her, "Boy, that's awful, but maybe it's getting better." Sounds lame as hell, but if she wants to continue spouting and get this off her chest, she will, and nothing you say can soften the situation. So there's my non-solution.

"Hey Princess, I have a suggestion. Ready?" She give it a 'yes' nod. "I think we should work on remaining parts of that 'muffaletta' since it is just screaming for attention." We munched on the two remaining fourths slowly, savoring a kaleidoscope of flavors ... a welcome change for our taste buds and a splendid way to end a gorgeous day.

CHAPTER 38

A CAPITAL MORNING

After waking at a decent time, and after brushing teeth, I went straight back to bed and wrapped my arms around my dear friend. And, as had been the usual response, she pulled my arms more tightly around herself. Three weeks had built some comfortable habits. We snoozed that way for perhaps another hour and began stirring. Each lost in our own thoughts, we dressed quietly and at a leisurely pace. Finally, she walked over to me, grabbed my ears, planted a gentle kiss on me, and asked "Coffee?" When I nodded yes, she said so softly, "Follow me" and took my hand. We walked out to the street and then a half block to a small restaurant. She asked if she should order for us. Thumb up. Soon we were sipping black coffee and I was rejoining the world in general.

We exchanged cups and Stella said, "You want to see some big ships this morning?" I said, "Well, at least one big ship, not just barges. And I want to climb up a big levee ... as a kid would do." She chuckled, saying, "You're always a surprise." "Hey Princess, you have something special you'd like to do?" She said "There is, in fact. I would like to stroll around a college campus. Just as an observer. There are two or three in this city, I think." That sounded good. Wanted to do that in Albuquerque and never got around to it.

We continued with breakfast, me with the usual pancakes, Stella with her usual feast, lumberjack size. We talked of various things, each of us probably trying to avoid what was foremost in our minds. Today would be our last day 'on the road' and it was a relatively short run ... less than a hundred miles. But it could not be avoided and Stella finally asked "What time should we leave Baton Rouge?" My answer was mid-afternoon, but we could be flexible. That would put us just north of New Orleans around six in the evening while it was still daylight. "Princess, after breakfast, let's check the hotel office to see if they have a decent map of the city we could borrow for a few hours. This is a busy town ... government stuff, refineries, factories, universities, and a good look at a map would probably help." Finished breakfast, walked back to our room, stopping on the way to ask for a map. They had an old one we could keep, a map of the state, with good city maps also, but it didn't show the latest highway changes. It would be fine for us. We readied ourselves for a morning out on the town. What would we do first? My suggestion: let's do a levee first, before the heat of the day takes hold, then the college campus thing ... they looked close to each other. Big ships could wait 'till later.

Stella and I did a little map research, decided to go a mile or two south to be near both a levee and Louisiana State University - LSU. We would take Route 30 which would put us in the middle of things. Onto Tony Lambretta, faithful scooter, a one-kick start again, a fragrance of exhaust with an oil highlight, and we were on our way. Route 30 was quite busy, after a mile or two, the navigator gave a 'slow down' signal and right turn pointer sign. A few blocks to the west and we intersected with South River Road. Looking west and directly in front of us was a levee, perhaps 30 feet high or more. We parked, locked up Lambretta and helmets in a parking lot of a University maintenance building. Let's have a good drink of water before we start our little hike across River Road. We guzzled what we wanted. And started, first crossing the road, then up a grass-covered hill or embankment. There was a paved service road running the length of this enormous, rather neat and continuous mound of earth. We crossed that little road and moving upward, we found ourselves in a woods. The Mississippi River was not yet visible, but we could hear an occasional distant horn from a ship or tugboat. Making our way through a wooded area on top of the levee seemed such a decided change from what we had been doing for all these weeks. Three or four hundred feet, maybe more, and the trees ended abruptly and we were looking down, it seemed almost directly, onto a collection of barges on the near shore of this tremendous river. Startling ... to me at least. This levee we were walking on was man-made and it was huge, much larger than what I had imagined. This river was also huge and man was trying to corral it and make it behave. It was the enormity of the now quiet struggle which struck me so profoundly on this warm, tranquil, apparently uneventful day. Downstream a short distance, perhaps a half-mile, was a ship, six or eight times larger than a barge and much taller. Very slowly it was moving upstream with two tugboats as company. My nautical knowledge was sketchy at best, but this was a very big ship, a tanker of some sort? Here it was, nearly 200 miles from open ocean. That seemed extraordinary to me. On the other hand, maybe not so unusual, considering the St. Lawrence Seaway, and other places 'round the world. Finding a place to sit, I just wanted to absorb the scene. Amazing stuff happening and as long as nature cooperated a little, everything seemed tranquil, orderly and in control. This enormous placid river, which provided so much to so many people, could strip the people and the land of everything just as quickly when angry. With surrounding terrain being so flat ... how many square miles would be covered with river water if this levee were to suddenly disappear?

There would be plenty of opportunity for me to see more of the river. My intention was to travel north toward Chicago along this river, and there would be time to witness and wonder. Stella sat next to me quietly, just holding my arm, not trying to get my attention, just being near. In time, I said "Hey Princess, I've accomplished both of my sightseeing goals with one stone, does that make sense? Anyway let's do your thing and take a walk at the University as long as there is some coffee involved somewhere." She smiled and said, "OK, White Knight, lead the way." A nice hug and a small kiss were my rewards for being so thoughtful, but of course, we White Knights were supposed to be that way ... just normal for us. Small rewards are always welcome.

Back through the woods, down the slope, across the roads and onto our scooter once again. Just a few blocks east was part of the LSU campus. Found some parking and locked up. I was always a bit reluctant to move any distance from the scooter, especially for any extended time. To my knowledge, nothing had ever been tampered with. The unusual appearance of the scooter with larger than normal 'trunk' attracted a few people to examine it more closely, but only occasionally. Before leaving the scooter, I took a drink from the water bag, offered it to Stella, along with two aspirin I had taken from my jacket. She looked at me, took the aspirins saying, "Thank you." I said, "Sorry, it didn't occur to me that the hill would affect your leg." She said she didn't think so either, but it wasn't bad at all and walking on the level was comfortable. OK, but we'll stroll, we'll take it easy, and I'd be honored if you took my arm in yours. And that's what we did.

Walking with this beautiful woman on my arm attracted a few stares from pedestrians we encountered, though most people smiled, nodded a greeting, or said "Hi' or "Good Morning". Most enjoyable to me was walking on a college campus without freezing my ass off. Not yet 21 years old (about a week short of it) I had sufficient memories of walks through bitter winter weather, or slushy and sloppy springtimes. I just hated winter, every damned part of it. But now I was with Princess enjoying a splendid morning walk thru a lush, green college atmosphere. Stella was walking normally with no trace of limp, so that was a good thing. Also, I could sense she was gathering impressions of the academic atmosphere, filing them in some cranial niche. Eventually, we wandered our way toward the student union. We sat outside, watching people going to and fro, went inside, got two coffees, sat down again and just observed a changing scene. "Rosano, what are you thinking right now?" That was the question. My answer: "These students look awfully young. And I'm not an old man yet." She laughed a little, saying "I had exactly the same thought. So strange to feel such a big difference in age for a very few years actual difference." We hadn't had a smoke yet and I pulled the pack from my jacket. We lit our cigarettes and talked more about schooling with me suggesting she not consider going to a college in the South. You have a great school right up there in Boulder, Colorado. A degree from a college in Alabama or Mississippi just doesn't carry the clout as the same degree from the University of Colorado. We exchanged coffee cups, eventually finishing each other's coffee, and she said "Let's walk back to the scooter and then go back to our hotel. OK?"

We drove the few miles back to the room, I was thinking this was a very active town. Into the room, she said "Naptime? I could really use one. Rosano, you going to join me?" Me: "Ma Certo!" We snoozed some, loved some, and showered. By then it was time to get ready for our afternoon run down to New Orleans. We dressed and started packing. Stella took our snack foods out to the scooter, and packed them. We got our clothing bags ready. Hey Princess, should we snack or are you ready for a real lunch? Real lunch was her choice. Do we need to come back to the room? Didn't think so. Ready when you are. I'm ready. Then let's adios. We'll get some lunch for us and some for Tony Lambretta and we'll be on our way. Route 30 heading south along the river, then to Route 61 which would take us all the way into New Orleans.

So this had been Baton Rouge (translated from the French it becomes 'red stick' or 'red pole'), a town dating from the early 1700's, and now a busy city. Lots of different things happening, most connected in one way or another to the famous Mississippi River. To me, it seemed peculiar that the presence of the river was so powerful, but a person didn't actually get to see the river often with the height of levee construction. I had no idea of how many miles of levee existed, but even if it were along one fourth of its almost 2400 mile length, it would be one of the biggest constructions in the history of mankind. Well, anyway, the levee system was impressive. What were the effects and consequences? As with other projects which attempt to tame nature, there are good effects and bad. Benefits can be seen almost immediately, the bad effects might take years and years to show themselves and by then, damage often has gone too far. An opinion formed after a one day visit would lack credibility, but for now, I was impressed with Baton Rouge.

CHAPTER 39

THE LAST HIGHWAY RUN

Our last hour in Baton Rouge was used for a good little lunch at a restaurant ... a children's size fish and chips plate for me and Miss Beauchamp ordered a big meal and finished it easily. While I was near an ocean, I would always get seafood if I could ... not freshwater fish, creatures from the ocean. East Coast upbringing showing there.

The next stop was for scooter fuel. Checked tire pressure - holding fine. Gently washed the windshield. The attendant, an older guy, looked at Stella and then at me, and repeated that about six times, I felt he was viewing us as he might observe animals at a zoo. Heeding that warning from Princess a few days ago, I said very little, but of course, was polite. This man just continued to look back and forth and said not a word while he was fueling. Somewhat creepy, I thought. When I asked how much I owed, he said some amount which was correct, and then asked me "Where are you people headed?" I said "North to Shreveport, if we're lucky we'll get there by nightfall." From the corner of my eye, I caught the tension in Stella's stance and then a relieved look on her face when I indicated a town in the opposite direction of where we were actually headed. Leaving the gas station, Stella, as navigator, directed us in the wrong direction, and I followed her directions knowing her intent. Again, that compatibility thing. We did a bit of 'go around the block' driving and then, several blocks from the gas station, got onto Route 30, heading south through some rather busy traffic on this warm and sunny afternoon. Just a few miles later traffic had thinned out and soon we were traveling into more agricultural areas with a bit of industrial mixed in. We had traveled less than an hour when the navigator gave a slowdown signal followed by the two-fingered clipping sign meaning a break was requested. That was fine and I slowed down and stopped near a small section of woods alongside the road. She said she just had to pee. I reached into my trusty jacket/attic and pulled out two café paper napkins and handed them to her. She walked into the trees a few yards. I pulled the pack of cigarettes out and lit one. On returning, the Princess said, "Rosano, I have to give you two compliments, small ones, but real ones.

First, you're such a gentleman to carry napkins for your lady. Thank you. Second, you handled that guy in the service station so perfectly and smoothly. Bravo!" I said, "That guy had a strange look and peculiar manner about him, and I disliked and mistrusted him immediately and not just a little bit. And I noticed that you also noticed and you were very good yourself." I offered the cigarette pack to her and she took one and lit it from mine. "Where are we staying tonight?" I asked. She said she had the name of a place on Route 61 in Metairie, about five miles from the French Quarter in New Orleans. We smoked without saying much. I believe we were both downspirited a bit. I field stripped our smokes and we got back onto the Lambretta and continued on our way. Route 30 bent to the east and fifteen or twenty minutes later, we intersected with Route 61, much busier this afternoon than the road we had just left. We had not quite two hours of driving, even with traffic, before reaching Metairie.

A few miles south of the intersection the road went straight, very straight across a bayou for more than a dozen miles. Peculiar feeling to know that pulling off the road meant you'd be in the water, along with the Creature from the Black Lagoon and its buddies. So I was relieved to finally get to almost solid ground as we reached a place called Gramercy, and headed to Laplace. We were still crossing bayou-looking stuff, sometimes very wet looking, sometimes not quite so wet, I knew none of the terms used to describe these variations ... swamp, bayou, bog, marsh, murk, morass, glomp, and on and on. In a short time, though, I didn't have to worry about that terminology because we were in the city, as in urban, and this bunch of urban stuff was called Metairie. Time to stop for a few minutes for fuel and some two-stroke oil for the Lambretta. We had hardly gotten back into the traffic flow when Stella gave me a slowdown sign, then pointed to our left at a motor hotel. I had to wait for some traffic, then took the left into the driveway, and then towards the lobby canopy. We had made it. From Denver to New Orleans. We had made it!

Stella, after some minutes, came out of the office, held up six fingers and pointed. I drove to Unit #6, found a suitable, lockable scooter location and shut the scooter down. I gave it a little kiss on the handgrip and said, "Goddammit, my friend, you did a splendid job!"

As Stella caught up to us, I noticed her walk was normal, so the leg problem had subsided or possibly vanished. That made me happy. We gathered our things into the room, a rather luxurious room. Stella held up the room keys, gave me one and said, "In your pants pocket please, not in the jacket. We've got the place for two days, paid in advance." Then she gave me a big hug and she held on and she said, "It's almost unbelievable ... three weeks ago, you said we would be OK and we are. Honestly, I didn't think that would happen, but you never had a doubt, did you?" I answered, "We were charmed from the beginning. I felt that, I knew that. You know those Fates that I don't believe in? Well, they were on our side, and they made sure we'd be OK. So, I'll continue unbelieving in them." Stella moved her head side to side, saying "There will never be another." Laughing I said, "So you do know that song?" She smiled that lovely smile and said, "Sometimes, I have no idea what you're referring to, and that means I'm going to learn a little something in the next minute or so. What song, Rosano?" Explaining, I said she had used that phrase three or four times during our journey, usually while moving her head side-to-side ... 'There Will Never Be Another You' is a song I remember from early childhood. Nice song. Stella said, "No, I never heard the song, but it's the truth in your case." And that got me another great hug. "What next, White Knight?"

"Principessa, I'm really pretty worn out. I'd like to shower with my friend, with shampoo and all, and then snuggle, snuffle, snooze, or whatever. After that, we can make plans. Are you OK with that?" She kissed me so softly on the schnoz, saying "Ma, Certo."

And so we washed deliciously, loved desperately, and slept delightfully. We knew our together time was short and unspoken emotions of the day had exhausted the two of us. Having slept for an hour or more, we woke as the sun was setting and spreading some patches of redness across the sky. We lay awake, looking at each other without talking, just gently touching until I said "It's rough isn't it?" She nodded 'yes' and her eyes grew watery. I said, "I really do love you and don't want to lose you, and yet I know I can't keep you." Again she nodded yes and said. "That's it exactly. That's the way it has always been, from our very beginning." Trying to be more positive, I said. "But Princess, always remember and know in your heart ... we've had a splendid run of it. Very few people have done anything similar to what we have ... Denver to New Orleans on a putt-putt. A fairy tale. A part of us now. And we can still enjoy the next few days here in New Orleans. I don't want to say this and I do want to say this ... if either of us, in the future sometime, desperately feels the need to contact the other, and I assume we are both smart enough and know enough to find the other, then we can make contact with no expectations." She almost smiled, but almost not.

To move off the subject, I said, "Princess, I really need a cup of coffee, as any coffee addict might, and there are coffee makings right here in the room. Will you join me?" She said, "Yes, I'll join you and I got half a dozen extra coffee packets to last the two days here, and also diverted tomorrow's maid service." So I fiddled around, got the coffee cranked up and asked "What about food? Shall I bring in some snacks?" She said, "There's a good restaurant less than two blocks away. Let's go there, have a nice meal together, but not right now, in a little while." I told her that sounded just fine, but I was ready to pour coffee, food or no food. There was a small table and two chairs near the window. "Come sit down," I said, and put the two chairs close together, not opposite each other. We sipped coffee silently, exchanged cups, and continued touching, as we always had. Always had ... it had only been three weeks. After some minutes of quiet, Stella talked, saying "There are so many many things to remember about our trip together. It's by far the richest experience of my life. And I know I have changed so much. And one thing truly amazing to me ... you haven't changed at all ... you are still the same person." I said, "Yep, just as aimless as ever, but getting you safely to New Orleans is something I've completed, and I'm proud of having been able to accomplish that and you made it possible by being a risk taker and accepting my offer, faraway back there in Denver. What an excellent navigator and enjoyable companion and exciting lover you have been! Listen here, my dear and beautiful friend ... your caterpillar days are over. You're ready for your butterfly wings." Standing up, she gave me a big smooch and said "Let's rinse off and go to dinner."

And so we washed again, dried again. Dressed, we walked through the warm evening the two blocks to a small seafood restaurant. I had my hand on her waist as we strolled. At the door of the restaurant, she turned into my arms, gave a little hug and said "You're still protecting me. I thought about that on this afternoon's final highway run and realized how much I needed that protection. It wasn't just nice and comforting, it was crucial and I suspect you knew that. So ... thank you. Now, let's eat. Hungry? "

After ordering our food, we talked quietly of various things. She asked about camping. Did I really enjoy it? Answer ... sometimes it was great, sometimes a disaster. I intended to buy a directory of US camping sites to finish my trip to the East Coast. If a place had showers, that was a big plus, a laundry was luxury. The major value in camping was in teaching a person to really appreciate a motel room, but only if it was clean. If not clean, camping was a better choice. Also there was usually no rigid check-out time in a camping site. For me, now, there was little novelty left in camping. I had camped in the snow, in a boat, on a beach, down in Mexico, in a cave, and on and on. So, if I were to be truthful with myself, I'd admit that the more camping done, the less the enjoyment of it. Though a big exception was sleeping and camping with a Princess I happened to meet not long ago. But of course, with the Princess, hotel rooms were magnificent also, especially the showering part. So the real value in camping was to enhance appreciation of the condition called 'not camping'. Then that beautiful smile appeared ... the one I had been seeking and trying to prompt for the last few hours. She asked, "What do you want to see in New Orleans?"

What did I want to see in New Orleans? Certain items I was sure to try to see. To see the French Quarter was one (though from the few photos I looked at carefully, it seemed as much Spanish as French). Basin Street was another on the list ... a street that a famous song talked about. Bourbon Street and Rampart Street are also famous, and all within a few blocks. Wanted to see the Mississippi River just before it started to fan out into its delta. And now I wanted to see a Dixieland band while I shared a drink with the Princess ... maybe be able to point out and explain a few things in the music so she could better enjoy it all. I asked if there was anything specific she wanted to do or see in town. She thought my list was a good start.

Our food had been served. We ate slowly and talked softly. Stella asked if I still wanted to go out that evening. I thought it better to save it 'till tomorrow when I wasn't so tired. Not being on the highway had allowed me to unwind. Finishing our meal, we passed on having dessert and coffee. We walked the two blocks back to our room. Stella asked if I had my key. I reached into my back pocket and used the key to unlock our door. The two travelers were crumping. In fifteen minutes, we were horizontal and deeply asleep, my arms around her.

CHAPTER 40

NEW ORLEANS TOUGH

In my sleep, in the middle of the night, there was vague awareness of Stella being up, moving around, doing things, and then being back in my arms. Later, struggling to wake, I knew she was not next to me. Able to open my eyes, I saw that she was in one of the lounge chairs, reading. Got myself up and over to the bathroom, did all the necessary maintenance and went out to the living room where the gorgeous lady was closing her book. She stood and moved to me and there was a strong hug and a smooch and a question. Coffee? "Badly needed." Do you want me to make some?" She said, "They have a Continental Breakfast room and I'm a little hungry. Can we go there?" "A minute to get dressed and I'll be with you, Miss Beauchamp. You're so pretty this morning, I wouldn't miss it for the world."

For me, the breakfast was coffee, nothing else. The small selection of foods was basic and looked quite good. No appetite at all at the moment, I took an apple and stuck it in my jacket pocket. Stella had a modest breakfast, smaller than usual. We sipped coffee, exchanged our cups. I talked of finding one or perhaps two bars or venues where we could find some bona fide Dixie for that evening. We could use today for sightseeing just as ordinary tourists might, but we could, at the same time, consider ourselves to be on a reconnaissance mission for the evening. One of the hotel staff announced the breakfast room would be closing in fifteen minutes. Wow, was it that late? Stella said, "Let's go brush our teeth and go into town for this scouting mission." I said, "Ma Certo, Principessa."

A beautiful morning was well underway as we returned to the room. Taking turns in the bathroom, we readied ourselves for the day. Stella neatened the room. As we left, she asked, "Got your key?" I patted my hip pocket, saying "Indeed I do." Helmets on us, then we were off to explore this famous town. Back onto Route 61 with only a few miles to travel. Quite a lot of traffic and going was slow. While temporarily stopped for some construction vehicles, she leaned forward, speaking loudly over the traffic, "The French Quarter is less than two miles that way" and she pointed forward and to the left. A block later, she signaled for a right hand turn and we took the next right onto Loyola Avenue. A mile later, the slowdown signal and a right turn into a wide driveway aimed at a building called the SomethingorOther Passenger Terminal. We approached the curb where she pointed and gave the closed fist 'hold' signal.

She dismounted from the scooter while slipping her helmet off, allowing her hair to fall free and surprised me with a big kiss and a fierce hug. Then she said, "Rosano, dear Rosano, this is killing me now. In the bottom of your trunk is a note from me which I don't want you to read for at least a week. So this is it, Rosano. We're saying goodbye right now. My dear, my precious friend ... you have been the miracle in my life." She was crying openly. Turning away, she walked toward the building. It was only then I noticed she had carried her clothing bag with all her things. The square corners of books showed through. So she was, in fact, gone. That quickly. It was over.

So surprising the finale. I was trying to process this, and a man in dark clothing with wide yellow cross straps approached the scooter. "You can't stay here, buddy. You have to move on out of here, buses coming in." Out of my trance, I merely said "Yes Sir, thanks." Putting Tony in gear, I drove out toward Loyola Avenue. Turned left to retrace my route. Four or five short city blocks later, on the left, was a small city park. Head still fuzzy from the surprise, I crossed Loyola and pulled up in the shade of some trees. Time to settle down, time to regroup, to reason and repair. I was a wreck.

It was the manner and swiftness of our parting that truly stunned me. I knew the last two days had been so tough for her. A few items began to make sense now ... her paying two days for the room, making certain I had the key to the room, the big food purchase in Baton Rouge, etc. In as many ways as she could, she had tried to take care of me. Maybe I should cry a little, but I couldn't allow that. Stayed in the cool of the shade for perhaps an hour, a long, long hour, had a couple of smokes and drank from the water bag. Wedged in the scooter seat was the map we had been using. My navigator was gone. The Voice talking in my left ear, the good ear, was saying "Can't sit all day in the park, Rosano. Go ahead, feel sorry for yourself, but only for another ten or fifteen minutes. After that, get off your ass and do something. How many times have you told other people 'all love ends in sadness'. So now, Rosano, enjoy your own personal misery ... then go get a cup of coffee and get your brain unscrambled. You're well enough to manage a cup of coffee. Beside, you're going to need to take a leak sometime." Removed the Louisiana map from its wedged place, found it already folded to show the New Orleans insert, and decided to find Basin Street and the French Quarter.

Onto my Lambretta, again started on the first kick, I traveled back up a block or so to a minimarket to take a leak and buy some coffee. Bought a large one, and a pack of Parliaments, and sat outside on the scooter, reviewed a few thousand little details of this journey I had half completed. I wanted to see Chicago and wanted also to touch foot on Florida, just to be able to say I did, and then make it to Connecticut in time, but not too early, for my sister Phyllis's wedding. There were no shortcuts if I wanted to do that. Three places in three very different directions. After drinking as much coffee as possible, I headed back down Route 61. Where Stella and I had taken a right turn, now it was a left turn instead. It required a few minutes before I realized I was already on Basin Street, which actually seemed rather ordinary. Driving around the block, I found myself on North Rampart Street (it was South Rampart that hosted the parade in the Dixieland number). Heading into the French Quarter, I encountered Burgundy and then Bourbon Street. Famous Bourbon Street, noted for strip joints and bawdy shows, none of which was of interest to me today. Bourbon Street reminded me that I hadn't had a drink for quite a time. While I knew the street name celebrated a French royal family and had not been named for the American whiskey, I thought the mistaken identity still served my purpose. Began to do a bit of noodling, driving at a moderate pace this way and that, saw an impressive bunch of wrought iron decorative treatments on balconies and elevated walkways. Ironwork which I cared not a hoot for today. Generally, I was moving closer to the river. From the map, this turn in the river was about as far downstream as I wanted to go. At this point, the Mississippi had to be a half-mile wide. For a confirmed desert rat, it seemed almost beyond belief. The huge amount of water flowing so peacefully past. Stopping the scooter where I could watch the river activity, I lit up a smoke and tried to enjoy the fact that at least one of my minor goals had been achieved – to see the river near the Gulf. I watched one or two moderately large ships moving with the flow toward the Gulf and one larger ship moving upstream. Pleasant to watch, tranquil, but my mood was very down. Did I want to seek out music this evening? No, a decided no. Listening to the blues was not a needed thing today. Deciding what I wanted to do next seemed important in pulling myself out of this mental sinkhole. Having seen what I had intended to, it was all diminished considerably ... no beautiful lady with which to share. Bummer. Big time bummer. I'd go back to the motel, maybe snooze, and decide something later. Started up and found my way back through the French Quarter and then back to Route 61 headed to the motel. So that was my big day in New Orleans. Not very impressive. A big fizzle, in fact.

Perhaps a mile from the motel, I pulled off the road to stop at a bar. I would have that Bourbon, after all. Dismounted, locked up the helmet, scooter, and a convenient lamp post all together. The bar had a small price guide posted outside the door. That was something I had never seen previously. At a glance the prices seemed ordinary. Out of the warm, bright afternoon, and into the darker, cooler pub. Nice feel to the place, not at all dingy as so many are. Nice smell, too. Sat down at the bar, put a five dollar bill on the counter and ordered a Jack Daniel's On the Rocks, side of soda, please. Drink served, some beautiful stuff Jack Daniel's is. The first few tiny sips tasted so incredibly fine. Three guys seated at a table at the far end of the bar to my left were having a good laugh at something. I couldn't catch much of what they were doing, but my immediate impression from the voice sounds, was that they were Brits. Things quieted down. My thoughts had just started to turn to my lost companion. In through the front door came a huge, muscular man almost shouting, "A Lammy, can you believe it? A Lammy! Who is here that pilots a Lammy? (referring to the Lambretta).

Reader's Note: It turns out the three guys at the table and the fourth one who came in shouting "Lammy" were not Brits, but Aussies from a cargo ship somewhere in port getting repairs. In my recounting this little story I will not attempt to imitate accents or speech patterns. Just know: the Australian accent added to their genuine overall coolness. For my entire life, I have been strongly prejudiced in regarding the Kiwis and Aussies with great favor.

The three at the table all gave loud greetings at seeing the fourth, while I raised my arm and turning, said, "That would be me." He walked right up to me, stuck out his hand, which I shook, "Jesus, I do love Lammys. And from Arizona, did you drive it here?" I laughed and nodded yes. He grabbed my drink and the five dollar note in one hand and grabbed my arm with the other, saying "Right this way, if you please," almost dragging me over to the table of three, now suddenly become the table of five. He said, "My name is Collin, and yours?" I said "Rosano, the name is Rosano." Almost shouting he said, "Friends, this here is Rosano, he drove a Lambretta motor scooter from Arizona to New Orleans, so show the man some respect and introduce yourselves." And with lots of noise, comments, and congratulations, they did. Collin continued enthusiastically, "Rosano, you Italian?" I nodded yes. "Fine,' he said, "You must be one tough sonuvabitch. I am so goddamn jealous. How long did it take?" I answered "About five weeks, but I went to Denver, Colorado first." One of the others jumped in and said, "But that's a thousand miles out of your way." I said, "Nine hundred, actually." "How many miles have you traveled to get here?" Answered "Twenty-five hundred." Collin, hearing this, said "Wait a moment.

He looked at the ceiling, in the universal body language for unwritten calculation, and announced, "That's equivalent to this crazy bastard driving from Sydney to Perth on a Lammy, can you imagine! Now, that is truly stupendous! You might be a wee runt of a Dago, but you have big balls, my friend. Could you take the time to tell us about your trip?" I asked, "Are you serious?" At least three, maybe all four of them, agreed rather rambunctiously, "Goddamnit yes!" and so forth. It seemed so peculiar to have four grown men, older than I, want to listen to me. I laughed and said "How about I take a leak first?" One of them said, "Absolutely, at least it shows you're a human being." Saying "Excuse me, Gentlemen," I left the table and headed to the restroom. On my return, the Aussies were getting seated again ... they had gone outside to see the scooter. There was a second Bourbon on the Rocks alongside my first, and the five dollar note tucked under it. Before I could protest, Collin said "Your American money isn't acceptable here. First tell us why and how you came to be the owner of that scooter." I said, "OK, but don't hesitate to interrupt me with questions or shouts of disbelief or cries of dismay or just plain heckling if you get bored." That got a laugh out of them, one saying "he's really asking for it," another saying "big balls, indeed."

And so the tale began. I talked of going through the Salt River Canyon, the Petrified Forest, the little dog taken by a coyote (one of the Aussies saying "American dingo"). And there were many questions, about the scooter, the countryside, about my food and water supply. Easy to see these guys were truly interested and I would not unduly abbreviate the telling. Told about the rainout and the flooded tent and they had a good laugh over that. Then the party in the trailer with the four knockout women from the University. I mentioned Enrico up in Pueblo, then Stella, and our journey together across some of the prairie, which they thought had to be magnificent compared to their 'outback'. Recalled the East Texas part of the journey and the disappointment of that area. Then talked of the last few days coming south to New Orleans and the parting with Stella. It seemed they were as surprised as I was. I had spoken for nearly an hour and these guys had been drinking steadily all the way through. Finally, one Aussie said, "That was just a few hours ago. You can't just let her go that easily. Goddamit, man, she is suffering ... you could find her if you tried." Another chimed in "No, he's not going to try regaining something that no longer exists. He's right to just leave it be." They got into a wildly animated discussion while I finished my first drink, and took the first little sip of the second. The comments were flying back and forth. These guys were loud, fun, and seemed rather intelligent and thoughtful in their verbal exchanges, not at all ignorant or unschooled. The conversation turned to some of the comparisons of US geography with that of Australia. I mentioned always being interested in going there some time in my life.

Collin asked my age. When I said twenty-one in just a few days, he asked if I had any skills. Cooking, I can cook creatively and make very tasty stuff, most of it with an Italian flair. He eyes got a big as saucers and he asked "So you think you could cook for 20 people?" I answered, "With a decent helper, it would be 'piece of cake.' He asked, "How would you like to go from this bar here to Australia? "You and your scooter, free passage, plus some reasonable pay and guaranteed return passage." Taking a sip of my drink, I said 'You are being serious, aren't you." He said "If you knew how sorely we need a decent cook on board our ship, you would promptly weep." I said I had no passport. He came back with "Our captain can get you a valid US passport in two days. We're in port for a week with repairs. So there's time." This was sounding interesting. I said, "Tell me about your ship, in terms I might understand, because my knowledge is close to zero." And he did, describing a medium-sized cargo carrier, heading to Asia, after passing through the Panama Canal. Oh wow, sounded exciting. Collin said, "Let me get you another drink." I said "No, for sure no, but thanks. I'm already past my limit. Collin, I think you're being up front and honest with me, so I want to seriously think on this for a night. How can I get in touch with you when I decide?" He shook my hand saying "The exact way you did today ... tomorrow afternoon, the four of us will be here, maybe another one with us. If you decide 'yes', you be here tomorrow same time, and we'll get the process moving." We talked more, and I did enjoy these raucous Aussies. They had a life force and spirit I absorbed and admired. We talked for at least another hour, with me answering more questions about myself, the trip, the scooter. From bits of conversation, I learned a fair amount of the cargo would be construction explosives. Explosives. Would that influence my decision? It may have already. Three hours, a heartening and uplifting three hours with some good-natured, and rambunctious Aussies, combined with two whiskeys, went a good way in helping me lift my mood. Finishing off the watery remnants of the second drink and standing up, I stuck my hand out to Collin, thanking him for his consideration, saying I had enjoyed this time with them, would seriously think about joining them, but right now, it was time to leave. This huge man grabbed me in a strong hug, saying "You little bastard, you are fine company. If you say 'yes,' we'll put you on payroll tomorrow." The others gathered 'round, slamming me on the back, shaking hands, hugging me, saying they hoped I'd come aboard. Of course, they were a little drunk, and that had to be weighed. I was working my way toward the door, but they were just hollering one thing or another and followed me out to the scooter in the bright late afternoon. Unlocking and donning my helmet, gave the scooter a kick, and it didn't let me down, starting with the customary blue puff of exhaust. Those awesome Aussies gave me a round of applause and were still talking as I put the 'Lammy' in gear, waved a 'goodbye' and putted over to Route 61.

A few minutes later, I was at the motel office, asking if there were any messages for Room 6 (None. Was I hoping my beautiful lady had a change of heart?) and asking the opening time of the Breakfast Room (usually open by 6:30AM). The morning paper was on one of the lounge chairs. Could I take it to the room? No problem.

CHICAGO

ILLINOIS

SPRINGFIELD

MISSOURI

ST. LOUIS
DESOTO
POTOSI
IRONTON
FREDERICKTOWN

CAPE GIRARDEAU

TENNESSEE

MEMPHIS

CLARKSDALE

HOLLANDALE

LOUISIANA

MISSISSIPPI

VICKSBURG

NATCHEZ

BATON ROUGE

NEW ORLEANS

PART THREE

NEW ORLEANS TO CHICAGO

CHAPTER 41

GOODBYE, NEW ORLEANS

At 6:30 AM, my nose was pressed against the door of the breakfast room, waiting for the official opening. Not quite true, but there was a hunger in my bones. Yesterday's entire intake was black coffee, two bourbons, and an apple I had taken from yesterday's Continental breakfast. This morning I would really tank up on food and coffee. And that I did. It was sorely needed. Finished, I filled my jacket with fruit. Back to our room, now my room, unloaded the fruit into my clothing bag, did bathroom maintenance, packed my few personal things, and packed the extra coffee packets. There was her shampoo. She had left it for me after hearing that I liked it. No, it wasn't an oversight. That woman knew exactly what she was doing. A marvelous person.

Vacated the room and drove back to the Breakfast Room. More coffee, another Danish, two more pieces of fruit in the jacket. Then into the lobby to surrender the key. Noticed a small post card rack. Did they have stamps? Yes. Paid for cards and stamps and quickly scratched out four or five postcards. Back onto the scooter. I would use Route 61. To head north.

Those fates that I didn't believe in had nudged me into the sphere and influence of those Aussies yesterday afternoon. How fortunate. Such a good group. Probably a bit on the wild side and that's perfect. Probably kept me from dwelling on the loss of my companion. The decision had been made sometime during the night ... I would stay with my original adventure to cross the USA and not be sidetracked into yet another adventure, this time to Australia, abandoning the first not completed. That had happened too often in my life already. So there was that reason. There was also my family obligation. It was my only younger sister getting married. It was my duty, as her older brother, to be there, but also my pleasure ... she being a kind, easy-going person as well as a genuinely stunning beauty. There would be no return to that bar, there would be no Collin and companions, and no trip to Australia, not just yet. But damn, I loved those Aussies.

From the map, I had seen Route 61 went north through Baton Rouge and then to someplace off my map ... North Pole? Before hitting the North Pole, there were a few miscellaneous things in the way, such as the states of Mississippi and Tennessee, maybe Canada, too. I'd have to get another map on the way. Should I stop in Baton Rouge? No, too early in the morning. Next major city going north would be Memphis, Tennessee, more than 500 miles from New Orleans. Without my lovely navigator to be concerned about, I looked more intensely at the landscape going past. Still flat, but more interesting than prairieland. Having my gorgeous friend riding with me had softened the prairie's impact and later, made unbearable East Texas bearable. This morning would be devoted to putting some miles between me and New Orleans. For two weeks, New Orleans had been a shining goal off in the distance. Now it was a sad place in my mind, a place to leave behind. This Southern segregation thing was also troublesome and now it seemed important that I travel to more northward places, however far off they might be. As I neared Baton Rouge, I planned to gas up on the far side. North of there was Louisiana's boundary with Mississippi, with damn little north of Baton Rouge, except agriculture and woodlands. The same seemed true of territory north of the Mississippi line until getting to Natchez, right on the River. Route 61 traveled east of the congested Baton Rouge downtown area and was easy going despite a fair amount of traffic, and some road construction thrown into the mix. The interstate highway system was just getting built and there were significant disruptions at intersections. 61 bypassed much of the heavy activity of Baton Rouge. Again I was impressed with the robust feel to the place. Stopped for fuel as the city fell behind. That strange-acting attendant the last time I fueled up in Baton Rouge came into my thoughts (was it only two days ago?). I wondered if that creep ever went chasing after us. Today's guy was fine. I was not trying to engage people, rather playing it close to the vest as I promised Stella I would. A self-preservation thing, I suppose. Her influence would not disappear, for a while at least. Let's face it ... today I was a little screwed up, feeling comfortable only when the scooter was running and we (Tony Lambretta and I) were anonymously eating up miles as we made our way northward. Somewhere in the remotes of my memory, Route 61 had significance beyond ordinary, but I could not drag it out. Back to the highway, there were suburbs, and then a bridge over Thompson Creek. I pulled over for a break. Found a place to pee privately, then reached in my jacket pocket for a peach from the morning's harvest. Rinsed my mouth with water from the water bag. Then pulled out a smoke and watched waters of Thompson creek head toward the Mississippi, just a few miles away. What Louisianans call a creek, Arizonans would call a river. Back to the drive, going thru agricultural countryside with an endless stream of settlements with names, none of which I would try to recall. Small houses tucked into niches here and there, some hardly qualifying as houses. Soon I was leaving Louisiana behind, crossing into Mississippi, a state of which I had preconceived ideas, but no real knowledge.

One idea was that Mississippi was a rural state, but I had no concept of just how rural. Between Baton Rouge, Louisiana and Natchez, Mississippi, there was about 100 miles of farmland and forest. Natchez would be the next decent sized town encountered and it had less than 25,000 people. Along this route were many cultivated plots of land, everything so green, with woods bordering pastures or croplands. The terrain was very flat, any depression having water in it. Wherever ground had been laid bare, the soil was a yellowish tan color. Miles were easily disappearing behind us and it seemed Natchez would be gained by noon. It would be a fuel stop, and a break time. Maybe some food. As we (again we ... the scooter and I) neared Natchez, there seemed to be an exponential growth of church spires. It surprised me that the Roman Catholics seemed to have their fair share of the worship pie. Just didn't expect that, but should have, since French and then the Spanish cultures had considerable influence in the area, both groups being strongly Catholic. A sign said "Welcome to Natchez, the Friendliest Town on the River." My sour thought was to respond by thinking, "Sure. If you're white." Then I edited that to "Sure. If you're the right shade of white." I was on the dark edge of that deal. And despite being rather conservative politically, I was disguised as a beatnik or hippie, beard and all. Short hair, though. Pulled into a gas station. Did my fueling routine and as I paid for fuel, I asked the attendant about the bluffs. He pointed and said to go about a half mile and then up the hill. I'd find them. They were big and the view of the river was pretty. Not a huge endorsement. I thought time off from driving would be good. Oh what the hell, give it a try. And I did. Not a big hill, but it was real and I had to downshift for climbing, something that hadn't been necessary for weeks, it seemed. Saw a family of four obvious tourists walking uphill. Parked Tony, my faithful Lambretta, locked it up, and followed these tourists. The woman was reading aloud small parts of a book, to her husband and to two kids, a travel book of some sort. From that I learned the Spanish had established this Promenade back in 1790. Finally, getting to the top of rise, I looked down at the abrupt descent to the Mississippi, perhaps 150 feet below. That was so visually surprising. But then, looking westward, across the river, toward Louisiana and points beyond there was a genuinely gorgeous panorama of river, a few barges, reflections on water, greenery, and sky. So very stunning. An incredibly soft and tranquil landscape today. Quietly, I ate the other piece of fruit from my jacket. Then, lit up a smoke, eventually finishing it.   Looking at this unbelievably peaceful scene very nearly hypnotized me. This was something I should have been able to share with my friend, now gone. There was no one touching my arm or pressing against me or pulling my earlobe. My mood was changing. Looking back on this morning, I realized I had been in a foul mood, about half pissed off, since waking. Now, pissed off was being replaced with a quieter sadness, but an accepting sadness. I would get over it. I'd be OK. Those beautiful Aussies got me part way out of the hole, the Bluffs at Natchez pushed me a little further in the right direction. I would leave now and head upriver to Vicksburg and find a place to camp for a night. And read something for a while … to focus on something new. That would help.

Turning my back to the splendor of that river scene, I returned to the scooter and prepared to leave. It had been a good moment for me … a healing interval. Down the hill, back to Route 61, which, with a few turns made its way through Natchez and then aimed us northward toward Vicksburg, about two hours away. Port Gibson, a town of 2500 was about half-way. I'd stop for a cup of coffee there.

Thinking back to the Louisiana part of this trip, I realized each of what I called the 'postcard moments' involved water … of course the Mississippi River, but also the bayou or swamp scenes. My general opinion of Louisiana was more favorable than my feeling toward East Texas (from Paris, Texas eastward). It was the segregation thing … to me the East Texans had less of an excuse than did the Louisians (my word) or the Missippans (also my word), maybe the Alabams, too.   Those people had been raised with totally segregated societies and had never known anything different. I felt that wasn't as true for the Texans, who should have been exposed to a wider focus. Though my knowledge was sketchy, I could see that this segregation thing was unsustainable, would have to end, and it would be a long painful transition. This would not be solved this year, this decade, but maybe this century would see an end to most of this absurdity. The Lost Princess (that's how I thought of her now) had warned me 'to be an observer and not a participant' and that seemed the wisest approach for me, at least temporarily.

Traveling though woods, and more woods, a mixture of pine and some hardwoods. This place was green, and where the forest had been cleared, it was still green with pastureland or cropland. It seemed there were so few housing units in view. But I could understand that ... with a state population of only two million scattered over a large land area. Jackson, the state capital had only 150,000 people. Reaching Port Gibson, small town, with café, I stopped for a fifteen minute break, drank two cups of coffee and had a smoke and was back on the road to Vicksburg, reaching it in an hour, where I followed the sign for Business Route 61, since it traveled closer to the Mississippi River. Stopped at a little diner for pie and coffee, despite having had coffee not long before. In addition to pie, camping information and a restroom break were needed. A young girl, my guess 16 or 17 years old, was behind the counter. As she served me, I asked about campgrounds. She asked where I was headed. Memphis, Tennessee. "So you're heading north and there are two or three little camping places right on this same road, the Business Route, but on the north end of town, you'll see them." When I asked about the bluff, she said to just keep going uphill and I'd find a good view very easily. Then, when I was done, just keep going downhill until I got onto this road again. And head north. I said I'd take her advice and do exactly that and thanks very much. Still sipping coffee and halfway through my pie, I wanted to switch plates with my navigator, but that wouldn't work any longer. The young waitress came back to me and asked if I was an artist, with the beard and all. Told her about my small part in a western movie starting in September and that seemed to satisfy her curiosity. That would be my story for this trip. Beards seemed to provoke an aggravated stance with a few people, and a cautionary stance in most people ... for those who had to look at them, not those who wore them.

Leaving the diner, it was uphill in lower gear, finally reaching a high point in town and there was a fine view of the river and land beyond. Though not as dramatic as that of Natchez, it was a beautiful scene. There was the realization that part of feeling of drama was inside me, the viewer ... it was the visual relief of not having trees always defining what I could and could not see. In our Sonoran Desert, we were accustomed to viewing things ten, twenty, fifty, even a hundred miles away. To my eye, all these trees were a kind of visual pollution that I constantly tried to see around or over or through, without realizing the extra effort to do so. Trees, as wonderful as trees can be, always seemed to be in my face and were the source of a very mild claustrophobia. It was the openness of views from the elevated bluff that was so welcome and refreshing. Now, down the hill and back on Business 61, stopping for fuel, asking again about camping and getting a repeat of the waitress information. Northward now just a few miles. Found one campground that looked rather shabby and neglected. Drove in and out without talking to anyone. Less than a mile further was a very neat camping area with a daily fee of fifty-five cents per person. Running water, toilets, but no showers. Perhaps one day, the owner said. Since today was a Monday, there would probably be wood and charcoal left by other campers. Help myself. Fair enough.

Did I need retraining to set up my tent and campsite? No, but it seemed like a short eternity since I had done so (was it only four days ago, or five?), but I managed. Refreshed the water bag, got a coffee pot fire assembled, readied the coffee pot with two extra motel packets, went into the trunk and dragged out a few small food items for later. Still had some daylight for reading and Stella had left the flashlight with me. At the 'door' of the tent, I began to read 'I, Robot', my third or fourth try at reading this fine collection of short sci-fi stories.

When time came to end the day, I crawled into my compact tent, which seemed so spacious now with only one person's baggage and one person alone. That would be me and it was time to get past the lonesome stuff. There would be damn little wallowing.

CHAPTER 42

ON TO MEMPHIS

It had rained sometime during the night in Vicksburg. Hearing the sound of rain on the tarp told me it was a gentle rain. Having taken two or three aspirins before trying to sleep had good results. Since childhood I had always dealt with periods of insomnia and through that had learned the value of aspirin as a sleeping aid. Through the tent opening, there was no daylight to be seen. Not carrying a watch meant it could be midnight or 5:00AM ... or something in between. Well, whatever the time, I was done sleeping. Pulling my boots on (a bit weird without socks), grabbing the flashlight and the toothbrush, I emerged from the tent into the cool, damp, dark and made my way over to the toilets. On the return, I decided to make coffee no matter the time of night. I had covered the prepared fire the night before. Soon, the pot was making that splendid 'almost done' gurgling sound. There was enough air movement to keep mosquitoes at bay and a promise of daylight began to show through the trees. How's that for perfect timing? Two cups of coffee would take me close to daylight.

After coffee pot cleaning (so easy with motel coffee packets), I packed up camp, putting two pieces of fruit in my jacket pockets. Refreshed the water bag, restroom again, and then putt-putting out of the campground and heading north on Business 61, which rejoined state route 61 a few miles later. Early morning, cool, very little traffic, and comfort to be had in the scooter purr. We weren't eating up miles ... with a top speed of 43 mph, it was closer to gnawing at miles. And that was on flat ground. If hills were involved, it would be more like nibbling at miles. The Mississippi was somewhere on my left, two miles or ten miles, I didn't know. Crossed Yazoo River, a tributary to the Mississippi, and then there was lots of farmland, cultivated pastures, very few houses that I could see, but, by God, there were churches. No wonder they didn't have houses ... they spent all available money on holy pews. Little snide comment, there. Mile after mile of cultivated rectangles, punctuated by ponds, creeks or brooks or drainage ways. Decided to take a break at an intersection called Leland. No real town that I could see. Peed in a little stand of trees. Had a welcome smoke. Walked around for a few minutes and then back to the road. This countryside was not as boring as prairie, but not much better either, the prairie being tan and this being green. In time, I knew I was approaching the town of Cleveland, Mississippi, by the number of church steeples poking their way into the sky like pointed white mushrooms after a rain. Pews and steeples, steeples and pews! This morning's run so far was just over 100 miles in just under two-and-a-half hours. Time to get fuel for the scooter and caffeine for the driver.

First the faithful scooter: fuel, check the tires, clean the windshield. Then me: coffee, add a doughnut, take a leak, have a smoke. Pay for it all and smile and say thank you (no conversation ... I'm not trying to meet people right now) and I'm on the road again. Most comfortable place for me right now... on the road. There seemed to be an endless scene of cultivated rectangles in every imaginable shade of green. Similar to my thinking on the tan-colored Colorado and Oklahoma prairies, I wondered about young people in all these little agricultural towns. Was television their primary exposure to anything outside the tractor barn? Of course, these kids could catch a bus and get some of our world's finest music, either in New Orleans, or Memphis and Nashville in Tennessee. In that regard at least, they were far better off than Boise, Oklahoma kids. Various churches were probably primary social centers, but in my experience, churches were not a welcoming force (they only pretended to be), trying instead to 'protect' their flocks from outside influence which might be tainted. There was no telling what havoc a deranged Lutheran or a violence-prone Congregationalist might precipitate. And please, let's not even speak of R. Catholics, Jews, J. Witnesses, or God Forbid, Crazy Ass Quakers. Of course, my reasoning went, each church (or fragment thereof) was entitled to create its own special brand of lunacy to sell to its victims.

All these thoughts were a sign that my brain was returning to its old sweetly cantankerous status and would not long slop around in an emotional morass just because some beautiful woman was no longer with me. And all this thinking in the past hour had caused me not to remember anything of a town called Clarksdale, which I had just passed through, so our next major stop would be Memphis, Tennessee. My plan was to either find a campground with showers or an inexpensive motel. No real feeling as to whether I should spend one or two days in Memphis.

Traveling through yet more agricultural stuff, a pickup truck passed me and someone gave a 'rebel yell.' The bed of the truck had a half-dozen confederate battle flags in the stake slots. I had seen many of these displayed in Texas, Arkansas, Louisiana, and Mississippi. People were evidently more proud of their Confederate emblems and displays than I would have guessed. Mentioned before, my knowledge of our Civil War was very spotted, that is, a little spot here and a little spot there. One 'fact' I had read was that less than five percent of the southern whites were actually slave owners. I had no way of verifying that, but assuming it was true, and putting myself in place of an average white working man, my age twenty, in the South, not in 1960 , but in 1860 ... why would I want to defend a system that was not doing as well as a system not too many miles north of me, and a system that used slaves and their so-called 'free labor' to keep MY wages down? So that was simple practical consideration. Maybe peer pressure would cause me to take up arms, but (in my 1960 thinking) if I were single (no wife, no kids,) I wouldn't join the North, but I might just decide to go elsewhere (California? Nevada? Europe?) to try a life there. Or, if I had a wife and kids, that might be a greater incentive to pack up and head for the West Coast. But now, today, in 1960, the Confederate battle flag was really a puzzlement to me. Something I probably could never truly understand. It was a battle banner of the side that lost. Why continue to celebrate it? Then again, my view was formed from a New Englander's upbringing and a Westerner's mindset with a goodly amount of ignorance tossed into the mix. My thinking was that somewhere on this trip, I would stop at a library and try to find a book about the Civil War ... not the various battle and military maneuvers, but more about economic and philosophical and psychological elements. These Southerners and Northerners had been, less than 100 years before the Civil War, allies against British forces. Now, today, another battle had started and was ramping up ... the Battle for Civil Rights. In my mind, the end result was inevitable ... the Southern mindset could only delay things temporarily, causing more hurt along the way ... what a mess! A mess I would try to sidestep during the remaining weeks of this cross-country exploration.

While all that pondering was holding my mind's attention, the scooter and I were passing a place called Mud Lake, rather a pretty spot within sight of the border of Mississippi and Tennessee, which meant I was on the outskirts of Memphis, and it also meant I was very nearly out of fuel, and also out of map. Time to stop. And at the next gas station, I did. Wow, I had already traveled about 225 miles today, a record for me and for Tony, too. Went through the mixing thing with the two-stroke oil, still maintaining that 4% mixture as closely as possible since the scooter ran so incredibly well with that ratio, and the spark plug stayed clean. Asked about any campgrounds. Didn't know. This was his second day on the job and he was from Kentucky. Did they have a map of Tennessee, specifically Memphis? No, the only map they had was an Alabama state map and they had about twenty of those. Did he know where Beale Street was? That he did. Just continue straight and when you get to downtown, Beale Street would be a cross street. You can't miss it. Well, that was something, at least. Sometime in the past, I had gotten an idea that Beale Street was very near Basin Street and Bourbon Street in New Orleans. I was close ... they were in the same nation and only 500 miles apart. Got a restroom I could use? He handed me a key attached to a thin flat board. Before leaving, I cleaned the windshield so gently. It was fabricated of some plastic which would scratch if cleaning was too vigorous. With a "Thank You, Sir", I waved 'Goodbye.'

Back on the road for a mile or two before I spotted a small bookstore. Aha! They would have a map of Memphis, for sure. Bookstores are never a quick stop for me. Locked up, spent a minute or two stretching arms and legs, had a smoke, field-stripped the butt, and went into that special little place in heaven called a bookstore. At last, trees on shelves ... just as God intended them to exist. Smell the wonderful scent of books ... of paper and ink ... a breath of fresh air, no?

When the older woman at the front of the store asked if she could help me, I said I'd like to wander a bit and then perhaps she could help. Poked around here and there knowing I should select something. Now traveling solo, I'd have beau coup time to myself. Having a companion does take a fair amount of time. Reading would cover some of that. Browsed through the comedy section, then sci-fi, then political, back to sci-fi. Kurt Vonnegut ... The Sirens of Titan. From where did I know of his writing? I'll read it. Moved toward the front of the store, book in hand. The woman looked up from behind the counter. "Vonnegut? You know of Vonnegut?" I said I almost did. Had I read some of his work in Saturday Evening Post.? I wasn't sure, but the name rang a very favorable bell in my brain. She said "Yes, you may have. He's a fine writer. This is an excellent selection." As we talked, a guy about my age walked into the shop, saying, "Hi Mom!" Then to me he said, "Is that your scooter out front." I said it was. "It's a Lambretta. You hauled that here from Arizona? I noticed your license plate." No, I drove it. "Really? I'd love to hear about it, but I have to run off to practice." He grabbed a bag from behind the counter and started for the front door saying "Bye, Mom." She turned to me and asked if there was something else. Yes, as a matter of fact, I'm out of maps. I'd like to see a map of Memphis, but I was planning to head to Chicago as well. How long did I plan to stay in Memphis? Only one or two days. I was pretty tired, but I wanted to spend some time with the music scene. She asked if I liked the Rock and Roll stuff. I said I preferred Jazz, but I acknowledged I was a misfit and knew Rock and Roll was kicking everything else off the popularity charts

... jazz, pop, everything. But I also enjoyed the Blues and particularly enjoyed Blue Grass and I knew Memphis had both. She said I could get all three, Rock 'n' Roll, Blue Grass and Blues in various clubs along Beale Street. They started about 8 in the evening and a few went 'til dawn. She had a small map of Memphis, it was a freebie. After Chicago, where was I headed? Well, I was thinking Florida and then New England. She came from behind the counter and from the front window, she looked at the scooter. She turned around and said "That's simply marvelous! You are to be congratulated!" And somewhere, she said, she had a small road Atlas hidden, give her a minute or two. It took five minutes, but she had it in her hands, mentioning it was out-of-date. I said I'd buy it ... anything was better than what I had. She said the printing was so small, most people wouldn't want it. I said I'd buy it. She said No, I wouldn't buy it. If I bought the Vonnegut book she would give me the atlas no charge, but, she warned, no Crazy Wandering Gypsy discount ... full price on Vonnegut. It's a deal. I paid for Vonnegut and asked if I could spend a little time in that lounge chair by the window, to look at the map. Please, be seated, young man.

"We'll be closing pretty soon," she was saying as she tapped my shoulder. I had fallen asleep. Such a comfortable chair. How long had I slept? She said, "Nearly two hours, and if you missed any appointments, you can blame me." I was waking up and said whom shall I blame? She said "Edith, just call me Edith. And you're the first person I have heard use the word 'whom' in a long, long time, and use it correctly." As I prepared to leave, I asked if she could point out a reasonably priced motel. She said they were all too expensive on this side of the river, but if I followed the signs to West Memphis, on the other side of the river, the Arkansas side, there would be something more reasonable within a few miles. Thanks, Edith, you have a good heart. Thanks so much. Arkansas? Better look at my atlas more carefully.

Still had some daylight. I'd get some coffee and dig into the trunk for food Stella had purchased back in Baton Rouge. Stopped at a doughnut shop for coffee, not for pastry. Of course, one would help my mood a bit. I did tank up on coffee. Used the restroom before and after. Drove to what looked like a little park. Opened the trunk and started to explore my food stash. There was some hard salami, crackers, dried figs, dried apricots. That was a good start. As I dug around, I saw a corner of Stella's envelope left for me. It had only been a few days. I'd leave it be for now. Finishing my little picnic, I put the little bit of trash into my jacket pocket, back onto the scooter, and directed the scooter and my thoughts to Beale Street.

In no time at all, it seemed, I was at the intersection of my route and Beale. While there was daylight remaining, I'd explore the street with an eye to where I could park Tony Lambretta securely. I turned left and slowly cruised along Beale, trying to look at every club, business, sign and doorway. Have to be careful. Easy to run into things when you brain is occupied with things other than traffic. Drove about a mile until I came to Riverside Drive and the Mississippi River. So that was one end of Beale Street, I supposed. Turned a 180 and retraced that mile, continued across my highway for another mile or so until Beale ended again, this time in a residential area. So Beale Street was only two miles long. Might have figured that out from the map if I hadn't fallen asleep in the bookstore. Still driving slowly and trying to be observant without killing any old ladies walking across the street, and seeking a good scooter spot, I spied a perfect place in an alleyway not far from Fourth and Beale to stash Tony. Which I did, using the cable tightly around a concrete-filled post.

So the scooter was within a walking mile of just about everything on Beale Street. My plan was to walk purposely, neither in a hurry nor strolling, close to the River, cross the street, walk all the way up the other side, then cross the street again and walk back to the scooter. That would be a half hours' walk or a bit more and night would be upon us. My intent was to find someone of knowledge to direct me to the bar or club for the music I wanted to hear. As I did that walking circuit, I noticed that Beale Street looked a little on the touristy side (of course, tourists had to be catered to for financial health) and somewhat on the seedy side, a little rundown. But that was OK, too. Finally, near a club advertising "the best in Rock 'n' Roll", I stopped at a sidewalk trash barrel to rid my jacket of major debris. Threw away some wrappers and came across a five dollar bill. How the hell did that ... oh, I know, it was that beautiful bunch from Down Under ... the Aussies in New Orleans. Those sneaky bastards slipped my fiver back in my jacket as I left the bar. Well, I'd have a drink on them and quietly toast them. So, "the best in Rock 'n' Roll" pulled me in. Recorded music going right now. Just a few people at the bar. Sitting on a stool about halfway down its length, I put my five dollar bill on the bar. A group of musicians was doing a sound check on the small stage and a bartender named Moretti (from his badge) came over. Before he could say anything, I said "Ciao, Signor' Moretti, come stai 'sta sera?" He laughed and said with a big smile, "Buona Sera and that's all I know in Italian, and no, I wasn't named after a beer ... it was named after me. Now what'll you have?" I said, "That's a good line, keep using it. First, I'd like a dark draft beer if you have one and second, I need a little advice. He said, let me get your drink first, then we can talk, it's slow in here right now, but another hour and it'll be busy." As he served my beer, he said "The advice?" I explained being on the road, that I wasn't really 'into' the whole Presley thing, but wanted to witness some of it. Told him I really did like the Blues and also Bluegrass. Which of these places should I try? He then asked what kind of music I listened to the most. I answered with Stan Kenton, Benny Goodman, Louis Prima, Miles Davis, J.J. Johnson, Dave Brubeck, ... he interrupted me with "Jesus, you are a Jazz man. OK, just hang on" and he left to serve another customer. I took a sip of that refreshing beer. The band was going through the sound check and damn, they were loud. A few minutes later, Moretti returned with a 4 by 6 card. On it, he had written two club names, their street addresses, and the numbers 1100 and 200. He explained this was the best I could do this evening. Stay in this bar until about 10:30 and endure the music, although this group did have some good stuff. Go to this club (and he pointed at the upper address) at 11:00PM to catch some pretty good blues until about 1:30AM, then (pointing to the other) go to this place, give the doorman a dollar, tell him you're a friend of Moretti, and listen to some excellent Bluegrass until the sun comes up and you don't have to buy any booze there ... just listen to the best Bluegrass in the world. "Can you handle an 'allnighter', paisano?" You bet I can and I stuck out my hand, saying, "Moretti, my name's Rosano." He responded, "Rosano, my pleasure, I'm an old Jazz Man myself, used to play trumpet quite a bit, studio work, gigs in Nashville, St Louis, Chicago ... but there isn't much for a Jazz man today. We are obsolete. Rock 'n' Roll has really kicked our asses." I knew that. It was sad, but it was true. Finally the band started their first set and Moretti was right, it was to 'endure' for. I listened carefully and I could see the appeal, but for me the lack of finesse was a powerful force. The two guitarists (one on bass guitar) were young, sounded like they practiced and worked at it, and both had some good moves. The drummer was loud, but that's about all. It was the bass guitar keeping the beat, not the drummer. After an hour, with the band taking a break, Moretti came over and said "One of my other customers ordered a coffee. I can't make less than two cups at a time. If you don't want the other, I'll have to toss it. You'll need it tonight." I gave him a thumbs up and said "Black, please." He brought it over, took my five, returned with five ones. I said, indicating the money, "wha ... "he interrupted and said "I got you covered, Mr. Jazz Man." The place was getting busy, I stayed for a few more pieces, then putting a dollar under the coffee cup, I caught Moretti's attention, waved and went out onto Beale Street. A little too early for the Blues location. If I were going to stay up all night, I wanted to have a clear head, and yet felt almost obligated to have at least one drink in each place. No biggie, but I'd walk around between stops and get some stretching. Purposely I went past the scooter to see if it was OK. And of course, it was.

Walking, observing, catching bits of music now and then, I could see Beale Street was a bit tired, a little bit worn. And yet, this was a genuine music focus point, really a national treasure if someone cared enough. Walking past a small eatery triggered some growling in the depths of my soul or was it my stomach? I'd have some food to go with my beer. Barbecued beef burger and a cup of coffee. By the time I finished lingering over a coffee refill and a couple of smokes, it was time for my Blues venue. Found it easily with Moretti's note as guidance. Walked in, a moderately-filled place, music already started, sat at the bar, got some dark beer in a bottle, put money on the bar and stayed with that beer and that music for two hours of nonstop Blues. One number was not sung, but rather was a Blues poem spoken in rhythm with the music background subdued, and, at the same time it was conversational. Heartfelt. Remarkable, I thought. Had never heard anything quite like it. Quietly sensational. I was witness to a unique American art form, the Blues, diverse in its origins but certainly it was its own form. The musicians seemed so honest in their performance, whether the lyrics were sad or playful or downright dirty, they were sincere. As a fifteen minute break was announced, I paid for my drink, tipped the bartender and returned to Beale Street.

Back to the little diner for a quick cup of coffee and then toward my Bluegrass address. Found it with no problem, followed Moretti's instructions, giving the doorguy a dollar and mentioning Moretti. He gave me a big smile and said, "That Moretti is someone special. He's my buddy." The place was very basic, a room with folding chairs, a stage elevated by no more than six inches. Three or four microphones, not much else. At the back of the stage, against the back wall, was some sort of curtain. On stage were five or six bar stools, some ordinary wooden chairs, a small bench, in a casual arrangement, no, a haphazard arrangement. The men, standing or sitting, were tuning a couple of fiddles, some guitars, at least one banjo, a mandolin, two bass fiddles. This was going to be a jam session. There was no band, it was a group, a gathering. One of the guitarists walked up to a mike and said simply, "Well, here goes." He began playing, and was soon joined by one bass player who carried his fiddle forward. Next came the violin and a banjo. So within a space of sixteen bars of music four musicians were performing as a quartet. For more than an hour, these guys, so extraordinarily skilled, came forth in different combinations and provided such excellent music. Started and ended selections with almost no conversation. I had no idea how they decided who would play what tune and when. I marveled at not knowing. The musicians had their own telepathy. Each musician had multiple chances to display his dexterity with his instrument. Various people walked onto and off the stage and performed. Completely mesmerized as someone stuck a beer in my hands. When I reached in my pocket for money, they waved no-no and said "Friend of Moretti". Sometime around 3:30AM, a guy sat next to me and banged into me. I looked at him. Big smile on his face. I said, "Moretti, how the hell are you?" We shook hands and slapped each other on the back. The Bluegrass started up with another tune. Moretti talking into my ear asked, "Good stuff, eh?" I said, "The absolute best." He said, "No. Not yet, but soon. Scruggs is coming by. That's why I'm here." Me: "Scruggs, Earl Scruggs?" Moretti nodded yes. Oh Man! Two or three more tunes and then a few hollers and some applause and Earl Scruggs, who had to be the premier banjoist in the world, stepped away from the curtain, where he had been half hidden (maybe tuning up), into a group that was already deeply involved in a breakdown. So splendid, so quick, really a blazing banjo rendition which sounded like he was picking with eleven fingers. So, without pause, Scruggs played along with various combinations on four or five different tunes and then waved and said, "Thank you everybody!" And people gave him a big cheer and they started the music again. Moretti said "So paisano, what do you think?" I said, "I'm stunned. Completely stunned." Moretti said as he offered his hand, "Good. Gotta go. See you around, my friend, and Remember the Moretti!" And he was gone. The music never stopped for more than a few seconds. What has always fascinated me was the musician mindset. Their brains are indeed different. How they talk to each other and understand one another and anticipate each other's moves, and do this through their magnificent music ... well, to me, it's just miraculous. I stayed to the end. They wound it up, someone on stage announced that his instrument couldn't work when the sun was up. I went and took a leak before the crowd lined up behind me. And that was it. People milled around and slowly moved out into the dawn of Beale Street and dispersed. Every other place on the street looked closed.

    Returning to Tony Lambretta in the cool of dawn, happiness glowed all around, surrounding me. It had been a marvel. And I was one happy clam. The scooter seemed untouched. Unwound the cable and got the helmet onto my head, so filled with the magic of music. More than wide awake, I started the Lambretta, headed back to pick up my old Route 61. Then with sunshine at my back, a slight breeze in my face, I crossed the Mississippi into West Memphis to begin a new day. Someone should make a movie which uses a scene like this for its beginning or its ending or both.

CHAPTER 43

CLOSE TO THE OZARKS

Well, that was something I hadn't planned on. Halfway across the bridge as I left Memphis and headed to West Memphis, I entered Arkansas, or rather re-entered. I had traveled through the southwest corner with my special lady friend while on our way to New Orleans. Now I was traveling through the diagonally opposite northeast corner, but alone, without my friend. There had been that beautiful nap in the bookstore, but other than that, no sleep at all in Memphis and I wasn't the least bit tired. My head had been stuffed with fantastic music, and I was really jazzed, so to speak. In West Memphis, I followed Route 61 northward. My intent had been to cross the river and find more reasonably priced motel rooms. Now, surprise surprise, I was back in Arkansas, and was in no need of a motel room, maybe later in the day. Oh well, time to go with the flow. Still very early morning as I left the northern edge of West Memphis. Driving conditions were perfect and that was good since my mind was still back in Memphis. The Rock 'n' Roll had been somewhat better than expected, and that's where I met Moretti, who led me to excellent blues playing later, then topped it off by joining me for short time for the most splendid Bluegrass I had ever heard or witnessed. What an experience! I was aglow with good feelings. Musicians, as screwed-up as they can be sometimes, are remarkable people and should be nurtured.

Being totally enveloped in a cloud of fine music doesn't prevent one's bladder from filling. Approaching a town called Blytheville, it was time to stop for coffee. Maybe pancakes, too. Café open and they had dollar-sized. Can't pass that up. Two cups, small order of dollar-sized pancakes, take a leak, pay the bill, walk outside and smoke and stretch. Then one-kick the scooter and back on the road going north. A few minutes later and we leave Arkansas and enter the state of Missouri. Here we are, on the west side of the Mississippi, traveling through unending farmland, my mind still in Memphis. Damn, I better pay attention. Another hour and forty miles later, we (Tony Lambretta and I) reach Portageville and it's time to gas up. Where in hell am I headed? Better take some time and check the road atlas, a gift from Edith at the bookstore. Pulled into a station, did the whole fuel mixture routine. Attendant was an older guy. As I paid for the gas, he glanced at the Arizona license plate, paused for just a moment and asked "Did you drive that to here?" At least semi proudly, "That's right, driven it all the way." He then asked "Why would anybody do such a thing?" I said I really didn't know. He said, "Well, I don't know either." So I said, "Fair enough, neither of us knows, and neither of us is afraid to admit it." He said "Yep."

Not wanting the old guy to see me reading a map for some reason, I got onto the scooter and drove northward again. A half hour later, in the town of New Madrid, there was a view of the Mississippi. Pulled off the highway and traveled less than a half mile to a great observation point. This town was located on the north side of what is called the Kentucky Loop, a big reverse bend or loop in the river. Lit up a smoke, took out my new atlas and settled down for a spell. Flipped through a few pages, familiarized myself with Middle American geography (to which I had paid little attention throughout my school years). Made a decision that for this day, my goal would be Cape Girardeau, (a town whose name I'd never heard before) which was north of New Madrid about 60 miles. I'd find a motel there and take a better look at maps. Grabbed a few pieces of dried fruit to keep me occupied. This river was so interesting, its farmland was the opposite. Enjoyed a smoke. Now again to the highway and head north. With the exception of a few small wooded areas, and a few little settlements, it was farmland all the way to Cape Girardeau.

Drove slowly into the town, did a fuel stop(less than a gallon), got the "I always wanted to do something like that only I got married" thing from the attendant. Then drove past some commercial businesses, car repair shops, and a coffee shop where I decided to stop. A little bit hungry and getting fatigued, I had driven more than 600 miles in three days. So it was black coffee and a small hamburger. Asked the waitress about an inexpensive motel. She said directly behind me, outside on the corner, was a small sign that read Room $2.00, with an arrow pointing down the street, and that's all she knew about it. Enjoyed my coffee, burger and fries. Had a smoke, used the restroom, paid the bill, and said my Thank You.

Looked at the small sign and went in the direction of the arrow. Three or four small city blocks and I was in a modest residential area and soon saw an identical sign at the front gate of a house. The gate had an electric doorbell button. Rang the bell and a middle-aged guy came to the door of the house and said, "About the room?" I said, "Yes Sir." He said to just go down the driveway, the room was in the rear of the house. Did that and he met me there. "Basic room, separate entrance, double bed, your own bathroom, no tub, shower only. Want to see it?" I nodded yes, he opened the screen door and we walked into the small room. I looked very quickly, and said I'd take it. He asked "How did you decide so fast?" I said "The corners are clean as a whistle. If the corners are clean, that usually means everything else is, too." I reached into my pocket and handed him the two dollars. Before he took the money, he said "If you smoke, it has to be outside, not in the room. Agree?" I said "Absolutely" and he said as he took the money, "You can park right here," indicating a place in the driveway. I walked to the front, moved the scooter to its place. Soon I was settled into the room, boots off, quick shower and zonk ... horizontal.

How many times has the course of human history been altered by something as seemingly inconsequential as a full bladder signaling its owner? The question probably deserved some serious attention or research, which I didn't have time for immediately because I had to pee and that was what had awakened me from a long nap. The more immediate research project had to do with my new road atlas. The greater part of this entire trip had been plotted in an off-the-cuff manner. Taking stock of my situation, I was in the middle of the country, with three specific places to be visited ... Chicago, Florida, and New England. And there was almost five weeks to do it in. Chicago was less than 500 miles to the north. Assuming nothing went haywire, I could reach that in three days easily. However, less than 100 miles to the west lay the eastern-most parts of the Ozark Mountains, interesting geologically, and culturally as well. I had read something of the geology and knew that these relatively small mountains were probably some of the oldest rock formations in North America. Looking at the atlas persuaded me that it was worth the one-day side trip. Chicago would wait for me, and probably not miss me at all.

Late afternoon, went outside for a smoke, met the owner of the house. We talked briefly. Told him I would most likely leave in the early morning. I asked about the name Cape Girardeau, what cape were they talking about? He said the cape they were talking about didn't exist anymore due to changes in the river. OK. Into my trunk, took out food for the evening. Time to read and then sleep. Spent more time with the atlas, a small treasure. Ate a few snacks which Stella had so carefully chosen for me. Then began to read Vonnegut's 'Sirens of Titan' and realized that after six or seven pages, retention of the words was zero ... my eyes were doing the reading, but my receiver wasn't engaged. Time to sleep. A basic need.

Waking into a dark morning (assumed it was morning), got into the shower and did a thorough washing this time, not just a quicky. Still dark, decided to get at least half dressed and read a little. Reviewed the atlas for a short time before light began to show in the sky. Used the bathroom again, got fully dressed, packed the few things that were out. While tying my clothing bag onto the scooter, there were plenty of mosquitoes about seeking a small snack. I kept shaking them off and finally did a quick check of the room, shut the door, climbed onto the Lambretta and purred on out the driveway. Coming to the corner, and seeing the café open, I went in for coffee. There was a little brochure rack which I hadn't noticed the day before. Took one of those touting 'All About the Ozarks' which I would read while doing my holy morning ritual with the black coffee. Read a little paragraph about the origins of the Ozark people ... primarily from the Appalachians, they were descendants of Scots, Germans, English, and Irish, with some percentage of American Indian in the mix. A restaurant ad in the brochure extolled great qualities of special Ozark cooking, unmatched anywhere in the world. Hmmm. Being an ethnic food snob, I'd have to think about that. Finishing the second cup, I paid the tab, and told the waitress about the room for rent sign across the street, saying the room was small but had a bath and was very neat and clean. She said that was good to know. I had been the first to mention it.

Onto the scooter once again and off to a small adventure in the Ozarks. Made my way through and out of Cape Girardeau and within ten miles was driving through the small town of Jackson on my way toward Fredericktown on Route 72, about 2 hours away. Traveling through farmland for most of the first hour, I knew the terrain would get more hilly as we neared the mountains. These were low-lying mountains (estimated age I remembered was about a billion years), with the highest peak being 2,500 feet. The Appalachians, east of here, went to above 5,000, the Rockies, to the west ranged up to over 14,000. Hills slowed me down a bit, but were far more interesting visually than cultivated farmland. So the Ozarks were the only mountains in the middle of the US. That being the situation, there were probably a million amateur and student geologists there on the weekend and every square centimeter had probably been examined at least a dozen times a year. And darn it all, I forgot to bring my Estwing rock hammer which I had purchased in a hardware store in Boston three or four years before. I might do a bit of hiking, but no rock hounding on this trip.

Gave some thought to Ozark cooking. Had never heard of it before. If it had evolved from English-Irish-Scotch-German cooking, it probably was sustaining food, but my guess was it probably tasted like a high grade of cardboard. If it had any appeal whatsoever, there would be at least a few 'Ozark' restaurants in other parts of the country, and I was fairly certain there were none. My hunch said there was actually no such thing as 'Ozark' cooking, and if there was something like that advertised, I would certainly not seek it out.

The drive was going well and encountering a few hills was refreshing. I could also see rocks exposed on hillsides, rocks which I knew were igneous. Probably just tired of flatness, of swamps and farmland and sedimentary this and that. Doing a little downhill coasting, I reached Fredericktown. Saint Francois Mountain was a dozen miles further west, but I'd stop for coffee and pancakes at a café ... a nice break after almost two hours scootering. And they did dollar-sized pancakes, well-cooked, please. And they were perfect.

Leaving town, we crossed, not the Saint Francois River, but the Saint Francis River. Same saint, different language. Within a half hour, I was at the base of Saint Francois mountain. A gorgeous morning, time for a hike ... needed the exercise. Carefully moved the scooter into the woods and secured it to a stout pine tree. Just a short hike, but I would take the water bag, and put a little food into my jacket pockets (just in case). I would carry my jacket with the machete hidden down one sleeve (scabbard stayed with the scooter). All set. An hour's excursion would be good. Having a companion might be nice, but there was no problem for my being alone, except, of course if there was an injury or who knows what. This was not really a mountain in my mind, but rather a beautiful hill, having an elevation of 1500 feet or so, but it had been a fine mountain 700 or 800 million years before and was showing its age. Did my little tour and eventually made my way back to Tony Lambretta, patiently waiting in the woods. My hiking had been worth the day's drive. For me, this was a refreshing place, so enjoyable. The day had been designated as an 'exploratory' time, not as a day to eat up miles. Packed up, and saying Ciao, I started the scooter and instead of backtracking, continued on the same road, which occasionally had signage pointing to Ironton. That's where I would go and have yet another cup of coffee if there was yet another café. The narrow two-lane road wound thru hills northwest where it joined Route 72 into Ironton, where, Eureka!, a café appeared, and it was calling me. Coffee was served and as it was being sipped, a young couple at adjacent counter stools were talking enthusiastically about Elephant Rocks, not indicated on my maps. Asking them, they described it as a place not to miss and it was only five or six miles to the north. That was enough for me, it would be seen. Twenty minutes later I was there.

A splendid place ... huge granite boulders, rounded into gentle shapes by millions of years of erosion. Couldn't help thinking of the Christian teachings that the earth was 6,000 years old ... what a bunch of ignorami, that's plural, no? This outcropping could be walked on, walked through, walked around. These enormous volcanic stones just begged to be petted on this mild early afternoon. Being only semi-familiar with the geology of this old mountain range, I nonetheless felt an identity with it. How peculiar. These stones and I were both made of stardust, so we were kin. These were volcanic, igneous stones, very tough stuff, yet weathered by a number of forevers. Sitting on one softly-shaped stone, I tried to reach out with my mind into other universes. This sort of thinking can occur when one has spent too many hours on the road. But this was indeed, a magical place. Being an earthling, however, does have limitations. It was time to depart and without my thinking it, my voice said aloud "See you later!"

CHAPTER 44

THE OZARKS

Midafternoon, leaving that special place called Elephant Rocks, it was time to find a campground or camping spot for the evening. My eating and sleeping schedule was non-existent. One consideration was that I was about 100 miles from St Louis, Missouri where all highways seemed to converge to cross the Mississippi. If I attempted it today, I would reach St. Louis at dinner rush hour or maybe as the sun was setting. Those hours can be a bit treacherous for a scooter and rider. Listen, Rosano, just find a good place to settle down this evening. And don't get any funny ideas. OK, I'm in no rush anyway. That's an important rule ... never be in a rush ... never push it if you're on a two-wheeler, never push it if you're tired, that's when mistakes can happen so easily. This state of Missouri had been a pleasant and interesting place so far. Somewhere, while heading toward the St. Louis metropolitan area, there was sure to be excellent camping spots. Now traveling north on Route 21, the terrain was an intermittent mix of hilly wooded areas and cultivated pasture and farmland. Quite beautiful motoring as less than an hour later, I pulled into a town named Potosi, where from the map, it seemed about eight small highways converged. The scooter needed fuel. Attendant admired the scooter and noticed the Arizona plate, we talked four or five minutes about my adventure (as I moved north, I became less guarded in conversations with people) and asked about camping nearby. He said the best place he knew, and had stayed there himself, was a place called Washington State Park, not too far north of Potosi, maybe 15 miles. Good campground with showers. Just stay on Route 21. Can't miss it. Hold on for a second. He walked over to the little office building and came out with a partial bag of charcoal. A customer had left it behind about a month ago. Maybe I could use it tonight. Tied it to the trunk, said my thanks and my goodbye.

Half an hour later, I was at the campground. Just a few people around. No employees that I could see. No idea if there was a fee. A number of vacant campsites. I chose the smallest and did my little tent construction project not far from a small fireplace. Tied the scooter to a suitable oak tree, then scouted out the facilities, very clean restrooms, very clean shower stalls, no trash or debris to be seen on the grounds. And now, a round of applause for the State of Missouri. An excellent State Park. Time to refresh the water bag, brew some coffee, drag out a book.

Using a few twigs and the charcoal from the gas station, the fire soon had the coffee pot in its embrace, causing it to make loving sounds of coffee about to be born. Pulled all the food out of the trunk, took an inventory. Plenty of food available until after St Louis. There was that envelope from the Princess, still looking at me from the bottom of the trunk. How many days had it been? Still sad about it sometimes. Only four days. Seemed so very long ago. Cut a number of slices of hard salami, gathered the bags of dried fruit and nuts, sat down at a small picnic table with my book, coffee, snacks, and thoroughly enjoyed the next few hours of warm breezes and daylight strong enough to read by. And no mosquitoes ... probably the breezes keeping them down. Perfect.

As daylight lessened, I finished the last few sips of coffee and got the pot ready for morning, using two coffee packets from the motel in New Orleans. Remaining charcoal and some dry twigs went under the tarp to insure some chance at building a morning fire, even if it rained. There would be time to shower in the morning since I did not want to get to St Louis until mid-morning at the earliest. As I was putting things into the tent or back into the scooter trunk, a Missouri State pickup truck pulled into the campground, parked, and two young guys got out. They were wearing uniforms and began going from site to site, with a receipt book in hand. A few minutes later, they were saying hello, informing me the fee for a tent site was 50 cents per night, and asking how many nights I intended to stay. Just one, so we talked briefly, I complimented Missouri and the two of them as to what a pleasant campsite this was, paid my fee, and got my receipt. The breezes had almost stopped, some mosquitoes were hunting me, and it was time for my retreat into my tent after one more restroom visit. This had been a day, both exciting and peaceful, active and restful. A splendid day and I would call it finished.

Night had been long and tranquil. Awake for a short time, I was inwardly laughing at the young waitress asking "Are you an artist?" I had skirted that question in answering her, but gave it some thought. The answer was something like "Well, maybe I am." During those months in Tucson, my older sister, Janice, had introduced me to Italian glass mosaic tiles and was doing some beautiful work with those marvelous pieces of glass. I had completed one mosaic and started another using this splendid material. As a kid I had always fooled around with the idea of 'mosaicking' using anything available ... seeds, pebbles, leaves, feathers, bits of this and that. Maybe the word 'collage' would be more accurate for what I had done through my school years. No, it was mosaic, for sure. As soon as the Italian glass was in my hands, I was truly smitten. What a beautiful, and durable material. A well-constructed mosaic could last centuries with almost no maintenance. A half-finished mosaic was waiting for me when I returned to my desert town. Then sleep took over again and I snoozed until bird calls pierced the tent ... a beautiful way to wake up to a dawn just started.

First, get semi-dressed, then get coffee, then get in the shower, then get dressed for the day. That was the plan and that's what happened, in that order. Decent daylight now and still far too early to start for St. Louis. Take a small brisk hike, I needed that from time to time anyway. Three or four trails available, one having the word 'petroglifs' on a piece of cardboard. So, I'd go see the 'petroglifs'. Almost feeling obligated to view these, my thoughts said "you're only a few minutes away... you must see the drawings on stone while you're here." Walking strongly and after a time, I did find them, and truthfully I say petroglyphs have never excited me. My preference is to think of them as modern art, the forerunners to Klee, Picasso, Miro, and others. As decoration, they're only so-so. As messages, I consider them a big bust. As something to get excited over, a decided dud. Oh well, nothing lost, a little hike was invigorating. Back to the tent, pack it up it, make sure the campsite is clean, get ready to launch this ship on this new day. This day would see us going north and east to cross the Mississippi again, at St. Louis, Missouri, hopefully on our way to Chicago. Kickstart, then inhale the fresh bluish-flavored exhaust. Ah, Nature at its best, courtesy of Lambretta. Was I getting addicted to two-stroke fumes? Would I become dependent on a daily two-stroke exhaust fume fix? Tricky stuff. Ease on out of the campground, take a left onto Route 21 toward a town called De Soto for the morning religious services at any non-Mormon café. Any other denomination can handle a café ritual.

The town was less than ten miles away. Stopped for coffee, two large cups, and a smoke. Didn't feel like eating anything, especially since I had brushed my teeth carefully just before leaving camp. The last two pieces of fruit were put into my jacket pockets this morning. But I did linger over coffee. The town of De Soto, was named after Spanish explorer Hernando De Soto, aka Fernando De Soto, who is famous for having 'discovered' the Mississippi River. I can imagine him telling people who were already there "Hey you guys, yeah you, you Indians, can you just get the hell out of the way for a week or so while I discover this place? And I don't give a damn what you call yourselves, you are Indians and that's that." Of course that would all be said in Spanish or maybe Latin.

On the road to St. Louis, about 60 miles to reach it. I'd gas up before trying to get through the big city. Worked my way northward through a mix of farmland and small wooded sections. Got into some hilly country which is always interesting and does require more vigilance. Saw several small groups of deer, gorgeous animals, but something to avoid running into. Then down from the hills a bit and into the town of Affton, really a suburb of St. Louis, and a restroom and fuel stop. Afterward, putt-putted over to a little parklike area for a piece of fruit, a smoke, and a good stretch.

Now, back on the highway, on Route 30, where did 21 go? This is where so many highways routes begin merging to get across the bridge spanning the Mississippi and this is where traffic gets thicker, and the closer to the river one gets, the more hectic traffic becomes. Since so many motorists don't seem to see scooters, they pull in and out of a lane I'm in, without hesitation and without signaling. Noise and fumes, spinning tires and guardrails, tail lights and dust. Maybe not so bad while sitting on your butt in a comfortable auto, but pretty scary stuff for a rider with a putt-putt. Road signs and arrows and lane changes. Wild. Forty-five tense minutes of white knuckle navigation. Then, soon after I crossed a bridge ... a miracle. Jesus might have changed water into wine, but that's small potatoes compared to the people in St Louis who changed route 30 into routes 40, 66, 70 and who knows what else, along which I was traveling after escaping from the thickness of the city and beginning to see little pieces of space, in time, it turns out, to get to my old friend Route 66 as it headed north toward Chicago, where it originally began. We would pass through a number of towns, including Springfield, before we traveled more than 300 miles to Chicago.

Hey 66, old buddy, where did I last see you? Was is in New Mexico? No, no, didn't I see you briefly in Amarillo, Texas. Yes, that was it. Amarillo. Good to see you again. Now you have to take me to Chicago, but first, let me stop for an ice cream. Get a chance to wind down. Damn, that St. Louis is a rough stretch ... tense. In the peaceful Ozarks a few hours ago and now, it was medicinal ice cream that seemed most necessary.

Route 66 was busy, but not frantic. A straight stretch, going northeast through farmland, occasionally crossing over small creeks or drainage ways. Some nice-looking corn growing here and there. Back to the relaxed scootering I preferred. Route 66 had businesses strung out along its length probably all the way from Chicago to America's west coast. Now with the interstate highway system replacing it, and bypassing whole sections of it, I wondered how many businesses would close. There are always benefits and losses, never equally shared by those involved. Started thinking about petroglyphs again. From what I had read a few years before, there seemed to be no system or structure to the drawings or groups of symbols or figures, at least no system that I had read about. The petroglypher (my word) had to commit a fair amount of time and effort to creating a symbol, for example, a simple spiral, which could mean something. Of course, if it was something complex, it might require another day's work. Don't want to get too wordy when you're hammering out petroglyphs. To my knowledge, nowhere had a petroglyph grouping been translated into any message ... "that way ... water ... half day" or something even simpler ... "alert ... stone on head." The sign at the State Park said the estimated time for those particular rock drawings was about 1000 AD, if I remembered correctly. But I couldn't help but think that another thousand years before these were pecked out on a stone surface, Julius Caesar was writing 'All of Gaul is divided into three parts'. Writing it on an animal skin or parchment or who knows. The comparison with Roman accomplishments comes to mind because I know a little bit about the rise and fall of that society. I really pissed off a tour guide in Arizona, by doing a similar comparison. She was just marveling about a row of rocks and some slight depression in the land where the Hohokam tribal efforts had created an irrigation system for crops. They had abandoned the area in 1200 or 1300 due to drought, it was supposed. As the guide swooned over this irrigation trench, Big Mouth Rosano said, "Not such a big deal if you consider that 1500 years before that, the Romans had an aqueduct bringing fresh water to the city." Apparently she became irritated with that observation and abbreviated our tour somewhat, and everyone was pissed at me ... crowd, guide, girl I was with, and maybe Hohokam spirits, too. What got me started on this? Yes, the petroglyphs and the pe-TROG-luh-fers. Just not very impressed. 'Show me, I'm from Missouri.' I wonder who knows about that saying. Should I explain?

Early afternoon, slightly overcast and pleasant, scooter behaving superbly over this level terrain. Break time near some trees involved the other piece of fruit from my jacket, a smoke, doing a few exercises to keep body parts functional, and taking a leak to keep body parts dry.

Within an hour, I would be on the outskirts of Springfield, the state capital of Illinois. I would move through the city slowly, but was not intent on stopping for anything in particular except for fuel for Lambretta and I would wait until I was on the far side of town. Springfield was a town of 80,000. Government jobs were probably the biggest employment. Traveled through the center of town. Not terribly congested. Nice enough place, but not remarkable that I could see ... except for its famous resident, Abraham Lincoln. In one way or another, everything in town was connected to Abe. From the south to the north edge of town was about ten miles. Reaching the north side, I looked for a gas station and a place to take a snack break. Did the fueling routine for a third time that day, pushed the scooter over to some trees at the edge of the property, and then walked around while eating a few morsels of fruit and nuts (not very hungry ... the ice cream, maybe.) Was most comfortable riding, and this day was perfect for it. Back on the road, the tank full, the scooter purring along, with me placidly happy. I had not yet considered how to 'do' Chicago ... there would be time and there would be no rush. One day, two days or three. Continued north on Route 66 through three or four more towns, through Lincoln, Normal, Lexington, and was finally feeling fatigued as we neared Pontiac. Time to quit for the day. Long hours, many miles (most ever in one day), but leisurely traveling with exception of the congested St.Louis leg. Stopped at a café for coffee and a smoke, decided to have a bowl of soup. Talked to the guy behind the counter about campgrounds or motels. He pointed behind me and said that directly across the street was an old place, but he knew the owner, and knew it would be a clean place because the owner was always cleaning something even if it didn't need it. Since I had gotten myself more tired than expected, the thought of not having to set up a campsite was appealing. Finishing my snack, I paid the bill, said my thanks. Across the street, a little cabin was available for $1.50 a night, no TV, no telephone, just a clean place with a shower. Again, no smoking inside. It's a deal. I'm out of steam.

Secured the scooter and helmet. Got some food for the night out of the trunk. Went inside, took a good shower and would take another in the morning. Started to read and never got there.

CHAPTER 45

ALMOST CHICAGO

Sometimes, morning arrives when you least expect it. Looking out the wallet-sized window of the small motel cabin, there was some light in the sky which meant I had slept eight or nine hours. Stomach was empty and complaining, bladder was full and complaining, and as I switched the light on my eyes were constricting and complaining. "Hey, body parts, quit your bitching, I'll take care of things one at a time. Why all these complaints? Yesterday was a great day and today will be another. OK, bladder first."

After reconstructing myself, I decided to walk across the highway for coffee and pancakes. Still not really daylight, but soon. The café was open and I sat down. Black coffee please and an order of dollar size. Older woman said they didn't do dollar sized, they did three dollar sized. Both of us smiling, and she said we'll make some small ones for you. I asked "pretty well cooked, please?" No problem. When she had a moment, I asked if she knew much about Chicago. She answered that she and her husband went to Springfield more often. Chicago was too hectic for them. Finished my little breakfast, worked on a second cup of coffee. Lit up a smoke. Chicago was about one hundred miles away (three hours max). Maybe the first thing I would do, when I neared the city, would be to stop in a public library or in a bookstore. Those people have so much information. Two or three library hours as a starter for my exploration might be a good move. Paid the bill, said thanks and goodbyes and walked back across Route 66.

Consulted the atlas for a fix on where I was aimed. Before Chicago was Joliet, a good-sized town of 65,000 and a familiar name. They would have a public library for sure. Time to get in the shower and get squeaky clean and wash my hair and beard with shampoo from my Princess. Since there was only me, holding onto the diagonal ends of the hand towel, I was able to wash my back. I missed having company in the shower. Everyone should have a friend in the shower. Drying myself, I noticed my hair and beard were somewhat exuberant (how's that for a euphemism). I wanted to present myself at least as a well-trimmed person to distance myself somewhat from the shaggier elements of society, too often terribly misjudged and mistreated by police and belligerent members of our society. There were many changes brewing in this nation of ours. Some had been violent and others, in the future, would also be violent. For the duration of this journey I wished to be an observer only. Having well-trimmed hair might just be the differentiating factor.

No big rush as I cleaned out and reloaded my jacket pockets, repacked the clothing bag, then went out to the scooter to reload the trunk and tie everything together. From the sun, I would guess it to be 8:00 or 8:30 AM, which would get me to Chicago's center before noon. Just a rough estimate. Not important. Might as well get going. The faithful scooter named Tony Lambretta gave me the blue smoke incense blessing and we eased back onto Route 66, heading northeast again. Ten miles of farmland later, we were passing through a town called Odell, elevation: 700 feet above sea level. An additional ten miles took us through Dwight, at 650 feet, at least that's what highway signs said. Why had I assumed we were a thousand feet higher? Assumptions being wrong much of the time, I missed another guess by assuming the land would be hilly, not be quite so level or flat. Some ten or fifteen miles north of Dwight, we passed through what looked like a coal mining area. Just north of that the Kankakee River was crossed by a bridge. At this point the river flowed north and west and emptied into the Illinois River somewhere west of here. So this landscape was getting more interesting just as we approached Joliet. Now getting into the urban scene, I needed a restroom break to empty my bladder and some coffee to refill it. Looking for a café, I found instead a barbershop, with a small sign saying 'open' in neon and additional lettering saying 'ladies' and 'gents'. Hell yes, let's do it. My hair had been washed just a few hours before, and I had not yet had a chance to perspire much, if at all.

Parking in front, I locked the scooter to a phone booth which had ventilation holes in its frame. Walking in, I called, "Good morning" to whomever was at the back of the shop. A "Good Morning" came back to me. A blonde woman, maybe mid-to late thirties appeared from behind a partition. "How can I help you?" "Oh, I need a hair trim, a beard trim, a nose trim and an ear trim and maybe an eyebrow trim." She laughed at that. Walking to the front window, she asked how I had gotten there? She hadn't heard me. Did someone drive me there? No, no, and then I pointed to the scooter, saying that was how I got there. "Ah, a motorcycle, no, that's a motor scooter. Is that American?" I said no it was Italian, made in Milan. "Oh," she said, "... in that movie Italian Holiday, like that?" Nodding yes, I said, "Yes, Roman Holiday, with Gregory Peck and Audrey Hepburn, yes, just like that" (and both the movie Princess and my Princess Stella flashed in my mind). She took a little folded apron, shook it out, gestured to the barber's chair, and said "Please sit down." I asked if I could use a restroom first since I'd been on the road for a few hours. Sure. After that, I sat in the chair as she tied the apron around my neck.

She started with "You're not uncomfortable with a woman barber, are you?" Me: "Listen, both my parents are beauticians, back in Connecticut, and a good part of their business is haircutting. So there's no problem at all." I stuck my right hand up in the air and told her my name and asked hers. Her name was Edith. And we shook hands. Without thinking, I mentioned the wonderful librarian in Memphis was named Edith. Memphis? You came all the way from Memphis on that scooter? I said no, it was crazier than that ... I had come all the way from Southern Arizona on that. Of course, saying that got us into a lively discussion of my trip. So she was snipping and combing as we talked. Mustache and ear fur was taken care of, and I asked her not to shave the back of my neck, which became uncomfortable with the helmet. I was facing an aquarium, maybe forty-gallons, which had black mollies and black angel fish. There was a white ceramic structure in the water, surrounded by medium blue stones ... very simple, eye pleasing. Asking if she had assembled that aquarium, I said it was elegant, and beautifully designed. She said thank you and not everybody around there appreciated its simplicity. People seemed to want to put more stuff in there. She asked if I had ever had an aquarium. No, not really, I had a big goldfish for a while, but I had to get rid of it because it ate too much. And, as that goldfish grew, I had to keep buying new and bigger bowls, and then I had to buy a bigger leash if I was going to take it out for its daily walk. Not only that, but the neighbors started complaining about the noise. She was trying to do my nose hairs and she had started laughing, really laughing at my stupid little routine. I put my hand a few inches in front of my face and said maybe we should wait for the nose hairs. That's when she really cracked up. I maintained a concerned look on my face. She excused herself. A minute later, I heard the toilet flush. She was still laughing as she returned and wiping her eyes. She asked me to please be quiet while she finished the last minute of my hairdo. And she finished off the nose hairs and we were done. She said my hair was in good shape, was clean, and smelled so good. I asked how much I owed her. She ignored me and asked if I wanted some coffee. That would be perfect ... just black, please.

We sat behind the partition and sipped our coffee. She asked where I was headed, I told her that I wanted to see Chicago and knew very little about it and if it required one day or three days it would be fine. She asked about my parents' beauty shop. I asked about her shop. I was curious.

This was a Saturday morning and there weren't many customers. She said since her husband had been killed last year, this shop would be closed soon, at the end of the summer. She had been discouraging customers for a year, but the lease that both she and her husband had signed required that it stay open for business. And they were making her stick to the terms of the lease. Every Saturday, around noontime, three old men, sometimes a fourth, came in together to get their haircuts and as soon as she finished with them, she closed the shop for the weekend until Tuesday noon. They used to have a booming business, five chairs busy all the time, but she really wasn't interested in it and was just 'serving out her time' until the end of August. She was trying to arrange for a hairstyling salon in a high dollar neighborhood. Abruptly, she asked what I was doing that evening. I told her I thought I'd go see something in Chicago … I didn't know what … and then look for a place to camp out and also find a coin operated laundry. I was out of clean clothing. Time to do maintenance.

"Will you be my date tonight?" The question surprised me. She said, "I want to go to a small party tonight and it would be so good to have an escort for a couple of reasons. Many of the people there would be involved in some manner with the beauty shop or barber shop business. There were two guys she wanted to talk with, maybe for just ten minutes, regarding the possible new salon. There were two other guys who just would not leave her alone at previous meetings. She needed someone to act as a bodyguard or as a diversion or as a dissuasion. I told her I'd be honored, but my clothing was really unsuitable for such a gathering and since this was all I had, it wouldn't reflect well on her. She smiled and said "but you have a great haircut. And I can fix you up with some good clothing. You're the same size as my brother, I bet. Will you do it? And don't worry about Chicago. We'll work that out. More coffee?" I pushed my cup toward her and said, "Please." It seemed that I would be partying tonight. We sipped our coffee a while longer. She said she still had to do the old guys' haircuts. They would be here soon. For them, this was an important social event each week. I could wait there or elsewhere. It would take about two hours. I asked if there was a public library or a bookstore nearby. She took my hand, led me to the front window, pointed north, and said go that way for just one block, take a left and go three or possibly four blocks and on my left, there would be a library branch.

Back to the coffee for a final sip. I gathered my helmet, said "Two hours. Ciao." As I was unlocking the scooter, the older guys pulled up in two cars.

In the library, there was an immediate problem. There were slightly more than one million things I wanted to read about. At best, I could only recall five, but more immediately, it would be best to learn more about

Chicago and then try to cover other topics. Instead of my usual trance-like stroll through the shelves and displays, I asked the librarian at the main desk where I could learn the most about Chicago in an hour and a half. Librarians are the greatest. She suggested I divide my time between the special display they had at the other side of the main room and the newspaper section for today's activities. That seemed a good approach. The newspaper thing first, the special display next, and then I formed a rough, tentative list of things to pursue in the big city. Time up. Back to the barbershop and the handsome blonde woman named Edith. Parked the scooter, but didn't lock it up. She was finishing the last of the three gents as I walked in. The three looked at me without saying anything, but with big question marks on their faces when Edith said, "This is Rosano, my cousin from Arizona." They all said hello, and I said, "Hello, gentlemen." And they started out the door. When the door closed, I asked what those guys are going to do when you close your doors. It seemed a little sad. Edith said, "I hope they find a good place." Shutting off the lights and the neon sign, she said "Ready?" I said I didn't know ... what are we doing?" She said "You're going to follow me to my house, about six miles from here." I responded, "That's OK with me, but I can't go over 40, so take it easy, OK?" She said "Is that all ... 40? ... OK, easy it is." And it was.

Putt-putting into the driveway of what I assumed to be her house, a double-wide garage door (one of two) opened slowly. This was an upper middle income area, very upper. I stayed out on the concrete apron, but when she got out of her car, she indicated I should pull into the garage, which to me looked about the size of an average football stadium. I shut the scooter down, put it on its kickstand, and was taking off my helmet when she came over to me, rubbed my hair where the helmet had rested on it and said, "You can camp here tonight if you'd like. And I do have a washer and dryer, except there are no coin slots. Is that OK?" And I said, "Shucks! And here am I, at the Taj Mahal with a pocketful of change." She laughed at me and said, "First, get all the clothing you need to wash and we'll get that started. Then we'll have some lunch. I've got too much food. You can stay in my brother's room, he's in Paraguay or Uruguay, I forget which, doing some work with the local people down there on the tundra." I said, "Pampa, the prairies down there are called the Pampas." Getting my clothing bag, I followed her into the house, she led me down the hall and indicated a room. She went into the closet, pulled out a pair of pants, a belt, and a shirt, saying try these on and get your laundry together, and would I like a beer with lunch. I said that sounded so good, but only if I didn't have to drive anywhere soon. And could I ask one favor? Sure. I know this makes me sound like some sort of ungrateful wimp, but can I not have any onions in the lunch. Sorry, but I just can't stand them. Anything else is OK. The man says no onions ... no problem.

So I changed into the clothes, which fit pretty well, and emptied the pockets of my jacket, my camping pants, my regular pants, my shirts, my tee shirts. Every piece of clothing I had went into the pile on top of my clothing bag. It wasn't a very big pile, but it was everything. Carried the whole business to the hallway and put it on the floor. Then I sought out the kitchen and found Edith putting lunch on a little table. She said we'd get the laundry going and then sit down and eat. And we did. She poured our beers into glasses and made a toast to a good party this evening. And I toasted a beautiful evening to a beautiful lady. As she smiled she did actually become beautiful.

As we began to eat, she said, "Rosano, that's what I should call you, right?" I nodded yes. "Rosano, you're really a nice guy and I know that already because of four different things. Want to hear why I know?" I said sure, I couldn't wait, and ... could I record this? She said, "One, you made me laugh harder than I have since before my husband died, almost fourteen months ago, and you did it while you were making fun of yourself. Two, when I asked if you would be my date tonight, you didn't think of your own plans, you were concerned with how it would look for me, with your camping clothes and that sort of thing. Three, you asked about the old men and what would happen to them. And four, when you were going to leave the shop for those two hours, you asked directions to where? To the library or to a bookstore. Not to a bar or pub, but to a library, of all places. That's a good guy there. I know. You're made of good stuff. How old are you, Rosano? I'm guessing 25 or 26 years." I laughed, "You're too high ... I'm almost twenty-one." Looking a little surprised, she asked "How almost?" "Tomorrow, and that's as almost as you can get, isn't it?"

We continued lunching and talking and finally I asked how her husband had been killed, but if she would rather not talk about it that was fine. No, she would tell me briefly. Her husband enjoyed drag races and stock car races. Down in Kentucky, at a stock car race, a small crash occurred. A wheel with some front end parts flew into the crowd and her husband was killed instantly and several other people were injured. That was it. Both she and her husband had gone through barber and beautician training and had been in business for about five years. They had planned to start having children, two or three they hoped. First thing they did to prepare was to get life insurance policies on both of them to protect the kids. His policy plus the race track insurance settlement had set her up very well financially. And there were no kids. So that was it simply. I offered her my condolences and said it had to be truly traumatic. Her response was "I was not as devastated as I thought I should be. It was just something that happened." She said my wash had finished and she would get everything into the dryer. I carried dishes over to the sink, had the table cleared and wiped off before she was done loading the dryer. I was putting our few dishes into the dish washer. She said while the dryer was working we could go out on the veranda to just sit around and talk. The day was beautiful and the veranda was screened in. Did I want another beer? No thanks, one beer is pretty much my limit. Maybe later.

We talked on various topics ... her possible new hair salon (this would not be a little shop), her big five bedroom house, my scooter trip, my library visit (she was curious about that), and what might I want to see of Chicago. The Museum of Science and Industry was at the top of the list. Next might be the Art Institute or at least see a modern art gallery or two. I heard Old Town, near St. Michael's church was a pretty good area to capture the 'feel' of Chicago. I'd like to visit Little Italy, wherever that was, just to buy some great cookies. Then, maybe just do some 'noodling'. Edith said, "Describe 'noodling' for me. And I did. I asked if there was anything really special about Lake Shore Drive because several people, in different conversations with me, had referred to it.

"You gave up most of your day for me and the party tonight. So tomorrow, if you're willing, we'll do some of your Chicago things, but not on the scooter, in the Buick. Is that OK with you?" I said, "Sounds absolutely great! I could use a little vacation from being so absolutely self-reliant. Edith, you know you don't have to do that. Just having a nice place to sleep for a night, oh, and laundry, too, is reward enough for me. You have the mind of a businessperson and that's excellent. I enjoy smart people and hope the party tonight works out well for you. And don't worry about your two annoyers. They won't trouble you. But of course, you have to somehow point them out to me." She laughed gently and said, "We'll work that out." She said, "We still have a couple of hours before we have to get dressed for the party. Is there anything you'd like to do?" I said that just talking with her was nice because I certainly talked to myself enough as I was driving. It would always be good to get a different view of things. If there was something she needed to do, I'd just sit quietly and read one of my books and behave myself. Laughing, she said, "You're really funny sometimes, Rosano." I said, "And that brings up the old question ... funny ha-ha or funny peculiar?" Big grin on her face, "I don't know you well enough, but I suspect you could qualify on both counts. I've got a couple of little chores to do and I'll be back in ten minutes or so."

When she returned, she started with "Rosano, I'm sure we can't do everything on your list tomorrow and ..." I started to interrupt her, but she put her index finger across her lips and continued … "and I'd like to do that whole list with you if you think you can put up with me. It'll take two days and either way, I'm not sure if there really is a Little Italy anymore in Chicago. Taylor Street is as close as we get, I think. We'll check it out. Not like New York or San Francisco, though." I said I'd be delighted to have two days with her as tour guide, it would be a genuine honor and that I enjoyed her company. And if there was no longer a Little Italy, I'll bet we could find a good Italian bakery. To find one of those is a worthy pursuit.

She said, "Let's go get your outfit for tonight lined up." In her brother's room, she went into his closet , pulled out one item after another, including shoes and socks. Then she said "You're naked under there, right?" I said yes. Back into the closet, she came out with some jockey shorts and a tee shirt. "Here, put these on and then we'll try everything else." In just a few minutes, my outfit was complete. Shoes were a little big, but not too bad. She said "Just wear two pairs of socks. Now Rosano, I have a question for you and don't be insulted … do you mind if I wear high heels? I'm already a bit taller than you, and if you would feel uncomfortable being with a taller woman, I don't have to wear them." I said, "Taller is better for you, especially if you want to talk some business. I don't have a problem being a shrimp. Not only that, but your hair is beautiful, can you pile it on top of your head somehow? That would be better yet, a regal look, and sure to get some strong admiration from the crowd." She looked at me, gave me a quick, strong hug and said, "You're unbelievable! OK, if you want to shower, go ahead while I fix a small supper for us. After that, we'll get ready and then we'll go. What would you like to drink with supper?" Coffee, if possible. Black, please.

Showered, got partially dressed, then sat with Edith for a finger food supper. Supper done, I again cleaned up table and dishes while she went off and composed herself for the evening's appearance. I finished dressing in her brother's clothes. Everything fit well, except for around my neck, mine being considerably larger than her brother's, but I was OK, and slipping on a light jacket, was surprised at my appearance in the mirror. With the neatly trimmed beard, there was a touch of controlled menace to my look, and that would serve me well for the evening's task. Returned to the kitchen to finish my coffee, now gone cold, but no problem. Not very long after, Edith presented herself to me. She did look tall. "Wow!" I said, as I got up from the table, "You look stunning. Do a little pirouette if you would, please." And she did. "Very, very, nice," I said. "I will be proud to be your gentleman for the evening. You look radiant … splendid." And she did. "Would you like me to carry anything for you in my jacket?" Just the car keys. I suggested we sit in the living room for a minute or two, get our signals arranged, and discuss her plan of action for the evening. She asked if I would be drinking. I said I would have one wimpy bourbon and ginger, then keep refilling with ginger ale. I just wasn't into drinking, especially if driving was involved. She said she didn't want to stay there too long. That was great. We can go anytime. Out to the car. Would she like me to drive? No, she was OK driving.

The party was a happy gathering of people at a hotel. Edith and I were together for starters. After she pointed out the two culprits, we split up for a time. After an hour or so, we moved together again, with me following her lead, circulated a bit and finally said a few Goodbyes. I shook a few hands, and we were on our way back to her house. We had been at the party less than two hours. In the car, with no one listening, she said, "Rosano, you were quietly magnificent tonight. It was so good having you there with me, and being able to talk to my two good guys undisturbed, which worked out considerably better than expected, and the two nitwits didn't even come close to me the entire evening after introductions. How the hell did you arrange that?" I just laughed, and said, "I just did my job. Don't worry about it. They won't bother you anymore."

Arriving at the house, and into the garage, she was almost giddy, and making us walk arm in arm for those few steps from the car to the house, she kept saying, "C'mon, Rosano, tell me, tell me what happened, what did you do?" I just avoided her questions and thought it funny that she was so persistent. Finally she said. "Rosano, it's almost your birthday, your twenty-first birthday. What do you want to do next?"

"My twenty-first birthday. Hmmmm. Please don't be offended. Here's what I would like to do. I would like to get in the shower and wash your back. Then, if you're willing, I would like you to wash mine."

Unsmiling, she looked at me, then she said, "If you think I would fall for a trick like that, just forget it ... how about a nice bathtub instead?"

CHAPTER 46

CHICAGO, AT LAST

It was a luxurious master bathroom with a large tub. After washing and gentle playing for an hour, she said, "we're getting wrinkled, let's dry off." We left the cozy waters and she held up a towel for me and patted me dry and of course, the favor needed returning. Taking my hand, she led me to one of the other bedrooms, threw back the covers, saying "Let's go slowly, I'm not used to this." I said, "You be the leader this time … take us by the path most comfortable for you." Not an emotionally charged time, it was instead, a quietly playful, exploratory time of enjoyment. Later we slept peacefully.

Brightness of morning was pushing its way through the window curtains. She placed her hand on my cheek and in a low voice asked, "Are you having a good birthday so far?" I answered almost in a whisper, "best ever, ever. Are you OK with last night?" She said, "Perfect, you were perfect for me last night. Would you like me to fix some coffee?" I nodded yes. "Is last night's coffee OK or do you want fresh?" Last night's would be fine. She said "Then, see you in the kitchen in five minutes."

Five minutes passed while I peed, found my pants in the other bedroom, and made my way into the kitchen where I got a major hug, a minor grope, and a cup of black coffee, three primary ingredients of that thing called a perfect breakfast. She was having tea, I was sipping coffee, and she asked if I was hungry since neither of us had eaten much yesterday or last night. Yes, I could stand to eat something. Then she suggested we hold off eating, get dressed, and drive to Old Town for breakfast. That would allow us to hear the bells of Saint Michael's while we ate. Sounds great.

With me dressed in her brother's clothes, and Edith in casual dress, no high heels, we are just ready to go into the garage, when the phone rings. She pauses, backs up three or four steps, and picks up and says hello. After a minute or two of silence, she says "OK, calm down" … long pause … "very well, I accept." And then, "Goodbye."

In the car, heading into Chicago, she explains that everything I want to see is along or near Lake Shore Drive and that 'Old Town' isn't really marked off. Its boundary is the sound of the bells of St Michael's church ... if you can hear them, you're in Old Town. My thought was that could vary considerably from person to person. Seemed to work OK, though. It's an historic area, started in the late 1800s and that's where we'd have some breakfast. We drove toward St. Michael's, moved slowly through some traffic congestion near the church (this being a Sunday). Soon however, Edith found a place to park the Buick, and parked it efficiently despite its being as long as a bowling alley. Out of the car quickly and walked around to open her door, offered my arm for her taking and we did a leisurely stroll for three blocks through a 'very charming' neighborhood. Normally, I'm not captivated by 'charming' and 'quaint' is usually something I avoid, but this was a beautiful Sunday Morning, this was Chicago, this was a handsome woman on my arm, and this was close to a source of breakfast, and I was more hungry than a hyena.

She nudged me gently into a small restaurant and we were seated at a small table for two. The place was fairly busy. Coffee first, then order. Edith was having a typical American breakfast, I would have a standard order of pancakes with raspberries on the side. We sipped coffee (she preferred tea first thing in the morning, but coffee through the day). Breakfast was served, the coffee refilled, and we began to eat, Edith said that an interesting thing had occurred that morning. Of course, that was my cue to say "Oh?" And I did. She said that one of the men who had been at last night's get-together had telephoned her. Again, a cue, and again, "Oh?" Edith said "You know those two guys who had been pestering me ... well, the worst of the two, the real pain in the neck, called me to apologize for his behavior at all the previous meetings and further, assured me it would never happen again, that he realized he had been 'obnoxious' and then asked if I would please accept his apology ... and you heard me accept." There was an empty place in our conversation which was supposed to be filled with my response. I was a bit slow in my timing, but managed "Well, the man feels sorry for being a jerk. So that's good." Edith had a small, smirky smile going as she said, "At the party last night, I saw you talking to those two for a few minutes, and that was all. So what did you guys talk about?" I said, "Well, we talked about you. How really pretty you were and so forth." Edith said "Give me the details of 'and so forth', please. C'mon Rosano, I have to know what I'm dealing with here." Nothing was said for a minute or two and then I said, "You're right. I'll be leaving and you'll be here. One thing, though ... they never need to know that I'm not around. OK?" She said "OK, I understand." And I said that it was all very short and sweet, and we really did mention how nice you looked. I impressed upon them that this pretty woman should be respected and that I had seriously bad reports on the two of them. The nastier asspain interrupted me and asked if I was in the beauty shop business. I said no, I was in the health care business. He was acting a little snotty and said you mean you sell health insurance to beauty shops. I said no, I helped people maintain their personal health, that is, if they 'cared' enough to maintain their personal health, they would take my advice. Anyway, the less nasty asspain put two and two together and arrived at five, caught on quickly he did, grabbed more nasty one's arm and pulled him aside while I continued with my bourbon and ginger. You saw it from across the room, two minutes later, the lesser jerk dragged his buddy over to me and asked how they could make it right with you. I explained it was a very encouraging sign that he asked and was, in fact, rather simple to accomplish ... a sincere apology was needed for all past sins and there should be a firm promise to sin no more. That would be sufficient if it was done before I left town for a few days to handle a little problem elsewhere. Sometime Sunday would be a good time. "And that, dear Edith, is the whole story. You can see, never was anything said or done that was out of line. How's breakfast?"

She put her fork down and gave me a stare, but I could see her trying to suppress a tiny smile. Finally she said, "I thought he would have a heart attack on the phone this morning." She smiled a little more, sat back in her chair, and said "Just look at you, at yourself right now, darkened skin from your riding (don't forget I've seen the rest of you), pitch black beard, meticulously groomed, very well dressed in my brother's clothes. Rosano, you look dangerous, you really do." When I said, "That's true, I know I look that way, so don't blow my cover and let everyone know what a sweetheart I really am." She laughed pretty good at that one, choked a little bit, shook her head, and said "Oh, Brother" and continued laughing.

When we decided we were done with breakfast, I asked for the bill. When it came, she grabbed it immediately and said this entire day was part of my Birthday present. As we walked back to the car, the bells of St Michael's began their call. Something special about that. Back in the Buick, she asks, "What's Next?" I said if she was up for it, we could catch the Museum of Science and Industry. I didn't want to spend an entire afternoon there, but I was very interested in a captured German U-Boat that we could tour, since I was often reading material on World War II. If we could use perhaps two hours, that would be it for the day. She leaned over, gave me a kiss on the ear and said "Whatever you want, Killer!" Then she explained the Museum was south of us, but she would drive to the north end of Lake Shore Drive first, turn around, and head south so that I could see the whole Drive. That sounded excellent. Beautiful stretch of road, with parks, museums, bike paths, running paths, walking paths, whatever they were.

On the side farthest from the lake were apartment and commercial buildings. Ended up at the Museum, which was pretty active with people. We had to wait in line for our turn through the submarine. Well worth the short wait. So happy she didn't wear high heels. Many fine displays, so well designed, an astounding place. To do it justice would require a week. Two hours was just an introduction, but a fine experience. As we left, she said she had known of this Museum and heard some glowing reports, but it had far exceeded her imagination and she would certainly return. The building was a science education all by itself. Thanks for dragging her there. In the car again, she asked what next. I said let's go to the house. That was enough for today. We had seen Old Town, heard St. Michael's bells, visited the Museum, and seen Lake Shore Drive. An excellent day. She said she would drive the remainder of Lake Shore Drive on the way home.

The remote control signaled the garage door, commanding it to open wide. We rolled in. Out of my door and around the car to open hers. As she rose from her seat, I gave her a big hug and a few kisses and thanked her for an absolutely splendid Birthday excursion. We made our way into the house where she said "That was great fun. I had a ball. That Museum is mind-boggling and I'm glad you took me there. OK, Rosano, it's your Birthday, what's next?" Another hug. "My Birthday, my choice? Is that it?" She said "You got it, buddy." "Hmmm. First we should have a cup of coffee. Then we should have a bath." She said "Coffee, then how about a shower this afternoon and a bath later tonight?" Saying she was driving a hard bargain, I accepted. She put on a small pot of coffee. I asked if she could open the garage and let me start the scooter for a minute or two outside the garage. By then the coffee would be done. Said hello to the Lambretta, rolled it outside the garage a few feet and started it up. Ran it for a minute or two, then shut it down and rolled it back into the garage. Replaced the water in the water bag. Soon enough we were sipping and talking when she laughed suddenly. She mentioned that at the party last night, I had the look of a South American 'enforcer' of some sort, and she had not really noticed that until we were at a distance from each other. She guessed the pesty guy probably had not slept that night. He sounded pretty shaken on the phone. Edith also wondered what others at the party thought of her 'date'. My comment was, no matter what they thought, it couldn't hurt.

Into the shower and we washed one another. Just two people enjoying the luxury of tending to the other and being tended to. We were emotionally unattached, but enjoyed each other's company, had OK conversations and a fun time in bed. My need was to have a break from the driven intensity of the last week. Her need was a break in the relative boredom of her past year. And in that circumstance we were good medicine for each other. In that spirit, then, immediately after washing and drying, we got onto the bed in her brother's room and applied as much medicinal love making to each other as energies allowed, followed by a good snooze for an hour or so.

Strange noises were sounding loudly in my left ear, the good ear, difficult to identify until I could become more fully awake and concentrate. Noises that sounded like "Rosano, Hey Rosano, you hungry? I'm starving. Want some supper. I've got too much food in the house. Let's eat soon ..." and so forth. I pulled her over to me, managed a few hugs despite not being quite awake, and eventually was able to say, "You sure do take good care of wandering strangers." She laughed quietly and said, "Only if they're men ... and with big ... hearts. I'll get some food ready for us. Do you want coffee or beer or what?" Coffee sounded good. It almost always does.

Seated at the table, with food before us and coffee to drink, Edith asked, "How long do you want to stay here, Rosano?" Before I could respond, she said, "You're welcome to stay until the end of the summer as far as I'm concerned. Or beyond that, if you like." These last two days have been a bunch of fun for me." I said, "For me, too. How about we spend tomorrow together and I'll leave Tuesday morning and be on my way to Florida." She was saying "Are you sure? We could have a great time, and ..." And I was responding with "I know we could, I really enjoy being with you, but I have to do this thing called 'Seeing America'." Even though I still had many miles to travel in the South, I had to do it. She could understand that, right? Yes, she said she could. We ate a supper of finger foods slowly and talked. Edith said, "What a beautiful Sunday we had today. Only one thing, though ... we didn't go to church." I said, we heard the bells, that's close enough, and not only that, but the bells are the best part of church. Their message usually is some hocus pocus dreamed up by one of God's hired hands. And more often than not, it's about 90 percent bullshit." Edith cracked up when she heard me say that. She asked my feeling on a few religious-related topics, finally asking what I "believed in." Answering, I said as far as organized religion, none of it. It was all a scam. But in terms of religious morality, if you want to call it that, philosophers and great thinkers have worked over that one for so many centuries it would be impossible to have an original thought, but ... I embraced one quote, or maybe it's a misquote, from Marcus Aurelius, the Roman emperor and stoic philosopher, summed up everything rather neatly. It goes like this:

"Live a good life. If there are Gods and they are just, then they will not care how devout you have been, but will welcome you based on the virtues you have lived by. If there are Gods, and they are unjust, then you should not want to worship them. If there are no Gods, then you will be gone, but will have lived a noble life that will live on in the memories of your loved ones."

"So, that's the code I live by. In other words, 'Be square with everybody'. And even that simple idea might have to be modified to 'Try to be square with everybody'." She nodded in acknowledgement, but neither accepted nor challenged anything I had said. When I asked if she went to church, she merely answered, "Sometimes." No explanation, no details. That was a thing in our conversations that I found peculiar. If I tried to pursue any subject, no matter how gently, the feeling came upon me that I might be prying or intruding. For example, I might have asked which church she went to 'sometimes.' I didn't ask and she didn't offer.

And so we had some discussion on a half dozen topics, but it was noticeable to me that she was not enthusiastically investigating or strongly curious about any of the things which she, herself had asked about. One notable empty spot in this large, well-furnished house, was the lack of books … there were no books in this house that I could see. There were a few magazines, popular stuff, magazines for a doctor's waiting room, but nothing of any substance, in my judgement. I had noticed, however, that extra light and life came into her eyes when she would mention the new beauty salon. So that seemed to be her focus. And that was OK. I could get her to smile or laugh sometimes … that's when she looked her best. The two of us were entertaining each other, and that, too, was OK. Ahead of us was one more day of fun and new experiences in Chicago, and two or three more mattress encounters. She was a good-natured, generous, and pleasant person. I considered myself most fortunate to having been chauffeured around Chicago with one day yet to go. It seemed that I was suggesting this whole show, but she was directing it and buying the tickets. More than that, I was grateful for a vacation from my vacation … not having to drive, find street directions, or be alert to traffic second by second. Strange arrangement, but working rather well, for both of us I hoped.

Had there been enough supper for me? Oh, plenty. She said it was different being single. There always seemed to be too much food. You might have the best intention of eating the leftovers the following day, but there always seemed to be too many leftovers. Did I want dessert? No thanks, maybe later. I started clearing the table and putting the few dishes into the dishwasher. She laughed lightly and said she wasn't used to anyone clearing dishes or cleaning the table. A little more coffee, Rosano? Sure, half a cup more sounds great.

As we sat down once again, Edith asked, "Are you ready for the second half of your Birthday?" "Second half?" She clarified, "Yes, tomorrow," which wasn't exactly clear to me. She continued "Today was the first half, tomorrow will be the second." I said I thought today was both halves of a terrific birthday. She said, "Let's talk about it. Tomorrow it's the Art Institute and Little Italy. Is that all?" I nodded yes. She said she knew almost nothing about both. Is the Art Institute a museum? I said it's really an art college with museums as one part. I think it opens daily at 10 or 11:00AM for visiting. She said, "OK, that could be pretty good. But Little Italy, I hear, just isn't what it used to be, although there still is an old style bakery on Taylor Street. Want to try that?" My answer was, "Sure I do. Italian bakeries are the closest thing to heaven on this place we call earth and don't let any of those false religious prophets or preachers convince you otherwise."

She looked at the clock and said "Do you know what time it is?" I must have looked puzzled or surprised or both. She said "Bath time."

Walking into her brother's room I found all of my laundry neatly folded at the foot of the bed. I was still wearing his clothes. She followed me into the room and I thanked her for the great laundry service. She said to continue wearing her brother's stuff, that when I left, I should have a clean fresh start on my journey to Florida and that meant all of my clothing should freshly laundered. From her brother's closet, she then laid out clothing, underwear and socks included, for the following day. She said the bathtub was filling up. As soon as I brushed my teeth, I'd jump in with her. She said, "Get naked before you do."

CHAPTER 45

CHICAGO IS FINE

That's what I did ... get naked that is, and climbed into the tub where she was already soaking. And so we did some pinching and poking and prodding and petting and eventually washed each other and got squeaky clean. Got wrinkly and got out of the tub. Exchanging gentle towel rubs was exciting. She grabbed me by whatever was handy and led us into the 'other' room, where action-packed adventure unfolded and was met with some acclamation and light applause by all parties concerned.

"Would you like something to drink? I'm thirsty." That sounded just fine to me. Edith asked if I'd like a beer. How about if we split one. That sounded perfect to her. She'd be right back. As we sat and sipped the coldness, she asked "Well, what do you think of Chicago so far?" Answering, I thought it had a gutsy atmosphere, a great feel to the place, it was active, alive. I knew there was some pretty rough edges, but Chicago was a vibrant place, lots of good thinking happening here. Chicago had so many trains going through, airplanes overhead, and road traffic, and boats on the Lake, everything. And it had the nicest hair cutters right next door in Joliet. Strongly impressed with this city, I felt comfortable here, comfortable and 'at home.' I would enjoy returning, but only in the summer. For me the winter would be fatal. She laughed and said, "Don't be such a sissy!"

What were her thoughts for the new beauty salon? She talked enthusiastically for five or ten minutes, then asked what I thought of her ideas. My opinion was that her outlook was modern, far more modern than that of my parents. They had stayed with the tried and true rather than risk new techniques or newer styles. Of course, most of their business was for older ladies, who most likely wouldn't be interested in updating their hair-do look anyway. Edith's outlook was more glamorous, but also more viable, I thought. The business that my father built up, would, in time, become so outdated it could not continue unless newer more modern attitudes prevailed. On the other hand, my parents had done very well for themselves and their extended family.

We sipped our half-beers slowly. I thanked her again for a splendid day and we talked of various other things, played a bit more, had a few laughs, and eventually settled into sleep mode ... the end of a day which had been strongly on the plus side, if anybody asks.

Dawn had already begun its process when I got up, used the bathroom, and returned to the bed. She had done the same minutes earlier. After a decent interval, I used my knee to bump her bottom a little more firmly than gently. Another interval, another bump. Yet another interval, the third bump and she was laughing. "Rosano, what do you think you're doing?" In a complaining voice, I said, "How many times do I have to kick your butt for you to offer to make coffee for us?" Edith, still laughing, said, "Oh, so you are not Mr. Nice Guy. All of that was phony. Is that right?" I said, "Correct. Now you know. It was all a façade. Grumble, grumble, grumble." She said, "No! Rosano, you're supposed to really grumble, but not actually say the word 'grumble'. I get your message anyway. I'll go make some coffee."

Ten minutes later, as I walked into the kitchen, she asked "Would you rather have a good morning kiss or a cup of coffee?" I froze in my tracks and didn't move a muscle, not even an eyelash. I held that pose for a long enough time for her to finally say, "I think I would lose that one." Laughing and giving me a big kiss, she said, "OK, you can have both." I wiped my brow in relief, then sat at the table. She poured that first cup of coffee and I said "Thank you" very softly. After a decent time, she mentioned that no one seemed to enjoy that first cup more than I did. Nodding yes, I quietly explained the first cup of coffee in the morning is a holy sacrament, and I thought there should be candles burning and a Hallelujah chorus, but perhaps folks might think that a little excessive. Just some monks murmuring chants in the background would be enough. Along with candles, that is.

She said she had thought about the day in front of us. We should drive to Taylor Street, where there was an Italian bakery, Ferrara's, which had been there for half a century. Maybe have breakfast there, if they have coffee. The area used to be considered a Little Italy, but we'll see. We'll see if there's a good spot to have lunch there, too. So here's a possible plan. Little Italy for a small breakfast, scout out the bakery and maybe a place for lunch. Then, after breakfast (either there or somewhere else) we'll drive to the Art Institute (eight or ten blocks away). Spend some time there and then drive back to Little Italy for an afternoon lunch and if they have some good cookies, we'll get some to take home with us. How does that sound for a loose plan? I told her it sounded like heaven. She then said it would be the second half of my birthday present and there would be no arguing or there would be no going. Damn, this was the second woman on this trip wanting to boss me around. There would have to be something done about that ... one of these days, but until then ...

After a second cup of coffee, we got ourselves ready to go into town. There was no rush and this would be a leisurely day. And so it was as she drove toward Taylor Street. Edith found a parking spot just a few steps from Ferrara's and expertly drove the Buick battleship into a slot. A very competent driver for sure. I asked her if she had ever been in a genuine Italian Bakery/Pastry shop before. She shook her head 'No.' Well then, this will be a new experience.

Bakery airs were greeting us even before we opened the entry door. Just simply magnificent. An exquisite combination of freshly baked bread as a base, topped with a startling variety of pastry flavors and smells. It was an aroma celebration. Not only that, but the place had tables and coffee and could provide breakfast or lunch. This was a bonanza. How about some coffee and breakfast? Edith asked what Italians usually eat for breakfast. I explained that breakfast was not the big deal that Americans made of it. Normally, it was a very small affair, maybe with just coffee and some Italian or French bread roll, usually toasted. Something a little heavier would be a brioche or croissant, both of which were more buttery and I thought it was the brioche that used egg in its mixture before baking. I wasn't sure of that. I said I'd tell her a little story about breakfast later. But did she want to try some breakfast. Sure, she was hungry. I suggested we order both a croissant, a brioche, and a roll with some coffee and we'll sit down. They would bring the coffee to us. I said after our little breakfast we'd take a closer look at the cookies. She said the smell of this place was unbelievable ... she could smell yeast, citrus, coconut, almonds, pistachios, and it went on and on. I said that's what it's all about ... that 'on and on', that enormous variety, but each flavor- cherry, fig, apricot, pomegranate, etc., was treated with respect. Of course, I was trying to absorb as many pastry aromas as my skin and schnozz would allow. Then I asked her why she had never been in such a place before. The short answer was that she and her husband had grown up and spent most of their lives in Montana and Wyoming. I said that would explain it, and I didn't think there really was a place called Wyoming, that it was just a myth, something they used to fill a hole in the map. I knew people talked about it occasionally, but I thought the idea of Wyoming was just an imaginary place or maybe a ruse of some sort. She laughed at that and cautioned I ought not say that when Wyomingers are near. Let's go look at the cookie display. And we did. And it was pretty good. And she said then let's go to the Art Institute and we'll come back later.

A warm and beautiful day greeted us again. Back into the Buick. In less than ten minutes we were parked near the Art Institute. This was something special. Gallery areas were open. Where to start? I asked Edith where she wanted to start. She chose an exhibit of European and American Glass. Good let's start there. We walked into an area with an enormous display of glass paperweights, beakers, vases, all beautifully displayed. So many different styles of decoration, glass flowers of every description, swirls and curlicues, etc. The craftsmanship of each piece was impeccable. Glassworkers of enormous skill had crafted these pieces. While I greatly admired the workmanship, after the first twenty minutes, the years passed slowly. My personal taste could tolerate intricacy and foofiness for a limited time. Glass mugs and goblets were not my cup of tea (wordplay intentional). Of course, I would never say that to Edith (there would be no point to it), so I continued to scrutinize glass pieces for another twenty minutes until she approached and said "Your choice next." Ah, I actually have two areas I want to see … I'd like to visit their Typographic Arts Exhibition since I had done a fair amount of typesetting in Junior High School and understood some typesetting and blocking techniques. Just a brief look. After that, a more leisurely viewing of modern painting and sculpture. And that's what we did. The typographic show was extensive and varied. Excellent, but we almost skated through. The Painting and Sculpture show of modern art contained many pieces by well-known artists. How I wanted to absorb their spirit. This is where I levitated. Wonderful abstract pieces. There was never enough time. After a little more than an hour, I said it was enough for today. She said let's get some lunch back in Little Italy. On the way, she asked what kind of lunch we should have. I asked how hungry she was. Not starving. Howzabout we just get a pizza or Italian sandwich or both? That sounded good. She parked that big car into a place I thought too small. No problem at all. A very good driver for sure.

Into a pizza place not far from Ferrara's bakery. She suggested that I order. Would she like some wine or would she want to split a beer? Splitting a beer seemed just right. OK, so I ordered a Sicilian style pizza with light cheese and a couple of veggie toppings (no onions), and a hot sausage and roasted red pepper grinder roll. And a Moretti with two glasses and I remembered my friend Moretti in Memphis, only a few days ago, and I will always remember my friend Moretti in Memphis when I order an Italian beer. Edith noted that I didn't order the famous Chicago-style deep dish pizza. I said I've never had one, but it sounded like a portable pot of soup to me and very un-Italian. When the food arrived, I said this was roll-up-your-sleeves meal. We clinked glasses and I toasted her once more for being such a great guide. Edith took a small piece of pizza and a fourth of the enormous sandwich, which I had sliced into four pieces. She thought the pizza was nice-tasting, friendly, easy going down. Then, on taking a bit of the hot sausage and pepper, she almost swooned. What a great taste combination! Wowie! I said "Amazing, isn't it? I think it's a New York/New Jersey thing ... I'm not sure, but so tasty, whatever its origin." She said, "An eye opener, for sure. Wonderful." Finishing lunch, we had eaten only half the food. The waitress wrapped it up for taking home. Edith asked for the bill, pointing at me and telling the waitress it was my birthday, but I quickly cautioned both that there would be no singing that dreadful song, don't even think about it. The waitress laughed, said, "You got it, Hon." As I'm thanking Edith, she says "Not yet, we still have to buy you some cookies for your birthday." How could I forget? She said, "You didn't forget ... not for a second." I had to admit she was right.

We walked to Ferrara's and she asked how many cookies did I want to pack in the morning? No more than eighteen, a dozen and a half, any more than that would start going bad without refrigeration. What flavors? Surprise me. We'll try a few this evening, when we're not so full. There were too many desserts to try, but at least Edith had now been exposed to heaven. Whatever she did with this new knowledge was her business.

Back in the Buick, she asked "Anywhere else?" Shook my head no. We headed back to her house. This had been an excellent day. How did she feel about it? She said it was amazing that a stranger could open her eyes so much to her own city and she had really enjoyed these past three days immensely, starting with the haircut and the party on Saturday and she laughed again and shook her head. On entering the garage, I started the scooter for another minute or two. And refreshed the water bag, too. And finally settled into the house.

Again, I started to say thanks when she shushed me, just gave me a hug and said it was time for a snooze. Naptime. Within ten minutes we were asleep in her brother's room.

From a far distant shore, I recognized that smell. That smell of coffee would lead me to a friendly place. I tried moving in that direction and woke up. How long had we slept? She said, "I slept for an hour, you ... an hour-and-a-half. Want some coffee?" We sat at the little kitchen table with coffee cups. After a few sips, I asked "Well, how do you like Chicago?" She said she would see it through a new set of eyes. I said, "It really is a remarkable city. It has something of everything and we just touched the surface. I'd like to return some day." She asked what time I planned to leave in the morning. I explained that since I would be heading almost directly East, I would wait until about 8:30 or 9:00 AM to avoid the sun's glare. Then I'd head to Indiana. "Hey, let's try a few cookies." She went to the counter, opened a large bag, withdrew four smaller bags, brought one to the table with a dish and arranged the dozen cookies on the plate. "Oh my goodness, they smell so good," she said and took one from the plate. I did the same. I watched her eyebrows go up and her eyes open wide as she tasted. So enjoyable to watch other people 'discover' this 'new' phenomenon ... something I had enjoyed since childhood. Edith did not show emotions easily, but she couldn't help herself in this situation. Finishing her third, she merely said, "Unbelievable." I said it was worth driving to Chicago for, no? She nodded yes. Three cookies seems to be the perfect amount. We should wrap them in saran, three at a time, and then refrigerate them. If they were refrigerated they would be good for a week or ten days or maybe two weeks. If frozen, a month was probably the limit and only if wrapped tightly. The quality diminishes fairly rapidly. Let's do that right now. And we did.

    We sat with another round of coffee and talked of the cookies, the great sausage and roasted pepper sandwich, the simple, tasty pizza and then we talked of the modern art. She was somewhat baffled by it all. I said that was OK, a good deal of it was a mystery to me as well. Did she remember the Owl by Leonard Baskin which I had pointed out? Yes, she remembered that sculpture well. I said Baskin wasn't trying to give you every detail of an owl. Rather, he wanted to capture the spirit of that bird. Did she remember the Leroy Neiman painting, with all the blobs and spatters of paint. Yes, that too she remembered. When we stepped back a bit, then the motion of the man and his sport becomes apparent. Not only that, but if you, as the viewer, allow your imagination to go free, you'll start seeing other aspects of the scene ... the flags, the crowd, etc., and maybe catch the whole sweep of things. So, in the future, don't be baffled, enjoy the line and color of the art and try to grasp what the artist is feeling, and if you can't come up with it, don't worry. Just enjoy. Oh, and one other thing ... don't let the art critics 'get' to you. Most of them are simply bubbling over with verbal bullshit.

    She said she ought to wash my mouth out with soap, but to do that we'd have to get closer to the bathtub, wouldn't we. I agreed it was a problem which could be solved if we cooperated. So we cooperated and had a good time of it. Just two people getting along as best they can. After a most enjoyable romp we lay quietly, without talking, for quite a long time.

    She said, "Tomorrow morning, when you leave, I'll have your eighteen cookies, six little packages of three, and some pizza and some of that sandwich all ready for your scooter trunk. Think of me when you're finishing that food. You have made these three days a truly good, fun time for me. Every time I look at that aquarium I'll have to think of you. And I'll never see the two asspains without having to laugh." I interrupted her and said,

"Hey, listen. This has been so enjoyable and so fine and good a time for me as well. And you made my twenty-first birthday memorable. You fed me and sheltered me and chauffeured me. Who could ask for better than that. You know, every time I hear 'Chicago' or even think the name 'Chicago', your image will appear in my head. And that's a good thing."

She said now that we have had dessert, do you think we should have supper? Sure, but very small. Just a small piece of that pizza for me, warmed up or cold, it didn't matter. She'd warm up a couple of small pieces. Beer? Split one? Perfect. Just perfect. When we started on the pizza, I told her that my grandmother's thick pizza was quite similar to this one, but a little thicker. The leftover pizza was sometimes sliced in half, separating the top half from the bottom, then very thinly sliced ham or beef or salami was placed between them to make a sandwich. Italian kids in school always had very tasty lunches and everyone wanted to share, but we didn't want any of the Anglo kids' lunches, nor would we eat the cafeteria food. Bunch of food snobs we were. Edith laughed and said she could certainly understand that, especially after going to Little Italy. I said, but you haven't really tried the fantastic deli foods. Great stuff in those display cases. You'd really enjoy them. Next time you have a party, talk to one of the Italians delis, you'll be happy you did.

We were both yawning and getting sleepy. She took my hand and said, "Let's get ready for bed." So brush teeth and all that and lay down in the 'other' room. Before falling silent, she said, "Thanks for always being kind, and always being physically clean, and always being a gentleman." Gave her a little hug.

CHAPTER 48

GOODBYE, CHICAGO

It would be nice sometimes if morning waited until later in the day to get started. A bedside clock told me it was a few minutes after 7:00 AM. My outstretched arm said I was alone. A scent, newly-brewed coffee, was reaching out to me as Edith, fully dressed for the day, came into the room and said "Ready for your morning religious service?" "Good morning, Edith. How kind you are. Give me five minutes." I made my way into her brother's room, used the bathroom there, did a first teeth brushing (or is it tooth brushing?), got dressed in my own clothes and wandered into the kitchen, beating the five minute clock.

Gave her a big hug and quietly said good morning again. She served black coffee and asked what I would like for breakfast. My answer: "In addition to an array of candles, and a minimum of six murmuring monks, I would like three cookies, please." She laughed and said "I thought you would say cookies, but it's still a surprise." So we sat down to a cookie breakfast ... her first ... cookies and coffee, the perfect combination for good health, nature at its best. We talked about our few days together and I thanked her profusely for a perfect birthday. She said it had been a delight for her and now she would try to do more things and different things in the big city. My suggestion was that she should do something new in Chicago at least once every two weeks. It didn't matter if it were an art show, a concert, a tour of the newspaper office or brewery, a ballet ... anything. In time and in that manner, she'd be able to converse knowledgably with her new clientele in the new high falutin' beauty salon. After a cup-and-a-half of coffee, I said I should pack up, but I'd like to have another cup just before I left. Packed my clothing bag and toiletries, brushed teeth again, put the toothbrush into a jacket pocket, got ready to leave, went out to the garage, checked the scooter, tied the clothing bag on. Edith had my 'care' package ready. It almost didn't fit in the trunk, but with a little friendly persuasion ...

"C'mon Edith, let's sit down with a cup and say our goodbyes." She smiled, poured some coffee in each of our cups. She asked which road I'd be taking. Route 30 to the east and I'd probably be in Valparaiso, Indiana in a couple of hours. Do you know what Valparaiso means? She shook her head no. I said, "Heavenly Valley or Paradise Valley." Did she know anything about that town? No, she didn't. I was leaving her with a pile of laundry. She smiled again and said, "Yes, but you're leaving some nice sparkle and sizzle behind you, too." I stood up. She did also. "Time to go. For me it's been marvelous." She put her finger across my lips, put her arm in mine and we walked into the garage. A nice kiss, the garage door started upward and I rolled the scooter out of the garage, kicked it to start, and was on my way with a wave ... a beautiful three days in my life bank of experiences.

Man, oh man, I was back on the road again after a three-day Chicago interlude. Sure, we could call it an interlude. I fiddled and adjusted to reacquaint my butt and myself to scootering and its process. That required almost ten seconds. It was a comfortable place to be, on Tony Lambretta's back and in motion along the roadway. Early in this journey, way back there in Arizona, after not too many miles, this scooter and its spirit had started to become part of my body and spirit. I knew and felt its sounds and its vibrations, its reactions and its mood changes. I had always talked in a respectful manner to this tireless beast of burden. It had not yet ever let me down.

Fair amount of traffic with a few delays, but nothing serious. Beautiful weather as I headed east toward the Indiana state line, now with most traffic congestion behind me. Starting an entirely new leg of this zigzag scooter expedition, and couldn't decide if this was a zig or a zag. In later years, as I would recall parts of this trip, I'd always lean toward singing that Willy Nelson song 'On the Road Again' though it would be twenty years after my jaunt before that song became popular... 'like a band of Gypsies we go down the highway' ....

After an hour we cross the Illinois/Indiana state line and another hour takes us to Valparaiso. Time to gas up, then take a break. Stopped for fuel, restroom, and answered a few questions from a young guy who was tending gasoline pumps. I was in the Midwest, amongst ordinary people, and felt no need to be 'on guard' yet and so we conversed for four or five minutes, until another customer pulled in. I had asked about a park or picnic area where I might take a break. He said if I stayed on Route 30 for another mile or so, I'd see Valparaiso University, which probably had a number of places to sit down and have a nice break time while I watched some pretty coeds pass by. Not an attraction to me this morning. Another time, perhaps.

In fact, there was a nice wooded area, part of which was a cemetery which served my needs beautifully. Dead people didn't bother me and I was confident they wouldn't want to mooch any Italian cookies which Edith had packed. Three cookies and a waterbag and a smoke. That was my break ... alone except for the horizontal crowd around and below me. Thought about Edith. We two had been an unusual pairing. Certainly, after conversations we had, she knew far more about me than I knew about her. And she offered so little information and that was fine with me. While we had had good fun, there was little emotional involvement.

Having asked permission and receiving no negative feedback, I sat on Judith Hendlersen's gravestone. Occasionally commenting, but receiving little response, I decided that Indianapolis would be my goal for this afternoon. Find a camping spot, retrain myself in lost camping arts, study the road map and at least semi-plot my way toward Florida. Tonight I would open the note from Stella. That would be tough no matter what the written words were. So Judith, can you hear me? Should I get going? What do you think? She said, "Go ahead, Rosano, you'll be OK. And thanks for visiting." Or so I felt she said. I said, "See you later."

Back onto Lambretta, with Route 30 traveling through the southern part of the town. Pleasant looking town, but I couldn't discern a 'valley' part of 'Val-paraiso' or 'Paradise Valley.' But, no matter, someone did. Ten minutes east of town was the intersection of Routes 30 and 421, the route I would take southward toward Indianapolis.

Again, we were surrounded by cultivated, rectangular plots of land to the horizon in all directions it seemed. Was Indiana greener than the same sort of terrain in Illinois? Not an easy thing to compare shades of color from different days of viewing. There were many miles ahead of me. The amount of farmland in the US is just enormous. The amount of food produced must be simply astounding, mind boggling. How do we measure such production? Considering hundreds of miles of grassland and farmland I had passed through, any production number would be incomprehensible. Probably measured in tons, but if the number were something like 24,769,000 zillion tons, that info would still be meaningless. What would be a bigger unit of measure after ton. Megaton? Superton? How about a unit called rcar (railroad car) or sf (shipful)? Doing math in my head as we passed these miles of farmland was impossible, especially given that I had no useful information with which to start. But this sort of mental meandering kept my mind active through some mildly picturesque (change to boring) landscape divided by an absolutely straight highway.

We had crossed the Kankakee River, with its respectably large flow going westward. It was refreshing to see this river did not conform to rigid rectangular patterns in this area. Along its banks were trees, wild volunteer trees with no production goals, merely trying to live and reproduce, to duplicate themselves.

Route 421 intersected and cohabitated with Route 24 for a few miles, and headed into the small town of Monticello, Indiana where I'd get some coffee and take a break. Didn't need scooter fuel yet. The Midwest has a network of small towns that parts of the far west doesn't. Gas stations exist not many miles apart from each other in the Midwest. It seemed a bit embarrassing to ask a gas station attendant for less than one gallon of fuel, though other folks would have no problem with that, I suppose. Fuel would be available three or four towns farther down the road and then I could buy at least one gallon. I'd take a lunch break near the Tippecanoe River, then get some coffee in a café and use their restroom before I got back to the highway. Found a good place to stop near the river, opened my trunk, which now smelled like an Italian Pizza joint, removed Edith's package, blew a little kiss in her direction, sat down with the water bag and the sausage sandwich, and had a great solitary lunchtime. I would be soon enough into Kentucky and Tennessee where Italian food was not their forte. Perhaps it was bourbon and barbeque that was their strong suit. No problem with that at all, especially if the barbeque was not too fatty. Or maybe 'cornpone' was king, whatever cornpone actually was. Maybe it was hominy, another mysterious thing, at least to me. This river flowed south. "Tippecanoe and Tyler, too" was a campaign slogan which was used to help William Henry Harrison become the ninth President of the United States. This was the river referred to in that famous slogan, used in the middle 1800's when we were still actively engaged in screwing Indians out of land they lived on. Land, which they, of course, had screwed somebody else out of. Finished that beautiful sausage and roasted pepper sandwich and nearly wept at the thought there would be none until I reached New Jersey or New York or New England. Now it was time for coffee. Putt-putted to a small diner for a restroom break and coffee, not as good as my cowboy coffee, but adequate.

Route 24 had gone its merry way eastward while 421 was heading southward again, and after crossing the Wabash River, took us traveling a half-dozen miles east of Lafayette, Indiana, where thirteen years in the future, an exciting event for me occurred. Had I known in advance, I might have stopped by for a visit and to say "see you later". But now, I knew only that Lafayette was the home of Purdue University, and that was sufficient.

Another hour or two and another fuel stop and I was on the outskirts of Indianapolis, still on Route 421. I would find a place to set up camp, rest and read. Route 421 circled the city to the east and was quite busy with traffic. Just as I drove past Fall Creek Road, I noticed a fair patch of woods to my left. Fall Creek Road probably meant there existed something called Fall Creek, and … there was. I managed a U-turn and made my way to Fall Creek Road which headed toward the northeast. After a mile or two, a thick grouping of trees beckoned, offering privacy, a source of wood, and a nearby creek to play in, if I so desired. Very slowly and carefully, I drove the Lambretta in amongst thick trees. Despite being in the middle of an urbanized area, I was alone and shielded from it. Tied the scooter to one of the trees in case wind came along. I would not start a fire, but rather make a pot of that cold coffee similar to what Stella and I had done back on the Texas prairie north of Amarillo. Tent and tarp were set up quickly, dug a small latrine pit using the aluminum scoop. Prepared my cold coffee brew, pulled some food from the trunk which included some pizza, took Stella's note from the bottom of the trunk. Next, had a smoke, had some water, and had to settle down. Long drive today and I was fading. Far in the distance, or so it seemed, city sounds provided background.

Stella's envelope was ordinary, but felt thick. Not wanting to tear the envelope more than necessary, I used my knife to carefully slit along one edge. Total surprise, in the envelope was one of those small bank cash pouches closed with a paper clip. Pulling this out, I found a tidy sum of money. On that wrapper, Stella had written 'in case you tire of camping.' Inside the envelope was a second sheet of paper which I recognized as having been removed from her thick little notebook. On this page, she had written a note. The note read:

> Rosano my dear dear Rosano
> You will always be the miracle in my life
> Take care of yourself as you took care of me
> A part of me will forever be with you
> —Stella

Much tougher to read than I had anticipated. Our last few days together had been joyful and painful and tougher on that beautiful woman than on me. Or maybe not. The morning of her surprise farewell had been carefully and lovingly planned. Similar to a baby tooth which must be taken, done quickly is by far, best. She, that splendid woman, had done exactly that.

After having spent three days with Edith in Chicago, today I had sought solitude, with my first break in a cemetery, second break alone at Tippecanoe River, and now, not in a campground, but hidden amongst trees hoping for no visitors. Perhaps I was designed to be alone. I'd have to think about that ... tomorrow.

Most likely, tomorrow evening would see me sleeping somewhere in Kentucky. I had missed it on my journey up the Mississippi, but now I'd be heading south through what I considered to be northern edges of Red Neck nation. Perhaps that's not a fair assessment, but that was my impression. In any event, normally outgoing, while in the racially charged areas, I would play it very close to the vest. No involvement with women, no drinking, and polite to everyone, no exceptions. The Red Neck element, in my estimation, could be kind and generous, intelligent and inventive, with a unique sense of humor and wordplay. Yet, I also considered that element as being one-third of the way toward lunacy, the responsible parties being ignorant parenting and those hateful 'good Christians' who would skin you alive if they could convince themselves that Jesus might enjoy it. Not only that, but the mean-spirited bastards taught that stupid shit to their kids. Sometime in the future I might tell you my true feelings toward those ignoramuses. The entire package was to me, something to be very cautious about. Stella was on the money when she said, while in the south I would be a foreigner in my own country. Heading toward the Southeast corner of the US, the major southern city I would first encounter would be Atlanta, Georgia. The Atlanta metro area had a population of a million or more. Perhaps a stay of two or three days would be good there. Get some urban input, always refreshing after miles and miles of rural. We would see.

My intention to read final parts of my book "Sirens of Titan" was put aside. Into the tent, and asleep in moments.

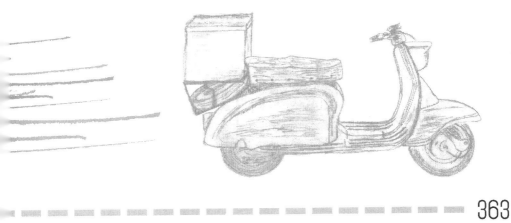

PART FOUR
CHICAGO TO JACKSONVILLE

CHAPTER 49

KENTUCKY GIRL SCOUTS

In my tent, in the middle of the night, in the middle of the woods, in the middle of Indiana, I was awake and I was alone ... not lonely, alone. Traveling across the US was doing what I had intended to do and I was more than half-way. This was not a painful 'alone', rather a sought-after, peaceful, contented 'alone'. In the quiet and darkness of my mountain tent, thoughts turned to a childhood throughout which I enjoyed company of a large, diverse group of people, typical of a gregarious Italian-American family setting, but where I could, at times, remain by myself without feeling the need for company. As a kid, I learned the value of being by myself from time to time, sometimes for many hours at a time and not being a part of someone else's doings. I knew how good it was to do as I pleased without having to consider reactions, feelings, or emotions of some other person ... to not seek approval nor fear disapproval of whatever it was I would be doing, whether it was singing off-key, reading, or making farting sounds with my mouth on the back of my hand. It seemed I had always been pretty good company for myself, and never experienced a deep 'lonely', as I knew other people did at times. Liking the person, oneself, that you're alone with, is a key to enjoying solitude, I supposed. But no outside person enjoyed my strange or illogical ideas or ridiculous little jokes more than I did. Being alone allowed time and space for dreaming. Vaguely, I remembered a day, perhaps at age five or six or seven years, when I realized how 'unlonely' being by oneself could be, but could not remember circumstances leading to that discovery. Being alone was a gift I gave myself from time to time. Occasionally, a friend or family member, would become

irritated at my self-containment, my not feeling need for contact. And I might act slightly remorseful when that occurred, but it wouldn't be a sincere reaction, since I so enjoyed vacations from people. Now a question in my mind concerned those few people I had known who could not stand being alone, even for short periods of time. If they found themselves in that situation, they would start the TV, and sometimes also turn on radio to produce the illusion of having company. A few past friends had that trait, which I had found so peculiar, a little pathetic in fact. Those friendships had fast faded, probably because of my need to seek distance. I wondered what kind of mental quirk had driven their need. Was that somehow similar to the incessant need to talk? This was getting too deep for me, having always felt that being in poor company was far worse than being alone, and further, that constant talking was far worse than silence.

Not having a watch was a plus. Time of night was unimportant. Getting more sleep was important. Having just experienced surging energy and positivity of Chicago, I had decided not to investigate Indianapolis or Cincinnati thinking they would pale in a comparison to that remarkable place, the Windy City, the nickname Chicago carried. Both cities, of course, were well-known. Both would have a number of interesting attractions. My decision was to bypass both. Whether that was 'fair' or not was not a consideration. It was my selection since I could not experience every city or town I encountered. Now on the outskirts of Indianapolis, I would head toward Cincinnati, but not explore it. An early morning start would face me directly into the sun. A later start would be better. Back to snoozing. And if any premature bird chirping awakened me, I would shoot that sweet little creature with my pointed finger and a verbal 'ka-pow' (since I had good aim it would require only one shot).

Eventually, Morning said "OK, you've had enough of that horizontal stuff. Let's see what you can do today." Morning had been delayed somewhat because of the thickness of my tree cover allowing dark to last a little longer. Dressed, dragged the sleeping bag out of the tent, flapped it around and draped it over the tent to air it out. Drank some cold coffee (better than last time) and ate three cookies (always an exquisite experience). Coffee and cookies, another well-balanced meal and a king's breakfast for sure. Packed up camp. Finished a few last swallows of coffee, dumped grounds on the ground and scattered them. Put the pot away unwashed (I'd clean it next time). Tied everything onto the scooter, covered up the latrine, and then a final look to insure the campsite was OK. Since no fire was used, I felt safe about that. Time to move out.

Back to Route 421 which intersected with I-70, part of that new interstate system, and a little farther south intersected with well-traveled Route 40. , both of which were part of a dozen or more highways radiating outward from Indianapolis. I was looking for Route 52 which would take me south and eastward toward southwest Ohio, where Cincinnati rested on the banks of the Ohio river, a little over 100 miles away. New I-70 highway roughly paralleled old Route 40. My guess was that devastation of businesses along Route 40 would be enormous. Small towns might wither and die also. It was probably a dirty political game which determined a new highway's routing, which towns might have an exit, which would be bypassed completely. Here was Route 52, which I would travel this morning. A moderately cool, slightly hazy morning, light breezes at my back. In the 100 miles before Cincinnati, there would be a dozen or more towns to pass by or through. How many would still exist after a major highway was installed? Initially, our new interstate highway system was justified on military alertness or preparedness grounds. Was that just a selling tool for the Eisenhower White House? My guess was that the military aspect was greatly compromised as politicians applied their sleaze-laced pressures to any plan.

About halfway to Cincinnati, was a town called Rushville, Indiana. I had never heard of it. There was a good indication that at least 7000 people had heard of it since they lived there. A stop for coffee. Temporarily at least, I was heading more eastward than southward in an effort to get closer to western edges of the Appalachian Mountains, which would have more variation than this flat farmland, of which I was a bit weary. Something so enjoyable, however, about some pastures, was seeing horses when they were frolicking. I would take a break, maybe have a smoke and watch these fine-looking animals. Never had much involvement with horses, but appreciated a picture they often presented. Remarkably powerful animals. A group of a half-dozen were dancing out there in a pasture, and jumping around. I pulled over to watch for a while. I was heading into Kentucky and then Tennessee and would certainly see horses there. Back on the scooter, and driving another few miles and I stopped at a small diner, where having pancakes and coffee was uneventful. Had a smoke and a stretch and was soon on the road toward Cincinnati, though I would turn southward before I reached it. That was the intent. Cincinnati took its name from one of mankind's 100 best people ever. Of course, that 100 number is my arbitrary number, but Lucius Quinctius Cincinnatus was twice given total control of Ancient Rome (about 500 years BC) and twice gave power back to the Roman Senate when his task was complete and returned to his farm. This splendid man is worth researching. That is in stark contrast to most politicians of our day, who seem to be primarily interested in making nice comfy nests for themselves and screw the public. My mini-rants would occur at moderate intervals as the reliable Lambretta made its steady way across the terrain. Sometimes I'd shout my opinions out loud with sufficiently bad language to give them some emphasis, but have never had any response from anyone on the highway. I could easily have avoided Ohio completely since I was just catching a small corner of it. I decided that it would be beneficial to be able, one day, to say, "Oh yes, I've really enjoyed Ohio and can appreciate the splendid efforts of those fine citizens there." Now, when would that sentence ever be used? Well, if I ever ran for Presidency of the United States, it would behoove me to have been in such an important state. Rather slim chance of my presidency, but one never knows.

Crossed into Ohio and found myself in Harrison County, named after our 9th US President. Time for a little road map and cookie break. Edith in Memphis had provided the atlas and Edith in Chicago had packed the cookies. Had previously considered taking Route 25 southward through Kentucky toward Lexington, but first I had to find my way across the Ohio River. Decided I would do that. First, savor three beautiful little cookies from Chicago. That convenient little road atlas was five or six years out of date, and showed none of the new Interstate system. Well, it would be just as easy to follow signs to Kentucky's Route 25 or signs to Lexington, Kentucky to eventually head southward to Atlanta, Georgia. That city was about 500 miles away, but my intent was to wander a bit in Kentucky and Tennessee. We would see, we would see. Following signs took me close enough to the center of Cincinnati to encounter a fair amount of traffic congestion, fairly fast-moving congestion at that. Time for a little tension and raising of blood pressure readings. Finally, on the bridge crossing the Ohio River and magically, I was in Kentucky's northernmost part.

After a little confusion of route numbers going through the town of Florence, I did finally find myself on Route 25, heading south into what I guessed might be Bourbon Country ... except there was no real demarcation, no specifically defined area of Kentucky or Tennessee which was legally designated as a 'Bourbon' area, though there was at least one county named Bourbon County. In my young life, previous to moving to Arizona, I had had some monumental encounters and legendary involvements with Bourbon or US corn-based whiskies. I had done most of my drinking while under-aged and genuinely enjoyed drinking whiskey. Now, at age 21 and finally able to drink legally, I had reduced my alcoholic consumption to one or two drinks per week, not quite a teetotaler but close. Still loved the taste of the US and Canadian whiskeys, but was no longer seeking the effect of alcohol to any degree. Still, I felt a natural affinity for any area that produced it. In truth, Bourbon can be made anywhere in the US as long as it is derived from mash which is at least 51 percent corn. There are other restrictions as well. In fact, I knew that one of the better-known bourbons, Jack Daniels Tennessee Sour Mash, was not officially a bourbon, but legal niceties are cast aside when holding a small glass with a fine-tasting whiskey casting that warm, honey-colored glow.

It had taken about an hour to make a transition from traffic congestion of Cincinnati to placid, now rural, countryside of northern Kentucky. The terrain was not flat farmland which I had forever driven across. This area had more texture, and because of it, roads were not nearly as straight. And there were hills to look up into, and down from. We were in Bluegrass country, not necessarily referring to the style of music (though that should not be excluded), but rather to the grass growing in this heavily limestone soil. Excellent quality grass due to its calcium content. And that, in turn, made for strong, sturdy, healthy horses. Leaving towns behind, horse farms appeared more frequently.

Now, how could anybody on tour, any adventurer, explorer, scooterist, manage to travel hither and yon in the state of Kentucky and not get to see part of the Red River Gorge, famous for its natural arches and cliffs of sandstone. Well, I managed to miss it completely. This was a rock climber's paradise and I had missed it by twenty-five miles, not knowing it existed. Of course, had I known and visited, I would have missed the girl scout troop. Tell you about that in a few paragraphs.

Lexington, Kentucky, toward which I was aiming, was named after the Massachusetts' Lexington, as were towns in perhaps a half-dozen other states. This Kentucky Lexington, about 60,000 population, was notable for a number of reasons, one being its efforts to preserve thoroughbred horse farms from being overrun by urban development. However, I first knew of Lexington as a place for alcohol and drug rehab efforts at The Narcotic Farm, rather than any horse farm. This was a federal facility for treatment of drug-addicts, some well-known, others not. It was a prison, some inmates sent there by court order, others just signed themselves in. It was among the first facilities to treat drug addiction as a disease rather than a crime. I had first learned of it because one of my favorite author/storytellers, Alexander King, had 'done Lexington' two or three times, and talked about it in his book 'Mine Enemy Grows Older.' Before that, in 'The Man with the Golden Arm' by Nelson Algren, character 'Frankie the Machine' goes through detox there in Lexington. I soon became aware that quite a few authors, poets, and especially jazz musicians, famous and obscure, went through the program at the Narcotic Farm. Started in the mid-1930s, there were musicians from several decades that had stayed there. From a saxophone player in Tucson, I had heard Lexington had witnessed some of the greatest jazz ever performed, with so many excellent musicians there for rehab, and encouragement to continue their music, often with instruments supplied by the hospital/prison. I asked if there were any recordings of these sessions. He said he didn't think any recording was being done, at least not while he was there in the middle 1950s. Why are musicians so prone to this sort of thing? Or ... is that not a valid question? Is addiction more noticed when an entertainer or artist or poet is involved rather than a cab driver or an accountant or a firefighter?

About 20 miles north of Lexington, taking a smoke break, I noticed a sign to Sadieville. That struck me as being an interesting name. Should I turn off and see? Hell yes I should. Field-stripping the cigarette, I got back onto Tony Lambretta and putted the very short distance to Sadieville, population 300, but ... believe it or not, it had a post office, which I supposed was one of the local points of interest. On that little road was a sign which said Eagle Crek Camp, shours, $0.50, cleen (sic). Now how could I possibly pass up that opportunity? I had already driven more than 150 miles that day. That was enough. Time to camp and to read while there was daylight. Putted through the gate and into the campground, which looked clean and orderly, each campsite area, about ten of them, having rake marks where it had been groomed. Turned around and putted over to a small house with an office sign out front. Middle-aged woman came out the door from her screened porch and said "Hello, how're you doing?" Pleasant lady. We talked for a minute or two, and she said before she took my money, she had to warn me there was a Girl Scout Troop that would be camping here and she could not guarantee a quiet place for tonight. Fair enough warning I thought, and told her I'd take my chances. She suggested any of the sites on my right since the girls would be on the left side. In less than an hour, my camp was ready, my shower was done, and a small fire had been started under a pot of coffee. Now, time to sit down, sip that coffee, and read from one of two books I had going at the time ... "I, Robot" and "Sirens of Titan." Digging into the scooter trunk, I noted the paper bag with what felt like a dozen Italian cookies, which meant that Edith had packed more than I had asked for. Maybe later I'd have a few. Don't want them to go bad. Had read "Sirens" for a little less than an hour, and had just finished sipping two cups of coffee, and preparing the pot for morning use when two large station wagons pulled into the campground. Must be cavalry coming to the rescue. No, it was the Girl Scouts.

Yes, except there were six or eight Brownie troops or the local equivalent of 'Almost a Girl Scout', two teenage real girl scouts, and two adults, probably a dozen in all. I couldn't help myself ... I had to watch as they started setting up one larger tent and two smaller ones. They had brought some firewood and charcoal, and got a good-sized fire going in one of the fireplaces. Some of the group had gone off to the Eagle Creek and their voices echoed back to the camp from somewhere in the woods. I continued reading and half dozed off, and started reading again. An adult, a teen, and one of the little ones walked toward my campsite and as I stood up, the teen said, "Hello. We were wondering if that was the kind of scooter which was in the 'Spanish Holiday' movie." I said, "Hello Ladies, yes, that movie is called 'Roman Holiday' and this scooter is almost exactly what you saw except that I installed this big metal box at the back, so it causes the scooter to look a little peculiar." The littlest of the three noticed the Arizona license plate, sounded out A-ri-zon-a, and asked if I had come from there. The other two moved around so they could see it. Of course, questions started and I answered as best I could considering there were three very different ages to talk to. Little one said she knew where Arizona was and it was far out west with 'real' cowboys and it was next to Mexico and did I ever go to Mexico? I answered yes, and, as a matter of fact, I had driven this scooter to Mexico a few times. She took the woman's hand and pulled her arm downward and whispered something, after which the woman said "What a good idea!" Big smile on the little girl as the woman in charge says "We are cooking some camp stew, will you join us for supper?" Laughing, I say "When three pretty ladies ask me to supper, do you think I could possibly refuse?" The little one says "Yippee!" and claps her hands. The teen says, "It'll be about an hour. Is that OK"? I answer "Excellent! Thank You!" Then she asked if it would be OK if the other girls wandered over to take a look at the scooter. No problem.

For an hour, I tidied up my campsite between visits from girls across the way, and brief explanations of what I was doing on this trip. Over to the bathhouse and washed my hands again, got the flashlight where I could reach it easily, dug the cookies out of the scooter trunk (exactly a dozen remaining) and put them in my jacket pocket, secured my tent opening to prevent any occupation by visiting critters in my absence. Sat down, had a smoke, then brushed my teeth once again. Just as daylight was fading into twilight, the teen and the one I now call Little One, walked toward my tentsite, and said, "C'mon Rosano, sir. Supper is ready."

Reaching their campsite, one of the adults introduced me to each of the others, and we gently shook hands all around. They had brought folding wood and canvas campstools, arranged now in a semi-circle, and I was directed to sit in one as they all took a seat. One of the teens made a few brief comments about our gathering, thanked the Lord for bringing them a guest to share their food, and then she mentioned that two young girls would serve. There would be a main course of their 'campground' stew, along with a platter of cut up vegetables and another platter of sliced meats and cheeses and bread. And the speaker said that somehow their signals got crossed and everyone thought someone else had brought dessert, so there was, unfortunately, no dessert. And through my mind goes the thought, Great! With my little sack of Italian cookies, the fit would be perfect. We were each given a small tray and utensils to put on our laps, then the two young servers went from chair to chair with bowls of soups, and then a small plate was distributed, and the platters of veggies and meat were passed. The food was simple, but nutritious, I guessed.

And as we finished, one of the adult women said that two of the little ones would gather up the dishes and while that was happening, the rest of the troop would sing a camp song to honor their guest. She explained to me that this was a newly-formed troop, only a few weeks old, and they hadn't had much time to practice, but they would try. One of the teens had a pitch pipe and got the song started. Someone put a few more pieces of wood on their campfire. The troop did a credible job of two-part harmony on the song which was totally unfamiliar to me. It sounded okay and, of course, I marveled at it and gave a one-man round of applause. The woman then asked if I would give a talk about my scooter and my trip across America. Certainly, I would. Standing and facing the semi-circle, I talked for no more than ten minutes about the trip, mentioning Tucson, Albuquerque, Denver, New Orleans and Chicago, saying that the next city to be visited was Lexington, just a few miles away. And they could find these places on a map when they got back home. Also there was a little surprise that had been carried all the way from Chicago just for such an occasion as this little campout. Reaching into my jacket, and withdrawing the paper sack, and removing the four little packages, I asked if anyone could guess what there might be inside. After two or three incorrect guesses, I announced that we really did have dessert and it was Italian Cookies, the best in the world. They were small and should be eaten slowly. Two packages to each of the teens for distribution. The young girls ate their cookies a nibble at a time and confirmed that they were the best cookies they had ever had. Did they have any questions ... about my trip or the cookies or anything? The Little One raised her hand and asked if I knew how to sing. Sure, I said, everyone knows how to sing. Some just do it a little better than others. She then said that they had sung a song for me, could I sing a song for them? Sure, but they had to promise not to laugh too much at me. She looked around and then said "We promise. Cross our hearts." So I sang the old song "When You're Smiling." (The Whole World Smiles with You). That earned me a little round of clapping and I bowed deeply. "OK, next, my turn." I said, "Do you girls know how to sing a round?" One of them spun in a circle and started singing and I said. "Close, but not quite. Want to learn?" A bunch of yesses. "Well, it's a simple tune and it's called 'White Coral Bells.' And you'll remember this song forever and ever and that way you'll remember the scooter and Rosano, too. So we began. Sang it once myself, then with the group all together two or three times. Then the group was divided into two parts, with me making sure an adult and a teen were included in each segment. In less than fifteen minutes, they knew it and were doing a beautiful job with it.

> WHITE CORAL BELLS
> Upon a slender stalk
> Lilies of the valley line my garden walk
> Oh, don't you wish that you might hear them ring?
> That will happen only when the angels sing.

Kids are the greatest. There is nothing on earth more rewarding than witnessing children learn something useful or interesting or learning something just simply beautiful. And so quietly thrilling to hear them. I suggested they try a three-part round, but not now, not this evening, maybe tomorrow, because now it was time for me to say goodnight, that I would start early in the morning, so I should return to my tent and get ready to sleep. I shook hands with the adults and the teens and a few of the kids gave me a little hug and Little One pulled me down to her level and gave me a quick little smooch on the cheekbone. Man, I thought I'd start getting emotional if I stayed, so I waved 'Good Night' and with my flashlight unlit, walked into the darkness.

CHAPTER 50

WANDERINGS AND INCIDENTS

While in no particular hurry to get back on the road, it would be better to be gone before the girls were up and about. Seemed more dramatic that way. It had been an evening of friendship and good vibes with that bunch of young girls and the sparkle in their eyes as they accomplished singing a 'round' and hearing themselves for the first time. So wonderful to witness well-behaved kids as they're learning and doing. While coffee was brewing, the tent, sleeping bag, and clothing bag were getting packed. Time to drink my coffee. The plan was to get to a café in Lexington, have some pancakes and make plans from there. Finished my coffee, packed everything, put out my small fire, and headed slowly out of the campground. And there was Little One, barefoot, in her pajamas, waving at me. Slowing further, I blew her a kiss, and said loud enough for her to hear "Goodbye, Sweetie-Pie". She smiled, waved again. And I returned to roads heading south, wondering if, in later years, she would remember the funny man who sang songs and had little cookies for everyone.

In less than a half-hour, Kentucky Route 25 took us through the center of Lexington, a town of 60,000 people with that many more in the suburbs. Before I did any noodling around, it was time to sit with my road atlas and a leisurely pile of pancakes and some coffee. At a café, I used the paper place mat for some calendar and mileage estimates, and a bit of trip planning, nothing too fussy or precise. Time not used in New Orleans when beautiful Stella said her tearful and prematurely surprising goodbye, and three or four high mileage days immediately after, had put me farther along than expected. Not wanting to arrive in Connecticut too many days before my sister's wedding, I would take a more leisurely, more meandering path to Atlanta, to Jacksonville, and then up the East Coast. Why not too many days ahead of time for Connecticut? Frankly, because my mother and I drove each other bazammi crazy in those years. So, three days at my parent's house was max ... and I would leave their home immediately after my sister's wedding. It was less than 400 miles to Atlanta from this café. Two days of scooter travel if I pushed. Instead, I would take four or five days or more and wander hither and yon on the way. So it was decided ... after I finished my pancakes ... I'd get on the Lambretta, noodle around Lexington a bit, then head toward the Daniel Boone National Forest, which seemed like an interesting place, with some dramatic terrain. We'd be going into the Appalachians. Daniel Boone was one of those heroes of my early childhood, along with Pecos Bill, Davy Crockett, Paul Bunyan, John Henry, Buffalo Bill, Wild Bill Hickok, and Superman. Can't ignore Superman, so I'll tell you a little story later ... about Superman and Me, the impressionable kid. Leaving the café, I drove slowly this way and that along various streets in Lexington, a clean and orderly city, lots of green spaces, some seemed to be pastures, unusual in the middle of a town. The two women last night had mentioned that Lexington was a pretty place, that I would enjoy the drive. My impression was that it was a well-ordered and moneyed place, a center of race-horse activities ... more manicured than most towns. Found my way back to Route 25 and putt-putted southward out of town headed generally in the direction of Daniel Boone's stomping grounds.

NOTE TO READERS: The next few days were days of noodling in Eastern Kentucky and Tennessee with a vaguely defined goal of reaching Chattanooga in southern Tennessee, then noodling my way southward toward Atlanta. Fifty-five years later, as I write this, I can recall a number of impressions and events, but cannot pinpoint locations associated with each. Over the years, I've always thought of these days in the Appalachians as traveling in Kentengia, my amalgam of KEN tucky, TEN nessee and northern G eorg IA. Following this reader's note is a disorderly blending of those days.

Before leaving Lexington, knowing that I would get into some remote rural areas, the scooter's gas tank was filled and two-stroke oil was purchased. The water bag was refreshed and refilled. Grocery stop next and a good supply of food stashed in the trunk. I had purchased a PayDay candy bar, never having seen one before ... a fairly simple combination of a caramel nougat sort of thing covered with roasted peanuts. Tried a bite outside the grocery. Good tasting, with no chocolate, so the melting problem was much reduced. Back into the grocery and bought half a dozen more.

Headed south for a spell, then east, and soon found myself traveling through some hilly, wooded, rocky terrain, interspersed with beautiful little valleys. The Appalachians can be so visually interesting. I was using all the gears of the scooter, climbing uphill, then coasting downhill, and climbing again. Oh yeah, give me hell, I know we're not supposed to coast or freewheel downhill. Well, screw that noise, coasting is the greatest if the grade isn't too steep. I always did as much coasting as feasible, occasionally for several downhill miles if terrain allowed. After perhaps an hour of traveling and as we, Tony Lambretta and I, topped a rise and started coasting downhill into one of the small valleys, there were three pickup trucks and four or five men not far from the road in a pasture. It appeared they were firing rifles, targets set up in the field. I slowed down and stopped the scooter. Then, from the sound and smoke, I realized at least two of them were firing flintlock, muzzle-loaded weapons (muskets?). Actually, none were modern rifles, but maybe one or two were percussion fired, I wasn't sure. I didn't know a great deal about these older firearms, but usually they were 50 caliber or more, and produced a loud explosion which seemed softer than that sharp crack of a modern rifle and along with it, a gorgeous cloud of white smoke. For an hour or so, I watched, each weapon being fired only two or three times in that hour. Maybe they were zeroing in, but I knew it was an involved process to get one of these loaded. Smoke drifted up toward me driven by a slow air movement, and I could actually smell burnt powder in the thin cloud drifting past. It had been more than an hour of observation and it was now time to leave. Started the Lambretta and coasted downhill quietly at a fast pace (presenting a tougher target) past the group, waving as I did so, and went on my merry way.

Taking several smaller roads as I wandered generally southward, I was either near or in (not sure which) the Daniel Boone National Forest. I saw signs announcing the forest and other signs warning that this was private property. A bit confusing until the road atlas showed the forest as speckled as a trout ... meaning they were as confused as I was. After quite a lot of wandering through this magnificent area of rough and rugged terrain, I came upon some sandstone cliffs. These were light-colored rock faces and at least one overhang. Four adults and two younger people with an assortment of ropes were in various positions on the rock face. Was this a rock climbing class or school? Or were they just practicing their rappelling, their ascents and their rock climbing? A few years before, I had done some elementary rock climbing, but never had become sufficiently interested to pursue the sport. I preferred horseshoes or bocce ball, something I might play if and when I turned eighty. I knew several rock climbers back in Arizona and all were genuinely good, kind people and crazy as loons.

Mid-afternoon somewhere near Manchester, Kentucky and pulled into the dirt parking lot of a small, well-worn café for a cup of coffee. A six stool counter was the serving area, with two stools missing altogether. So it now seated four rather dispersed patrons. The coffee was served without a word. Good strong-tasting coffee, better than most places I had tried in the last month or more. Thought I should get something to eat. To the short, very wide, moderately dark-skinned woman behind the counter, I said, "Excuse me, miss, but this coffee is excellent." She nodded a barely perceptible yes, but said nothing. So I continued with "Maybe I should get something to eat. Could you make a hamburger and maybe some French fries for me?" There were no displays of menu items or prices anywhere that I could see. Her low, soft, gravelly voice said, "No hamburger, no French fry ... we got bean soup." That didn't attract me, so I asked "Well, instead of that, could you just make something like a small ham and cheese sandwich?" Facial expression remained unchanged as she said, "No ham, no cheese ... we got bean soup." My third try was simpler ... "How about just a couple of slices of toast? Toast sounds great!" With no change in voice, and not showing any impatience whatsoever, she said "No toast ... we got bean soup." Well, it doesn't take me all day to do some basic problem solving. So, from out of the blue, came one final idea into my head ... "Would you happen to have some bean soup by any chance?" She said evenly, "We got bean soup, thirty-five cent." "Good, I'd like some bean soup, please." From some mysteriously hidden pot, she ladled out a generously-sized bowl of bean soup. And it was absolutely delicious. Glad I thought of it.

Went outside to have a smoke wondering who patronized this little diner if there weren't enough lost scooterists to support it. Having passed a dozen small campgrounds, I decided to choose one, settle down for the afternoon, read, and start noodling anew in the morning. Found a small campground, not terrific, but reasonably clean, with showers and firewood. Set up camp, showered, then read from my book 'Sirens of Titan' by Kurt Vonnegut. It's a sci-fi telling a story of an alien stranded on Titan, a moon of Saturn, who needs to a get a spare part for his disabled space ship. A sci-fi, but more of a comedy or farce poking fun at our normal images and understandings of religion, God, and the idea that we humans are the center of God's divine plan. Reading in late afternoon in these campgrounds was, for me, a slow process, as I was often side-tracked as I listened to and watched birds, squirrels, and occasionally, other critters. Enjoyable. But, in spite of all distractions, "Sirens" was finished. Savvy writer, Vonnegut. I'd read more of his stuff as I happened upon it. Now I'd get serious about Asimov's "I, Robot" and seek out yet another book to read since I always wanted a minimum of two in progress.

Thought about the girl scout/brownie group from last night ... too bad there wasn't another group of them tonight. Good bunch of people. On the other hand, there were no more Italian cookies. Got out a few other snacks, had a couple of smokes, drank a pot of coffee, tended to my small campfire for a few hours, and finally crawled into the tent for my beauty sleep.

After coffee, road atlas review, and 'decamping' the following morning, the Lambretta and I headed out, in no particular hurry, with the idea of viewing surrounding countryside and possibly seeing two rivers for no particular reason. The Laurel River, closer of the two, was about 25 miles away (as the crow flies) and since no crows capable of carrying the scooter and me were headed that way, we had to drive almost twice that distance on roads, but that was fine. The Laurel was a tributary to the second and larger river, the Cumberland River. It was about 100 miles distant and toward the west. My intent was a low-key effort to expose myself to a bit of Kentucky, which I had completely missed on the way from New Orleans to Chicago (and that meant no Padukah, and without a Padukah you're in big trouble).

There were caves in this part of Kentucky that were reported to be of interest to cave explorers (spelunkers) and of course, every advertised cave was supposed to have been a hideout or treasure stash for bank robbers or other tourist-attracting characters. The unadvertised caves and caverns were probably far more interesting. I had done rather extensive spelunking for ten or twelve days in my college days, just a few years before. The caves were in Virginia and West Virginia, none in Kentucky, and none were commercial. The only people involved were covered with a layer of batshit, just as I was. We had joined up with cavers from Brown University. I believe we actually crossed the state line between Virginia and West Virginia while underground. Not certain of that, however. In any event, it was a damn interesting couple of weeks. At the end of that trip, while fascinated, my curiosity had been satisfied and my choice was to not pursue it farther. I still wanted to do far too many different and diverse things and was just beginning to realize my limitations … just couldn't do them all, so caving was stricken from the list. Rock-climbing was probably next to be eliminated.

Mid-morning and I hadn't traveled far before approaching the town of London, Kentucky. Three or four miles before reaching that, a sign alongside the road read 'Hot Coffee and Other Things for Sale – 75 feet' in neatly painted lettering on thin plywood. Now how could any caffeine addict pass a sign like that? 75 feet later, in front of a very small, neatly-kept house and yard, was a trimmed grassy area with two picnic tables and a young, maybe 13-year-old negro lad, arranging his little store of 'Other Things.' As I stopped and removed my helmet, he greeted me with "Good Morning, Sir." I returned the greeting with "Good Morning to you, Sir. Is your coffee good coffee?" He responded, "Yes Sir, my mother says it is much better than good." "Well Sir, I would like to buy a cup of coffee, black coffee, no cream or sugar, please." He poured coffee from a thermos into a ceramic cup and taking a sip of blazing hot coffee, I said, "Your mother is right, it is, in fact, better than good. My name is Rosano, what name shall I call you?" He "Alex, Sir." "OK Alex, Sir, let me pay for this coffee. And then, I would like to look at your 'Other Things' for a few minutes." He spoke quite precisely as he explained this table carried miscellaneous items, while the other table was mostly books. I paid for the coffee and started looking at his collection of books. To be honest, I did not expect such a high level of reading material. Each book had a small slip of different colored construction paper with a price written on it. I asked Alex if he had read these books. He said he had read many of them. Mostly his father would read them first, then he would. A small, used, hardbound book titled 'Soul of the White Ant' caught my attention. Strange title. I asked Alex if he had read this one. "Yes Sir, it's about termites. Very interesting book, especially when they talk about termites in ... Australia I think it was, where termites will eat clothing off your body when you're sleeping." "Really? Well, Alex Sir, I will buy this book, for two reasons. One, because of your recommendation, and two, because I just finished my book, a science-fiction novel. So, let me buy 'White Ant' and I'll start reading it tonight." And I paid 50 cents. I finished my coffee. Opening the clothing bag, I stashed my new hardbound book, and at the same time, withdrew 'Sirens of Titan'. "Alex Sir, have you ever read any science-fiction?" He shook his head 'No' and I said "Let your father try this first and if he says it's OK, then you can read it. Consider it my addition to your collection." As I started putting on my helmet, his mother appeared at the door of their little house. Waving to her, I stuck one thumb in the air, said Goodbye to Alex, got a 'Goodbye, thank you sir' in return. Kickstarted Tony Lambretta and we were on our way again. Just a good feeling. Bright, polite young boy. I'll bet his parents were terrific people.

Putted into the town of London. Despite having had a great cup of coffee not too many minutes before, I'd stop for another and have some pancakes, too. Café stop, dollar-size pancakes, more coffee, a leisurely smoke and the thought I ought to learn a little more about the area and review the life of the local hero and national legend, Daniel Boone. After all, having a national forest named after you is no small potatoes. Having passed a sign pointing to the public library, I'd backtrack and visit. Finished at the café, onto the scooter and in a short time, walked into the library. Asking the older woman in charge for suggestions, she pointed out two or three books telling me about Boone, and areas of Kentucky he traveled through. He was an extraordinary hunter, explorer, soldier and woodsman. The number of stories featuring him was endless, many stories were myth, but nonetheless captured the unique spirit of this courageous man. Boone was one of my early childhood heroes ... some real, some fictitious. I had not read about him for a decade and therefore was doing an acquaintance renewal.

Mentioned earlier in this scooter trip account was the fact that during childhood I was an avid and continuous reader. Reading anything and everything. Of course, this fed my own imagination, which needed very little encouragement to run completely wild at times. Reading about Daniel Boone triggered memories of other characters, including Pecos Bill, Paul Bunyan, and Superman. As a child I could vividly imagine the exploits of these men and could, in my mind, almost live these events myself. Occasionally I would actually try to imitate them. Pecos Bill was a difficult one. He could ride a mountain lion and could tie a rope around a tornado. That was a tough challenge, too tough.

Paul Bunyan, the giant lumberjack, seemed easier. He was big and strong. I was small and, I thought, also strong. He had Babe the Blue Ox as his companion. I had Mittens, our black and white cat. I believed that Mittens and I could approximate Paul Bunyan and the Blue Ox, but on a smaller scale, of course. That day (I was about seven years old), there was, unfortunately, an ample supply of blue, water-based, poster paint available to me. Using my hands directly in the paint, while Mittens was lounging and half asleep, I was able to 'pet' this animal until most of her white fur was mixed with blue. Eventually, she realized that whatever was happening, was not a good thing. Mittens placed some rather prominent scratches on my arms before running around in circles while distributing flecks of blue paint rather evenly around the room, while blood from my scratches mixed with blue paint to create a muddy purple color. So ... Paul Bunyan and Babe the Blue Ox were put aside.

Superman fascinated me. Superman captivated me. What a guy! Sure, he had weaknesses .... he couldn't tolerate Kryptonite, he couldn't see through lead, and he had a weakness for Lois Lane. But he was enormously strong, enormously fast, and with his x-ray vision he could see through anything except lead, (which meant he could probably see Lois Lane's underwear) and, most importantly ... he could fly! Without any aids, he could fly! And I knew, if I were determined enough, and concentrated enough, I could fly too. Superman could just leap into the air to start flying. I was not stupid. I knew that I needed a little help getting started. With a little start, I was certain I could succeed.

The window ledge of my parent's upstairs bedroom was 12 or 13 feet (4 meters) above the level of the garden outside. I balanced on the ledge, holding firmly onto one of our large, black umbrellas, ready to point with my right hand in the direction I would fly (naturally, a person could not fly well if he could not point). Slowly, I moved to the edge, pointed ... and then I jumped ... son of a bitch ... the umbrella turned inside out and I hit the ground. A shock! Oh Jesus! It was a good thing the ground was soft, my foot prints were four inches (10 centimeters) deep. Damned umbrella ... I felt the pull, but lost all the lift because of the damned umbrella. Why didn't

I think of that first? Still in shock, but determined (a person needed determination to fly), I calculated that a large pillowcase would hold air much better. It would allow me enough floating time to begin my flight. Back to the ledge, with four corners of the pillowcase held in the best possible position by some wire, I again moved to the edge of that same ledge. I launched outward and plummeted to a point very slightly beyond that first set of footprints, but Lord in Heaven, this was beginning to get painful. I had felt a strong pull on the pillowcase, however, and had, in fact, traveled further. Should I try again? With a large bedsheet instead? Determination … that was the most important factor … Determination. There would be a third attempt. I was indeed determined. I fell nearly as swiftly on this third flight. Now there was noticeable pain in my legs. No one could say that I wasn't determined. No one could say that I wasn't persistent. But this planet called Earth, with its relentless gravity, can be a cruel place for those of us who wish to fly. I would have to wait for some other day to join Superman in the sky.

To the librarian, I said my thanks and complimented her on knowing exactly what I sought. Leaving the library, it was time to travel south and westward to the countryside, the Cumberland River, the town of Monticello, Kentucky, not Jefferson's Monticello, that, of course, sits in Virginia. After that, it was back into the hills of the Daniel Boone National Forest, where I became very wetly involved in some strong lightning and thunderstorm activity. Tried to find a motel room. Everything filled for miles around. Some sort of livestock show happening for the next few days. One B&B said I could hunker down for the night on the screened-in porch and wait out these storms. If I was still there by morning, I could buy a breakfast. Spent the night watching a lightning show and listening to a thunderous concert echoing from a hundred hills. A relaxed day with a roaring, long-lasting finale.

CHAPTER 51

TOUGH MORNING IN TENNESSEE

The night had been a mixture of magic and misery. The surrounding complex array of hills and valleys made for multiple echoing booms and loud rumblings of thunder ... a gigantic percussion concert. That was the magic part. The misery part was the half-wet clothing along with stickiness. I had been at least half awake through the entire night. Decided not to wait for people in the house to start their day. I'd start mine by getting onto the scooter, driving to the first coffee source and trying to dry out a bit more. Missing a few highway signs during the rainstorms meant I wasn't sure of my location. Distant thunder sounded as I started southward in growing daylight. It was a much slower pace with wet pavement. After an uncomfortable half hour, the town of Pine Knot came to my rescue with its mini-market and an aroma of precious coffee. Asked the woman if she minded that I stay inside for a time to dry out. She said, not at all, and indicated a stool I could sit on, pointed to the restroom, and said it was good to have company. We chatted for over an hour as she straightened shelves and then split a packaged sweet roll while we both sat and sipped coffee. Customers began to arrive. Said my thanks and goodbye to my hostess and went to the scooter for the atlas to figure out just what the hell I was doing. I did admit to myself that I was tired from lack of sleep and probably shouldn't travel far today. Thought about heading westward about 150 road miles to Nashville for more music. But my magnificent night of music in Memphis (thanks to Moretti the bartender jazzman) could never be equaled. Decided to 'noodle' eastern Tennessee in much the same manner as eastern Kentucky ... that is ... with a 'Let's just see what happens' attitude. The store was just a few miles north of the Tennessee state line. I'd aim generally toward Knoxville, about 100 miles away, and then perhaps toward Chattanooga.

Rain or shine, the Lambretta seemed to do its job whenever asked. Heading southward, there began appearing some dry spots on the road meaning rate of travel could be increased a bit. Morning was starting with a few cloud gaps allowing sunlight to leak through and fall to earth. With such a long wet night past, sunshine was welcome as I crossed the line into Tennessee heading toward the town of Oneida and from there, traveled eastward again, back across mountainous roads. Beautiful scenery on all sides. Had to reduce speed to avoid a group of deer. A few hours and a few breaks later, we eventually rejoined Route 25, an old friend. Got some fuel and some coffee in a place called Rocky Top. Was it a town or a village or just a settlement? Population about 1000. Fatigued, I was beginning to not trust my own driving and attention span. Not long after noon, near Clinton, not far from Rocky Top, I took a cabin for the night. Sign said "Small Cabin, clean, $1.25. Vacancy." Stopped, took a quick look. The sign was accurate. Very small, but clean, with a shower and hot water, sorely needed. Tucked way back into the trees, it was perfect. A luxury it was to strip off all the sticky clothing and get myself washed, hang up all the wet clothing, and immediately after, it was time for snoozing.

Four or five hours later, I shot up out of bed before I was awake. What the hell? My little cabin was bouncing up and down. Earthquake. Earthquake. I'd never been in one before. Not severe. But … just a minute … the place was still trembling, but too steady and too long for a quake, I guessed. Looking out the small window, and through the trees, the pulsing light of a train, and now the sound with it. A train was headed directly toward this cabin. To avoid disaster, either the train or the cabin had to change direction. It was the train that finally turned away, but not by much. It seemed that the space between the cabin and the moving train would allow perhaps a coat of paint, but not much more. Later, I took a closer look. The distance was less than six feet. Who builds a cabin within six feet of a railroad track? Strange, crazy, and funny. And loud as hell. I still had not ever been in an earthquake. Maybe I should look forward to it. Someday.

It was late afternoon. There was enough food in the trunk, though I'd have to do some grocery shopping tomorrow. Prepared a pot of coffee to brew itself uncooked for the morning. Decided to begin reading that book I had purchased from Alex. Was that two days ago? No, that was only one day past. Another quick soap and rinse and then some snacking and reading. And again, some snoozing.

Waking the next morning (there were no trains during the night), the two cups of cold brewed coffee helped me transition to daytime mode. The road atlas occupied me for a short time before one last shower was decided on. Then it was time pack up, vacate the cabin, and drive to Knoxville, about ten miles distant, where I'm sure they'd have some hot coffee, even on a Sunday morning.

The Lambretta took us into Knoxville in less than a half-hour. This was a good-sized city, about 100,000 people. A café offered a 99 cent breakfast

— an egg (prepared in any manner), toast, bacon, and coffee. Imagine starting a day with no pancakes, was it possible? This was a big adventure, I'd give it a whirl. Exciting, no? Ordered that breakfast (hold the bacon, please) and I survived. The coffee and refill were perfect. Decided I'd noodle around this city a bit during late morning. Started the scooter, got my dose of blue scooter exhaust and headed eastward ... arbitrarily. This was not a sleepy Southern town. It was a city, for sure. Driving this way and that, my feeling was this city had a certain liveliness to it. Noodled my way eastward and southward and dead ended near the Holston River or was it the Tennessee River? Stopped at a small park to watch the river and have a smoke. This Knoxville felt comfortable on first impression. I watched the river for a bit while two kayakers made their way. Next was a two-man canoe. Kayaks were good. Canoes were better. Just my preference.

Back at the scooter and ready to resume noodling when a beautifully customized 1951 Ford coupe parked in an adjoining parking spot. Driver was a young man, about 25. He got out of the car, looked at me and said nothing. As he was doing that another car pulled into the spot on the other side of the scooter. And this was a '49 Mercury coupe, also customized. I said to the Ford guy, "Man, that is one beautiful car. Did you do that chopping and channeling yourself? He paused, nodded yes, and asked "You know about that stuff?" I said I did, but had never attempted it myself, but I knew enough that this was excellent work he had done and mentioned that I had been in a hot rod club up in Connecticut a few years back. The Mercury had been chopped (the roof lowered) and looked as smooth as ice cream. Two more customs eased in and joined us. These four guys were looking at the scooter and started with the questions and I answered as fast as I could. Then I introduced myself and shook hands with all four. These guys would meet here just about every Sunday morning after taking their parents or grandparents to church. They would hang out for an hour or more and then drive back and pick up their people after services. Anyway they were intrigued by the scooter and the journey. One thing I found interesting was their question as to whether anyone had given me any crap about the beard. Not thus far, but I didn't know how long that would last. One of the four said he had a couple of distant cousins in Connecticut and he had been up there about five years ago in Middletown. I said you're kidding ... I know that town pretty well, had a lot of family there. He said he had been at one of their club meetings and there were guys from other towns, too. Like Waterbury and ... and I chimed in ... New Britain. His face lit up and I continued with "and the speaker that night was from Perfect Circle Piston Ring Company." He said "No shit, you're right, which town were you from?" I said "New Britain ... I was 16 years old and President of our club that year." Laughing, he said, "You guys were different, but suave in your own way. You were the ones with the quiet cars. Unbelievable. I told these guys about your cars. That they were so, so quiet, like a mouse", and he laughed softly. I said, "Yeah, we used to say "Quiet as a mouse pissing on a cotton ball. That was our 'thing' ... stealth ... and it made us 'different' than most other clubs. One of our guys had a souped-up Buick straight-eight with an engine so smooth one could lean against its fender and not know it was idling. It was quietest of all." We talked for nearly an hour and I admired their cars more. It was time for them to retrieve their people. Shook hands again with the four and they eased out of the parking lot. Small world.

Resumed my wanderings in Knoxville, now from east to west, mostly along Route 11, noticed a deli/market open for business and stopped to buy a few groceries for the next day or two. It was an OK place, not great, but adequate. It did have those PayDay candy bars, my most recently acquired addiction. Stashed the food in the trunk and went back to some serious noodling through town. Needed to stop for flashlight batteries soon.

Noodled my way along Route 11, westward through Knoxville and then southward, all the way to Athens, Tennessee, named after the Greek city/state (there is also a Corinth and a Sparta in the state). Just before Athens, a group of a dozen or more small craft displays were set up in a kind of impromptu fair. Time to take a break and look at stuff, not to buy stuff ... no room for stuff. There were displays of needlecraft, crochet, three woodcarvers, some food things. Watched the woodcarvers, all whittling away at one thing or another. They were set up adjacent to each other and appeared to be friends. One of the three was carving in a more sleek, modern style, while the others were doing their carving in what I might call 'hillbilly' style, very similar to what I had seen in the Ozarks a week or two ago. To the first carver I said "Afternoon, sir, can you tell me what type of wood these are carved from?" and I pointed to several that were grouped together on his table. He said hello and said they were carved from pignut hickory. I shook my head and said I had never heard of that, but it had to be a hardwood if it was hickory. He said it was about the most dense wood in these parts and picked up a stylized carving of a horse and handed it to me. It had more weight than one might expect. Looking at it carefully, I said the piece showed fine craftsmanship, and my compliments. He said "Well, thank you, sir." To the other two guys he said loudly "This fella noted the fine craftsmanship on that horse. He might be funny-looking (and he winked at me), but he's smart as hell and you two might just learn something." And he started laughing. After more peeking at this and that I waved goodbye, returned to the scooter, and putt-putted my way into the small town of Athens for some coffee and maybe some late lunch, it being mid-afternoon.

First, into a gas station for fuel and then to a small diner with an 'open' sign in neon. Closing time in one hour allowing time for a bowl of chicken noodle soup and a cup of coffee. Asked the waitress about camping spots. She suggested to drive east a few miles where the Cherokee tribe had several different campgrounds ... not far past Englewood. So I was right back into the Appalachians or were these just the foothills? The Appalachians are enjoyable ... scenic and varied, not vast sweeping vistas as in the west, but beautiful in their own, somewhat softer manner. About a dozen miles east of Englewood, a small campground in the Cherokee National Forest seemed a great place to spend an afternoon and evening. Small fireplaces, so I could brew hot coffee. So far I had greatly enjoyed not paying close attention to direction and just noodling around eastern Kentucky and Tennessee and would noodle my way toward Chattanooga the following day. Alone most of the time, my enjoyment came from observing, absorbing, admiring, and minding my own business. Set up camp (with time out for a PayDay bar), made some coffee, and did some reading while daylight was available, swatted a few mosquitos, put some detergent on my exposed skin. Before all the daylight was gone, I prepared my coffee fire for the morning.

No shower tonight, already had three washings in the last day. Don't want to overdo this cleanliness thing. We are taught that 'cleanliness is next to godliness'. So, my reasoning went, too much cleanliness might lead to godliness, and if that happened, it might turn into some deep-seated boringness. I'd rather die than have that happen. Best be careful of being 'too much' clean.

Very early in the morning I was awakened by shouting from two or three campsites away. Poked my head through the access of my tent and saw flames, a bunch of movement, heard more shouting, a few more flames appeared and then diminished amongst all the confusion. Finally, a flashlight lit up a small area. At least two people were moving about. In a short time, the campground was again quiet and dark. Back to some serious sleeping.

In this part of eastern Tennessee, morning comes pretty much on schedule and this morning was no exception. A full bladder dictated it was time to stir. Time to start the coffee fire, use the bathroom, brush teeth, that sort of thing. Time to return to the small fire, and sip some of my splendid cowboy coffee. After that, pack up camp and get on the road, noting the burnt corner of a tent, scene of last night's disturbance. How does a person set their own tent afire? Doing something stupid, I'm certain.

Noodling my way southward and westward, my 'maybe' goal was Cleveland, Tennessee, then possibly westward to Lynchburg (to take a tour of the Jack Daniel's Distillery), and then Chattanooga. Very little traffic in the warm morning. Topping a slight rise, I saw ahead of me a figure of a man waving his arms and then saw that he was in the middle of the road. I slowed, and slowed some more and glided to a stop. Before I could say anything, this young Negro guy was saying "Oh thank you, sir. Thank you for stopping. Please mister, could I please have a ride to the next town. It's about 6 miles. I'm supposed to be in court and I'm late already, and please etc." The guy had tears running down his cheeks and he clearly was desperate. I said "Sure, hop on, but this thing doesn't go very fast." And the poor guy was trying to thank me enough and was, I think, actually crying and saying "There was no one else I could ask." And, "Thank you so much, sir." And on and on. And I'm saying things like "It's OK. No problem. Don't worry about it. We'll be there soon. Everything will be all right." Just trying to get him to calm down a bit. The ten or twelve minutes seemed like that many years. We got very close to town and I said "Tell me where to stop, OK?" About four times he said, "Yessir, thank you sir." Finally he said, "Right over there, god bless you, and thank you, sir, thank you very much." As we were stopping and he was dismounting, I was saying "Good Luck." That's when a stone about the size of a golf ball hit the front tire of the scooter. Then there were several stones skittering across the road. My passenger was running toward a group of five or six teenagers (I guessed) throwing the stones. I caught a glimpse of him running between them toward a small white building that I supposed was a courthouse. The stones were coming faster and higher (the bastards were finding the range), one hitting my metal trunk box as I was pulling away as quickly as possible. One stone passed overhead as I headed away from that little town center. The speed limit was low and I was torn between breaking the speed law and getting the hell out of there or risking a speeding ticket by some half-assed legendary "southern sheriff" who might think that a negro guy and a white guy on the same scooter was a threat to world order. I went just a bit over the limit … that was my compromise. All this was absolutely insane and frightening as hell! After a short time, I took a smaller rural road, hoping no one would notice my change of route. Was I being followed or not? No idea. Went about four miles on that road and continued taking one turn after another, trying to confuse any possible pursuit by any of those goddamn redneck nitwits (may they roast in hell). My mind was cranking with all sorts of thoughts. First, my passenger … what kind of fear causes a man to run toward, not away from, a bunch of rock throwers? So my dark-skinned passenger had me as a white driver, or something like that and those dumbasses didn't like it. I remembered Stella's warning 'You're an observer, not a participant. You're a foreigner in your own country.' So today I was a participant and might yet pay a big price for it, but who wouldn't have helped this guy pleading and waving his arms in the middle of the road? I took one turn then the next, this way and that, with no regard to signs, just continued to try gain as much mileage as possible toward the south. No idea as to how much time was passing, but all of that time, I'm am so pissed off. Those sonsabitches should fry in Hades and so should their parents ... where the hell did they learn that shit? From the stupid adults in their lives, that's where. And why did no one stop them? And now I was a complete packaged tornado of helpless outrage and fear and curses and disgust. Those dirty bastards.

All these thoughts were ricocheting inside my skull as I was climbing a hill on a small road in a wooded area, and traveling at a much slower pace than I wanted. On the opposite side of this narrow, two-lane road were two cops carrying rifles or shotguns. Before my imagination could connect them to my dilemma, I saw about ten men with their ankles chained in a line. They were cleaning a drainage ditch on the far side of the road. I putt-putted on by, maybe 20 feet away, at far too slow a pace. The cops or deputies or guards kept a steady eye on me and the Lambretta. At the end of the line of men, another guy with a rifle or shotgun was stationed, also with a steady eye in my direction. This was a chain-gang! A real chain-gang ... the kind we sang about in elementary school ... 'workin' on the chain-gang, chain-gang, chain-gang, all the live-long day' kind of chain-gang. They still existed here in the US? This was 1960! First, I'm trying to escape a stone-throwing bunch of trash and now I'm crawling past a chain gang! This was supposed to be America, for Christ sake.

Took a few more roads, almost at random, but finally it was time to take a break, take a leak, time to calm down. Take a little side road a short distance and stop. And I did. Jesus, this was unbelievable! How long ago did all this start? One hour? Two hours? Less? More? Talk about a time warp. I took some water to cool my innards, and that was so keenly needed. Time to have a smoke, wind down, time to figure out just where the hell I was at the moment. I needed a reference point like a road sign to begin that process. Having paid zero attention to any road signs, only answering my guessing and instinct as to which direction to take to avoid my imagined, but possibly real pursuers (I imagined a pickup with two confederate flags on the sides and three jackasses in the cab, but it was just imagined, not real so far). Needed to find a highway sign after this rest stop. Fuel was next. Getting low. By this time, I felt reasonably safe there wouldn't be anyone in pursuit. Aside from knowing I was lost, all was well, considering.

Couldn't help thinking about my passenger, whose name would never be known to me. I hoped things went decently for him. Then … the chain-gang. Jesus, I'd have to think about that one. Break time was over and it was back on the road. I had just passed through two or three hamlets or groups of houses, though I couldn't recall any names. Started my beautiful little Lambretta and traveled only 2 or 3 miles before nearing a place called Crandall, Georgia. Vaguely remembered was a bridge crossing a river, but there was no remembering crossing a state line. So … surprise! I was now in the state of Georgia, in an agricultural area. Stop again, get out the atlas. If this was Crandall, then this had to be Route 411, and Route 411 had no idea how it had gotten me to travel along its roadway … all a mystery spawned by the stress of being a participant in a stoning … as the target, no less.

There was enough fuel in the tank of my friendly scooter Tony, to get me to Chatsworth for gasoline. A warm midday sun gave me a bit of a lift in spirits. Maybe crossing the state line did its psychological lifting also. The Jack Daniel's tour and Chattanooga had been bypassed in all the turmoil. I might return another time, but not on this trip. Atlanta, then became the next roosting place. It was less than a hundred miles away. I could approach it this afternoon, but first, time for a decent break. What an unbelievable morning! During this cross-country journey, I had sought some adventure, but these past few hours had been somewhat excessive. I'd have to have a serious talk with those fates that I didn't believe existed.

First things first. Fuel for Tony Lambretta. Checked it over visually for any damage. None. Next, fuel for me, in a small diner. Small order of pancakes, an order of spinach (recommended by Popeye), and coffee. Spinach seemed to make my teeth feel 'fuzzy' and I'd have to brush them outside after. Coffee and a refill and I was good to go. Outside, started up on one kick, putt-putted over to some trees, brushed my teeth and rinsed from the water bag. Had a smoke while consulting the atlas again and loosely plotting an afternoon in Georgia, hopefully a peaceful afternoon, since my turmoil tank was on overfill.

First, I'd have to stop at the minimarket across the road for the flashlight batteries, a bar of soap and more detergent. I was OK with shampoo and skin lotion for a while. I'd need to do laundry soon. Man alive, what a day! It would take approximately forever to calm down.

CHAPTER 52

AT LAST, ATLANTA

After the disturbing and tumultuous morning, the simplicity of ordinary and uneventful scootering was a welcome change. We were moving gently southward along Georgia's Route 411. My inclination was to find a campground somewhere near Atlanta, spend one night camping and then begin to experience that city, first by visiting a library for information. Then, maybe two or three days in town. Big city, Atlanta, the biggest I would encounter for a while, and probably the most progressive city in the southland. Mentally, I was in genuine need of some 'urban.' After an hour and a half of the most pleasant driving available, Route 411 decided it wanted to go west, but I preferred going farther south, getting closer to Atlanta and Lake Allatoona. From 411, I took Route 41 southward, through Cartersville and began searching for a campground. There were many choices all hoping to get business from the attraction of Lake Allatoona. Found an inexpensive place with clean bathrooms and shower rooms (I looked prior to paying for a space). After paying the small fee, I putt-putted into the campground area and picked a tentsite on the left side, away from the toilet/bathhouse building. Before setting up, I walked to a half dozen vacant sites and quickly gathered enough wood and charcoal leftovers to fuel my little coffee fire for this evening and tomorrow morning. Dropped that small fuel harvest next to my fireplace and then began to set up camp. Two or three tentsites farther in, was a young couple with a very fancy tent, with enough headroom for standing. Probably had a screen door and a picture window, too. Talk about luxury. All I needed was a good shower, after which I read for a short time, brewed a pot of coffee and consumed every delicious drop. Then setup for tomorrow morning's **coffee ritual**. The fancy tent folks were having quite an argument and few exchanges sounded fairly intense. He was a tall blonde guy, she was shorter with darker hair. That's all I knew at this distance.

As nighttime was making its way into the campground, I made a final run across the center open area toward the bathrooms. As I neared the little building, the woman of the spatting couple was leaving. I said "Hello" and she smiled without saying anything. At closer range, I could see she was a bit shorter than I was, a little on the plump side and quite pretty with chestnut-colored hair. After my return to my tent, my coffeepot and fire for morning sacraments had to be tended to. Too dark to read. While the couple continued their occasional arguing, I decided to just 'settle in' and think about the morning's craziness.

First, this chain-gang thing. My initial reaction was shock, much the way I reacted in Paris, Texas when I first witnessed segregation. But that had to be put aside if logical thinking was to prevail. I had to assume a few things: (1) these guys with ankle irons were jailed for some not-so-minor offense, and rightfully so, or maybe not. (I, of course, had no knowledge of how justified any of their situations might be). (2) Being outside the walls of a prison was probably better than being inside. (3) These chain-gang prisoners were getting some exercise and activity they might not ordinarily have been offered. Is that naïve? (4) Society, to some extent, was getting some useful work performed. (5) Maybe prisoners received extra pay or time credit for their work. So my question became, "How bad is a chain-gang situation compared to just being in a jail or prison cell?" No answers from me, that's for sure. Just questions.

The stoning or stone-throwing, whatever you might call it, was simply appalling. The half-wits sailing rocks at us or at me (I couldn't discern which, with only the briefest look at them) should have had their asses kicked. I had already cursed them and ranted enough for one day. Maybe tomorrow I'd try again to bring curses down upon their heads. Dimwitted numbskulls.

My thoughts were still churning with the day's events. Usually, taking an aspirin was helpful toward falling asleep. Tonight I would take two. There were a few mosquitos seeking a meal from me, and I thought it best to climb into the tent. If they didn't leave such a long-lasting, large, itchy welt on my hide, I might take greater risk.

In the darkness, I could hear a few sounds from surroundings. The clearest sound came from the couple who were still fussing at each other. The only real words I could distinguish were in her voice, saying rather loudly "The hell you will!" and "That is not going to happen!" Everything thing else, though loud at times, was unintelligible. My thought was that this was one tough lady. Wanted to read, but didn't enjoy reading by flashlight. Tomorrow evening I'd get a motel room somewhere closer to Atlanta itself.

In the middle of the night ... or was it early morning ... my bursting bladder woke me and I headed to the bath house. Yes, very early morning. Had already slept eight or nine hours. More than enough. Started the coffee, lit up a smoke, sat and waited for precious sounds of coffee on the make. The couple's tent to my left was lit up, and there were some indistinguishable words again being exchanged at a rapid pace and fairly high volume. My coffee was making those final delicious sounds and I started my 'count-to-100' coffee aging process. Now their tent was coming down and getting packed into the bed of their pickup truck. Other things were being tossed into it also. More angry sounding words. Some minutes later, truck doors are loudly slammed shut, and the truck's engine is revved up. Now the truck lurches forward, travels 50 feet and skids to a stop just past my campsite. Driver's door opens, cab lights up from the dome light, blond guy runs around the back of the pickup, opens the passenger door, pulls the woman out of the cab, sends her flying to the ground, runs to the back of the truck, pulls a suitcase out of the truck bed and throws it on the ground. I'm only beginning to react as he gets back into the driver's seat and takes off with wheels spinning, showering the woman with dirt and gravel, and exits the campground, disappearing into a still dark morning. Oh, Christ Almighty, what's happening now? What is the matter with you people?

Moving quickly to the woman, who is now sitting in the dirt, crying and holding her forehead, I take her arm gently and say, "Miss, let's just go easy. Let's see if you can stand up." And slowly, she did, with me steadying her. "OK, now come over to my fire, so I can see you," and I lead her to one of the little stone benches near my fireplace. "Please just sit still and let me get my flashlight." I got it, told her to close her eyes, and looked at the scrape and bump on her forehead. Not too bad. Told her to hold still while I rigged a cool compress. Took my last clean t-shirt, poured some water from my waterbag, placed the wet shirt against her forehead, and took her hand and pressed it in place. "You're OK. Now, just rest for a minute or two. Take some deep breaths, exhale slowly and try to be calm and wind down. I'll go get your suitcase out of the roadway." (I'm expecting the idiot driver to return at any moment). Sitting on the other stone bench, facing her with our knees almost touching, I reached up, took her hand from the compress, took it from her forehead, a small but noticeable 'egg' had appeared. Using my t-shirt, I gently wiped some of the dirt from her face. "Let's rinse your hands" and I got the water bag and trickled some water into her hands. One hand had a sizable abrasion, but not deep or serious. Do you drink coffee? She said yes, I gave her my cup, saying be careful it's hot. Do you take aspirin? She said yes. You should take at least one right now. I reached into my jacket and got the tiny bottle and gave her two. She returned one of them. I asked her to stand up and see if there are any other injuries. Ankles, knees, wrists, etc. She was OK, she thought. Now, sit down again and rest while I have a cup of coffee and do some thinking.

I finished her coffee and refilled with more hot coffee and sipped that for a minute or two, then drank most of it. Handed the cup back to her and said she could finish it – that I had only one cup. I asked for her name. Marie. The guy's name? Arnold. As I clean up this campsite, tell me about this argument ... not all the details, just generally. And she did.

They had just gotten engaged to be married. They had been heading to Nashville. And then back to the Atlanta airport in a few days. There was an argument over a past girl friend of his. He was moody sometimes and had a bad temper. She provided more details, but that was the core of it. Meanwhile, I was packing up camp. The tarp was folded and when I collapsed the tent, and rolled it up, she looked surprised. She said quietly "What should I do now?" So I sat on the bench again and took her hands in mine and said quite slowly. "Listen to me very carefully. You are OK physically. The bump on your head might hurt but it's minor and your eyes seem to be operating normally. So my best guess is that you are OK. Now you have a choice to make, more important than you might realize. I, personally, am not going to wait around for your boyfriend to return. In about fifteen minutes, I am leaving this campground and going to a café for more coffee and a little breakfast, and then I'm planning to spend two or three days in Atlanta, a place I have never been before. So it is your choice right now, this morning, in the next few minutes ... you can either stay here waiting for that piece of garbage to return and collect you or you can get on this scooter and have breakfast with me and decide what to do from there. By the way, my name is Rosano." She said "Arnold has a temper, but he's not garbage." I answered her. "Anyone who would do that to you is a piece of garbage. He doesn't really give a damn about you. His moodiness will increase and his temper will only grow worse. Don't think you can charm him and make it any better. Don't waste your life with that jackass. Whatever your decision, I'll be leaving in a few minutes." I walked across to the bath house, freshened the water bag, and purposely took a bit of time returning to the fireplace. As I approached and neared the scooter, Marie asked if it could carry both of us and the suitcase. I said, "Let me introduce you to Tony Lambretta. This will be awkward at first, when we have decent light, I'll rearrange things." I tied some cording onto the suitcase, told her to get onto the Lambretta seat, then handed her the suitcase, telling her to put her arms through the two loops and when I get on, hold onto me with her hands. The suitcase, fortunately, was only medium-sized. The whole deal was a little cumbersome, but functional ... OK for the short term anyway.

It took a few minutes to get back to Route 41 and from there we soon made it to a café. Parking out front, I locked up, grabbed the suitcase and we went inside. It was early enough and the place was just opening. As we entered, a waitress came over to us and I pressed a dollar into her hand and said "Marie, here, fell into the dirt and hit her head. Would you help her get cleaned up a little more, like get the dirt out of her ear, things like that?" The waitress said, "C'mon Honey, take your suitcase, we'll use the restroom that I use. Not the public one." I, on the other hand, used the public one. Eight or ten minutes later, they reappeared. Marie looked much better. Clean shirt. Clean pants. Clean face. We sat at a small booth. The same waitress took our order and we settled down to some serious coffee. With a short stack of pancakes for me. And toast for Marie. We ate quietly, not much talking. I wanted to smoke and asked her if it was OK with her. She nodded yes.

I said she might never see Arnold again. She thought she probably would see him, because she had his wallet and his money. She found them in the suitcase when the waitress helped her clean up. Arnold and she had matching suitcases and while they were arguing he had angrily thrown his wallet into her suitcase. I laughed and said it served him right, that shtik drek. He thought he was leaving you stranded.

When our waitress came over to refill coffee cups, I asked her the whereabouts of the nearest Greyhound Bus station. She started to explain, but Marie interrupted and said she knew where it was. As the waitress left, Marie asked me about the Greyhound Station. I said they usually had lockers where she could stash her suitcase while she figured out what she would be doing. Then I asked how she knew the Greyhound location. She said she had lived in Atlanta for almost a year, a few years ago. I asked where she was from originally, since she had no southern accent. San Francisco. And Arnold? Minnesota.

We drank coffee and talked for a half hour. Waitress very attentive with the coffeepot. Marie asked what I would be doing. First, I would like to go to the library so I could get information on what I might look for in Atlanta. Second, I needed to do my laundry today since these were my last clean clothes and I had already slept in them. Third, it was time to get a modest motel room for these two or three nights. Marie looked at me and tears started to form and then run down her cheeks. She said, "It's good that you know exactly what you're doing, but I have no idea of what I should do now? No idea at all. Where should I go? How do I get Arnold's wallet back to him without having a big scene. I'm really lost and I'm really scared." I stopped her and said "Listen to me. OK? No reason to panic. We are going to solve one of these problems right now. Where is Arnold's wallet? In your purse? Good. Take it out and open it. Money in there? A lot. Good. Take the money out of the wallet and put it in one of your pockets. Now, put the wallet back in your purse. How far is the Greyhound station? A few miles. Good. We can go there and stash your suitcase. Look for a post office box on the way and dump the wallet into the mailbox. The post office will take it to the address on his driver's license, but more important, you're done with it. You have to fix yourself now, and to hell with Arnold. What friends do you have here in Atlanta?" She answered she had none at the moment, but her closest friend, Ellen was flying in from England to Atlanta this Friday late afternoon. She could stay with her friend, starting Friday night. They were closer than sisters. "OK, that's a good start. That's three days from now and …" She interrupted me … "Rosano, let's stash my suitcase, but could I just stay with you for a few hours, for part of a day? Could you stand it for that long?" And she was a bit of a wreck, choking up, and about to cry again. I nodded and said, "Sure, no problem." And the waitress was approaching without being asked, and I asked for the bill, and that sweet woman said "Honey, you paid for breakfast the minute you walked through the door. It's taken care of." I protested a bit as she said gently "you just shush." So I said "C'mon Marie, let's go. Somehow this will all work out." Marie gathered her things, including the suitcase and started to the door. I put a dollar under the coffee cup, and took the suitcase from Marie. With Marie outside, the waitress said to me softly, "I know you guys just met, but take of that girl, she needs big help right now." I told her I'd do my best. Out in the parking lot, I said I wanted to do a better job with the suitcase. That took five minutes or so. "OK, Marie, the suitcase is secure. You don't have to hold it, but you still have to hold onto me." She said, "Rosano, we're still more than 20 miles from the center of Atlanta, with Marietta about halfway. How close do you want to get?" I answered that I really didn't know. What was reasonable? Marie said, "Rosano, would you do me a favor? Instead of going to the Greyhound station, could we just go to a good motel, at my expense? No it'll be Arnold's treat. I just don't want to be alone right now. God, I never thought I'd ask a stranger such a thing." Maybe I paused a bit too long, but I said "OK, but look for a mailbox on the way and since I don't know exactly where we're headed, you have to learn these hand signals." And I quickly instructed her on the 'left, right, slow down, point, and stop' signals. "See if we can find a place with a laundry or near a laundry, OK?" She said "OK" and gave me an almost hug, a thank you, and got onto the scooter. Started up and I could see the waitress watching through the window. I waved and gave her a "thumbs up." And off we went.

And I was thinking about and talking aloud to my dear friend, the Princess. Yeah, Stella, I know … just be an observer, not a participant. But Princess, this is not a 'southern' thing or a 'redneck' thing, this is just a 'people' thing. I still think of you sometimes. Where are you now? Chicago? Did you enjoy New York? Did you see 'Gypsy' and 'Fiorello'? Did you find any good cookies?

Ten minutes of scootering later, Marie signaled a 'right' and then pointed to a drive-by mail box and closed her fist. I stopped within reach of the opening and she shoved the wallet into the hopper and made sure it had dropped in. Driving through traffic, a half-hour later, she pointed to a hotel/motel and gave the closed fist 'stop' signal. She said "Give me a minute to see what this is like and she dismounted from the scooter." Less than ten minutes later, she was back, saying, "we'll be on the ground floor ... no public laundry area, but they'll do a load of laundry for us with one hour service. Breakfast room open 'till noon. Want to do it? I said yes, sounded OK. She told me to drive around and park near #16. Which I did. Semi-luxurious room, two double beds. She said "Is this OK?" I said it was far more luxury than I was accustomed to, but it would be just ducky.

Next she asked, should we have them do our laundry now? That would be great. So I did my usual thing and put everything in my clothing bag except one shirt and my pants. She added a few things from her suitcase, including the dirt-stained clothing from this morning's struggle. She said she'd take this down to the laundry and they would deliver back to the room in one hour. Tell them to wash the bag too, OK?

When Marie returned to the room, I suggested we visit the breakfast room, have some more coffee and maybe another bite to eat and we'll talk more. And we talked a great deal. She finally agreed that Arnold really was a jackass and she hoped she would not see him again. And Rosano what is 'stickdrick'? I said "Close, but it's 'shtik drek' and roll the 'r' when you say it. It's means 'shit head' in Yiddish." She laughed with surprise and asked if I was Jewish. I said no, but I was a sympathizer and admirer. I was, in fact, a liberated and recovering Roman Catholic from Italian parents. When she asked what we might do this afternoon, I said I would like to go to a few art galleries, hopefully with modern art. It would also get her mind off her troubles. First she said she wanted to call her mother in California, where her friend Ellen would be calling. They could relay messages through her Mom. OK. When the laundry comes back, we'll go out for the afternoon.

NOTE TO READERS: Marie and I spent an excellent and busy afternoon together, first buying a helmet for her. Then we visited a few galleries, went to a pizza place (Arnold's treat again) where I ate a half-acre of decent pizza. She had warned her mother about possible calls from Arnold and cautioned her not to reveal her location. We went back to the room as the sun set. We showered individually. There was no magic happening with the two of us ... strangers thrown together by circumstances. She did know Atlanta. That was an enormous asset for my purposes. In exchange, I was an available stabilizing element in her present world of turmoil. Without having a signed contract, that would be the exchange between us for days following ... her knowledge of Atlanta and, believe it or not, my stability. END NOTE.

We had two beds. In some of our conversation, she had referred to current TV shows. I suggested she take the bed closest to the television. She did. After more conversation, I began reading in my book, while she clicked the TV on. We were both exhausted and I started nodding off. My book fell out of my hands once or twice. "Marie, I'm done for the day. Time for sleeping." Got up for my bathroom break, brushed teeth, and returned to bed. Stripped and got under the covers. She came over to me, gave me a little hug, said she was just as tired. Took her turn in the bathroom, returned dressed in little pajamas and got into her bed and then, across the divide separating the two beds, thanked me for not pushing myself on her. Responding, I said if there was any 'action' with the two of us, she would have to initiate it ... I never forced myself onto a woman. She said, "Rosano, you're a good guy. Thanks for staying with me. I'm such a disaster. And I've used you as my safety net. Thanks." Well, I was thinking ... all that is nice and noble, but I was 21 years old, horny as hell, with a generously built, fine-looking sexpot of a nearly naked lady just a few feet away. But she had had enough mental disruption for one day and I did somehow manage to get into doze mode. Two hours (my guess) later, she was naked and in my bed, pushing her bottom against me and playing petting games. And we consummated her non-marriage to Jackass Arnold a few times before morning ... all still nice and noble. And that sort of thing happened for the next few days. Late start each morning. Go see and experience a good deal of Atlanta, then back to the room, rest a bit and rut around as if each day were the last day on earth.

Atlanta. What a mixture! For sure it was the Deep South, but not sleepy Deep South. There was racial tension at every turn it seemed, but there was a vibrancy of growth in the air as well. On our second morning, Marie and I had spent about two hours in the public library, (though I didn't think Marie was nearly as mesmerized by libraries as I was), and in that time, I looked through newspaper headlines and a few articles from three and four years back to get a more accurate understanding of recent happenings. There had been lunch counter 'sit-ins' just a few months before my visit. A federal court (one of them) had ended legal segregation of public transportation just 18 months before. The City of Atlanta had approved desegregating public schools just five or six months before, but that process hadn't yet begun. Martin Luther King was active as a pastor of Ebenezer Baptist Church. The NAACP was everywhere doing its work in a variety of ways. Aside from, or in spite of all this racial struggle, Atlanta seemed to have part of its soul which said "no matter the struggle, there will be progress." This was my interpretation, my bone marrow feeling ... that this was a far more progressive place than East Texas, for example, and more 'alive' than Louisiana. Atlanta had so many different businesses, many of them new. So many different cultural influences, not just the two major blocs. They were all going to have to adjust to changes and it seemed, change was being accepted, often reluctantly, but it was happening.

Doing some 'noodling' around town, we visited Georgia Tech, which had been started way back in 1885, but allowed women to enroll just eight years before, in 1952. Did segregation apply to females of all colors or just the darker-skinned ones? The population of Atlanta certainly was not 'one big happy family.' That would take another century or two. But it did seem to be one big 'painfully adjusting' group. And that's far better than totally entrenched groups. One important factor which few people discussed was that separate bathrooms, separate drinking fountains, etc, were an economic burden. Separate bus systems were unsustainable. But if we're all paying the same price for seats, then we should be able to choose any bus seat not occupied. Atlanta seemed up to the challenge, I was guessing and hoping. So ... these were my impressions, my feelings ... based on atmospheric pressure? On the pollen count? I had no idea if my feelings were accurate or not ... I was merely observing, not measuring.

At Marie's suggestion, we visited a deli and purchased enough food for an excellent picnic lunch (Arnold the Jackass was still picking up the tab) and putt-putted over to Stone Mountain. About 10 miles north and east of us. Picture a mushroom pushing its way up through the earth. That's Stone Mountain, but the head of the 'mushroom' is 800 feet high and five times as wide and made of granite. A truly impressive formation geologically. On the north face we could see the world's largest bas-relief sculpture, approximately one full acre (equal to about two football fields) of carved granite, and to my knowledge it still was not completed. Carved into the mountain are the images of Jefferson David, President of the Confederacy, and the two famous generals, Robert E. Lee and Stonewall Jackson, all three on horseback. Bas-relief is an art term which I translate as 'slightly elevated' meaning that material surrounding the images is removed, but not deeply carved. The beginning sculptor, Gutzon Borglum, (who later in life began work on Mount Rushmore) began the Stone Mountain project in 1916. Here it was, almost a half-century later and not quite completed. A staggering-sized artistic project.

We set out the tarp and had lunch far enough away to be able to see the entire sculpture, and talked briefly about the desegregation movements across the country. Marie thought the Negroes should probably go slower. I said the Civil War was supposed to 'free' them and that was almost 100 years before. How much slower should they go? She said she hadn't thought of it that way, but I made sense.

During lunch I suggested that she have Arnold the Jackass buy her a new light-weight collapsible clothing bag since hers had probably been scratched when he threw it to the ground. She asked what she should do with the one she had, which was quite expensive. I suggested she offer it to the maid at the hotel, who could probably use a good quality suitcase and besides, it matched Arnold's and she had to forget about him. On the way back to the hotel, we bought a clothing bag at the same sports shop where Arnold had treated her to a helmet for scootering with Rosano. Jackass Arnold was turning into an OK guy as he funded everything we were doing. On the way back, I couldn't stop thinking about the sculpture on Stone Mountain.

Artistically, I couldn't judge whether it was "good art' or not. Who could be the judge of that? Certainly not me. But it was certainly big ... I was qualified enough to say that. And just the mechanics of carving something so large that it couldn't been seen while one worked on it was another sign as to how clever this human species could be at times. It was impossible for me to imagine jackhammering on Robert E. Lee's nostril and not being able to truly see what the effect was.

This huge stone carving was going to be a granite can of worms ... forever was my guess. The fact that Ku Klux Klan seemed to regard it as their special place didn't help that situation at all. Knowing nothing about the maneuverings, political and social, and the funding to get this thing carved, I could indeed guess that the substantial Negro population of Atlanta would eventually have some say in what ultimately happened to Stone Mountain. In my mind, the desegregation move would inevitably succeed, especially with the US Federal Government exerting their slow but powerful push in that direction. When the dark-skinned population started using their votes, ballots and dollars, there would be changes. Stone Mountain would represent a constant insult to Non-Southerners as well. The Southern Whites, on the other hand, seemed to treasure the symbols of the failed Confederacy beyond any reasonableness. But that observation was made by my mind, which had grown up in New England. This would be, I felt, a long tough road for both sides, and for both sides, kind of sad.

During our days together, while good old Jackass Arnold had picked up the tab, Marie had given me an excellent tour of Atlanta. Can't ask for more than that. Our bodily contact sessions were a substantial added bonus. During those days, I tried to instill a sense of worth in Marie and more important, a sense of self-completeness and independence, judging that she relied too much on being 'part of a couple.' A number of times, I said "No matter whom you are with, no matter whom you might marry, you are always an individual. You might be part of a 'team' but you should always be aware that you're still an individual." There would be no knowing if I succeeded, or made any progress at all. She had stayed in touch with her friend Ellen, by phoning her mom in California every afternoon, relaying messages, and talking for a few minutes. Friday morning, our last day together, we had a small breakfast and a fun frolic back at our room. Took a scooter ride later. She thought I might like the Atlanta History Center. And I did find it interesting. Late in the afternoon, as we showered together, she asked "One more time, Rosano? You won't have to use any effort at all. Just lie down and look pretty." I said she was asking the impossible, but I would give it my best to look pretty. After, we showered once more. As we dressed, she said she would pack all her things, carry her new lightweight bag to an excellent Italian restaurant where we could have dinner, say goodbye and she would then take a cab to the airport to meet her friend Ellen. Marie got slightly tipsy on the wine while I took only a taste. Waiting outside the restaurant for her taxi, our goodbyes were casual, friendly, and matter-of-fact ... not at all emotional and with 'thank you' back and forth. When the cab arrived we had a last embrace, and went our separate ways. Returning to the room, opening the road atlas, I looked at the circle that represented Jacksonville, Florida, perhaps my next landing spot, though one could never tell.

    Atlanta had been an excellent choice.

CHAPTER 53

DEEPER INTO THE SOUTHLAND

Saturday morning, waking early. Some rainfall during the night, a little more this morning, but skies were clearing. Breakfast room, precious coffee, ate heartily, no hurry to leave the hotel, especially with the scattered rain. Thought a bit about Marie and hoped she had met her friend at the airport and that all was well. There was no emotional investment, however. We had been convenient for each other and pretty decent entertainment for each other as well, but that was all. Back to the room, I gathered laundry, went to the hallway, found one of the hotel maids starting on an adjacent room and asked if this laundry could be done this morning. She said, in one hour she'd knock on my door carrying cleaned clothes. I settled in, finished reading that wonderful little book 'The Soul of The White Ant' and would leave it for another person. After the laundry arrived, I packed as much as possible, pillaged the breakfast room once more, returned to the room, showered one last time and made ready to leave. Marie had left a generous tip for the maid. I had seen postcards at the front desk and would drop off keys, write a few cards, and be on my way. But, on the way out of town, there was one more critical stop to make ... a new and used book store, which we had passed two or three times in previous days. Each time we passed it, the scooter would, despite my efforts, lean in that direction.

Since there was no urgency to leave Atlanta, I spent some time browsing, eventually selecting two books ... 'The Fountainhead' by Ayn Rand, and a book I had intended to read a year or two before ... 'Guadalcanal Diary' by Richard Tregaskis. He had been a war correspondent with the US Marine Corps during the battle for that island in 1942 and 1943. I had read perhaps ten percent of this true story and gotten side-tracked. Since my intent was to learn more about World War II, this copy was a welcome find. Evidently, this book had won some notable recognition and was required reading for new Marine officers. Wasn't sure of that, however. The book would be with me on the next leg southward toward Florida.

Macon, Georgia, about 100 miles south of Atlanta, would be the next major town on this trip. If a map of Georgia were pasted on a clock face with Macon as its center, and a line drawn from 8:00 o'clock (where the town of Columbus, Georgia was on the border with Alabama) to 2:00 o'clock (where the town of Augusta was on the border with South Carolina), that line would closely approximate a line called The Fall Line. I had read about this when Marie and I had spent that little time in the library. The Fall Line is where the foothills area of the Appalachians meets the much flatter terrain of the coastal plain. Macon was in a transition zone with hills on its north side and flat lands on the south side of town.

Leaving Atlanta, Route 41 would take us to Macon in three hours, that is, if no diversions presented themselves along the way. Three hours or three days, either was OK with me. Three days at a leisurely pace would get the Lambretta and me to Jacksonville, Florida. At this time in my journey, I was not deeply interested in exploring Florida, but felt compelled to set foot there for an hour at least, if for no other reason, to say I had done it. After Jacksonville, it would be approximately 1000 miles up through the coastal states to Connecticut to end this zig-zag trek across the US. Rain permitting, I had decided to camp each night until reaching Florida, conserving my money. Despite having more than enough money from my dear friend Stella, I wanted to make the journey with the original $400.00+. That seemed reasonably doable, especially since the three women I had been 'involved with' during my trip had footed much of the bill during our times together. Camping would be OK as long as there were showers available in the various campgrounds. On starting this trip, the thought of taking small jobs here and there across the country was in my mind, and it might have been necessary, except for the good fortune of the ladies' companionship and contributions. I'd been a very lucky man so far.

Driving deeper into the South, though determined to do so, I did not feel socially comfortable, and had pretty much resolved myself to being alone for the duration of travels in the South. The segregation thing had affected me far more than anticipated. Inquisitive looks from people encountered were noticeable and a bit unnerving. Until I looked in a mirror, I would forget that I was darker-skinned from the sun, and bearded. People seemed unsure as to how to react ... was I part of the white group or not? Well, screw 'em, if they didn't have the balls to ask, they could just continue guessing. For three days, driving southward through Georgia, being an observer, I was certainly not a participant ... except for the coffee stops and the refueling stops, where I was cheerful and polite, but did not initiate, invite, or encourage conversation ... in contrast to my natural inclination.

The coastal plains were one of nature's biological stewpots. While bird life was often visible and remarkably beautiful, who knew what lurked in these rivers, below the surface in swamps and wetlands. Camped a few miles south of Macon and the following night a few miles north of Valdosta, always keeping to myself, doing a fair amount of reading in late afternoon and evening. It had been more than two hundred uneventful miles of farmland, small towns, woods, swamps, and small rivers ... a mixed bag, for sure.

Closing my book and before getting into my tent in a campground north of Valdosta, I observed a bobcat observing me. Beautiful creature, perhaps not quite as yellow in coloring as bobcats in Arizona and maybe their ears were slightly longer or more pointed. The cat and I watched each other for some time in the fading light and then it was gone.

Waking, bathrooming, making and drinking coffee, and packing camp were all routine by now and there seemed to be some comfort in that routine. This afternoon, most likely, Jacksonville would see us and I would find an inexpensive motel room for a night or two. Route 41 avoided the town of Valdosta. Tony Lambretta and I would do the same. A faded tourist pamphlet had pointed out the Elk's Lodge as a 'Place To See' in the town ... not a good indication of an 'action' place. Route 84 intersected with 41 and headed east 50 miles through half a dozen small towns before entering a town called Waycross. Then I would take Route 23 southeastward, giving me a look at Okefenokee swamplands. That was the nebulous plan, always subject to change, but how could anyone pass up a chance to see a place called Okefenokee? Finished my coffee, rinsed the pot, did final packing, started up the faithful scooter, got my morning fix of blue two-stroke exhaust, and began making my way back to 41 to circumvent Valdosta.

Off to the side of this narrow two-lane rural road, just a mile after leaving the campground, I spotted two black bears, one larger than the other. The larger looked up and of course, I tried to shrink away from all the disastrous possibilities, and kept the throttle to 'fully on, let's get the hell out of here' setting. How fast can a black bear run? Well, if they can catch a deer, they would have little trouble catching me and could probably do so without breathing too hard. Damn, I truly was vulnerable. If a bear visited the tent at night, for example, I would be like a tamale prewrapped in fabric. Yummy, mmm, good. There was some relief in reaching the main highway, where there was more traffic. Took 84 Route eastward and looked for a café with coffee and pancakes, griddle cakes, flapjacks, or whatever they were called in this area. Needed scooter fuel, too.

The day was warm and steamy and the area was certainly fertile for growing things, and growing things were everywhere. Crops of all descriptions, many I didn't recognize, some I could. Every speck of dirt had at least five things growing in it. With all this greenery competing for its time in the sun, there was one important scarcity that had become increasingly noticeable to me ... the colors maroon, violet, the darker magentas, and the purples. They were not to be had in landscape or sky. No purple layers of rock, no purple-smeared cloudscapes. The group of purple colors had always been my favorite, and seemed entirely absent. A simplified definition of purple is a range of hues between red and blue. For centuries, purple was the rarest and usually the most expensive coloring that mankind could obtain ... from plants, from rocks, from seashells, etc., and came to represent luxury and royalty. Why did I like purple? Perhaps because purple has elements of both cool and warm. To me, for some reason, purple seems to have a wider selection of variations ... lighter shades looking playful, floral, and frolicsome, while darker shades seem more dignified, more intellectual, more solidly founded, and more noble. Scientifically, of course, all that doesn't make sense. These are some of the profound thoughts which ran through my mind while purring along at 40 miles an hour.

    Two or three miles west of a town called Waycross, on the south side of Route 84, rested hundreds and hundreds of railroad cars of various descriptions, flat cars, tank cars, etc., on perhaps two or three dozen sets of track. This was where trains were assembled or changed and reassembled for various railroad routes. Two or three miles long, it seemed enormous far beyond that. Is this called a marshalling yard? That was the term rattling around in my head. Waycross, about 20,000 population, was at the northernmost reaches of Okefenokee Swamp. I'd stop for coffee and pie and to ask a few questions about it, referred to as a 'blackwater' swamp, which meant that decaying wood from the forest it occupied gave a dark coloration to its waters, a dark coffee or mahogany coloration. Okefenokee is almost a half million acres in size and extends 80 miles or more from this town southward and across the Florida state line. In a small diner, I asked about getting a good look at the swamp without having to take one of the airboat rides or guided tours. The guy next to me at the counter suggested I drive about 15 miles south along Route 23 to a place called Racepond. There would be some small side roads, on my right, leading to the swamp. But, he cautioned, be careful, don't try to get too close. The alligators love having tourists for lunch. Good word play, and I thanked him.

    Route 23 was, in fact, the road I had chosen to Jacksonville, Florida about 85 miles southeast of Waycross. So Route 23 it would be. Had a smoke at the diner, said my 'goodbyes' and 30 minutes later, I was at that place called Racepond, taking a little side road toward Okefenokee, then going onto a road called Swamp Perimeter Road, which I would trust as being accurately named. Not too many feet away are two alligators, of approximately equal size. One appears to chewing on the other's head. Was this a feast or was it foreplay? There are about eight 'gators' in view. How many more hidden? My eyes, not being trained for swamp duty, didn't pick up signs of other gators, others which might be hidden. All of this seemed in strong contrast to the desert environment ... this idea of many critters being hidden right under one's gaze. A much greater percentage of desert creatures could be easily seen, even with their clever camouflage techniques. Keeping my distance, I could only guess this swamp would be heaven to botanists, swampologists, herpetologists, murkymologists, actually 'ists' of almost any kind. Most likely, this swamp was teeming with life in every biological niche. From that standpoint, Okefenokee was a phenomenal place. Watching wading birds held my attention for nearly an hour. Had a smoke, field stripped it, and had a drink of water from my water bag. Onto the scooter, faithful old friend, and on to Jacksonville, about two hours in the distance.

Traveling south about 20 miles put us on the state borderline separating Georgia and Florida and by crossing a bridge across the St Mary's River, we had reached Florida, a mini goal of sorts. Continuing on Route 23 would take me into Jacksonville's center ... that much I knew. We reached the northern suburbs of the city. Time to take a break, drink some water, have a smoke, and consult my trusty road atlas. If I continued, I would eventually cross St. John's River and be in some area called Southbank. Once there, I should look for signs to Atlantic Beach, Neptune Beach, Jacksonville Beach, or Ponte Vedra Beach ... I didn't know of differences between them, if any. That would put Tony Lambretta and me at the seashore ... the Atlantic Ocean. Now I was gripped by an urge to see true ocean. Sometimes cattle (in the old western movies and maybe in real life) would stampede to get to water. Suddenly, that's close to what I felt about getting to the ocean.

A hot afternoon in the summer in Florida was probably not the most popular time and place in the world at the moment, but the lure of an ocean was strong. Road traffic was moderate. In some manner (road signage was confusing or missing, don't know which is worse) I found a bridge crossing the river and made my way to Southbank. In less than an hour, my feet were enjoying sand, sun, and salt water of Neptune Beach. The scooter and helmet were locked up to a power pole. My jacket, shirt, tee shirt, boots and socks were cooking on the sand and I was sloshing in water half-way to my knees and it was a growing and glowing euphoria. Laughing at myself, and surprised for being so excited, I splashed around and was hugely content. I had discovered another planet. This was water that moved around and made bubbles and waves and noise. So much better than murky, silent, nearly stagnant stuff I'd been seeing far too much of. And my eyes could see into the water and if I aimed higher I could view a horizon many miles away. So welcome was this change with vision not constantly interrupted by a wall of greenery. The Connecticut in me celebrated a return to the ocean while the Arizona savored a wide expanse of sky and huge white clouds as visual expressions. Magnificent.

Sat on the sandy beach next to my stuff for some time thoroughly enjoying doing nothing. Temporarily at least, I couldn't get enough of nothing. With my back to the sun, I could see my shadow getting longer and thought it best to get dressed and find a place to stay for the night ... much easier a task in daylight than in darkness. On the way in, there had been some pretty rough neighborhoods toward the northwest, so I wouldn't head in that direction. On with my socks and boots and stood up to do the rest when I was almost immediately on my butt again, having been knocked on the head by something. Trying like hell to regain my footing and my thinking, and suddenly three people were surrounding me and reaching for me ... and a male voice, from a great distance, was saying, "Oh, so sorry Mister, it was an accident, oh shit! Beth, get a cloth. My apologies. My apologies. Marge, get his t-shirt and wet it. We'll buy him a new one. Goddamn, I'm so sorry ... " And it went on and on as I regained my senses, and the voice got closer, and Beth or Marge was dabbing at my forehead and I could see that my t-shirt was pink, no, it was more than pink.

In time, I began thinking almost normally, I took Beth's or Marge's hand with the shirt and pressed it against my forehead saying, "No more dabbing, just push." And she did. Another minute or two, I lifted her hand away and asked "Has it stopped?" She answered, "Almost", and pressed again. Another few minutes. I lifted her hand once more and she nodded and said "It's stopped."

The three had stayed with me, and were making sure I was OK. I asked what had happened. He said they were just being stupid and using a pie pan as a Frisbee, an old-fashioned steel pie pan, not an aluminum type. Wind had caught it, and here we were. And he started with apologies again and I waved him off. We talked as our shadows grew longer. Beth or Marge asked where I lived. I answered Tucson, Arizona. She said no, where was I staying in Jacksonville. I said I hadn't found a place for the evening, but I was just about to seek one out when someone mugged me and stole my shirt. That lame little joke seemed to relieve the three of them. Finally, the guy said his name was Richard, and did I want to stay at the commune with them? That was a new one for me ... the commune? What was I driving and was I OK to drive? I thought I was and mentioned the scooter. He said their house was about a dozen miles from here. They were on bicycles and could I just follow them home? That would be great. They walked me back to the scooter and said to wait right there. They'd come by and I could follow. Good. My head was hurting a little, but I was OK and slowly I putted along behind their cycles, following them to a house in an area called San Marco. Nice place with a garage where I could lock up the scooter. Quite an introduction to Florida … no?

CHAPTER 54

THE COMMUNE

Jacksonville, Florida had become the 80% mark of my journey, the end of the fourth leg of five ... first: from Tucson, Arizona to Denver, Colorado, second: (unplanned and spur-of-the-moment) from Denver to New Orleans, third: from New Orleans to Chicago, and now, I had just completed the fourth ... from Chicago to Florida. The final leg would be from Jacksonville, Florida to New England, another 1000 miles or more.

The three of them ... Beth, Marge, and Richard were very attentive, but there really was not much to be done. I had a bump on my forehead, with a cut across the middle of it, but I was OK except for a sharp headache. Was there anything they could get me? I asked about the possibility of a cup of black coffee. Beth or Marge said she knew how to make coffee and would get some started right now. So now I said I had an important question, which of you is Marge and which is Beth? After it was explained, I said tell me about yourselves and then about your 'commune.' I would just sit quietly and listen. They were all 18 years old and all were students at Jacksonville University (which had just been upgraded from Jr. College) in a summer study program. The commune was comprised of 20 students sharing this fairly large house and they all paid into a common rent and food kitty. Right now, during summer, there were only six or seven people, but everyone had to 'kick into the kitty' no matter where they might have gone for the summer. They tried to have a balance of freshmen, sophomores, etc. so the commune could continue indefinitely at twenty people (they always had applicants waiting for a vacant spot). Richard said maybe we should get some pizza for supper and the girls agreed as long as the wounded guy agreed. I nodded yes. Richard asked what kind of toppings would everybody like. I quickly said as I was taking some money out of my pocket, anything but onions. "We don't accept donations from the injured", Beth said, "Let me get your coffee. Then Richard and I will go for pizzas." Marge asked if I would be OK by myself for a few minutes as she had chores that must be tended to. So I sat back in the kitchen chair, with my eyes closed, just to rest. House so quiet, though there were background city sounds. Some minutes had passed when I thought I sensed movement near me. I opened my eyes, then probably opened them wider as I saw a naked and decidedly voluptuous young woman staring at my forehead. She said "Hi, I'm MacKensie, I heard they conked you on the noggin. Would you like me to get a bandage for that bump?" Before I could gather my wits for an answer, she said "I heard you were from Arizona, but what's your name." Well, just inches away, gorgeous and generous parts of a very handsome lady were in full, unobstructed bloom and my name could not seem to make its way to my tongue. Instead I pointed to my forehead and nodded 'yes.' So MacKensie left the room saying she'd be right back. I struggled into consciousness and was able to drag my name out of some dark closet in my brain, where it had gone to hide. She returned with a large bandage and proceeded to apply it ever so gently to my wound. I finally was able to say "Thanks, MacKensie, my name is Rosano." This Rubenesque young woman was certainly something of a prize, as well as a surprise.

Marge came into the kitchen and began washing her hands while saying, "Arizona, we didn't have time to tell you about nudity and the free love parts of our commune. Everything here is voluntary and allowable as long as there is no objection from any other member. Just so you know. Are you OK with that?" My first thought was 'if this is communism, I'm all for it', and 'right now I'll be an undercover capitalist.' But I said ... "I vote yes!" MacKensie said, "The injured party has a name and his name is Rosano." Marge asked how many would be having supper. MacKensie thought there would be six, with Stephanie just getting off work. They took out six serving trays and 'set' each one with a fork, knife, small plate, empty glass, and small cloth napkin. Soon there was noise of Richard and Beth coming back with pizzas accompanied by Stephanie, a tall, slim, pretty, light-haired girl. Three or four small pieces of pizza were put on each plate. Marge announced everyone should carry a tray into the main room, MacKensie was taking drink orders. Coffee and water were fine for me. A couple of people had a beer. Everyone was sitting in a group on twin-size mattresses, each having its own metal-framed platform to keep it off the floor. I was introduced to Stephanie. The pizza was decent, not great, but welcome. Richard said he would tell what happened this afternoon and why the guy from Arizona was here. And he told the story accurately with no embellishments. Then he said "And now our guest should tell us what he's doing in Jacksonville on the small Italian scooter." Introducing myself, I said before I talk about the scooter stuff, I'd like to ask where all of you were from, because none of you has a southern accent ... at all. None of them was from the south, but from everywhere else ... New England, the Midwest, the Far West. They were all going to school, at least part time.

"I'll talk quietly about my trip for a short time, and then you guys can ask all the questions you want." I just didn't want to bore anybody. And that's what we did. And questions poured in. Topics ranged all over the place. I split a beer with someone. When we talked about food, Richard said that none of them knew how to cook, though a couple of their 'winter' people did fairly well in the kitchen. MacKensie said she had a good herb garden in the back yard, but didn't know much about using them. I said, "Look, it seems I'm the old man of this group, and I'm a pretty good cook. I'll cook breakfast for everyone tomorrow morning if you're willing to risk a slow, painful death. I'll need an assistant or apprentice. Who will it be?" MacKensie and Beth raised their hands simultaneously. So I said, "Good. Two is better."

This group of six talked for a long time touching on every subject imaginable. We talked of the 'beat' generation which was dispersing and a new 'hip' group gathering in California fueled by psychedelic mushrooms, banana peels and drugs. Summer evening in Jacksonville was warm and Marge had nodded off to sleep. Pert little Beth, who was now wearing only denim shorts, asked how my head was doing and could she get anything for me. Just a glass of ice water if she could. My head would be fine in the morning, I thought, but I'd like to take a shower if I could, since I still felt sandy and gritty from the beach. Beth said she'd get some water for me and MacKensie, could you show Rosano our shower room. MacKensie got my clothing bag from the corner of the kitchen and said to follow her. Through a hallway. She pointed out a door saying "toilet there." Adjacent was the bathing room, that is, a room with one bathtub against one wall and four shower heads arranged along another wall. She put my bag up on a built-in shelf, started a shower going and said to go ahead and here was a washcloth and a towel and there's liquid shower soap right here. This group of young people had remodeled this house to serve twenty people, hence multiple shower setups. I was impressed. They were quite serious about this commune. It was non-political and had nothing to do with Soviet communism. From their conversation this evening, that was evident. It was a mutually beneficial housing arrangement, with no other intent. As I began to soap up, MacKensie started the adjacent shower and started doing the same. "Your ice water is next to your bag." That was Beth, now naked, starting a shower on the other side of me. This was a definite 'first' for me. MacKensie walked into my shower stream saying "Here, let me do your back." And she started. Oh Man! Excited, my reaction was becoming more apparent by the moment. Beth then said, "His head might be hurt, but part of him is working rather well, I would say." I could only laugh helplessly while MacKensie worked on my backside. She said I still had sand in my hair and that she would wash it. Please sit down on this bench. Let me remove this bandage. We'll get a new one for you. Beth was holding the shampoo. Jacksonville might be a rough town, but, so far, it was an exciting paradise for me.

Done washing, Beth handed me a lightweight, terrycloth bathrobe, saying let's go back to the main room. And we did. Richard and Marge had already fallen asleep. Stephanie came over and joined us for some conversation. She had made some iced tea. Anyone for tea? MacKensie showed up with my ice water and a smaller bandage. She carefully placed it on my wound saying the swelling had gone down somewhat, and then kissed me lightly on the other part of my forehead. I just softly said "Thank you." We talked for another hour since the ladies were asking more about the scooter trip ... what prompted it, wasn't I scared, etc. I asked what food was in the house for breakfast. Beth said she'd wake us up in plenty of time and we could look in the morning. If we needed anything, she could bike to the grocery store and be back in a jiffy. OK. MacKensie opened some cabinets, took out some sheets, pillows, and light blankets. She pushed three platform beds together and made up places to sleep. She said, "C'mon everybody, brush teeth, go pee, and let's go to sleep." Stephanie said she was going to write a letter for a while and might join us later. In a short time, the three breakfast cooks were asleep.

During the night, there was some gentle, but stimulating exploration by MacKensie which I answered in kind, with soft squeezes and tender pettings added. The conclusion was quiet, comforting, and complete.

Morning started early with Beth giving me a little kiss on the cheek and whispering in my ear "Good morning, chef. Do you drink coffee in the morning? I've got some ready, if you do." "I do, I do, thanks." She said to go get dressed and come to the kitchen and we could start the day there. The three of us drank coffee quietly and then I asked what food we had available. Beth said she had it arranged on the counter. Good. A quick survey and then I asked for a tour of the herb garden. MacKensie's eyes lit up. "Right this way, chef Rosano." We went outside into the warm very early morning, with MacKensie pointing out this and that, and new mint she had planted two days before. She had forgotten what this other stuff was, but it was pretty. I told her she had a pretty good garden, but she should dig up the mint and put it in a pot separate from the garden because it would take over and drive all the other stuff away. Did she know she had a really nice Rosemary bush at the corner of the garage?

Back in the kitchen, they had two dozen eggs, a small canned Danish ham, some Velveeta cheese, grated parmesan, sliced black olives, a few other items, and some sliced sandwich bread. I said, OK, are any of you vegetarians? No. Good. Let's make a huge omelet, which I call a frittata, but we need a few things from the grocer. Beth was there with a small pad and pencil. "OK, two loaves of decent bread, French or Italian, two full loaves or four baguettes. Some decent cheese, Asiago or Parmesan or Romano Pecorino (not grated), or any firm cheese that sounds like that. A can or jar of roasted red peppers, any other color is OK, too. A can of garbanzos or red kidney beans or black beans or all three. OK, that's it. Beth disappeared. MacKensie and I sat down with our coffee for a minute or two. She asked about the feathery beautiful plants in her garden. I said after breakfast I'd tell her as much as I knew. I got up, leaned toward her and gave her a gentle smooch, and said she had been pretty sneaky during the night and I enjoyed every second of it, but now it was time for her to go to work on breakfast. She said last night was so very nice, but breakfast looked like it could be really exciting, too. I had MacKensie crack the eggs, and beat them with the grated parmesan, go to her garden and get some of that oregano she had grown and chop it very fine or use scissors and cut it up that way, and the same with needles of a small branch of rosemary. I preheated their oven, got the large cast iron frying pan buttered. Beth returned from shopping, they did have Asiago, and the beans, roasted peppers, and baguettes. Good. This was fun for all of us. The kitchen was hopping. Everybody learning and doing. The assembled frittata went into the oven with a cookie sheet for a lid. It would be ready in an hour or less. Let's clean up the kitchen and we'll sit down and have more coffee. In time, the other three in the house started wandering into the kitchen, drinking and making more coffee or tea. None were naked or topless. That allowed my eyes some welcome rest. Two people alone and naked ... I was used to that, but the possibility of six nude people would be a wild new experience for me and just then, I was responsible for breakfast. Beth asked what more was there to do. I said throw out the sliced bread they had, it was garbage. And the Velveeta, too. Disgusting stuff. Both she and MacKensie laughed at me. Going over to the counter, I took one slice of that balloon bread, similar to Wonder bread. I squeezed it in my hand, then released it. It remained completely mushed, and I said that was because it was full of phony stuff. It was like glue. You wait and watch. I asked Beth to cut two baguettes in half the long way, giving us four long halves. Looking at the rosemary, I asked MacKensie to try to cut it finer. A platter was ready and I inverted the frittata onto it. Everyone was watching and oohed and aahed, and I sprinkled the whole thing with the rosemary, and damn, it did smell good. I had melted some butter on the top of the stove. Stephanie and Marge had gotten the individual trays ready. Beth said the toast was perfect. I showed Beth how to lightly paint the toast with butter, sprinkle a tiny amount of sugar, and then dust them with cinnamon and asked her to finish them and serve everyone half of a half. Carrying our trays to the main room, we sat down to a simple, savory, satisfying breakfast. To these young people (only two or three years younger than I was), the whole deal seemed like magic. You know, it was magic. For sure.

As we finished breakfast, Beth asked what I had planned for today and what my plan was generally. I wanted to see some of Jacksonville and for sure wanted to go to the beach again, and maybe visit the public library. Marge spoke up saying "Rosano, you really don't want to see much more of this town ... it's really kind of dumpy, and not only that, some places are pretty dangerous." I said I knew that, because I had been mugged at the beach yesterday by some crazed person with a boomerang. And now Richard almost spit his coffee out laughing. To Richard, I said "All is forgiven, and I have to congratulate you, more than anybody. Here you are, alone in a house with four beautiful ladies. My compliments." Marge said, "You have a wedding in Connecticut. And you want to get there on June 26 or 27, right?" A yes nod. "You spent three days in Chicago, four in Atlanta, and we'd love to have you for the rest of your life if you can cook like this." "Marge, Thank you," I said, "to stay at least one more day here would be so beautiful for me, all of you treated me so well after the beating." They all laughed again. "Here's what I'll do. I'll cook a supper for you that will knock your socks off, but better than that, it'll be a simple supper that you guys can learn in one shot and repeat with variations for the rest of your lives." Richard said "A Done Deal" ... and offered his hand as a welcome. Thanks, Richard. Beth said she would be my guide for the day. Everyone was carrying their things into the kitchen, Stephanie was washing dishes. People were getting ready for the day and as they dispersed, each thanked me for a delicious breakfast.

Beth asked, "more coffee?" "Sure, let's sit down and have another cup and make some plans for today." Beth poured coffee and sitting down she said, "Rosano, I think it would be best to do this: First we go to the library. Next we go to the market for food for tonight's supper and tomorrow's breakfast because we don't have enough food in the house for either right now. After that, we come back here, take care of groceries and do some serious love-making. Next, we have a little nap, and then, we'll go to the beach. When we get home, we can cook. How's that?" My response made her laugh. "I like your thinking, and I believe you should be the President of the United States." Laughing she said, "Does that mean Yes?" I nodded. She gave me a little smooch.

We needed a large canvas bag, or a laundry bag, or maybe a couple of pillow cases for groceries, since paper sacks were too fragile. She had two large canvas bags. Let's just take one. We were standing at the scooter as I taught her basic hand signals. I complimented her on wearing a helmet when she was on her bicycle yesterday and if she ever wanted to do Marge and Richard a big favor, she could get helmets for them as well. And so we putt-putted to the Southside Branch Library, where I read of the causes of the Civil War. In the articles I read, chosen at random, it seemed every possible cause was explored thoroughly except ... preservation of slavery. Was this the library's subtle censorship? I didn't know, but viewed all that reading I had done with a jaundiced eye. In addition, my reading covered some descriptions of other areas of Florida. Also read a few minutes each for the major southern cities along the coast, from Georgia to DC. With the exception of the ocean and Miami, the whole state of Florida sounded a little boring, unless you were a boater, a fisher or a golfer, but I really knew so little about it and was merely guessing.

Beth and I made our way to the grocery store, which was an independent food store and not part of a chain. They had some pretty good stuff, not a huge selection, but better than I had expected. Beth said the commune had an account there. We did our shopping. For meat, I got six each chicken breasts, thighs, and drumsticks. Also asked the butcher for some lean, very thinly sliced beef (across the grain, please). The butcher said "Oh boy, these kids will eat well tonight! Glad to see it." We picked up a number of other things including a bottle of good olive oil. Time to go back to the commune (I couldn't get used to saying that word).

"Rosano, that was a fun morning. I love giving signals and having the scooter respond ... gives me a sense of power. Let's put this stuff away and what do you suppose we should do next?" I had an idea ... we should have a little coffee, then brush teeth, then get naked, then wash each other meticulously, then see what happens. She said, "Yes, yes, yes" and began warming two cups of the morning's coffee. It wasn't long before we were washing each other, being especially attentive, then drying each other and having Beth show the way to one of the platforms. Giving her a big kiss, I told her to take the lead this first time, and be comfortable with anything and everything. She said if anyone else comes in, she could cover us with a light blanket if I wanted. "Not important", I whispered. It was a glorious time for both of us. Then, a nap in each other's arms. Sometime during our nap, people walked through, but I didn't know who or how many.

Afternoon sometime. Awake. Now, Beth stirred, rolled a little closer, gave a kiss and said "That was really something." I said, "Yeah, you really were." We were quiet for a few minutes and she asked if I still wanted to go to the beach since it was still early. Sure. Dressed. Back out to the scooter. We were off to the seashore with the sun at our backs. It was twenty minutes to the coast. Locked up everything to the same power pole, and we went out to the water with my pants rolled up above my knees. I wasn't interested in swimming, as much as I was in just experiencing. A warm afternoon and I loved it. And again, the water, the wet sand, a little bit of splashing, the sounds, everything. After sloshing through the shoreline for a while, Beth and I sat on a small blanket she had packed, and we talked. She said that almost all members of the commune were misfits and that their families were glad to have a place to 'ditch' them. Beth was from near Bend, Oregon. I said Bend is on the dry side of Oregon, no? She said yes and that her family was a ranching family, very conservative, fine citizens, deeply involved in their church. A few years ago, Beth had spent one weekend in San Francisco, 500 miles away, and was forever changed. Returning to Bend, she rebelled against the church stuff (which she had wanted to do for at least a year or two before), refused to go to services, and became an embarrassment to this straight-laced family ... to the point where she and they worked out an arrangement in which they would send her a check each month for the next five years and she had to get her education or her profession and at the end of five years, she was on her own. As soon as high school graduation was over, she was on a bus to Florida. She knew her family would never welcome her returning to the ranch. I asked why she came to Jacksonville. Her answer: It was diagonally opposite from Bend, Oregon on a US map. I then told her how I had used a map and ended up in Tucson, Arizona. She laughed loudly and said "We're so similar. That's why we were so fine together in bed today." I said, "You think it's in the charts, eh?" Still laughing, "Rosano, so you, too, are a misfit, no? That's why everyone in the commune wants you to stay. They sense you're one of them." Mentioning our age difference, I said it was OK to be a misfit and that I had arrived at that conclusion just before starting this trek across the country. So it was nothing to worry about. Further, I felt comfortable being a misfit, though my family was wringing their hands over my lack of direction. Misfits are interesting people. Let the 'normal people' cook the meal, but it is the misfits who provide flavor and spice. She gave me a big hug and asked, "How long would you stay if we begged you?" "Truthfully, I was going to stay only one night in Jacksonville and then start north. Today is Wednesday. I would leave Friday morning at the latest, and only if invited. Then I would head north to Savannah. You people are the only reason I would stay. You guys are good people, so savvy, and fun, and I really admire what you have done. And Beth, you're a beautiful person, and I have so enjoyed being with you." She gave me a squeeze and said, "Let's go back for another cooking lesson. That frittata was a marvel ... so simple and so good tasting."

Riding back to the commune, Beth reached up and held onto my ear lobes for a few seconds. My mind instantly went back to that splendid three weeks with Stella. But I had to put that remembrance aside ... I was with other exciting people, in the present, right now, and Stella would always be a memory, a treasured memory, but a memory nonetheless.

Into the kitchen and we began preparing for supper. Beth got the chicken pieces from the fridge, and I had her push a garlic clove under the skin of each piece. MacKensie showed up, wearing a skirt and no top. And I'm telling you, Brother, she was stunning. I set her to getting about six lengths of rosemary, the width of our roasting pan, and the same with the oregano from her garden (she was quietly thrilled to use the things she had grown). I showed her how to arrange the rosemary in the bottom of the pan. Now put the chicken pieces on top of those little branches. There were two pieces too many for the pan. Next, while Beth was dicing the thin skin of a tangerine, I had MacKensie wash and then score the 16 or 18 small sweet plums we had found at the grocer, and arrange those between the chicken pieces. Sprinkled the tangerine and we placed the oregano branches on top, drizzled some olive oil over the whole mess, then a little salt and pepper. Ladies, preheat the oven to 375 deg. F. One hour before serving, we pop this into the oven. MacKensie, sweetie pie, when the oven or the stove top is active, you should put a blouse or shirt on ... for safety of your goodies. She laughed, said, "You're right," left the room and returned now wearing a shirt and a skirt. OK, m'ladies, let's clean up our little mess and get ready to make another one. Here's a big soup pan, let's put about a quart of water in and we'll put it on the big burner. While that's happening, Beth, I found this platter. We'll make a big veggie platter, so you can start washing the veggies we bought this morning and cut them in some decorative fashion. For instance, the red cabbage can be cut into some good-looking wedges, but that'll be your choice. Now MacKensie, let's get a good knife and go to your garden, and I'll show you some magic that you've already grown. And all this time, I'm occasionally touching them gently and the two of them are doing the same to me and we're having a ball. Out to the garden, and I say to MacKensie, take some of these feathery leaves and roll them between your fingers and then sniff. She does that and smiles. "Licorice? No, it's anise, right?" I shake my head no and she looks disappointed. Then I tell her it's better than that. It's fennel. You have grown eight or ten very nice fennel bulbs. My congratulations! And she looks puzzled. C'mon, I want you to harvest two of these bulbs. I showed her where to cut. We had two big beautiful plants. Let's wash them with the garden hose and then we'll take them in the house. As we're doing that, Beth leaned out the door to tell us the water is boiling. OK Beth, put the two pieces of chicken in the pot and we'll be right there. Beth had a good start on the veggie plate. Now we cut all the greenery and the stalks from the fennel bulbs, we slice the bulbs to create rings of this wonderful vegetable and give the rings to Beth for her plate. They have a splendid taste and I don't understand why so few people know about fennel. MacKensie can chop up all the greenery, thinly slice all the stems and toss the whole pile into the soup. Whatever veggies Beth has left over are also sliced up and put into the soup. I proposed we name it 'kitchen sink soup.' It was time to put the chicken into the oven. In an hour, it could be served. Looking through cupboards, I found some rice, which was still good. Into the soup. A small can of mushrooms ... into the soup. MacKensie can slice the two remaining baguettes just as last night's were, except this time, we'll toast them, paint them lightly with balsamic vinegar, sprinkle with shredded cheese and retoast quickly and serve. Marge and Richard caught a whiff of the chicken and started hanging around. Pretty soon Stephanie would show up. While the three cooks took a break, the other two began setting up the trays. I wasn't seeing much of Florida, but was having a grand old time with these great young misfits.

Let's turn the soup pan off. We'll finish cooking it tomorrow. The kitchen was flooded with mixed aromas. Stephanie showed up just in time. I announced the chicken would be done in five minutes or less. Everyone should wash their hands and get ready. The chicken came out of the oven, I removed the oregano branches from the top, scattered some of the oregano leaves back onto the chicken. Popped the pan under the broiler for a few minutes to brown the chicken. Come and get it!

Supper was a decided hit. They had never eaten chicken this tasty ever before. Never heard of combining plums, and branches from the bushes, with chicken, etc. After the conversation became a little more subdued, I said my two lovely apprentices knew how to do this, and they could teach the others. And my question was, "Do you see why most Italian-Americans do not cook turkeys for the holidays?"

CHAPTER 55

THE LAST LEG

As we finished supper, conversation turned from one subject to another. Marge asked if I was comfortable with the nudity and free love atmosphere. Admitting it was a little unusual at first, my feeling was of easy acceptance and thorough enjoyment. My opinion was that the idea of "free love" was a shocker for most of the US population, and it was "the pill" which made it a viable lifestyle, so unencumbered with hang-ups. However, could you imagine your commune group without the pill, with 10 women and 10 men, and half the women pregnant. Not so fun. Now a few children are born. Do you kick those women out ... while they're still trying to go to school? But kids in the house would change the whole dynamic so dramatically. So, embracing "free love" suited me, but there are responsibilities attached. And that's OK. As far as the immorality of it ... let the church mice stay in their churches and keeps tabs on their own moral failures. Judge not ...

In the kitchen, Beth accidentally poured chicken drippings on her leg and on the floor. It wasn't hot, so no injury, just a bit of a mess. She headed to the shower. The three non-cooks began doing dishes and kitchen cleanup. It was good to see people just pitch in and get things done without being assigned or it 'being their turn'. MacKensie got my hand and said "C'mon Rosano, let's go join Beth." In short order, we three were back in the shower, this time gently fooling around with each other while getting squeaky clean. A stimulating experience. Any more stimulation and I wouldn't have had enough skin on my body to close my eyelids.

Back to the main room in our light terry cloth robes. "Are you two going to be my breakfast helpers?" Yep, same as this morning and MacKensie would be my companion/guide for tomorrow. Did she have a helmet? No, but she'd find one in the house somewhere. Marge joined us for conversation and then Richard and finally Stephanie. When we were all together, I said Friday morning, sometime after breakfast, would be my leaving time. Richard said he was glad to have met me and knew, from the beginning, that if he hit me hard enough I would have to stay a day or two. Again, our conversation was varied and lively, but evidently not sparkly enough to keep Beth awake ... she had fallen asleep right next to me. In time, the others began to wilt and so did I. Time to say goodnight. Use the bathroom, brush teeth, and return to the platform bed. MacKensie did the same, returning, putting a sheet over the sleeping Beth, and lying on my other side, saying so quietly, "Rosano, you ready?" Me: "Ready?" She: "Right ... ready, because I'm so horny for you that I'm gonna push my goodies in your face and jump your bones." Me: "I'll bet you get a lot of guys with that slick little approach." Giggling, she pulled a sheet over the two of us and began to do what she had threatened, despite there being one or two other people still walking around. Of course, I tried to fight her off, but for some odd reason, was unable to. Beth slept, undisturbed ...

... until too early in the morning. Whispering in my ear ... "Rosano, (pause) Rosano. Want some coffee?" Automatically, I nod yes. More whispering ... "Well, you can have some after you're done." Now I'm waking up, glancing at the window, still nighttime, and Beth is taking her turn with me ... and this was a slow, dreamy, luxurious joining, and then ... back to sleep.

An hour or two later, after presenting me with some of that promised coffee, and having a cup of her own, Beth went out on her bicycle for more baguettes, six of them, and three dozen eggs ... enough for two mornings. We'd go out for supper stuff later this morning. MacKensie brought some basil and parsley in from the garden and using scissors, cut both spices into fine pieces. So breakfast was a scrambled affair, scrambled ultra-thin beef, scrambled with olive oil and flavored with a little bit of pressed garlic and chopped basil. A dozen eggs were scrambled with little chunks of cheese, black pepper, and parsley. Toasted baguette halves painted very lightly with melted butter and a teaspoon of good quality cherry jam placed on one end (if someone doesn't want jam, they can slice that end off and give it to someone else). OK, my young friends, time to eat. My helpers couldn't believe how fast breakfast had been cooked. Look, you two, now you've seen it done. When you guys do it for yourselves, you'll find that the food sometimes dictates that you move quickly as hell, and that you keep moving. As soon as you've picked up the technique, you should pass it on to others in the commune. Evidently the scrambled breakfast was OK ... not a bit of food was left on plates. They had never heard of scrambling meat and it was delicious, so said they, the young misfits, the young communers.

While I drank another cup of coffee, people cleaned up, then went their separate ways. This morning I got a little hesitant hug from Stephanie and a warm and quiet thank you, as well.

Within the hour, MacKensie and I were alone, making up a grocery list for the night's supper and tomorrow's breakfast. She asked what I wanted to do today. Aside from grocery shopping, this morning I'd like her to direct a little scooter tour of the San Marco neighborhood. Evidently there were some ties to famous Venice in Italy, and it seemed to be a desirable place for noodling around. Maybe stop at an art gallery or two. Then to the beach for a little while. I had noticed a clothes dryer in the house. Did it work? It did. Good, because I'd surely like to do my laundry before I left. Possible this afternoon? That is, after we have another bone-jumping session. She laughed and asked "You like that?" Me: "I could get used to that in an eye blink. Thank you, thank you." She: "you're welcome, very welcome."

MacKensie and I headed out to the scooter. She had her headgear on while getting instructions on basic hand signals. She needed to find the canvas bag for the groceries. Trying to carry paper sacks or other packages gets fairly tricky when traveling by scooter. So ... off we go to the grocer first. Complimented the butcher on the thinly sliced beef he had cut for us before. Now, did he have any hot Italian sausage? He had made four pounds this morning, but only moderately hot, and not in links. We'd take the four pounds if he put the approximate amount of red pepper flakes in a little bag ... enough to make the four pounds qualify as hot. No problem. We'd also like four pounds of ground round steak or other very lean beef. He'd get it ready while we picked up a few more items, including a box of corn flakes and some sliced almonds. I asked MacKensie to get a large bunch of grapes, taste them first to make sure they're ripe, not too tart. Picked up a few more things, scooter started on the first kick, and we headed back to the house. Put the food away, we'll deal with it later.

Time for a cup of coffee and then she could conduct the tour of San Marco. I described my process called 'noodling' and she thought it as valid as any other way to get a feel for a place. After that, I'd enjoy the beach again if she also could. We started out and within a few minutes, we were noodling. The area was touted as being allied with Venice, Italy. Though I hadn't been to Italy, I had seen enough photography of Venice to know that San Marco in Jacksonville being similar to Venice was far more tout than truth. Aside from that, it was a decidedly pleasant area. And there was an art gallery we might visit. It had modern paintings including two by an abstract artist named Gino Severini, the first 'real life' works of his I had seen instead of mere photographs. So that was a good little tour of San Marco. Now, down to the beach. Very few people, the sand was warm, the water clear and refreshing. Huge white cotton clouds overhead. Pant legs rolled up, walking in the shallow water, good-looking lady with me, and all was right with the world.

It was early afternoon when we got back to the house, the commune. We showered together again, ridding ourselves of beach sand, then down for some downright immoral playtime, then a nap. In time, I realized Beth had joined us and was deeply snoozing beside me and snoring lightly.

Later in the afternoon, we began stirring, coffee was made for the three of us. The two beauties got laundry started after I got into my camping pants, a shirt, and my boots. Everything else went into the laundry pile. We then gathered supper stuff and I became a chef once again, with two apprentices. How splendid was that! I had found a large roasting pan and tried it for size in the oven. It fit. OK, MacKenzie is going to use her hands to mix the meat while we toss in various things. Eight pounds is a fair amount to handle, but it gets better (or worse) as other ingredients are added. While Beth crushed the cornflakes, to make them finer, I added the whites of a dozen eggs, (the yokes saved for tomorrow's breakfast), some olive oil, and spices, including the butcher's additional red pepper. Now the cornflakes went into the mix and the entire mass needed to be kneaded for a few minutes. Next, form the ground meat combination into twelve equal-sized loaves and arrange in the large roasting pan. We prepared the green beans and cooked them three-fourths of the way, toasted the almond slices lightly to be combined later with the green beans. So that was it, with bread added, it would be a simple supper, but with a good degree of that most important culinary ingredient ... pizzazz.

Time for another cup of coffee. The three of us sat and I said they would be responsible for breakfast tomorrow morning. They would do the whole thing without me being there ... I'd be packing. I suggested they put toast and a small bunch of grapes on each plate, then serve scrambled eggs (don't forget to add the leftover yokes) fixed however they determined in a bowl on a common platter with cold slices of the meat loaf. Let each person help themselves. Simple breakfast, without much fuss. I'd be leaving shortly after breakfast and I wanted both of them to know what splendid people they were and that I would surely miss them and the others too, but especially my dear apprentices. We sipped coffee and it was a weepy, heartfelt time. These days in Jacksonville had been so beautiful for me ... for the ocean, yes, but primarily because of them. I wanted to check on a few scooter things before we cooked the evening's supper. Typically, as soon as women are involved, old friends get pushed aside. I didn't want Tony the Lambretta to feel neglected. Sensing the scooter was eager to get going, I went out, fiddled around a bit, and talked to it, reassured it, saying we would soon be back on the road, doing our usual purring along.

Richard arrived, and then Marge. Not long after, Stephanie showed up and we began supper cooking saying it would be about an hour before food was served. Richard brought a bottle of something in a plain paper bag, and stashed it in the fridge, with a note on it saying 'Private, don't touch.' Supper was ready to be served, the trays were ready, and we put a final minute under the broiler onto the loaves of meat. The green beans were ready with the almond slices scattered on top. The bread was the last component and we all carried our trays into the main room. Supper was a solid success, gaining compliments from all concerned. Meat loaf was usually pretty bland. Not this ... this had some zam and some character and was delicious. I said these two great apprentices knew how to make this and that it was, in fact, an ingredient, and could be served a hundred different ways ... with tomato sauce, sliced as a cold cut, on top of pasta, broken up into soup, etc. And all of you should learn some of this cooking, and these two could show how it's done. It just makes life more interesting. For me, sitting for supper with five young and open-minded people, alive with good conversation, was comfortable and rewarding, especially when I saw everyone go for second helpings on meat loaf and also green beans. Cleanup began, MacKensie disappeared for a time, then returned with my laundry neatly folded, including my combination jacket and storage room.

The three cooks gathered onto the platform beds. One at a time, the other three joined us and we talked of so many things. They asked about my trip through east coast states to Connecticut. I suggested it might be fairly anticlimactic, after what I'd already seen and done these past two months, and because I had already seen much of the east coast, especially north of the Carolinas. Catching up on my reading would be a priority. Since six hours per day on the road was about max, the rest of the time was occupied by other activity, reading being at the top of the list. I explained that no reading had been done during my time with them ... and that was the highest compliment possible from me ... that they were interesting enough people to pull me away from a good book. Of course, they had worked my ass off in the kitchen, but that had been fun, as well. I would probably camp out somewhere near Savannah that first night out. Savannah is 150 miles away ... and doing some math, if I averaged 25 or 30 miles per hour, it would require 5 or 6 hours plus break times to get there. Asking that each of them tell me a little more about the path they had taken to Jacksonville and to this commune, discussion became philosophical as, one at a time, they told as least part of their stories. In one way or another, we were indeed misfits, but now it all seemed OK. We had split a few beers and in time, people became sleepy. MacKensie was the first to fall asleep and Beth covered her with a light blanket. That seemed to signal everyone to get up, brush teeth, etc. and settle down for a night's sleep. Putting my arms around Beth, she quietly said, "Rosano, let's get naked." She pulled a sheet over the two of us, and I rolled over to be side by side with her. As we enjoyed each other, no one else was stirring, not even a ...

Oh Man! Here was morning again and I was alone and there were noises from the kitchen. Got myself dressed in freshly laundered clothing and made my way to the bathroom. Next was a critical kitchen stop where the two new cooks were getting ready for breakfast as I sat down at the small table. Coffee was placed in front of me. I whispered my thanks and had a few sips, then a few more. MacKensie gave me a big slow smooch and said "Good Morning, you splendid little man." Beth was next with another kiss, a hug, some tears, and "Thank you so much for you." We three embraced together. The others gathered for breakfast. Richard went into the fridge, took his secret package out, went to the kitchen counter. Bam! The sound of a champagne bottle and he poured six little glasses of champagne and they toasted me. No big words, just thanks, little hugs, little kisses, handshakes and MacKensie said "Breakfast is served." They had done it all, the two apprentices, and done an excellent job of it. Gave them my compliments and mentioned not to forget the soup which was half complete.

Breakfast being done, they began cleaning up. These people were starting their day, and I would start mine. Another bathroom visit to make sure I wasn't leaving anything behind. Packed my single bag, got my water bag from the kitchen and headed out to the scooter. While I secured my clothing bag and the water bag, these lovely misfits, one at a time, came out to say goodbye. MacKensie was crying now, but had to leave. Beth and Marge remained. Rolled the scooter out of the garage, kick-started it, got my morning two-stroke fix, waved and headed out, to begin the last leg of this journey.

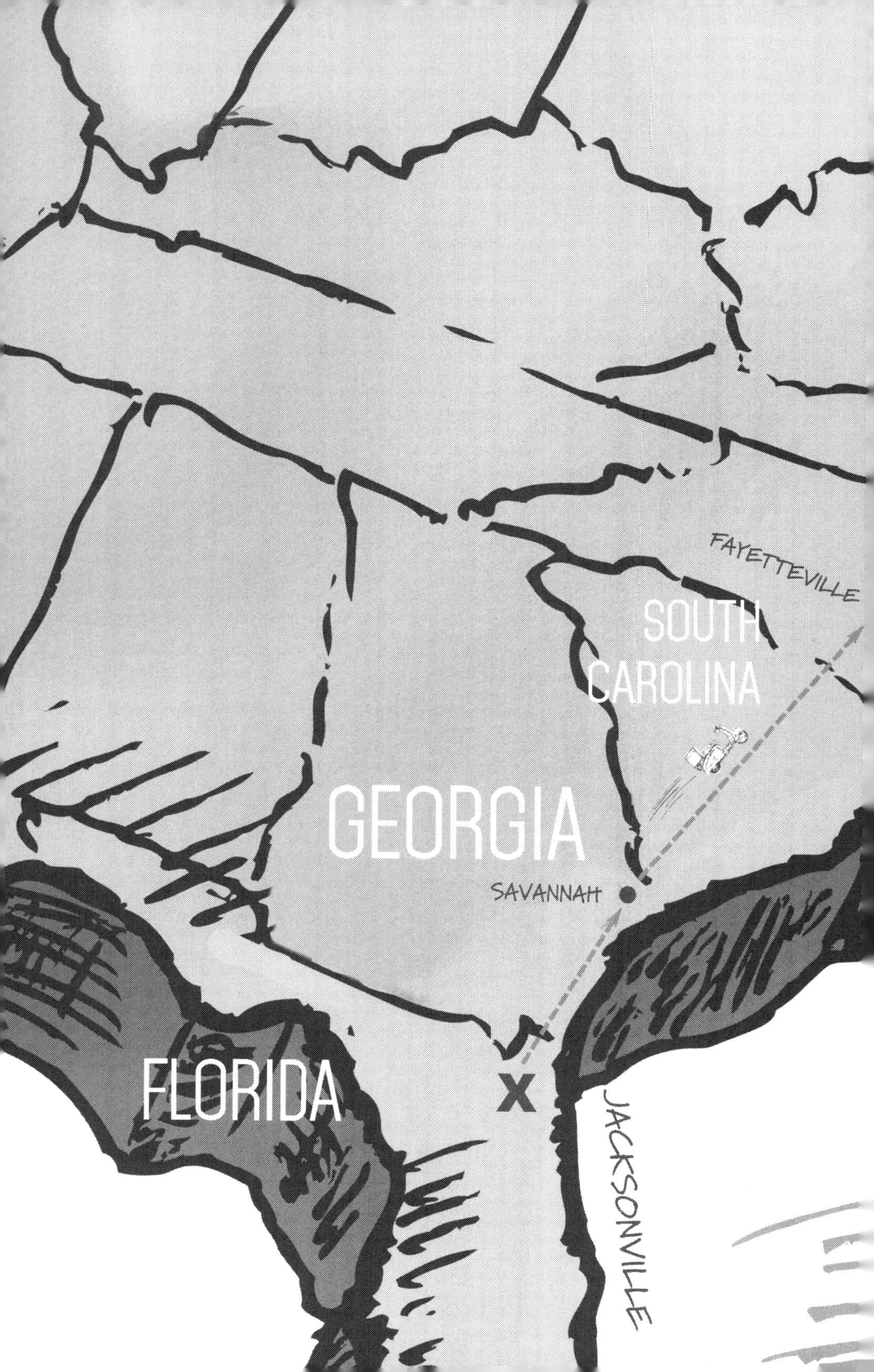

FAYETTEVILLE

SOUTH
CAROLINA

GEORGIA

SAVANNAH

FLORIDA

X

JACKSONVILLE

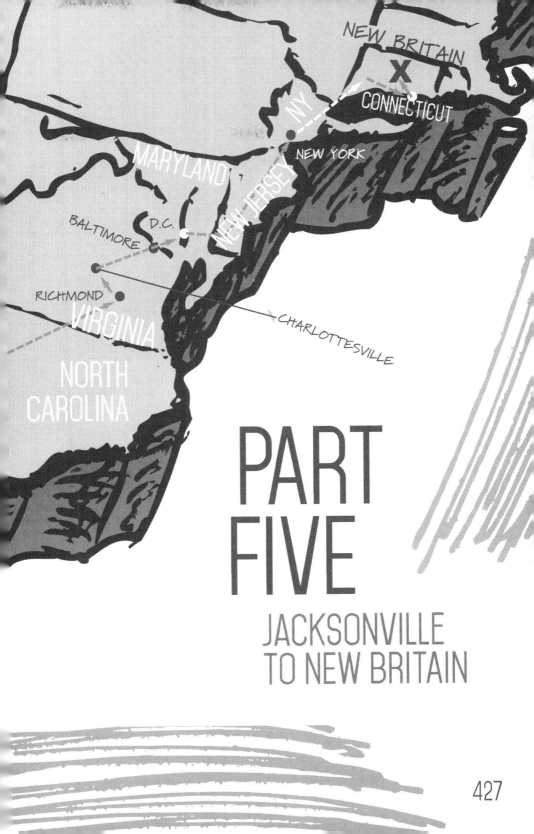

PART FIVE

JACKSONVILLE TO NEW BRITAIN

CHAPTER 56

OASIS AT BALTIMORE

Within a few minutes of leaving the commune, we ... Tony Lambretta and I, were crossing St John's River going northward back into the southland. Jacksonville, not the city, but the group in the commune, had been a stroke of good fortune. Looking back, my intent had been to spend as little time as possible in northern Florida. Instead, three full days of active cooking, and teaching, of love making and beaches. Now I was headed to Savannah, then possibly Myrtle Beach. During my Jacksonville stay, there was hardly a thought or acknowledgement that I was in the south. This morning, it wasn't long before my attitude change began. As if it were a tangible object, my open attitude toward people was retreating as once again a more guarded stance was assumed. Intentionally, I would limit myself, as far as possible to pleasant, but necessary exchanges with people in gas stations, cafes, grocery stores, campgrounds, motels, and such ... at least until I was north of Washington, D.C. or Baltimore. This was going to be a long, lonely ride northward. An hour after leaving my new and now former friends, I was back in the state of Georgia, heading to Savannah. The terrain was slightly sloping and draining to the ocean, mixed forest, grassland, and marshlands. And that's what it would be for most of the next 500 miles. Leaving the commune and those beautiful people was disappointing, but left me feeling so lucky to have been smacked on the forehead by that pie pan ... all of us had enjoyed a good time because of it. The hope was this final 1,000-mile leg of the journey would not just become a task. Part of my problem was that I was, at best, only faintly interested in the historical preservation districts of Savannah, or

Charleston, Fayetteville, or the other towns. My resolve then became to simply enjoy the scenery and natural beauty of these coastal states, and maybe visit the seashore again, maybe not.

In the next four days of travel, this fine machine called Lambretta, took me from Jacksonville, Florida to Richmond, Virginia, by way of Savannah, Florence, Fayetteville, and 100 other towns, covering about 600 miles or more. Campgrounds were used the first three nights and then a motel near Richmond as rain had begun that afternoon and threatened to continue into the night, according to the weather report from the waitress in a small diner. Other than necessary stops for fuel, food, breaks, or camping, there were only two, the first being a bookstore in a strip mall near Savannah, the second was a car show near Fayetteville, part of it having restored vehicles of every make, the other part featured custom cars and hot rods of every description imaginable. While critical of the southerners in some ways, as far as their work on cars, they are certainly in the top echelons. Just magnificent workmanship and design and a pleasure to see.

The small, simple motel room was a welcome landing spot, a relief, with a real reading lamp and a chair and small table. A coin-operated laundry (open 24 hours) and breakfast shop (breakfast 'round the clock) were within walking distance. Way back in Savannah, four books were added to my baggage. That wonderful book by Tregaskis, 'Guadalcanal Diary', which I had purchased back in Atlanta, had been finished and surreptitiously left in a café in one of the Carolinas with my little note written on an inside page, highly recommending it and asking the next person to pass it on. Maybe this book thing could start little chains of reading interest here and there. Also had read more than half of 'The Caine Mutiny' by Herman Wouk. I might finish it this night. There was more than enough snack food in the scooter trunk to get me through the night. After Atlanta, my idea was to buy smaller quantities more often. In the next day or so I would spot a good Greek, Jewish, or Italian deli, and then, being so weary of beef jerky, I would load up on real food. Food with pedigree. The domestic chores were done as far as was possible … fueled up the scooter, refreshed the water bag, pulled food out of the trunk for the evening, gotten the laundry ready for morning, showered, and then settled down for some reading and snoozing. Feeling some weight loss since Jacksonville, I would try to regain it in Baltimore's Little Italy, and almost anywhere in New Jersey and north of that. These past few days, while gnawing on jerky or other food, my thoughts had often turned back to the commune, my two apprentices, and my guesses as to what food they might be attempting, preparing and teaching to others. The three of us … MacKensie, Beth, and I had done some good cooking and enjoyed some great loving. And damn, the three of us, we had fun. And we three would remember.

Since there was no time crunch to reach Connecticut, Jefferson's Monticello would see us the following day. It was an added ninety miles of traveling, but Jefferson was a genius (many people agreed), and I would 'pay homage' and see some of his 'stuff', before I made my way to Gainesville, Virginia. I had spent a few hours at the Jefferson Memorial in DC a few years before. An exquisitely beautiful place. Gainesville, about 30 miles west of Washington, DC, seemed to be a natural stopping point between the rural southern solid green landscape and the far more intensive road traffic and congested mid-Atlantic and Northeastern cities ahead of me. From Gainesville, I would head to Washington, DC and enter that huge urban stretch running Washington, DC to Boston, Massachusetts. For that run from Florida to Virginia, there were very early morning starts. Mid-afternoon I'd settle into a campground and read for two hours or more while I made and drank a pot of coffee. Tomorrow would probably also be an early start, laundry and breakfast and then Monticello, but after that, in the cityscapes, I would try to avoid the very heavy traffic of early mornings or late afternoons.

Settled down to read. 'Caine Mutiny' held me to its final page and there would be a good feeling leaving this book for someone to find. I'd write some sort of note on an inside page. Neon light filtered through the curtains and I slept.

There were no coffee makin's in the motel room. Just had to tough it out, get dressed, get the small bag of laundry onto the scooter, drive it the very short distance to the 24 hour breakfast place. All of this was accomplished with no fatalities. Then, coffee and pancakes ... what a surprise! Time to wake up and return to my human form. Then back to the coin-op laundry, with my washing machine nearly finishing its work. Transfer to a clothes dryer. Have a smoke. "Caine Mutiny" was left on a chair, and I began Steinbeck's "East of Eden". The clothing finished. Back to the motel. Another shower, then pack things up for a drive to Monticello (which can be translated from the Italian as 'heavenly mountain'), about 70 miles or two hours distant, barring the unforeseen, as they say. Got a firm grip on Route 250 out of Richmond and headed northwest toward Charlottesville, near Monticello. There had been some rain during the night, but morning was splendid and the sun was behind me. Mentally reviewing my road experience these past nine weeks, there had been such good fortune in several ways: (1) weather had been kind ... no tornado, no severe storms, no severe heat, and not too much rain; (2) thus far, Tony Lambretta had been the most reliable beast of burden and deserved a hearty pat on the side panel; and (3) there had been no road mishaps, and very few close calls ... only in cities, with motorists not paying attention.

At Monticello, I took the little tour of Jefferson's plantation house, then walked over to the graveyard. That was the moment when I most admired that brilliant man. On his gravestone was the inscription claiming only three accomplishments: authorship of the Declaration of Independence, authorship of the Commonwealth of Virginia's religious freedom clause, and being the father of the University of Virginia. Of course, so many historians have examined every facet of Jefferson's life. The man and his work is worth the study, for sure. One of the most brilliant of our national founders.

In Charlottesville, I refueled the scooter and stopped for coffee. Found my way to Route 29 and started to the northeast toward Gainesville, I'd stop for a snack and a smoke about halfway there, it being about 90 miles from Monticello. Another splendid afternoon with the sun again at my back along with a light breeze, no real rush, and the driving through the countryside was easy. It would be city driving for much of the remainder of this journey, starting the following morning.

Halfway to Gainesville, at Culpepper, it was snack time for me on this gorgeous Virginia afternoon. Gaining Gainesville, an inexpensive room was available near a semi-industrial area. Took it. I'd have to check my money supply to see what remained of my original $400.00 plus whatever was in my pocket (maybe another $30 or $40) on that morning back in April when Tucson saw me wave goodbye temporarily. This was the first time actually counting my remaining dollars and it was $99.00 exactly. I had traveled more than 4/5 of the distance and spent about $325.00 or 3/4 of the money. Not bad.

Fell asleep reading "East of Eden."

Did the Capital have rush hour traffic like other cities? Didn't know the answer to that one, but decided not to start until a little later to drive into DC. Time for coffee and to gas up the Lambretta and get ready for the day. Had been in Washington several times in previous years and knew parts of it were just simply beautiful. Yet, there was no urge to be the tourist that morning, rather to just enjoy passing through, find Route 1, and head northward toward Baltimore. There was moderate traffic, but still it was taxing to remain ultra-alert and not get run over. Route 1 was not particularly fast paced this morning, but I couldn't complain because I was the slowest thing on it. Not quite true ... because I did actually pass a horse and buggy (maybe some lost Amish).

A little over an hour after leaving Washington, and approaching Baltimore, a stop was made at a corner market. Use the restroom, ask for directions, and buy anything (usually coffee, but this time only a Payday bar). Got clear and easy directions to Little Italy. Understand that if a town has a Little Italy, it will have good food. Baltimore's Little Italy was, to me, like an oasis after a desert ordeal, but tempered by knowledge that from here northward, there would be delicious food always available. No more shortages of Italian cookies or tasty panini or... or ... For the first time on this journey, there was a feeling of 'getting close to my origins.' Now there was a pretty fair chance I could actually do that which I had started more than two months ago. There was an added bonus of knowing that I needed to regain some four, five, or six pounds of weight. Surely, that would be a pleasant task.

Following the clerk's direction, I continued on Rt. 1 to Pratt St, turned right, went a dozen blocks and there past Inner Harbor, to the right again, was Little Italy. It was time to noodle around. The sights and sounds, but mostly the aromas announced this small chunk of heaven. Stopped at a bakery. It had been a long, dry spell, but here at last ... Italian cookies in at least a dozen varieties. Bought only a dozen, knowing I would be able to get replacements in New Jersey, New York, and Connecticut. Took my little treasure with an espresso (for variation) to a little table outside along the sidewalk. Sat down and thanked bakery gods for the blessings in a bag ... a paper bag. And here's a middle-aged couple, carrying coffee cups, looking around for a table. I gestured to two vacant chairs at my table. They smiled and walked over. We introduced ourselves and began a conversation. We starting talking about the baked stuff and then started joking about withdrawal pains when pastry wasn't available, etc. It was in Chicago with Edith, when last I could get cookies. That brought up the scooter trip. The scooter was parked at the curb, 20 feet away in plain view. The woman asked how I could possibly have survived without cookies. I said it was touch and go for a while. We began with little dumb jokes and the jokes got dumber and we got louder and had a helluva time ... strangers but understanding friends. Time to say goodbye, but not before I asked them to recommend a deli. They were local people and directed me to the one they thought best. That's where The Lambretta and I went. Bought some good tasting, sustaining, and inspired food things to carry with me. To where? Toward Wilmington, Delaware ... about 75 miles north of Baltimore, Maryland on Route 40.

A truly enjoyable stop in Baltimore, an important seaport city, and now back on the road for another few hours. Moderate traffic on Route 40. It was reassuring to see a pizza joint every so often (one never knew when they'll need an emergency pizza), an occasional bookstore, signs of more urban life. While viewing nature over thousands of miles of my journey was appreciated, the urban scape and its potential was more a magnet to me.

Now crossing the Susquehanna River and a few miles later, entering Delaware, coffee and fuel break, then bypassing Wilmington, by following Route 40 across the Delaware River into New Jersey. A happy, but very long afternoon. And somehow, with all that ground covered, I missed Pennsylvania completely. Onto New Jersey's Route 130, traveling along northeastward and near a place called Cinnaminson (believe it or not) found a thick growth of trees. Stopped for a snack break, sampling some very welcome wine-cured hard salami, a few gorgeous olives, and of course, a few heaven-sent Italian cookies. Since I was getting very short of daylight, the decision was to move deeper into the grove of maples, and set up camp. It would be cold-brewed coffee in the morning, but I was tired enough not to care. There were some strange industrial smells in the air, but I was exhausted and crawled into the tent and went directly to lala land as available light after sunset was dimming.

CHAPTER 57

NJ, NY & ?

There was no moon at all. Up above. Wide awake and hungry and thirsty and needing to pee. Out of the tent, take a leak. By flashlight, get the coffeepot with the precious two cups of not-too-bad cold brew coffee and ahhh, the Italian cookies will make everything better. And it was true. They don't tell you that stuff in the doctor's office or the church now, do they? It was indeed dark and I had no idea of clock time, but sleep time was past. Finishing coffee and cookies and looking toward what I thought was east, there was no hint of sunrise. Didn't like driving the scooter at night, but to hell with it. Give it a try. A warm, pleasant night, and I could hear some traffic on Route 130. Packed up camp in darkness. Using the flashlight, I would make my way to the road and then check to see if everything had been tied decently near a street light. The scooter's headlight was so faint I had to use the flashlight to see if it was working at all. A little joke there. The tail light seemed bright and that was a plus.

Out onto the highway and giving everything a glance over, my intent was to stop at the first café or diner available in an attempt to rejoin the world. Here we were in New Jersey and headed for New York City. There would be no avoiding traffic congestion. No matter the time of day or night, there were always people moving. It never stopped. Café open in Bordentown. Just black coffee, please. Clock said 5:10. Back onto to the scooter named Tony. When was sunrise? Was that a hint of it over there? Wasn't sure. Today, if fate allowed, we would pass through NYC and make our way to the Connecticut seashore. No longer a tourist, now just a traveler. Since I had already seen much of what was about to be seen, my intent was to stop only for important things, like gasoline, peeing, good food, or ice cream. I'd have to be patient and work my way through all the traffic, just as everybody else had to. Sure, the smaller width of the scooter might offer some advantage in stopped traffic, by driving between lanes, but that was a dangerous game I would not play. There was about 175 miles to go to get to my secret temporary goal.

Let me explain: Earlier in this accounting, I have written that at this stage of my life, my mother drove me absolutely nuts and I probably did the same for her. She was certainly a loving little Italian mama and would do anything possible on earth for me, her only son, anything except ... she would never cease asking me and then directing me toward life paths I should follow. It never stopped. It never even slackened. Tough on me, because I hadn't the foggiest idea of what I was 'doing' in life, aside from trying anything and everything which might interest me. The good career and secure retirement path seemed deathly dull and held zero attraction for me and that drove mom crazy and probably drove my father only half crazy. Now, here was their kid, their hope, having crossed the country on a putt-putt. In their eyes, probably just a waste of time and money and no accomplishment whatsoever. So, rather than spend much time at my parents' house I would arrive no more than three days before my sister's wedding and leave their house right after the wedding. Their being occupied with the wedding would help avoid a major blow up, I thought. My secret interim goal, then, was to travel from NYC to Hammonasset Beach, near Clinton, along the Connecticut shore, use up excess days camping at the shore and just screwing around, and then travel the final forty miles to their home, the house where I grew up, in New Britain, Connecticut. That was the plan.

At 6:00 AM on the button, as if they had an appointment, Route 130 merged into Route 1 at New Brunswick, NJ. I would follow Route 1 across New York City, New York State, and into Connecticut. More coffee and refuel the Lambretta in Newark, another hour from now. This part of New Jersey was heavily populated and heavily industrialized, kind of stinky, raucous, and noisy, but if I had to choose between this urban turmoil and a pristine prairie town, I'd pick this mess.

Northward toward Elizabeth and putt-putting through so many towns, one smack up against the next, all the way to Newark. Getting close to Newark, I was imagining one of those fantastic grilled sausage and roasted red pepper grinders (sometimes, a submarine or hero sandwich was called a grinder, though I believed that use was being lost). In my mind was the idea that New Jersey Italians did that sandwich better than anyone. But it was not yet 7:00 AM, so instead, it would be some hot coffee and the last of the cookies for me ... and a refuel for my buddy, Tony Lambretta. Getting into Newark, traffic was heavy, but moving, sometimes more quickly than I preferred, but moving. Time to take a decent break. Stopped for scooter fuel first, walked all around and made sure everything was secure and that the handle of the machete was hidden (as it had been the entire trip.) Next was coffee from the corner mini-market and a smoke. No hurry. Route 1 and Route 9 had begun running together and following that path for 10 more miles would take me to the George Washington Bridge, where a dozen highway routes converged to cross the famous Hudson River and land in the more famous New York City. Crossing a bridge or passing through a tunnel invariably causes me to marvel at the ingenuity of the human species. No exception this morning. Fortunately, while traffic was slow, it was almost continuous, making the scooter driving somewhat easier than expected, having anticipated a white-knuckle frantic stop and go procedure. A major problem was getting boxed in by trailer rigs, which meant I couldn't always see traffic signs far enough in advance. At the east end of the bridge, Route 9 disappeared, and looking for Route 1 was finally rewarded with a sign which I could actually see. I was OK. Being a scooter amongst eighteen wheelers was like walking in the land of giants, a bit scary, somewhat dirty, and bigtime noisy. At last, I was in the Big City. I had been in NYC a number of times, for NY Yankee ball games and some splendid Broadway shows, but never felt certain of my directions.

So many dazzling things to see and do here. In the distance there's the Empire State Building, there's the Chrysler Building, there's Yankee Stadium (how I loved Yankee Stadium when I was a kid, having seen Casey Stengel, Phil Rizzuto, Billy Martin, Yogi Berra and Joe DiMaggio many times), but what I wanted now was a good sausage sandwich. Somewhere in the West Bronx, as I putt-putted along Route 1, now a city street with traffic lights and crosswalks, I spied an Italian deli that displayed a blessed sign. The sign read : 'Fire Roasted Sausage - Pepper'. That was enough for me and I did a quick U-Turn, found a parking spot. "Too early for a sausage sandwich?" "Never too early!" was the response from a young guy behind the counter, "What else do you want on it, buddy?" Me: "Just the roasted peppers would be just fine." "You got it ... two minutes, all the sausage is precooked, but we grill it, too." A woman was putting a tray of great-looking cooked veggie mixture into the deli case. Eggplant, olives, some large beans, green peppers and more. The guy said, "Here? Or To Go?" Almost directly from the George Washington Bridge, I had landed in heaven, and I left that ordinary, but beautiful deli with half the sausage sandwich in my belly and half all wrapped up. That, and an equally large cooked veggie sandwich for later in the day. Leaving, I said "Mille Grazie e Ciao!" Got a "Prego!" and a "Ciao!" in return. Gotta love New York! And I thought of Enrico, back in Pueblo, Colorado. He certainly would have enjoyed this, too. Two or three doors away was a small Italian bakery, which I smelled before I saw. Have to make a house call there. Got a dozen and a half cookies. Heaven indeed. Food for the spirit! Food for the soul!

Traveling on Route 1 again, passing the well-known Jesuit college Fordham University (so that's where it was all this time) and then the Botanical Garden, started in the late 1800s, great place to spend an afternoon, which I had done four or five years before. Continuing north and east out of the city through some miles of housing and toward New Rochelle, a wealthy suburban city on Long Island Sound.

Driving was markedly more relaxing now, having left the rambunctious pace of NYC behind. A little bit of slack for daydreaming allowed me to think of the few tolls I had paid during my trip, the latest at the G. W. Bridge. Imagining a conversation with the manager of the toll booths, saying I had a question as to why they overcharged me for the scooter toll. If an eighteen wheeler had to pay a toll of five dollars, and an ordinary car was charged one dollar, why shouldn't the scooter just be charged maybe a dime, since it only weighed a tenth as much as a car. And what if I wanted to cross on a pair of gasoline-powered roller skates. Shouldn't that be less? And what if I could do it on just one gasoline-powered roller skate? The manager, while imaginary, became irritated, said I was being ridiculous and further, that there was a minimum toll for anything that wanted to use the bridge to get across the river. Oh yeah, well, what if a squirrel wanted to cross? Would you guys take acorns as payment? NOTE: At this point, the reader can see possible damages caused by too many hours on a scooter or maybe from too much traffic exhaust.

New Rochelle was a high-dollar suburb of New York. Everything in New Rochelle was perfect. The careers, the marriages, the children, the schools, etc. And that's OK, if that's your choice and if you can afford it and if you can possibly tolerate it. Staying on Route 1, also called the Boston Post Road, would take me to my interim goal, Hammonasset Beach State Park, a beach for common folk. First though, I had about 80 miles to travel. Through Port Chester, Greenwich, Stamford, Bridgeport, New Haven, and a dozen or two dozen smaller towns in between. Persons growing up in the Western states often have difficulty imagining traveling through 7 different towns in 20 miles. After New Haven, another three or four towns and fifteen miles would get me to the beach. The 80 miles might take two or three hours, depending on traffic. I would take a leisurely approach and probably piss off a few drivers, but that's one of life's risks. Good fortune occurred in New Haven, where there suddenly appeared a gelato shop and inside that, there suddenly appeared a bowl with three different flavors. Certainly, today was a day of miracles.

When a child growing up in Connecticut, the three families from my mother's side would rent a beach house for the summer and that's where all the kids from the three families stayed. It might be at Westbrook,

Saybrook, or Clinton, or another area, but it was always a fun summer. Got pretty good at catching the blue shell crabs and damn, they were the warriors of the crab set, but I don't recall ever being bitten. Traveling through one little shore town and then another, triggered all sorts of childhood memories. The time passed quickly and we turned off Route 1 toward Hammonasset Beach State Park where I rented a campsite for two nights. Stopping the Lambretta, I gave it a warm pat on the side panel and said, "Well, Partner, we did it." Walked toward the water, sat down, took off my boots and socks, rolled up my pants and walked into the little waves at the shoreline. We had, in fact, scooted across the USA! No one with me to share that moment, but I had no problem with that, not at all.

CHAPTER 58

THE LANDING + LOOSE ENDS

Here we were, the scooter named Tony Lambretta and I, at the Connecticut shore, having made it across America. For me in normal life, a day was filled with activity, always trying to do a dozen different things. For relaxation, there was reading or going to a movie or play with one girlfriend or another. However, when I concentrated, I was also accomplished at doing nothing, which was my intent for the next two days. Time to sit, read, think, and accomplish as little as possible. Oops, forgot, I'd have to shave.

Set up my little tent at my little rented campsite, tied Tony Lambretta off to a tree, walked around and picked up six or eight partial bags of charcoal and some leftover firewood from the previous weekend's campers. In previous years, I had visited this beach, Hammonasset, visited friends who camped here regularly, but had never done so myself. Prepared my little coffeepot and a fire and got it started. My delicious 'cowboy' coffee and half of that veggie sandwich would be enjoyed quietly. The ruler of the kingdom could not have eaten better food than I had in my hands. And cookies would be the icing on the cake, so to speak.

Knowing that my arrival on a scooter at my parents' house in New Britain would be a shock to them, I expected a very mixed homecoming ... warmth and shock, since they had been deliberately misled into thinking Tony Lambretta was a human friend, not my mechanical buddy. They would have been petrified with worry had they known the truth. To add to the drama was my trim, but very black and noticeable beard. That would certainly be overwhelming. My sister's wedding was the occasion and I would not be stubborn about the hair on my face. Well, maybe a little, but only temporarily.

Reader's Note: Remember this was 1960, and this was conservative, uptight, constipated New England and an extra quarter-of-an-inch of hair on a man's head in those days, but especially on his face was grounds for drastic measures. Having a beard was akin to showing your fangs. Obviously, people with beards were weird, probably some type of deviant or criminal, who knows. They represented non-conformity and without doubt, were, at the very least, disruptive elements. For shaving, the following morning, I would drive into Clinton or a nearby town to a barbershop for hair surgery, with a haircut as a side order. Remember, both my parents were beauticians, and my father, who had started as a barber, would always want to cut my hair and always wanted to cut it too damn short. At age twelve, I began to dislike his haircuts. When a freshman in the first college I attempted, and just before Thanksgiving break, I went to a barber (other than my father) for the first time in my life. And he wasn't Italian, he was a Swede or a Dane, and do you know what that guy did? No, of course you don't. That crazy so-and-so did what I asked him to do and not what he thought should be done. In other words, he was trying to please his customer. How revolutionary! From that point on, my father cutting my hair was avoided. It never happened again.

The coffee was gurgling its readiness. Off the fire and give it a 100 count for aging. The sandwiches from New York were exquisite and half of each remained … the half with sausage for later that night, the veggie mix (schiacciata) half sandwich for the next morning. Sipping at the coffee gave me opportunity to review some of what I had seen and done during this journey.

Considering money, I believe expenses were underestimated, but not by much. It was those beautiful women on the trip who had made life easier, socially and financially. Had my funds run too low, I would have worked at one job or another for a few days at a time (since little kidhood, I had always been able to scramble and find some sort of odd job or paying employment), but because of those splendid females, I was able to travel with little cause for worry. In some manner or another, I would show up in time for my little sister Phyllis' wedding. I would arrive in New Britain, with $30 or $40 dollars still in pocket. There was another $100.00 stashed in my stuff in the basement of the house in Connecticut, about $200 in the bank in Tucson. And … Stella's gift had not yet been touched. While not in great shape, I was OK for the ending of the journey.

As far as my scooter named Tony Lambretta … The complaints first: (1) Personally, I would have preferred a foot throttle rather than hand-operated, (2) the headlamp was really a joke, could never get the damn thing to be of any use at all, and (3) an additional 20% power added to the engine would have been a decided blessing. Finished with complaining. Now, outweighing complaints many times over is praise: very comfortable and easy to handle, surprisingly economical, unmatched reliability … most reliable machine I have ever owned. This beautiful little scooter, designed and built in Italy is now (December 2015) no longer produced. As a testimonial, one should know, there are Lambretta clubs and associations all over this world of ours. Lambretta has many thousands of fervent fans, restoring and remodeling the old machines. Today, prices of these Lambretta scooters are astronomical.

The Women: While I was always 'on the prowl' in those years, there was no advance clue as to how important women would be in the course of my trek across the country. In the ten weeks of traveling, there had been involvements with seven women. In those days, arguably, that would be considered promiscuous. We were young and pumped up on raging hormones. The birth control pill was being used extensively by young women, at least partially freeing them from fear. And most importantly, this was a time before HIV or AIDS or other fairly nasty STDs became so prevalent – in short, it was a great time to be alive and horny. In 1960, to be alive and horny ... and ... to share a shower with a beautiful young woman (which I did as often as possible) was a celebration of life and good clean fun as a bon ... us.

There is a chance one or more of these women might still be alive and actually stumble upon the telling of this journey. The two college girls in New Mexico were unusually handsome and daring people and the party in a storm-damaged mobile home remains, for me, more than a half-century later, the best impromptu party I've ever experienced. Beth and MacKensie, my two cooking apprentices in Florida, were attractive and delightful people, in a remarkable setting that served the three of us admirably. So pleasant to witness the two of them being kind to each other, as well as to me, as we enjoyed ourselves immensely those three days. Marie in Atlanta: good-looking? Absolutely. Sexy? Certainly. She showed, however, no interest or curiosity in anything other than the most superficial things. But Atlanta would have been a much different experience without her and the support of her ex-fiancé's cash. Edith in Chicago was a splendid and lucky encounter and I genuinely enjoyed being with her for those days in Chicago. She would be in her mid 90's now ... hard to believe, but simple math can be brutal. Of course, I've saved the best 'till last ... my dear Stella, from Denver. Indeed, for me, the finest companion ... so easy to fall in love with. An intelligent and remarkably beautiful woman. And Damn, the two of us were so good together. My thoughts turned to her many times after we parted in New Orleans. Stella would be in her early 80's today. There was only one small disappointment with Stella (aside from our having to part ways) ... I had wanted to show her how to find the North Star and that was never done. For the rest of her life, I wanted her to remember us every time she saw or heard of that important little star. Sappy, right? But sappy is OK ... sappy is a vital part of our soul.

With the exception of Marie, each of the women had enough information, and with the most casual bit of sleuthing or searching, could have found me in Tucson in later years. None ever did. Nor did I seek out or hear of any of them. While these were such sweet times, they soon after became history. Best remembered as sweet ... the women to remain forever beautiful and vibrant.

Traveling across the country gave me opportunity to view many of the warmer parts of the US. As I was leaving Florida, there was strong indication that I couldn't have chosen a more suitable place for myself than Southern Arizona. That was not quite a closed issue ... for I had not yet experienced any of Nevada or Southern California. Way back in January, when I gave away the northern half of the US map, I had done myself an immense favor. That was certainly apparent now. And so a great value was gained by this journey across the country ... now I knew where I would start my life ... in the scorched deserts of Southern Arizona. I might bump into a better location, but there would be no further energy spent purposely seeking a suitable place for myself. Southern Arizona would be my start.

It was a Thursday evening at Hammonasset Beach, and I could see cases of beer being transported here and there, even a keg of beer came by on a medical stretcher with three young guys bearing the load, one in front and two holding the handles at the rear. Seemed that there would be parties nearby. After this long day on the road, there would be no parties for me, being committed to a 'wind down' mood. I would keep to myself. Spent an hour finishing the second half of the sausage and pepper sandwich. As the day darkened, I walked over to the bathrooms, returned to the tent, had a smoke, brushed my teeth carefully, prepared my coffee fire, and crawled into my portable cave, thinking to shower and shampoo in the morning, to avoid offending the barber.

Only vaguely aware of party sounds around me, I slept with no interruption until just before dawn. That's when I heard a few raindrops against the tarp. Time to rise. Started the coffee fire, walked to the bathhouse, showered very quickly, and returned to the tent as the eastern sky began to glow. For some reason, there was the expectation of full sunshine my first morning in Connecticut. That was not to be. Maybe it was nature's reminder that we're not as important as we might think. Cloudy, about 70 degrees, and the sea was quiet and slightly textured with an almost drizzle, and no other people in sight. The coffee was done, and the sacred morning ritual of two cups worth began. Had a few bites of that superb veggie sandwich from NYC. Excellent. No need for pancakes this morning, perhaps more coffee, but no pancakes today, thank you. Traveling across this country, coffee had been a constant companion ... somewhere between 400 and 500 cups and only half were mentioned. Such uncharacteristic restraint. Certainly the best of the coffee was that which I shared with my dear friend Stella.

Weather permitting, the plan was to do some 'noodling' in shore towns along Route 1 from Guilford northeastward to Old Saybrook, with three or four towns in between, a total distance of ten or fifteen miles. I'd wait 'till mid-morning to start, then look for a barbershop and a library. And for the hell of it, I'd try to find one or more of the houses that our family rented when we were kids. First, I'd begin a new book ... 'The Day of the Triffids' by John Wyndham, an English author. The sci-fi tale of an aggressive plant species made for wild reading for early in the foggy morning. The fog gradually dissipated and it was time to begin the day in earnest. Neatened the tent area, wrote one of those ambiguous notes to 'Big Louie,' and tied it to the tent string. A trusting soul, I am, I am, but never quite completely. You can say that last sentence with rhythm if you like.

Got onto the scooter, made my way to Route 1, took a left and headed to Guilford, a town just loaded with historical houses, which was OK, but better was the large, and beautiful green in the center of town. Today, however, was the day for a barbershop, which I found easily (not certain, but I felt people subtly pushing me in that direction without their being asked). In the shop, with two guys working, the older one already occupied, the younger guy greeted me, said he was an apprentice, and if I didn't mind, he could give me a haircut. An apprentice barber in Tucson usually cut my hair and I had no problem with that. Gave him instructions for trimming my hair, and for the shaving ... to leave a solid mustache, but no handlebar and a good-sized, but trim goatee. As the apprentice finished, I was surprised by my own appearance and laughed out loud. The guy had done excellent work, and I said so, and gave him a pretty good tip. My thought with the goatee was to offer it as a sacrifice in an effort to keep my mustache when I finally reached my parent's place. Guilford had a good-sized library and had the weather been worse, I might have gone in, but the sky seemed brighter and I'd take advantage of it for putt-putting around. I noodled my way toward Madison. Not familiar with it, and I continued toward Clinton, where we had stayed at least one summer, and where I found the house we rented. Of course, it looked different with a different paint job. Had it grown smaller? Or had something else changed? Stopped for an order of fried clams at a stand along the highway. Hadn't had those for a while. Delicious. Explored my way to Old Saybrook and then returned to Hammonasset Beach, but not before stopping at a pizza joint where I ordered a large pizza, but would they cut it up into pieces to fit two smaller boxes for scooter travel. At Hammonasset, I used the remainder of the afternoon and the evening to watch the ocean, read, eat pizza, watch people, drink coffee, read more, eat more pizza, and mind my own business ... all honorable pursuits. Since weather had been marginal all day and more marginal was expected, that evening I decided not to extend my campsite rent and return to New Britain late Saturday afternoon instead of Sunday.

Saturday loomed, much the same as Friday had loomed ... dull and grey. Not unusual for New England. Again, the coffee was brewing, but this morning I would have hot pizza for breakfast by putting pizza slices on the grille near the coffeepot, but not directly touched by the fire. There was a mental balancing game being played in my mind ... I was anxious to leave this campground, but not anxious to arrive in New Britain. My parents would be staggered by the foolishness of crossing the US on that two-wheeled contraption, but faced with the fait accompli, there was nothing to be done but accept it. Now the goatee and the mustache ... something could be done about that. It was just too radical for the upcoming wedding, giving my mother enough excuse to start her nagging about something. I would tolerate that for the next two days (with the dim hope of retaining the mustache, as it turned out, not a chance at all) but after the wedding, I would never listen to nagging again and would only laugh when she started in later years. I knew that 98% of New Englanders would agree with my mom, but that was their problem (fifty years later, they've become a bit more tolerant ... maybe).

My sister's wedding was beautiful and I was clean-shaven. Immediately after, I scootered around Connecticut and Massachusetts for a few days. That, then, was the finale of my little excursion. A fair chunk of the country had been seen since my decision to 'scoot across the USA' and I returned by auto (driving a Nash Rambler Station Wagon pulling a trailer with the scooter aboard) ... in time for an exciting monsoon season in the blazing desert of Southern Arizona.

PASS IT ON ...

When you've finished this book,
or have simply enjoyed all you can possibly stand,
pass it on directly to a friend or relative.

You can also pass it to another person
anonymously and surreptitiously (two cool words) ...
by quietly abandoning this book on the subway,
in a coffee shop, in the dentist's office, or in a taxicab.

The blank area opposite this page
can be used to write a comment
(example: "good reading, this guy is a nutcase"
or something else equally flattering)
before you secretly leave this copy somewhere.

The book will find a new owner.
Hope it's a kind one.

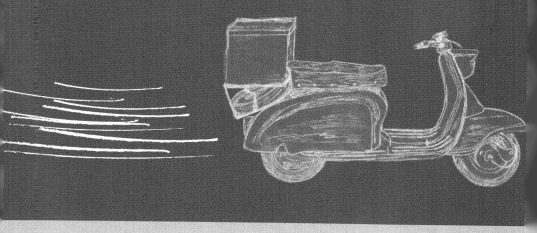

SCOOT ACROSS THE USA • 3RD EDITION
by Aureleo Rosano
© 2016, 2017, 2020 • All Rights Reserved
Book Design by Dominic Arizona Bonuccelli

AVAILABLE FOR PURCHASE ON LULU.COM
For more on the author, visit: www.rosano.org

Made in the USA
Las Vegas, NV
12 May 2023

71904790R00259